D0275255

Provincial Families of the Renaissance

PROVINCIAL FAMILIES

THE JOHNS HOPKINS UNIVERSITY PRESS

BALTIMORE AND LONDON

James S. Grubb

OF THE RENAISSANCE

Private and Public Life in the Veneto

This book has been brought to publication with the generous assistance of the Gladys Krieble Delmas Foundation.

05 04 03 02 01 00 99 98 97 96   5 4 3 2 1

The Johns Hopkins University Press
2715 North Charles Street
Baltimore, Maryland 21218-4319
The Johns Hopkins Press Ltd., London

Library of Congress Cataloging-in-Publication Data will be found at the end of this book.

A catalog record for this book is available from the British Library.

ISBN 0-8018-5321-4

CONTENTS

ACKNOWLEDGMENTS

IT IS A PLEASANT DUTY to thank those persons and institutions who have so greatly aided me in writing this book. Because its production extended over a decade and a half, as professional obligations and other projects constantly pushed ahead of this work, my debts are many.

An empirically based study requires long stints in archives. I discovered the Arnaldi and Repeta memoirs, and collected the bulk of Vicentine data, during a year's stay funded by a Fulbright fellowship. The Gladys Krieble Delmas Foundation provided a summer in Venice during which I uncovered the Freschi memoir and explored the Marciana and State Archives. During a summer trip sponsored by a National Endowment for the Humanities grant, I located Veronese memoirs and worked through the holdings of the State Archives and Biblioteca Civica. Grants from the UMBC administration permitted me to complete research in the cities in the Veneto. Back home, the excellent librarians of the Johns Hopkins University and UMBC tracked down secondary sources. A year-long NEH fellowship provided the tranquility I needed to produce a preliminary draft. Without the generosity of these bodies and the help of their staffs this book could not have been undertaken.

The compilation of a monograph requires, as well, extensive personal assistance. Scholars here and abroad, consistently friendly and forthcoming, have immensely enriched my sources and arguments. Gian Maria Varanini, who shared his unmatched familiarity with Veronese records and propelled my interest in memoirs, merits special thanks. I am grateful, as well, for the leads and comments of Stanley Chojnacki, Elisabeth Crouzet-Pavan, Michael Knapton, Patricia Labalme, Paola Lanaro Sartori, Edward Muir, Anthony Molho, Reinhold Mueller, Dennis Romano, and Giuseppina de Sandre Gasparini. My colleagues at UMBC, too, have been congenial and collegial.

The protracted and often wearying writing of a book requires, finally, a good frame of mind. Patricia and Thomas Crawford provided a splendid research base in Verona. My parents, Anne and Edward MacBurney, have always encouraged an eccentric choice of vocation. I once dedicated a book to my wife Anne and son Thomas, and to do so again may seem super- erogatory, but they are still centers of my own private and public life, and I offer them this look at bygone lives as token of my appreciation.

INTRODUCTION

IN THIS BOOK I investigate a cluster of unremarkable people who lived in two midsized Italian cities five hundred years ago. This study is based on texts that they produced and records that others generated about them, and seeks to uncover their priorities and strategies: what engaged them sufficiently to write, how they arranged their lives within the possibilities (and limitations) accorded them, the choices they made and the choices made for them.

Three features shaped the project. The first was controlled serendipity, when in the course of thorough archival searches a colleague and I discovered rich documents of an unexpected type. The second was my growing conviction that these texts might serve as the basis for an examination of experience in settings that the historical literature has seldom considered. Third, the writing of the book has been conditioned by a newfound sense of freedom to apply an eclectic, primarily empirical methodology.

The Sources

Some years back I found the memoir of the Arnaldi family of Vicenza. I was surprised by the work's existence, because my professional training had never mentioned domestic chronicles in any region except Tuscany. On a subsequent visit, I was informed that the Vicentine state archive had acquired a massive multifamily cache of documents that was thought to contain Arnaldi material. The staff's intuition proved accurate, and officials graciously permitted me to photograph the 1,500 parchments and several account books in the Arnaldi trove, along with two thousand notarial documents relating to the family. Later I determined that another memoir from Vicenza, by Manfredo Repeta, was in the original an equally revealing source for private life; a poor and partial nineteenth-century edition had obscured many of its best features. Further search uncovered Bartolomeo dal Bovo's family chronicle in Verona, Ruggiero Cortusi's annotated account book in Padua, and the Freschi memoir in Venice, as well as brief or fragmentary entries by the Trento, Guastaverza, da Romagna, and Feramosca families.

Meanwhile, Gian Maria Varanini found comparable manuscripts from the Verità, Fracastoro, and Stoppi families of Verona, and drew my attention to the miscellany of Bartolomeo Muronovo, which had been cited for other reasons but never examined for its copious domestic notices. The Veronese archivist Gloria Maroso showed me the uncatalogued *memoriale* of Bonaventura Bovi. Varanini and I are preparing a critical edition of the Veronese and Vicentine memoirs.[1] These memoirs, supported by evidence from tax rolls, testaments, notarial registers, and family archives, provide the documentary basis for this study.

It has been remarked, accurately, that the genre of the memoir does not exist in the Veneto.[2] The term itself, as well as its synonyms "family chronicle," *ricordanza*, and "domestic chronicle," is a catchall label rather than a precise descriptive. Heterogenous in format and content, the family texts of Verona and Vicenza share only what has been called an anagraphic feature: the recording of births, marriages, and deaths within domestic units. Bovi's *memoriale* alone is freestanding, dedicated solely to the writer's immediate family.[3] The rest fall into two main groupings. Some began as property account books with inventories and summaries of transactions, into which authors inserted anagraphic material: this was the case in the Stoppi, Cortusi, and (perhaps) Fracastoro manuscripts.[4] Others began as *zibaldoni*, miscellanies of classical, spiritual, poetic, prophetic, political, medical, and astrological writings, into which authors entered domestic notices: this was the case in the Verità, Muronovo, and dal Bovo manuscripts. The *catasto* of Manfredo Repeta is a hybrid, originally a land account book that Repeta gradually turned into a *zibaldone*, recording the careers of his children along the way.

Because the genre does not exist in terms of uniformity or autonomy, can these texts sustain a monograph? I think so, on three grounds. First, the anagraphic material is remarkably constant in format throughout, and provides a common core of commensurate demographic data. Second, the heterogenous quality of the nonanagraphic texts enhances rather than throws up an obstacle to the study of family life: the variety of information allows commentary on a wide range of topics. Third, the memoirs of Verona and Vicenza are no more miscellaneous than the Florentine *ricordanze* that have supported several recent studies. As I shall argue in the introduction to the critical edition of these works, virtually all that *libri di famiglie* have in common is their rich personal and domestic record.

The Subjects

It is meaningless, as Lucien Febvre and Thomas Kuehn have charged,[5] to justify the writing of a book on the grounds that its documentary base is interesting or novel. Interesting to whom, besides the author? And what greater purpose can new information serve? Equally dubious is the premise that a book fills a gap: some topics have been overlooked deliberately and justly, as Girolamo Arnaldi has said, because they are of little importance.[6] The very notion of filling gaps smacks of the positivist program of a Great Wall of History that will someday be completed as historians multiply substudies, a scheme that has lost currency.

Bringing long-forgotten families from two semi-important cities to light, then, requires justification. It could hardly be argued that we know little about domestic life in the fifteenth century: the bibliography is now too vast for anyone to master. The geographic basis for that bibliography, however, remains slight indeed, as the field rests on case studies from a very few metropolitan centers. The family history of Italy is the history of great houses in great cities. At a rough guess Florence has claimed about 85 percent of scholars' attentions, the rest of Tuscany a further 5 percent, Venice another 5 percent, and Milan and Genoa combined the remainder. Of late there has appeared considerable work on lesser centers—collaborative histories of Brescia, Prato, Vicenza, and Vigevano, and monographs on Bergamo, Pescia, and Brescia—but these retain a traditional focus on politics and administration, economic structures, and political elites, with little regard paid to the domestic and the ordinary.

This imbalance has understandable historiographic roots. The preference for major urban units is very old: as the fourteenth-century jurist Bartolus of Sassoferrato commented, "It is better to be a middling citizen of a noble and honorable city than to be a leading citizen of a moderate city."[7] When the field of Renaissance studies was founded in the nineteenth century, few found cause to alter that judgment. Partisans of the Risorgimento and the nation-state located appropriate historical models for unified, sovereign polities in the free city-states of the past, and left fragmented, unfree little cities to local antiquarians. Evolutionary historians of the left and right located advanced social and economic change in metropolitan centers, and thought provincial cities backward. Cultural historians looked to centers of innovation and production, and saw no reason to examine backwaters. That legacy has persisted to a surprising degree in the twentieth century.

Too, it can hardly be denied that archives of the capitals are incomparably richer than those of the provinces: Florence, above all, provides copious evidence for questions that cannot even be posed for second-tier cities. There is, as well, the inescapable fact that a few centers set the tone for the rest. In the exercise of power, or high culture, or economics, capitals never eradicated localism but continued to provide overall direction; local societies resisted the hegemony of their masters only at the cost of remaining marginal. It has been reasonable, then, to look at the sites that gave cues to others.

The metropolis's near-monopoly on historical writing is, however, a risky proposition for social history, however that field is defined. Recovery of the quotidian and nonelite cannot be achieved with confidence if only a few major locales provide models and evidence. The overriding assumption for a metropolitan focus must be either that Florence or Venice constitute worlds unto themselves, such that there is no need to look beyond, or that we can safely extrapolate from the center to the periphery. Both propositions make those of us who work in the provinces nervous. One of my mischievous graduate students likened the situation to studying American society by looking at Manhattan alone: the one great borough might indeed offer a representative sample, but we would only be sure if we looked at Jacksonville, Dayton, Tulsa, Tucson, and Seattle as well.

Verona and Vicenza were fair- to good-sized cities: the former counted about 35,000 residents by the late fifteenth century, the latter about 21,000, compared with Venice's 100,000, Florence's 55,000, Genoa's 60,000, Milan's 100,000 and Naples' 120,000. Both ranked with cities such as Ferrara, Bologna, Mantua, and Perugia, and both were considerably larger than the second tier of Lombard and Tuscan cities. Neither was independent, having been incorporated into the Venetian dominion in the first decade of the century. Neither was a center of extraregional exchange, though Verona in particular enjoyed prosperity on a local scale and sent merchants abroad. Neither exercised much political or cultural influence beyond its borders.

These provincial settings were, then, rather different in their formal characteristics from metropolitan centers. They are considered here because they offer perspective on the Florentine and Venetian experiences. It is not claimed that they were somehow more typical of Renaissance Italian societies than were the big cities: as nuanced case studies proliferate, it becomes difficult, even futile to claim that any one experience is representative or unrepresentative. Nor does this book intend to mount a frontal assault on Florentine- and Venetian-based historiography, most of which is cited here with approval. Provincial towns are not good bases for thorough revisionism. Instead, the experiences of Verona and Vicenza provide an additional, alternative viewpoint. At some junctures they replicate metropolitan patterns, and so help universalize hypotheses generated from major centers. At some junctures they do not, and so suggest that the social history of the peninsula is more variegated than we would otherwise suppose.

NONE OF THE PEOPLE who emerge from the Veneto memoirs accomplished anything significant, good or bad, which might warrant fame on more than the local level. This book is not an attempt to rehabilitate the unjustly overlooked: its subjects are indeed obscure. They attract our attention only because, unlike their fellow citizens and for reasons that remain unclear, they chose to write about themselves and to record texts that mattered to them.

Here, too, I hope to provide a novel perspective, that of the solid but unconspicuous citizen of the lesser center. This figure has not received much attention. Nineteenth-century bourgeois did not wish to study the middling sort critically because to do so might call themselves into question;[8] the left viewed them as unprogressive, Romantics viewed them as dull, and the right viewed them as ignoble. When social history detached from traditional political-administrative-diplomatic concerns, scholars moved in new directions, but these, too, have seldom been concerned with the established but pedestrian. Many have looked at elites, to discern mechanisms by which the upper ranks of Florence, Venice, and Genoa acquired, consolidated, and perpetuated their prestige, power, and wealth. Other historians swung to the other extreme, examining artisans, urban underclasses, and peasants. Lately, many have studied outgroups: the miserable and the abused, criminals and rebels, and those classified in their time as deviants. Partly these categories have received attention for their own sake, as unfairly neglected in traditional history, and partly because marginality can furnish clues to the boundaries of the conventional.

This book, once again, does not even implicitly condemn those concentrations: the experiences of the mighty, the low-ranking, and the dispossessed should indeed be made known. Instead, the Veneto memoirs can contribute to social recovery by examining a stratum that remains nearly unknown: the middling sort, those who lived their lives in relative quiet and passed quickly into obscurity, neither powerful nor powerless, well fed but not outstandingly rich, neither victimizers (to any major extent, at least) nor victimized, literate but not cultured. The people who appear in these pages were modest in their victories and local in their ambitions. If the subjects of this book fall into the "abyss between the rich and poor, the well-connected and the isolated,"[9] it is also the case that to scorn and/or ignore them is to miss a significant portion of the historical landscape.

I do not claim here that these families of Verona and Vicenza were in any way more representative of fifteenth-century experience than were metropolitan elites, the poor, or marginals. Indeed, as the many people without history are increasingly recovered and put at the center of the historical stage, any effort to establish typical experience seems futile and even undesirable. Rather, I make a more modest claim: that the middling sort, too, had a voice, and that if we undertake the task of hearing all voices we should listen to theirs as well.

Methodology

The Veneto memoirs cannot by themselves support a thorough history of the provincial family in the early Renaissance. On many issues that presently engage historians they are, alas, silent. While that silence at least indicates that the priorities of these authors were not those of contemporary historiography, it cannot be used as the basis for substantive comment. For other topics they provide brief and tantalizing bits of information, suggestive but insufficiently dense to permit confident conclusions. Furthermore, the Veneto offers little corroborating literature such as treatises, sermons, moral prescriptions, or spiritual guides, and the secondary literature on family history in the region is scant.

How, then, to put the data of the memoirs into a larger context? The strategy adopted here is that of the gloss, a point-by-point exegesis of the texts using comparison with and explanation from other sources. Some of these sources are commensurate (e.g., the memoirs, notarial instruments, and testaments of other cities). Some are not: to establish the prescriptive and theoretical field for memoir entries, I have drawn upon works of law, theology, pedagogy, demographics, spirituality, and ethics that were produced elsewhere. For example, memorialists in the Veneto demonstrate an understanding of an intricate theory of nobility but did not articulate it. They wrote for descendants who shared their culture and did not require elaboration. We, on the other hand, have not inherited that culture and require explanation for what seem murky but critical issues. Because the texts are laconic, and

fellow citizens provided little commentary, the only available guides are treatises of jurists and humanists, most of whom wrote elsewhere.

The nature of the gloss requires a leap from the discrete case to a much
larger setting. The leap may at times seem ungainly and will invite challenge, but it should be kept in mind what the gloss tries to do. There is no
suggestion here that the modestly educated writers of the Veneto actually
knew and used the works of Alberti, San Bernardino, Bartolus, or Francesco
Barbaro. Still, ideas and models circulated widely in Quattrocento Italy, detached from the works in which they were most famously articulated: humble memorialists in provincial cities shared some elements of a cultural
patrimony with learned authors. For example, memoirs and testaments frequently mention orders for postmortem Masses, which responded to a belief in purgatory. Veneto citizens probably knew little of that highly technical and contentious doctrine firsthand, but they addressed generalized
notions about easing the afterlife; so the high texts discussed in Le Goff's
magisterial *Birth of Purgatory* can shed light on their actions.

Sometimes, on the other hand, the gap between the treatise and provincial
experience is very great. Yet that fact alone measures the distance between
high and middling culture. It is frequently the case that observed behavior in
these outlying cities did not correspond to the dictates of prescriptive literature. People in everyday life did not always do what theologians, canon lawyers, and moralists thought they should do. Learned writers and preachers, for
example, urged audiences to put penitential and Marian themes at the forefront of devotions; memorialists paid little heed to contrition and the Holy
Family. Here the normative literature, precisely because it is remote from
praxis, reveals the extent to which people in the Veneto went their own way,
resisted authority, and so exercised considerable freedom in shaping their lives.

THIS BOOK is decidedly empirical. I have gathered available data, drawn
conclusions that I judge supportable and plausible, and borrowed historians'
insights to provide reinforcement for or contrast with those conclusions. Both
sources and techniques are borrowed in eclectic, "ecumenical"[10] fashion:
whatever sheds light on the core evidence has been deemed useful. Notes are
copious, so that those who wish to follow up leads or query interpretations
will have the resources to do so. The language is as plain and straightforward
as possible, shorn of highly theoretical phrasing, so that the book can be understood by specialists in other fields and even by that perhaps mythic figure,
the general reader. The overall approach is thus rather traditional. At any rate,

the task at hand requires both conservatism and eclecticism: to provide comparatives with and perspective on secondary studies from other regions, I must at least in part replicate their methods.

I only hope that this book is not naively empirical. Many criticisms of "dig and muddle through" history are entirely justified. I am aware, too, of the profound contributions of allied disciplines that have enriched the writing of family and social history. Indeed, many of the questions posed here are drawn from allied disciplines. But I have chosen not to take the lead of multidisciplinarians, and little is based on firsthand reading in other fields. Partly this is due to personal inclination. Partly, too, this is due to the nature of the sources. The accounts of Veneto families are never thick enough for social anthropology, nor sufficiently compact and linear for microhistory or the "new narrative"; the serial data cannot support more than rudimentary quantification. The texts are not sufficiently revealing to be closely deconstructed, and the web of signification is patchy rather than dense.

Empiricism is also possible because the triumph of pluralism in the historical community has cancelled any notion of a single inherently superior approach. The field of family and social history began with a two-part program: an attack on traditional interests and methods,[11] and a willingness to borrow alternatives from neighboring fields. Both were largely successful, but there has been a price to pay. Appeals to allied methodologies have become so numerous as to be cacaphonous. With traditional history pushed to the background, champions of new histories justify their appeals partially on the grounds of merit but largely through criticism of competitors. Interdisciplinarians have fallen out among themselves.

The present internal self-examination in social history resembles the scene in the Chinese folktale of the War of the Five Armies, in which equally matched factions march down from mountain strongholds to join in chaotic and inconclusive battle on the plain below. Much criticism has indeed been telling: that sociology and structural anthropology impose rigid, functionalist categories; that quantification and collectivist social science are reductive and deterministic, denying variation and choice, and force aggregate analysis upon evidence that was never intended for such purposes; that nonquantification can only fall back upon the anecdotal; that most subfields ignore the technicalities and conventions of the texts that carry (but also condition) information; that overconfident social anthropology is blind to the degree to which texts are made to answer presentist questions (as ethnographers hear only responses to questions they themselves ask) and cannot speak for their own ages, hence becoming mere vehicles for historians' projections. Many defenses are equally convincing, and most historians would acknowledge that there has been masterful work in all fields. In consequence, no approach is beyond reproach, but no approach is eliminated altogether. If all techniques distort the past in some manner, no single methodology can claim inherent preference and none—including the empirical—is inherently without promise.

Granted, empiricism can only rejoin the ranks of the acceptable by assuming a degree of reserve seldom found in earlier generations, which were blithely confident that the data spoke in a straightforward manner. Current thinking rightly teaches that words are unstable and often defy understanding; that the formulas and literary conventions of texts construct (and so partly conceal) rather than directly reveal events; and that the historian is inevitably active transformer rather than passive reporter. There must always be kept in mind the question posed by Anthony Molho: can we, at five hundred years' distance, understand what people in the fifteenth century meant by their words?[12] An unequivocal yes is indeed naive. An unequivocal no, however, allows only two unpleasant alternatives: the despair and paralysis of those who see only the radical otherness of the past and thus find historical reconstruction impossible and ultimately pointless, or else the cheerful anarchism of those who, likewise denying the enterprise of seeking to understand the past on its own terms, justify its use as raw material for purely topical inquiries.

Staking out a middle ground among the fruitless varietals of blind optimism, nihilism, and abandon, insisting that foreign cultures can become somewhat familiar and that partial recovery of the past is indeed within our reach, demands extreme care in reading documents and limits expectations that we can establish their meaning. Occupying that middle ground, a cautious empiricism that tries to remain close and faithful to its sources may at least avoid the more obvious distortions.

Provincial Families of the Renaissance

CHAPTER ONE

MARRIAGE

$\mathcal{V}$ ERONA'S BONAVENTURA BOVI opened his *memoriale* with an account of his union with Isabeta Paulino. In Vicenza, Gaspare Arnaldi the elder initiated his *liber* with his marriage to Caterina Zugliano on 23 November 1407. Son Andrea continued the book with an account of his marriage to Caterina Botarini, and grandson Gaspare II entered as author when he "touched the hand" of Giovanna da Schio. Verità I, Bartolomeo Antonio, and Verità II Verità succeeded their fathers as writers with notices of their own marriages, as did Contino and Girolamo Stoppi.

Authors assumed a personal voice when they took wives. That is not to say that marriage constituted a moment of liberation. Authors of memoirs married while still under the paternal roof and remained there until their fathers' deaths. Many thereafter lived in fraternal households. Nor did writers stake a claim to personal autonomy: the very genre of the memoir testifies to their desire to maintain solidarity in the patriline by inscribing their share of its collective memory. But, in Bolognese[1] as in Veneto memoirs, assertion of personal identity within the memory of the lineage began with *matrimonium*. In a small but telling irony, writers claimed full membership in the historical family by an act that established horizontal rather than vertical connections.

Realistically, no other rite of passage could mark the individual's coming of age. Few Veronese or Vicentines were formally emancipated from the father's authority *(patria potestas)*. Tax rolls did not accord separate fiscal households to sons while their fathers still lived. The reaching of economic maturity at age twenty and legal maturity at age twenty-five[2] did not evoke notice. In Vicenza, political maturity at age eighteen[3] mattered little since a seat on municipal councils could be had through inheritance or purchase at any age.

Most of the Arnaldi, for example, obtained council membership in childhood. In Verona, as will be seen, young men usually failed several times in eligibility scrutinies before they gained a council seat: the drawn-out process for securing political access did not offer a single threshold.

Marriage was given centrality because the region lacked other rites to mark a transition into adulthood. In the terms of social anthropology, marriage transformed the dangerously ambiguous status of youth—sexually mature but socially indeterminate—into one that called for responsibility and settlement. The primary ritual of social integration and equilibrium,[4] marriage also reordered the family and the community in a way that no other event in the life cycle, not even birth or death, could accomplish. Writers of domestic chronicles knew that instinctively, and began their accounts with marriage. It is fitting that we do the same.

The Formation of Marriage

Who Marries?

In March 1440 Andrea Arnaldi's wife died in childbirth, leaving three daughters and a newborn son, who died the next day. His younger brother Battista had produced only daughters, and anyway was estranged from his siblings. Youngest brother Tommaso immediately took a wife. The sequence of events suggests that Tommaso had been destined for bachelorhood, but was called to matrimony in a last-ditch attempt to secure an heir. For the second time in as many generations the Arnaldi had limited their sons' marriages; this time, too, the strategy pushed the patriline close to extinction.[5]

The incident raises the issue of nuptuality: who, in any given pool of sons and daughters, was to marry? Populationist pressure, at this low point of the demographic curve, urged high rates of marriage: so humanists praised the union of man and woman as the source of civic rejuvenation, and several cities passed laws to promote nuptuality—denying public office to unmarried men, for example.[6] Spiritual pressure worked in the same direction. St. Paul urged those who could not accept the higher calling of celibacy to marry. Augustine and others thought marriage a vehicle to spread *caritas* through the community and to generate future citizens for the city of God. Moralists noted that marriage promoted civic pacification by channeling lust into acceptable relations, reducing the rowdiness of young men, and expanding alliances between lineages.[7]

Yet there were strong counterarguments for limitation. Lawyers identified the family with its collective wealth—"familia, id est substantia"[8]—and over-production of heirs jeopardized that patrimony. The Veneto's custom of partible inheritance, by which all legitimate sons received equal portions of the family wealth, increased the risk. Daughters received a further share of the patrimony as their dowries, which would usually pass to their children or otherwise out of the direct male line. For the propertyless, the absence of a consistent patrimony could relax restraints on marriage,[9] but for families who held and wanted to conserve wealth the consequences of high nuptuality were acute: dissipation of *substantia* would reduce the *familia* to economic oblivion within a few generations.

The imperatives of repopulation and *caritas*, then, might well conflict with strategies for preserving wealth. Most families tried for some middle ground. Evidently the Arnaldi had initially adopted a tactic once favored in northern Europe: allow one or a small number of sons to marry, leaving some or most of their brothers to fend for themselves or remain in the household as celibates and reserves.[10] But the medieval feudal nobility had enjoyed a climate of demographic prosperity: the family was likely to survive even though a small proportion of sons married. High mortality and low fertility in the fourteenth and fifteenth centuries rendered that strategy highly risky. Of the thousand or so Vicentine families prominent from 1200, more than half were extinct by 1500.[11] Still, patrimonial imperatives induced Italians of the Quattrocento to continue the very delicate game of limiting the number of sons who married. Only some 60 percent of Venetian patrician males married.[12]

Calculation was much the same for daughters. The old feudal nobility had tried to marry off all girls, certainly in the interest of spreading alliances and perhaps in the interest of spreading *caritas*. That strategy, too, could endanger a patriline's wealth, given the inevitable outflow of dowry monies. The price was evidently worth the risk in the economically expansive eleventh and twelfth centuries. In fifteenth century, however, the economy was relatively flat while dowries were shooting upward at a frightening rate. The wealthy found it virtually impossible to provide all girls with the high dowries necessary to maintain or improve social status. Keeping down dowry costs by imposing spinsterhood on daughters, a prominent feature of the famous "European marriage pattern" of the sixteenth century on,[13] was rare in Quattrocento Italy:[14] an unmarried woman in the household posed a danger to family honor.[15]

Increasing numbers of parents responded to the dowry crunch by sending some of their daughters to convents, which required lower dowries and equally served to spread *caritas*.[16] Among Veneto memorialists, the case of

Manfredo Repeta is the best documented: four daughters married and two became nuns, in line with the figure of 31 percent of noble girls in the Lyonnaise who entered religion.[17] Only a few families still married off all their daughters. The Arnaldi, a family on the make, did so: they were hungry for alliances and were willing to pay the price in dowries. But they were among the minority rich enough to afford universal female nuptuality.

Age at Marriage

Figures for the age a male in Florence married vary with the data and test used, but a general figure of thirty-one to thirty-two years may serve here for comparison.[18] Fewer than half of men were married by twenty-five, and only three-quarters by the age of thirty-three. While data for Venice are less secure, patrician men apparently married on average at twenty-nine to thirty years, with the averge rising over the course of the century.[19] Florentine women married at around seventeen or eighteen, with the figure rising by a year or two over the course of the century. Between 75 percent and 90 percent were married by their twentieth birthday.[20] Wealthier Florentine women married younger than the norm.[21] The actual age of women at marriage cannot be calculated for Venice, but dowry provisions in wills often set an expected age. If these orders were respected, noble girls in Venice would have married earlier than Florentines—at fifteen in the first half of the century, at sixteen in the second half.[22]

The smaller cities of the Veneto offer a strikingly different picture. In the families that produced memoirs, men married for the first time at about age twenty-five. The age of men for all marriages, including some late second unions, is about twenty-eight (see appendix, table 1.1). If men married more than a half decade earlier than their counterparts in metropolitan centers, women married two or three years later, at about age twenty. Child brides were rare, with only 4 percent married at sixteen and none younger. Only half were married by their twentieth birthday. Thus the age gap between spouses, up to thirteen years in Florence (and about fifteen for wealthy couples),[23] shrinks to less than six years for first marriages in the Veneto and seven years for all marriages. For Verona as a whole, the age difference between spouses stood at seven years in 1425, shrinking to 5.8 years in 1502.[24]

The Veneto data cease to look anomalous if the focus shifts to nonmetropolitan Tuscany and to areas beyond Italy. Florence, in marriage patterns as in many aspects of demography,[25] stands at an extreme even within its own region. Herlihy and Klapisch-Zuber have posited a spousal age gap of ten years or less for Prato and five other midsized cities. Lucchese men, like those of Verona and Vicenza, married at about twenty-five; they were on average less than a decade older than their brides.[26] Even so, figures for Tuscany as a whole might be on the high side: men in southern France married rather earlier, the women married a shade later, and the age difference between spouses was seldom over seven years.[27]

The extra-Florentine data, while hardly definitive, suggest some broader hypotheses. Hajnal, attempting to locate the development of modern marriage patterns in northwest Europe during the sixteenth through eighteenth centuries, noted a relatively high percentage of (especially female) celibacy and a late age at marriage for both women and men. He guessed that the situation in southern Europe in earlier times would be rather different.[28] The evidence noted so far supports his intuition. The percentage of women who did not marry was, indeed, quite small, and women overwhelmingly married before age twenty. Only the marital age of Florentine men—but not that of men elsewhere—lines up with the later northern model. The experience of most of fifteenth-century Italy and southern France belies any claim to modernity, as Hajnal defines it, and suggests Florentine precociousness.

The Italian figures also suggest broad regional differences in the cultural norms that determined when men and women would marry. Delayed marriage among Florentine men, for example, has been associated with a long apprenticeship and the need to establish economic independence and security before assuming the burdens of wife and children.[29] The argument is based on the assumption that marriage depends on economic and perhaps residential autonomy. This is not inevitable. The Veronese and Vicentine men who left memoirs—notaries, wool merchants, a physician—all faced periods of training comparable to those of patrician Florentines, but married significantly earlier. They were willing to marry before having accumulated enough capital to set up a separate household, and accepted a period in which their own conjugal nuclei were subordinate to the authority of a father or older brother.

Early female and late male marriage in Florence has been linked, as well, with the norms of prescriptive literature. Maffeo Vegio, for example, held that men should not marry before the age of thirty-six, when their bodies would be at full strength and more capable of producing healthy children. Giovanni Morelli recalled that in the golden age of the twelfth century his male ancestors had commonly married at forty or older, and he noted without surprise or dismay that his own father had married a girl of thirteen or less. Michele Savonarola cited with approval Albertus Magnus's preference for men to marry at thirty, and Aristotle's comment that men should marry at thirty-seven. Florentine moralists wished girls to marry young because they would incline to dishonorable behavior if not safely married, and because the husband would find a young wife easier to teach and control.[30]

Veronese and Vicentines did not heed that opinion. They drew, instead, on a local tradition that offered another emphasis. In the Trecento, Fra Paolino da Venezia had counseled women not to marry before eighteen, lest they bear sickly children; in the next century Padua's Michele Savonarola, citing Aristotle, agreed. Venetian humanist Francesco Barbaro looked at the constitution of Sparta and reached the same conclusion. Bernardino da Feltre even thought that couples should be the same age. Marriage, he said, was like a yoke, and the team had to be equal if the plow was to be pulled effectively. The puzzled onlooker might well ask, equal in age, or status (conditione), or kinship ties (parentade)? Bernardino would not distinguish: "Make it that they are equal."[31]

Differing regional patterns in marital ages suggest a final comment. Sympathetic historians have noted the traumatic effects of marriage on the bride, thrust suddenly into a foreign household at a tender age and subjected to the authority of a husband who, much older and preoccupied with business and civic obligations, might well prove emotionally distant. Images of the Florentine bride of seventeen "in tears" and the "terror-stricken child brides" of Venice, thirteen to fifteen,[32] indeed command our pity. Still, evidence for distress is purely speculative.[33] One might argue that girls had been trained throughout childhood for that very moment. Even if such were the case in the big cities, the shock must have been much reduced in Verona and Vicenza, where brides were nearly twenty and grooms about twenty-five; in Verona as a whole, some 70 percent to 80 percent of women married after the age of twenty-two.[34] Husbands were not much older, were not heads of household, usually were not launched on political careers, and did not travel on business. Because they were roughly at the same stage in the life cycle as their brides they were likely a good deal less remote.

Choice of Spouse

When the Arnaldi family began their memoir, in the early years of the Quattrocento, it was just emerging from the obscurity of earlier centuries but was still far from prominent. The Arnaldi lacked the patina of ancient lineage, they were not judges or lawyers, and they did not sit on elite magistracies. As notaries and all-purpose merchants, they were in a position to know a good deal about the economic resources and political standing of potential in-laws throughout the city. Their marital horizons, however, were more restricted than their business and political perspective. They deferred to neighborhood solidarity: seven of the first eight spouses lived in or next to the *sindicaria* of Carpagnon, where the family had long resided.[35] It is tempting to suggest that nonpatricians preferred residential endogamy; such was the case of the laboring classes in Florence.[36]

The early Arnaldi preferred, as well, spouses from a similar occupational and status group, even at the cost of economically disadvantageous unions.[37] Like the Arnaldi, the Revese were wool merchants and notaries.[38] The Fracanzani, Zugliano, dal Gorgo, Cardino (Feramosca), Botarini, and Clivone families—all Arnaldi in-laws—also placed sons in the College of Notaries.[39] The Botarini similarly were large-scale grain and land merchants. The Fracanzani and Zugliano joined the Arnaldi in the merchants' guild, and the Cardino, Fracanzani, and Zugliano were fellow members of the wool guild.[40] None of the in-law families were particularly old or possessed of bygone heroes, and none were yet sitting on the city's top councils.

In the first generation, marriage was the product of long years of association and sealed rather than created relationships between families. The Arnaldi used marriage not as an instrument of upward mobility, to effect a change in status, but as a means of consolidating their position within the upper-middle range. The situation changed around 1470, with a second generation. By that date the Arnaldi sat on the highest municipal councils, and had amassed lands so extensive that they could give up the notariate and retail trade. Indeed, they had begun to call themselves noble with some frequency.

They also arranged marriages with a new pool of partners. The families that now furnished spouses were near (Repeta and Poiana) or at (Sesso and Thiene) the top of Vicentine society. If new in-laws had once engaged in commerce or the notariate they had long abandoned any connection with dishonorable manual trades. Their economic bases were large rural estates, supplemented with income from usury and passive investment. They came from older families that could claim martial ancestors and were continually represented on executive magistracies. They were also the economic equals of the Arnaldi, as measured by tax assessments: the Arnaldi now had no need to sacrifice economic parity to accomplish social ends. Four of five spouses lived outside Carpagnon: when the Arnaldi moved up socially, they shifted focus from the neighborhood to a topographically diffuse, exogamous patriciate.[41]

Creating the Marriage

The Sequence of Rituals

The memoirs of the Veneto provide a fair overview of the "series of cere-monial stages" that created a marriage.[42] At the completion of preliminary negotiations, the father or close kin of the prospective bride met with the prospective groom, usually in a church, to establish a betrothal with words of future consent (*verba de futuro*). After a pause that varied from days to months, the couple met for the first time, usually in the bride's house, for a cluster of rites that included the exchange of words of present consent (*verba de praesenti*) and either the placement of a ring on the bride's finger or a sim-ple touching of her hand. Finalizing arrangements occasioned a further delay (about eight months on average) before the groom or members of his fam-ily led the bride to the marital house (the *ductio* or *traditio in domus mariti*). The Veneto sequence does not deviate much from that of other cities.[43]

Taken as a whole, the memoir notices seem clear enough. Each entry, though, recorded different components of the sequence, omitting some and emphasizing others, and placed those components in different order. The lack of uniform description suggests that observers did not perceive a single mo-ment that effected the union or a standard sequence of rituals. They were not sure, for example, that the exchange of words of present consent was necessarily the operative rite. Gaspare II Arnaldi "touched the hand [of Gio-vanna da Schio] with words of present consent" on 13 March, but "married" (*sposai*) her three days later; seven weeks separated the hand-touch and the *sposai* in one Stoppi marriage. Other notices called the *verba de praesenti* a promise only, and indicate a time lag between exchange of present consent and the moment when the groom actually married (*desponsavit*) the bride. The exchange of *verba de praesenti* might take place before or after the ring ceremony, and several days might separate the two. Manfredo Repeta, un-certain as to what signified what, retreated into generic language: daughter Lucrezia "married" (*se marida*) on one day and "was wed" (*fu spoxada*) on another.[44]

Veneto authors were not particularly ignorant. The many English court cases validating or disqualifying marriages show that their northern coun-terparts were equally unclear as to which ceremony established a binding marriage.[45] Confusion reigned in Italy as well, and occasioned grievous loss of honor to humble women such as the Feltrines Fiorenza dalla Croce and Elena Cumano and the Tuscan Lusanna di Benedetto. They pointed to some exchange of word and gesture as proof of valid matrimony; their upper-class seducers convinced authorities otherwise.[46] The variety of marital rituals, and widespread disagreement concerning their precise meanings, might well bewilder the well-intentioned and give opportunity to the devious.

Doctrine, it is true, seems to show more certainty. Agreeing that mutual consent alone could legitimize a union, canon lawyers and theologians in the twelfth century worked to uncover the moment when valid consent had been made. The Bolognese jurist Gratian argued that the betrothal *(desponsatio)* established an "initiated" but valid marriage *(matrimonium initiatum)*, which was then "perfected" *(perfectum* or *ratum)* by consummation. He was countered by a group centered in Paris and headed by Peter Lombard. Exhuming and transforming Roman law, northern writers divided the *desponsatio* into stages of *verba de futuro* and *verba de praesenti*, downgraded the former to a promise, and gave operative value to the latter. Exchange of words of present consent by the bride and groom alone created a "perfect" marriage; consummation was a consequence but not a cause of a valid union. When the canonist pope Alexander III, following a stay in France, shifted his position to support the northern model, the triumph of Peter Lombard's position was assured. Local synods, church courts, pastoral manuals, penitentials, sermons, and guidebooks for confessors spread the word to the faithful.[47]

The triumph of present-consent theory did not, however, eradicate alternatives. Both Peter Lombard and Alexander III reluctantly admitted that future consent combined with consummation created a legitimate union, though they preferred the *verba de praesenti*. Gratian's stress on consummation, though dismissed in France, remained normative in Italy.[48] Contemporaries noted a considerable admixture of usages on the local level, as strains from Roman, Lombard,[49] and several sorts of canon law liberally combined with purely popular rituals.[50] If there can be a covering doctrine, it might be the canonists' dictum "A marriage is legitimate if contracted according to legal form or provincial custom."[51]

The profusion of alternatives gave provincial fathers considerable discretion at each stage in the marriage sequence. For example, canon law held that betrothal by *verba de futuro* constituted a "mutual engagement," expressing the full consent of both parties for eventual union.[52] Veneto memoirs indicate, however, that the girl's consent to a future union, if indeed it was even sought, was not regarded as worth recording. Males alone effected betrothal: the prospective bride "was promised to me by words of future consent," or her father promised her to the intended groom.[53] Ancient Germanic usage, after all, allowed the man who held legal authority over a woman (the *mundualdus*) to establish betrothal on her behalf; some canonists held that a father could betrothe his children, though such betrothals required eventual ratification by the actual parties.[54] If the girl did not raise an explicit protest, her silence was taken as tacit consent and she was obliged to marry, under penalty of excommunication.[55]

She might not have much say in the next stage either, as fathers and brothers claimed the right to exchange words of present consent on her behalf. In Andrea Arnaldi's memoir, for example, Caterina Botarini "was promised to me by *verba de praesenti*" in 1432; he used exactly the same words for his second marriage in 1441. His daughter Margarita "was by me promised by *verba de praesenti*" to her husband Simone Revese. The formula violated canon law on two counts. First, Arnaldi regarded the words of present consent as a promise only, not as actually creating the union. Matrimony was not complete until the bestowing of the ring or touching of the hand, a separate and sometimes later ceremony. Second, he insisted that someone other than the bride actually uttered the words that bound her to the union. Bartolomeo Muronovo did not use legal language, but his words, too, suggest an authoritarian approach to daughters' marriages: "I had her married," or "I gave her as wife."[56]

Here, too, custom sanctioned the father's directive role. King Saul, after all, gave (*dedit* in the Vulgate) his daugher Michal to David (I Samuel 18:20–27). Under Roman law, marriage was made by consent, but consent might be made by parents or whoever held *patria potestas;* only much later, and without complete success, did the Church reinterpret the principle to demand "consent by the partners themselves."[57] Germanic law held that the father holding the *mundium* of a girl could *desponsare* her without her consent, and Hincmar of Reims wrote that a lawful marriage was created when a free woman was given by her father. Furthermore, strict application of the doctrine of mutual consent would admit the validity of clandestine marriages, which were universally reviled. So Gratian and Cardinal Ostiensis argued that betrothals and marriages were not valid without the consent of fathers, and statutes in Vicenza and Verona (and elsewhere) imposed hefty fines on men who contracted marriages without the approval of the bride's kin.[58]

The final stage in the marital sequence, the ceremonial transfer of the wife to her new home, is the common denominator in the memoirs' records of marriage. Nearly all mentioned the time and circumstances of the procession; in several cases, entries provided more detail about the transfer than about any of the preceding ceremonies. We are told, for example, that Tommaso Arnaldi's aunt and cousin accompanied Elisabetta dal Gorgo because of the illness of his brother Andrea, that six women accompanied Angela Chiara, that women accompanied Lucia, and that Gaspare II personally led his wife to the Arnaldi house.[59] In Germany, England, France, and other regions as well the procession to the husband's house was given ritual emphasis equal to that of the exchange of consent and the conveying of the ring.[60]

It is not hard to see why writers gave that emphasis. The *ductio*, not the wedding, reconfigured the household and the family at large. Since the dowry had to be settled if not actually paid before the *traditio* took place, transfer also marked the reordering of the patrimony. In the Veneto, as was the case at Rome and Augsburg and (at some periods) Florence, transfer alone, and not the exchange of *verba de praesenti*, authorized sexual relations between husband and wife. In only one Veneto case out of about fifty was a child born less than nine months after the *traditio*.[61] Amid uncertainty regarding the sequence and the meaning of marital rituals, the *ductio* was the end point, the moment when there could be no doubt that a valid marriage had been established.

Mainstream lawyers, it is true, so stressed the exchange of present consent as creating a "perfected" union that they gave little value to subsequent acts. Even they might acknowledge that the *ductio* made public and unmistakable demonstration of consent; Bartolus thought that the *traditio* had the effect of proving publicity and "rendering effective the consent," whereas his pupil Baldus regarded it as one of the proofs of a valid marriage. And, of course, there remained many who persisted in the view of Gratian and Bernard of Pavia that consummation—authorized only by the *ductio*—was the constitutive act in forming a marriage.[62]

The public passage of the bride from paternal to marital house equally served a social imperative: as marriage reassembled the social order, it was necessary that the community at large witness the critical act of transfer. Moreover, because the words of the ceremony were susceptible to misunderstanding and abuse, they required ratification by physical gestures such as the *ductio*, which were public and blatant.[63] This was particularly important in Italy, where the exchange of consent usually took place in a private dwelling before a handful of close relatives and friends. The Veneto families that produced memoirs respected that belief: some 60 percent of transfers took place on Sunday, which was not only a holy day but a holiday, when the greatest proportion of the populace might be on city streets to view the passage (see appendix, table 1.3).

Authorities took that reasoning a step further, demanding that not only the transfer but the ceremony itself receive witness. To remove all doubt that consent was coerced, a notary, judge, or priest should interrogate the bride and groom as to their true intentions. A spiritual rationale held that, as a marriage constituted a sacramental union before God and his people, the community of the faithful should serve as witness and the community's spiritual director should supervise the proceedings. Clandestine marriages escaped all controls; if sustained, they threw the serious issue of the dowry into turmoil; if overturned, they threatened dishonor to the spurned party. Both Church and lay authorities wanted positive proof of the wedding, preferably by an official and at least by neutral parties.[64]

Florentines largely respected these desires, and a notary usually presided over and/or recorded the marriage; Lusanna di Benedetto's failure to obtain the services of a notary was both anomalous and ruinous to her case. Legal norms in the north pushed in the same direction: Paduan statutes required a public instrument of marriage, Trevisan law required interrogation by a judge, and Bolognese ordinances ordered registration of marriage in municipal books. Venetians commonly married before notaries, or at least an early Quattrocento traveler thought they did.[65] Still, local usage was not uniform. Milanese law, for example, made no provision for a notary at any stage in the sequence. While people in Vicenza and Verona ordered notaries to record dowry confessions, which is another matter altogether, they did not order a record of marital rituals—or at least notarial registers and family archives preserve no such instruments. Memorialists married in a private world of words, not in the public world of legal agents.

To secure public attestation of free consent, and to underscore the sacramentality of marriage, Alexander III and the Fourth Lateran Council of 1215 urged Church bans before marriage, a wedding presided over by the parish priest before the church door ("ante facie ecclesie"), or at the very least a nuptial blessing during the procession to the groom's house. Reformers from the twelfth century on offered model liturgies for church weddings. A proper wedding, declared San Bernardino, began with a Mass in which both man and woman took Communion.[66]

Because mutual consent alone made the marriage, and because the couple mutually administered the Sacrament, neither priest nor holy setting could add anything to it. Thus the Church enjoined a religious matrimony but could not nullify a marriage contracted otherwise.[67] Until the Council of Trent, the sacralization of marriage proceeded at a slow pace. In northern France and England, marriages might be concluded before church doors, with priests presiding, though recent studies conclude that a majority of English marriages were made out of church and French evidence for church weddings derives from model *ordines* rather than praxis.[68] In the rest of Europe, private or civil marriages remained the norm. Constant reiteration of synodal statutes prescribing marriages before priests, for example, suggests that the dictates of the Fourth Lateran were widely ignored. In fourteenth- and fifteenth-century Toulouse, the "church ceremony was not an essential feature of matchmaking."[69]

The same was true in Italy, with a few exceptions in the marginal phases of the marriage sequence.[70] Florentines, notably, manifested "indifference to the recommendations of the Church." Marriages at the bride's home, absence of priests, and omission of benediction or wedding Mass indicate a casual attitude to ecclesiastical ratification and a determined resistance to the messages of Church-sponsored myths and images glorifying a sacralized matrimony.[71] Memorialists of the Veneto also preferred to marry at home, without benefit of clergy. Girolamo Stoppi, it is true, *sposai* Claudia Boldero after a priest's benediction. But this took place seven weeks after he "took her as wife" and "gave her my hand"; it but sealed an already legitimate marriage. It also took place in 1565, when the strictures of the Council of Trent were beginning to be felt.[72]

Prior to Trent, memoirs make only two references to religion in the marriage sequence. First, the *verba de futuro* for Andrea's marriage to Marcella Fracanzani was pronounced in the church of Santa Maria dei Servi. Andrea and Nicolo Fracanzani needed a church, however, not the Church. Sacred space gave greater solemnity to the promises, but did not signify recourse to ecclesiastical authority; no priestly presence is recorded. A church also represented neutral space, appropriate for the conclusion of negotiations. Second, Simone Revese took Margarita Arnaldi to the marital house "in the name of our Lord Jesus Christ, and with his benediction."[73] Evidently Simone and Margarita detoured the *traditio* procession past a church, where a priest blessed the union. But they were not married before or in a church. None of the Arnaldi were. Anyway the blessing came a full ten months after the marriage, ratifying but hardly creating the union. This is the only notice of its kind among fifty marriages mentioned in the memoirs. If couples in Verona and Vicenza went before a priest with any frequency, they did not regard the event as worth recording.

Seasonality

The timing of marriages was not random. Canon law counseled against matrimony during penitential seasons: Advent through Epiphany, Lent, and Pentecost through the feast of St. John the Baptist. At least a third and as much as 40 percent of the year was off-limits. Failure to observe these guidelines would not invalidate a union, but might require penance and temporary separation before the Church would bestow its blessing.[74]

Families of Veneto memorialists sometimes respected and sometimes ignored ecclesiastical prescriptions. In twenty-seven cases in which a core moment—exchange of *verba de praesenti*, conveying of rings, or indefinite "married" *(nubsit, desponsavit, sposai)*—can be dated, they indeed obeyed the Advent prohibition: a single marriage was made during that season, but eleven (41 percent) clustered immediately before and after it (see appendix, table 1.2). They also avoided Pentecost, with only a single possible instance (the exact day in June was not specified, and might have fallen after the 24th). Lent, on the other hand, was actually a favored time for marriage: six (22 percent) were made then, compared with the 13 percent of marriages that would have fallen during Lent if matrimony had been spaced randomly throughout the calendar. Of fourteen Freschi marriages, one took place during Lent and none during Advent; five clustered around Advent.

The moment of marriage was not the target of Church restrictions. Ecclesiastical intent was to banish distractions from penitential observance: raucous feasting and sexual union. Marriage could well take place during reserved seasons, because the bride remained quietly and chastely in the paternal home for some time. *Traditio* to the marital household alone brought celebration and consummation. To gauge respect for canonical prohibitions, then, we need to look at the day of *ductio* rather than the day of matrimony. The number of dated cases is not great, only seventeen, but the pattern is clear: not a single bride went to her husband's house during Advent, Lent, or Pentecost. The greatest number of *traditiones* (47 percent) took place in January and February, between Advent and Lent. A further, purely secular cluster of transfers is found in September and October (29 percent), when harvest markets filled cities with foodstuffs for feasts.

Marriage was specific to day as well as to season. Wednesday and Friday were discouraged because they were days of abstinence. Sunday was encouraged, perhaps to share in the sacrality of the day and certainly to maximize publicity. Venetians called the husband's postconsummation present to the bride a "Monday gift," in expectation of a Sunday *traditio;* indeed, they considered any day except Sunday cursed. Gaetans and Florentines typically conveyed the ring on Thursday or Sunday, and, like Romans, most commonly transferred the bride on Sunday.[75]

Here, too, the Veneto memorialists followed norms more closely with regard to transfer than to marriage itself (see appendix, table 1.3). Matrimonial prohibitions were relatively weak: while Sunday was indeed preferred (44 percent of cases) and Friday avoided (4 percent), there was no particular dislike of a Wednesday wedding (22 percent). Again, the wedding would not violate rules of abstinence since the bride remained in her house. What did violate those norms was feast or consummation at the time of the *ductio;* here Veneto families scrupulously respected the rules. Because the bedding of bride and groom would occur in the evening, after the sundown that marked the beginning of the next day, it was licit to transfer the bride on Wednesday (20 percent of cases) and even better to transfer her on Sunday (60 percent). Tuesday transfers (with consummation on penitential Wednesday) were rare (13 percent), and Thursday transfers (with consummation on forbidden Friday) unknown.

Folklore, too, set rules for the seasonality of marriage. On twenty-four "Egyptian days," declared "all Greek authors," terrible things would befall a person who married: "if he takes a wife, he will have little good thereby, and he will stay only a short time with her, in poverty." A second list of twenty-nine "unhappy or unfortunate" days does not specify the curse.[76] Authors recorded these texts in the belief that they possessed merit. Families also, it seems, gave them credence in scheduling marriage. The two lists deemed some fifty-one days inauspicious, or 14 percent of all days, but only 7 percent of marriages and transfers took place on unfavorable days. The figure would decline to 5 percent if we exclude the Stoppi, who were newcomers to the region and perhaps unfamiliar with local beliefs, and would drop farther to 3 percent if we exclude one marriage on Epiphany Sunday, when the holiness of the day might be expected to counteract bad fortune. Gaspare II Arnaldi, at least, apparently relied on the lists in arranging his marriage, splitting its stages between March 13 and 16 to avoid unhappy days on the 14th, 15th, and 17th.

Dowries

Dowries were universal in Verona and Vicenza, at least among those who documented their marriages. Intended to "sustain the burdens of matrimony" and support the widow thereafter,[77] they also ratified the social and moral legitimacy of the bride and her family: thus Tommaso Arnaldi provided dowries for the daughters of brother Battista because he was avid and eager *(cupidus et amator)* for the honor of both brother and nieces.[78] The dowry represented the daughter's share of the patrimony:[79] when Veneto women confessed receipt of their dowries they renounced further claims to the inheritance. Their share was to be a "fitting" *(congrua)* proportion of the patrimony, though it need not be equal to brothers' shares; in a few cases, daughters received portions equal to those of sons, though this was not the norm.[80] The dowry constituted the lion's share of goods exchanged at marriage; extradotal goods brought by the wife were seldom mentioned, and then were not substantial,[81] and if husbands brought gifts to the marriage these were not recorded.[82] Dowries could not be squandered during marriage and were to be restored to a wife upon her husband's death: he pledged goods as "counterdowry" as security for eventual restitution of the dowry.[83] If the wife predeceased her spouse, without children, he received a half share of the dowry.[84]

The striking feature of Veneto dowries is their inflation. The first marriage of the Arnaldi memoir, that of Gaspare I to Caterina Zugliano in 1407, brought in 200 ducats.[85] His sons' marriages in the 1430–40 period brought in an average of 317 ducats.[86] Three dowries averaged 433 ducats in the 1450s,[87] and the figure rose to over 500 ducats for the five dowries of the 1460s.[88] When documentation resumes in 1496–1502, three dowries averaged 3,167 ducats.[89] That hypertrophy is the more remarkable because the tax assessments of the Arnaldi and their in-laws did not rise in absolute value or relative to those of fellow citizens: families committed progressively larger shares of the patrimony to dowries. In similar fashion, Bartolomeo dal Bovo raised the dowries of his four daughters by 50 percent in a short time span, from 300 ducats for the eldest to 450 ducats for the youngest, while Freschi dowries rose by 138 percent between 1452–77 and 1520–32.[90]

Dowry inflation has been noted throughout Italian cities. The phenomenon was not new, if literary commonplaces are any guide: Dante perceived fathers of daughters in distress well before his time.[91] The hardships posed by inflation were so severe by the fifteenth century as to preoccupy civic leaders, who worried that increasing demands would ruin families and/or reduce nuptuality. In 1425 Florentines created a municipal dowry fund which, because of its social importance and vast cash flow, remained central to marital strategy and public finance for over a century. The Venetian *scuola* of St. John the Evangelist did the same three years earlier, though the nature and scale of the fund's operations are unknown.[92]

Why dowries rose so dramatically has been the source of considerable speculation. Susan Mosher Stuard, for example, has taken growing dowries as an indicator of greater aggregate wealth and liquidity among the well-to-do in Ragusa.[93] Indicators in the Veneto suggest an economy that was indeed growing, but not sufficient growth in personal incomes to sustain skyrocketing expenditures on marriage. David Herlihy has offered a demographic reading: high age differentials at marriage, coupled with normal midlife male mortality, produced a surplus of marriageable women whose families had to compete for husbands with progressively higher dowries.[94] In the Veneto, however, the much lower age gap between husbands and wives would reduce the applicability of the model. Stanley Chojnacki has attributed Venetian inflation to a snowball effect and changes in women's attitudes: widows possessed of ever-larger dowries increasingly dowered their female kin, fueling self-perpetuating upward pressure on dowries.[95] Women in Verona and Vicenza, however, left only small amounts to dower other women, assigning the bulk of their dowries to sons.

The single factor supported by the Veneto evidence is status competition. Ambitious and well-off families bid up dowries to attract husbands from higher social strata, and the rest of the population followed suit simply to maintain their positions. Those aspiring to the patriciate absorbed short-term losses; if they were successful, the balance sheet corrected itself when inferiors bid for their offspring and equals matched their dowries. Alternately, patricians accepted high dowries as obvious markers of their distance from the masses. In any case, the economic burden on any one family balanced itself out because dowry exchange is a zero-sum game, and in the long run as much would flow in as would flow out.[96]

Moralists, it is true, decried the use of marriage and dowries for social advancement. Giovanni Dominici regarded the inflation of dowries as a form of selling oneself, and warned darkly of the disasters that awaited those who married above their station. Alberti, too, wanted equality of husband and wife: marrying too high incurred obligation and cast one's own family into the shadows. Giovanni Conversino wanted economic equality of spouses: a wealthier wife would boss her husband around, and squandering the patrimony to secure a prestigious husband was "insane." Bernardino da Feltre extended his metaphor of marriage as a yoked team to urge that husband and wife be of the same rank *(conditione)*. Fathers such as Giovanni Morelli, though, felt that marriage strategies should be directed to "raise yourself up," and the fact that the Morelli gave more in dowries than they received indicates that they were willing to pay for socially advantageous unions.[97]

Strategies pursued by the Arnaldi in the two phases of their social development suggest that if dowries paid and received were comparable, a family was marrying within a generalized social grouping; if a family gave daughters greater dowries than it received from daughters-in-law, it was investing capital to attract a better sort of alliance. The first generation of Arnaldi, up to about 1470, intermarried with families that came from their occupational group; the dowries they paid out roughly equaled those they received from in-laws. The Arnaldi seem not to have aspired to upward mobility, and set commensurate dowies to consolidate their position among the notarial-commercial ranks. The second generation, however, openly aspired to nobility. In 1502, when Silvestro Arnaldi simultaneously married a daughter and son to offspring of the very great Thiene family, he used differential dowries as an inducement. Silvestro paid 4,000 ducats for daughter Laura's dowry, but took in only 1,500 ducats from son Andrea's bride.[98] That 4,000 ducats was about double or triple the prevailing rate among the city's nobility. The Thiene needed money; the Arnaldi needed ratification of newly acquired standing and were willing to pay the price.

So, too, the Veronese Pietro Verità acknowledged that dowries had to be calibrated with the quality of the groom, giving his testamentary commissioners power to augment his daughters' dowries "according to the status and rank of their husbands." In turn, social climbers sought unions with the well-established Verità, and paid handsomely for the privilege: the 1,500-ducat dowry paid by Filippo Pindemonte to Michele Verità was nearly twice that given in any other Pindemonte marriage.[99]

THE LAMENTATIONS of fathers and city councillors might, however, be taken with a grain of salt. Those who decried inflated dowries were the same men who arranged inflated dowries for their own daughters. Neither the weak authority model (patriarch-politicians were helpless before upward pressures) nor the hypocrisy model (they preached one position in public and practiced another in private) is convincing. Perhaps, instead, high dowries were not so disruptive as they appear at face value. Three types of evidence from the Veneto suggest that we might question the degree to which sharply higher nominal dowries truly jeopardized patrimonies, the marriage market, and brides' families.

First, dowry confessions can be fictive documents. When it is possible to compare dowry confessed to dowry actually received, the gap is often considerable. In one extreme case, the Vicentine patrician Gaspare Monza acknowledged receipt of six hundred ducats for the dowry of his wife Jacopa Rabi; he later admitted that "in rei veritate" he had received nothing. Verona's Pietro Verità formally declared that daughter Ginevra had been given a dowry of six hundred ducats, and her husband confessed to receiving two hundred ducats as a first installment; "in veritate," Pietro admitted on his deathbed that the dowry totaled only five hundred ducats and the husband received but a hundred.[100] In such cases, the husband's family was obliged to restore the sum stipulated in the false confession, though it had received less: the husband's family agreed to contribute a share (or, in the Monza case, the entirety) of the dowry.[101]

Second, dowries were seldom conveyed at a single moment. In 1496, for example, Silvestro Arnaldi promised four thousand ducats as the dowry of his daughter Cassandra, but stretched payments over fifteen years.[102] The obligation would have been unbearable if demanded in a lump sum, but installments averaging 267 ducats annually would not wreck the family's wealth. The cash portion of the dowry often consisted of credits owed by third parties, which still had to be collected by the husband's family, often over several years.[103] In yet another form, Domenico Uberti designated the dowry of daughter Caterina as part of the capitalization of a commercial company formed with her husband and brother-in law: he assumed a long-term obligation, but did not have to come up with any cash at the time of marriage.[104]

Third, a chronic shortage of liquidity in the Veneto led to widespread assignment of land and land rights rather than cash.[105] Property in the region was capitalized at 6 percent, so that a dowry of fields valued at fifty ducats would produce rents of three ducats annually. The immediate monetary loss to the bride's family did not remotely approach the sum stipulated in dowry confessions, and the husband's family accumulated the dowry only over a decade or more. Moreover, in land dowries the bride's family generally conveyed not full title to the property but only the right to collect rents. Her family invariably retained the capacity to reclaim ("francate") that right of collection for the nominal value of the dowry, over an extended period. For example, the Arnaldi in 1456 assigned forty *campi* of land in the village of La Longa and half of their house in Vicenza to Marco Clivone, to cover most of the dowry of Angela Chiara Arnaldi. Over the next fourteen years, the Arnaldi produced small sums of money and assigned miscellaneous lands until they recovered both properties.[106] Francating portions as funds became available, they could promise inflated dowries without jeopardizing short-term fiscal stability or long-term patrimony. And they cemented a close alliance with the Clivone family, binding debtor to creditor in mutual interdependence and risk.

In practice, then, newly married men did not enjoy a sudden infusion of ready money. The income from dotal lands was paltry, and long terms of payment meant that the dowry was an annuity, not a lump sum.[107] The dowry could not fund a new household or launch a business career, and so belied the classic definition that it was intended to sustain the burdens of matrimony. Nor were brides' families suddenly drained of wealth even when, as with Silvestro Arnaldi, the stipulated sum was very great indeed. Nonliquid dowries, protracted payment, and the possibility of francation also suggest modification of the thesis that the dowry represents a one-way, one-time cash flow from bride's family to groom's family, complementing the brusque separation of the girl from her natal family and her definitive integration into the marital family.[108] The amount stipulated in the dowry confession thus had symbolic rather than purely economic consequences. It measured not wealth actually transferred but such intangible factors as the social valuation of the union and the contracting parties, good faith, and reputation, or, in other words, status itself.

Constante matrimonio

Spousal *affectio*

Marriages among the Veneto memorialists lasted, on average, somewhat over two decades before the death of a spouse sundered the union.[109] While perfect strangers at the moment of marriage, husbands and wives had plenty of time to get to know each other. The memoirs even hint at what men, at least, eventually thought of their partners, provided we resist overconfidence in our abilities to penetrate the emotional world of the past.[110]

The meaning of their words is uncertain. When Bonaventura Bovi noted the death of his "sweetest" *(dulcissima)* wife Isabeta,[111] and when Andrea Arnaldi mentioned his "fondness" *(dilectio)* for his recently deceased wife Caterina Botarini and called her the sharer of his fortunes *(consors)* rather than simply wife *(uxor)*, neither may have intended sentimentality. Andrea left other clues, however, which suggest at least a deep respect for Caterina. He twice spoke of her in the superlative: she had been a *dilectissima consors.* Usually a spare writer, he carefully recorded the date, day, and hour of her death, noted the date of the onset of her "infirmity" (a fatal childbirth), and commended her body and soul to Christ. As if deflecting and thus alleviating sorrow with a flurry of details, he recalled the date and duration of their marriage, and the birthdates and present ages of their surviving children.[112] He never devoted such saturated attention to any male in the family.

The writers of Verona and Vicenza were far less eloquent than many Florentines who wrote movingly of their wives' deaths. They offered no equivalent to the Bolognese Gaspare Nadi's lament that "I loved her more than seemed possible, because I don't believe there is or has ever been a woman better than she."[113] Yet Veneto writers did not waste words: when they recorded a fact we can be certain it mattered to them, and they scrupulously noted salient information about their wives. Three times in a single page, for example, Andrea Arnaldi recorded the date, saint's day, and hour of his second wife's birth, repeatedly giving Marcella a concrete identity by locating her in worldly chronology and celestial patronage. He felt that posterity needed reassurance that sister-in-law Cassandra Revese had "died to our Lord Jesus Christ, with all the comforts of the most holy mother Church, with a sound mind to the end."[114] Each time a child was born, the Verità and Arnaldi repeated the name of both mother and father: wives were partners in procreation, not mere agents of parturition.

There is nothing surprising in such expressions. Venerable tradition, after all, had expected a warm and trusting conjugal union. Jesus himself told men and women to leave their families and cleave unto their spouses, to become one flesh. St. Paul required that husbands show love *(caritas)* to their wives; when he set the union of husband and wife as analog to the union of Christ and his Church, he defined the bond of both unions as unswerving love. Hugh of St. Victor interpreted the Epistle to the Ephesians to require mutual *caritas,* solicitude, affection, compassion, consolation, and devotion, while the canonist Alexander III took the *maritalis affectio* (intent to treat each other reciprocally as husband and wife) of Roman law, which had lacked emotional connotations, pushed it toward our "affection," and made it requisite to a binding marriage.[115]

Renaissance Italians, too, expressed high ideals. Alberti valued the good wife as a "constant companion," and devoted long passages to the mutual pleasure, benevolence, intimacy, good will, and shared emotions of the conjugal union. Poggio defined marriage as a "bond of concord" by which "two wills, two souls are joined in one." Francesco Barbaro extolled the joys of having a good wife; his and others' high valuation of procreation, nursing, and domestic management equally honored the virtuous spouse. Civic humanists saw the family as microcosm of society and marriage as foundation of the social order; moralists stressed reciprocal service, concord, respect, and *dilectio,* while enjoining men to remain sexually faithful and not beat their wives. Even the misogynist Bernardino da Feltre thought the good wife the most honored of humans, "half the life of her husband"; she wears the Virgin's crown of twelve stars, and is a radiant sun. A good union was the "most beautiful" of the human relationships pleasing to God. Paolo da Certaldo, who otherwise found women "empty of head and frivolous of heart" and authorized an occasional beating, ranked the love of a good wife among "the greatest loves that exist," and thought a "good wife the crown and honor and fortune of a husband."[116]

Whether people in the Renaissance expected or experienced romantic love must remain an open question. Historians have concluded that their medieval forebears had known both doctrines of sentimentality and episodes of sincere, even passionate love within marriage. It is tempting to infer the same from the Veronese Leonardo Montagna's *Zampolina,* a sprawling collection of prose and poetry mourning the loss of his wife.[117] At the very least, respect, trust, and companionship flourished in some later marriages. Contino Stoppi, for example, mused on the death of his *dilettissima consorte:* "she passed from this mortal to a happier life, leaving behind many who were disconsolate and in great tribulation over her death." Contino himself died within two months, his final sickness "fed by a melancholic humor contracted from sorrow for madonna Valeria his wife."[118] What wives thought of their husbands was seldom recorded, but trace indicators such as wives' preference to be buried in the tombs of marital rather than natal families, and scattered episodes such as one Veronese woman's bequest of two hundred ducats "to her beloved husband,"[119] indicate occasional high regard.

Affection cannot be proven, but trust certainly can. A wife who successfully supervised the domestic regime and raised children to physical, moral, and spiritual maturity commanded appreciation that frequently carried over into testamentary hopes that she continue as manager in widowhood.[120] Gaspare I Arnaldi named his wife Caterina Zugliano as executor of his will, and demanded that his heirs honor and reverence her and obey her warnings and advice. Son Tommaso's will ordered that his sons and daughters marry only with the approval *(scientia)* of his widow Elisabetta dal Gorgo, and that she be treated well, loved, and honored by stepson Gaspare II if she chose to remain in the house. Aventino Fracastoro wished his widow not only to live in the house but to be *domina* over the household, and threatened to withdraw his blessing upon his sons if they did not show reverence and obedience to her. He once called her frugal, and once *frugalissima:* she could well be given responsibility over goods and children.[121]

It is true that such testamentary provisions are colored by family self-interest. Keeping the widow happy at home ensured that she would not take her dowry and go elsewhere. In the more fulsome Venetian and English wills, however, historians have seen signs of husbands' high regard for and trust in the wives they were leaving behind. Venetian husbands increasingly made wives the sole or decisive executors of their estates, used personalized language to express affection, and made significant bequests to wives over and above their dowries. Warm feelings and self-interest are not, after all, mutually exclusive. Even if expressions of love and trust were merely formulaic, that does not alter the argument: formula itself demonstrates that "affection between spouses had become normative."[122]

Women's Dotal and Property Rights

Battista Arnaldi, the prodigal who never returned, was already in debt when he demanded his inheritance and left the fraternal household at the age of twenty-two. For two decades he sold pieces of land, and brothers Andrea and Tommaso provided relief from creditors. Perhaps he was a compulsive gambler: in 1443 the brothers offered an allowance if he would give up chess. His life continued to unravel. Relations bought his land, rented him a house, took in one daughter, and eventually dowered both daughters. By midcentury his behavior was unsupportable: Andrea and Tommaso cut him off, and a prospective son-in-law refused to negotiate with him. The family memoir does not record the date of his death.[123]

Semiramide Thiene at first acted the model wife. Shortly after her marriage in 1437, with Battista's consent, she named her brother and her husband procurators to collect lands and monies owed her. Less than a year later, she bought a small piece of land for herself and her husband, but she then acted without Battista's consent and specified that the purchase price come "out of the money from her dowry." In 1445 she bought land independently, without reference to her husband. A year later the break was complete. Semiramide began her will with the request that Battista could not undo *(contrafacere)* its provisions, then commanded that he not impede alienation of her goods after her death.[124]

This exceptional case hints at several norms. Semiramide's first transactions are entirely conventional, reflecting the economic and judicial limitations on married women. She required a procurator in court proceedings, as did Florentine wives. She could not act or defend in court without a surety; at least she was better off than Florentine women, who needed consent by a male guardian to effect legal transactions. The husband, here and throughout Italy, administered the dowry and reaped all profits from it. Under normal circumstances a wife in the Veneto and elsewhere could not alienate her dowry or extradotal goods during marriage. Local statute declared that goods purchased by a wife were presumed to belong to the husband. Custom also worked against her. Jurists such as Baldus had advised women to secure notarized inventories of nondotal goods they brought to marriage, but this seldom happened in the Veneto and a widow would find it hard to prove that household goods did not, in fact, belong to her late husband. Finally, the wife could bequeath goods to her husband or anyone else only if she left an equal share to her children.[125]

Semiramide's recovery of control over her dowry is no more remarkable. If women were deemed "weak and feeble," likely to jeopardize their own or their families' interests by light-headed decision, and therefore required male protection from their own poor judgment,[126] they equally needed protection from errant husbands. Vicentine law sanctioned a woman's right to sue her insolvent husband for an equivalent of the dowry, and further gave her the capacity to assign a tutor to children if her husband dissipated their goods as well; he could not then touch their patrimony.[127] Julius Kirshner has concluded that later medieval legal opinion not only revived but reinforced the Roman law remedy of lawsuit against a husband verging on poverty *(vergens ad inopiam)*.[128] Nor did women find it a merely theoretical resource, as the case of the peasant Flora attests. Appearing before a judge in 1451, Flora charged that her husband "through mismanagement of his goods was verging on poverty," thus endangering restitution of her dowry. The judge granted her the right to sequester agricultural goods from her husband's lands up to the value of 213 *lire*.[129] Many Toulousaines and some 460 Florentine women secured similar rulings.[130]

Lawyers and legislators, in fact, widened the entire range of protections afforded dowries. Statute in Vicenza and elsewhere was clear: during marriage the wife held a hypothec on the husband's goods for her dowry, and he could not alienate it even with her permission. She, in turn, could alienate her dowry if threatened with starvation, but only if a judge ascertained that the husband had not pressured her to claim poverty. When another Flora in 1483 petitioned to sell land to feed herself and her nine children, the podestà himself questioned her privately and took testimony from her kin to determine that the request was freely made.[131]

Dowries, declared the law, held preference over claims by creditors.[132] In 1422, fearful that women might be forced to obligate or even alienate their dowries to pay husbands' debts, Vicentine councils ruled that women could only cede dowries and *parafrenalia* in case of hunger, capture of husbands by foreign enemies, or husbands' physical disabilities.[133] Owners disliked the principle that dotal claims constituted a hypothec on husbands' lands, because tenants possessing *dominium utile* might refuse to pay rents or repay loans on account of dowry commitments—one piece of Verità land had been obligated for three dowries, and the family had to forgive considerable arrears to regain full control[134]—but they could not alter it. Creditors and lawyers worried that devious couples might shelter assets behind the wall of the wife's hypothec, but here, too, the law stood firm.[135] Further, a husband's testamentary bequests supplementing the dowry fully belonged to his widow and could not be impounded by his heirs. Attempts to safeguard patrimonies in the male line by imposing a blanket entail suffered defeat with the ruling that Chiara Squarzi's dowry, at least, was excluded from her brother's inheritance.[136]

. Even the ever-hungry Venetian fisc made no headway against dotal claims. Early in the fifteenth century the Senate specified that a portion of goods seized from mainland rebels be designated for return to wives after the deaths of their exiled husbands. Later magistrates not only upheld that law but allowed wives of rebels to petition for the return of dotal goods during their husbands' lifetimes.[137] In midcentury tax officials complained that subjects who owed the fisc for gabelles *(dazi)* had accepted large dowry hypothecs so that their lands could not be confiscated for arrears. The Senate apparently misunderstood the issue, and passed an irrelevant law that land purchases from the fisc be made with ready cash, but at least it did not downgrade dotal rights.[138] Such protection of dowry rights may, in fact, have provided a stimulus to dowry inflation.

WHEN WOMEN APPEARED not to require assistance, male controls could be relaxed. That appears to be the lesson of Semiramide Thiene's later transactions. No law prevented her from buying and selling without the consent of a male; statutes assigning the wife's purchases to the husband seem, at least in her case, to have been ignored. Notarial registers contain thousands of records of women, acting alone, engaged in commerce. Nothing prevented them from suing or defending themselves in court, provided they could obtain surety, and statutes did not demand that they have a procurator. Court records show many women going to law on their own. Nothing prevented them from freely bequeathing their estate once they paid due respect to children. The Vicentine rubric "That the masculine category shall encompass the feminine," applying the male voice of statutory language to both sexes, set the principle that men and women should enjoy substantially the same rights and obligations.[139]

Semiramide Thiene did not declare independence. She asserted freedom from an irresponsible husband, but only with the support of her husband's kin. When she bought land in 1438 and 1445, brother-in-law Andrea Arnaldi witnessed the transaction. When she shut her husband out of her will, she entrusted her estate to the priest who had baptized Andrea's children and the notary who had redacted Andrea's will; an executor who appears in later documents was an Arnaldi cousin. Apparently lacking natal kin, she was not prepared to go it alone, and instead relied on a loose network of affines to protect her interests.

The Arnaldi, in turn, were ready to help. Respectable men had little to gain in the long run from the victimization of a wife or the mishandling of her dowry. They were fathers and brothers as well as husbands and in-laws: if the assets of any vulnerable woman could be plundered with impunity, so could those of their own daughters and sisters. With so much money tied up in dowries, corruption of the delicate mechanisms for the orderly devolution of dotal wealth between families and between generations would throw the domestic economy into chaos. So public authorities provided remedies such as *vergens ad inopiam* for dysfunction, and guarded against competing claims which—civic councillors were also landowners, creditors, and tax collectors—might otherwise have worked to their benefit. And so, when Semiramide discovered that her husband's irresponsibility threatened her property, she found no difficulty in securing protectors from among his kinsmen.

Affines and Cognates

Giovanni Rucellai of Florence twice mapped the boundaries of his family. In 1457, near the start of his *zibaldone*, he stressed its vertical dimension with a genealogy of the male line of descent. After two decades of practical experience, he redefined the family in horizontal terms, to include those *parenti* whose families had provided brides for Rucellai men.[140]

This second dimension is characteristic of the Veneto memoirs. Writers' vision rested not on the patriline—genealogy is nearly absent—but on a wider, contemporary kin group and particularly on *parenti* related by marriage. When Bonaventura Bovi listed deaths in the family, for example, he included those of his father- and mother-in-law, his father's father-in-law, and a maternal aunt who lived with him for thirty-five years.[141] So, too, the Arnaldi noted the divorce of cousin Bartolomea, the broken engagement of cousin Cardino, the deaths of aunt Guglielma and uncle Nicolo, the birth of a child to what might have been a second cousin once removed, an aunt's pilgrimage, and her *ductio* of an Arnaldi bride.[142] All these kin were related through marriage or the female line. Writers largely ignored agnatic uncles and cousins.

A striking feature of the Arnaldi family archive and notarial documents is the frequency, intensity, and variety of relations with marital kin. The Arnaldi bought and sold land with their affines, used their shops to transact business, chose them as arbiters, executors, and tutors, lent them money or borrowed from them, hired them as notaries, and employed them as agents and procurators. Members of the Revese family, which provided two brides for Arnaldi men, redacted a score of documents, witnessed a dozen transactions, seven times served as escrow agents, sold them land, and acted as partners in the farming of episcopal incomes. The relationship lasted over three generations, from 1434 to at least 1508. Over a longer span the Zugliano served as arbiters three times, executors three times, and partners in the wool business two times, and made two important testamentary bequests to the Arnaldi.

That concentration runs up against stock historiographic images. On the personal level, historians note tearful brides brusquely removed from natal families and thrust into husbands' households, objects passed from one proprietor to another, or, more poetically, "cuttings to be carefully grafted onto new stock."[143] On the general level, historians note the European transition from bilateral or cognatic kin groups to patrilineal or agnatic kin groups. In both models, marriage constitutes a merely momentary touching of lineages, with ongoing affinal relations unnecessary or even harmful to each family. Yet stock images look less secure in the light of recent revisionism, notably Herlihy's assertion that the agnatic lineage system may have been superimposed on the bilateral or cognatic lineage but by no means replaced it.[144]

A cluster of spiritual and civic-ethical imperatives pushed patricians of the Veneto into sustained and intimate relations with their in-laws. These have been little studied: family history has been markedly materialistic and structural, identifying self-interested strategies for maximizing wealth and maintaining social networks. But fifteenth-century Italians were also dutiful Christians and good citizens for the most part, and they were heirs to less cold-blooded belief systems. Augustine had powerfully defined marriage as instituted to spread *caritas* within the community. The supreme law of love demanded that "bonds of social relationships" be "distributed as widely as possible, so that a common social life of the greatest number may best be fostered." Marriage, wrote Jonas of Orleans, creates an *amicitia* that constitutes the very basis of the polity; Peter Damian thought marriage a "seedbed of charity" that reunited the dispersed descendants of Adam and Eve in love and social harmony. Fifteenth-century writers as diverse as Francesco Barbaro, San Bernardino, and Matteo Palmieri viewed marriage as promoting charity, pacification, and mutual assistance, and expected close bonds between affines.[145]

Memorialists in the Veneto were certainly aware of more utilitarian imperatives. Family self-sufficiency in public life was out of the question. It will be seen, for example, that young Veronese men faced a rigorous *cursus* of eligibility scrutinies before they entered councils; the well-connected might secure a seat in only a few attempts, but the isolated waited a decade or more—if indeed they ever gained favor. The Arnaldi lacked any political presence until maternal uncle Antonio Zugliano left Andrea his seat on the municipal council. Gaspare II and Alvise Arnaldi each received from maternal greatuncles positions in the closed lists of notaries eligible for government employ, thus placing the family among the elite of the College of Notaries.[146] In Venice, maternal uncles frequently advanced the political careers of young patricians, sponsoring them for early election to the Maggior Consiglio. When voting on issues involving individual patricians, Venetian councils excluded in-laws from participation: they expected affinal collusion as a matter of course.[147]

Statute required that disputes between family members be settled in a compromise worked out by two or more "common friends."[148] Although any citizen could serve, affinal relations were especially prized—they had a general interest in the family, knew the facts of cases, and also stood neutral with regard to individual family members. Thus when Battista Arnaldi left the household in 1437, the arbiters of the patrimonial division—Alessandro Zugliano, Nicolo Cardino, and Gaspare Tomasini—were all maternal cousins. The first two helped rework the division in 1439, and the latter two adjudicated Battista's protest of the settlement in 1443.[149] In 1451 Tommaso protested that dowries to Andrea's many daughters drained his share of the common wealth, and *communes affines* Cardino, Tomasini, and Zugliano again served as arbiters.[150]

Statutes ordered that no one under the age of twenty could alienate or obligate goods without the consent of two close male relatives *(proximi)*, one from the paternal side and one from the maternal side.[151] Maternal or affinal kin, then, were given equality to patrilineal kin in protecting the patrimony. The principle respected customary lines of property descent: because most or all of a woman's dowry usually passed to her children, at any given point a family's wealth derived in large part from the mother's natal family. Furthermore, marriage did not end the father's paternal authority *(patria potestas)* over his daughter, and he retained a residual interest in the administration and devolution of her property.[152] The fact that the payment of dowries might stretch over a decade or more, with exchanges of cash and land rights throughout, further entangled the economic interests of the two families.

Mutual cooperation and shared experiences in political, economic, legal, and patrimonial affairs may also have engendered mutual respect, even warmth, between natal and marital families. The memoirs of the Veneto, paying vigilant attention to events in the lives of maternal kin, bespeak at least a close concern. Recurrent selection of affines as arbiters and executors—after a marriage in 1407, the Zugliano handled Arnaldi estates in 1433, 1463, and 1499[153]—certainly indicates long-term trust. Evidence from other cities goes a step further. The Florentine agnate system excluded married daughters from the patrimony but not from the collective memory of their natal families, and women in turn kept close "sentimental ties" with fathers, brothers, grandparents, and maternal uncles.[154] Female Venetian testators made widespread bequests, indicating strong affectionate ties, to members of both families. Some men, too, were close to their affines: Gasparino Morosini left fifty ducats to each of the brothers of his deceased wife "because of the great love and respect which I have always had for that house."[155]

Soluto matrimonio

Divortium

Two unions mentioned in the Veneto memoirs were dissolved not by death but by an entry into religion. In 1448 Lucia Colzè broke her betrothal—a *matrimonium initiatium*—to the Arnaldi cousin Cardino Feramosca, and entered the convent of Santa Chiara. Five years earlier cousin Bartolomea and her husband Nicolo had gone before the bishop in the episcopal palace and separated ("fecerunt divortium"). Both immediately entered the order of the Observant Franciscans, Nicolo at San Biagio and Bartolomea at Santa Chiara.[156]

At least they bothered to go through the formalities. The persistent view that marriage was a purely secular arrangement, regulated by the couple itself and without need of Church sanction, led—in England, at least—to frequent "self-divorce" in which husbands and wives simply divided and felt free to contract new unions. Few there sought formal dissolution of marriage, even though the Church offered several grounds (consanguinity, crime, coercion, impotence, insufficient age) for claiming that the marriage had not been valid in the first place.[157]

Lucia Colzè was on fairly firm ground. Strengthening of the *verba de fu-turo* had led some canonists, notably Alexander III, to deny that even entry into religion could override a betrothal, but after Huguccio most theorists accepted this exceptional case. Gratian thought that an unconsummated be-trothal could be dissolved by entry into a "better life"; Albertus Magnus re-garded monachation as a death to the world which, as much as corporal death, effectively sundered the relationship. Peter Lombard even argued that a per-son joined by *verba de futuro* could enter the religious life without the con-sent of the other party.[158]

The *divortium* of Bartolomea and Nicolo, however, was less certain. Early authors such as Gratian and Peter Lombard had taken the hard line that any complete or "perfect" matrimony *(matrimonium perfectum)* could not be bro-ken. Alexander III softened the position to permit dissolution of unconsum-mated marriages in the case of monachation. Writers such as Huguccio and Innocent III ratified his position, and Bonaventure and Thomas Aquinas en-dorsed it by repeating the metaphor of entry into religion as death to the world. But these authorities allowed the dissolution only of an unconsum-mated matrimony, which they regarded as a spiritual union that one or both parties could exchange for a higher spiritual marriage to Christ. After con-summation, most agreed, man and wife were joined in physical union, which could be dissolved only by physical death.[159]

Bartolomea and Nicolo were well into middle age, and the marriage had almost certainly been consummated: their *divortium* required counterlogic. Scripture offered two possibilities. First Corinthians 7 reluctantly admitted separation as long as both parties remained unmarried in a worldly sense, and the injunction "whom God has joined let no man separate" (Matthew 19:6) could be interpreted to mean that God—or vicars such as the bishop of Vicenza—could separate couples. The very purposes of marriage, Augustine's triptych of procreation *(proles)*, mutual fidelity *(fides)*, and binding obliga-tion *(sacramentum)*,[160] allowed some flexibility. Bartolomea and Nicolo had already had their chance to produce and raise children to populate the Chris-tian community and spread *caritas;* they preserved *fides* if they remained true to their vows in a carnal sense. Scholarly consensus removed the obsta-cle of the *sacramentum*, affirming that the desire to enter the monastic life released the obligation if there was mutual consent to separation. The latter provision was adequately respected if both parties entered convents, as hap-pened in Vicenza in 1443 and in several hagiographic models.[161]

Still, divorce was unsettling. It could not be accomplished casually if the parties involved wished to keep faith to the Church and to the community.

To heal those breaches of ecclesiastical tradition and the social order, divorce required spiritual blessing and public confirmation. So Bartolomea and Nicolo made their divorce before the bishop, and Andrea noted carefully that he had witnessed both their entries into convents.

Widowhood

In the Veneto memoirs, twenty-three men and eighteen women lost spouses to death; widowed males also appear with frequency in Veronese tax declarations *(anagrafi)*. With a spousal age gap of only six years (compared with twelve to fifteen years in Florence) upwards of a quarter of Veronese men would outlive their first wives. Like their Tuscan and Genoese counterparts, widowed women in the Veneto rarely remarried: only 11 percent are known to have done so. The assumption that men nearly automatically remarried, however, is not supported, as only 44 percent of widowers in memorialist families entered a second union. The *anagrafi*, too, indicate that most widowed men in Verona raised their children alone (see appendix, table 1.4).[162]

The first of the Arnaldi marriages presents a model case of female widowhood. By the will of her husband Gaspare, Caterina Zugliano was left, in addition to her dowry, food, and clothing, the income from a hundred ducats and the use of a room with a bed in the family house "as long as she lives a widow's life in a chaste and respectable manner." Gaspare's heirs were to honor and reverence her as their *domina* and mother, and acquiesce to her advice and warnings, if they wished to receive her blessing. If she chose not to live with her sons, they were to provide her with a sufficient dwelling, clothes and food, and a servant. During the nine years of her widowhood, Caterina indeed remained in the Arnaldi house, and she did not reclaim her dowry.[163]

Men took considerable pains to ensure that widows remained safely and honorably in the marital house. Powerful reasons, moral and material, dictated that they do so. Honor thy mother, said the commandment; St. Paul ordered respect and provision for those widows "who are real widows" (I Timothy 5:3–16). His fear that unsupervised widows would stray into wanton behavior, bringing condemnation upon themselves and their families from God and the community, was widely echoed by fifteenth-century Italians. Widows were classified among the *miserabiles personae* whom Christians were obliged to protect and succor. Continued widowhood showed respect for the deceased spouse and prevented the neglect or abandonment of children from the first union. The son who honored his mother, said Giovanni

Dominici, piled up great treasure for himself, but if he treated her badly, her curse would tear down the foundations of the house. Financial interest, too, induced men to keep the widow close and happy. Her property would stray from the male line if she was discontent or produced a second set of children: thus the Bolognese Cesare Nappi's harsh words for his stepfather, thief of his own goods.[164]

The tacit bribes for widows to remain were sometimes considerable: Pietro Verità granted his widow a lifelong usufruct of all of his goods, providing she lived *vidualiter et honesta* with her children and did not demand her dowry. Bonaventura Bovi ordered his heirs to show all "obedience, *caritas*, reverence, and love" to their mother, and granted her "all power and freedom of ruling and administering the entire family, because he has great trust in this madonna Isabeta."[165] Appointing widows testamentary executors and tutors of children likewise served to bind them to the marital household. Husbands in Venice, Florence, Genoa, and elsewhere offered much the same inducements.[166] Their strategies evidently worked: most widows did not leave,[167] most widows did not remarry,[168] and most dowries eventually passed to children.

This is not to suggest that there might not be friction. Because fraternal households were common in the Veneto, widows might find themselves under the authority of an in-law: Marcella Fracanzani, widow in a household headed by her brother-in-law Tommaso Arnaldi, moved out and eventually placed her son Silvestro under the tutelage of her own brothers. Second wives might be subject to the authority of offspring from the husband's first marriage: Elisabetta dal Gorgo, widow in a household headed by her stepson Gaspare II Arnaldi, also left to live on her own.[169] When a widow sought to leave the household, heirs might refuse to restore the dowry or nondotal goods; Florentine archives abound in lawsuits against recalcitrant offspring.[170]

Still, dysfunction was the exception; none of the other Veneto widows are known to have departed. There were perfectly good reasons why, in the absence of friction, a widow might choose to remain in the house of her late husband. After a decade or more of marriage her ties to her children were probably stronger than those to her family of origin. If she returned to live with father or brothers she would occupy a peripheral place in their household. If she went out on her own, she exposed herself to depredation and social opprobrium. If, on the other hand, she stayed put, she was guaranteed shelter, food, clothes, and servants,[171] and had little vested interest in claiming her dowry. She also, as tutor to her children and executor of her husband's estate, might still administer that dowry without formally reclaiming it. In moral and material terms, then, the stay-at-home widow gained an authority she was denied in any other situation. She still retained freedom of movement and association if, like Caterina Zugliano, she joined an order of tertiaries and traveled across town to spend time in their house.[172]

Historians who argued for the victimization of wives once romanticized widowhood as the time when a woman was at last free and economically independent. More systematic study of the Italian situation presents a darker picture. Tuscan widows in 1427 were poor and isolated, so economically marginal that they may have been seriously undercounted. Herlihy speaks of "social immiseration" of widows, and concludes that "the Florentine marriage pattern did not treat them well."[173] Vicentine tax rolls seem to support that contention: most widows were given the lowest assessment, five *solidi*, just above the poverty line.

Some qualification is in order, however, at least for patrician widows. Vicentine tax records provide imperfect indexes of true economic standing and actual residence. If, as usually happened, a widow remained in a son's house, keeping her personal nondotal goods but not separating out her dowry, she would be listed in a separate tax household but would go on record as having little of her own. A tiny *estimo*, then, indicates neither isolation nor poverty. Many widows from wealthy families, widows of very rich men, did not appear in the tax rolls at all, because they did not take the minimal step of holding personal property in their own names. Marcella Fracanzani in 1460, Elisabetta dal Gorgo in 1477, and the unnamed widow of Girolamo Repeta in 1505 were all eligible to reclaim their considerable dowries and appear in the *estimi* as heads of distinct households, but they did not do so. They preferred to merge their financial interests with those of their sons, keeping honorable chastity and material comfort within the family house.

CHAPTER TWO

CHILDREN

*L*EON BATTISTA ALBERTI most famously articulated the rationale for recording births: "immediately when a child is born one should record in family records and secret books the hour, the day, the month and the year as well as the place of birth, and this record should be kept with our dearest treasures."[1] Writers of memoirs in the Veneto went further, fixing the birth in spiritual as well as mundane time. They specified the patron saint of the day, the liturgy celebrated at the hour of birth, the day and place of baptism and chrismation, the presiding priest, and the godparents. As if calendrical and ecclesiastical reckoning were inadequate to locate the event, they frequently added the imperial indiction and the day of the lunar phase. They never said why they took such care: the need to keep anagraphic records was so self-evident or widely shared that it did not require explanation.

The Demographics of Birth

Conception and Childbirth

The spacing of births largely followed a seasonal pattern. The Church enjoined abstinence from sex during Advent and Lent, and some writers and local synods also commanded abstinence during the forty days after Pentecost.[2] Penitentials ordered expiation by parents who had sex during prohibited times, and a famous vision of the monk Alberico da Settefrati threatened errant husbands with dire punishments in the afterlife. A child conceived in transgression of sexual prescriptions, it was widely believed, would suffer deformity or death.[3]

The Veneto families that produced memoirs accepted that counsel: their 174 legitimate births were indeed spaced at predictably irregular intervals around the calendar (see appendix, table 2.1). They especially respected Advent prohibitions. Fewer children were conceived in December than in any other month; conceptions fell by 36 percent from November's figure, then rose by 67 percent in January. The Lenten prohibition was only slightly weaker: conceptions in February (part of which usually fell in Lent) were very low, while those in March (which almost always fell in Lent) were below average. April, about half of which usually fell in Lent yet which produced the highest monthly rate of conception, is an ambiguous case: couples may have tired of abstinence and risked spiritual punishment by having late-Lenten sex, or they may have adhered to prescriptions and concentrated sexual activity in the weeks immediately following Easter. On the other hand, they altogether ignored post-Pentecost strictures.

Other cities reveal a similar pattern. Births of girls registered in Florence's Monte delle Doti declined in September and nosedived in December–January, indicating respect for Advent and Lenten prohibitions; a high incidence of births in February—also the case in the Veneto—indicates accelerated conception in May, due to increased post-Lenten sexual activity. The 1,760 births recorded in Milan in 1470, and forty births recorded in late medieval Limoges, are spaced in much the same way.[4] Venice's Freschi conceived most often in November (15.6 percent) and January (18.8 percent), bracketing Advent; Lenten conceptions were very rare.

The Church did not possess a monopoly on the making of sexual timetables. Medical lore offered alternate norms. Authorities from Aristotle on advised against sex in summer. Winter was controversial: Hippocrates held that the woman's body was warmer and healthier in winter, but Soranus of Ephesus asserted that her body was "condensed" in winter and thus less likely to conceive. All agreed that spring was favorable, even, for Soranus, the "supreme season" for conception.[5] Veneto memorialists appear to have respected that advice. Women seldom conceived in summer: the rate fell by 57 percent between June and July, and rose by 23 percent between August and September. Late spring was the best season for fertility, with April, May, and June posting the three highest monthly figures. These families preferred Soranus to Hippocrates: winter rates were well below average.

PREGNANCY AND CHILDBIRTH were dangerous: two of the twenty-four women whose reproductive history can be reconstructed from the memoirs died immediately after giving birth, and the new bride of Contino Stoppi probably died of complications from pregnancy.[6] In Venice, two of eight Freschi women died in or immediately following childbirth. The frequency of widowers in Veronese *anagrafi*—a quarter of male heads of household—suggests that these are not isolated cases. Furthermore, as will be seen, some 26 percent of women in the 20–39 age group died, compared with only 8 percent of men of similar age. Obviously many young wives died of other natural causes, but a high incidence of postpartum hemorrhage, puerperal infection, and sheer exhaustion cannot be discounted.

Medicine offered little to reduce the risks of pregnancy, though Bartolomeo dal Bovo did write down a recipe for an unguent to alleviate the kidney pains of pregnant women. Memorialists, instead, placed their trust in faith and magic. St. Anthony was a special protector of pregnant women; dal Bovo offered him a poetic prayer. He advised pregnant women to wear next to their skin a leather belt inscribed with the words of Psalm 1:3, referring to the godly and upright person, who "shall be as a tree which is planted beside a water course, which will bring forth its fruit in due season, and its leaf shall not fall, and all that it does shall prosper."[7] The Athanasian Creed (the *Quicumque vult*) was frequently recited over women in childbirth; Bartolomeo Muronovo and dal Bovo copied it into their manuscripts. Grafting Christianity onto magic, as well, was the incantation that the latter advised reciting "over a virgin boy, when the woman is in labor," complete with prompts for making the sign of the cross: "+ Anne brought forth Mary [who] brought forth the Savior + Elizabeth brought forth the precursor + Creature come forth because Christ is calling you + and the light desires you."[8] The baby, he claimed, would be born without pain to its mother.

Fertility

The 24 Veneto women in the memoir sample bore an average of 7 children, as did 6 Freschi women in Venice. The mean spacing between births was about 25 months; the average span of childbearing was 12.5 years (see appendix, table 2.2). Individual women's experiences varied widely. Cassandra Bevilaqua bore 11 children at a rate of one every 17 months, while Caterina Zugliano bore 4 at a leisurely rate of one per 4.6 years. Bonafemina da Montalban produced 3 children in a 2-year span, while Margarita Buzzacarini produced 14 over 24 years. Indeed, the number of offspring clustered around the mean (6–8 births) in only one-third of cases; the interval between births clustered around the mean (23–27 months) in only one-sixth.

Fertility rose sharply between the later Trecento and the early Cinque-cento. Ten women born before 1420 produced a mean of 5.8 children at in-tervals of 30.4 months; 9 women born in the 1420–60 period bore an aver-age of 7.1 children at intervals of 23.3 months; 5 women born after 1460 had an average of 9.6 births at intervals of only 20.7 months. Later women in the Veneto had 66 percent more children than earlier counterparts, with 32 per-cent shorter space between births. Contributing to demographic success, women remained fertile for ever-longer periods: while the earlier cohort bore children over a span of 143 months on average, the later group had re-productive careers of 178 months.

It cannot be known if an average of around seven offspring represents maximum fertility. Seasonal patterns of births indicate that couples practiced sexual discipline; whether they practiced family limitation is another matter. David Herlihy has concluded that birth intervals recorded in Tuscan *ricor-danze* "suggest that Florentine wives were about as fertile as biology allowed." On the other hand, tax records indicate differing rates and timing of fertility among groups of roughly comparable economic and social status, suggesting that biology was not the sole determinant of fecundity. Some cohorts clearly restricted or timed conception, and not simply by hastening or delaying mar-riage. How they did so remains unclear. It is hard to know what to do with the condemnations of preachers such as San Bernardino of Siena, who thought that 99.9 percent of marriages were "of the devil" and hinted darkly at wide recourse to abortifacients, contraceptive potions, and "unnatural" sex.[9] Celi-bate monks might be dismissed as out of touch with reality; yet they were also confessors and privy to information about everyday behavior.

Calculation of 701 births recorded in Tuscan *ricordanze* indicates that the average couple produced six children, one fewer than was the case in the Veneto. The difference can be attributed to the higher ages of Florentine men at marriage, which would result in a higher incidence of unions cut short by the death of the husband. The same calculation gives a median interval of 17.8 months between births at Florence, or about 22 percent less than the overall rate for the Veneto.[10] Here, too, age may be a factor. Florentine women married younger than their Veneto counterparts, and may have been phys-ically more capable of conceiving soon after childbirth; women in the north were often still bearing children in their mid-thirties, when natural rates of conception decline. Mothers in the Veneto, in sum, devoted a greater share of their lives to childbearing, but enjoyed several months' longer respite be-tween pregnancies.

Illegitimacy

Manfredo Repeta, at least, acknowledged his illegitimate offspring. Indeed, in the *catasto* he lavished more detail on his three illegitimate sons than he gave to any of his ten legitimate offspring. The first, Nicolo, was brought to the paternal house soon after birth; Manfredo noted the boy's early death— dropped by his mother—with evident irritation. Second son Zuane Alvise was put out with a wet nurse, where he, too, died. The third, Riccardo, was born in the Repeta family house in Vicenza, a sign of acceptance. Manfredo provided the details of the boy's baptism, which he did not do for legitimate children. He also found it noteworthy that Riccardo's maternal grandfather was killed in Venice by a co-parent, who was then quartered.[11]

Though only Repeta spoke of illegitimacy, a total figure of three such children out of about 175 births recorded in the Veneto memoirs provides a point of comparison. Various Florentine data report a slightly higher incidence of illegitimacy, in the 2 percent to 3 percent range.[12] One in twenty testaments in the Lyonnais mentioned a bastard. In one Genoese guild scrutiny, on the other hand, 18.6 percent of notaries' sons were qualified as illegitimate and 35.5 percent of fathers reported at least one bastard.[13] The memoir of Venice's Freschi listed thirty-three legitimate births and six illegitimate births. Bernardino da Feltre, for one, thought that illegitimates were rife in Italy, though he may have exaggerated for greater moral impact.[14]

Manfredo Repeta's extramarital episodes seem typical. He was rich; the overwhelming majority of reported Florentine bastards were born to wealthy families, and nobles in Lyon were more than three times as likely as common citizens to mention bastards in wills. The mothers of his natural sons were domestic servants, one a girl *(fantescha)* and the others apparently older (each a *massara*). In Florence, too, household dependents were the main source of nonmarital sex partners.[15] Manfredo's three partners in six years suggest brief liaisons; long-term concubinage seems to have been rare in the Veneto.[16]

Repeta's natural sons were born after he ceased to produce legitimate offspring. That is not to suggest that marriage and extramarital sex were regarded as incompatible. Both Repeta and Florence's Paolo Niccolini had natural offspring while married. In each case, however, their wives had ceased to bear children. Rather, marital and extramarital pregnancy were incompatible: when they had wives capable of conceiving, patrician men in Florence and the Veneto produced few illegitimate children. They bracketed satellite families before, between, and after their marriages, with serial but not simultaneous sexual relationships.[17] The Bolognese Cesare Nappi's two bastards were born before his marriage, as was the illegitimate daughter of Simo d'Ubertino of Arezzo.[18] Of six Freschi bastards, two were born before marriage and two after a wife's death; the others were born to an unmarried man. Verona's Girolamo Guastaverza wanted it publicly known that he had been free from marital bonds for twenty-two years before he took a mistress and sired a child.[19] As Gregorio Dati remarked of his bastard son, "maybe he isn't legitimate, but I didn't have a wife."[20]

Repeta was conventional, too, in his open recognition of his natural offspring. Fathers felt little shame in acknowledging paternity, though moralists such as Bernardino da Feltre condemned their double standard ("you want her to be an angel, but you want to act like a pig").[21] Well-to-do Italians were willing to accept the legal obligations incurred by acknowledgment, such as the duty of feeding and clothing bastards and dowering natural daughters. They accepted them into their households, started sons in careers, arranged marriages for daughters, and—though bastards could not hope to inherit[22]—provided for them in testaments.[23] Even women made such bequests.[24]

A bastard son had considerable value as a potential heir in case no legitimate sons survived; he could be legitimated by the simple act of an imperial noble.[25] Perhaps this is why the Florentine *catasto* reports many more male than female bastards.[26] Perhaps this is why Manfredo Repeta was so supportive of Riccardo: two of his four legitimate sons had died in infancy, and he needed a reserve. He certainly sought to integrate Riccardo symbolically into the lineage: the name repeated that of a heroic ancestor, and the boy was given the additional name of Bartolomeo, which had been conferred on each of the ten legitimate children. This is certainly why the Arcimboldi family of Parma legitimated several bastard sons: they had placed too many legitimates in the Church.[27]

Female bastards were not so favored. Tuscan fathers often neglected to report them in tax returns, and consigned them to foundling hospitals in disproportionate numbers. Patricians were a little more generous: Donato Vellutti grumbled, but eventually fetched his illegitimate niece from Sicily and arranged for her marriage. The Freschi twice welcomed bastard nieces into their house. Still, fathers set much lower dowries for illegitimate daughters than for legitimate daughters—among the Freschi, about 24 percent of the value of their half sisters' dowries—and married them down the social scale. They also sent bastard daughters to convents at five times the rate of legitimates.[28]

The Child, God, and the World

Baptism

Memoralists set an absolute priority on noting the newborn's entry into the Christian community. First, the child's eternal fate depended on baptism: John 3:5 made it clear that those not reborn by water could not enter the kingdom of heaven, and medieval doctrine destined the unbaptized dead to hellfire or, at best, to grey oblivion and eternal longing.[29] Second, the child was not born to the parents and the world, but was lent by God;[30] baptism made due acknowledgment of the source of all life. Finally, birth alone did not make the person: only ceremonial rebirth into the family of the faithful created true identity. Hence many children in the Veneto and elsewhere were assigned only a provisional name at birth, and were given their real names at baptism. The Verità and the Freschi went further: they mentioned only the gender of the newborn, and specified that the name was conferred only at baptism when the child was reborn (*regeneratur* or *renatus est*).[31]

Margarita Bona, the first of Andrea Arnaldi's children, was baptized on the day of her birth "because it was feared she would die." In fact, she survived to maturity, but the fate of some of her siblings and cousins proved the wisdom of Church rules that allowed baptism without a priest, without a set formula, and with words spoken in the vernacular. Of the four other Arnaldi who were baptized immediately—about one-fifth of all children in the family—one girl was so sickly that, in the confusion of the impromptu ceremony, she was given a male name. She lived only four months. The rest died within a day of their baptisms. In total, about 16 percent of children mentioned in the Veneto memoirs were baptized within two days of birth, and just under a half within a week (see appendix, table 2.3).[32]

Sources from other regions inform us that, when the birth of a healthy child afforded more leisure, the feasting and gift giving that accompanied baptism could be elaborate and costly.[33] Veneto memorialists, however, regarded social rituals as not worth recording, and focused the attention of posterity squarely on spiritual matters. They wished, in the first place, to locate the event in sacred time. In 71 percent of cases, nonemergency baptisms fell on Sunday. The only other days recorded are Tuesday and Thursday; Wednesday, Friday, and Saturday, penitential days when the faithful were enjoined to ponder their sins, were clearly inappropriate for the joyful washing away of the newborn's sins. The holiest of days, when God would give special audience to prayers, Sunday was also a day of leisure when parents found it most convenient to assemble godparents. Sunday was also a public day, with citizens gathered in churches and squares. It was well that the community witness the entry of the child into the body of the faithful.

Aside from listing godparents (who will be considered below), the memorialists also noted the name of the presiding priest. In an age before systematic record keeping, his testimony might have judicial value in proving both the identity and the authentic Christianity of the child. Furthermore, the priest would probably predecease the child, and serve as witness and intercessor in heaven as well. Not just any priest would do. Thus while their children were baptized at the cathedral, which had a large staff, the Arnaldi were careful to maintain long-term bonds of clerical patronage. During the 1433–55 period, the priest Cristoforo baptized no fewer than thirteen Arnaldi children; Zanfrancesco da Cologna baptized the remaining two.[34]

ANOINTING WITH CHRISM, a consecrated mixture of oil and balsam, sealed the new Christian in the grace bestowed by water and blessing during baptism. Chrismation, not a required sacrament, did not confer but only ratified spiritual initiation. It was an ancillary ritual and, not surprisingly, was infrequent. The Arnaldi and Bovi each mentioned it four times, Bartolomeo dal Bovo once, and other memorialists not at all.

Chrismation possessed considerable strategic value since, in the Veneto, it was detached from baptism and might be performed at any time. On average, children were chrismed forty-four months after birth, precisely the figure for twelve Freschi in Venice. The rite celebrated survival of the dangerous first years of life. In the case of Silvestro Arnaldi, the ceremony had particular poignancy: his two older brothers had died in infancy, and father Andrea finally was assured of an heir. In two other cases, chrismation also compensated for a baptism that had not fulfilled the desired aim of publicity. Sister Margarita Bona was baptized hastily, in fear of death, and sister Ursula Imperatrice was born and baptized in the countryside, where her parents had fled in fear of the plague: later chrismation provided the opportunity for a regular public ceremony, this time with full trappings. In all cases, chrismation allowed parents to secure a second set of godparents for their offspring.

Socially, chrismation was even more powerful than baptism. Expanding on ancient tradition that only bishops could consecrate the chrism, the Roman liturgy declared that only a bishop should anoint;[35] Veneto custom respected the rules. The ceremony was thus one of the very few moments in which a midranking family could secure the personal patronage of prelates—in the case of Silvestro Arnaldi, under the portico of the episcopal palace. Bartolomeo dal Bovo was delighted at the honor and neighborhood prestige he obtained when Verona's suffragan, who had laid the first stone of a family chapel, deigned to stay for dinner and chrismate at the site before a crowd of "many persons."[36]

Names

Rules for naming accommodated a wide variety of meanings. A name refreshed the memory of ancestors or remade a recently deceased relative; sought celestial patronage or cemented a social alliance; augured good fortune or invoked a civic hero; honored a saint or recalled a figure from antiquity; expressed a personal characteristic or repeated the name of the lineage. Given the many strategies for bestowing names, it is not surprising that the stock was large: each of the Vicentine tax rolls (estimi), listing some 2,300 heads of household, offers about three hundred different names.

The personal name was a "public statement,"[37] but whose statement? Personal choice or public commentary determined purely descriptive names— Hunchback, Black, Strongarm. Personal names remained unstable in the Quattrocento and beyond, and the individual might change names completely in the service of a spiritual or humanist ideal: one Vicentine of the Volpe family was known variously as Nicolo, Battista, and Enea.[38] Even those who retained baptismal names might customize them. Giovanni Andrea Nicolo Arnaldi shed his first and third names; brother Giovanni Battista and the chronicler Giovanni Battista Pagliarini dropped their first names; and many with compounds—Margarita Bona Arnaldi and her brother Silvestro Francesco—dropped the second.

On the whole, however, most people in the Veneto kept whatever parents named them at birth or baptism. That feature contrasts with custom in northern Europe, where the godfather often gave his own name to the child or at least determined the name.[39] In Florence, however, the natural father conferred the name,[40] and this was the case in the Veneto as well. No child mentioned in the memoirs received the name of a godparent, and reiteration of personal names amid changing godparents suggests that the name was above all a statement of the natal family.

Italian patterns of naming had changed in the recent past. A plurality of names in medieval Tuscany referred directly to the child, without invocation of lineage or patron saint. Some recalled time of birth, place of origin, or physical qualities; some welcomed the child into the world, wished it good fortune, or called for God's aid.[41] Veneto families shared that preference. One list of Vicentines in the thirteenth century includes a Red, a Cat, an Iron-head, a Goodman, a Well-behaved (Bonagente), and an Uglychild (Bruto-fante).[42] Arnaldi ancestors included a God Aid Him (Deolavanzio), a No Trouble (Senzabriga), a Little Famous One (Chiarello), a Welcome (Ben-venuto), a Goodfortune (Bonaventura), a Pilgrim (Pellegrino), and an All-good (Ognibene).

Quattrocento nomenclature, as indicated by the 8,853 names of heads of household in the Vicentine *estimi* of 1453, 1460, 1477, and 1505,[43] demon-strates the growing preponderance of saints' names and the decline of de-scriptive, augurative, and chivalric names (see appendix, tables 2.4–2.5). This feature has been noted in several other cities and regions of Italy and Europe at large.[44] Among Vicentine men, the ten most frequent names, twenty-three of the top twenty-five and forty-four of the top fifty, were those of saints. Other favored names included reference to angels and figures associated with Jesus (the three Magi), which also expressed a desire to secure a heavenly patron. The Christianization of nomenclature, however, really demanded as-signment of the name of a specific saint. Angelo, Gaspare, Melchiorre, and Baldassare declined in frequency, as did archangels Raphael and Michael. Generic Christian references such as Grazio, Perdono, Pellegrino, Evange-lista, and Cristano were never given to more than a handful.

Of the stock of pagan names only Zanino (but perhaps it was a derivative of Giovanni) and Rigo were found in the top fifty in 1453, and both nearly disappeared by 1505. Augurative and descriptive names were rare (no more than one percent), and many of these were but augmentatives of saints' names (Belpietro, Bongiovanni). Pagan Germanic names, frequent in the Duecento, seldom recur two centuries later. That disappearance of non-Christian names largely accounts for the growing concentration of Vicentine nomenclature. In 1453, 2,195 men shared 286 names (7.7 per name); in 1477 the ratio rose to 8.4 per name; in 1505 only 228 names were given to 2,344 heads of house-hold (10.3 per name).[45] Christianization produced uniformity, since the pool of saints' names was limited.

Not just any saint's name would serve. The names chosen for Vicentines clustered in two polarized groups: those derived from apostles, Evangelists, and figures of the patristic era,[46] and those of recent saints (Francis, Domenic, Anthony of Padua, Bernardino, Clare).[47] The saints of the High Middle Ages (William, Albert, George, Blaise, Gregory, Margaret) were not popular to begin with and gradually fell out of favor. Biblical saints maintained or im-proved their positions; apocryphal or legendary names (George, Christopher, the Magi) declined.

Political allegiance was not a priority for Vicentine parents. Names associated with former rulers (Galeazzo and Ambrogio from Milan, Zeno from Verona) remained infrequent: none appear among the fifty most common. Parents honored the patron of the current ruler, the Republic of Venice, but his cult did not grow in favor: Marco appears in fourteenth place in 1453, 1477, and 1505. Perhaps more surprising, local patriotism seldom dictated the choice of name. The nearly homonymous Vincenzo, focus of a civic cult in earlier years, never gave his name to any great number of Vicentines: the name ranked eighteenth in 1453, and rose only to sixteenth place by 1505. Just eleven of 8,853 heads of household bore the names of saints whose relics graced urban churches (Leonzio, Carpoforo, Felice, and Fortunato).

Vicentine nomenclature does, however, demonstrate a growing sense of regional identification. Apart from those entirely associated with the Holy Land, saints buried wholly or partially in Italy predominated: Francis, Anthony (buried in Padua), Peter, John the Baptist (skull in the Lateran), Mark, Nicholas (relics at Bari), and Domenic (buried in Bologna) ranked among the top fifteen names, while Paul (buried in Rome), Bernardino, and Augustine (buried in Pavia) grew in popularity. Saints whose cults lay elsewhere in Europe—Martin, Michael, William, and George—declined in favor. The cult of the Magi, centered in Germany, also faltered.

Naming patterns were sensitive to changes in religious sensibilities. Shifts in cult popularity would take time to show up in tax rolls, of course, since a quarter century or more would elapse before a child became head of household, but if we accept some lag time those changes are still apparent. Francis, moving from sixth place in 1453 to second place in 1505, was preferred to Domenic (declining from eighth to eleventh), reflecting attitudes in the city as a whole: the Conventual Dominicans of Vicenza suffered growing opprobrium until their expulsion in 1463, and their Observant replacements did little more than stabilize the convent. The Conventual Franciscans, on the other hand, were reputable, and Observant Franciscans made spectacular strides with successful preaching missions and the establishment of male and female houses. Bernardino, who took the city by storm in 1423 and 1444, was an immediate favorite: unrepresented in the first two *estimi*, his name occupied twenty-thirdth place in 1477 and rose to fifth in 1505. The other great success story was that of St. Jerome. Growing in popularity in art and devotion throughout Italy, and patron of the Jesuati order, which established a house in Vicenza in 1445, his name ranked forty-first in 1453 but rose to eighth in 1505.

Parents could resist as well as embrace current fashions. The cult of the

Holy Family, in particular, never gained much favor in the city's nomenclature. Much has been made of Marian devotion, but parents were not inclined to dedicate their daughters to it: Maria occupied only seventh place in 1453, and seventh place again in 1505. Only four heads of household out of 8,545 males were named Joseph. Plague saints protected the city, not individuals: Vicentines honored Sebastian with two churches and Rocco with one, but gave the former's name to only twelve children and the latter's name to only one.[48]

Only 3.5 percent of heads of tax households in Vicenza were women, and the 308 names recorded do not permit exhaustive analysis. Still, some broad patterns are evident. Among women, too, the names of saints predominated. Of the auguratives and descriptives, only Bona and Bonora ever ranked among the ten most frequently found names; the former slid to tenth position, and the latter disappeared. Vicentines preferred Christian names for daughters, above all, the names of specific saints: the generalized Angela held only seventh position in 1453 and 1505. Nomenclature for women, too, was sensitive to new cults: parallel to the success of Franciscan-related names among men, Chiara did not appear in 1453 or 1460, but entered in tenth position in 1477 and reached fifth in 1505. Domenica, on the other hand, was never popular.

Daughters were named, above all, for female saints. Parents increasingly discarded feminized forms of male names: Bartolomea, Tomasina, Giovanna, Antonia, and Tadea disappeared, or nearly so. Fathers displayed growing gender sensitivity, securing for their daughters a patron saint of the same sex. Consistently popular names for women—Caterina, Magdalena, Elisabetta, and Lucia—established a strictly feminine spiritual community. In this the Veneto differs from Florence, where just over half the saints' names given to daughters were those of male saints.[49]

The clustering of women's names was weak, declining from 2.1 women sharing any given name to only 1.7 per name in the 1453–1505 period. This contrasts with the growing concentration of men's names, which rose to a mean of over ten men sharing each name. Vicentine parents reached relatively weak consensus on appropriate names for daughters, which suggests that they exercised greater freedom in naming daughters than in naming sons. Boys' names perpetuated the lineage stock, which dictated a conservative strategy: the Arnaldi, for example, repeated Tommaso, Giovanni, and Andrea in every generation. Girls married out of the direct line of descent; as was the case elsewhere in Italy and parts of Europe at large, their names could be chosen without regard for ancestors because they were not fully a part of the patriline.[50] So girls' names were constantly more exotic, drawn from legend, romance, classical mythology, or simple whim: Isota, Laura, Amia, Lucrezia, Ginevra, and Diamante are found in the memoirs, for instance, and Galatea and Diana in the 1505 *estimo*. Little Ursula Arnaldi was given the additional name of Imperatrice ("Empress") in 1438 because of a recent imperial passage through the city. This pattern also disadvantaged daughters, who were less likely to receive spiritual patrons.

The wealthy, with access to higher learning, felt increasingly free to look beyond Christian worthies and invoke the heroes and authors of antiquity. Vicentines heeded, too, the humanist plea that names be beautiful and magnificent rather than merely respectful of ancestors.[51] Extremely rare in the 1453 and 1460 *estimi*, pagan worthies suddenly appeared in some force in 1477: Eneas, Centurion, Fabius, Justus, Octavian (two), Patricius, Tacitus, Valerius, Virgil, and Dionysis (two). They were even more common in 1505: Aurelius, Caesar (two), Camillus (two), Dionysis again, Julius (two), Hannibal, Lactantius, Octavian (four), Troilus, and Ulysses. The memoirs offer an Octavian, a Claudia, a Pantasilea, a Medea, several Cassandras, a Tullius, a Faustina, a Semiramide, an Achilles, and an Hippolytus. Verona's Pindemonte family named sons Tullius, Seneca, Pliny, Hector, and Demosthenes, while Vicenza's Clivone named sons Hippolytus, Virgil, and Centurion.[52] Classical names never reached statistical frequency in the population as a whole, but were overrepresented in councils and palace salons.

TWO PRIMARY STRATEGIES guided the memorialists in their choice of personal name. The first, and stronger, was to repeat the name of a deceased relative. They respected the basic principles that Florentines revealed in their memoirs: perpetuation of names bound "the community of the living and the dead of a lineage," remade a dead child, reinforced the collective person of the lineage, and honored an ancestor who might provide heavenly intercession for the living.[53] Ruggiero Cortusi in Padua, for example, named firstborn Zuan for paternal grandfather Giovanni, Maria Lucrezia I for her paternal grandmother, daughters Maria and Lucia for their sister Maria Lucia, and Isabella Maria "la secunda" and Maria Lucrezia II for sisters. In each case the deceased relative's name was bestowed on the next child born.[54] The Florentine priorities noted by Christian Klapisch-Zuber also applied in the Veneto, with preference for siblings over grandparents, immediate kin over lateral kin, paternal side over maternal side, recently dead over remote ancestor. They never reused the name of living kin, as this would contradict the twin aims of perpetuating the dead and securing heavenly patrons. In Florence the name of a first wife was often given to the first daughter of a second,[55] which was also Veneto usage (hence Caterina Chiara Arnaldi, after Caterina Zugliano).

Once relatives had been duly remade, the next strategy was to honor a saint.[56] Children born sickly were often immediately named Giovanni or Giovanna to secure the protection of the Baptist, as happened frequently in the Veneto.[57] The rest were named according to a hierarchy of priorities. Most important was reiteration of the saints of a family cult, such as Francesco-Chiara-Bernardino among the Arnaldi and Bartolomeo among the Repeta. Slightly less commonly invoked was the saint on whose day the child was born.[58] This was the case with eight of the Arnaldi: Marcella Fracanzani, Angela Chiara Antonia, Ursula, Silvestro, Paola Martina, Tommaso Salvatore, Cassandra Antonia, and Michele Agostino. This practice offered the additional advantage of infusing new names into a family's stock and preventing the petrification of nomenclature. Least important for the memorialists, as for the population at large, were civic, plague, apocryphal, medieval, and foreign saints, as well as the Holy Family.

Over time, however, names were not constant. It has been said of Florence that "given names formed a sort of family patrimony, no part of which should be neglected or lost"; over time the name was a constant and the individual was "interchangeable."[59] In the Veneto, while families were no less concerned to establish a strong and continuous lineage, they were less respectful of tradition. The Arnaldi ceased to name children after the Magi, perhaps because in the second generation Gaspara and Melchiorre died in infancy. The cult of St. Francis proved equally ephemeral: only two of the dozen Arnaldi named Francesco, Chiara, or Bernardino survived to adulthood, and after 1460 the name was not repeated. The little Jeromes proved healthier, as did the Magdalenes, and these names stuck. The Stoppi dropped the name of the patriarch Bartolomeo, who had moved the family to Verona, and Girolamo Stoppi left one uncle and four deceased brothers un-remade when he named his third son. Verità Verità had eleven children, but gave only one a family name. Nomenclature, after all, is in some measure contractual: the saint was expected to repay the honor by protecting the little eponym. If he or she did not, substitutes were available.

Godparents

The child was born to the flesh, to blood mother and father, but as baptism constituted a second birth in the spirit the infant required an additional set of parents. In metaphoric terms, as the midwife had lifted the child from the womb in physical birth, the godparent lifted up *(levavit)* the child in its spiritual birth.[60] Thereafter, biological and baptismal parents were jointly responsible for raising the child. They were, in the terminology of the day, co-parents.

Spiritual parentage was analogous to and hence was to mirror natural parentage. The Church wished spiritual parents to be of about the same number as blood parents, and disliked multiple sponsors.[61] Memorialists in the Veneto respected this norm and gave children, on average, two godparents (see appendix, table 2.6).[62] Only five of seventy-five children were given four or more sponsors, with five—a single case—the maximum. Figures for the Veneto are below those of Florence, where *ricordanze* demonstrate a mean of nearly three godparents per child.[63] The mob scenes occasionally reported for very great families in Florence and Venice—the later Freschi averaged nine—find no parallel in Verona and Vicenza. The number of godparents was not constant among children: Veneto sons had on average 2.2 godparents, and daughters only 1.8, just as Florentine boys received more sponsors than girls and Freschi boys received on average two more godparents than their sisters.[64] Cementing social ties for sons, who would remain within the patriline, was more important than for daughters, who would marry out of it. In godparentage as in names, girls began life with fewer spiritual resources than did their brothers.

Further, theorists urged that the child have one godparent of its own sex, and ideally one male and one female godparent.[65] In the fifteenth century in the Veneto, however, gender symmetry and parity were little respected. Some 85 percent of godparents reported in the memoirs were male, about the figure reported for Florence[66] and precisely the figure for twenty Freschi baptisms. This is no surprise: co-parentage, after all, incurred reciprocal obligations and services—political support, mediation, loans, and gifts—which were largely public and denied to women.[67] More surprising, the imbalance was more pronounced for daughters than for sons: girls' godparents were 89 percent male, compared to boys' 82 percent. A third of sons were given godmothers, but fewer than a fifth of daughters (see appendix, table 2.6). Among the Freschi, too, a higher percentage of boys received godmothers than did girls (19 percent versus 11 percent).

Baptismal and natural kinship were to be complementary, not duplicative: godparents should be chosen from outside the body of blood relations. The injunction, while never absolute, was largely respected.[68] As a corollary, no one should serve as godparent to more than one child within a family. As

St. Augustine preached, sacraments spread charity through spiritual kinship, and the Christian family should extend as widely as possible.[69] Serving as godparent to several children wasted an opportunity to extend bonds of mutual amity, and anyway was redundant since the godparent was already related to all siblings. Memorialists of the Veneto paid little heed to this norm. Bartolomeo d'Avanzo and his wife Caterina raised at the font six of Alvise Stoppi's seven children, and Tommaso Lavagnoli seven times sponsored a child of Verità Verità. Marco Mironi was godfather to seven of Andrea Arnaldi's children, while his wife was twice chosen and his son served as godfather to a great-nephew. Antonio Scroffa was five times a godfather to the Arnaldi, and Pietro Valmarana four times. Five other men each sponsored two children. In consequence, the pool of co-parents was small. Among the Arnaldi, for example, about two-thirds of all spiritual relationships were established by individuals or families who accepted more than one godchild.[70]

Diffusion of spiritual kinship was not, then, a priority. Neither, it would seem, was spiritual mentorship: no memoir mentions godparents' roles in the moral or religious education of children. Giovanni Dominici, indeed, thought that the entire spiritual dimension had disappeared from the institution of godparentage, and that baptism now served to create purely social alliances—a development that he condemned in the strongest possible terms.[71] Recent historians have agreed with his perception, and note, for example, that there is little evidence of ongoing relationships between adults and their godparents. Instead, as Giovanni Morelli noted with approval, godparentage formalized advantageous friendship (*amicitia*) between co-parents.[72]

For the Arnaldi, best-documented of the Veneto families, co-parents occupied a place distinct from the family's other systems of linkages. They did not provide husbands and wives.[73] They did not order or receive testamentary bequests, and were not chosen as heirs.[74] Only rarely were they business partners. They were not executors of wills or guardians of minor children. Godparents, instead, widened the social range and created new clusters of alliance and obligation. For example, the early Arnaldi married strictly within their neighborhood and occupational group; they chose co-parents who lived elsewhere in the city and practiced trades other than commerce in wool and the notariate. They also chose spiritual *amici* who were unlike themselves, forming patronage and clientage bonds with superiors and inferiors— those with whom marriage would have been unthinkable.[75] This strategy ran contrary to ecclesiastical teaching, which viewed *amicitia* in terms of an egalitarian rather than a unsymmetrical relationship and thought that birth parents and spiritual parents should hold a rough parity: the *patrinus* (god-father) was not a *patronus* (patron).[76] The Arnaldi did not see matters that way, however, and selected godparents for their children from somewhat higher or much lower strata of the population.

The Vicentine social order can be established with some precision from Pagliarini's *Cronicae*, which ranked the city's "noble houses" in order of importance. The Arnaldi occupied the thirty-sixth position, which fell in the 87th percentile. The Mironi family, ten times godparents, ranked seventeen places and six percentiles higher. The Mironi had owned palaces in the city from at least 1222, and had supplied several civic martyrs to the city's vain efforts to overthrow past tyrants: by any standard except wealth they counted for more than the Arnaldi. The Valmarana, six times godparents, could trace their family back five centuries and had produced several lawyers and titled nobles *(equites aurati)*; they ranked twenty-two places and eight percentiles above the Arnaldi.[77] The family of Bartolomeo Loschi, godfather to Andrea Giovanni Arnaldi, occupied the first position.

The Arnaldi also, on several occasions, looked downward. An additional set of godparents ranked so low that they appeared in neither tax records nor Pagliarini's chronicles. All were women, just as upwards of 70 percent of Florentine godmothers were drawn from the ranks of artisans, the poor, and the *miserabili*.[78] Lucia Spira and madonna Palma were midwives or nurses, pressed into service as godmothers in emergency baptisms. The relationship may not, however, have been ephemeral, since the *baila* was often kept on as a domestic servant: the employer-employee relationship might be cemented with ties of spiritual kinship. Two other godmothers, Benvenuta, who lived in the hospital of San Marcello, and Caterina, the mother of Thomas the carpenter, were apparently poor or marginal: extending *caritas* to the fringes of society was a Christian duty often fulfilled at baptism.[79] Finally, two godmothers were wives of important rural tenants. It will be seen that the Arnaldi, as all landowners, faced constant obstacles to collecting rents; cooption of Maria da Setteca and Bona della Longa would certainly intensify their husbands' sense of obligation.

Parents and Children

After baptism, and before marriage, the record grows faint. A scant half dozen notices, amid hundreds of pages of written memory, tell us that some mothers, particularly in the Bovi and Guastaverza families, heeded the advice of moralists and physicians and nursed their children. Other parents, particularly in the Arnaldi family, resisted that advice[80] and sent children out to be nursed. Weaning came at seventeen to twenty months.[81] Northern Italian memorialists, concerned only to document salient points in the life cycle, made no comment on subsequent socialization, education, or training. If little can be gleaned concerning childhood proper, memoirs at least provide indicators as to how parents, particularly fathers, regarded their children. When the writers of Verona and Vicenza lifted their usual reticence to note exceptional moments in the lives of offspring, they came as close as they ever would to revealing their emotions.

With uncharacteristic loquaciousness Andrea Arnaldi embroidered the account of his daughter Giovanna Gaspara's life and death, and thus personalized the child. She was born prematurely, at seven months in the opinion of her mother, so ill-formed in body that she was believed to be a boy and was baptized with a male name. The family entertained hopes for her survival, as she was given the playful nickname Valvina as a mark of a distinct identity. She died within four months, however, and Andrea allowed himself a rare comment: "she suffered great pain before she migrated from this life, and she suffered for two straight days." The birth of his next child was a happier event, and prompted the sort of quirky detail that suggests a delighted father: Angela Chiara "brought with her at birth two teeth in her lower gums, towards the back."[82]

So, too, Bartolomeo Muronovo, who rarely devoted more than a few lines to each offspring, relaxed his taciturnity but once: daughter Elena, long sick of an infirmity that the doctors despaired of curing, was miraculously healed through prayers to St. Peter Martyr. That day she pledged to wear the Dominican habit for a year, and more than fulfilled the vow. Manfredo Repeta, not one for emotional outbursts or commentary, briefly noted that on the death of son Girolamo from flux and fever "all the city was greatly sorrowed, because he was comely and robust in body and heart." Silvestro Arnaldi offered a vignette of grandson Renaldo's four days of "sickness of the body" and the boy's death at the auspicious moment of the ringing of the Ave Maria bells. A garland was placed on the child's head and the servant Francesco Veronese, arms uncovered as sign of grief and humility, carried the tiny body to the cathedral for burial in the family tomb. This was the only time Silvestro put pen to paper.[83]

Surely it is not forcing the evidence to conclude that some writers dearly loved some of the children in their midst. How representative are these anecdotes? The problem with formulating an answer is that the debate that has swirled around the famous thesis of Philippe Aries, that "in medieval soci-

ety the idea of childhood did not exist," and around oft-repeated conclusions
that medieval parents were indifferent or downright harsh to their children,[84]
has drawn from prescription rather than experience.

A considerable body of writing might support a view of non- or anti-affec-
tionate parent-child relations. Francesco Barbaro, for example, advised parents to show *gravitas* to children. More than one author suggested that parents should resist emotional investment in newborns because of the likelihood
of early death.[85] Giovanni Dominici deplored parental displays of affection
because Ecclesiasticus 7:26 forbade parents to show a "glad face" to daughters and because excessive cuddling planted the seeds of later immorality. He
and Bernardino da Feltre thought children weak in mind, sinful, and prone
to vice, better served by parents' stern vigilance than affection.[86] In Matthew
10:37 Jesus declared that "he who loves son or daughter more than me is not
worthy of me," and medieval commentators hammered home the point that
inordinate love of children distracted from love of God. Augustine, in one of
his more Manichaeist moments, concluded that "The coming of Christ is not
served by the begetting of children."[87]

Counterprescription is not lacking, however. Augustine elsewhere counted
offspring a positive consequence of marriage. Others offered a vision of childhood innocence and purity. Fifteen-year-old St. Agapitus, in the *vita* copied
by Bartolomeo dal Bovo, modeled Christian eloquence and fortitude. Dominici's authoritarianism came from conviction that children were the
greatest gift that God committed to humans, and that parents had a fundamental obligation to raise children in a solicitude born of *caritas*. Barbaro,
even at his most reserved, was animated by concern that children turn out
well. Salimbene of Siena counted children the first of "those things dearest
to a man." Petrarch declaimed against women and marriage, but mourned
his daughter Francesca and a little grandson who bore his name. Boccaccio,
too, attacked marriage but expressed tenderness to his daughter in one
eclogue, and in the *Ninfale* he vividly portrayed parents' grief at a son's
death.[88]

The bachelor stoic of Alberti's *Libri della famiglia*, urging indifference to
a child's death, is brusquely rebutted by a married opponent who dismisses
his advice as hopelessly theoretical; interlocutors who endorse parental love
are not contradicted. "Who could believe, except by experience of his own
feelings, how great and powerful is the love of a father for his children?"
asks the married Adovardo, and Lionardo answers that "a father's love is indeed immense." Paolo da Certaldo located love for children among the four
great loves of a happy man, second only to love of God.[89] Funeral orations

for children owed their genre to the ancients, but their impetus to actual events; Gianozzo Manetti found grief at the death of a child a natural and even necessary response, and thought that stoic repression of love brutalized the soul. Salutati and others rejected stoic commonplaces. Back in Verona, Giorgio Bevilaqua da Lazise's *Excusatio* has been termed an "epic record of parental grief."[90]

On both the learned and popular levels, the cult of the Holy Family promoted a vision of childhood innocence, parental devotion, and mutual warmth. The earlier image of a foolish or irascible old Joseph gave way to one of a model head of household, protective and fond. In a Paduan sermon, for example, Bernardino da Feltre embroidered the account of the Presentation in Luke 2:22–35 with an invented dialogue: Simeon says to Joseph, "Let us die together happily, I wish to die with you because I have seen the Messiah"; Joseph prefers to experience the Christ in family life, saying, "I wish to live and work with him, to stay with him and enjoy his presence."[91] When Joseph died and ascended to heaven, a cross appeared over his head to signal divine approval of his words.

Nor was close bonding viewed as the exclusive province of fathers. The mother "very much loves her infant, embraces, kisses and lovingly nurses and feeds it," said Bartholomaeus Anglicus. To Jacopo da Voragine, a woman would mourn the death of a child more than would a man, because she had worked harder to bear and raise it, spent more time and was more intimate with it. Jurists assumed that maternal love was stronger than any other bond that could guarantee a child's well-being, favoring mothers as guardians of minor children "by reason of maternal obligation and presumed affection" ("ratio pietatis materne et presumpte affectionis"). Christine de Pisan celebrated her own mother's affections and stressed the great pleasure that mothers took in their children, especially in their daughters.[92] In Venice, one Freschi mother was thought to have died of sorrow over the death of her daughter.

Moving the discussion from the literary and prescriptive to the everyday text confirms that parental tenderness was common: Tuscan memoirs echo the intense attachment suggested in Veneto counterparts. The most vivid account is that of Giovanni Morelli, whose grief at the death of sons Alberto and Antoniotto dominates the last hundred pages of the *Ricordi*. He recorded Alberto's final days in excruciating detail: "no one could be of so hard a heart that he would not have had pity, seeing him in such pain." Mother and father were so consumed by "inestimable sorrow" that they left the house for a month, and they could not bear to enter the boy's room for a very long time. A year afterward, unable to put his sorrow to rest, the "afflicted and tribulated father" reproached himself for harshness to Alberto, endlessly recalled the boy's death and his own incessant prayers since, and swung wildly between spiritual comfort and bitter suffering.[93]

If Morelli was extreme in self-analysis and expressiveness, he was far from unique in his solicitude. Other diarists, noting with bookkeeper's care the details of infant deaths, wet nurse contracts, apprenticeships, unruly sons' misdeeds, and negotiations toward marriage alliances, demonstrate a more businesslike but no less intense engagement in raising offspring. Recent writers who have worked through the prosaic documentation of wills, memoirs, and letters have remarked on the consistent intensity of parents' emotional responses to children: joy at birth, sorrow at death, tenderness, anxiety, and pleasure in childraising, and solace in the domestic circle. If Venetian testators showed "coldness" and "stoniness" in disposing of daughters in marriage, for example, they also showed considerable tenderness. One referred to "my most sweet daughter, my very heart," whom "I love as my own soul."[94]

IN FLORENCE IN 1427, on average, a baby was born to a mother aged approximately twenty-six and a father of around forty. The extreme age gap between fathers and children has supported a string of hypotheses regarding family dynamics and the psychological development of offspring. Fathers, according to this model, were distant from their wives and children in age and experience, and were preoccupied with business and political commitments. They were likely to be emotionally remote from children, and death often removed them from the scene altogether. Mothers, therefore, were primary figures in the moral upbringing of children, and likely were the focus of their affections. Moralists worried that maternal care produced spoiled and effeminate boys; insufficient paternal control may have resulted in young men's lawlessness.[95]

Distance in age does not, however, automatically translate into emotional distance, and it is not certain that older fathers might not enjoy close bonds with sons and daughters. Indeed, the many paintings of a doting St. Joseph and portraits of older men exchanging fond glances with children and grandchildren (Ghirlandaio and Perugino provide examples) suggest that the Quattrocento did not see age as an impediment to affection. Moreover, prescriptive and prosaic literature assumed that fathers were active parents, even the principal agents of children's moral formation. Vegio, Dominici, and Alberti addressed their remarks on childrearing to fathers, demanding but also presuming paternal guidance. Writers of *ricordanze,* too, laid down precepts and *exempla* for sons to follow when, in turn, they headed households.

Even if the general lines of the age-gap thesis are accepted, its effects would have been blunted outside Florence because the gap was much less. Again, the Tuscan capital stands at an extreme: fathers in the rest of Tuscany were considerably younger than their Florentine colleagues. In the Veneto the age gap was still less, since men married much earlier and women married slightly later than did Florentines. In 1425 fathers in Verona were two years younger than Florentines when their children were born, and mothers were two years older. By 1502 the gap had shrunk farther, with fathers and mothers only six years apart.[96] By the logic of the age-gap model Veneto fathers would have been more capable of emotional engagement and guidance. They also were less likely to die during their children's childhood, leaving upbringing solely to the mother. Indeed, the memoirs indicate that a child would more likely lose its mother than its father (see appendix, table 2.7). The demographics of marriage and birth in the Veneto offered the likelihood of relatively symmetrical parenting, without the wide variation in treatment that has been presumed for Florence.

DAUGHTERS LEFT less trace in the record. Fathers often noted the marriage of the eldest, but did not document the fate of the younger. Among the Arnaldi, what became of Ursula Imperatrice, Caterina Chiara, Chiara Julia Martina, Paola Martina, and Maddalena? Probably they died young, because they do not show up in wills or dowry documents, but the fact that they could die without notice indicates disregard. Veneto memoirs, in general, noted the deaths of many more men than women; the imbalance is especially pronounced for the young, with 61 percent of entries recording the death of a son.[97] Those daughters who survived warranted a notarized dowry confession, but only occasionally a place in family memory: what befell them after marriage was seldom noted. Fathers, as has been seen, gave fewer baptismal sponsors to their daughters than to their sons, and by giving daughters fanciful names deprived them of sponsors in heaven. Tommaso Arnaldi listed the godparents of the sons of his second marriage but did not fill in the blank space allocated for godparents of daughters; he was disinterested in spiritual kinship through the female line. Antonio da Romagno openly acknowledged that he loved his son Tullio more than the boy's twin sister.

A considerable body of prescriptive writing confirms differential attitudes to children. Padua's Michele Savonarola, for example, revealed techniques for conceiving sons with the assumption that this was what readers wanted. Alberti thought it a good sign in a prospective bride that she had brothers but not sisters, that is, that her family was disposed to produce males; his model newlyweds offered prayers for sons.[98] Dominici thought that girls, because of their "imperfect nature," were more inclined to shameful luxury. Maffeo Vegio counseled parents to supervise daughters closely since women as "fragile and vain vessels" were "more subject to danger." Paolo da Certaldo found it unnecessary to feed girls beyond the level of subsistence, and thought there was no point in teaching daughters to write unless they were destined for convents.[99] Bernardino da Feltre was even more brutal: "By woman is signified vice and guilt, by man good works; by woman leaves and chatter, by man fruit and deeds. . . . A girl is merchandise which should not be kept in the house, for it spoils easily, and when it is spoiled and corrupted it cannot be sold."[100] Daughters in Milan, Florence, and San Gimignano were consigned to foundling hospitals and convents far more often than sons.[101] Tax returns grossly underreported girls; more frequent rounding off of their ages indicates that fathers were relatively indifferent to their anagraphic standing.[102] In Vicenza, no one knew or cared how old Ursula Imperatrice Arnaldi was.[103]

The pendulum should not swing too far. There is little evidence that daughters were systematically or exclusively ignored, or that girls received lesser or even detrimental care. The most serious charge, that childraising customs produced a sort of female infanticide, rests on conjecture.[104] Claims that fathers refused to present a glad face to daughters or gave them unequal nourishment rest on the assumption that fathers actually obeyed the unpleasant prescriptions of misogynists such as Dominici, Vegio, da Certaldo, and da Feltre. Denying daughters access to higher learning, restricting their training to domestic management, and limiting their movements in the interests of chastity offend modern sensibilities, not those of the fifteenth century. None of the claims of deterioration in the treatment of girls is plausible, since the sorts of evidence adduced do not allow for measurement over time and, in any case, the whole notion rests on a mythic and undemonstrable golden age for women sometime in the past.

There is some good evidence to the contrary, albeit of an anecdotal and nonquantifiable sort. The voluminous Datini correspondence reveals one case of a girl "lovingly cared for and taught to read, dressed up and indulged by both parents and finally married off in style"—and she was an illegitimate daughter. The childless Margherita Datini "borrowed" a niece for extended periods of time. The girl gave such pleasure to aunt and uncle, and in turn received such fine clothes and education, that only with difficulty did the parents reclaim her.[105] Alessandra Macinghi Strozzi may have been in a hurry to marry off her daughters, but she also cited the proverb that "as long as there are girls at home, nothing is done that isn't for them," admitting that daughters more likely experienced a surfeit than a deficit of affection. Da Certaldo, in a kinder moment, urged parents to love sons and daughters alike.[106] Among recent historians, Gavitt has strongly denied that female foundlings in Florence suffered especially harsh treatment or higher mortality rates. Chojnacki concludes that Venetian daughters increasingly enjoyed the capacity to make a choice among marriage, convent, and—a novelty—an unmarried life in the world.[107]

To return to the Veneto: Bonaventura Bovi, with three sons living, singled out a daughter as "most honest and modest, most sweet and well-loved" of his children.[108] Andrea Arnaldi lavished detail only on his daughters Giovanna Gaspara and Angela Chiara: they received effusive welcomes and sorrowful farewells while sons were born and died with spare narrative. He noted the birth of a daughter to his daughter Margarita Bona, but failed to record the birth of grandson Antonio. Arnaldi sons, too, frequently disappeared from the record: the fates of Giovanni Francesco Bernardino, Tommaso Salvatore, Andrea Giovanni, Alvise Giovanni, and Girolamo are mysteries. The bias of the memoirs is not really very strong; several of the authors—Alvise and Donato Stoppi, Bartolomeo dal Bovo, Bartolomeo Muronovo, and Manfredo Repeta—showed strict impartiality in recording the lives of sons and daughters.

CHAPTER THREE

DEATH

The Demographics of Death

Mortality

*T*HE MEMOIRS OF THE VENETO allow reconstruction of the life span of fifty-eight women and seventy-six men (see appendix, table 3.1). The death toll began early, as 6.7 percent of children did not survive their first week. A further 5.9 percent died between one and four weeks of age. Nearly a quarter (22.3 percent) did not celebrate a first birthday, and nearly a third (31.3 percent) did not live beyond age three. While mortality rates for young children (four–twelve years: 5.9 percent) and adolescents (thirteen–nineteen years: 3.7 percent) dropped steadily, losses remained high. Overall, four children in ten did not reach age twenty. This figure is, if anything, on the low side.[1]

Boys were far more vulnerable in the early years. About 17 percent of males died within a month of birth, compared with about 7 percent of females. The gap then closed slightly, but the first year still favored girls (17 percent of whom died) over boys (26 percent), as did the one–three year age span. Boys fared slightly better than girls in the rest of childhood and adolescence, but their success could not compensate for much higher losses in the neonatal and infant stages: about 5.5 percent more of the female cohort survived to age twenty than did male counterparts.

These data seem to support the demographic argument for dowry inflation: a paucity of eligible males forced the fathers of girls to bid for husbands by offering ever-larger dowries. Simple survival to physical maturity is only part of the story. During the stage of reproductive maturity (twenty–thirty-nine years), the sex ratio swung brusquely back into balance: some men died (7.9 percent), but at less than one-third the rate for women (25.9 percent). Men were frequently widowed while able to produce children, and they reentered the pool of eligible husbands. Marital pressure on the families of young women was only significant if they sought young husbands; if they were willing to accept older or widowed husbands, their chances were much improved.

The Veneto data also belie the common image of Renaissance cities replete with older women. The higher death rate for women between the ages of twenty and thirty-nine actually tipped the sex ratio of the middle-aged and elderly in favor of men. Nearly half of men lived to the age of forty (48.7 percent), compared with little more than a third of women (36.2 percent). Among the old, those who survived to age sixty, the preponderance of males is also pronounced (34.2 percent versus 22.4 percent).

Figures from the Veneto match up well against those of other cities, though differences between types of data can never allow a precise match. The 22.3 percent of Veneto children who died in their first year falls between the 17 percent and 18 percent of Florentines who died at wet nurse and the 26.6 percent of foundlings who died in that city's hospital of the Innocenti in a normal year; in Milan, 20 percent of all deaths were those of children under a year.[2] In the Veneto, as in Milan, a third of all children died before their fourth birthday. In Milan, too, death rates were highest in the first year of life, declining throughout later childhood and adolescence, and in the early age groups Milanese boys were more vulnerable than girls. The Veneto's slight reversal in gender fortunes about the age of four finds some confirmation elsewhere: in four of five years tabulated from the Milanese books of the dead, more girls died in childhood and adolescence than did boys.[3] Overall childhood mortality, though, may have been slightly lower in the Veneto than elsewhere: children below the age of twenty suffered 50.6 percent of deaths recorded in Florence's books of the dead, and 52.5 percent in a similar source in Milan, compared with 41 percent for those recorded in Veneto memoirs.[4] In three generations of the Freschi in Venice, girls fared better than boys in infancy, but not in adolescence; 43 percent of all children died before age twenty; a high incidence of female death in childbearing years reversed the sex ratio in favor of men, more of whom lived to old age.

Veneto evidence for longevity does not swing far from the mark. Florentine men who reached the age of twenty-five, like their counterparts in Verona, Vicenza, and Padua, could usually anticipate another three or more decades of life. So, too, could men in Perigeux and the Limousin.[5] Indicators that Veneto men were reaching old age in greater numbers than women by the later Quattrocento can be partially corroborated: in the tax records of Verona and Florence, elderly men outnumbered elderly women at the end of the century.[6] Even an apparent anomaly in the Veneto memoirs, a slump in survival rates and life expectancy for those born after 1450 (in an era when most historians see a rising population), finds confirmation in Florentine *ricordanze*, which indicate a dip in life span for the 1476–1500 period.[7]

DEATHS, like other events in the life cycle, were not scattered randomly around the calendar. Seasonal mortality was particularly sensitive to epidemics, which hit hardest at specific times of year: gastrointestinal infections in high summer, plague in late summer and early autumn, influenza in winter, and typhus in winter and early spring. The breakdown of deaths into monthly totals can, therefore, be used to track mortality crises. An unusually high death rate in July through October, for example, seems a strong indicator of plague and its co-contagions.

The 119 dated deaths in a dozen Veneto families have some indicative value (see appendix, table 3.2). As was the case in Florence and among Venice's Freschi, the summer death rate was by far the highest (36.1 percent of all deaths), with fall and spring far healthier (21 percent and 16.8 percent of deaths, respectively). The major difference is that winter, by far the healthiest season in Tuscany, was second-deadliest in the north (26.1 percent), perhaps because winters are colder and wetter there. Veneto deaths exhibit more intense swings between the seasons than do the relatively flat Tuscan curves of "normal" years, and more closely approach the violent fluctuations of plague years on a regular basis.[8] In particular, the Veneto figures for August (10.1 percent of deaths) and September (16.8 percent) drive the summer rate up to a level well above the norm elsewhere.[9]

Seasonal mortality, broken down into age groups, furnishes evidence for a crucial but vexing question: did the very young suffer disproportionately from the plague?[10] In the Veneto, deaths of the mature were spaced fairly evenly throughout the year. Deaths of the young, on the other hand, concentrated in March and April, suggesting difficulty in surviving the winter, and especially in the summer, perhaps indicating a lack of resistance to the epidemics of the hot season. Half of children and adolescents died in the plague months of July, August, and September,[11] compared to a third of their older kin.

Timing of female deaths roughly echoed that of the population in general, male deaths that of the young. Unfortunately, sex-specific calculation does not find corroboration elsewhere, as historians have not looked at this aspect of gender demography. In the Veneto, at least, women died fairly evenly throughout the year. Summer rates were the highest for women, but were well below that of the overall population, and if September was again the most perilous month it only tied with November and barely exceeded August. Men, on the other hand, were struck down overwhelmingly in the summer, with a sharp spike in September; perhaps they were more vulnerable to plague.

Veneto memoirs support the thesis that the plague lost potency over the course of the fifteenth century.[12] Before 1450 some 57.7 percent of deaths were recorded in the July through September period when bubonic plague raged most fiercely. The summer figure for deaths after 1450 fell to 30.1 percent, and deaths in the later Quattrocento exhibit gently rising and falling curves, with mortality spaced more evenly over the calendar. Perhaps people after 1450 had acquired resistance, or perhaps plague pathogens grew more feeble. Perhaps, too, the growing incidence of typhus, smallpox, tuberculosis, and associated co-contagions smoothed out the sharp seasonal clustering of death characteristic of an earlier age of virulent bubonic plague. Mortality peaks in the later Quattrocento came at times—October–November, January–March—which earlier had been relatively safe.[13] In any case, after 1450 people had less reason to fear sudden and overwhelming surges in mortality—except in September, when no era found safety.

Family demography hints at general demography. The number of tax households reported by Vicentine memorialist families rose by 69 percent between 1453 and 1505, while Veronese memorialists show a 170 percent rise in the number of tax households in the 1425–1502 period (see appendix, tables 3.3–3.4). The size of Veronese memorialist families reported in *anagrafi* (another sign of a healthy population), grew from a mean of 4.7 persons before 1460 to 5.3 persons in the final decades of the century (see appendix, table 3.5).

Over the Quattrocento, the population of urban Verona nearly tripled, while that of Padua doubled in the century after 1430.[14] Circumstantial evidence for Vicenza points to a demographic resurgence there as well. Urban leaders perceived saturation and tacitly dropped inducements to repopulation: the city encouraged immigration into the 1430s, offering tax breaks and citizenship to artisans who came to live in the city, but in the later part of the century progressively tightened immigration requirements and after around 1480 placed formidable obstacles before those who wished to become citizens.[15] Placement of the new church of S. Rocco in a suburb may reflect a municipal attempt to ease increasing density in the urban core by directing settlement to the periphery. By 1471 there are indications of rural overpopulation as well: the commune forbade construction of houses on smaller holdings in order to discourage continued fractioning of land. After 1504 rural communes could not concede tax immunities to immigrants. The latter measure may be part of the city's battle to maintain economic superiority by preventing the influx of skilled workers into country towns, but it is equally likely that reversal of pro-growth policies reflects a perception that the countryside was overcrowded when measured against food supply and economic opportunity.[16]

How can we account for population growth? It seems likely, as mentioned above, that plague virulence was attenuated in the second half of the fifteenth century, and that new epidemics were never as lethal as the earlier plague had been. The memoirs of the Veneto offer three further explanations. First, the average female age at marriage declined by about two years, from just over twenty-one to just over nineteen. Second, female mortality during the childbearing years also declined: before 1450, about 28.1 percent of women in the 20–39 age group died, compared with 23.1 percent of women born after midcentury. Third, the interval between pregnancies dropped by a third, from thirty months to twenty months. More women enjoyed full reproductive careers, and those careers were longer and more productive. From the first third of the century to the last third, the period spent in childbearing rose by thirty-five months, and the average number of children born to each mother increased from 5.8 to 9.6.

The population grew throughout late-fifteenth-century Italy,[17] but with significant local variation. The higher rate of incomplete or truncated (i.e., biologically unproductive) households in metropolitan centers, coupled with higher mortality, may have reduced the replacement rate to below the point of equilibrium in some larger cities. In some cases, the persistence of social strategies reduced opportunities for demographic expansion. In Florence and Venice especially the imperative of conserving family patrimonies led to a high rate of celibacy (monastic and otherwise) and a higher age of males at the time of marriage. Government efforts to encourage marriage were not successful. More efficient cities with new health and security laws, sanctioning expulsion of vagabonds and restricting the influx of people from infected areas, suffered the trade-off of slower demographic recovery.[18] As a consequence, the pace of Italian repopulation varied widely from place to place. Among the big cities Milan offered strong inducements to immigration and a successful annonary policy, and showed signs of recovery by 1410–30.[19]

Venice, Siena, and Florence, on the other hand, hit bottom in the first decades of the fifteenth century, and rose substantially only after 1450.[20]

The Veneto was particularly well placed. Relatively larger rural hinterlands guaranteed a pool of potential immigrants; protectionist obstacles to immigration, constantly repeated, were apparently ineffectual. Celibacy was rare, and the age of males at the time of marriage was considerably lower than was the case in Florence. Moreover, Herlihy's calculations for Verona indicate that biologically unproductive households—measured by the number of marital nuclei per household—were also more rare than in Florence. Indeed, provincial cities in general fared better than metropolitan counterparts. The smaller Tuscan cities reached their demographic nadir earlier and then grew faster than the center. As the population of Verona tripled that of Florence grew at a more modest rate—modest in relation to other regions as well—and the Tuscan capital declined in the overall Italian ranking.[21]

Pathology and Piety

A majority of Veronese and Vicentine citizens simply died (*morì, decessit, mortua est, morite*, or the like). Sometimes memoirs located their deaths in terms of day, hour, and place, but fewer than one-fifth of entries noted the cause. The very purpose of a memoir would render the final illness a lesser concern: the fact of death alone was sufficient to trace genealogy and to assure posterity that ancestors were available as heavenly intercessors. All ancestors had to die sometime, and the precipitating cause was of little account. When memorialists wished to be expansive they concentrated, instead, on the afterlife. Several Arnaldi, for example, "fell asleep in God" (= Acts 7:60), "died to our Lord Jesus Christ," or "flew up to the heavenly kingdom." Valeria Bevilaqua da Lazise, wife of Contino Stoppi, "passed from this mortal to a happier life."

Memorialists were not insensitive to the mortality crises that hammered these cities throughout the century. Indeed, *peste* or *morbo contagioso* was by far the most frequently mentioned cause of death. Still, etiological aspects of death did not occasion much comment before midcentury. When they did so, the stress was still on spiritual consequences. The epidemic that swept away Giacomo Verità in 1428 was less important than the fact that he "left this life and gained a life which is true life." When Andrea Arnaldi in 1438 noted that a daughter was born in the country because of the "plague which raged in Vicenza," his concern was not with rampant disease but with the fact that Ursula Imperatrice had to be baptized away from home. The flux that killed his brother received less attention than the fact that Tommaso received the last rites.

Early writers were not simply fatalistic before mass contagion. Manfredo Repeta offered a recipe for pills, compounded from herbs and white wine, to combat *pestilentia* and several other illnesses. Less pleasant was the "optimal medicine" suggested by Bartolomeo dal Bovo, largely concocted of the afflicted person's urine: "give it secretly, because it's really bitter."[22] But he little trusted his own remedy: when the plague struck Verona in 1438 dal Bovo immediately left town.[23] He and other memorialists paid little heed to the moralists and theologians who held that escape constituted a breach of charity to neighbors, or that any effort to escape God's judgment was futile, or that stoic resignation was the preferred response to contagion.[24]

Before midcentury, governments, too, had little to offer. Most municipalities, like that of Vicenza, simply reiterated ancient and ineffectual injunctions against depositing offal and waste in the streets, keeping unpenned beasts in the city, washing skins or throwing dyes in rivers, selling diseased animals, or admitting lepers.[25] Equally time-honored was appeasement of God's wrath through public charity, Masses, and processions of miracle-working images. Suffering continuous plague for twenty-four years, Vicentines honored an appearance by the Virgin with foundation of a great church on the Monte Berico overlooking the city. The strategy worked: a chronicler noted that the plague immediately ceased.[26] Authorities, too, gave priority to the spiritual consequences rather than the pathological agency of death. Statutes of Vicenza (1425) commanded that no physician or doctor could visit a sick person more than three times "unless first the infirm person accepts penance or is confessed of his sins with a priest."[27] Disease posed less danger to the city than the possibility that citizens might die in a state of sin.

Only by about the mid-Quattrocento did memorialists regard disease as worthy of attention, and governments look on the more virulent forms of disease as requiring specific intervention. The memoirs' earliest attempt at diagnosis came in 1438, with the note of Giacomo Verità's "contagious sickness which was hidden and not apparent on the body." A decade later Girolamo Arnaldi "fell asleep in God," as was formulaic, but his father noted that the boy "had been sick for 13 days with a flux in his body, without blood however, and with fevers and an intense heat in his body, and with worms." Thereafter, medical commentary became commonplace. An Arnaldi uncle and aunt died in 1456 "from the plague," Tommaso in 1463 went to the heavenly kingdom after fifteen days of flux, and little Renaldo fell asleep in the Lord after four days of "sickness in his body"; others died of flux, fever, a disease of the head, and mysterious illnesses such as *postimation* and *rioma*.[28] After midcentury, in fact, physical explanation of death is more common than spiritual comment.

These diagnoses could hardly have been anything more than vague descriptives, given medical knowledge at the time. Moreover, contagions of the later Quattrocento were more etiologically complex, with newly strengthened diseases such as tuberculosis, influenza, dysentery, typhus, and smallpox mixed with various forms of plague: not even experts could distinguish an underlying cause of death. Yet at least memorialists were making an effort to look directly at sickness and attempt an analysis. Manfredo Repeta, for example, associated terrible weather, meager harvests, and high food prices with the *grandissima pestilentia* of 1464 and a lesser *peste* the following year. His ecological-annonary argument, widespread in Italy and England,[29] indicates a newfound empiricism and attention to the body.

So, too, if learned doctors remained stuck in Galenic miasmic theory, blaming epidemics on "corruption of the air," pragmatic legislators began to work from a vague, poorly articulated, but accurate theory of contagion. Progressive cities passed measures to isolate the infected from the healthy and to seal off entire provinces from surrounding areas of high mortality. Already in the early 1370s the Gonzaga and Visconti experimented with travel restrictions and expulsion of plague victims; Ragusa imposed the first quarantine in 1377. Shortly afterward the Visconti required entry and exit permits during plagues, in 1399 (perhaps) set up the first permanent health commission, and in 1401 ordered the listing of all those sick with the plague (extended in 1438 to all the sick). Venice in 1422 established the first permanent plague hospital, and the next year ordered daily accounting of plague victims. By 1450 Milan was keeping agents in several cities to warn of approaching contagion.[30]

Venice, Mantua, and Milan were ahead of their time. Even Florence did not systematically address the problem of epidemics until midcentury, when it founded the hospital of S. Maria Nuova, granted the Otto di Guardia new powers to isolate the infected, and, in 1463 or 1479, set up a Lazzaretto for the infected. Most cities did not institute plague hospitals or refound temporary health commissions on a permanent basis until later in the century.[31] For the cities of the Veneto, too, the mid-Quattrocento marked a turning point. By 1449 Veronese councils were regularly electing officials to deal with the plague *(provisores super morbo)*. About that time the Vicentine commune set up a plague hospital named "the Nazareth" in the city's suburbs, and deemed the project important enough to require notaries to ask testators for a bequest to finance construction. About that time, as well, the commune began to hire public physicians, and the Venetian government granted them a tax exemption to make the job more attractive. Padua's Lazzaretto dates from 1453.[32]

Public health measures may indeed have reduced mortality during subsequent attacks.[33] Epidemics were no less frequent, however, and on occasion proved lethal enough: contagion theory could not supplant belief that the ultimate cause of epidemic was God's anger at human sin. The Veronese could draw on the *exemplum* of San Bernardino, who arrived in the plague-swept city in 1444: he urged citizens to give up usury, and when they did so the disease promptly ceased. When a later citizen forgot that lesson and opened a shop for lending, the plague returned until he closed the business. There was no reason to abandon old remedies. Artists throughout Italy continued to paint banners and panels of Jesus hurling the arrows of plague upon cities, with only the Virgin mitigating divine wrath. The Vicentine commune sponsored a new church, dedicated to the plague protector Sebastian, just after the *pestilentia* of 1464–65. The other major plague saint, Roch, was honored by a Paduan confraternity in 1468 and by inclusion in 1480 among the official cults promoted by the commune of Verona. A few years later, after an epidemic that ravaged northern Italy from Venice to Milan, Vicenza sponsored a convent dedicated to Roch.[34]

The Disposition of the Body

The Moment of Death

Memorialists assumed that their deceased kin were destined for eternal bliss, but they were of two minds regarding the timing of entry into paradise. In some entries the soul passed directly into heaven—"sailed up to the celestial kingdom," "passed from this mortal to a happier life," or "left this life and gained the life which is truly life."[35] Others, however, assumed an intermediate period between death and attainment of the beatific vision. The phrasing here suggests sleep or dormancy until the end of time, when the blessed would see the Savior face to face ("fell asleep in God" or "died and rests in peace"[36]).

Uncertainty as to when the soul would end its journey reflected the ambiguities of Scripture itself. The Gospels offered three very different interpretations of the moment of death, each authorized by a direct statement from

Jesus. At Calvary, in Luke's account, the good criminal was promised an instant reward: "Truly, I say to you, today you will be with me in Paradise." But Luke earlier presented a different reading. The beggar Lazarus "died and was carried by the angels to Abraham's bosom": he received the promise of paradise, but with an indefinite delay before reunion with Christ.[37] Throughout the Gospel of Matthew, on the other hand, Jesus preached that all souls await a final moment of judgment, when "the son of man comes in his glory," and in the Gospel of John he promised to raise believers on the last day.[38] In the first reading (the good thief), the soul's fate was determined at the point of death, and judgment was individualized. In the second reading (Lazarus), judgment was also individualized and immediate, but execution of that judgment was left to the future. In the third reading (the second coming), judgment was future and collective. It would appear that the first reading gradually prevailed among theologians and pastoral writers after the fourteenth century,[39] but memorialists were not sure.

In any case, the deathbed was the ultimate arena in the battle for salvation, the last opportunity to atone for sin and resist the pull of the devil. Several memorialists found it comforting that their kin had died "supplied with all the rites of holy mother church." Bartolomeo Verità, indeed, thought that such *ordini* were required of the faithful Christian.[40] The dying participated in the increasingly elaborate cult of the good death, guided to assurance of forgiveness by prayer sequences, litanies, confessions, absolutions, examinations of conscience, Communion, and unction. The text known as the "Art of Dying" *(ars moriendi)*, which fixed the choreography of the deathbed, proved enormously popular; though South German in origin, it was quickly translated into vernaculars, and Italians made it their own by attributing it to Bishop Domenico Capranica (died 1458). Verona, Vicenza, and Venice produced at least six printed versions before 1500.[41]

Such rituals emphasized what could be done to secure the redemption of the dying. That positive reading, in turn, offers contrasts with two themes frequently associated with the moment of death. First, the optimism of Veneto texts stands at odds with the obsessive concentration on physical decomposition common to peoples north of the Alps. Italy may have pioneered macabre imagery, with the fresco of the Triumph of Death in the Campo Santo at Pisa, but the peninsula thereafter showed little taste for graphic illustrations of death and the putrefaction of the flesh. Its writers preferred the relatively calm theme of *vanitas* and the transient quality of earthly existence. In the visual arts as well, the predominant Italian figure was the skeleton with scythe or hourglass, a simple reminder of physical impermanence, not the morbid dances of death with horrific images of mass slaughter, or the Three Living and the Three Dead theme, in which corpses confront the living with the "As you are now, so once was I; as I am now, so you will be" warning. The double-decked *transi* tomb, with healthy effigy above and worm-ridden carrion below, is a primarily northern phenomenon.[42]

Second, one strain in late medieval thought doubted the efficacy of deathbed heroics. Girolamo Savonarola, for example, emphasized living well throughout life, and distrusted penance at the end. Indeed, the Christian who waited until the deathbed for atonement was probably lost, unable to remove a lifetime of hardness of heart amid the distractions of family and the final snares of the devil. Paolo da Certaldo was more homespun: "Those who don't repent when they can, can't repent when they want." Bernardino da Feltre thought that deathbed charity could not atone for a lifetime of egoism: "*Now is the time to rise from sin, and begin to do good.*" Deathbed acts of devotion, he thought, were possibly insincere; prayers made in the full of life were more powerful than those ordered at point of death. The fact that Bernardino had to preach five sermons downplaying such last acts, however, suggests that he had trouble making his message felt by the faithful.[43]

Funerals and Tombs

The theme of an individualized death dominates discussion of mortuary rituals. Recent students of testaments, the major sources for funerals, note expansion of the individual's desire to glorify his or her own life, proclaim kinship and community solidarities, and improve chances in the afterlife. Wills became more widespread, to the point where even the lower strata of society often spent the few coins necessary to redact a testament. Easing the strictures of notarial formulas, these documents grew in both loquacity and personalized statement. Wills became increasingly specific, as testators devoted folio after folio to minute orders for preparation of the body and lamentations over the corpse, the dress and constitution of those in the procession, the number of priests, candles, drapes et al. at the requiem, tomb construction, and commemorative liturgies. The rites themselves grew far more ostentatious between the Middle Ages and the Renaissance.[44] Florence's Giovanni Morelli counted funeral expenses among the calamities that might befall young heirs, but he and many neighbors gladly paid the price.[45]

The Veneto offers some corroborating evidence. The 1476 will of Marco Thiene, newly created count of Quinto, is as voluble and self-serving as those of Tuscany or southern France. His body was to be carried by six members of the Gesuati order dressed in red cloth bearing the family arms, preceded by thirty "pauper peasants" from Quinto dressed in black capes and thirty more in white. All of the city's guilds, religious orders, parish priests, and bishop's chaplains were to be present, at his expense. Six servants "dressed in military style," along with relatives and friends, were to accompany the body to the cathedral. In the family chapel—in which Thiene endowed a perpetual chaplaincy—his heirs were to erect a marble tomb with statues of his patrons, the emperor and the doge, flanking the sarcophagus. Bequests to clergy attending the rites, provision for a yearly cloth for the tomb, and endowment of Masses ensured that he would not be forgotten in Vicenza or in heaven.[46] The sons of Verona's Ireco Aleardi spent 1,248 *lire* on his funeral and immediate legacies, which was 251 *lire* more than the estate held in cash.[47]

Legislation might also corroborate the perceived trend toward conspicuous consumption. Vicentine sumptuary laws thought mortuary rituals wasteful and/or indecorous, and attempted to curb display. No funeral could convoke more than the cathedral chapter, the brothers of one convent, and the personal chaplain of the deceased (substitution of flagellant confraternities was allowed); only bells of the burial place could be rung; only close relatives could wear *funebres vestes;* no more than eight candles of two pounds each could surround the body. In 1441, in a similar vein, Veronese councils complained that funerals were unseemly and squandered the resources of the citizenry, and set thresholds on the number of candles and attending priests. Ordinances in Padua, Venice, Florence, and elsewhere imposed comparable strictures.[48]

If policy in the Veneto confirms recent studies that stress individualization and self-proclamation, custom does not. Marco Thiene's testament is exceptional. In a sample of 150 Vicentine and Veronese wills, from the great Thiene and Monza down to humble cultivators of the countryside, only a very few made provision for funerary rites beside a simple order of place of burial. A few of the rich and some of the humble mentioned a monument or a stone, but they passed over in silence the composition and adornment of the procession, the attendant clergy and mourners, and the decoration and sequence of the requiem. That is not to say that funerals were not, in fact, elaborate. They may have been. Testators found disposition of the body a low priority, however, and left funeral arrangements to heirs and executors. Funerals were not, then, individualized statements. Nor were people in the Veneto idiosyncratic: Milanese wills, too, rarely specified funeral rites, and samplings of Tuscan wills indicate much the same pattern.[49]

Memorialists were much like their fellow citizens: at most they specified placement in the family tomb. The Arnaldi, to take one example, were as wealthy as the Thiene and Monza, and could have commissioned ostentation. They were also socially ambitious and aware of the value of tangible display in working up the social ladder: their two urban palaces testify to strategic expenditure. Yet the family wills made no reference to the clothes, candles, marching orders, priests, or mourners of their funerals. Perhaps they could assume that members of their confraternities and guilds would accompany their bodies,[50] but they did not mention corporate participation. The Arnaldi did not find funerals an appropriate occasion for parading their pretensions. The single instance of detailing works in the opposite direction. Silvestro, who otherwise was quick to claim prominence (he was the first in the family consistently to call himself noble, arranged marriages with oligarchs, and engaged in vendetta with a mighty clan to prove his arrival in top circles), buried a grandson with simple dignity. A single servant carried the body of little Renaldo to the cathedral, with a garland being the only decoration.[51]

Indeed, a strong countercurrent in Veneto wills regarded glorification of self or lineage with hostility. If Gaspare Monza and Marco Thiene made opulent provisions, the wills of their kinsmen demonstrate that austerity and self-effacement were closer to the norm. The illustrious Giovanni Thiene wanted to be buried in the church of whatever place he died in, and did not specify any type of funeral. Another noble Thiene ordered burial in a small rural church. Gaspare's cousin Francesco Monza wanted to be buried humbly (*humiliter*), without any "solemn funeral."[52] In Verona, Gabriele Verità sharply restricted the number of attendants, candles, and mourning clothes at his exequies. Alvise Stoppi wished only the friars of S. Anastasia and "whatever number of priests is customary in the city" to participate in his burial. The "magnificent knight" Verità Verità went further: "because nothing is more seemly than humility, he has renounced all pomp for himself at his funeral and burial." Isabeta Paulino, wife of the memorialist Bonaventura Bovi, desired burial wherever her heirs thought best. When the "opulent and well-beloved and commendable" Bonifacio di San Michele died in 1409, he desired only a parish priest and an associate (*socius*) at the funeral, with three small candles; he was to be buried naked.[53] A considerable number of people in other cities, even those as great as Niccolo d'Este and Cosimo de' Medici, also preferred simplicity.[54]

The Arnaldi did have a family tomb, by the right corner of the altar in the cathedral's chapel of St. John the Baptist.[55] The location was superb. The chapel was the baptistry for the entire city, the place in which rebirth in the spirit was celebrated daily; the power of the liturgy might transfer to their bodies simply by osmosis. In metaphorical terms the Arnaldi could also hope for rebirth into heaven, since baptism into Jesus was also baptism into Jesus' death and resurrection, just as St. Paul had conflated initiation into faith and initiation into paradise: "We were buried with [Jesus] by baptism into death, so that as Christ was raised from the dead by the glory of the Father, we too might walk in newness of life" (Romans 6:4).

Burial in a baptistry was not only burial *apud sanctos,* but *apud Christum,* and elsewhere was reserved for the very great: Florence restricted burial in its baptistry to worthies such as the ex-pope John XXIII, while in northern Italy only two doges in Venice and the Carrara rulers of Padua were buried near the font. Moreover, in Vicenza the chapel of the Baptist was nearest to the high altar, constantly filled with words of eucharistic celebration; here, too, the departed were touched by transforming words of death and resurrection. The chapel was also located at the east end of the cathedral, the first to be touched by the rays of divine light at Christ's second coming.[56]

But it was a family tomb. Neither the very rich Andrea, nor his assertive son Silvestro, nor anyone else in the family ordered a personalized monument. Gabriele Verità made detailed requests for the construction of his resting place in Santa Eufemia in Verona, including an image of himself, but he wished it known that the monument simply be added to a complex built "per quondam illos de Veritate." When other Veronese made reference to tombs, they emphasized that the bones of ancestors also rested there.[57] The persistence of collective interment argues against historians' assertion of highly individualized mortuary rituals, as does the Veneto tendency to leave funeral arrangements to heirs and executors. In a similar vein Alberto Tenenti has noted the quasi-pagan humanist cult of glory which, achieved on earth and indicative of a surging love of life, required commemoration of immortal fame in a one-person tomb; but this was fashionable among a restricted elite.[58] In the provinces, custom dampened any impulse to self-glorification. Marco Thiene might have wished a gaudy monument to himself, but his family did not share that sentiment and the tomb was not built. Most testators, noble and humble, preferred anonymous burial in the ancestral sepulchre.

The Disposition of the Soul

The Living and the Dead

The theme of individualized death and judgment must be qualified by the participation of the community of the living in determining the experience of the afterlife. The "solidarity of the dead and the living" did much to mitigate the potentially baleful consequences of individual responsibility and free will.[59] Indeed, the individual in purgatory could do little to affect his or her fate; the intervention of friends and family was a primary determinant of both time and degree of pain during the intermediate period between death and paradise.

Provincial wills were concerned less with burial than with provisions for the afterlife, particularly for charitable and pious bequests, prayers, and Masses to win heavenly intercessors and speed the soul through purgatory. The effect was not exclusively spiritual, of course, as even the most other-world-centered orders sought to control descendants' expenditures of time, money, land, and liturgy from beyond the grave. More important, however, legacies deliberately erased the divide between the here and the hereafter. Requests for postmortem suffrages bound the living and the dead into community by reciprocal obligations, and gave urgency to the fulfilment of mutual service by imposing high stakes of honor in this world and salvation in the next. The living received consolation that they had rendered *pietas* and *caritas* to proximate kin. They could hope that if they dutifully performed suffrages for the dead, the same would be done for them; and they were given pointed examples of the harsh fate of those who refused to assist the deceased.[60] The souls of the departed, once redeemed, would intercede for the living: "They will not be ungrateful." The dying, in turn, gained confidence in easier purgation and hastened entry into paradise.

Postmortem suffrages presuppose a fully developed belief in purgatory. Whatever the evolution of that doctrine (still much debated) during the first millennium of Christianity, its basic outlines were no longer in question after the councils of Lyon (1274) and Ferrara-Florence (1438–39).[61] By the fifteenth century, purgatory was a familiar place. It was not yet frequently depicted in art,[62] and Dante's magisterial geography did not much resonate on the popular level, but travelers' accounts gave it shape and substance. One of these was told in Verona in 1407. On the first of July, two foreigners with swarthy faces and unkempt beards arrived in the city and revealed that they had been to purgatory (whether in or out of body, they did not know), whose entrance was found in Iberia. They had heard the groans, cries, and wailing of its inmates, and had seen the serpents that lived there.[63]

By itself, however, belief in purgatory would not provide much stimulus to postmortem commemorations. Both learned opinion and popular usage had to overcome powerful obstacles posed by early doctrinal statements. First, the scriptural text that stood at the center of belief in purgatory (I Corinthians 3:11–15) implied that each individual had to answer for his or her own works: the poor foundation had to be burned away, and nothing done by the living could change that punishment. But conviction grew that the individual was not, in fact, alone in purgatory. Early Christianity accepted the efficacy of prayers for the dead, even before the formalization of belief in purgation, and most writers thereafter made the utility of prayers, alms, fasting, and Masses central to their comments on the afterlife.[64]

Second, Augustine had been convinced that the number of souls eligible for expiatory purgation "was not very numerous." If that were the case, there was no point in routinely ordering suffrages. Later writers, however, opened purgatory to greater as well as lesser sinners. By the later Middle Ages, theologians such as William of Auvergne and popularizers such as Jacopo da Voragine held that nearly everyone had to endure postmortem purification.[65]

Third, several authorities, including Augustine, held that expiatory punishments would cease only at the day of judgment. If that were the case, the suffrages of the living could not alleviate the duration of purgation, though they might alleviate its severity. This was, however, increasingly a minority view. Pope Gregory recounted anecdotes of shades of the dead returning to report that their souls had entered the communion of the saved because of earthly intercession. Systematic theologians, taking up Paul's distinction among the foundations of wood, hay, and straw on which individuals based earthly life, noted that these elements had different rates of combustion and concluded that souls would undergo different lengths and intensities of purgation. Hugh of St. Victor thought that souls that completed purgation were released to a state of resting or waiting (refrigerium); the stronger view of Bonaventure, Albertus Magnus, and Thomas Aquinas held that they gained immediate access to the beatific vision. In either case the good works of the living shortened penalties.[66]

Growing inclusion of indulgences among the works that could aid the souls of the departed also supported the notion of variable terms spent in purgatory. Initially intended to remit earthly penalties only, in the High Middle Ages time-specific indulgences were applied to souls in purgatory as well. The principle that spiritual merit was transferable led in 1457 to the issuance of indulgences strictly for the dead. In addition, it was widely held that the recitation of certain prayers constituted a sort of indulgence which, like those issued by popes, obtained remission of a fixed term. The Precor te copied into the Repeta memoir, for example, conferred 6,666 days of indulgence.[67]

Individualization of death must be qualified, as well, by a closer look at testaments. The assumption that wills testify to personal spiritual mentalities has become almost axiomatic.[68] A will, however, is a committee document, a product of several sources of input, many of which were beyond the testator's control. The individual dictated basic terms that the notary rendered into Latin, copied into rough notes, and eventually drew up in definitive form. The language and constructs that actually conveyed testamentary bequests were dictated by formulas derived from custom, statute, and the broader *ius commune;* the repertoire of mechanisms for disposing of property, and thus the individual's freedom of action, were in fact limited.

The testator did not enjoy complete freedom even in the early stages. Family tradition strongly conditioned choices: the collective sanctity of the lineage required a few strong cults rather than dispersal of heavenly patronage by many scattered bequests. The fact that nearly all the Arnaldi favored the Observant Franciscans, for example, indicates that none of the Arnaldi exercised purely personal options. When Caterina Zugliano endowed postmortem Masses with a donation of three *lire* in annual land income, the terms of the bequest were not her invention: they echoed a stipulation of her husband for his own commemoration, in a will drawn up eight years previously.[69]

Municipal governments, too, exercised a voice in determining legacies, ordering notaries to ask testators if they wished to leave anything to officially favored projects. Testators, often at the point of death, were subjected to an increasingly lengthy interrogation. In the mid-fifteenth century the Vicentine list consisted of the hospital of saints Mary and Christopher near the church of S. Marcello, and the hospital of saints Mary and George (or S. Gottardo). Councils added the city's plague hospital in 1451, the church of S. Bernardino by 1456, the church of S. Rocco by 1489, and the Monte di Pietà by 1492.[70] Testators could refuse these suggestions, of course. Still, to do so they had to resist considerable pressure to keep bequests within a narrow range.

Pious Bequests

In Verona, Vicenza, and elsewhere, lay and ecclesiastical authorities sought to encourage pious donations by ensuring citizens that their bequests would be honored. Verona's *domus pietatis,* operated by a confraternity and directed by council-appointed governors, distributed alms and offered shelter to the indigent; at least by 1443 the commune appointed two *sindici pauperum* to administer pious legacies in conjunction with the bishop's vicar.[71] Vicenza's bishop appointed a syndic to distribute bequests to the poor, and the urban commune after 1431 annually chose two citizens to expedite testamentary gifts *ad pias causas.*[72]

Rationalization and government oversight of charity did not, however, stimulate largesse. There were exceptions, of course, and we would be unduly harsh to conclude that Veneto testators were altogether lacking in Christian love. Among the families of Verona's memorialists, Ognibene Guastaverza gave four thousand pieces of cloth and Bonmartino Verità gave a hundred ducats to "Christ's poor"; Aventino Fracastoro ordered food and wine distributed to five religious houses, and wished his heirs to support three paupers for three years.[73] These were exceptions: most wills did not mention pious legacies, and the remainder usually donated money to convents strictly in return for prayers and Masses. In the sampling of 150 Vicentine wills, only a third ordered disinterested legacies—those for which no services were expected—to paupers, hospitals, convents, confraternities, and parish churches. Less than a tenth ordered bequests to two or more charitable or ecclesiastical foundations.

In this regard citizens of the Veneto resembled those of some other cities. In Lyon, 83.8 percent of testaments made pious bequests in the 1300–1320 period, but only 35.4 percent did so in the 1480–1500 period. Some 78 percent of wills in the early Trecento specified gifts to the poor, but only 21 percent in the later Quattrocento. The average number of pious legacies dropped from 7.8 per testament to one per testament. The early Lyonnais made many scattered bequests; their descendants made fewer though larger bequests, and overall levels of giving dropped sharply from the earlier time. Sienese wills demonstrate the same broad movement, despite frequent spikes: a drop in the frequency and value of legacies to pious institutions, as the Quattrocento ushered in a "great age of selfishness." In one sample Venetian parish, bequests to the poor were never frequent or substantial, and declined during the fifteenth century.[74]

Measurement of changes in charitable giving would be difficult for the Veneto, since patricians were not particularly generous at any time. The 100 ducats that Giovanni Thiene left for dowries of poor girls in 1415 seems expansive, but seen against the vast landed patrimony mentioned in his will the bequest probably constituted a smaller share of wealth than did the 50 and 10 *lire* that two peasants of Quinto gave to the poor and sick about the same time. Verona's Gabriele Verità appears generous, with a bequest of 300 *lire* to the *domus pietatis*, prisoners, a confraternity, and poor girls, but the long inventory of lands left to his heirs belies any perception that he made a great sacrifice.[75] Gaspare I Arnaldi left 20 *lire* to the poor in 1433, out of an estate whose value was calculated at around 7,800 *lire*. Tommaso Arnaldi left 220 *lire* to 6 different convents in 1463; he had inherited 10 times that sum

4 decades previously, and had since grown rich enough to rank among Vicenza's 10 wealthiest citizens. At the very end of the century Gaspare II Arnaldi left nothing at all to the poor or religious, though tax assessments placed him among the city's wealthiest 10 percent.[76]

Where it can be measured, the drop in pious largesse was inconsistent across the charitable map. In general, the marginal and disadvantaged were particularly hard hit. Some 85.7 percent of early Lyonnais wills funded Christ's poor, but only 21.6 percent did so at the end of the fifteenth century. The average bequest to the Sienese poor suffered a ninefold decrease during the Quattrocento.[77] Anecdotal evidence from the Veneto suggests that there, too, testators regarded the merely indigent with some disdain. The successful Paduan artisan Nicolo da Fabriano did leave one hundred *lire* to paupers, but obliged them to make public (and no doubt embarrassing) testimony of their want: the indiscriminate charity of an earlier age had given way to suspicion. Verona's Cristoforo Lanfranchini compared the poor to crows who descend upon a corpse, though he did specify a distribution of grain.[78] In two wills the memorialist Bartolomeo dal Bovo provided for the feeding and housing of an indigent nephew, but then changed his mind and ordered cancellation of the bequest if this Battista Panzeri did not make dal Bovo's children his heirs.[79]

By the later Quattrocento bequests to hospitals in Lyon were less than a third of what they had been in the previous century; the slide in Siena was equally pronounced.[80] Hospitals did rather better in Florence, but the older charitable institutions such as Orsanmichele suffered a sharp drop in legacies.[81] Bequests to confraternities, always rare in the Veneto (two cases in 150 testaments), fell to negligible levels in San Sepolcro.[82] Hermits and the imprisoned virtually disappeared from Veronese and Vicentine testaments, which mentioned *pauperes carcerati* only four times.[83] Among religious houses in Tuscany, the older Benedictine foundations and those in the countryside suffered a precipitous decline in the frequency and amount of donations. Female convents were the worst off. Vicentine testators, too, showed little regard for rural monasteries, and abandoned the ancient Benedictine house of SS. Felice and Fortunato until monks from the reformed congregation of S. Giustina took over around 1430.[84]

Changing patterns of endowment did bring favor to a few. Mendicants, concentrated in cities, did better than older and rural orders in Toulouse, Lausanne, and Tuscany, and Observant houses did best of all.[85] In Vicenza, the Observant Franciscans at S. Biagio and S. Chiara outdrew the Observant Dominicans at S. Corona and S. Domenico, but both sets of observants prospered in absolute terms and relative to conventuals.[86] Construction or rebuilding of urban churches for new orders such as the Gesuati, the Servites, and the Girolimini attracted considerable patronage. Veronese wills, similarly, preferred Observant Franciscans at the new house of S. Bernardino to conventuals at S. Fermo, while the cathedral and the old Benedictine house of S. Zeno received little mention.

The favored few were closer to home. Early Lyonnais bequests were spread throughout the region, but later bequests directed gifts to institutions within city walls.[87] In a similar vein, pilgrimage to distant sites virtually disappeared in the huge sample of Lyonnais wills analyzed by Lorcin; the same has been claimed for Toulouse, Milan, and Provence. While Vicentine testaments ordered pilgrimages with undiminished frequency, they now directed heirs to nearby shrines—Monte Summano in the northern hills, and especially Monte Berico, a short walk from city gates.[88]

Testators left money and food to persons and institutions they knew firsthand, whose expenditures and prayers could be directly witnessed by heirs. Servants in Siena received a derisory proportion of bequests in the 1301–25 period, but a healthy 5 percent in the 1476–1500 period. Bequests to fund dowries rose from zero in 1300 to become, by the early Quattrocento, "the principal form of social charity."[89] Both categories were much favored in the testaments of the Veneto. Gabriele Verità, for example, gave cash grants to, boosted the salaries, and forgave the debts of household servants and rural workers; Giovanni Thiene bequeathed a hundred ducats and Francesco Monza assigned a permanent income "to marry poor maidens."[90] Many such dowries were assigned to servants, nieces, or granddaughters, literally keeping charity within the house.[91] Rewarding kinship or faithful service, and so expecting future loyalty and hard work, simply made more sense than expending money on the indigent.

There was another category of pauper, the "shamed poor" (poveri vergognosi) of eminent families who were not so much impoverished as unable to maintain a tenor of life consonant with their social station. These might be well off by most standards, but the offense to their honor made them worthy recipients of aid, and in the Veneto—as in Florence and Milan—they were given relief. If Alberto Bilanth founded a Vicentine hospital in the Trecento for "pilgrims, the infirm and other begging and miserable persons," Giampietro Proti's hospital in 1412 targeted assistance to distressed nobles.[92] The Veronese aristocrat Spinetta Malaspina, four decades earlier, established a hospital to assist those of his own class. Verona's Donato Stoppi bequeathed some bread to paupers, but left the considerable legacy of one ducat weekly to a "worthy person."[93]

Masses

In the general shift from charity to liturgy, more people wanted Masses; they wanted more Masses, with more clergy in attendance, and they were more precise regarding the timing and format of those Masses. Here, too, quantification of wills indicates changes in collective sensibilities: from 1300 to 1500 the proportion of Lyonnais rustics ordering postmortem services rose from 37.2 percent to 69.4 percent. In Siena, bequests for Masses as a proportion of all pious bequests rose from 11.6 percent to 38.1 percent, and the value of Masses rose twelvefold.[94] Lower-class wills in Vicenza demonstrate a clear trend away from gifts to burial churches toward endowments of commemorative Masses. The shift began around 1420, but was not general before midcentury. The upper ranks had already arrived at that point: Gaspare Arnaldi in 1433 left a one-time payment for Masses of St. Gregory and a perpetual income for *missa mortora*. In total about 36 percent of Vicentines before 1450 ordered Masses compared with about 64 percent after midcentury. The proportion of those giving land, money, or goods to churches, without strings attached, fell from 42 percent to 24 percent.

Testaments in the Veneto may, if anything, underestimate the incidence of liturgical endowment. Elsewhere, the will largely replaced other mechanisms for funding postmortem suffrages,[95] but this was not the case in Verona and Vicenza. Caterina Zugliano, for example, set up elaborate cycles of Masses some fifteen months before she dictated a will, with a *donatio inter vivos* of land to the sacristy of the cathedral, and she ordered a postmortem pilgrimage in a vow rather than a will. If her experience was at all representative—and there is corroborating evidence—testaments tell only part of the story.[96]

The shift from charitable bequest to postmortem Mass especially affected clerical status and duties. Priests were no longer passive beneficiaries of largesse but active participants in the collective effort to alleviate punishments of purgatory. Their work shifted from inward contemplation to outward service, from prayerful remembrance of past generosity to labor for the patron's future release into paradise. In theory remote from bonds of kinship, priests now provided linkages for extended spiritual families. Intermediaries between God and humanity, they now also mediated between life and afterlife.

Their endowments no longer depended on their own reputation for piety, but on the degree to which they fulfilled the tasks set by others.

At the same time benefactors became more demanding consumers of religious benefits. Charity was now contractual rather than philanthropic,[97] as support for convents was made contingent upon specific acts demanded of their priests. Testators' focus shifted from giving to receiving, from the bequest of money to the receipt of sacraments. They changed the nature of suffrages, from prayers to the more powerful Masses. Patristic authorities had sanctioned alms, fasts, prayers, or liturgical observance, without preference, as providing solace for the souls of the departed. In the sixth century, however, Gregory the Great's *exempla* showed Masses alleviating torments in the afterlife, and later canonists and theologians established that implied priority in rigorous terms. In the fifteenth century, for example, Jean Gerson declared that sacraments were more beneficial than other forms of intercession.[98]

The timing of Masses was a delicate issue. When, precisely, did souls in purgatory require assistance? No one knew precisely because there remained uncertainty regarding the moment of the soul's judgment and the duration of purgation. If judgment was immediate and entry into purgatory began at the point of death, there was no time to be lost: hence Francesco Monza's order that friars of the Observance celebrate a hundred Masses even before his burial.[99] The individual needed ongoing solace as well. By the thirteenth century the period of purgation was estimated at a few days or months, at most a few years, since punishment was so intense that a relatively short span seemed like an aeon;[100] this would prompt short-term suffrages. There remained the possibility that purgatory would endure until the end of time, as Augustine had asserted, and the possibility that judgment was rendered only on the final day, as Matthew and John had written. Thus, many testators opted for perpetual Masses.

In the sample of 150 Veronese and Vicentine wills, the number specifying postmortem Masses is small (thirty-one), since most testators left the details of suffrages to be worked out by their heirs. About a third of these were concentrated in the short term, clustering Masses within a year of death; most common was the thirty-Mass cycle of St. Gregory.[101] A fifth, less hopeful of quick release from purgatory, spread Masses up to ten years from the time of death. A further fifth looked to the end of time, endowing perpetual Masses. A final fifth of testators, generally the wealthy, hedged their bets and ordered both short- and long-term Masses. Gabriele Verità, for example, desired a hundred Masses said within a week of his death, plus monthly Masses in perpetuity.[102]

Veneto wills show growing confidence that purgation involved a calculable period of penance and was not, after all, an enduring experience. Three-quarters of Veronese and Vicentine testators before 1450 sought perpetual Masses for their souls; the figure drops to 30 percent in wills redacted after midcentury. Some 13 percent sought Masses within a year of death in the early period, but 39 percent did so after 1450. Studies of Milan, Lyon, and other places also note a movement toward short-term commemoration.[103]

The number of Masses requested in the Veneto also demonstrate reassurance in the power of liturgical suffrage. Testators in France have been termed obsessional, so anxious over the pains of purgatory and the possible inefficacy of postmortem celebrations that they ordered hundreds and even thousands of Masses, with hypertrophy reaching 25,000.[104] Their contemporaries in the Veneto showed no such fears. Even counting the cycle of St. Gregory as thirty separate Masses, that figure is the median number requested; the most nervous testator ordered only 132.

Finally, provision for the afterlife can roughly measure the degree to which testaments advanced self-interest. Testators in the Veneto were indifferent to the broader community of the dead. None ordered prayers or Masses for all the souls in purgatory, as happened in France.[105] But they seldom regarded the lineage either: only 5 percent wished suffrages for "myself and all my predecessors." Less than one-fifth of wills requested intercession for immediate kin such as spouses, children, or parents. More than three-quarters, on the other hand, made pious legacies or sought Masses exclusively "for my soul and the remission of my sins."

Women and Death

Caterina Zugliano, like her husband eight years previously, devoted three *lire* annually in land income to endowment for anniversaries and monthly Masses. She sought approximate parity with his testament, to ensure that they would have comparable chances in purgatory—but she put the odds in her favor. Gaspare Arnaldi had demanded a single anniversary Mass; she specified a sung Mass and four "small" Masses; his monthly Masses were to run for four septenaries, hers for five. She ordered pilgrimages, which Gaspare had not.[106] Predecease gave her husband a head start, but Caterina set out to secure an earlier release into paradise.

She was no religious rebel—early in widowhood she became a tertiary of the Observant Franciscans, the order favored by her marital family[107]—but she had her own mind when it came to the afterlife. Gaspare ordered burial in the family tomb in the cathedral's chapel of John the Baptist; Caterina's request for Masses in the chapel of John Evangelist hints that she chose burial apart from her husband. Her order that son Andrea visit the tomb of blessed Giovanni Cacciafronte, which males in the family did not venerate, also indicates cult and patron distinct from that of her marital kin. The site of her requested pilgrimage, too, suggests independent-minded spirituality. Monte Ortone lay thirty-five kilometers from Vicenza; the Arnaldi supported only cults in the city. The shrine was run by Augustinian hermits, who were not present in Vicenza and were not beneficiaries of her marital family. It may not be coincidental that the other known pilgrimage to Monte Ortone was ordered by a woman. Vicentines knew that certain holy places were specially favored by women, notably the altar in S. Pietro in Campiglia "where women adore."[108]

Her case points to a general principle: the experiences of women in and around death did not always resemble those of the men in their families. Their deaths were less conspicuous, for one thing. Veneto memoirs noted the deaths of many more men than women: aunts, sisters, and married daughters passed on without comment. The imbalance was particularly pronounced among the young, where 61 percent of mortuary entries describe the decease of a son. In a number of cases we surmise the death of a daughter only because her name was reused for a sibling: she clearly had died without her father taking written notice.

Second, women left far fewer wills than men. Among the families of Veronese memorialists, for example, seventy-four men produced testaments, compared with only forty-four women. These figures are consistent with data from throughout Europe.[109] Indeed, a woman in the Veneto had little impetus to make a will at all because law predetermined the flow of much of her wealth. If she predeceased her husband, he automatically received half her dowry. If she survived him, she could only make bequests if she left an equivalent amount to her children. Her goods automatically passed to children unless she specified otherwise, and even then she could not choose alternate heirs unless she explicitly disinherited sons.[110] Husbands at times offered effective incentives for widows not to reclaim their dowries, and many widows did not, in fact, choose to control significant resources. A woman whose bequests were conventional and small, and who followed custom in leaving the bulk of her goods to her children, scarcely needed to order a will.

Third, women played a different and lesser role in the rituals surrounding dying and interment. In the Veneto, as elsewhere, law imposed gender distinctions on the spatial configuration of funerary rites. Women directed mourning in the house, while public commemoration was largely reserved for males. Women were too inclined to weeping and lamentation, thought Petrarch and others; allowing women on the streets in a volatile state posed risks to honor and decorum. Veronese women could not join a funeral procession unless the deceased was a child under seven. Vicentine women could not accompany bier or body to the church, and though they could attend the immediate requiem no woman from the house of the deceased could attend the public Mass on the following day.[111]

Fourth, women might or might not choose burial with their marital kin. The Church sanctioned women's right to elect interment separate from husbands at least from the time of Urban II. In Siena, 83 percent of women's wills specified burial apart from marital or natal kin.[112] That, however, seems an extreme case. Elsewhere it was far from certain that women would consign their bodies to solitude, and in general women divided their attentions between natal and marital kin. Most Florentine women were buried with their husbands. In the Veneto, as many chose husbands as chose other kin as companions in eternal slumber. Four Freschi women opted for burial in the vault of marital families, and three did not. Still, provision for separate burial should not be automatically taken as a sign of estrangement or autonomy: Libera, wife of Jacopo Guastaverza, chose burial with another woman but made her *dilectum maritum* executor; and Caterina da Quinto, who wished interment with her father, made her husband universal heir.[113]

CHAPTER FOUR

HOUSEHOLD

AND FAMILY

*T*HE WORD *familia* might refer to persons, or to collective economic resources *(substantia)*, or to lines of authority.[1] In purely human terms, *familia* demonstrates "shifting criteria of membership"; to Alberti, the family might encompass only household residents, or it might extend to the entire body of blood kin. The Veronese Aventino Fracastoro defined *familia Frachastorum* as anyone possessing that surname, including both lateral and lineal relatives.[2] The quasi-synonym *domus* was equally elastic, applied sometimes in a constricted sense to the co-residential household and sometimes in an expanded sense to all descendants of those who co-resided in an ancestral house. Veronese councils forbade more than one member of a *casada* to sit on key magistracies,[3] defining the *casada* as those inclined to use political influence on behalf of kin but refusing to set boundaries. In other contexts, membership in the family was based on agnatic or cognatic ties, marriage, or co-parentage. "Family" might include servants or, in the case of Bonaventura Bovi, someone as remotely related as his wife's uncle's widow.[4] What held that shifting and disparate body together has been variously defined as blood ties, material interest, co-residence, *caritas*, patrimonial succession, or honor.[5]

Lawmakers, too, declined to fix the dimensions of the family. When Vicentine legislators forbade more than one member "de una domo, familia, sive agnatione" to sit in councils, for example, they regarded house, family, and agnate group as roughly synonymous but not quite the same, and refused to settle on a single standard.[6] Elsewhere, they set standards on a case-by-case basis. Each subdefinition applied to a precise setting—political influence, fiscal liability, mutual assistance—and constricted or widened the perimeter according to the needs of that context. In general terms, statutes defined priorities in concentric ranks outward from the protagonist, with preference for the male line. Intestate inheritance went first to children, in their absence to ascendants, in their absence to collateral agnate relations, and, failing all of these, to *propinqui*, defined as agnate relations beyond the third degree. A man having sex with an honest but unmarried woman had to amend the insult to her family "through the fourth degree," the same compass allowed for alienation of property to noncitizen kin.

Other sorts of exchanges brought affines or cognates into the legally defined family. Alienation of property by minors, for example, required consent by close kin *(proximi)* from both the paternal and maternal sides. The boundary widened in public jurisdiction: no one could syndicate anyone of the *familia*, or agnate group, or personal descent group *(stirps)*, or brother (from father or mother), or paternal cousin, or son of brother or sister, or brother-in-law, or father-in-law, or son-in-law. Wider still, no litigant could appear before a judge of the same house, agnate group, *familia*, or "anyone connected by a similar degree of consanguinity or affinity." Widest of all, compromise rather than adjudication was ordered between ascendants, descendants, collaterals to the third degree, in-laws, and the distant "leviros sive leviras, glores vel ianitrices," and this miscellaneous category was to be construed as broadly as possible *(largo vocabulo)*. Only illegitimates consistently fell outside the bounds of effective kinship.[7]

Households Paternal and Extended

Household Composition

Snapshots of the Arnaldi household at regular intervals demonstrate incessant recomposition, and indicate that no classification type was valid for more than a few years at a time. In 1430 seven of the Arnaldi lived in the house in the Carpagnon neighborhood: Gaspare, his wife Caterina Zugliano, their four children, and an unmarried brother. In 1435 son Andrea presided over a group consisting of his mother, uncle, wife, daughter, and two brothers. A decade later the blood ties of those who remained were if anything more tangled: Andrea had four children by two wives, and his brother Tommaso was now married with three children of his own. By 1455 the thirteen residents of the house counted Andrea's widow and children, Tommaso's second wife, two sons by that remarriage, and the two daughters of brother Battista. In total the household counted ten children by five mothers (three deceased) and three fathers (two deceased). Although death and division later simplified matters, no grouping of the Arnaldi was ever reduced to a single nucleus. Indeed, in eighty-one of the 111 years covered in the memoir and family archive, Arnaldi brothers shared roofs and patrimonies. Only two men split off to set up house elsewhere.

The Arnaldi experience was not altogether typical. Other fathers in the region guaranteed a limited period of sibling communion by predividing their patrimonies and assigning portions to each heir. Gabriele Verità took a dozen folios to parcel not only lands but furniture, clothes, and jewelry, declaring that he wished to prevent future discords between his universal heirs. Grandson Verità Verità split his wealth into four parts well before drawing up his will. In Vicenza antemortem division was made not only by the noble Giovanni Thiene but also by the humble Zambono da Cremona.[8] Those fathers, demanding the separation of wealth, virtually ensured that their sons would go their separate ways. Documents of division are common in family archives and notarial registers, suggesting that brothers normally divided wealth, though only after a variable period of co-residence.

On the other hand, the Arnaldi predilection for fraternal households would not have been unrecognizable to contemporaries. Manfredo Repeta was married for a decade and had produced seven children when he and his brother Bartolomeo went their separate ways. Antonio Trento was born when father Giacomo lived with brothers *in communiae fratrum*. Bonzanino and Bartolomeo Muronovo lived and held patrimonies together from at least 1429, when the latter began to write, until their division in 1466; kinsmen Giovanni Antonio and Bonadomane remained together for at least two decades after the former married.[9] Adult brothers headed some 15 percent of fiscal units in Vicentine *estimi*, and 10 percent of Veronese households in ninety *anagrafi* returns from memorialist families.

Complexity, too, was frequent if not the norm (see appendix, table 4.1). True, by standard typologies some 83 percent of Veronese households in the sample were either truncated or consisted of a single nucleus. This figure, however, belies the fact that households were varied and often elaborate. A quarter of households extended over three generations. About 17 percent had multiple nuclei, either vertical (parents and married sons), horizontal (married brothers), or, in one case, both vertical and horizontal. More than one in ten had taken in stray relatives: sisters, wife's parents, aunts, cousins, and one daughter of a deceased daughter. Adults lived with married uncles, grandparents, nieces, and nephews. Sons commonly remained under the paternal roof until their fathers' deaths, even after their own marriages. Francesco Bovi still lived with his father at the age of fifty, although he had been married for two decades and had produced at least five children.[10] Indeed, there scarcely existed a typical domestic unit.

How do Veneto patterns of domestic structure—often complex, filiolocal, and fraternal—fit in the larger context? The prescriptive literature of Florence, to take one sort of evidence, frequently offered injunctions for sons to live with fathers and for brothers to live together. Most famous is the position of the senior Giannozzo in Alberti's *Books of the Family:* "I desire all my family to live under one roof, to warm themselves at one fire, and to seat themselves at one table." He pointed to the comfort, company, and prestige that accrued to a *paterfamilias* surrounded by kinfolk, and to the economies of labor and money that co-residents enjoyed. Furthermore, fathers should not permit filial division because "through division, the family not only is reduced in size and the number of its youth, but its authority shrinks and its importance and standing so decline that a good part of all the fame and honor accumulated over the years is lost." He was proud of his own record: "I am not pleased with this division of families, this coming and going from separate entrances, nor has my spirit ever allowed my brother Antonio to live under a roof not my own."[11]

Matteo Palmieri and Gino Capponi equally urged an undivided patrimony and household. Marsilio Ficino thought that the "union of the father with his sons in one residence" was prerequisite for the "good and honest life." To Matteo Palmieri, a united *parentela* offered mutual protection against enemy houses. Memoirs constantly invoked the ideology of the large family, and pointed to the disasters that could befall those who scattered.[12]

Florentines appear to have paid little attention to that advice. The evidence from the *catasto* of 1427 is straightforward: a mean household size of about 3.8 persons, with 92 percent of households consisting of a single conjugal nucleus and unmarried offspring. In Tuscany as a whole multinuclear households were rare; fraternal households were infrequent (under 8 percent) and short-lived.[13] At most the fraternal joint household was an ephemeral aspect of the domestic cycle, between the father's death and the division of patrimony by his heirs. Community usually lasted only until the youngest reached maturity, but many heirs did not wait even that long: the eldest of the Niccolini took his share and departed within a year of the father's death, and his two brothers split up shortly thereafter. The household might expand vertically as children and grandchildren were born, but usually contracted laterally as sisters married out and brothers moved out.[14] In England, too, "the nuclear family household constituted the ordinary, expected, normal framework of domestic existence" from the Middle Ages to the Industrial Revolution.[15]

Were the households of Veneto memorialists, with a preference for multigenerational arrangements during the life of the father and for fraternal co-residence thereafter (Andrea and Tommaso Arnaldi, for example, lived together for twenty-one years after their father died) simply idiosyncratic? A more careful scrutiny of the Tuscan situation reduces the apparent gap between northeast and central Italy: schematic presentation of Florentine data exaggerates the small size and simplicity of households there. The *catasto* of 1427 measured fiscal households, not residential units. The patrimony, not the domestic group, was liable, and distinct patrimonies might receive separate entries even though their holders lived under the same roof. Working out who actually lived together would require scrutiny of street addresses in sixty thousand tax returns and thousands of notarial registers, which no scholar has yet attempted. After decades in the archives Klapisch-Zuber concluded that *catasto* registers set a "documentary trap" and seriously underestimated the number and extent of complex households: "we should not be fooled by the statistical predominance of the conjugal family."[16]

Too, the Veneto families that produced memoirs were wealthier than the norm. Their counterparts were not Florentines as a whole but only the well-off among them, and this group more closely resembles Veneto patricians in extended and expanded household configuration. Wealthy families in Florence were considerably larger than those of the poor: if two-thirds of Florentines lived in households of under three persons, the richest had households twice that size, with more nuclei and more lateral extensions. Their development cycle was more stable: fewer sons moved out, and greater life expectancy ensured a larger number of long-term patriarchs. They more commonly gave shelter to lateral relatives, orphans, and strays; greater reliance on a landed patrimony gave brothers impetus to keep collective wealth undivided.[17]

Furthermore, the *catasto* year of 1427 marks the nadir of Florentine demography. Repeated disasters in previous generations virtually ensured that the city would be filled with "truncated or incomplete families."[18] The timing of the survey strongly depresses the calculation of the domestic unit's size and shape. But times were getting better, in Florence and elsewhere. More children survived, more parents lived to old age, and outmigration did not increase. In little more than a century the average urban household rose in size to 6.2 persons. The proportion of single-nucleus households remained steady, but those containing two or more married couples became more common.[19] The large Veneto households of the mid- and late fifteenth century were not, then, out of line with their Florentine contemporaries.

Finally, Florence, once again, presents an extreme case. Even in 1427 "the city favored solitude," with higher rates of solitaries and biologically unproductive unions than were found in the countryside; the rate of isolates was 25 percent higher in Florence than in Prato, and the incidence of multinuclear households 50 percent lower. Smaller Tuscan cities had considerably larger and more complex families than did the capital. Towns and villages, for example, held up to twice the proportion of three-generation families.[20] If the fraternal joint household was rare throughout Tuscany, brothers in Genoa and Montpellier had long shown a proclivity for co-residence and economic communion.[21] A household average of 5.7 persons in Verona in 1473 corresponds roughly to the average of 5.2 persons in the *menages* of Carpentras in 1473. Some 79 percent of Veronese lived in households of five or more persons, as did 72 percent of the people of Carpentras. Figures for the Polesine show 6.4 persons per domestic unit in 1510, not far from the Veronese calculation of 5.8 in 1502.[22] Looking not at Florence but at the second tier of urban centers, the large and composite units of families such as the Verità, Muronovo, and Arnaldi no longer appear an oddity.

Across the Generations

The younger generations of Bonaventura Bovi's family posted dismal records. Son Francesco was murdered in his twenty-sixth year. Grandson Francesco junior contracted a clandestine marriage that Bonaventura denounced fiercely. Nephew Pietro, too, was murdered. The *memoriale* ends with notes on "incorrigible" son Girolamo, who left the paternal roof to live with his "crazy wife" amid goods stolen from Bonaventura's house. Misadventures are found in other memoirs as well: a Mantuan provoked nineteen-year-old Zuane Stoppi into a fight and then killed him with a stab wound to the throat, and Repeta youth committed murder in 1475 and 1493.[23]

Contemporaries noted a youthful proclivity to violence and insubordination, deemed youth a period in the life span when passion ruled over reason and restraint, and thought that arrogance and overindulgence were defining characteristics of the wealthy young. To that perception David Herlihy added a demographic reading, based on the configuration of the upper-class Tuscan family. Delay of marriage extended a male's adolescence over nearly two decades; youth not subject to domestic responsibilities might expend energies in antisocial directions. Since fathers were near forty when their sons were born, they were possibly emotionally remote and certainly distracted by commercial and political commitments, and could offer little guidance and discipline. Many died before sons reached maturity. The primary burden of raising children fell on mothers who, thought commentators, were inclined to spoil their children and were less able to control the errant.[24]

The model does not entirely work for the Veneto. Since patrician men in Verona and Vicenza married much earlier, they were thus, by Herlihy's reckoning, more likely to be engaged in the raising of their children, and were less likely to die when their children were young and thus deprive offspring of paternal control. Even when children were left fatherless, widows did not bear sole responsibility for their upbringing, since families without fathers usually lived with a mature male.

Another aspect of the Tuscan model does apply to northern cities: upper-class males passed through an extended period without significant responsibility or autonomy. Sons of artisans might split off to form separate households and establish independent careers; they had little economic incentive to remain.[25] But older patricians in the Veneto, as was the case in Tuscany,[26] did not retire, divide or liquidate business assets to launch sons on independent careers, or divide lands to give sons a separate income. Sons who married did not set up separate households; fathers commanded the dowries and dotal goods they received from wives.[27] Growing life expectancy and reduced infant mortality increased the force of patriarchy, since more fathers reached a ripe age and more sons survived to maturity under paternal tutelage. Even the father's death might not change the situation much. When testators granted wives large usufructs of land or movable goods to induce them not to demand dowries and leave the household, sons had to await the deaths of their mothers as well before they secured financial independence.

Veneto custom particularly strengthened paternal controls. Young men in Florence and Venice often trained in foreign branches of commercial or banking houses, and young Venetian nobles regularly received minor offices on the mainland and positions in the fleet. In Verona and Vicenza, while patrician apprenticeships were not unknown—Zuane Stoppi met his death while an agent in the family business—the infrequency and small scale of extra-regional partnerships sharply reduced opportunities for youthful employment. Most young men, as far as we know, grew up at home, and none appear in the records of paternal businesses.

Emancipation might have freed sons and eased father-son tensions, but faced increasing disapproval throughout Italy. Fear that shifting assets could be used to protect the patrimony from creditors produced laws hedging the capacity of sons to achieve a capitalized independence; fathers, moreover, showed growing reluctance to share the wealth. In fifteenth-century Florence the incidence of emancipation declined sharply, which "increased the likelihood of competitive tensions."[28] In the Veneto emancipation was never popular in the first place, and was subjected to strong statutory disapproval.[29] Restive sons such as Girolamo Bovi might simply pull up stakes and go elsewhere, but they seldom received either formal permission or a portion of family wealth to live on.

Nor did thresholds for coming of age, which merely established minimum standards for different types of legal capacity, sanction independence. Indeed, these norms tended to reinforce paternal or familial authority. For example, the good will of fathers, senior relatives, and allies entirely determined political access. In theory any Vicentine aged eighteen could secure election to the city's Great Council; in fact there were no elections. Since inheritance and alienation alone distributed seats—as Andrea Arnaldi inherited his seat from uncle Antonio Zugliano, and passed it to son Silvestro—a rebellious son would see the place pass to someone else. In any case, in 1498 the minimum age for election to the elite Council of One Hundred was raised to thirty.[30] Any Veronese could stand for election to councils, but first had to pass rigorous eligibility scrutinies: councillor fathers could ensure that disloyal cadets did not enter.

In theory, too, any qualified person over the age of eighteen could enter Vicentine guilds. However, places in occupational corporations were patrimonialized, secured by family connections and transferred by alienation and inheritance: so the Arnaldi brothers entered the College of Notaries and the wool guild when their father and uncle were prominent in its leadership, and the family regularly bequeathed places in the elite lists that provided communal notaries. Here, too, family influence cut both ways: it allowed fathers to advance good sons but equally to cut off the disobedient. Anyway, in a region without banks, young merchants relied on fathers and allies for startup capital: here, too, the suffrance of seniors determined access.

Finally, the law set strict limits on the ability of the young to act in a public capacity, further reinforcing dependence on elders. No Vicentine under age twenty could alienate or obligate real property without the consent of two close relatives; none under age twenty-five could appear in court without a guardian or procurator.[31] Even so, coming of age conferred theoretical rights only: a man could seldom dispose of much property while his father still lived, since fathers held their lands closely until the end. Some children received bequests from mothers or grandparents, but testaments indicate that fathers actually held these during their lifetimes. At death, parents retained the capacity to reward or punish their offspring through unequal bequests: so Maddalena Fracastoro privileged one son over another "because he has always been most obedient towards her and has shown the greatest obedience and reverence towards the lady testatrix, his mother."[32]

The degree to which patriarchal strictures and retarded independence had disruptive consequences is difficult to assess. Elsewhere, intergenerational tension between son and father frequently erupted in ugly confrontation when matters of honor or property were at stake.[33] More often, youth directed energies and frustrations outside the family, into factional violence, rape and assault, carnival, and political rowdiness.[34] Still, criminal registers measure only deviations from expected behavior; dutiful offspring would not leave many traces in the record. Anecdotes of the Bovi, the Stoppi, and the Repeta must be placed against the careers of the several hundred boys in Veneto memoirs who waited for independence, perhaps with annoyance at delay but without such overt manifestations of frustration as to attract attention. After all, they were raised from childhood not to expect autonomy until a later age. They certainly did not find the system odious enough to loosen controls when they in turn assumed leadership of a household.

MANY TESTATORS granted their widows a strong position with regard to property and children. Gaspare Arnaldi ordered that his sons honor and revere their mother as their *domina*, and that they acquiesce to her warnings and counsel, threatening to withhold his blessing from heaven if they did otherwise. Bonaventura Bovi granted his widow full power *(potestas et libertas)* to govern his family "because he holds great confidence in the lady Isabeta"; his heirs were to demonstrate obedience, charity, reverence, and love to her if they wished a blessing. The practical Aventino Fracastoro desired heirs to show reverence and obedience to their mother "because she is frugal and gives good advice." Pietro Verità's "beloved wife" Benedetta was to serve as tutrix of her children and co-commissioner of his estate. Several others named their wives *gubernatrix* or *domina* of minor children; those who imposed maternal authority ranged from the humble Domenico da Quinto, whose widow Vincenza was to govern "without contradiction by his heirs," to the noble Giovanni Thiene.[35]

Legislators felt strongly enough about guaranteeing widows' tutelage that they set aside ancient doctrine. Roman law had assigned the burdens of tutelage to those who held the right of succession to a minor's estate, which was not normally the mother, and preferred a male agnate as tutor. Even in the time of Baldus the idea of a woman as tutor was anomalous. But the principle was challenged by the perception that tutors with a personal stake in the inheritance might prove predatory. Choosing the mother or maternal kin as guardian best assured impartial management and decent care. Public magistracies then sought to safeguard that choice.[36] In the Veneto, cases involving widows and minors received summary judgment in order to forestall legal obstructionism by male relatives, and municipal officers such as syndics and advocates received special jurisdiction to protect *miserabiles personas*, a category that included widows and the fatherless. The Venetian appellate magistracy of the Auditori Nuovi was repeatedly ordered to give special favor to these *miserabiles*, hearing their cases in preference to more lucrative lawsuits. Statutes and testaments made the widow's job easier by releasing her from the obligation to draw up an estate inventory.[37]

In practice, however, widows did not normally govern either estate or children. Even when named tutrix or executrix, they seldom appeared in the documents that recorded transactions of property, marriage, and movable wealth. Despite Gaspare Arnaldi's injunctions, for example, his widow Caterina Zugliano did not control his wealth and his offspring: eldest son Andrea managed wealth and household for his brothers for over two decades. In the next generations, too, widows less frequently served as tutors of minor children than did adult males. Brother Tommaso managed the patrimony for Andrea's widow Marcella Fracanzani and son Silvestro; he figured in some 150 transactions as the boy's tutor, while Marcella remained in the shadows. After his death, Silvestro's uncles served as guardians in five of six transactions.[38] Tommaso left a widow and two sons of his own, with the order that older son Gaspare serve as "tutor, curator, rector, et gubernator" of his brother; his widow was merely given maintenance.[39]

Other testators in the region gave guardianship to mature sons rather than widows, and documents show brothers rather than widows acting on behalf of minor children.[40] Of the Veronese families that produced memoirs, eleven widows appeared in the *anagrafi* along with an adult son; in seven cases the son headed the fiscal household. Vicentine law actually encouraged male guardianship, at least in property transactions: no minor under the age of twenty could alienate or obligate land or land rights without the consent of two close relatives—and those *proximi* were to be men.[41]

Moreover, minors did not necessarily respect tutelage. Silvestro Arnaldi, for example, came of age early and threw off all guardianship. Despite the threshold of age twenty, he made a land investiture as sole proprietor in January 1466, when he had just reached the age of sixteen. While his uncles appeared occasionally as tutors for the next two years, Silvestro—described as *factus adultus*—engaged in large transactions after November 1466, and after late 1467 his documents made no mention of supervisors.[42] In a similar vein, Gerardo dal Gorgo in 1451 acted as tutor for his younger brother Francesco, but the middle brother Gian Maria, aged sixteen, acted for himself.[43]

Strays and Servants

For thirty-five years Bartolomeo Bovi resided with the widow of his wife's uncle. After living with a paternal uncle for nearly three decades, Tommaso Arnaldi headed a domestic community that included a widowed sister-in-law and two sets of nieces and nephews. Battista Guastaverza lived with his wife, children, a former wet nurse, a man identified as "cousin or partner," and an aged woman "whom he keeps for the love of God." The Veronese jurist Cristoforo Lanfranchino kept house with four brothers, a widowed sister-in-law and her sister, plus a nephew. Zaccaria Freschi's mother-in-law lived with him for twelve years (and was buried in the Freschi tomb); his mother's sister lived with him for twenty-eight years.[44]

Decades of studies have underscored the small size and simple configuration of the premodern domestic group; in fact, the composite family was common in the fifteenth century, in the Veneto and beyond. It has, however, been overlooked for two reasons. The first is the nature of the documentation. A tax system such as Vicenza's, where the fiscal unit as a whole was liable, gave no incentive to mention co-resident relatives whose patrimonies were insignificant. In Florence's *catasto*, separate patrimonies required separate declarations, and co-resident kin often appear apart. *Ricordanze* were concerned to trace lines of agnates, and ignored the miscellaneous kin who took shelter with the family.[45] Testators found little impetus to mention co-resident kin who would not inherit.

The second problem is that, despite disclaimers, aggregation oversimplifies data. Peter Laslett, for example, reminded his readers that despite the "relatively small average size and uncomplicated structure of the domestic group in England," that fact did not preclude the constant, even considerable presence of complex households;[46] even so, his refusal to include "inmates" and the "houseful" in his calculations inevitably obscured nonnuclear but co-resident relatives. In a similar vein, the reminders of Herlihy and Klapisch-

Zuber that Florentine households show huge variety in domestic configuration are overshadowed by their figures of mean household size (3.83) and percentage of noncomplex nuclear households (92.25 percent).

When the vantage point shifts from the aggregate to the individual family, however, exceptions to the norm multiply to the point that they dominate impressions of the household. At any given moment in the 1410–65 period, for example, the Arnaldi were living with one or more stray relatives. Uncle Pietro died but was replaced by nieces Isabeta and Bartolomea, who in turn married out but were succeeded by sister-in-law Marcella and cousin Silvestro. Standard schemes would classify the domestic group as a simple alternation of vertically extended mononuclear and fraternal joint families, whereas it was in fact a hodgepodge, more a concertina than a succession of tidy boxes.

Most of the strays came and went with little fanfare, and we scarcely know more than their names and relationships. *Why* they were taken in is not always self-evident. For the Veneto the best case is that of Semiramide Thiene, married to the wastrel Battista Arnaldi. After her death in 1446 Andrea and Tommaso accepted at least one and probably both of her daughters into their house; later Arnaldi arranged their marriages and guaranteed their dowries.[47] It is true that the Arnaldi did not intend to lose materially because of their kindness. Andrea specified that the expenses of Isabeta's food and clothing were to come from her mother's estate and whatever was left of her father's money. The maternal inheritance was likewise designated to fund most of the girls' dowries. But the Arnaldi did not stand to gain either, since anything beyond expenses would flow to the girls' dowries and thus out of the male line. They did give shelter in an already crowded house for several decades and, since the girls' father was perpetually insolvent and Semiramide was not wealthy, probably never recouped the expense of maintenance and dowries.

Material interest was secondary to more vital considerations of *caritas* and public standing. An undowered daughter had no future; so Tommaso dowered Bartolomea because he was "avid for the honor and wellbeing" of the girl. He was equally avid for the honor of the Arnaldi house. Abandonment of Semiramide or her daughters would have seriously breached social imperatives and rebounded to the harm of the male line, since men's honor and thus family honor was at least in part associated with protection of their women. Semiramide Thiene was their brother's wife, thus by the doctrine of *uno carne* their sister; and the Christian who did not provide for relatives "has disowned the faith and is worse than an unbeliever" (I Timothy 5:8).

Moreover, by hard-headed and worldly calculation, failure to care for them would impugn the family's good faith, respect, and *publica fama* in the community at large. As Paolo da Certaldo put it bluntly, "If you have poor relatives, don't treat them badly or kick them out, because if you treat them badly you open yourself to charges of cruelty. Therefore love them and maintain them as best you can, so that those who hear about it won't be as cruel to you as [they would if] you were [cruel] to your kin."[48] Doing the right thing might also repair some of the social damage that Battista had caused. And if the Arnaldi did not care for the helpless in their midst, they could scarcely be trusted in future marriages, alliances, or business dealings.

WHEN GIANNOZZO ALBERTI declared that servants were to be reckoned as members of the family, he simply drew on traditional definitions.[49] To Romans, the family encompassed all those under the *patria potestas*, including servants and slaves; the *domus* was defined as a community of shared resources and mutual obligations that extended beyond blood relationships. Servants too, thought medieval writers, were owed the *caritas* that bound the household.[50] But one did not need to be steeped in legal and patristic writings to know that domestics were integral to the family. Their service extended beyond mundane tasks of provisioning and maintaining the physical fabric of the house, to acts of intimacy and personal risk: to cite but two examples, Francesco Veronese carrying the body of little Renaldo Arnaldi to burial, and the *famuli* of Ludovico Thiene and Matteo Toso refusing to surrender arms and brawling with the night watch.[51]

Three demographic conclusions can be assayed. First, the number of household dependents grew over the course of the Quattrocento. In Veronese *anagrafi*, which record both domestics and some of those hired to work on rural properties, the wealthier counted an average of 1.23 dependents in 1423. That figure rose sharply, as did the number of Florentine servants: rich Veronese in 1502 employed an average of 3.87 subordinates.[52] In the *anagrafi* of Veronese families that left memoirs, the average household employed 1.7 persons before 1474, 2.2 in the following quarter century, and 3.1 in the first half of the sixteenth century (see appendix, table 4.2).

Second, the sex ratio of dependents, which initially favored women and girls, shifted steadily until males constituted some 62 percent of employees after 1500. Overall, 54 percent of dependents were male, the reverse of the Florentine and Venetian experiences in which female employees were always in the great majority.[53]

Third, employment patterns were different for men and women (see appendix, table 4.3). Women servants were five years younger than male counterparts, taking the median. Nearly half of women domestics in the Veronese sample were under the age of twenty, compared with less than 30 percent of men. More than twice as many very young employees were female than male: girls were more highly regarded for the simple tasks of carrying and tidying. Men were more prized in maturity. Women served during childhood and adolescence, earning dowries and learning domestic tasks; their brief time in service marked a temporary stage in the life cycle.[54] Men more commonly made a career of servitude, entering patrician households after adolescence and remaining in service for some time.

Writers regarded servants with distrust: Alberti advised wives to protect household goods with "fear and vigilance."[55] Vicentine statutes on servitude mirror that suspicion, directing rubrics against servants who departed before the stipulated time—they forfeited salary and were fined—and against those who carried off family goods.[56] More seriously, they perceived servants as likely sources of the sexual pollution of the *domus*. A domestic who opened the house to someone attempting to rape or commit adultery with the mistress or her kin was not only executed but burned; this was the most severe of penalties, imposed on those guilty of heinous crimes such as heresy or treason. Anyone having consensual sex with a serving girl was ordinarily fined a mere ten *lire,* but the penalty was quintupled if the act took place in the master's house.[57]

Servants were placed firmly under the *patria potestas* of the employer: Andrea Arnaldi was obligated to "rule and govern" little Margarita Scremini "just as citizens are accustomed to do to their daughters."[58] Servants, however, by no means received the same protection as other members of the household; recent studies stress exploitation of servants' labor as well as their sexual victimization.[59] Predators had to be punished, but servants were deemed victims of little account and penalties were basically token. In Vicenza, sons, nephews, grandsons, and close kin of the master were fined a derisory ten *lire* for consensual sex with a servant girl, and other males were fined fifty *lire* for the offense; these penalties should be compared with the five hundred *lire* levied on those convicted of fornication with a respectable wife. The attempted rape of a married woman rated a fine of three hundred *lire,* but that of a servant only twenty-five *lire.*[60] It comes as no surprise that the mothers of Manfredo Repeta's three illegitimate children were one *fantescha* and two *massarie.*

Terms of employment also seem to support an image of servants' vulnerability. Vicentine notaries, like counterparts elsewhere in Italy and France, did not possess models for hiring contracts. They found substitutes in formulas of land transactions: the father of the young girl, declaring himself acting under the *jus locationis*, actually leased *(locavit)* her for a specified period and payment.[61] In legal terms, these children were regarded as little more than real property, conveyed by their fathers just as a landowner transferred a field or a house.

But a different interpretation may be in order. The Vicentine law of domestic service offered no guarantee for the personal well-being of employees. Highly detailed land law, on the other hand, was designed to preserve economic assets. Several rubrics ordered tenants to preserve the integrity of property, prohibited treatment that might harm future income, and set stiff penalties for nonpayment. Procedures for redress clearly favored owners.[62] Vicentine employment contracts, explicitly invoking that *jus locationis*, extended the guarantees of the land law to little girls in domestic service. Fathers of abused servants had little recourse under the law of servitude, but abundant redress under the *jus locationis*. In a curious way, servant girls received better protection when considered as leased property than they would have received as mere hirelings.

Servants may not, in fact, have been consistently mistreated. Good relations, after all, would not occasion notice in the documentary record. A few flagrant cases cannot establish a norm or even an appreciable frequency, and normative indifference to the sexual victimization of domestics does not mean that men habitually took advantage of the situation. The contrary notion, that employers commonly appreciated service, receives some confirmation in testamentary largesse. In Siena, orders to provide dowries to young girls rose throughout the period, with a large proportion of these directed at servants; in Lyons, legacies to servants were regular and stable. Venetians commonly left objects and art to servants, as well as dowries, and there are even cases of servants making bequests to their masters.[63]

In the Veneto, dowry bequests to servants were frequent and generous. The hundred *lire* left to servants by Giacomo Guasterverza, madonna Libera, Cornelia da Valmarana, and Francesca d'Arzignano, the 150 *lire* left by Bonaventura Bovi to a *pedisequa* and Alvise Stoppi to an *ancillae*, and the two hundred *lire* left by Giacomo Thiene to a *massaria* should be measured against an annual salary of around eight or nine *lire*.[64] When the Arnaldi gave two hundred *lire* to a former servant in 1433, half was deferred salary but half was a free gift.[65] Those who had served faithfully might be supported in old age: thus Pietro Verità ordered that *famulus* Pietro Viadana be clothed, fed, and kept in the household for the remainder of his life; heirs in fact respected the provision.[66] Several families of Veneto memorialists made domestics godparents to their children: self-interest was a factor, as those bound by spiritual kinship might be expected to exercise good care, but the fact remains that these servants were deemed worthy of deep trust.

Succession and Inheritance

Veneto sons inherited "equally and in equal portions," and the sons of a deceased son assumed their father's share. Roman and Germanic law discouraged the *melioratio,* the favoring of one son at the expense of others, and indeed it was little known; northern Italians scarcely knew primogeniture before the mid-Cinquecento.[67] Sons received the core of the patrimony: fathers seldom dowered daughters with outright grants of land. When shortage of liquidity forced them to bestow a few fields in dowry, they ceded only miscellaneous lands and retained contiguous blocks for sons; they reserved the right to francate dotal lands and so recover them for the patrimony. When daughters confessed receipt of their dowries they renounced any further claim to family wealth. Lest there be any residual question of daughters' rights, many Vicentine fathers left them five *solidi,* and Veronese left them a few *lire,* with the order to be "silent and content" with this token.[68]

In the normal course of events testators with sons seldom deviated from this formula. They made bequests to siblings, daughters, cousins, affines, cognates, and other blood kin—preference for patrilineal devolution did not eliminate alternate strategies—but these nearly always consisted of cash and anyway did not amount to a significant share of disposable wealth. The lion's share of patrimonies, and the overwhelming proportion of land, passed to sons and grandsons. In the background, however, was ancient Germanic custom, which established a broad category of "natural heirs" from the larger kinship group, who might present a claim. To be on the safe side, to protect their sons from grasping relatives, many testators also granted *attinenti* the formulaic five *solidi* with the request to be "silent and content."[69]

Rules for intestate succession most clearly articulated priorities of devolution. In Vicenza, for example, males inherited according to their degree of distance of kinship to the deceased, as reckoned by canon law: sons were preferred to brothers, brothers to first cousins, and so forth. Women of the same degree, and male offspring of these women, "should on no account be admitted to succession." If brothers were deemed the closest kin, sisters did not inherit; if nephews inherited, nieces did not. Indeed, women only succeeded to the patrimony in the absence of male kin within the third degree.[70]

None of this was either new or peculiar to the Veneto. Dugento and Trecento statutes of Verona, Padua, and Treviso excluded dowered women from the paternal inheritance. Earlier medieval Italy, whether governed by Roman, Lombard, or Frankish law, showed preference for agnates *(favor agnationis)* and for males over females; equal inheritance by sons was likewise the norm in Florence and Genoa. The Veneto's rules for intestate succession largely repeated those of Italy at large, as did the prejudice against giving land to women.[71] At most it can be said that the Quattrocento tightened up the rules, particularly in pushing cognate, female, and collateral agnate inheritance to the margins. Both Verona and Padua, for example, sharply restricted the rights of female agnates and their sons to inherit. Lyonnais wills equally demonstrate declining bequests to lateral kin and a decreasing incidence of daughters as heirs, and exclusion of collateral relatives with a token bequest can be found as far afield as Siena and Avignon.[72]

But normal succession requires a conventional family, which occurred in no more than a plurality of cases. Some 40 percent of all couples had no surviving children or only daughters; hence "female succession was a statistically frequent possibility."[73] Anyway rules of inheritance were more socially and legally approved guidelines than fixed requirements, and had to allow for personal preference. Deviations from the norm were so constant that they must condition any image of relentlessly patrilineal devolution.

Even those with eligible sons claimed the right to deviate from custom; social penalties for nonconformity were insufficient to deter the strong-willed. Caterina da Quinto, for example, cut off her sons and daughters with the five *solidi* token, and left her estate to an apparently unrelated woman. Bonmartino Verità gave his two sons and two daughters equal shares in his wealth. The aged Bonaventura Bovi revised his will, adding a good chunk of land to the portion assigned to "most honest and most modest . . . , most sweet and most beloved" daughter Lucia. Ignoring hostility to the *melioratio*, Maddalena Fracastoro left a hundred ducats to her beloved *(dilecto)* son Battista but named obedient and reverent son Ludovico universal heir.[74]

If fathers without legitimate sons had inclined to a strictly agnatic approach, they would have found heirs among their brothers, brothers' sons, or sons of paternal uncles. In practice, however, men without direct issue often preferred miscellaneous relatives and friends, connected by marriage or affection, to lateral agnates. This was the case even when relations with male kin were not, apparently, strained. Zampietro Piva of the little village of Setteca had a brother, to whom he left some land, but named as universal heirs his sisters Elisa, Lucia, and Romana. The Veronese Ognibene Guastaverza had a brother, to whom he bequeathed land, but made his daughter primary heir in his first will and the sons of that daughter heirs in his second. Venetians, too, preferred daughters and daughters' sons to collateral males.[75]

Other wills established as heir a stepson, a daughter, the godfather of a child, and a son and stepson equally. Roman law allowed succession between spouses, but as a last resort only; men in Lyon rarely named their wives as heirs. Testators in the Veneto (and Milan), on the other hand, not infrequently left the bulk of their wealth to spouses. One ser Giovanni fu Francesco in 1431 left his estate to his wife, son-in-law, and stepson. Men's choice of residual heirs, too, might disregard conventional priorities. Count Giovanni Thiene did have sons, who were named universal heirs in customary fashion; but if their lines died out the will substituted his daughter—not his brother or nephews.[76]

Women with children usually left their goods to those children. To some extent their choices were limited: Vicentine and Paduan statutes allowed them to make bequests outside the line of descent only if they left an equal portion to children.[77] But if most respected that clause, they then chose secondary heirs from a wide pool of relatives: so Dorotea Verlati named her son heir, but left her dowry to her sister.[78] Women without children showed even less inclination than men to seek heirs among agnates or cognates. "All good works expect a reward," noted Caterina Verità, and she left almost everything to the unrelated couple who had provided "many and infinite services" during her illness. The Vicentine Elicha da Legnago left goods to Andrea Arnaldi and the aptly named donna Bonità out of gratitude for *multa beneficia*. Dorotea Malasi vacillated among Christ's poor, a "spiritual daughter," and a niece, but did not consider male kin. Antonia da Quinto wanted the daughters of her daughters and the sons of her sister to succeed.[79] Some did show preference to spouses and their kin: a second Caterina da Quinto chose her husband, as did Maria da Lisiera, and Romana da Lisiera gave the disposable half of her dowry and all residual goods to a father-in-law who had cared for her in sickness. Tadea Fracastoro, however, ignored her husband and named her mother universal heir.[80]

Pressures for male succession might be resisted when sons were less than beloved. It was difficult to exclude them altogether: Roman and Germanic law granted sons a portion of paternal goods by natural right and limited grounds for complete disinheritance to a few dreadful offenses. Girolamo Bovi, who looted the parental house and went to live with a wife that his father thought crazy *(prava)*, was guilty of disobedience in contracting an unapproved marriage, perhaps sufficient cause for cutting him off. Still, his mother acknowledged, the boy was owed a legitimate portion "by the law of nature," and his father would not withhold a blessing. They would not, however, grant him equality with his "dear and beloved" brothers Agostino and Francesco. Their solution was to grant him a hundred ducats, for which he was to be content and silent.[81] So, too, Bartolomeo dal Bovo provided a hundred ducats for chronically indebted son Giovanni but excluded him from the list of universal heirs.[82] Effective disinheritance through bequest of a token came cheaper to the less well-off: five *solidi* only went to the sons of Domenico da Quinto, Marco da Bolzano, and Caterina da Quinto.[83]

Testaments offer a final category of exceptional bequests: those to children in convents. Technically, taking religious vows constituted a sort of civil death; and only the living could inherit. Moreover, such legacies reduced the resources available to the lineage. Veronese legislators in 1450 echoed long precedent with a provision that those in monasteries could not be admitted to inheritance as long as agnates or cognates were available. Veronese parents disagreed. Benedetto Verità and his wife left a large sum to their daughter Caterina, which her brother Antonio converted into a maintenance payment. At her death, nephew Verità covered the cost of her funeral, medicines, and other debts, and he and the noble Maddalena Fracastoro made bequests to daughters who were nuns. These legacies were doubly dubious, since they paid for personal needs and so contravened the Justinianic requirement that gifts to the religious enter the patrimony of their convents,[84] but testators showed no hesitation.

IF DESCENDANTS lacked the *substantia* to keep up an appropriate tenor of life, remain in the good graces of public reputation, and expend the all-important symbolic capital, the family would cease to exist in any social sense. Moreover, the income from commerce or professions alone could not maintain status, and required supplement by inheritance. Accordingly, testators increasingly sought to guard against dissipation of landed patrimonies by inserting nonalienation clauses into wills. In its mature form, often but not always labeled *fideicommissum* (vernacular *fedecommesso*),[85] this mechanism forbade heirs to alienate the core of the estate to anyone outside the patriline; the share of any branch without legitimate male issue should pass to other branches in the patriline.

Fedecommesso is crucial to the development of a sense of lineage, and to the evolution of mechanisms for keeping the lineage intact over the decades. Yet it has suffered misconceptions and a paucity of studies linking doctrine to practice. First and foremost, it should not be connected to primogeniture, as means to counteract the dissipating effect of equal inheritance.[86] In fact, *fedecommesso* and primogeniture are very different mechanisms. They were distinct in timing: *fedecommesso* was common by the later Middle Ages, while primogeniture was rare or absent in Italy until the mid-sixteenth century. More to the point, testators did not use the former to establish the latter. Instead, in the Veneto as in Tuscany, they granted equal portions to each son and then imposed collective nonalienation clauses on all sons, aspiring not to reserve wealth for the firstborn but to preserve wealth among the entire male line of descent.[87]

Veneto examples come, as we would expect, from families that had the most lineage self-consciousness and wealth to preserve. But *fedecommesso* was far from universal even in the wills of patricians: mechanisms for entail were still in a formative state, and varied widely in format. Often the testament forbade alienation only until minor sons came of age, or for a generation or two.[88] Nonalienation clauses were not yet strictly enforced. Gaspare Arnaldi, for example, forbade his sons to touch their inheritances before the age of thirty; soon the twenty-three-year-old Battista withdrew his share and began to sell off pieces. His brothers could not legally block his squandering of the patrimony, and could only maintain its integrity by buying the lands themselves.

Lineage

At the end of a very long and stern testament, after binding his heirs with an eternal *fedecommesso*, Gabriele Verità broadened his efforts to ensure the solidarity of the lineage as a whole. Invoking symbolic patrimony, he commanded "that the arms and insignia which are placed above the house of the testator shall never be removed or deleted, but shall always be preserved: because these insignia shall be the *stimata* of those of the Verità."[89] *Stimata* had a dual meaning. In simplest terms it was the neo-Latin form of the vernacular *stemmata*, referring to the heraldic device painted or sculpted above the palace portal: Verità demanded that all sharing his name adopt common insignia. The word also referred to the verb *stimare*, denoting public esteem and estimation, and so pointed to the arms as emblem of the Verità's high social standing. To efface them would in a metaphoric sense delete the lineage's claims to eminence and thus efface the lineage itself. Moreover, surname[90] and heraldry alone did not bind the family: *these* insignia, the ones on his palace, were to serve as focal point. Collective identity required tangible expression in stone and bricks and mortar. Bartolomeo dal Bovo, likewise, fixed the "memory of the house" by erecting a pillar upon which were carved the family arms and texts recalling great events in history that had touched the ancestral village of Bovo.[91]

The law, too, invoked the house as principle of family aggregation. Prohibition of sitting in judgment on someone from the same *domus*, and statutes against the presence of more than one individual from any *domus* on a council, assumed that broader family connections had palpable force in everyday life, and in turn strongly fostered the individual's consciousness of membership in the extended family group. Statutes that imposed arbitration upon close relatives, reinforcing the principle that the broader family community should settle disputes internally, defined the *domus* to include ascendants and descendants, collaterals up to the third degree, and a miscellaneous category to be reckoned "broadly" *(largo vocabulo):* their intent was to extend the frontiers of effective kinship.

Still, apart from symbolic and normative statements, there remains the question of how effective that broader kinship was in everyday life. For example, the archives of Veneto families hold no records of collective association. Genoese *alberghi* met to set rules for membership and conduct and appointed officials to keep peace between participating households, and Florentine houses such as the Peruzzi met to swear self-disciplining pacts,[92] but Veneto patricians did not claim corporate identity for their houses. The wider family was not a *consorteria,* a judicial entity with norms and structures, and the lineage remained unformalized.

Testaments were firmly patrilineal and seldom paid much heed to the larger agnate group. *Fedecommesso* clauses named collaterals as residual heirs only when the testator's direct line failed; Gaspare II Arnaldi, to take one example from many, established cousin Silvestro as heir of last resort.[93] Testators without sons preferred daughters and miscellaneous kin—including affines and spouses—to lateral males, and testators as a whole did not regularly order bequests to nephews, cousins, or lateral male relatives. Venetian and Genoese testators bound extended kin through gifts and expressions of gratitude, and some 80 percent to 90 percent of testators in Lyon made bequests to the wider family;[94] Veneto counterparts offered few incentives to agnate solidarity, and more often remembered servants.

Executors of estates were relatives or nonrelatives, with no consistent pattern. Gaspare Arnaldi and his son Tommaso chose executors from among maternal relatives, Bonmartino Verità wanted Verità cousins to handle his estate, and Gabriele Verità opted for public officials and friends.[95] Alberto Monza chose six friends; Marco Thiene, Gabriele Monza, and Gaboardo

Monza mixed paternal and maternal cousins and nonrelations; Clemente Thiene recruited a cousin and a brother-in-law. Gaspare II Arnaldi elected a friar, three friends, a distant affine, and his cousin Silvestro.[96] This assortment demonstrates weaker reliance on the broad family than was the case in Genoa and Florence, where testators regularly chose commissioners from the agnate pool.[97]

The community of the dead, in similar fashion, occasionally but not invariably extended laterally. The entire Verità *gens* gathered in a sepulchre in S. Eufemia, and the Bovi, Muronovo, and Stoppi owned collective tombs in S. Anastasia; generations of the Arnaldi rested under the right side of the altar of S. Giovanni Battista in Vicenza's cathedral. As many testators, on the other hand, mentioned *sepoltura sua* or noted construction of a personal tomb, indicating that lineage solidarity in death was no great priority. A few testaments, such as that of Gabriele Verità, ordered prayers and Masses for *parenti;* most, however, desired suffrages for the testator alone or, at most, for spouse and children. Nor did testators regularly intend funerals to proclaim the unity of the larger family. Marco Thiene ordered that a flock of relatives be dressed in mourning clothes to accompany his body to the tomb, but the case is exceptional; more representative was Gabriele Verità, who provided mourning only for wife, son, daughter, daughter-in-law, and grandchildren. The many who stipulated an austere burial were more representative still.[98]

The family at large seldom functioned as an enduring economic community. Testamentary provisions might bind the generations for some time: Bartolomeo dal Bovo ordered his descendants to supervise jointly the family *juspatronus* of a rural church, and Gaspare Arnaldi bound his heirs to give yearly alms to the hospital of S. Marcello in perpetuity.[99] Land rights held in fief from the bishop were impartible; one such *decima* bound Arnaldi cousins together for at least thirteen years after they separated assets.[100] These contacts, however, did not tie up any significant proportion of the patrimony. For seventeen years cousins Gaspare II, Girolamo, and Silvestro Arnaldi held some lands and investments as a jointly owned reserve, but this constituted a small part of total family wealth and anyway was divided once Girolamo reached maturity.[101] Other cuginal transactions were low-grade (Gaspare once named Silvestro his procurator, and the cousins twice rented land to each other.[102]) or merely completed unfinished business, winding down investments made many years before and completing the dowering of uncle Battista's daughters.[103] With the exception of the Stoppi, newcomers to the region, cousins or lateral agnates never formed commercial partnerships or held large blocks of land in common.[104]

Brothers often held goods in common, but uncles and nephews, cousins, and stepsiblings usually divided patrimonies at the first opportunity. Convenience might dictate separation, and most divisions seem amicable enough, but some documents hint at indifference or even tension: as a Florentine noted dryly in 1519, "communions of goods frequently produce divisions of souls."[105] When Andrea Arnaldi died in 1454, leaving four-year-old Silvestro and eighteen-year-old Angela Chiara in brother Tommaso's care, the family evidently suffered a shortage of liquidity. To provide Angela's dowry, Tommaso ceded a half share in the family palace in Carpagnon—Silvestro's share. Somewhat later Tommaso bought Silvestro a house in the outlying neighborhood of Santi Apostoli, exiling his nephew both from the family's traditional center and from the municipal center; the two branches thereafter remained residentially and fiscally divided.[106]

Further, there is the test of residence: were lineages cohesive enough that their households sought to live in proximity? In Florence, judging from anecdotal rather than systematic study, those with a common surname often clustered in a few neighborhoods. Thirty-one Strozzi filed returns from a single *quartiere* in 1427, and the Salviati concentrated their properties and residences in six contiguous blocks; twenty-four sets of Buondelmonte lived near each other in the early Cinquecento. In Genoa, *alberghi* formed residential as well as economic and legal communities; in Rome, Perugia, and perhaps Venice, residence patterns demonstrate the "effective topographic cohesion of lineages."[107]

Veneto tax rolls, however, indicate the opposite. Dividing the number of a family's households by the number of neighborhoods in which they resided produces an index of residential concentration; a ratio of one indicates dispersal (five households in five neighborhoods), while a higher ratio indicates solidarity (five households in a single neighborhood). For the later fifteenth century and the first decade of the sixteenth century, the index for the Veronese families that left memoirs is 1.6, which is virtually the figure for Vicentine families as a whole.[108] On average, eight households of a given family lived in five different neighborhoods, which indicates weak clustering. Both samples indicate a slight trend toward concentration, as indexes rose to high points of 1.9 early in the Cinquecento; even then, on average, over half of a household's kin were not immediate neighbors.

Nor were Veronese and Vicentine families attached to ancestral centers. Even when one branch of the family remained in an original neighborhood, other lines scattered throughout the city (see appendix, table 4.4). Furthermore, outlying branches moved frequently and did not establish new clusters: the Bovi kept continual residence in only one of thirteen neighborhoods in which they resided. By 1502 only one Verità household remained in the ancestral neighborhood of Falsorgo, and the family had households in eleven other sites. If they heeded the patriarch Gabriele's words to gaze on the common insignia, they would have had to walk a considerable distance to do so. The Dionisi, Bovi, and Muronovo went a step further, and abandoned their original homes entirely (see appendix, table 4.5).

To return to the memoirs: with the exception of the Stoppi, writers were little concerned with anyone except their parents and progeny. Manfredo Repeta, for example, began his account of the *agnatio* with the common ancestor, but when he reached his own times he ignored the wider descent group and noted only the births, marriages, and deaths of his own children. He later mentioned the deaths of a brother and a cousin only because these had made him a residual heir.[109] In the multigenerational memoirs of the Arnaldi and Verità, each writer noted salient events in the lives of his own offspring, with a glance upward to record the deaths of parents, but did not follow the life cycles of those uncles, aunts, nieces, nephews, cousins, or stepkin whose births were recorded by earlier memorialists. Glances sideways were faint and occasional, and most lateral agnates disappeared after a single notice. If the memoirs are any guide, Gabriele Verità's thunderous injunction for family unity sounds more like a plea than a realistic expectation.

CHAPTER FIVE

WORK

*J*TALIAN ECONOMIC HISTORIOGRAPHY, anticipating the world economy and modern business structures, privileged great merchants and bankers, international commerce, and metropolitan centers. Even Gino Luzzatto, who in a pioneering 1931 article urged attention to lesser traffickers and the "small, isolated economies" of cities such as Padua, Perugia, and Bologna, soon returned to familiar terrain.[1] Only recently have revisionist scholars noted the exceptional nature of cosmopolitan finance and trade. The Tuscan economy, they conclude, was overwhelmingly driven by regional exchanges;[2] elsewhere, save for Venice and Genoa (and, to a lesser degree, Milan), small scale and limited range were the order of the day. This was certainly the case for the second-tier cities of the Veneto. The Arnaldi made forays into the markets of Padua and Venice, the Guasterverza sent cloth to Apulia, and the Stoppi had business contacts in Lombardy, but few traders set up enduring, highly capitalized companies to market local production beyond the regional level. Provincial cities scarcely knew sophisticated mechanisms of credit and exchange. Indeed, their economies were only partially monetarized.

Further, a growing body of case studies suggests that properly "modern" specialists may have been rare, even in the metropolis:[3] Genoese notaries had important sidelines in trade and insurance, and aristocratic colleagues served as apothecaries and "loansharks" as well as merchants;[4] a Roman lawyer-courtier invested in wool, silk, warehouses, and wine; a midlevel Venetian patrician dealt in a wide range of goods, and directed the sale of vegetables and fruit from his mainland estates; Florentines, albeit on a larger scale, kept a "portfolio of diverse investments."[5] In the provinces, too, diversification was the norm. Andrea Arnaldi, for example, was simultaneously a notary, wool merchant, silk retailer, organizer of livestock raising, tax farmer, usurer, professional surety, leather broker, legal agent, and dealer in agricultural commodities. The Giacomo Guasterverza who sent cloth to Trani was also a *fornaserius* or tile-maker; the Verità were spicers and goldsmiths as well as rentiers and government officials.

Commerce

The Cloth Trade

The most prominent activity of Veneto memorialists, and the most important sector of urban economies, was cloth production and marketing. The Arnaldi were wool merchants from at least 1417, and more often styled themselves *lanarii* than notaries or retailers. Bartolomeo dal Bovo, Antonio Bovi, and several Guastaverza were drapers. The Stoppi traded in Lombardy as well as locally; their very name (Stoppa in the documents) refers to tow or oakum, the coarse, broken fiber used in the warp threads of cheaper cloth.

The Arnaldi brothers joined the guild of cloth merchants (*mercatores* or *mercatores pannorum lane*) probably in 1425, and the guild of wool cloth producers *(fratalea lanariorum)* in 1434.[6] Verona, too, had separate corporations for production and marketing although, as in Vicenza, individuals often engaged in both trades.[7] The status of those guilds, however, differed in the two cities. Occupational bodies in Vicenza were largely autonomous, their statutes and matriculation registers subject only to periodic pro forma ratification by civic magistracies. In Verona, on the other hand, an overarching corporation known as the Domus Mercatorum regulated nearly every aspect of production, distribution, litigation, legislation, and jurisdiction; city councils passed statutes for all eleven corporations in the wool trade.[8]

Structural differences aside, cloth guilds set similar policies. They sought above all to concentrate more lucrative operations of production in the city, in particular, to forbid weaving of fine cloth *(panni alti)* in the countryside and to ensure a monopoly on cloth finishing for urban workshops. To concentrate marketing, they obliged rural producers to bring cloth to city fairs and obtain the seal of the urban guild. Opposing municipal governments, which offered inducements to immigration, guilds protested any influx of foreigners.[9] *Arti* in Padua, Verona, and Vicenza tried to block importation of all but the finest foreign cloth—Vicentine consumers complained until Veronese cloth was allowed—to prevent importation of cheap wools from

Puglia and to force imported wool to be subject to urban tolls and guild fees.[10] Efforts to block the export of fine wools and to prevent shepherds from grazing sheep outside the dominion were less successful but at least reserved most good local wool for urban producers.[11]

Cloth manufacture in the Veneto did not follow the putting-out system of Florence, where the merchant-entrepreneur directed the production cycle from raw wool to finished cloth, retaining ownership of goods throughout. Salaried workers performed some steps in the merchant's shop, and outside subcontractors further processed materials for a per-piece payment.[12] Veneto organizers such as the Arnaldi, instead, bought and sold semifinished goods from independent artisans at each stage in production. Even when Andrea moved warps or cloth from one artisan to another—from a napper to a tailor in 1439, for example—he worded the transaction as a purchase and resale rather than as a transfer of materials that he held in continual ownership. Scores of commercial transactions mention but one case of putting out, and that was in the silk industry, which operated under special rules.[13] All processes were performed off-site, since the Arnaldi held only a small shop in the city square.

Only in obtaining raw wool for eventual sale or distribution to artisans did Veneto merchants attempt vertical integration. In the *soccida* or partiary husbandry contract, the merchant consigned sheep to an inhabitant of the countryside for a fixed term, usually two to four years, to be kept at the tenant's risk. During the term of the contract, the merchant-owner received a portion, usually half, of the wool from the March *(marcege)* and August *(avostane)* shearings. At the end of that period the owner collected the capitalized value of the flock, or the animals themselves, and owner and tenant divided profits from the sale of lambs. At any given time the Arnaldi were involved in several *soccide*, each covering between thirty and two hundred sheep, ensuring a constant and considerable supply of wool.[14]

Small trading companies handled the sale of cloth. The single exception is striking: in 1476 Alvise Stoppi in Verona formed a *compagnia* with his brother Contino and the latter's father-in-law, both resident north of Como, which was capitalized at 7,000 ducats and wound up in 1494.[15] The case, however, is atypical. Of the 100 Veronese contracts studied by Michele Lecce and the two dozen in the Arnaldi archive, none were joint family ventures. The capital in each *societas* was far smaller, ranging from 21 ducats to 600 ducats in Trecento Verona to 21 ducats to 400 ducats in Quattrocento Vicenza; the Vicentine mean was around 50 ducats. Duration was shorter, usually between 9 months and 5 years, never above 10 years, and never open-ended. All were made with fellow citizens; Veronese contracts often specified that commerce was to be restricted to the city itself. Finally, the generalized *mercancia* of the Stoppi companies finds no counterpart: other Veneto contracts specified a single product line for each partnership. The Stoppi and other companies shared only a general structure, with passive investors providing the capital and traders supplying *industria;* profits or losses were split between the parties.[16]

By the token of great Florentine companies of the thirteenth and fourteenth centuries, the commercial economy of the Veneto—characterized by brief, small, local partnerships—appears either primitive or a backwater. But a note of revisionism has crept into Tuscan economic history: in the fifteenth century, smaller firms with limited capital and short duration (to compartmentalize risk) replaced the massive, multigeneration trading company of earlier centuries. Production companies, too, were many and small, with few permanent employees and little capital investment in equipment. Regional rather than international commerce dominated the economy. The sprawling, enduring Medici company, often held up as a model, may have been accidental and certainly was atypical.[17] In Milan, too, companies were small and lacked foreign branches; single households generally supplied their capital.[18]

The Veneto may not have been a barren region in which to do business, either. Caterina Uberti took 10 percent profit from the Stoppi company, and her brothers boosted their share to 16.7 percent by waiting a few years. The Arnaldi brothers made 128 percent profit on one three-year wool venture, and although they could not recover the cash they still gained a house and two fields. An eighteen-month *societas* in cloth more than doubled another Arnaldi investment, with profits taken in wool and hides. The more modest return of 34 percent on a three-year leather company was still respectable, and compares well with Tuscan profits in the 10 percent to 15 percent range.[19] There was money to be made in small businesses in small cities.

Verona was the undisputed leader of the region's exporters, though cloth from Vicenza and Padua may have been subsumed under the generic category of *panni veronesi*.[20] Most was of top quality: judging from available figures, *panni alti* constituted 95 percent of urban production (see appendix, table 5.1). Indeed, Veronese made some of the best cloth in the peninsula: by Jacopo Bardi's 1427 reckoning of goods on the Constantinople market, it was only slightly inferior to the finest wares of Florence, England, and Venice.[21] The city's cloth enjoyed such a high reputation that merchants from nearby centers, particularly Mantua, tried to pass off their wares as Veronese.[22]

The Venetian government, not surprisingly, wished goods to flow through the capital so it could collect transfer taxes to support the merchant fleet. As early as 1414, in anticipation of increased revenues, the Republic set up a new customshouse to handle mainland trade. Its sporadic efforts to force the passage of wool and cloth through Venice, however, met with resistance from Veronese merchants, who preferred the southern route via Ostiglia and the Po and who could easily evade Venetian strictures by smuggling through the extensive network of rivers and canals in the southern flatlands. In 1455 the central government abandoned its 1421 policy creating an obligatory entrepot, and though the order was reimposed in 1475 its success was limited.[23]

Much of Verona's production went south. Apulia had imported Veronese and Vicentine products since the Trecento, and in the mid-Trecento Tuscans favored unwashed Veronese wool. Exports were apparently strong in the next century. Veronese cloth was sold in Perugia after 1468 and Salerno in 1478, and in midcentury the city's wares in Rome and Aquila were exceeded only by Florentine cloth. In 1472 communal orators claimed that the city was accustomed to send three thousand cloths annually to the kingdom of Naples. Though Veronese merchants resisted mandatory shipment through Venice, they found its markets of considerable value for re-export to eastern cities such as Damascus and Alexandria; from 1474 on they had use of a house in the capital.[24] Verona sent cloth to Brescia, Crema, and Parma, as well as to the Tyrol and Germany, and it has been said that the Veronese monopolized the Hungarian market.[25]

References to Vicenza's trade are more sparse, but the city's low profile may actually have been due to favorable trade conditions. Vicentine merchants had long enjoyed the right of free export to Venice and exemption from Venetian taxes, and the Republic renewed the privilege in 1404.[26] In consequence, they oriented their business to the Venetian re-export trade: they kept a house in Venice, and municipal councils modified regulations of cloth size and quality to match Venetian standards. By the mid-Quattrocento they were sending semifinished fine cloth to the capital for dyeing and eventual export to Syria, and the city's cloth appeared with some regularity in tariff schedules of the Marche, Abbruzzo, Puglia, and Rome. In addition, much Vicentine cloth was smuggled out of the district (the Arnaldi may have been involved), shipped down the Brenta, and sold clandestinely in Venice. Vicentines, then, shared in the prosperous Venetian wool industry and trade, even though their cloth lost its local identity in the process.[27]

They could not, however, rival their neighbors' cloth in quality. While Vicentines were enterprising—they placed more kinds of cloth in Constantinople than did any other city—their wares commanded lower prices than those of Verona, and competed only with goods of second-rank cities such as Bergamo and Treviso.[28] Here the Vicentine guild had made a grave mistake, defending a monopoly on *panni alti* that was little prized and leaving the making of cheap cloth to rural producers who at least found a market for inferior goods.

The degree to which the region actually reaped the profits of cloth commerce is uncertain. Veronese merchants were resident in Rimini by at least 1460, and fellow citizens held a warehouse and workshop in Pesaro; the merchant Matteo della Torre was in Rome in 1478.[29] Much if not most of the export trade was handled by foreigners, however, with only production and first-level marketing in local hands. Florentine companies had agents in Verona and Padua during the Trecento;[30] unfortunately account books of the fifteenth century have not been published, so it is hard to know if the practice continued. It is certain, however, that Pistoiese traveled to Verona to purchase cloth for re-export in the early Quattrocento, that the Venetian Marino Gritti conveyed Vicentine "three-thread" cloth to Calabria, that Florentines and Venetians sold Veronese cloth in Aquila and Apulia, and that Venetians sold a dozen types of Veneto cloth on the Constantinople market.[31] Probably, like their Milanese counterparts, merchants in the Veneto left the risks and profits of international exchange to others.[32]

The industry as a whole flourished during the first three-quarters of the fifteenth century. Vicentine provisions of 1416 spoke of the wool industry's great utility to the city and noted its honorable place among the urban *artes;* the twin guilds of merchants and producers, which once held only middling rank in the city's corporate hierarchy, occupied the premier positions in 1425.[33] The peak of Vicenza's industry has been dated to 1430–70; Verona's may have had a slightly longer run.[34]

Students have noted a crisis in urban industries later in the century, with competition from rural producers and northern Europeans the most frequently mentioned causes.[35] The intensity of that crisis, however, is difficult to assess. Tagliaferri, looking at tax returns, noted that Veronese drapers declined both in number (from ninety-four to seventy-one) and in median assessment (from sixty to twenty-three *solidi*) over the course of the century. The number of lesser wool workers rose steadily, and the total number employed in the industry grew by 50 percent in the 1409–1502 period; but the urban population tripled over that span.[36] Some 343 of 555 wool workers were unemployed in 1477;[37] another source, however, suggests that the year was an unusually poor one (see table 5.1). Communal officials in 1473 claimed that the urban economy as a whole was declining relative to other economies in the dominion, but the lament was made to support a petition for tax relief and its validity is uncertain.[38] If indeed production of wool cloth fell off, the growing felt hat industry may have provided compensation.[39]

The rapidly expanding silk industry at least partially offset a perceived or real decline: while the numbers employed never approached those of the wool trade, profits were high. In the later Trecento the Veneto began to produce raw materials locally, making the industry competitive with import-dependent cities such as Venice and Florence. By the end of the fifteenth century, silk was integral to Veneto economies: in 1488 the doge supported a Vicentine request that Ludovico Sforza be denied permission to bring mulberry trees into Lombardy, lest competition harm the "livelihood of our people" and the "treasury of the commune." A similar provision for Verona in 1505 used precisely the same language.[40] Furthermore, because the silk industry was largely unregulated—neither Vicenza nor Verona had a silk guild until the mid-Cinquecento—wool manufacturers could easily establish sidelines in silks. The Arnaldi, for example, identified themselves as silk merchants as early as 1431, even as they built up a prosperous wool trade.[41] Nor, it seems, were Veneto producers greatly harmed by competition from the booming silk industries of Venice, Milan, Florence, and Piedmont;[42] rising demand brought plenty of business for everyone.

Retail

The commercial center of Vicenza, like that of Verona, occupied the site of the old Roman Forum. In Vicenza, the three contiguous spaces of the Piazza Maggiore, the Piazza delle Biade (for grain), and the Piazza Erbe (for fruits and vegetables) wrapped around the communal palace on the north, east, and south; smaller *piazze* dedicated to sale of fish and wine stood to the west and southeast. Strung out on the east-west axis of the broad Piazza Maggiore was the double file of shops of Vicentine retailers. These were conceived as impermanent, as seen in a map of 1480, which portrays the commercial district as unoccupied. They were in reality substantial, as evident from a document of 1443, which describes an Arnaldi-owned *statio* with five external and two internal doors with locks, a protective grille *(canzela)*, a second story *(solarium)*, and a balcony.[43] Gaspare Arnaldi set up business toward the west side of the row sometime around 1431.[44] Eight years later heirs Andrea and Tommaso moved to the other end of the *bina apotecarum mercatorum*, opposite the column of San Marco, where they rented a shop from the noble Valmarana family, renovated it with new wood- and ironwork, and paid a considerable rent of nine ducats annually.[45] Toward midcentury the brothers apparently moved back to the western edge, "towards the cathedral."[46]

The shop was most frequently called a *statio scapizarie*—*scapizare* is the local verb for selling cloth, retail or wholesale[47]—and, as befit their guild memberships, cloth was the most frequently mentioned product. They sold whatever the market wanted: upwards of fifty different types moved through the shop. *Scarlatini*, the better "three-thread" *(ad tres liceos)*, better blue *(celeste)*, and black *morello* cloth were most costly, at slightly more than three *lire* per *brachium*. Cloth worked with gold or silver threads—*pano frixo aureo* and *planecia*—must have been equally expensive.[48] Lesser blue *(azuro)*, common three-thread, and "mixed" cloths *(panni miceli)* cost between two *lire* and three *lire* per *brachium*.[49] Bed-cloth *(fodre a lecto)* cost about a *lire*, as did good fustian (made of a linen warp and wool or cotton weft) and felt for hats *(beretini)*.[50] Ordinary fustian and *pignolato*, a largely cotton mix, sold at around ten to thirteen *soldi* per *brachium*.[51] Each type of cloth was further subdefined: *alto* or *basso*, native or foreign, dyed or plain, finished or unfinished, ordinary or worked with precious threads. The Arnaldi also sold raw or semiworked goods such as wool, cotton, warps, and thread.[52]

Completing the textile end of the Arnaldi business was the trade in silk. Here, too, the Arnaldi carried on a diversified trade in all phases of production and marketing. They bought materials as well as finished cloth, put out raw silk to be spun into thread, set up at least one company in the *arte*, and sold cocoons *(bacini)*, thread, warps, and finished cloth.[53] In addition they kept a stock of luxury items made from silk, such as cords or the boots *(stivos)* with gold fasteners, enamel, and gilt work that they sold to the patrician Bartolomeo Baldanucci in 1439.[54]

Within a half year of Andrea's death in 1454, brother Tommaso sold the shop's stock for 3,879 *lire*, equivalent to the dowry of a noblewoman or about four times the price of a large urban house. About two-thirds of that sum was inventoried. Of that, 42 percent consisted of fustians, and another 25 percent of other types of cloth. Silk goods were 18 percent of assets, cottons 4 percent, and a catchall category of warps and raw silk a further 4 percent.[55] All of these goods logically fell within the purview of the *mercatores pannorum*, but many of the products sold at the Arnaldi shop infringed on the monopolies of other guilds. The final 7 percent of goods liquidated in 1455, in fact, consisted of silver, which fell under the goldsmiths' jurisdiction, as did the accessories such as silver buttons, enamel fastenings, and rings that Andrea and Tommaso commonly sold.[56] The vair-trimmed overmantle *(pelanda)* worth sixty-five ducats and the less valuable *proponte* should have belonged to tailors or furriers.[57]

From an early date the Arnaldi were active in the trade of agricultural goods. Debt confessions, the most common business documents, show that Arnaldi clients had received wheat, wine, sheep, millet, beans, rye, mixed grains *(granate)*, cows, sorghum, seed wheat, cotton, spelt, hay, wool, and pasture rights.[58] When the Arnaldi entered into *soccida* contracts—which involved cattle, horses, and pigs as well as sheep[59]—they often found themselves in receipt of skins, and so entered the leather trade.[60] From sheep *soccide* the family received, and put up for sale, half of the cheese produced; from all their *soccide* they acquired and sold newborn animals. When Andrea contracted to collect the city's taxes on meat, he collected quantities of salted and dried tongues from the butchers, as well as skins.[61] The list of products received at or sold from the little shop also includes oak beams, cartloads of firewood, haystacks, and fifty beehives.[62]

In the early and mid-Quattrocento their sale of agricultural and comestible goods was occasional and small-scale: the Arnaldi sold goods that they had accepted in lieu of cash payment for rents and shop-goods. Around the middle of the century, as they wound down the cloth business, they began a more systematic trade in agricultural commodities. The occasional woolsack sold for a few dozen *lire* gave way, in 1454, to the sale of some 7,360 pounds of wool valued at nearly 1,900 *lire*.[63] Wheat sales rose by similar degrees, from a few *staria* early in the century to 200 *staria* in 1455, to 634 *staria* in 1477–78.[64] To obtain these quantities, the Arnaldi could no longer depend on *soccide* and rents in kind, and became major buyers on the urban market. In fact, the incidence of *soccide* dropped sharply: the family found incomes in cheese and skins an inconvenience, and preferred straight sales of animals and wool. Finally, the very purpose of Arnaldi commerce changed somewhat: to turn a profit, as always, but also to barter food for land.[65]

The Arnaldi, then, replaced diversified retail with specialized wholesale. Cloth and luxuries disappeared from the inventory around 1455, and silk a little later. The social as well as economic priorities of an upwardly ambitious family appear to explain the shift. Andrea Arnaldi could scarcely press a claim to nobility while peddling rings, boots, and bolts of cloth. Son Silvestro, a self-styled *nobilis* who contracted marriages with aristocratic houses, had to abandon retail—reference to a family *statio* disappeared after 1470—but suffered no opprobrium for selling entire herds and cartloads of foodstuffs.[66]

An Economy of Debts and Credits

Silvana Collodo, studying Paduan wills, was struck by the volume of outstanding loans, uncollected credits, and unredeemed pledges that testators passed on to their heirs. She concluded that Paduan merchants were consistently small-scale lenders and small-time borrowers, with transactions left incomplete for years on end.[67] In like fashion, the commercial records of Verona and Vicenza are remarkable for the degree to which sales concluded not with payment but with a promise to pay. The Arnaldi's *Liber Actoris*, the region's best record of daily transactions, consists largely of summaries of debt confessions, in which clients acknowledged arrears and agreed to terms for repayment. Some entries were cancelled (a sign that the debt was extinguished), but most were not. The document served not to record income but to pursue future payment.

The constancy of debt may indicate artisans and cultivators mired in poverty: while wage and cost of living figures are wanting in the Veneto, evidence from Tuscany points to a large proportion of the population at or below subsistence level.[68] Poverty alone, however, cannot explain a debt-saturated economy. It is difficult to believe that the Arnaldi and their colleagues were such poor businessmen that they made a habit of selling to paupers with few prospects for repayment. Moreover, debt obligations were as widespread among patricians as among the lower classes: the Arnaldi themselves often took years or decades to pay for land purchases, and lent goods and money as often to the well-heeled as to workers.

Rather, an economy of debt resulted from a chronic shortage of liquidity that affected all social categories. Widespread recourse to nonmonetarized exchanges such as barter, delayed payment, and future sales was also a response to and compensation for a lack of circulating money. To be sure, evidence for a monetary pinch is purely anecdotal: for example, Veronese councillors complained in 1456 and 1461 that textile workers were being paid in goods because of a "penury of money" as well as "the greed of the drapers."[69] The hypothesis does, however, receive some corroboration from other regions. While there is controversy over the availability of specie in Florence,[70] it seems certain that the smaller cities and the countryside of Tuscany were persistently short of coinage. Even in Florence, the necessity of assuming debt may account for the fact that 31 percent of the population reported liabilities in excess of assets in the 1427 *catasto*, and that half the population had obligations equivalent to 50 percent of declared wealth.[71] Milan and Piedmont suffered a lack of liquidity in midcentury due to rising state expenditure and a bullion shortage. Economic historians of Europe as a whole point to a "general retreat from a money economy," and conclude that "contracting exchanges were indeed one of the fundamental characteristics of late medieval economic life."[72]

Venice was not the only capital to drain specie from its dominion, but its magistrates may have been more systematic. They demanded taxes in gold and better silver money, and required that subject cities pay for the minting of cheaper coins with superior coinage. A shortage of bullion in the 1430–71 period further increased the rapacity of the capital, especially since the Levant trade required constant export of precious metals. Recurrent devaluation of lesser silver and alloyed "black" money relative to better coins—recall of some currency and depreciation of the rest in 1472 was shock enough that Manfredo Repeta noted it at length[73]—especially hit merchants, who suffered loss of buying power, rising real cost of taxes (paid in gold and better silver), and falling real value of long-term debt repayments (collected in lesser monies). Adding to economic instability were monetary wars that put counterfeit and severely alloyed monies into circulation: in 1472, for example, Venice protested that the duke of Milan had flooded the *terraferma* with eighty thousand ducats' worth of silver coins with a false Venetian stamp.[74]

Smaller cities in the Veneto possessed none of the advanced credit mechanisms that might compensate for a cash crunch. They enjoyed neither locally owned deposit banks (as smaller Piedmont cities and Tuscan towns such as Arezzo and Pistoia did not)[75] nor the presence of foreign bankers. Bills of exchange, bank monies, deposit accounts, transfer letters and lines of credit, which allowed big-city merchants to avoid recourse to coinage, did not exist in the provinces. Jews licensed to take pledges provided only small consumption loans. At best, Silvestro Arnaldi made periodic deposits with a friend or relative, who then paid for his land purchases.[76] These were closer to escrow payments and did not constitute a sophisticated way to move money.

The sole means by which merchants could convert outstanding credits into cash were the municipally operated Pledge Offices (Camere de' Pegni). In theory, creditors could obtain a court order for public messengers to collect a pledge equivalent to the debt; the money from redeemed pledges was remitted to the creditor, and unredeemed pledges were sold at auction. In the Veronese Camera, business was brisk early in the Quattrocento; the number of *viatores* nearly doubled in the latter part of the century. But the Camera's operations fell short of expectations, as local and Venetian magistrates repeatedly complained of insufficient oversight, slow operation, endless litigation, corrupt officials, and overall dysfunction. Debtors delayed or resisted the taking of pledges: those in Verona, who had a legal right of refusal pending final adjudication of lawsuits, exercised that *vetatio pignoris* in some two-thirds of cases and bogged the system down with multiple refusals. Recusants in Vicenza were subject only to a token three *lire* fine, which they often evaded: rustics claimed that their assets were obligated for dowries and could not be seized for debt, and many sent women—who could not be jailed, and who would receive lesser fines—as their representatives before urban tribunals. Here, too, the prevailing lack of liquidity prevented collection of arrears, as unredeemed pledges often failed to sell or received derisory bids.[77]

Markets without Money

With fairs concentrated in the autumn, customers could not pay throughout most of the year: weavers who bought the March clip, for example, would not see much income until November; rustics who needed wheat in the spring could not repay until the harvest. Barter, payment in kind, and long-term schedules for repayment gave the moneyless a chance to enter credit markets in a modest fashion and to buy needed goods from urban stalls. For rural debtors, cashless transactions saved liquidating assets to make restitution. Thus when Tommaso da Enego owed the Arnaldi two hundred *lire* from a *soccida*, he paid with sixty of his own sheep that he regained in a further *soccida*, in effect rolling over the debt and avoiding recourse to the urban market.[78]

The elite also found advantages in exchange without money. Employers with cash flow problems could maintain production by paying workers with goods, even though Venetian and Veronese authorities tried to forbid the practice.[79] Merchants conserved their stocks of coin by trading for other goods that they needed: so the Arnaldi gave cloth in partial payment for a horse, and warps, skins, and foodstuffs in partial payment for land.[80] They, and Veronese counterparts, frequently formed trading companies by providing working materials in addition to or instead of money, promoting commerce without extensive capital investment.[81] With grain prices rising in the latter half of the century—they nearly doubled in Florence[82]—merchants found strong impetus to make loans in return for future payment in crops.

Stretching compensation over a long period of time did not, in the long run, harm the local economy. Since merchants both bought and sold products, artisans both bought raw materials and sold semiworked goods, and cultivators both bought urban products and sold foodstuffs, long-term credit and long-term debt tended to balance out and no single group was the loser. In fact, the economy as a whole was stimulated because issuance of debt in effect expanded the money supply. Sellers of goods could simply build the delay into the purchase price. Sellers of land were often indemnified by a clause that gave them a mortgage on and income from that portion of the land not yet paid for. It mattered little to Giovanni Pirli that Silvestro Arnaldi took eleven years to complete payment for land in Bertesinella, since Silvestro paid a fixed rent all the while.[83] A similar clause specified that a title to land would pass to the buyer only at completion of payment, with the seller enjoying all income in the meantime.[84]

Debts and credits were themselves fungible, and could be bought, sold, or assigned to a third party. To give a relatively simple example: in 1439 Andrea Arnaldi owed Andrea del Meze *lire* 81/11/3 for wool, and del Meze owed Zano da Schiavon *lire* 74/0/5; Andrea Arnaldi paid the latter debt directly to Zano.[85] Most cases were more complex, involving transfer of credits among four or more parties. The Monza brothers owed fifty ducats to Giordano Trissino for their sister's dowry; the Arnaldi bought the credit from Trissino and assigned it to Bartolomeo Giulia to retire a previous obligation; the Monza brothers settled the account by transferring land to Giulia. Not a single coin changed hands. Debts owed by third parties, investments in *societates*, and land incomes were regularly reassigned to pay for dowries, land, and merchandise.[86]

Alternatively, an individual could pay a second person's debt to a third person in return for a debt confession, transferring the original obligation to him- or herself.[87] Cash-rich merchants such as the Arnaldi made a considerable business of covering others' debts. Respecting usury prohibitions, they seldom mentioned discounting or interest: Andrea Arnaldi once bought a thirteen-year-old debt for its face value plus *lire* 5/14 in notary's fees.[88] Still, many documents record payment for unspecified "services" *(patrocinia)*, suggesting that payment of others' debts was not an act of charity. Occasionally a notary's blunt honesty hints at potential profits. When Andrea paid 150 ducats for the right to collect 180 ducats in debts, he stood to make 20 percent on the deal.[89]

Rustics usually had but a single asset they could transfer in compensation for debt: their lands. In the simplest transaction, the *datio in solutum* (transfer in payment), the debtor acknowledged the obligation and ceded an equivalent value in land to the urban creditor. For example, Giovanni Pavanato owed some Arnaldi cousins 232 *lire* and made satisfaction by assigning a house and a field in Malo.[90] When cultivators owed several parties, the preferred format was a document of sale, with the purchase price used to extinguish the various obligations; little or no money went to the seller. When the Arnaldi brothers bought land from Tomeo da Enego for 406 *lire*, for example, 43 percent of the price retired a debt owed to the Arnaldi and 37 percent was paid to another of Tomeo's creditors; the Arnaldi satisfied the remaining 20 percent by assigning wool in their common *soccida*.[91]

Both wealthy and humble citizens, women as well as men, knew how to move obligations around until a single transaction cleared the books. Provided with such flexible and efficient means of transfer, merchants in particular may not have been much hindered by the prevailing lack of currency. They did not have the means to pool capital on a significant scale or to launch interregional trade, but as long as their ambitions were limited they could hope to pile up considerable assets. The Arnaldi made a small fortune on the credit market in the 1430–55 period, in the midst of a gold drain, a silver drought, and a scarcity of small coins.

Genteel Usury

In an economy strapped for cash, those with ready money exerted enormous leverage. Few of these, apparently, were specialists: the number of Veronese styling themselves banker or moneychanger or moneylender in tax rolls declined from thirteen to one in the 1409–1502 period.[92] Rather, usury was a sideline for men with diversified portfolios in land, commerce, the professions, and public office. Since most owned their homes and received food from land rents, their income from trade and office was never consumed in day-to-day expenses and could be deployed on the credit market.

Few documents record outright loans of money. Most are known only from later debt confessions; discreet silence covers terms of repayment and possible interest. Andrea Arnaldi's *mutuum* of *lire* 27/5/9 to Chiarello Zanini, for example, was mentioned only when the latter promised to pay an equivalent value in the August clip. At other times borrowers repaid precisely the sum said to have been loaned, implying that no interest was charged.[93] A common formula shows explicit respect for usury prohibitions, specifying that a loan was made "out of mutual service and love" ("ex causa mutui servicii et amoris").[94] Clearly notarial fictions are at work: Veneto lenders had long known that inflating the actual loan amount could disguise real interest.[95]

Documents also record loans of foodstuffs and agricultural equipment out of pure *caritas*, but these are less ingenuous. They often did not mention the quantity lent but specified the amount to be repaid, which could mask an increment. Alternatively, stipulation of future payment of goods, in return of a loan of the same quantity, could disguise real interest since prices varied throughout the year. Wheat was scarce and costly in the late spring (ca. twenty-eight *soldi* per *starium*), and abundant and cheap after the July–August harvest (seventeen to twenty *soldi* per *starium*). When Jacopo dalla Longa borrowed sixteen *staria* of wheat in October, and repaid the same amount in late March, he technically paid no interest but he returned goods more costly than those he received. Men of La Longa received two hundred *staria* of wheat in October, and promised to repay the monetary equivalent of two hundred *staria* at the May price: differential prices between fall and spring built in an interest rate upwards of 50 percent. The Barcellari brothers were allowed to repay a loan after the harvest, but at the higher May price, and Filippo di Franceschino's loan in December was assigned a value according to the May price.[96] Most agricultural loans, in fact, were made in the fall, with a six-month term for repayment. If the loan was not repaid, it stayed on the books at the higher spring price, or the lender accepted land in its stead.

Merchants of the Veneto, preferring not to demand open interest, shared widespread unease at demanding outright profit from loans. They had heard the fierce injunctions of preachers such as Giovanni Capistrano, who in the Lenten sermons at Verona in 1438 condemned any sort of usury, and Bernardino da Feltre, who took an ever harder line throughout the region for the better part of a quarter century. San Bernardino of Siena, visiting plague-wracked Verona in 1444, had urged citizens to give up their usury; when they did so, the plague ceased. Four decades later a citizen returned to usury, and the plague returned too until he realized his breach of Bernardino's teaching and closed the business.[97]

Usurers of the Veneto also felt cold blasts of disapproval from Venice. In 1456 the Senate railed against those who bought wheat on future contracts (*ad terminum*) for a "dishonest price," driving the poor into debt that they could not escape.[98] Punitive legislation then failed to pass, but the next day the Senate ordered that "subjects and countrymen" buying wheat *ad terminum* appear before the local podestà to explain terms of the deal, and that the podestà remind them that they were not obligated to pay a higher price than was in effect at the time of sale.[99] The omnibus Lex Vendramina of 1477, extended the next year, blasted the iniquity, malignity, and moral sickness of any usurious contract, especially grain sales at illicit prices. In 1494 the doge extended a ban on hoarding to those lending grain, ordered investigation and trial of the guilty, and demanded restoration of money thus extorted. Closing a loophole, the Maggior Consiglio in 1499 noted that documents of sale often concealed interest by stipulating prices up to one-third above the just price; the buyer was henceforth allowed to pay just a "reasonable price."[100]

Some merchants heard and obeyed: the Venetian Guglielmo Querini forbade his agents to make possibly dubious exchange deals "because I do not wish to profit that way, nor have I ever done so, because it is less than honest."[101] Others softened the terms of future sales, inserting a clause in contracts that buyer or seller would offer compensation if the price of goods changed between sale and payment.[102] A few, but a very few only, felt the prickings of conscience enough to order heirs to make partial restitution, through charity, of illicit gain.[103]

For those who persisted in lending, it was safer not to make an open loan at all. Preferred was a more roundabout transaction. In one entirely conventional agreement it worked this way: Tommaso Arnaldi and his nephews bought a field from Zambono Ziliotti for one hundred *lire*. They promptly leased the land back to Ziliotti at a yearly rent of six *lire*. In addition, Ziliotti had the opportunity to regain *(francare)* the land within ten years, for the same price of one hundred *lire*. The hundred *lire* represented the sum loaned, the rent constituted a 6 percent annual interest, and the period for francation was the term for repayment. Between "sale" and possible redemption, the land itself was held as collateral by the "buyer"/lender. If Ziliotti could not francate within ten years, the Arnaldi kept the field, with Ziliotti as tenant.[104] This was not, formally, a loan, and "usury is not committed except in a loan."[105]

This type of transaction was not only licit; it was infinitely flexible. "Prices" ranged from a few *lire* to hundreds of ducats, property ranged from city houses to single fields or vast rural estates, and borrowers ranged from humble cultivators to urban patricians and clerics. The price (or loan) was paid outright or applied to offset preexisting debts; it could be paid on the spot or over time, and repaid in cash or in kind. The land value could be made to correspond to a round figure—multiples of ten *lire* or ten ducats were preferred—by shaving off a few *campi* from a property. The term for repayment varied from one to ten years, with possibility of an extension at the lender's discretion.

It was not, of course, a Veneto invention of the fifteenth century. In Milan of the eighth and ninth centuries, land was frequently given in pledge for a debt, but was still held by the debtor at a rent equivalent to the interest; if the debtor paid the loan, he recovered the land. Slightly later Milanese documents show a form of sale/leaseback that is not far from that of the Veneto, and Tuscans established the mechanism by at least the thirteenth century. Paduans, who earlier preferred outright loans, responded to anti-usury campaigns by switching (in the Dugento) to sales followed by *livelli* or *affitti*.[106]

Purchase and leaseback with right of francation remained a common means of making loans throughout the Cinquecento; the sole variant was that later lenders usually collected rents in kind to protect against currency devaluation and/or to profit from rising agricultural prices.[107]

What was extraordinary in the Veneto of the Quattrocento was the stability of the institution. The structure and terms of the loan did not change over the seventy years of documents held in the Arnaldi archive. In a very few instances the interest rate rose to 7 percent,[108] and even less frequently fell to 5 percent, but deviations from the 6 percent norm amounted to no more than a twentieth of all such transactions despite recurrent currency fluctuations, economic cycles, and demographic upheavals. Lenders were not able to challenge custom by raising their rates in periods of high demand or penury of coinage, and borrower-sellers made no concerted effort to modify the system, as they did in the next century.[109]

This type of loan was also cheap, because it was backed by real collateral that would produce a steady rent/interest and would provide a safe asset in case of nonpayment. That may have been small consolation for borrowers who, unable to repay, remained on their former lands as tenants. The fact remains that, in other times and places, borrowers would have regarded a 6 percent land loan as a good deal. The similar *vendita/pegno* of early medieval Milan charged 18 percent to 25 percent, and that of later medieval Tuscany carried interest rates of 25 percent to 50 percent. Trecento Paduans charged a median of 12 percent, down from 20 percent in the previous century, as did Veronese and Vicentines.[110] Furthermore, loans unsecured by land were far more expensive. Quattrocento Venetians accepted a rough norm of 10 percent for commercial loans, with sharp spikes for short-term or risky ventures. In Florence, returns ranged between 8 percent and 10 percent on time deposits, between 7 percent and 15 percent on merchants' loans, and between 20 percent and 30 percent (or higher) on loans from licensed lenders. Jewish lenders in Vicenza demanded 15 percent to 20 percent on money loans, which was on the low side: their counterparts in Bologna and Florence took up to 25 percent to 30 percent interest.[111] In the Veneto of the Cinquecento, many "grain loans" were in the 10 percent to 20 percent range until local statutes returned the ceiling to 6 percent.[112]

The Notariate

Memorialists, habitual recorders of private worlds, and notaries, professional recorders of public transactions, were often one and the same. The four Ar-

naldi memorialists were members of the local college of notaries, as was Manfredo Repeta.[113] Among Veronese writers, Alvise Stoppi, Bonaventura Bovi,
and (perhaps) Bartolomeo dal Bovo were notaries, and Bartolomeo Muronovo
and the Guastaverza brothers were sons of notaries. The Fracastoro and Verità families were often present in the college.[114]

Membership in a corporation of notaries brought the rewards of participation in a high-ranking status group. Its very name *(collegium)* associated
notaries with lawyers and physicians, and ranked them above the artisans
grouped in mere guilds *(artes* or *fratalee)*. In municipal processions, notaries
marched ahead of guilds and gathered with top civic officials, Venetian governors, relics, and banners in the center of ritual display.[115] The Vicentine
college provided, as it had since the thirteenth century, a member of the elite
council of the Anziani.[116] As will be seen, collegiate notaries possessed a
plausible claim to nobility by right of technical skill, legal authority (a notary was also a *judex ordinarius*), and freedom from the taint of manual trade.

Were notaries guilty of incompetence or indecorous behavior, the profession's reputation for expertise, impartiality, and honor would suffer. To preserve that status, colleges set rigorous standards to ensure that notaries were
professionally and morally sound. The college of Verona, for example, set a
strict threshold of age twenty for candidates, required two years of study
(and hired a lawyer to give lessons), and imposed stiff entrance examinations. Members could not fight, blaspheme, gamble, or frequent taverns or
brothels under penalty of fines or, in extreme cases, expulsion.[117]

In practice, however, colleges were self-serving corporations, concerned
to secure an occupational monopoly for a privileged membership, and their
actions tended to subvert more high-minded claims. Collegiate notaries might
be altogether untrained: brothers Andrea, Battista, and Tommaso Arnaldi
entered Vicenza's notariate aged thirteen, seven, and six, respectively, when
a hard-up college assumed fifty new members in order to collect fees. Places
in the elite lists of *module* notaries, which supplied communal officials, were
alienable and heritable, and could be conferred on friends or relatives: the
Arnaldi brothers gained access to the *module* aged seventeen, thirteen, and
fourteen.[118] A second generation of Arnaldi entered the college as infants,
and the *module* aged nine, four, and two.[119] Accepting custom though con-
travening statute, the college after 1454 kept separate lists of the sons of *module* notaries, who would enjoy early entry and pay a reduced fee.[120] Open
nepotism appeared about the same time, as Andrea Arnaldi and Cardino Feramosca, elected leaders *(gastaldi)* of the college, enrolled an infant nephew
and a five-year-old son.[121]

Compounding problems of quality control was the fact that colleges virtually had to accept those with imperial privileges, qualified or not. Counts palatine held an unchallenged right to create notaries, even outside their own cities: Vicentine rural notaries owed their positions to aristocrats from Treviso, Padua, Lucca, Verona, and Milan. Technically, as was the case in Florence, imperial notaries had to pass ordinary tests, but the 8 percent failure rate in a 1429 Vicentine examination indicates that scrutiny was derisory. If the Modenese count Tommasino Bianchi could raise to the Vicentine notariate a boy of fourteen, a soldier of fortune, and a seller of horoscopes, the office was clearly devalued.[122]

Corporate standards, rather, aspired to keep out those without good connections. In 1443 the Vicentine college charged that some palace notaries lacked "civil habits" (mores civiles) and showed disrespect for God and good manners: no countryman could be admitted unless he or his relatives had paid taxes with the city for twenty-five years. Four decades later the college extended the ban to new citizens and those whose family members had practiced a manual trade. Even so, notaries perceived a growing influx of undesirables who threatened their privileges. The Veronese college in 1478 complained that those enrolled in the rural notariate (the cronaca minor) too easily passed into the upper body eligible for public office (the cronaca maior), and raised promotion standards from a majority vote to two-thirds approval. In 1499 the Vicentine college complained that outsiders were buying their way into the module; henceforth those who were not sons of notaries could enter the module only after a special (and rigorous) test of learning and comportment. The cursus of admission remained a polite fiction for the well-born, however, as reflected in the nonchalance of one Vicentine, son of a notary and a shoo-in candidate, who cast his petition for admission in facetious rhyme.[123]

Verona and Vicenza both had multitiered colleges, a feature of many Italian cities. The "major" and "middling" categories in Verona elected college officers, leaving the two lower ranks of rural and "extraordinary" notaries without an institutional voice. The maiores of Verona, like those in Treviso, filled approximately one hundred annual municipal offices.[124] The Vicentine system was slightly different but operated in much the same manner. Only notaries in the five module, lettered A through E, were admitted to the regular college sessions, and they held all major offices. With module of sixty members each providing sixty "ordinary" municipal notaries in four-month turns, 60 percent of the Vicentine notarial elite could expect public employment each year. Below them the vacantes, notaries on the waiting list for the *module,* received twenty-nine offices yearly. Several additional positions in the municipal government, urban guilds, charitable commissions, and other corporations were reserved for college members. Only rural notaries were denied office.[125]

The best effort of college and municipal legislators could not insure competent and reliable employees in government service. The Veronese college, it is true, made strict provision for technical expertise, and several times prohibited the buying and selling of public office. Notaries chosen for office were to serve in person, and if they declined the job the college selected a substitute.[126] Surviving evidence, however, is insufficient to indicate whether these norms were respected. In Vicenza, better documentation shows disregard for idealistic criteria. The college's rule that the letter of a deceased or retiring notary pass to the first on the list of *vacantes* remained a dead letter. Andrea Arnaldi gave his place to son Silvestro, Gaspare Arnaldi inherited a *modula* letter from a great-uncle, and Alvise Arnaldi received the letter of another great-uncle at the behest of cousin Cardino Feramosca. The Fracanzani brothers passed places around as one or another needed a job, while Manfredo Repeta gave a place to his aged father as a pension.[127]

Public offices assigned to members of Vicenza's *module* could also be transferred to other notaries. In the register of ordinary offices, in fact, most entries specified substitution. The going price for a sublet was between six ducats and seven ducats per term in office, plus a bonus of one or two ducats for a choice office, which was a considerable sum—about the cost of ten cartloads of wood, or a mare and foal, or a year's rent on a house.[128] That was why a nonpracticing notary such as Silvestro remained in the college for year after year, drawing a steady income from his place in letter B. In return, he suffered only the minor irritants of college dues and the obligation to turn out for processions and funerals. For its part the college, despite pious words in its statutes, did not supervise the qualifications of those who actually exercised offices. Indeed, the college organized the auction of several jobs annually, demanding only that winning contestants actually pay the agreed fee.[129]

Municipal statutes anticipated abuses, sternly enjoining notaries to write up their notes into complete documents in a timely fashion, not to remove records at the end of office, not to encroach on the offices of other notaries, to show up on the job, to enter documents into official registers, and not to take extra fees.[130] Still, evidence of scandalous performance is not hard to come by. Complaints of excess fees were legion. Notaries often held onto council provisions, neglected to copy legislation into official registers, and forced interested parties to pay to see public records. They illegally wrote up judgments concerning their relatives; some tried to serve simultaneously as court notary and advocate. Bored and inattentive counterparts in Treviso filled judicial registers with poetry and maxims, and once sprayed an audience with a prototype water pistol.[131] The fact remained, however, that notaries constituted a law unto themselves. When individual notaries were dilatory, inept, or peculative, their superiors had little recourse.

Many frustrated magistrates, in response, tried to regain control over their offices by bypassing local notaries. Chief among these, in the eyes of the jealous Vicentine college, were the Venetian-appointed chancellors who directed correspondence. With monotonous regularity chancellors imported their own notaries to handle business, drew up and copied documents personally, and otherwise cut into the fees of college members. But, while governments in Florence, Bologna, and Milan reduced employment of notaries and replaced them with more cooperative secretaries and scribes,[132] the Venetian Republic declined to contravene entrenched privilege. On twenty-six occasions the Vicentine college protested interference by chancellors, and each time central authorities confirmed its rights. In 1452 the college even organized a job action when the Republic tried to cut salaries and fees, forbidding its members to hold any office "for a limited price." Public offices, the college's ambassadors then declared, were *bona patrimonialia* that could be bought, sold, or willed to heirs: offices belonged to notaries, and were not subject to government control.[133] Venetian magistracies accepted that assessment.

THE NOTARIAL ARCHIVES of Verona were destroyed by fire in the eighteenth century, and the private notariate in the region can only be known from Vicenza's substantial holdings. These show little consistency to careers. For most notaries, only one or two registers survive: private practice was not a full-time job. Andrea Arnaldi, for example, drew up only 375 transactions over an eighteen-year span.[134] Others simply could not drum up enough business to make much of a living: many practicing notaries received the minimum tax assessment of five *soldi*. On the other hand, some made the notariate a solid profession. The high end is represented by the excellent Bortolo Bassan—he wrote clearly and provided accurate indexes—who filled forty volumes of around two hundred pages each over a forty-two-year span.[135]

Working conditions were not easy. Notaries were peripatetic. Andrea Arnaldi possessed a shop from which to base business, but even he walked around the city and suburbs to meet clients. Bartolomeo Scroffa and several notaries in his family were always on the move: they worked in thirty-one hamlets in a fifty-mile arc from the southeast to the northeast of the city, even venturing into Paduan territory, and seldom remained in any one place long enough to draw up more than a single act. In summer and winter, rain and shine, they gathered parties at casual locations—on a stairway, under a tree, on a road, under a doorway, on a bridge. Only testators and major landowners gave notaries shelter.

Time pressures, in the midst of constant travel to take on other jobs, were considerable. After making rough notes *(minute)* on the spot, the Veronese notary had eight days to draw up a semifinished legal document *(imbreviatura)* in registers, and between fifteen days and sixty days to make a parchment version *(instrumentum)* if this was requested.[136] Land sales required an inventory of properties, identifying field size, crops, borders, and neighbors; major sales might require hundreds of entries. A document such as Gabriele Verità's will, which occupies over twenty folios, could take a day or more to redact and copy. The original notary had to draw up all three types of document, since the use of scribes was not permitted. Throughout, the notary had to take great care because he was personally liable for mistakes. In Verona and Vicenza, moreover, documents of more valuable transactions had to be presented promptly to the communal Registry Office for copying into official volumes; the notary of record received nothing for this service.[137] In both cities, as well, notaries had to present a copy of testaments to public archives within a few days of completion of the *imbreviatura*.

Notaries might use assistants to speed things along. In an illuminated manuscript from the Veronese College of Notaries, for example, two men are shown working in tandem, one reading from notes and the other copying into a register.[138] Andrea and Tommaso Arnaldi were once described as exercising a joint notariate within their joint household.[139] As long as the lead notary actually wrote and took responsibility for the *imbreviatura* and *instrumentum*, no one could complain. Other devices for convenience and efficiency, however, were plainly dubious. For a notary—a "public person" and in theory an impartial public witness—to draw up transactions to which he or relatives were parties was highly irregular, but the Arnaldi and their circle did so frequently.[140]

Less savory shortcuts multiplied during the Quattrocento; the internal discipline of the notariate seems to have declined. Even the upright Bortolo Bassan sometimes used a scribe to record the body of an instrument, though he was careful to put his mark at the top and his signature at the bottom to preserve authenticity. He did so rarely, and mostly in old age,[141] but his son Cristoforo often appeared as putative notary of a document that is not at all in his handwriting.[142] By the end of the century scribes were commonplace, and the Arnaldi's chief notary Antonio Saraceni often did not bother to fix any mark testifying to personal supervision. His registers abound in grammatical mistakes, elision, and confusion of names and formularies, indicating haste or carelessness.

Cristoforo Bassan habitually did not bother to draw up his rough notes into legally valid *imbreviature*. Saraceni, in turn, commonly saved spaces in the registers for transactions previously noted, heading a blank folio with a quick cross-reference back to his *minute*; if the transaction was contested or required a full version, he could turn back to the notes and resurrect the details for after-the-fact redaction. Even when he did start to fill in a page, the document often petered out partway with a reference back to notes or a formulary.[143] This was not only lazy, but quite illegal; it left close to half of all transactions in a legal limbo, summarily noted but never turned into authentic documents. *Minute* had no legal standing, and many were so cursory that any later effort to reconstruct the act would have been futile. If later Arnaldi had faced litigation, they would have been hard pressed to supply uncontestable evidence.

Amid deteriorating standards, a growing number of citizens chose not to secure notarial services. The first such case from the Arnaldi archives is late (compared with Tuscany), with the first-person debt confession of *ego Franciscus de Gualdo* in 1440.[144] Thereafter, the incidence of such declarations rose sharply, and secondhand references to *scriptura privata* and "chirographs" also proliferated. The legal standing of these private writings was doubtful, since they lacked witnesses and the *publica fides* of a notary, but many people preferred them to sloppy notarial work.

The public standing of the corporate and public notariate never received direct challenge, but key indexes indicate that the private notariate lost ground. The mean *estimi* of Veronese notaries fell by nearly 50 percent in the 1409–1502 period, and the mean tax assessment of practicing notaries in Vicenza dropped from 1.89 *lire* in 1453 to 0.86 *lire* in 1505, from well above the mean *estimo* of about one *lira* to well below. If 73 percent of Vicentine notaries lived in prestigious central neighborhoods in 1453, only 52 percent did so in 1505.[145] Collodo perceives a similar decline in the state of Paduan notaries—poor, unable to gain access to urban councils, and ranking only with the "inferior strata."[146]

Other Ways to Make a Lira

Shuttling among a variety of professions, Veneto patricians found myriad little ways to add to family coffers. The shadow zones of the urban economy have received little attention, but were far from insignificant: the upper ranks as well as the marginal and semiemployed were active in the all-purpose service sector. The Arnaldi, for example, knew their way around the courts and the markets, and gladly lent their expertise for a price. Municipal statutes forbade lawyers to act as syndics or procurators.[147] As notaries, then, the Arnaldi were among the best-trained legal agents available, and they served as procurators to those who could not press claims in person. Andrea held a general retainer from the villagers of La Longa, who gave him open-ended authority to appear before any court or agency in Vicenza or Marostica on their behalf.[148] He also served as procurator in specific lawsuits. In a 1437 dispute between men from Molvena and the commune of Marostica, both twenty miles from Vicenza, Andrea represented the losing party and paid the judgment, in return for a fee. He then turned around and sold cloth to the winners, taking profit on both sides.[149]

Debtors and creditors, too, found it inconvenient to come into the city to settle accounts. The Arnaldi, financially astute and usually on the spot, were ideal middlemen for the collection or payment of obligations. They also served as agents for rural communes and tax collectors, forwarding monies to the city treasury.[150] The municipal government was slow to make payment, and its more humble creditors required legal leverage to collect their due; Andrea Arnaldi used his insider's influence, for example, in forcing payment for several cartloads of bricks used in building up the city's walls.[151] The Arnaldi helped lease or sell land on behalf of women owners unable or unwilling to manage property personally, and toward the end of the century they both served as and used third parties to buy and sell land.[152]

Any debt or contract of even moderate size required a surety or guarantor (fideiussor), who assumed joint responsibility for the obligation. Friends and relatives usually agreed to serve, but solitaries and major debtors sought outside paid assistance. The Arnaldi brothers, experts in credit markets and experienced in extracting collateral from impecunious debtors, frequently agreed to assume the risk of default. In one example of many, two brothers of La Longa, owing a considerable sum to the noble Battista da Porto for loans and foodstuffs, made Andrea Arnaldi their guarantor for the debt. Andrea had to pledge his own goods for eventual restitution, but was covered by the stipulation that he would receive rights to the debt if he had to pay off da Porto.[153]

What did this gain them? Documents recording payment for service *(pa-trocinium)* are scattered, but hint at a miscellaneous income which, while never huge in individual transactions, might mount up over the course of a year. Representing Daniele and Maredolo da Meledo brought in a fat lamb at Easter and two ducats at Christmas. The brothers from La Longa ceded eight pieces of land in partial payment for Andrea's surety; the retainer from the commune of La Longa was worth three ducats annually. Andrea once earned ten *lire* for accounting services. He was promised thirty *lire* in return for paying someone's twenty-five *lire* debt—a tidy 20 percent profit. Poor clients contributed a few carts of wood.[154] If the take seems meager, the Arnaldi thought it not to be scorned.

THE GOVERNING BODIES of Church and commune regularly entrusted the collection of their incomes to private subcontractors. They were guaranteed a fixed return with a minimum of personnel and overhead costs, which offset the fact that they would fail to reap maximum profits in good years. Further, by letting out contracts in public auctions, authorities forced competition among would-be collectors and kept the quota high. The Arnaldi had long found it worthwhile: ancestor Giovanni had collected the wine tax of Treviso in the 1350s (he lost a lawsuit there, and was assessed the then-considerable sum of three-hundred *lire*), then returned home to collect the urban wine tax and the tithes of the village of Brendola.[155]

In 1440 great-nephew Andrea began cautiously, collecting the meager sixty *lire* that a few villages owed for wartime carrying services. Within a decade, he was confident enough to promise 1,200 *lire* to the Venetian Camera Fiscale for one of its taxes; nor was he deterred when he was still paying off the obligation nine years after the *colte* were to have been collected. In 1450 he and two partners successfully bid 3,400 *lire* to collect tolls on goods passing through city gates. The next year he won the contract to supply the city with meat, and financed a *societas* with urban butchers in return for skins, salted tongues, and fees.[156] His profits are not known, though they must have been sufficient to bring him back to the auctions several more times.

While Andrea had no more guarantee than old Giovanni that he would collect his quota, he and later Vicentine contractors enjoyed partial protection if they could not (or simply did not) pay authorities in full. As early as 1413 central magistracies returned control over tax auctions to local governments, and reconstituted the Vicentine tribunal of the *judex datiorum* to hear prosecutions of collectors.[157] This informally indemnified tax farmers, since municipal tribunals had no reason to be aggressive in prosecuting those in arrears to the central government. In 1454 the doge forbade the Venetian Camera Fiscale to impose penalties on *daziarii,* and another Venetian magistracy in 1460 upheld the inability of the Camera to impose penalties on collectors in arrears.[158] The Senate charged in 1467 that the monies of its Vicentine treasury were "most negligently collected and badly handled," but its remedy ordering payment of arrears within eight days (with a penalty of 10 percent) was probably ineffective since, as the Senate admitted, tax collectors were not subject to penalties for late payment. The magistracy of the Auditori Nuovi, charged (among other things) with bringing outstanding fiscal cases back to the capital, was forbidden to interfere with collectors or their sureties.[159] Tax farmers could pocket their profits, but did not have to worry too much about shortfalls.

Church incomes, too, were for rent. Nonresident clerics found it necessary to have agents collect the proceeds of their benefices, pay local expenses, and forward the surplus. Since they regarded incomes as private property, they did not have to work within the ecclesiastical machinery: professor of canon law Girolamo da Monza walked over to the Arnaldi shop, lay notary Bortolo Bassan in tow, to record a purely civil transaction when he wished to lease the revenues of his six benefices. The Arnaldi brothers were glad to pay forty ducats annually for the privilege of handling Monza's finances, especially since Girolamo promised that they did not have to pay in full if the current war cut into their collections. They also collected the income from a midlevel canonry in Lonigo, even though this brought them a suit with the local apostolic representative over payment of annates. They also contracted to collect the tithes due cathedral canons despite a two-year dispute with a former collector.[160]

A generation later, Silvestro Arnaldi in 1482 served as a revenue collector for the bishop himself.[161] In 1496 he formed an alliance with two other nobles to collect the entire episcopal income—in one candid document of the transaction, Cardinal-Bishop Battista Zeno declared that he had "leased and rented his episcopacy"—for the great sum of 3,300 ducats annually. Zeno's faith was well rewarded when, ensconced in his Paduan palace, he received final payment with only slight delay.[162]

CHAPTER SIX

LAND

Patrician Acquisition

*T*HAT LAND OWNERSHIP passed from small cultivators to urban proprietors is commonplace in studies of Tuscany,[1] Lombardy, and other regions.[2] By consensus, accumulation by the urban well-to-do was already advanced by the early Quattrocento—in 1427 Florentines controlled two-thirds of the land value of their contado, and contadini only 18 percent—and accelerated over the course of the century. Scholarly commentary on the decline of peasant ownership ranges from the cooly analytical to the scathing, and the transition has been characterized, variously, as "erosion" "expropriation," and "proletarianization." But divergent interpretation takes place within agreement about overall trends, and study of tax records and notarial instruments by a small army of scholars puts the matter beyond contention. Veneto studies support the thesis of patrician accumulation,[3] and examination of the memorialists' archives would not challenge it either: the Arnaldi, Repeta, Verità, Muronovo, Guastaverza, and Stoppi owned more land in 1500 than in 1400.

Still, the phenomenon may not have been as drastic as is usually concluded. For starters, historians are overinclined to accept documents of acquisition at face value. Contemporaries, however, freely acknowledged that many instruments were fictitious, to disguise loans or protect assets from creditors.[4] Four of Silvestro Arnaldi's purchases, for example, should be removed from the balance sheet: the instrument of one was later admitted to be *fictum et simulatum,* and in the three others the actual buyer—a countryman—used Silvestro as a front.[5]

Further, it is necessary to take into account the biases of extant documentation. Families generally preserved parchment records of incoming land, since these were necessary to sustain future claims. They had no reason to keep records of land that they alienated. If they sold a field to a cultivator, the new owner would order the instrument—but the archives of smallholders have not survived. Silvana Collodo has noted that Paduans only drew up documents when their loans could not be repaid and they assumed the borrower's land in compensation, but did not bother to do so if loans were repaid. Surviving records, then, document a citizen's successful acquisition of land for debt, but not a cultivator's successful retirement of debt. We can conclude that land invariably passed from cultivator to urban lender, which is what the archives seem to show, only if we make the dubious assumption that all loans resulted in default.[6]

In the widespread concealed loan transaction, a borrower "sold" land to the lender; he was then reinvested with the land for a fixed rent (the interest) and given the chance to redeem ("francate") it within a few years. Archives of the elite only rarely indicate that the cultivator repaid the loan and recovered title—two of fifteen cases in Lucca,[7] two of several hundred cases in the Arnaldi archive. But, again, family parchments do not tell the whole story. Several dozen humble paper documents in notarial registers record cases in which the borrower did, in fact, francate the land.[8] In many other cases, though these too never appeared in the family archive, the Arnaldi sold land outright.[9] A reverse flow of ownership, from patricians to rustics, is revealed when the evidence base is notarial *minute* and *imbreviature* rather than private archives—but that is not where historians usually look.

Roberto Greci, examining the patrimony of the Rossi family of Parma, confessed an inability to track the history of individual properties. A given field appears once, in a lease or purchase document, then disappears from the record.[10] The evanescence of land equally characterizes the copious Arnaldi documentation, where only a handful of fields can be firmly identified within the family's patrimony over the long duration. It is possible, of course, that missing lands were combined with others to form compact holdings that bore new boundaries and names. But land reconfiguration is not a completely satisfactory explanation, for the Vicentine at least, because (as will be seen) owners faced considerable obstacles in consolidating scattered fields. As the *imbreviature* hint, it is entirely possible and logical that many of these ephemeral properties were ceded to peasants through sale or francation. It will also be seen that land rights had become fearsomely tangled by the Quattrocento, such that an inattentive owner might lose track of dues and eventually lose the land to a peasant's prescriptive right or simple occupation; one hospital's land survey notes that "these six pieces of land were in the old inventory as they are listed here, but at present they can't be found." In the single village for which ownership has been systematically studied (Lisiera in the Vicentine), the percentage of fields owned by urban patricians actually declined over the course of the Quattrocento, from 61 percent to 46 percent, while that owned by local residents rose from 5 percent to 18 percent.[11]

Furthermore, it is far from certain that Veneto patricians built up landed patrimonies exclusively or even predominantly at the expense of small cultivators, who had only dribs and drabs of widely scattered property to cede. More significant accretions came, instead, from the goods of ex-rulers, from other patricians, or from ecclesiastical corporations. Early in the fifteenth century the fisc sold vast Scaligeri holdings in Verona and Vicenza, and Carraresi holdings in Padua; the Verità acquired land in Soave, Mozzecane, Nogara, and elsewhere for 15,870 ducats.[12] When Alvise Dal Verme's rebellion failed in 1441, the fisc confiscated his enormous estates and sold them to Venetian and mainland patricians. Listing his holdings in Verona required sixty-two dense folios; while the extent of his property in Vicenza cannot be known, it is certain that the Arnaldi picked up a large bloc in Agugliaro. Fellow patricians eventually acquired much of the Dal Verme land originally bought by Venetians.[13]

Citizens of Padua and Verona had earlier amassed large estates in the Vicentine. With the cities separated jurisdictionally and fiscally in the Quattrocento, absentee ownership became a nuisance and many liquidated their Vicentine holdings. The Arnaldi, for example, paid 1,200 ducats for the Veronese Antonio del Cozza's land and land rights in Nuvoledo and Porcileto in 1447, and soon purchased Bartolomeo Giuliari's possessions in Villabalzana and Leonardo Nogarola's property in Poiana.[14] At the end of the century Padua's Dotti family sold the Arnaldi a variety of urban and rural lands.[15] Vicenza's Monza leased 1,419 *campi* in Dueville from the Veronese Cortese Serego in 1407, purchased the land outright in 1435 for 900 ducats, and provided a further 560 ducats in 1446 to retire Serego's right of repurchase.[16]

Within the city, straitened patricians such as the Orgiano, Garzatori, and Schitini sold chunks of land to the Arnaldi and their prosperous colleagues, or borrowed money and subsequently defaulted on land pledges.[17] When older houses failed biologically, which frequently happened (Pagliarini listed many more extinct noble families than the 271 extant), their patrimonies passed to others of their class. While outright sale of ecclesiastical lands was uncommon, citizens of Vicenza and Verona (as did counterparts in Tuscany and Lombardy) obtained church property in perpetual lease for a nominal rent.[18]

ACCORDING TO another commonplace, later medieval merchants progressively pulled capital out of commerce for investment in land, responding to a highly volatile and stagnant or even contracting commercial economy.[19] For the Veneto, Angelo Ventura modified the thesis considerably: while accepting "a general tendency to abandon mercantile activities for landed investment," he denied that capital for land acquisition came from liquidation of commercial and industrial interests. Rather, he argued, public office, professional careers, ecclesiastical benefices, fiefs and land rights granted by rulers, and tax farming provided acquisition capital. Thus land represented not a diversion from trade but simply a new sector for investment of noncommercial income. Further, his demonstration of considerable profit from land reclamation and intensified exploitation indicates that agricultural investment was not due to slumping trade or fear of commercial risk.[20]

The archives of Veneto memorialists confirm his position: as notaries and lawyers, ecclesiastical feudatories and tax farmers, all enjoyed sufficient noncommercial incomes that they did not have to liquidate businesses to build up landed patrimonies. Nor did they see business and land as incompatible. Land rents might maintain a lifestyle but could not expand a patrimony, and the merchant who tried to liquidate commercial interests to fund property accumulation would soon run out of money. The Guastaverza were simultaneously wool merchants and landowners; the Stoppi styled themselves *mercatores* into the sixteenth century, well after their campaign of land acquisition reached maturity. Those who abandoned commerce, such as the later Arnaldi, did so for social reasons—ceasing "vile" trades to ease access into the nobility—and not because business was poor. Even they remained active in farming ecclesiastical incomes, cash and agricultural loans, and the wholesale food trade.

The careers of Veneto memorialists do suggest a slight modification of Ventura's position: income from office and the service sector was not directly invested in the land, but passed through the intermediate sector of the credit market. Default on loans, not purchase, was the most common means of accumulation.[21] That feature, in turn, raises the issue of the land market. Here, too, there is an ulterior historiographical debate: the degree to which land transactions were governed by an open market, an accumulative ethic, and the forces of supply and demand, setting the stage for capitalist agriculture in the early modern period.[22]

For the Veneto, the notion of rationalism in the land market is open to two objections. The first is that urban owners found it difficult to mount programmatic campaigns of land acquisition and consolidation because the credit market rather than the open market was the usual mechanism for acquisition. Patricians picked up land by defaults on loans, but had to be satisfied with whatever was offered as collateral. Most commonly, pledged fields lay not adjacent to their own but in another village altogether: the Arnaldi owned land in seventy-seven different jurisdictions. Irregular opportunities for accumulation and the prevalence of scattered and small fields prevented or at least retarded the rationalizing schemes of even the most enterprising owners.

Second, Veneto evidence supports Wickham's thesis of noneconomic pricing. It is impossible to establish more than a rough range of land values— the value of a single *campo* of arable land might be rated at anywhere from eight ducats to twenty-five ducats—because acquisition most commonly came not from purchase but as a consequence of the sale/leaseback concealed loan. In such transactions, the stated value of the land was determined not by market price but by the need to preserve a 6 percent ratio of rent (the interest) to nominal value (the loan). Land values were usually rounded off to multiples of ten or twenty-five *lire* or ducats, even for fields of varied dimensions and types. In another type of transaction, the buyer declared a global per-*campo* value for miscellaneous fields: so the Arnaldi bought the large Pirli holding at a flat price of twenty-five ducats per *campo*. Here the land value was set high to conceal interest charged on long-term amortization.[23] Credit needs, not the land market, determined the stated value of property.

Tenure and Cultivation

The secondary literature has focused on Tuscan sharecropping. In schematic form, agriculture under *mezzadria* shared several features: loss of peasant ownership; formation of compact holdings; short-term leases; owner's obligation to provide or lend working capital, seed, and equipment; tenant's obligation to live on the *podere* and cultivate its lands exclusively (and consequent breakup of villages); introduction of mixed-crop cultivation *(coltura promiscua)*; and partition of the harvest between owner and tenant.

Though sharecropping was everywhere a minority tenure in the fifteenth century—even in Tuscany, where it was earliest and most common, only 29.6 percent of rustics in the Florentine dominion were *mezzadri* in 1469, and the system was nearly absent in Pisa, Lucca, and Arezzo[24]—its actual incidence is beside the point. Near-obsession with *mezzadria* and other partiary tenures has been driven not by historical but by historiographic concerns: by a revisionism that blasts the paternalist "myth of the *mezzadria*," with images of progressive owners and deferential, contented peasants;[25] by those who, noting the dominance of sharecropping into contemporary times, trace the medieval origins of a more "modern" or "rational" tenure;[26] by the thesis that sharecropping represented one aspect of a "feudal reaction" and bourgeois "return to the land" that stunted the transition from feudalism to capitalism.[27]

Given the amount of attention historians have devoted to *mezzadria* and its various subtopics, it is difficult to evaluate a region in which much of the debate is inapplicable. True, several large holdings in the flatlands of the Veronese and Vicentine countryside come close to the perceived norm. Lands of Gian Pietro Proti in Bolzano Vicentino, for example, were largely given out in partiary contracts in which tenants yielded half of the major grains and a third of lesser grains, hay, and grapes. In addition, the owner furnished seed and agricultural implements to tenants. Use of written, short-term contracts, formation of *poderi*, intensified investment, land reclamation, and the introduction of new crops moved several swathes of the Veronese countryside close to *mezzadria*.[28]

But the Proti estates and Veronese counterparts were studied because they were well established and highly organized, and left particularly rich archives; they do not, by that token, represent the norm. When, as in the majority of cases, ownership was more recent, management less systematic, and holdings less consolidated, Veneto lands bore little resemblance to those under *mezzadria* in Tuscany. Outside a few aristocratic estates, fields were small: 70 percent to 80 percent were less than two hectares in the holdings of S. Maria in Organo and the parish of Isola della Scala, and less than a hectare in the patrimony of the Veronese hospital of SS. Giacomo and Lazzaro.[29] The nearly five thousand fields described in the Arnaldi archives averaged under a hectare and a half, and those in the Vicentine villages of Lisiera and Dueville were even smaller.[30]

Most land was held in traditional twenty-nine-year and perpetual leases, by tenants who lived in nucleated settlements and paid fixed rents of cash or kind. As Veronese councils proclaimed in 1478, "In all Italy no place is more leased out *(livellata)* than ours."[31] The Arnaldi, who owned land throughout the countryside and thus managed a wider variety of lands than did the Proti, set partiary leases in only 6 percent of their holdings, with an additional 2.5 percent given out for a mixed rent of money, produce, and a share of the harvest (see appendix, table 6.1). Even that figure is misleadingly high, since their partiary tenures were almost always perpetual. Only three of 366 transactions indicate true *mezzadria,* with the Arnaldi providing seed in exchange for a fixed share of the harvest throughout a short-term contract.[32]

Both the twenty-nine-year and the perpetual lease, known as emphyteusis,[33] were grounded in the notion of a dual ownership of land: the overall proprietor held *dominium directum;* the tenant possessed a *dominium utile,* which guaranteed substantial autonomy in land management. As long as he paid rent, the holder of *utile* determined crops, rotations, and techniques. He could, moreover, bequeath, pledge, or mortgage his rights to the land, or even sell the *utile* outright, subject only to the proprietor's right to match the sale price (by *prelazione*) and reclaim the *utile.*[34]

Initially, emphyteutic land was held by an unwritten, customary arrangement, which could prove dangerous to inattentive owners. Several jurists, particularly Bartolus, noted that the cultivator might acquire *dominium directum* by not paying rent for a generation or two, by right of prescription, if the owner of the *directum* did not offer formal challenge. To guard against inadvertent alienation of land, owners by around 1400 insisted on a written contract that demanded renewal every nine or ten years. Governments, too, sought to replace customary with more firmly defined tenures: Vicentine statutes in 1425 and Venetian doges after 1451 required that cultivators without a contract should be regarded as holding their land in emphyteusis. In a similar vein, Veronese statutes of 1450 set the principle that, on all lands purchased from the Scaligeri or Visconti fiscs after 1387, tenants should be regarded as "true emphyteutics and leaseholders in perpetuity," as should their heirs and successors; owners were obliged to renew the tenures at an unchanged rent.[35]

Contracts ordering regular renewals may have brought greater discipline to landholding, but left the basic relationship unaltered. Renewal was automatic, a formality usually allowed to lapse; documents of renewal are extremely rare except when death and inheritance introduced new owners or tenants, and none changed the terms of the arrangement. Contracts did not give owners any greater control over cultivation; indeed, by ratifying the tenant's possession of *dominium utile,* they established the tenant's freedom from interference in actual management. They spelled out the perpetual term of the *locatio,* and so protected the tenant against arbitrary eviction. Further, a rent fixed on parchment could not easily be increased.

Not only was ownership divided, but the rights and obligations of each party could be subdivided and separately alienated. For example, an intermediary might receive land from the owner of the *dominium directum,* then grant the land to the actual cultivator in a perpetual sublease; alternatively, this middle figure might purchase the *utile* from the cultivator and lease it back to him, promising to forward rents to the holder of the *directum*. This offered considerable convenience for absentee owners, priests, and ecclesiastical corporations, who were freed from direct management, and offered profits for entrepreneurs such as the Arnaldi and the Verità, who made part-time careers as owner-agents of the *utile* of others' lands.[36]

Because the rent *(fitto)* established in the emphyteutic contract was fixed and in theory certain, Baldus had said, the proprietor could mortgage the land with the income as surety.[37] The principle was thus established that the *dominium directum* and the income of the land were two distinct assets, and could be owned by separate persons. By the Quattrocento people bought, sold, pledged, and mortgaged *fitti* freely, without, however, alienating the *directum* itself. When on several occasions Silvestro Arnaldi paid considerable sums for *fitti*, he bought rights to an income, almost like buying an annuity, but the land itself was peripheral. Indeed, the income was no longer directly connected to the land, and the notary usually did not bother to list the pieces.[38]

The proliferation of tenants and subtenants did, however, play havoc with owners. With rents owed to one person and ownership held by another, with several intermediaries between cultivator and proprietor, and with one peasant owning the *utile* and another actually working the land, who exactly bore liability for dues? If one link in a chain of subleases did not pay rent or taxes, what were the obligations and rights of the others? The problem was exacerbated by the fact that tenants often did not notify owners when they alienated, divided, or sublet land, though the law said they had to do so; and tenants did not have to notify owners when they mortgaged lands of which they held the *utile*.[39] A careless owner could easily lose track of an obligation altogether and eventually lose the land itself. Fear of the unwitting dissipation of ecclesiastical property led the Venetian Senate to prohibit leases of church lands beyond a three-year term without its permission, and the pope in 1467 forbade any leases for more than three years.[40] Even careful managers such as the Arnaldi might lose their way in the maze of rents, subtenants, and divided obligations. When Silvestro Arnaldi tried to buy a tiny field from Matteo Nascimbene in 1498, neither party could determine the precise status of the land and the notary inserted a battery of clauses to cover contingencies. Silvestro might or might not own the land outright, he might or might not owe a *fitto*, and he might or might not be liable for taxes.[41]

Improving the Land

From the later Trecento into the second quarter of the Quattrocento, evidence for the ruinous condition of the land is episodic but overwhelming. Vicentine communal petitions in 1388 complained that Paduan raiders torched the countryside and carried away animals, and asked for a debt moratorium to halt depopulation. Another petition two years later lamented that citizens "had not a penny to buy wheat" and that cultivators "were moving away lest they perish from hunger." By 1407 most villagers of Gambellara had fled their homes, and the "eight or nine families" that remained petitioned for tax relief.[42] Land inventories commonly listed fields without tenants, houses without occupants, and fields "once arable and now waste." In the Veronese village of Colà, around 1400, 42 percent of the land was partly uncultivated and 10 percent totally *vigra*. Some 45 percent of Dueville's land was uncultivated or abandoned in 1407, and only 29 percent of house lots were inhabited. When Lisiera hit bottom slightly later, only half of its land was intensively cultivated, with the rest waste or given over to labor-extensive use such as forest and pasture. The Paduan countryside, too, suffered "ecological degradation" from sharp depopulation, and much of Friuli reverted to forest.[43]

Similar conditions in Tuscany[44] allowed owners to consolidate fractioned holdings, buying and merging vacant lands into *poderi*, setting the stage for improvements in crops and changes in tenures later in the century. In the Veneto, however, a variety of factors combined to reduce owners' ability to take advantage of the crisis. Many of these have been noted. Lands acquired by loan default, dowry transfers, and debt were scattered (the Arnaldi, for example, owned land in seventy-seven villages). Patrimonial divisions did not create coherent holdings: while the Arnaldi held clusters of land in and around the villages of Setteca, Nuvoledo, and Meledo, brothers usually received a portion of each. Since proprietors had several perpetual tenants in any given village, each holding several small and separated fields, owners faced considerable practical obstacles to overriding the integrity of fields and tenancies to effect integration.

Emphyteusis itself posed obstacles to increased exploitation. Classic definition of the tenure assumed that rent was both monetary ("pro nummo annuatim solvendo") and fixed. This soon became true in practice as well. *Fitti* in money grew as a proportion of all rents—on the Arnaldi lands, from 20 percent to 71 percent over the 1400–1499 period, simultaneous with a decline of rents in kind from 26 percent to 15 percent (see appendix, table 6.1). Among mixed rents of money and produce, which fell from 45 percent to

6 percent, the share of produce declined to the purely symbolic—a pair of chickens at Christmas, a dozen eggs at Easter. Owners consequently suffered a slow erosion of income, as coinage devaluation and inflation reduced the real value of monetarized rents, and they could not benefit from strong agricultural prices later in the century. Over the long haul, cash *fitti* became exiguous, even nominal. Giovanni Bertrachini, professor at Padua, noted that returns from emphyteusis were "modest" and bore little relation to the market value of crops produced; they might constitute little more than formal recognition of the landlord's rights.[45]

When the tenant of an emphyteutic holding was removed by death or old age, the proprietor could neither recover control nor raise rents: tenants enjoyed the right to bequeathe their *dominium utile*, and heirs received the *utile* under the terms of the former contract. Furthermore, the doge declared in 1466, if the *utile* were sold and the new holder expressed willingness to pay the original rent, he could not be disturbed in his tenure.[46] On four occasions the Arnaldi were obliged to accept a new tenant at reduced rent, and only once commanded a slight increase.[47] On hundreds of occasions the *fitto* remained constant.

Even when an emphyteutic tenant simply gave up the land, the owner did not regain control, since local custom allowed an outgoing cultivator to name his successor. So, for example, Giovanni fu Pietro resigned his *jus utile et livellaria* in a suburban field to Gaspare Arnaldi in 1433, on the condition that Jacopo fu Gabriele be invested with the land. Jacopo indeed received the field, at the same rent. A decade later, in Verona, the Guastaverza brothers renounced an episcopal fief with the stipulation that a cousin be invested in their stead. Examples of substitution persist into the later Quattrocento, even though a burgeoning rural population might in theory have reduced tenants' leverage.[48] In every case, the new *fitto* was the same as the old.

Emphyteusis could not, however, deny change altogether. Owners in the Veneto seldom, it is true, matched the advances of counterparts elsewhere in building huge nucleated estates (Lombard *cascine* and Tuscan *poderi*), or undertaking massive land reclamation and irrigation projects (as in Lombardy), or diffusing intensive, mixed cultivation (as in Tuscany).[49] Smaller, recent proprietors were less able than aristocrats and ecclesiastical corporations to effect fundamental alteration. But obstacles were never insurmountable, and even heavily emphyteutic areas of the Veronese and Vicentine countryside experienced modest reform.

The most obvious course was simply to rationalize and intensify management. Progressive owners began to keep systematic records and insist that documents detail tenants' rights and obligations. Gaspare Monza, for example, demanded that tenants actually make ten-year renewals of their contracts, recognizing his ownership and rehearsing the terms of tenures, an act very rarely performed in previous generations.[50] After midcentury newcomers such as the Arnaldi followed the lead of traditional holders such as the Thiene, Valmarana, and the Ospedale Proti by employing factors or *gastaldi* to oversee their lands.[51]

Concentration of the patrimony was also a priority. The early Arnaldi, for example, acquired land wherever possible. But collection of rents from seventy-seven locales was inefficient, and the second generation focused their attentions. They alienated fields in distant villages where they owned only a few *campi*. In one characteristic transaction of 1483, Silvestro Arnaldi traded scraps of land in Tretto, Liviera, and the city for plots in Marola and Bertesinella, where he already possessed substantial holdings. He lost income and had to apply to the pope and the Venetian Senate for permission to make the exchange, but in return he reversed his father's tendency toward diffuse accumulation.[52] Simultaneously, Silvestro abandoned the indiscriminate lending habits of his father and uncle, and made loans mostly to his own tenants and to cultivators in clusters of villages—Nuvoledo-Porcileto, Setteca-Bertesinella-Marola—where the bulk of his property was concentrated. When insolvent debtors yielded their fields, Silvestro had more compact holdings.

Owners also encouraged more intense exploitation through labor-intensive cultivation on mixed-use lands. The key innovation was the spread of viticulture. Grapes could be grown on the margins of arable fields, on hillsides, and on miscellaneous scraps of land unsuited for arable crops. Since peak periods of labor demands (harvest and crushing in September–October, trimming in the winter) fell between the times when workers were most occupied with arable crops (sowing winter wheat in late fall and summer wheat and legumes in the spring, harvest in mid- to late summer), viticulture also did not require additional human resources. The percentage of Arnaldi fields described as purely arable declined from 30 percent to 16 percent over the course of the century, and the percentage of fields that supported a mixed cultivation of arable crops, vines, and fruit trees rose from 40 percent to 61 percent (see appendix, table 6.2). In the hamlet of Lisiera, similarly, the percentage of *campi* combining arable crops and vines more than doubled, while single-use cultivation fell sharply.[53]

Reclamation of waste began about the same time. The Proti had systematized rivers in Bolzano Vicentino since the later Trecento, and contracts and tenures designed to bring land into cultivation had been known throughout the peninsula for several centuries.[54] But for the most part Veronese and Vicentines had neither the labor nor the capital to undertake the work of cutting watercourses, building dykes, and clearing forests before about 1440. After that point, however, constant reference to land "once waste and now arable," "formerly pasture and now with vines," "previously forest and now planted," and "lots once empty and now with houses," demonstrates that a once-derelict countryside was experiencing strong recovery.[55] The forests of Lisiera disappeared by 1500, and the proportion of land described as uncultivated or waste shrank to a fraction of the total. By the last quarter of the century, repopulation of the countryside reached the point of overcrowding, and the Vicentine city council tried to block house construction by those with smaller holdings. The Venetian government, needing oak timbers for ships, grew concerned about deforestation. On the positive side, boasted Giorgio Sommariva in 1478, Verona could now export a quarter of its wheat harvest.[56]

To put land into cultivation and to encourage viticulture on purely arable lands, owners began to experiment with partiary and/or short-term contracts. In 1427, for example, Pietro Boni invested cultivators with a large field on a ten-year renewable lease, in return for one-third of grain harvested. The tenants could use the pasture for their own animals, but were obliged to spread manure on a *campo* of arable land yearly; Boni, for his part, agreed to pay half the cost of digging ditches and building terraces. Beginning in the 1440s, improvement leases demanding deforestation or drainage of low-lying land became common.[57] These contracts had in common a short duration (usually ten years) and a partiary rent (usually a third of produce).

In contrast with emphyteutic contracts, improvement leases often imposed specific conditions that sometimes approach the stipulations of *mezzadria* contracts. The Barcellari brothers, for example, were forbidden to work other lands and owed labor services; their Arnaldi landlords promised to furnish wheat, rye, and beans for sustenance and to lend seed grains. Seeking to bring an eighty-*campi* forest into cultivation within five years, Gaspare Monza required his tenants to clear ten *campi* annually, plant vines and trees, establish rows of willows along watercourses, and create fields and pastures from reclaimed land. In return, he was to receive one-third of the crops.[58]

Some ecclesiastical corporations in Verona and Padua were equally aggressive in promoting reclamation, improvement leases, short-term and partiary tenures, investment in infrastructure, direct management, and a salaried workforce.[59] Clerics in Vicenza were more conservative, remaining loyal to emphyteutic tenures, but they too brought wasteland into cultivation. They possessed incentives unavailable to lay proprietors: by the terms of a papal bull of 1444, the bishop of Vicenza could grant tithes on reclaimed lands to the entrepreneurs who organized deforestation and drainage of "swampy and nearly sterile" lands. Other ecclesiastical owners gave exemptions from tithes to offset "great labors and expenses" of *bonifiche*. Monasteries and the cathedral chapter could also offer much larger chunks of land than the laity—150 *campi* in Noventa, 367 in Villaruina, and 1,200 to 1,500 around Villalta.[60]

In yet another respect, progressive landlords made headway against the immobility of emphyteutic agriculture. From the middle of the fifteenth century on, many owners of *dominium directum* recovered the *dominium utile* of their lands. Consolidating title was neither simple nor cheap, since new owners had to buy out tenants as well as former proprietors. In one typical case, Nicolo Colombi renounced his *jus livellaria* in the village of La Longa to his landlord Bartolomeo Fava in exchange for a hundred ducats. Andrea and Tommaso Arnaldi had supplied Fava with the money; they then paid Fava an additional hundred ducats for the combined *dominia* of the land.[61] The transaction was typical, as well, because the cost of the *utile* was the same as the cost of the land: in the twenty-five cases in which calculation is possible, the value of *jus livellaria* and the value of *dominium directum* were about the same. Breaking a perpetual lease, in other words, cost as much as the land itself. But this was virtually the only way to raise rents, introduce partiary tenures, combine small fields, or shorten the term of the lease on extant lands, and owners were willing to pay the price.

Owners and Tenants

Peasant Misery and Resistance

Reading Tuscan rural history can be a grim experience. Peasants, pushed into debt by usurious loans, grasping landlords, and mounting taxation, ceded their lands to the urban rich and remained only as tenants and/or salaried workers. Owners imposed increasingly harsh terms on cultivators, demanding labor services and reducing the proportion of capital and equipment that they furnished. Creation of *poderi*, and sharecroppers' obligation to reside on the farm, broke village solidarity and imposed isolated habitation. Short-term leases denied security to cultivators and robbed them of incentive to make improvements. The aged and infirm were simply discarded. The sole alternative to grinding poverty was flight into the uncertain, often hostile urban environment.[62]

Much of the published work for the Veneto echoes Tuscan themes, particularly in demonstrating cultivators' debt, the buildup of estates, and the reduction in owners' contributions. Looking at seventy-six Friulan cases, for example, Paolo Cammarosano noted that only 21 percent of cultivators were able to pay anything close to what they owed. As in Tuscany, wealthier smallholders emigrated into and paid taxes for the city, leaving villagers with a much-reduced tax base.[63] Vignettes from the archives are as poignant as those from Florence. The case of the Dueville widow, forced to sell her last field to raise the cash to bury her son, is perhaps melodramatic but no less telling; so was Giovanni della Grana's flight to avoid crushing arrears. The *impotentia* of Madonna Flora, unable to feed her seven daughters and two sons, won a judge's permission to sell her single *campo* to Silvestro Arnaldi. The Venetian government tried to block alienation of common assets by rural communes, but villagers of Longare were in such "extreme poverty and urgent necessity" that they were allowed to sell pasture rights to the Vicentine noble Domenico Scroffa.[64]

Still, what are we to make of recurrent debt? When a tenant acknowledges unpaid rents for year after year, his economic status may indeed have deteriorated, but he may instead have proven resistant to eviction. Some caution is due. To take one lead example: by mid-1449 Michele Revese had not paid rent for five years, and the Arnaldi went to court to force payment. Six months later the Arnaldi were still trying to seize an equivalent value in two pieces of land. Four months after that a judge ordered that Revese not impede the Arnaldi in taking possession of the fields. Revese continued to resist, despite a restraining order in the spring of 1451. When he finally acknowledged both his debt and the Arnaldi version of the story in the spring of 1452, his claims actually triumphed: the Arnaldi brothers leased the land back to him at the original rent. After three years of legal maneuver, matters were back to square one. None of the arrears had been paid. Revese's heirs were still on the land a generation later, and still far behind in paying the rent.[65]

Verità Verità, too, left the courts with small satisfaction. He had sued a man of Tregnago for back rent and a judgment of twelve ducats for poor cultivation, but the defendant denied the obligation in part by pointing out that it had been incurred by his father. In a compromise, Verità cancelled debts and expenses, and in return the tenant renounced the holding on the condition that he be reinvested with the land. Verità gained only a new and presumably more ironclad contract, plus clarification of the tenancy.[66] Tenants knew how to use the legal system to fend off creditors. Eviction, confiscation, and seizure of goods required long, drawn-out, and frequently futile litigation; as was the case in Tuscany,[67] lawsuits were usually unsuccessful in forcing payment and were used primarily to force out-of-court settlement.

It should not, in theory, have been that way. Municipal law provided owners with apparently sure mechanisms for collecting debts and shedding unwanted tenants. In Vicenza, rent cases received summary judgment, avoiding the laborious *cursus* of civil suits. The city's entire police force was put at the disposal of the official delegated to oversee the collection of debts and debt-pledges *(pegni)*. In Verona, debt cases were heard on any day the courts were open, tenants could not leave property until their rents were paid, and immediate kin were obligated for a tenant's dues. Nonpayment of rent for two successive years automatically cancelled the tenant's rights of *dominium utile,* as did alienation of the *utile* without the owner's permission.[68]

But a legal system stacked in favor of landlords did not provide failsafe means of obtaining satisfaction. Eviction, the most serious penalty, was also the most difficult to effect. Owners, in fact, seldom enforced the two-year rule, and allowed unpaid rents to pile up well beyond that point. Faced with a depopulated countryside, they found it difficult to secure new tenants, and they might have to accept a lower rent when bidding for cultivators. Anyway a new tenant was not necessarily preferable to a proven debtor, since nearly everyone seemed to owe something. So, when Zampiero Bule ran up the considerable debt of 424 *lire* in goods and rents, he received his lands back in lease on the usual terms.[69] Only when matters got out of hand did landlords in the Veneto—as was the case in Lucca—actually remove those in arrears: the Arnaldi absorbed fifteen years of nonpayment before evicting some tenants in Meledo, and even then the former *livellari* successfully claimed the right to ratify the new investiture.[70]

Documents ordering eviction or substitution of tenants are rare. Owners preferred legal action to collect arrears, but even here their hand was weak. Recalcitrant debtors delayed judgment by failing to appear when cited, sending representatives to challenge every stage of the procedure, and simply refusing to comply with judgments. Silvestro Arnaldi won a judgment against the Viti family of Setteca in 1485, and a second judgment the following year; only in May 1489 did the podesta's vicar declare that the disputed grain belonged to Silvestro, and another three months passed before he ordered actual execution of his sentence. Somewhat later Silvestro failed to collect some rents in the village of Poiana for sixteen years. When he lost patience and went to court, his petition to sequester some hay required fifteen court hearings. Between nonappearance in court and formal protest of each citation and sequestration order, the tenant dragged the affair on for eight months. At that point the register falls silent, and we do not know if Silvestro ever received anything.[71]

Tenants knew, as well, how to exploit the system for demanding debt-pledges. In Verona, most debtors exercised their right of *vetatio pignoris* and refused to provide debt-pledges; at that point the judge reviewed the case and, if the original sentence was upheld, imposed an additional fine, but the outcome was often yet another unpaid pledge. Sheer poverty may have been the reason, but Varanini suspects that "obstructionist anticitizen boycott" played a major role as well.[72] Vicentine village chiefs routinely ignored orders to bring *pegni* to the city; thousands of prosecutions of *decani* in the five surviving registers equally suggest rural collusion against citizens' demands. In a single year (1452) the hamlet of Lisiera, counting at most 170 inhabitants, twenty-three times failed to deliver pledges. Recusant *decani* were summoned before urban courts and fined three *lire,* but it is uncertain that they could then be forced to execute the original order.[73]

Countrymen based one effective strategy for resistance on women's distinct and protected legal status. Up to a quarter of village chiefs prosecuted for not producing pledges recruited wives or female relative to represent them before urban tribunals. They knew that women faced no personal risk, since statutes forbade the incarceration of women or their sureties for debt; by custom, a pregnant woman could not be forced to appear at all.[74] Moreover, judges found it difficult to force a woman to pay a debt on behalf of others since her own goods were presumed to derive from her dowry, and hence were protected from creditors. Anyway the fines levied on women refusing to pay a pledge were only half to two-thirds of those levied on men.[75] The original debtor and the village as a whole reaped the benefit of women's partial immunity.

Neither arrears nor back taxes could be seized from goods secured for the eventual restitution of a dowry. Landlords and tax officials complained that tenants piled up dowry obligations and other hypothecs to withstand creditors;[76] the man of Tregnago claimed that his lands were obligated for no fewer than three dowries—a point Verità was forced to concede. Owners could not, however, remove this obstacle without undermining the dowry system as a whole. Strongly rooted legal theory gave dowries priority over other claims to a patrimony, and since (by the authoritative opinion of Baldus) a wife's dowry constituted a general claim on a man's property, a tenant could argue that all his goods were so obligated.[77] At best, owners obtained a decision that their claims held priority over those of all creditors except the fisc and anyone holding dowry hypothecs.[78] After all, judges and patrician owners were also husbands and fathers, with vested interests in protecting the dotal goods of their own womenfolk. But they had, on that account, to accept the fact that tenants could use general dowry protections against their own claims.

The Venetian government came down on the side of rural debtors. Fearful that impoverished cultivators would be driven off the land, with consequent harm to tax revenues, food supplies, and military conscription, central magistracies mitigated the seizure of goods for debts and past rents. In 1444 Paduan rustics complained that tax officials seized pledges from any villager if they could not find the actual debtor; the doge forbade the taking of pledges from anyone except the *debitor principalis*. The ruling soon extended to cover the entire mainland and all debts: in 1448 the Senate forbade the jailing of *decani* or other rustics for the debts of fellow villagers "because it is not right that the innocent should suffer punishment for the offender."[79] A decade later the Senate issued a thunderous decree against the taking of work animals as debt-pledges, and later extended protection to carts, plows, and agricultural equipment.[80]

The Avogadori di Comun, meanwhile, supported the right of tenants to receive compensation for improvements, which raised the cost to owners of evicting cultivators. A ducal letter of 1476 went further, declaring that tenants who improved holdings could not be deprived of their rights of *dominium utile*, though they could be compelled to pay back rent.[81] Later doges, in rulings addressed to specific cases but regarded as general precedents, blocked eviction of tenants for nonpayment. A Paduan abbess, for example, was prevented from expelling a tenant who had not paid rent for two years, the term established by law; a Ravennese landlord could not evict a tenant twenty-five years in arrears "because we do not wish that anyone who for a decent reason cannot pay the rent should be deprived of rights which he holds by lease or emphyteusis."[82]

Deeply indebted cultivators, then, were neither thrown off their land nor reduced to landless laborers. The last document in any series is likely to show them as deeply entrenched as before, despite mounting arrears. Their capacity for survival may have been partly due to a distinctive land system: where, as in Pisa and Lucca as well as Verona and Vicenza, *mezzadria* and *poderi* were relatively rare, and holdings were scattered and fractioned, cultivators' capacity for resistance was relatively strong. Those holding land from several owners were never dependent on any single landlord, and fellow villagers were better able to offer support because they, too, were not subject to an overwhelming proprietor.[83] But the phenomenon may not have been purely local. Speaking of Tuscan *mezzadri*, Klapisch-Zuber has concluded that "On the balance sheet, the rustic never seems to win. In reality, he knew how to make the best use of his work potential in a period of demographic penury that encouraged landlords to be more accommodating."[84]

To the demographic factor must be added tenants' capacity to make the legal system work on their behalf: to leverage debt and dowries, to exploit dowry protections, and to use tortuous and inefficient legal procedures to fend off creditors. This is an unexpected source of assistance, and one suspects that patrician legislators were frequently annoyed to find their laws and procedures used against them as landowners. In any case, peasants were far from hapless before the law. Perhaps they were not so badly off as a grim Tuscan historiography wishes to demonstrate.

Resistance and Patronage

Friction between tenant and owner was episodic but recurrent, and frequently violent as well. Verona experienced some unsettling outbreaks: the 1425 assassination of a Venetian trying to collect rents, murders of rural vicars in the 1420s and 1442, and widespread arson in 1471. Anti-landlord sentiment came to a head in 1461–62, with murders of Venetians and citizens, assaults on owners, and attacks on property. Veronese countrymen made constant and highly organized protest against the erosion of the rural tax base, grants of citizenship to rural immigrants, and innovations such as the taking of rent in money rather than produce.[85]

Their Vicentine counterparts undertook no collective action, but individual towns sent endless embassies to Venice to dispute urban privileges. Rustics there also showed readiness to use force against landlords and urban officials. In 1456, for example, the Vicentine commune moved against the "audacity" of residents of the district who used threats and assaults to prevent owners from putting new tenants on their lands. The "impious" torching of a notable's barn in Barbarano drew the wrath of the Venetian Senate, as did the murder of a factor of the great Loschi family, the ambush of the noble Gabriele Anguissola's servant, and the killing of Antonio Giovanni Thiene.[86] Villagers of Mason so harassed their landlord, the Paduan convent of S. Giustina, that its clerics gave up the fight and petitioned to sell the land; Jacopo da Poiana so terrorized the village of Campolongo that neither landlords nor even the local governor dared move against him.[87]

Ruling bodies and the upper ranks of society perceived a hostile rural population. Rustics were not, probably, more inclined to violence than other social categories, but they were numerous, distinctive, and inclined to mass tumult: the rash of arsons in Cogollo, the wave of riots in Mason, and internecine slaughters in Marostica gave periodic reminders to an already nervous urban patriciate. Cultivators were not responsible for the private armies with which patricians carried on feuds, or for the endemic depredations of urban exiles who gathered in remote reaches, but authorities lumped the innocent and guilty together in general suspicion of all inhabitants of the countryside.[88] Thus much anticrime legislation was targeted at the rural population. Early in the century Venetian councils forbade any *rusticus vel districtualis* to bring arms into the city of Vicenza. In 1444 Veronese councils, attempting to eradicate organized violence, outlawed rustics' wearing of partisan colors; four decades later the Vicentine commune complained of the "many scandals and infinite brawls" of countrymen, increased punishments for carrying arms, and forbade the wearing of "devices." City dwellers received a short term of exile for illegal gatherings; rustics suffered the same penalty, but with public flogging as well.[89]

Fear is evident, as well, in literary genres that satirized peasants. Mockery and suspicion were but two facets of a single attitude: if rustics were animallike and stupid, and thus the butt of tricks played by clever citizens, they were also brutish and inclined to violence and fraud. Watch tenants carefully, advised Giannozzo Alberti, for "you can't believe how much wickedness there is in cultivators raised among the clods." An anonymous Paduan of the Quattrocento summed up the prevailing view of the countryman:

> Impious, cruel, enemy of all humility,
> Crude, rough, full of every rottenness,
> Born of chestnut stock,
>
> Backward, outside humanity, rustic,
> Lacking any good, son of a bitch.[90]

The poems gathered in Maffeo Vegio's *Sequentia rusticorum*, which circulated in Verona, likewise mixed derision with an undertone of fear for the peasant's explosive anger. Only Giorgio Sommariva's *sonnetti villaneschi* sought to temper abuse with sympathy, putting into the mouths of his peasant interlocutors some valid complaints against the oppression of fisc and army.[91]

SUCH JUDICIAL and literary records are vivid and abundant, and tend to command center stage. They also tell only half the story. More genial relations between owner and tenant certainly existed, though they produced fewer and less memorable documents and have attracted less interest. One pleasant exception comes from Dueville, near Vicenza, where villagers gathered in 1488 to toast their landlord: "The noble lord Gaspare fu Alberto of the House of Monza, by his labor, industry and vigilance, has brought the lands of Dueville (which were sterile and uncultivated) to the greatest fertility."[92] Many documents in notarial registers, in fact, attest to close working relations between owners and cultivators. When the people of Longare suffered from the fiscal tricks of the noble Domenico Scroffa, for example, they found a champion in the even more noble landowner Nicolo Valmarana. When villagers of Negrar in the Valpolicella sought to exclude foreigners from their common woods and pastures, they invited the landowner Bartolomeo Verità to their assembly to lend strength to their deliberations.[93] For at least nine years the villagers of La Longa hired as their representative Andrea Arnaldi, who owned considerable land there; they clearly did not bear him ill will. The Arnaldi also served as agents to the commune of Setteca, where they had a villa and many fields.[94] They frequently preferred *patrocinium* to individual countrymen, appearing in court, collecting debts, and handling tax payments. Many clients were also their tenants. Granted, the Arnaldi took fees for their work, but the greater point is that their workers trusted them with important business.[95]

Owners had strong self-interest in keeping the good will of rural dwellers. By allowing long-term debt and by extending loans that could not be repaid, the urban elite suffered economic loss but acquired clients who might further their other interests. Credit and debt markets thus functioned not strictly for financial gain, but rather for accumulation of social capital.[96] The benefits that accrued from patronage were less tangible than profits from forcing payment through the courts, but—given peasants' effective techniques for legal recalcitrance—might prove more effective in the long run. The Arnaldi, for example, carefully cultivated close ties with wealthier peasants such as the Piva and Bucellari, the "big men" of villages in which they had land; in return they gained increased leverage over all tenants. Veronese patricians frequently managed to have their factors and overseers listed in urban tax households, thus reducing dependents' fiscal obligations; the reward, in all likelihood, was greater loyalty and vigilance. Long-term reclamation projects required stable tenancies, and farsighted owners might tolerate arrears or grant extensions of a francation period in return for a steady labor force. By showing mercy to debtors and not proceeding to eviction, Veronese and Vicentine proprietors collected labor services in busy months and thus avoided paying salaried labor.[97]

Cordial relations had other potential advantages. Tenants, for example, frequently appeared as witnesses to landlords' transactions. Most of the time this participation was a mere formality, but if the deal went sour and/or the document was disputed those witnesses were critical to proving a case in court. It says something, as well, that tenants and other *districtuales* were willing to support urban proprietors, even to the extent of offering testimony against fellow villagers. A further benefit came from the custom that the holder of the *utile* of land could be obliged to resell it to a former owner at the original price. By giving that former owner the capital to reclaim title, then buying the *utile* from him, the Arnaldi were assured of a low price; buying directly from the holder of the *utile* offered no price restrictions and they would have to pay a premium. First, however, they needed the former owner on their side. Alternatively, a tenant could renounce *utile* rights but specify a successor at the same rent; the Arnaldi acquired considerable *utile* cheaply by paying for the renunciation and having themselves named successor. Here, too, they needed a compliant cultivator.[98]

Reluctance to initiate eviction proceedings until debt got out of hand indicates that Veneto landlords preferred to carry insolvent tenants rather than disrupt the favor they enjoyed in the countryside. They were not unusually soft touches. Under Tuscan *mezzadria*, as David Herlihy has noted, uncollectable loans served to build up utilitarian friendship. In Lucca, too, debt was a key component of a fine network of relations binding owner and tenant. Proprietors, unwilling to jeopardize loyalties through lawsuit, found it socially and in the long run economically advantageous to leave smaller debts alone. The Rossi of Parma, in like fashion, preferred a light hand and built up a stable core of clients.[99]

Business and Pleasure

The thesis of the urban bourgeoisie's "return to the land," a staple in debate over refeudalization and the failed transition from feudalism to capitalism, has received trenchant criticism lately. Revisionists, led by Philip Jones, claim that citizen-merchants had always owned extensive properties in the countryside; the economic importance of landed patrimonies was no greater in the fifteenth century than it was in the thirteenth.[100] Even if we accept that position, however, we are left with the question posed by Sante Polica: was ownership of land qualitatively different in the later period?[101] In cultural terms, amid villa construction, the vogue for neochivalric trappings and the diffusion of pastoral poetics, did patricians of the Renaissance look at the landscape differently than had their predecessors?

The georgic hexameters of the Veronese Antonio Cipolla suggest that they did. He derived twofold joy from his estates around Porcile: pride in successful improvement of agriculture and pleasure in cultured leisure. Between *negotia* and *otia*, Cipolla felt that he had attained the ancient ideal of combining the active and contemplative lives in a single productive career.[102] The twin themes of pleasure and utility are not, of course, his alone. Most famously, Alberti put into the mouth of one interlocutor the assertion that the primary function of land was alimentary self-sufficiency, but the same speaker also offered a graceful little discourse on the esthetic pleasures, good exercise, spiritual refreshment, and mental stimulation to be derived from a well-sited and well-run farm.[103] The very study of literature deemed *otia* and *negotia* complementary. Reading the ancient treatises of Palladio, Varro, and Columella, as well as recent derivatives by Pier de' Crescenzi, Pagano Bonafede, and Michelangelo Tanaglia, the proprietor learned new crops and techniques while Horace, Theocritus, the later Cicero, and the Virgil of the *Georgics* and the *Bucolics* taught the delights of rural leisure. Moreover, he could draw on newly found justifications for rural life: Tanaglia's opinion that cultivation of the soil ranked only behind letters and arms in the hierarchy of honor, or Leonardo da Chio's definition of true or "Roman" nobility as based on agriculture.[104]

Pleasure was at least a secondary priority for some Veneto proprietors. The Proti *domus dominicale* in Bolzano Vicentino was host to banquets and home to peacocks and hunting birds, and the Monza house in Dueville was decked with sumptuous decoration of fine cloth.[105] Of the 263 Quattrocento Veneto villas catalogued by Martin Kubelik—70 percent of which lie in the Vicentine—a few are quite splendid. Still, for Kubelik and his sources, the definition of a villa is very broad indeed. Two Arnaldi villas in Setteca, for example, could most politely be described as farmhouses; both are today used as barns.[106] Like most in the region, their architectonic forms relate to "practical-economic" functions and do not demonstrate a learned or esthetic vocabulary.[107] With five or six rooms each, some clearly intended as byres or storehouses, the villas were a good deal less hospitable than the family's urban palaces. Spending time in the country meant roughing it.

Giving the label of villa to an edifice introduces anachronistic implications from the rich tradition of later centuries. It also begs the question of what the edifice was used for. The documentation suggests that patricians did not primarily view country living as a source of *otium*, a soothing haven from the heat and tumult of city life. They fled to the country to escape the plague, as did the Arnaldi in 1438 and the Ferretti in 1455. Manfredo Repeta was almost continually resident in Campiglia in the 1469–86 period, but as manager rather than occasional vacationer. *Villeggiatura*, the spending of summer months in otiose splendor, was not part of his agenda; he apparently lived year-round in the city for the last fifteen years covered in the *catasto*.

The Arnaldi spent heavily to refurbish one of their country houses, in the village of Nuvoledo. Payments indicate a substantial complex: for twenty-seven cartloads of lime, two hundred cartloads of stone, twenty thousand bricks, six thousand clamps, eight thousand roof-tiles, construction of a well and barn, and the labor of plastering.[108] The timing of that campaign, just when the family had acquired great wealth and political access and was beginning to call itself noble, would be appropriate to aspirations to gentility. A daughter was born there in August 1464, and Silvestro Arnaldi is found there in August 1471,[109] so there must have been some summer residence.

Residence was not only in the summer. Andrea did business from the Meledo house in January, while Silvestro stayed in Nuvoledo in the months of November and January. Overall, the Arnaldi were more commonly recorded in their country seats from November through February than in the summer. Bartolomeo Verità made a land investiture in Lavagna in January, and great-grandson Verità Verità did the same in Bardolino in February.[110] These are rainy, cold, and blustery months, not the time to be out in the countryside if one had any choice in the matter. But business was business, and no amount of discomfort would justify passing up the chance to pick up a few more *campi*. Indeed, the buying and leasing of fields, and the collection of rents in kind, seems to have been the primary activity in the rural seats.

Even the Arnaldi *domus dominicali* in Meledo, substantial enough to draw the attention of a curious traveler, did not inspire much affection for the rustic life. Not long after he came into his inheritance, Andrea II Arnaldi leased the complex to a consortium of six men and retired to the old urban palace in Carpagnon. What he wanted from the country was neither ostentation nor repose, but 450 ducats, two plovers, eight carts of firewood, a hundred pounds of linen, a haystack, two and a half cartloads of wine, two hundred eggs, three loads of fruit, two cheeses, several hundredweights of oats, sorghum, millet, and wheat, a sack of nuts, a calf, and the carrying services to transport all these goods to the city.[111] A subsequent Arnaldi repented and hired Palladio to design a villa in Meledo, but that is the story of a later era.[112]

CHAPTER SEVEN

PATRICIATE

AND NOBILITY

Defining the Patriciate

*T*HE ARNALDI ENTERED the fifteenth century respectable but outside the Vicentine civic elite: they had been notaries in past generations and had owned some property, but had never been noteworthy in public affairs. Andrea Arnaldi, however, secured political access and eventual election to high office. He and brother Tommaso grew rich: in 1453 their assessment of ten *lire* ranked in the wealthiest one percent of tax households. The brothers gained investiture as episcopal vassals. In the second generation, Gaspare II was elected to the leading civic magistracy and built a substantial palace in the new Renaissance style. Cousin Silvestro, styled *nobilis vir* in most documents, married into the old feudal nobility and found spouses for his children in the great house of the Thiene. Within a century, the Arnaldi had joined the local patriciate.

A working definition of the patriciate—a restricted body of families monopolizing high municipal office, possessing great and honorable wealth, and eventually effecting "aristocratic transformation"[1]—would hold true for other cities in the Veneto, and indeed for most cities in northern and central Italy. For the later sixteenth century that definition would not be hard to sustain. By that time, councils were usually formally closed and highly resistant to newcomers; their seats were passed down by hereditary succession. By then, too, nobles possessed fabulous genealogies, reams of documents, and unimpeachable titles to ratify their standing. After 1575 the Arnaldi were papal *cavalieri,* and traced their origins from the mythic Germanic warrior Arnaldus.

For the fifteenth century, however, "patriciate" remains a term of convenience, a piece of historiographic shorthand. It is not entirely satisfactory, since in every case save Venice boundaries were indistinct. Armando Sapori, for one, wished the term driven from the lexicon, since it does not reflect contemporary usage, means different things to different people, and lacks sufficient precision to be useful.[2] Few have followed his lead, however. Most historians of most cities perceive a consistent leadership group and a movement toward a consolidated elite on the basis of prosopography: in membership lists of inner councils and embassies, the same names appear over and over, from generation to generation. Still, unable to give firm definition to bodies that were not formally isolated, historians have resorted to generic labels such as *ceto dirigente, gruppo oligarchico,* or *ceto dominante.* Even Sapori acknowledged exclusion and coherence, and commonly spoke of the *dirigenti del Comune.*

Some cities, it is true, possessed lines of demarcation between the powerful and the powerless, but even these tended to lose effective meaning. From at least 1277, with a matriculation list established a century later, Milan had a formally constituted body of nobles that controlled cathedral benefices. Visconti and Sforza rulers, however, had their own favorites, and the proportion of benefices that went to *ceto* members declined from 93 percent in the fourteenth century to 29 percent in the sixteenth century. Moreover, matriculated nobles sought ecclesiastical, not municipal office. In any case, numerous Milanese merchants acquired noble status by other means.[3] In Siena, to take another example, five formalized factions *(monti)* taken together constituted a "definitely privileged body" that controlled public office. Still, matriculation in each *monte* was open and not hereditary, and Mario Ascheri concludes that the effective political leadership was both composite in membership and growing in size until 1493.[4]

Closer to home, Treviso's College of Nobles supplied town councillors and higher officers. But places in the college were elective rather than strictly hereditary; anyway the college's significance declined after the council was abolished in 1407.[5] Vicenza, too, once possessed a corporation of nobles, the *coetus nobilium,* but that body dissolved in the thirteenth century; as early as 1213 a "Description of noble families" listed a generous proportion of *popolares maiores, popolares de medio,* and *popolares minores* among the nobles.[6] Vicenza has also been held up as an example of precocious aristocratization since after 1311 seats in its Great Council were restricted to current holders, their heirs, and assigns. Even then, however, the political class was far from closed: only a quarter of families represented in the 1314 council were still active in 1346, and two-thirds of those holding seats in 1337 disappeared from public life within nine years.[7]

Florence, again, provides a standard by which the experiences of other cities can be measured. Throughout many permutations the municipal constitution remained, on paper, open; elections by lot and the obligatory presence of guildsmen ensured that common folk regularly obtained places at least on lesser magistracies. In consequence Nicolai Rubinstein, charting the ways in which electoral commissions effectively excluded those unacceptable to controlling factions, discerned substantial continuity of families in highest offices and so accepted the notion of a patriciate, but he also noted the constant admission of new families and expressed doubts about the possibility of charting anything more than a de facto and highly permeable leadership. Accepting his overall conclusions but also his reservations regarding membership, many successors avoid typological rigor and use descriptives in the loosest possible sense—oligarchy, aristocracy, patriciate, "cadre of prominent citizens," "inner circle," "traditional ruling elite," "political class," and the like.[8] Prosopography reveals who the privileged few were, but, in the absence of firm principles of demarcation, simple identification may be as far as the issue can be pushed. As was the case in cities as varied as Padua and Lucca,[9] formation of a *governo stretto* was effected by collusion rather than by normative exclusion, and was far from absolute. But if principles of patrician membership and separation remained informal and permeability remained constant, the entire notion of a municipal elite dissolves into impression.

Historians can hardly impose clarity where none existed. Contemporaries, no less, were unwilling or unable to articulate criteria of rank. Managers of the Quattrocento had a hierarchic view of society, but chose not to draw precise lines. That councillors and officials should be chosen from among the "best and most respectable" citizens ("de melioribus et praestantioribus"),[10] that testimony or a petition to bear arms or the seriousness of a crime should be evaluated according to an individual's *conditio* or *qualitas*,[11] acknowledged stratification but left determination of the individual's standing to on-site evaluators such as judges and electors. Those who set the rules, operating within ostensibly open political systems, either did not wish to risk the shocks of imposing formal demarcation or did not find consistent boundaries.

Writers of the time shared their reluctance. Several Paduans produced col-

lective family chronicles which, while aspiring to trace all the city's important lineages, declined to indicate criteria for inclusion. Giovanni da Nono
set the model early in the Trecento, declaring an intent to trace the "origins
of some citizens of Padua, both noble and ignoble." He preferred the noble,
among whom he ranked his own house, but included some descended from
notaries, millers, usurers, innkeepers, tailors, and even rustics, paupers, and
people of "vile condition." The bland "some citizens" of his title sidestepped
the problem of defining membership in Padua's elite; copying and imitation
of his chronicle left the problem open throughout the Quattrocento and beyond.[12]

The Vicentine Battista Pagliarini was even more catholic. He found precedent in a simple list of 165 families;[13] research in private and civic archives
allowed him to expand the number to nearly three hundred and to provide
copious historical commentary. He also pinned a more precise, socially descriptive label to his survey: "On the noble citizens of our city." But Pagliarini
was not sure what constituted nobility. Listing patrician families in descend-
ing order of importance, he had no problem with the top ranks: high municipal office, great deeds, antiquity of lineage, imperial title, and leadership of
the *patria* were unassailable markers of prominence. Toward the bottom,
though, some families were "now descended into agriculture and manual
labor" or "of lowest condition." He did not, on that account, omit suspect lineages from the list.[14] Faced with an uncertain lower edge to the local elite,
he opted for inclusion rather than risk insulting those whose claims might
yet stick.

IN THE PAST generation two historians in particular have addressed issues of permeability and closure. In 1978 Philip Jones' "Legend of the Bourgeoisie" attacked the traditional assimilationist position, which posited composite patriciates of upper merchants and feudal nobles, as well as its
Braudellian corollary of the "betrayal of the bourgeoisie," which held that
the later medieval Italian commercial elite broke ranks, abandoned trade for
land, intermarried with the ancient nobility, and made common cause with
former enemies in a true aristocracy. Jones denied that capitalism ever
wrought fundamental changes in Italian society, or that capitalists ever constituted a distinct class or successfully seized power at the head of the medieval *popolo*. Neatly turning the venerable topos of the "conquest of the
contado" on its head, he argued that the later Middle Ages saw the advance
of rural and agricultural interests at the expense of trade and finance. The
traditional nobility, never completely pushed from power, reaffirmed its an-

cient authority. Like Braudel, Jones attempted to demonstrate Italy's failed transition from feudalism to capitalism and consequent decadence; unlike Braudel, he so downgraded the achievements of merchants that no significant passage into nobility would have been possible.[15]

Slightly earlier, and from a different point of view, Marino Berengo denied assimilation in the Veneto. He acknowledged that elsewhere in Italy families of mercantile origins earlier acquired political power and by the Quattro-Cinquecento successfully claimed noble status. In Verona, though, ruling classes uniformly derived from an ancient feudal nobility. A few newly rich families did make it onto councils, but were never amalgamated with great aristocratic houses. By the sixteenth century the old nobility had closed its ranks even more firmly and now ruthlessly resisted the claims of upstarts.[16]

For the purposes of the case study, these revisionist models converge. To Jones, the Stoppi and the Arnaldi would have been too weak to hope for advance; to Berengo, they would have stood little chance of vaulting the barriers to aristocracy. Yet both families did rise from obscurity (and, in the case of the Stoppi, from the ranks of recent immigrants) into full membership in their cities' elites. Were they among the handful of lucky families, the exceptions that prove the rule?

A core of powerful families indeed dominated municipal councils in each city in the Veneto at every juncture between 1200 and 1600—but they were not always the same families. As bare chronicles of the early period give way to more saturated lists of officeholders, it is evident that turnover was both consistent and massive. A few grand dynasties recur, but they were always flanked by newcomers. The surplus nobility of neighboring cities could only partially supply recruits; the rest came from the upper ranks of commoners. Positing continuity *of* elites is not the same as positing continuity *within* elites.

Biology alone required permeability and forestalled closure of patriciates. E. A. Wrigley once estimated that in a "stationary preindustrial society" 20 percent of couples would have no surviving children, and 20 percent be survived only by daughters, such that male-descent lineages would invariably suffer a 40 percent extinction rate.[17] Empirical study confirms his expectations. Recurrent epidemic also eliminated many families. Low numbers of surviving children—in Florence, well below the replacement rate[18]—doomed others and forced social mobility. Using good data from the Lyonnaise, Lorcin calculated that, of all families mentioned before 1340, fewer than 20 percent survived into the late fifteenth century.[19] The situation in the Veneto could not have been much different.

The patrimonial strategies of the upper ranks made them especially vulnerable to extinction and/or social climbing. Limiting marriage of sons worked against survival; it will be recalled that only 60 percent of Venetian patrician males married. The Arnaldi, after two experiments of this sort, barely survived the fifteenth century. The nobility of Lyon put 31 percent of daughters into convents but only 23 percent of sons, and the resulting shortage of girls in the aristocratic marriage pool forced many young men to marry down.[20] If patricians in the Veneto at all resembled their Florentine counterparts—who sent many more daughters than sons into religion[21]—the situation would have been much the same.

Patricians were also more susceptible than commoners to political upheavals. Ezzelino da Romano decimated elites in all Veneto cities in the first half of the Dugento. When Vicentine Ghibellines several times failed to throw off Paduan lordship later in the century, many suffered death or exile. The della Scala of Verona broke Guelph partisans in Vicenza and Padua, and the Visconti in turn excluded Scaligeri and Carraresi partisans. Mighty Paduans such as the Dalesmanini, Scrovegni, and Bibi fell to Carraresi persecution. Debt, often imposed for political vengeance, forced many Paduans of note to cede their lands and leave the public arena during the Trecento. Repression of anti-Venetian revolts in the early Quattrocento removed a further section of Padua's notables.[22]

Due to a combination of infertility, disease, execution, and exile, seven of ten Vicentine "noble houses" listed in 1259 were no longer on the scene two centuries later. An anonymous chronicle from around 1400 noted that the twelve original comitial families in Vicenza "are all extinct, such that there remains hardly any memory of them." At the end of the fifteenth century Pagliarini borrowed the phrase as title for his account of family losses, counting over four hundred surnames that had died out within memory of his documents; fewer than three hundred worthy families were extant.[23] Vicenza, with five changes of regime in two centuries, may have suffered unusually severe patrician decimation, but the overall conclusion that "aristocratic extinction rates were often high"[24] seems to hold true for the region generally.

Changes of ruler brought new houses to the fore. Signorial favorites arrived as governors and put down roots; loyal natives from formerly obscure families—the Thiene in Vicenza are a good example—were coopted into signorial administrations and acquired permanent prominence. Further, all cities encouraged immigration to offset depopulation, and several newcomers arrived with or eventually achieved prominence. One of the themes of Pagliarini's prosopographical study, in fact, was the degree to which much of Vicenza's upper crust was relatively recent. A half century of Paduan domination brought in the Conti, Ovetari, Brusomini, Ferreti, Litolfi, Polcastri, and the chronicler's own family. The Nogarola, Bevilaqua, Sarego, Cavalli, Borselli, and Fracanzani arrived during the next half century, under Veronese control. Visconti rule introduced the Anguissola, Cavalcabo, Monza, Nievo, Muzani, Soardi, and Roma. Reggio Emilia contributed the Angiolelli, Ghellini, Gislardi, Sesso, and Macchiavelli; Tuscany, the Pigafetta, Baldanucci, della Zoga, Provinciali, and Saraceni; the Romagna, the Faella, Zuffatti, Scarioti, Cerrati, and Toso.[25]

The municipal elite of 1400 was very different in membership from its predecessors a century or two before. Even then, although mortality crises abated and Venetian rulers declined political persecution, wholesale change in the Vicentine patriciate did not cease. Infertility, incapacity, and misfiring marital strategies continued to take a toll. Several cases of Quattrocento mobility into the patriciate cast further doubt on extreme assertions of a "closed aristocratic caste." The Arnaldi made it into the top ranks, as did their Feramosca kinsmen, the Braschi, the Volpi, and the newly arrived Trento. Some families that came to the city in previous centuries but were not then prominent also rose into the oligarchy—the Nievo, Pigafetta, Macchiavelli, Zugliano, and Monza come to mind. Strict closure would have led to eventual class suicide, and patricians were too smart and too protective of long-term interests to adopt such a policy.

Political Elites

The Arnaldi had held seats on Vicenza's Great Council in the Trecento,[26] but that fact alone means little. Many councillors were not exalted—a majority lacked family names, and several exercised humble occupations—and, as seen above, turnover was massive even in the quarter century between extant council lists. The Arnaldi were not then prominent, as they had not been previously: chronicles by Maurisio, Smereglo, Ferreto, Conforto da Costozza, and Antonio Godi, which detailed the city's public life in the thirteenth and fourteenth centuries, do not mention them.

The situation changed dramatically during the Quattrocento. In 1426, eighteen-year-old Andrea Arnaldi succeeded his late maternal grandfather Antonio Zugliano on the council. Just shy of his twentieth birthday, he was elected notary to Vicenza's College of Notaries, and quickly rose to serve as syndic, councillor, and *gastaldis* of the college. In 1439 he was elected to manage the commune's church of San Vincenzo, and served at least two more terms in the following decade. A year before his death, Andrea won election to the elite Council of One Hundred.[27] In 1482 nephew Gaspare II served as communal deputy, the chief magistracy in the municipal hierarchy. He and kinsmen may have held other posts: scanty public archives provide no lists of officeholders for the period. When records become regular (in 1510) the Arnaldi were holding four seats on the Great Council. In the next decades they were territorial vicars, governing small towns in the hinterland. The job must have been uncomfortable and was certainly badly paid, but it marked acceptance into inner circles and served as threshold to high municipal careers thereafter.[28]

Their experience stands in opposition to a historiographic consensus of a progressive restriction of access to political office throughout the Veneto. In the classic statement of that thesis, Angelo Ventura argued for passage from "broad government" in the communal era to a "rigid aristocratic arrangement" in the early modern period. Trecento *signori* reversed a previous trend toward "democratic broadening," pushed popular corporations such as guilds from power, promoted smaller and exclusive councils, and denied the mass of citizens a share in government. Venetian dominion, in turn, accelerated "crystallization" of political elites and "reconstitution of hierarchic structures," and stripped the vestigial traces of popular representation of real authority.[29]

Some details of Ventura's interpretation have been challenged. Historians of Verona, for example, deny a Venetian role in the emergence of a political elite: initiative for constriction was purely local, and effective replacement of a Great Council (of five hundred) by a Council of Fifty predated 1405 although it was only formalized in that year. In the dominion as a whole, Venetian governors, in fact, frequently intervened to prevent constriction of municipal structures. Responding to complaints that Vicenza's eight deputies were too powerful, the Republic in 1422 flanked them with a new Council of One Hundred. Nine years later the doge blocked the Vicentine oligarchy's attempt to replace councils of one hundred and forty with a single body of forty councillors. The Senate in 1446 forced an increase in Paduan council membership from sixty to one hundred. In 1455 the Senate ordered enlargement of the Veronese electorate, and in 1461 the Council of Ten ordered its governors in Verona to select twenty members of the local Council of Fifty because many able and loyal citizens had been excluded. Veronese patricians effected moderation of the former order and revocation of the latter, further indication that the impetus to exclusion came from native forces rather than the capital.[30]

Still, the Venetian role aside, research confirms Ventura's overall thesis of the constriction of the political base. The Veronese case is particularly clear. Already by the mid-Trecento a Council of Twelve held real power, and the Great Council of Six Hundred was soon moribund. Corporate representatives, once dominant in central magistracies, lost real power and finally, around 1390, were replaced by twelve deputies. Around that latter date the Twelve (actually seventy-two, with six bimonthly panels of twelve members) began to coopt fifty citizens as a *zonta*, which in 1405 replaced the Great Council. Councillors simply passed from one body to the next in alternate years—in a sampling of electoral lists, some 88 percent to 100 percent of members of the Fifty were drawn from the outgoing Seventy-Two, and 88 percent to 98 percent of the Seventy-Two were outgoing or former members of the Fifty—leading Varanini to acknowledge "the extreme compactness and stability of the ruling class which held administrative power in the city."[31]

The Vicentine case presents variants that are both precocious and (apparently) conservative. Vicentines were involved early in formalizing mechanisms that turned nominally elective office into personal patrimony. Statutes of 1264 specified election of councillors from among the "best and brightest men" of the city; 1311 statutes, followed substantially in 1339 and 1425 revisions, reserved seats in the Great Council to the heirs and assigns of current councillors.[32] Vicenza may have been the first city to perceive office as property, but Padua and Bergamo were not far behind in allowing outgoing councillors to select their successors.[33] Outright assignment made a mockery of the notion of civic councils as assemblies of the most talented and committed citizens. Silvestro Arnaldi, for example, inherited the paternal seat a few weeks shy of his fifth birthday, and his son Andrea II entered the Great Council at the age of seventeen.[34]

The Vicentine constitution was, on paper, backward in continuing to assign a major role to guilds and colleges. The thirteen corporations that provided a Council of Anziani received automatic seats on the Great Council, and the Anziani held a high-sounding charge to assist the podestà, act for the utility of the commune, and preserve civic prerogatives and honor. Still, the Anziani were given no means to enforce that jurisdiction, suggesting a largely symbolic or ceremonial role. Four of the guilds that named Anziani—the Judges, Cloth Merchants, Notaries, and Wool Merchants—were controlled by the wealthy and powerful, and scarcely provided a voice for the *popolo*.

Further, a member of the College of Judges presided over the Anziani, and assumed their task of registering membership in the Great Council. Anyway the council is not known to have met during the Quattrocento. In 1520 a delegation of *popolani* complained that guild officials were excluded from meetings of the Great Council.[35]

Vicenza was also behind the times in its retention of a Great Council. Verona's Five Hundred was replaced by the Fifty in 1405, and Treviso's large council by six *provveditori* two years later. The Paduan council, once among the largest and most broadly based in the region, shrank to sixty members before the Venetian Senate raised the number to a hundred; a few deputies held day-to-day authority. Brescians reduced their municipal council from five hundred to seventy-two members.[36] Vicenza's Great Council, on the other hand, expanded from a nominal five hundred in 1425 to an actual 626 in 1510.

But Vicentines were abreast of the times in vesting executive power in smaller and more exclusive bodies. The eight deputies and the Council of One Hundred drafted legislation, supervised charitable bequests, set taxes, managed communal property, revised statutes, heard petitions for citizenship, elected fiscal officers, and appointed ambassadors. Because the deputies and One Hundred elected the following year's One Hundred, which in turn elected that year's pool of forty-eight from which the eight deputies were drawn for two-month terms, important citizens could simply shuttle between elite panels. The Great Council basically ratified laws already approved by higher bodies, and made appointments to lesser offices.[37]

Shifting power from councils of many hundreds to councils of a few dozen, and eliminating guilds from serious tasks, did not itself close off political access to the middling and lower sorts. Veneto constitutions did not erect explicit barriers between the powerful and the disenfranchised. Local notables could, however, adopt strategies to restrict if not prevent upward mobility. One was to tighten up the rules for acquiring citizenship, to keep rustics and foreigners from gaining that minimum prerequisite for political access. In 1425 petitions for Vicentine citizenship required hearing by eight commissioners; within sixty years the rules changed to require additional approval by rectors, deputies, and five separate sessions of executive councils. Not surprisingly, grants of citizenship dropped off sharply. At the same time, authorities challenged the standing of those who had acquired citizenship but refused to adopt mores appropriate to civil life. The Venetian Senate in 1448 summed up several decades of local laws requiring urban residency with a decree that stripped the citizenship of those who practiced a rural trade or refused to reside in the city; in 1500 the central government made universal a Paduan ordinance denying citizenship to anyone working the land "with his own hands."[38]

Nor could those who still managed to acquire citizenship hope for easy political access. Vicentine councils in 1437 passed an ordinance blocking immigrants from holding top positions for thirty years after acquisition of citizenship. Brescians were even more hostile to newcomers: a 1488 law declared that no citizen could hold office unless he or his forebears had paid taxes from 1426 or 1439.[39] Both rules stopped short of outright exclusion, but delay and discrimination served notice that outsiders were not welcome.

MEMBERSHIP IN municipal councils closely mirrored cities' economic elites. By the time *estimi* become available to measure the wealth of the politically active, the humble had been pushed from councils. Lanaro Sartori concludes that artisans were well represented in Veronese councils in 1406–8, but had largely disappeared by the later 1420s.[40] Once again, elites effected exclusion in an informal manner. The constitution of Verona, for example, continued to insist on proportional representation by the "less," the "middling," and the "great," as defined by tax assessment. The system hardly guaranteed that councils reflect the actual distribution of wealth in the city, however, since the top threshold for *minores* was set so high (three *lire*) that some very rich citizens qualified for the seats reserved for the "less." Varanini's comparison of the 1407–9 councils with the city's 1409 assessment reveals that 99.4 percent of councillors had more than one *lire* of *estimo*, which put them in the top 29 percent of the population. Around 87 percent of councillors were assessed over two *lire*, which ranked them in the richest 14 percent of the citizenry. Ventura's calculations for 1495 councils reveal a similar coincidence of wealth and political standing. Two-thirds of councillors were still drawn from the "middling" and the "great," with their assessments placing them among the city's richest 6 percent. Three-quarters of all councillors were estimated over two *lire*, which ranked them in the wealthiest 9 percent of assessed households. Ventura notes, as well, that less well-off councillors generally came from families whose other households received high assessments: the rich were merely granting positions to needy kin.[41]

The Vicentine counterpart of these elite councils, a Council of One Hundred whose membership is known only from a 1453 list, would appear at face value to be more economically variegated (see appendix, table 7.1). While the two cities had about the same proportion of citizens assessed above two *lire* (9 percent to 14 percent in Verona, 11.7 percent in Vicenza), the proportion of councillors falling into that category was considerably lower in Vicenza (63 percent) than in Verona (77 percent to 87 percent). But Vicentines were not, in fact, more inclined to permit entry by the middling and poor. Rather, systems of assessment were slightly different. Verona measured the relative wealth of all citizens, while Vicentine assessors assigned *estimi* until they reached a quota of 2,500 *lire;* the poorer half of Vicenza's households did not appear on the rolls.[42] So Verona's councillors are measured against the taxpaying population as a whole, while Vicenza's councillors are measured only against the wealthier half of the population.

In all likelihood, then, Vicentine inner councils were drawn from just as wealthy strata as their Veronese equivalents. The mean assessment of the members of the 1453 Vicentine Council of One Hundred was 4.4 *lire,* which falls in the 96th percentile of overall assessed wealth; the median was 2.5 *lire,* which falls in the 91st percentile. By another reckoning, 90 percent of Vicentine councillors ranked in the top quarter of estimated wealth, and half ranked in the top decile. Only 5 percent received the lowest assessment, which was assigned to over half of the taxpaying population.

Vicenza's Great Council also drew from the city's economic elite. Councillors' mean *estimo* ranked in the 90th percentile of assessed citizens, and the median *estimo* in the 82nd percentile. Members of the Great Council, as we would expect, were less wealthy than were those on the more important Council of One Hundred (see appendix, tables 7.1–3). Mean and median assessments of the smaller council were twice those of the greater. Some 10 percent of the Hundred were very wealthy (*estimo* over *lire* 10), compared with 3.3 percent of the Great Council. Only 39.6 percent of the larger body were assessed at or above *lire* 2, compared with 62.9 percent of the Hundred. On the low end, 8.6 percent of the Hundred were rated under one *lire,* but over a third on the Great Council were. The percentage of the Hundred given the lowest possible assessment (4.9 percent) is under half that of the Great Council (11.3 percent).

A NUMBER OF little families and virtual unknowns crept into the municipal councils. Some councillors in Vicenza in 1510—the Pietrobelli, dalla Banca, delle Canove, Capasanti, Bussioni, and Mantegna—were so minor that they were not counted in Pagliarini's contemporary list of notables, even though Pagliarini strained hard for inclusion. Percolation into the council was, in fact, a regular event: even as the 1510 list was being prepared, two seats changed hands.[43]

Veneto cities indeed saw consolidation of political classes in the Quattrocento, but there is no need to exaggerate exclusion. The Paduan council, described as the "monopoly of a restricted group of families," experienced at least one phase of "modest opening" in the mid-Quattrocento. Newcomers had to be admitted simply to keep up numbers, since 41 percent of council families dropped out of public life in the 1372–1446 period.[44] In like measure Varanini argues for the "aristocratization of governing bodies and the institutional consolidation of the ruling class's predominance" in Verona, but acknowledges that thirty-four of 131 conciliar families in the later Trecento disappeared from the political scene soon after 1405, and offers examples of several families—the Saibante, Miniscalchi, Emilei, Giusti, dal Borgo, and Fregoso—who entered councils over the course of the Quattrocento. The Trivelli, inactive in the Trecento, consistently appeared in councils after 1407, and the immigrant Stoppi joined them after midcentury.[45]

Even within the charmed circle of the patriciate it is possible to point to a broadening of the Veronese political base in the fifteenth century. After 1408 a commission of 24 citizens, which included the 12 deputies, directly elected the councils of Fifty and Seventy-Two. Statutes of 1450 changed the system. Henceforth a similar commission (now composed of the current 12-man *muda* of the Seventy-Two, 6 members of the Fifty, and 6 others) instead elected a pool of citizens eligible for office; from that pool were drawn the 122 councillors for the following year. Further modification in 1456 allowed all 122 current councillors to determine the body of those eligible for the next year's council seats.[46] The electing group, that is, was to increase fivefold. This in fact happened: the average yearly number of electors was about 20 in the 1450–56 period, but rose to 93 in 1457 and exceeded 100 after 1481 (see appendix, table 7.4). More significantly, the number of candidates for eligibility scrutinies also rose dramatically, from 225 annually in the 1450–56 period to 311 annually in the 1500–1509 period. Expansion of the pool of candidates reduced chances that any one aspirant would be elected and hence actually secure a seat: 54 percent of candidates were selected as eligible for councils in the mid-Quattrocento, but only 39 percent in the early Cinquecento.

Vote totals indicate a contentious political process, with a growing proportion of candidates rejected in the first scrutiny. After 1457 the rejection rate was so high that a second ballot was usually held to attain a sufficient number of eligibles, and by the early Cinquecento as many as five scrutinies were sometimes needed. Few candidates were elected in the first attempts: the young gained experience in several futile bids before they were deemed ready for inclusion. Even established families did not find election to municipal councils a mere formality. Verità Verità, for example, lost eight elections before joining councils in 1466.

Eligibility scrutinies, then, belie any image of cozy collusion between insiders. Electors looked for qualified individuals, and did not grant blanket favors to preferred families: Antonio di Benedetto Verità failed in every election between 1481 and 1488, while his brother Giacomo passed with huge majorities. Individuals' vote totals often changed sharply from year to year as their popularity rose and fell. Election one year did not guarantee success the next: Girolamo Fracastoro lost nine times in his apprenticeship, then alternately won, lost, won, lost twice, and finally won eleven times. Memorialist Bonaventura Bovi won seven elections, then lost four. Many, despite a good last name, never secured election to the pool of eligibles: Giacomo di Michele Verità failed thirteen times in the 1495–1507 period, then apparently gave up the effort. Winners were usually wealthy, but the wealthy were not always winners: Giovanni Poeta Verità, from an offshoot line, received tax assessments averaging twenty *lire*,[47] which ranked him among the city's richest citizens, but he failed in seventeen of twenty elections, and in thirty-one scrutinies his sons never won eligibility for councils. Ancient and proud lineages such as the Fracastoro and Verità did not enjoy a higher success rate than did newer and relatively humble houses such as the dal Bovo and Bovi; none of the four families that produced memoirs placed more than two-thirds of their candidates on councils (see appendix, table 7.5).

The thesis of Vicenza's "ruling class, now become an aristocracy" through "rigid caste exclusiveness,"[48] likewise does not hold strictly true. Statutes of 1311, restricting Great Council seats to the heirs and assigns of current councillors, actually cut both ways. The law allowed patricians to keep seats within their families, but also allowed councillors to assign positions to outsiders without subjecting their assigns to the risk of a general council election. The modest Arnaldi joined, thanks to grandfather Antonio Zugliano; so did the Feramosca and immigrants such as the Monza, Trento, Anguissola, Soardi, and Cavalcabo.

It is true that in Vicenza, as in Verona and Padua, major offices remained in the hands of long prominent lineages. Varanini's intuition, that Veronese newcomers might rise to just below the level of the very great, may fairly be extended to its neighbor. But even that inner barrier, between traditional oligarchs and the main body of the patriciate, was far from impermeable. The Arnaldi, Feramosca, and Trento made it through, even if they required a half century of seasoning after joining the Great Council: by 1500 they were scarcely distinguishable from the da Porto, Trissino, Thiene, Loschi, and Bissari.

Perhaps they made it just in time. By all accounts, the gates slammed shut in the Cinquecento, though the political prosopography of that century is still in infancy and may yet provide some surprises. In Vicenza, for example, councils in 1567 forbade entry to those whose families had not been citizens for a full century, and to those stained by their own or their parents' manual trade. Few outsiders could qualify after that date. Verona's aristocrats, for their part, undertook ruthless persecution of upstarts who claimed seats in councils.[49] But overt political closure was still in the future when the Arnaldi and a few colleagues would begin their rise to the top.

Patriciate into Nobility

At the outset of the fifteenth century the Arnaldi were simple citizens, and at its completion they were nobles—at least, that is what the redactors of notarial documents perceived. They provided aristocratic title rarely in the 1430s, commonly in the 1460s, and almost unanimously in the 1490s (see appendix, table 7.6). Still, Arnaldi status changed very slowly (over eighty years and two full generations). Documentation at best provides incidents that pushed the family along the path: acquisition of a council seat in 1426, investiture with an episcopal fief in 1452, accumulation of a great fortune at least by 1453, election to high civic office in 1453 and the highest office by 1482, retirement from the active notariate and retail trade. No definite moment of ennoblement, no single threshold, moved the family from *cives* to *nobiles vires*. The long passage from commoner to aristocrat status suggests that the Arnaldi and their notaries held no one standard for nobility.

The stakes were high: nobility offered the one means by which a loosely defined patriciate could obtain status recognition, indelible superiority, legitimation of prestige, and distinction from the unprivileged. In practice, however, definitions and criteria of nobility were nearly as imprecise as those of the patriciate itself. Theory did not offer much certainty—or, rather, different theories supported and denigrated a variety of claims. Taken as a whole, these can be grouped into a rough hierarchy. As we move down the scale, claims were weaker and denials more fierce—but no qualification could be dismissed altogether.

Counts palatine and imperial knights held the only unimpeachable claim to nobility. Jurists said so, following Bartolus: "Nobility is a quality conferred by princely authority, by which an individual is shown to rank above honest plebeans."[50] Indeed, said Bartolus and his followers, "if a man lives for a thousand years filled with all virtues and the prince loves him greatly, he still remains plebean until there is conferred upon him some rank or nobility by which he is distinguished from plebeans."[51]

Doubtless society could have functioned perfectly well without counts' vestigial imperial jurisdiction (the capacity to create notaries and legitimate bastards) and the emperor himself held no real authority in Italy. But would-be nobles needed an unambiguous seal on their standing and so, during the half dozen imperial passages of the Quattrocento, they fawned over the emperor in hopes of obtaining safe title. They flattered him outrageously as "head of all the lands of the globe, chief of all human affairs," and the "sole light of the world," and they hoped that he would still unite Christendom and conquer the enemies of the faith. The patrician-led communes of Verona and Vicenza greeted emperors with flags, festoons, baldachins, musicians, speeches, and parades, and even Venetians, despite their professed immunity from imperial authority, sponsored lavish ceremonies of welcome; Andrea Arnaldi admired one such *magnum gaudium* in 1452. An ill-paid professor might sneer at a figure like Frederick III, noting that "writers have made little mention of him, since he has left little worth remembering," but patricians knew that the emperor had important symbolic capital to distribute.[52] Fortunate in securing recognition (or reconfirmation) were the Nogarola, Campagna, Lavagnoli, Cavalli, Spolverini, Malaspina, dalla Riva, Giusti, Guagnini, Pellegrini, Salerno, Bevilaqua, dal Verme, Montanari, Cipriani, and da Faenza in Verona,[53] and the Ragona, Pagello, Manelmi, Thiene, da Porto, Valmarana, Loschi, Cerrati, Serego, Chiericati, Poiana, Garzatori, Trissino, and Sesso in Vicenza.[54]

Many patricians, unable to vaunt an imperial privilege, looked farther down the hierarchy of qualifications and found confirmation of their status in knighthood. Here would-be aristocrats could exploit ambiguous terminology. *Eques* was a clear enough title, signifying imperial concession. A companion term, *miles,* was far from synonymous and far from straightforward. *Milites aureati* were also imperial grantees and hence unquestionably noble, but simple *milites* owed their title to purely local usage. Communes had long claimed the right to grant knighthood, and though the shift to mercenary forces made citizen cavalry obsolete the practice continued as a means of bestowing civic reward.

Were all knights equally noble? Emilio Cristiani finds no practical difference between imperial/feudal *milites* and communal *milites* in Pisa, as these "pretty indeterminate categories" first blurred and then converged. Amelio

Tagliaferri observes that the personal descriptive *miles* disappeared from Veronese tax rolls because all *milites* passed into the rank of true nobles and no longer required qualification by title.[55] Contemporaries, though, refused to allow amalgamation. As early as the twelfth century Otto of Freising scorned communal knights as being of inferior condition, even practitioners of manual trades. The stories of Boccaccio, Sacchetti, and others made the figure of the fat merchant with borrowed sword and ill-fitting armor, sitting unsteadily on a scrawny horse, a favorite target for ridicule. Satirists had good material to work with: Florentine knights of the Trecento included a four-year-old boy, a dying man, and a corpse, and the base Ciompi in one day created seventy-seven knights, including a spicer, grain dealers, a carder, a wine-seller, and a baker.[56]

Lawyers put disregard for the communal knighthood on a systematic footing. They could not here rely on Bartolus, who endorsed the principle that communes could grant office or rank *(dignitas)*, which itself conferred nobility, but then left the issue of whether the *militia* so qualified to local usage.[57] Left to their own devices, jurists offered a strict definition: a true *miles* was willing to risk death to defend the fatherland. On that basis, said Padua's Michele Savonarola, those who wore the insignia of knighthood, without any martial skills, did not merit the title. Verona's Cristoforo Lanfranchini went further, blasting those descended from "really vile parents" who girded themselves with swords, kept horses and servants and hunting birds, and then claimed nobility without exercise of arms:[58] "our knights are dedicated more to commerce or agriculture or private business. They stand daily in the squares and shops and practice quite vile occupations, and there are many who do not know how to put on armor." Unless they desisted from trade or cultivation, and gave themselves over to arms, they should not enjoy the privileges of the *militia*. Anyway, declared Lanfranchini and Ludovico Bolognini, the communal knighthood was an office, not a rank, and implied no nobility.[59] Verona's Bartolomeo Cipolla, more irenic, simply omitted knighthood from his list of the twenty-six possible qualifications for nobility. Furthermore, communal knighthood, unlike its feudal/military cousin, did not confer indefinitely transmissible title. When rank derived from an individual's appointment or election to office, said Bartolus, that rank lapsed with his great-grandson. He left a loophole, admitting that the nobility of office indeed passed to descendants by custom "in some parts of Italy." His successors were not so generous, and argued for a general disqualification.[60]

Aspiring aristocrats might find support in a third source of nobility—communal office. Looking to Roman usage, Bartolus had sanctioned the notion that participation in councils or high office might automatically confer rank *(dignitas)*, which itself ennobled. Cipolla suggested that those with high office in the *res publica*, or those born of an ancient lineage whose ancestors had held high office, could licitly claim nobility.[61] Councillors, for their part, seized upon Bartolus's oblique connection of Roman titles to nobility and began to style themselves *clarissimi* (for consuls), *spectabiles, illustres*, or *egregii* (for deputies and ambassadors), and *providi* or *prudentes vires* (for lesser offices).

There were, however, flaws to the claims of a conciliar or officeholding elite. Roman titles may have resonated powerfully, but they were self-proclaimed and honorific, not grounded in legal distinctions. More seriously, the issue of inheritance of title posed a problem for those who saw office as a springboard to perpetual aristocracy, since Bartolus's statement that the nobility of a *dignitas* could not be transmitted beyond the great-grandson still stood. Some of his other comments, however, offered comfort. He spoke, for example, of "a boy born of a noble, who immediately is noble" even without himself holding office, and here too custom "in some parts of Italy" had admitted "all descendants" to nobility. A century later Cipolla admitted the heritability of ancestral rank without qualifications: five of his twenty-six standards of nobility hinged upon descent from those with high office, and he did not mention lapse of title.[62]

Still, those inactive or unsuccessful in municipal politics could not borrow their forebears' prestige indefinitely, and they could not recycle bygone titles without some accomplishment of their own. Furthermore, it was all very well to claim nobility for councillors in cities like Verona, which elected only a hundred or so in any given year. Admitting the principle for the Great Council of Vicenza, though, raised the possibility of a seriously diluted nobility, because numbers were great (over six hundred members) and because the right of alienation allowed newcomers easy access. Battista Pagliarini, for one, doubted an intrinsic correlation of the political class and aristocracy. Of the 191 families on the council in 1510, only 156 (82 percent) appeared in his list of noble houses. On the other side of the coin, he listed 271 noble families, but only 58 percent of them held council seats. Acknowledging these disabilities, patriciates monopolizing offices and councils did not go so far as to put Bartolus's principle into law: only in the Cinquecento did commentators explicitly connect a council seat and nobility.[63]

A fourth source of nobility might be professional knowledge. Lawyers, with vested professional interest, seized eagerly upon the Roman law tag that "knowledge ennobles a man" *("scientia nobilitet hominem")* because it conferred a high sort of *virtus*. The principle could apply to physicians and, perhaps, to those trained in letters: when Verona's Spinetta Malaspina established a hospital for "poor nobles" in 1372, he extended eligibility to those qualified by any *scientia*. Jurists, however, reserved special standing for their own sort of knowledge. They also repeated Bartolus's conclusion that a law professor reading for twenty years was automatically ranked as a count.[64] Nor were lawyers hurt by the bruising side debates on which type of nobility was to be preferred—lawyers versus physicians, doctors versus knights[65]— simply because lawyers did most of the writing and did not give their opponents much of a hearing.

The legal profession offered practical advantage to would-be nobles. It was open to those with sufficient funds and talent to obtain professional education; hence upwardly mobile families such as Verona's Pindemonte and Verità and Vicenza's Arnaldi, Feramosca, and Repeta sent children to university.[66] Still, the status value of *scientia* had a drawback for the lineage as a whole: the lawyer's nobility was personal and could not pass to offspring who did not enter the profession. As a practical disadvantage, the Vicentine college accepted, on average, fewer than two new members annually.

Notaries, too, had specialized knowledge and sought to parlay their *scientia* into nobility. The Trevisan college staked that claim as early as 1395. Its counterpart in Vicenza forbade admission of those whose fathers practiced manual or "barbarian" trades, lest the honor and *nobilitas* of the profession be stained by those unfit "in nobility and learning." Verona's college recalled that the notariate had always been sought by the most noble citizens.[67] They faced an uphill battle, however. Bartolus had flatly declared that "the notariate is not a rank" and thus nobility was not annexed to it. "The work of writers," sneered Ludovico Bolognini, "is a really vile thing."[68] No citizen could fail to notice notaries such as Vicenza's Scroffa, who tramped from village to village recording miserable transactions. If a college accepted infants for membership, as it did for several Arnaldi, how seriously could anyone take its members' claims to *nobilitas scientiae?* The Arnaldi, declining a risky claim, retired from the notariate before they consistently claimed nobility.

Another qualification for nobility was simple wealth. As Pagliarini noted of the Fiocardi family, "Although earlier they were simple citizens, now they are numbered among nobles because of the enormous wealth which they possess."[69] He was right about their riches—Fiocardi households ranked second in the city in the 1453 and 1477 *estimi*—but his definition of wealth as sole criterion for nobility would have appalled commentators. Dante in the *Convivio* rejected outright the emperor Frederick II's assertion (from Aristotle's

Politics) that wealth plus ancient good habits *(boni antiqui mores)* conferred nobility. Some followers added the neo-stoic notion that poverty might be a positive factor, freeing the individual from material distraction and eliminating the stain of "sordid earnings."[70] Bartolus was inclined to agree. He repeated the comment from Aristotle's *Ethics* that wealth contributed to happiness and the cultivation of magnanimity, which was a virtue; hence wealth contributed to nobility itself. But he also endorsed Dante's position that wealth was at best a "remote cause" of nobility.[71] Quattrocento humanists and jurists, at best, assigned wealth a very low priority in determination of nobility: material resources could assist virtue by promoting *otium* for study, or contribution to the *patria*, or liberality and charity, but had only accessory value and by themselves had no standing.[72]

Even if wealth might contribute to nobility, it had to be of the right sort. Baldus denied nobility to those living by "manual trades," Bartolus denied rank to those trading in *artes vilissimas*, and both were quoted with approval. To Lanfranchini, commerce, agriculture, and "vile arts" disqualified individuals for knighthood. Humanists respected the accessory value of inherited wealth, but Poggio drew upon Cicero's polemic against the "sordid gain" and cupidity of merchants to denigrate those who themselves acquired riches.[73] Acting on widespread prejudice, Verona's College of Notaries created a special and privileged category for those whose fathers had not practiced a trade. The Vicentine college poured scorn on the ignobility of notaries imbued with "bad ways" from their fathers' "mechanical and abject arts and barbarian trades," and sought to purge *rusticos et villes* from its ranks. Treviso's College of Nobles excluded those whose father or uncle was a countryman or had exercised a mechanical trade.[74] Bartolus's more generous interpretation, that the stain of *rusticitas* could be purged within a generation or two, and that a rustic's children or grandchildren could indeed be counted noble "as we see daily,"[75] was studiously ignored.

The problem was that nearly all patricians had to work for a living. Equal inheritance by males fragmented family patrimonies, dowries and taxes constantly drained liquidity, and land rents were insufficient to keep up appearances. Few, however, could rely on the two professions that were, by common consent, entirely honorable: arms and the law. Most Veneto patricians/nobles were active in trade. By itself this did not disqualify someone from the nobility: investment in a holding company or management of a wholesale operation was respectable enough. But in the Veneto, lacking great trading companies, the line between detached management and active management, or between wholesale and retail, was difficult to draw. Jurists, otherwise scrupulous in definitions, chose not to address the problem of which occupation was vile and which was not.

On the everyday level, enrollment in a guild whose trade might or might not be manual did not necessarily disqualify nobility: four of the early Verità entered the Veronese goldsmiths' guild, with no damage to the lineage.[76] Nor did the earlier Arnaldi and Feramosca cease to be styled *nobiles* or *egregios vires* even when standing in their cloth shops. Their claims to nobility were, however, vulnerable as long as their hands were close to merchandise. The second generation, quicker to claim nobility and thus more sensitive to potential criticism, found it safer to retire to trade that could be maintained by contracts alone. Silvestro Arnaldi kept up the wholesale end of the business, and usury, but he gave up the shop and the draper's trade. Several documents find him in other people's shops, or in the tavern of the Ox, or in the open air: he deemed it better to suffer muddy boots and boorish company than be perceived as a shopkeeper.

A sixth criterion for nobility, descent and antiquity of lineage, derived from Aristotle's perception of moral development. Noble actions repeatedly performed became habit, then second nature; nature could be transmitted to offspring; and performance of good actions across several generations could reinforce or consolidate that nature. Given Aristotle's stature it is not surprising that few authors dismissed the position altogether, but none save the Venetian aristocrat Francesco Barbaro accepted it without reservation.[77] For Dante, in the *Convivio*, personal nobility or *virtù* could not be transmissible, rendering issues of descent and antiquity moot. Elsewhere, in the *Monarchia*, he distinguished between individually achieved nobility *(nobilitas proprium)*, which he took from Juvenal, and nobility derived from ancestors *(nobilitas maiorum)*, which echoed Aristotle; he preferred the former but did not reject the latter.[78] The other great authority, Bartolus, was also ambivalent. His insistence that nobility had to be conferred by princely authority demanded a personal nobility, and his insistence that nobility derived from descent *(ex progenie)* lapsed with the great-grandson denied long-term heritability, but elsewhere he validated local custom that permitted the nobility of "all descendants."

In the Quattrocento, the *sic et contra* format of humanist dialogues and jurists' treatises allowed writers to present both ethical/personal and hereditary/lineage qualifications without absolutely endorsing either. Those who aspired to synthesis could fall back on Baldus, who accepted nobility through ancestry when combined with personal *virtus*, and on Bartolus, who endorsed those who claimed their parents' nobility as long as they themselves lived in a *virtuosus* manner: "When a noble son is born of noble parents and lives virtuously, he shall be deemed noble according to all [authorities]; but when there is born a reprobate son who has bad ways, thereby he is infamous and so loses nobility."[79] This allowed hereditary nobility, which would support the lineage, but not simple nobility of blood, which turned nobility into a mere byproduct of reproduction. It was tidy, sensible, and useful. Still, even Bartolus's *via media* left practical issues unresolved. What qualified ancestors as sufficiently great to pass on nobility, how long did it take to establish *antiquitas*, and how eminent did descendants have to be? Surely the ancestral "virtue, fame, glory, power, high offices, wealth, and clientage" required by Salutati set too high a standard, and surely the decade or two proposed by Bartolus was insufficient.[80]

For would-be aristocrats such as the Arnaldi, whose archive stretched back only to 1300 and whose forebears were at best notaries, argument from ancestry provided a thin claim only. For most of Vicenza's notables, Battista Pagliarini, too, had little to offer. Sometimes he found a document or fable that located a great deed or an ancestor two or three centuries past, but more commonly he found scant backing for eminence and long descent. The Rusticelli, to take a typical example, were "ancient and noble citizens," but Pagliarini found only three names from the mid-Trecento. If the Revesi "shone with antiquity and noble blood, and produced men of wealth and friendships and noble marriages," Pagliarini offered only a single physician of 1370 as proof.[81] He tried hard—he gave the Arnaldi several ancestors who were not, in fact, part of the lineage—but his prosopography could not stand up to cursory scrutiny. In most cases he simply gave up the attempt, styling a family *antiqua* without dates and *nobilis* without explanation.

For many, like the Arnaldi, who possessed several claims to noble status but found no firm ground in any, episcopal investiture provided a qualification of last resort. By ancient tradition, backed by centuries of diplomas (some forged), the bishop of Vicenza was duke, count, and marquess;[82] his vassals were by definition noble.

On 17 September 1452, Andrea and Tommaso Arnaldi entered the bishop's audience hall and, on bended knee, declared readiness to swear fidelity and vassalage to the bishop. His lieutenant agreed to the request and invested them with a golden ring; they gave their oath. In return they were invested with a fief once held by Giovanni Volpe. The brothers then repeated the procedure, and received investiture of another fief once held by Antonio Cozzi. The fiefs were insubstantial—the right to collect tithes in the hamlets of Nuvoledo and Porcileto, and the right to put overseers in Porcileto—but they mattered less than infeudation itself. The Arnaldi held the title in sufficient regard to seek reinvestiture with every change of generation.[83] Their Veronese counterparts, for whom tithes were significant portions of patrimonies, regarded episcopal fiefs as important enough to warrant furious opposition to Bishop Ermalao Barbaro's efforts to regain control over them.[84]

The title was safer than most. Seldom mentioned in polemics or treatises, episcopal investiture was not burdened with theoretical disqualifications. Praxis overrode the few that remained. Sticklers such as Baldus had said that those who did not actually rule counties and marquisates should not be called counts and marquesses.[85] Common opinion, however, still regarded the bishop of Vicenza as duke, count, and marquess: chroniclers recalled that fact, the commune sponsored *tableaux vivantes* to impress it upon the citizenry,[86] and documents of investiture mentioned it incessantly. Baldus had said that "Nobility is not born in the blinking of an eye. Only an ancient fief makes for nobility, not a new one,"[87] but if the Arnaldi's investiture was recent, their fiefs were ancient. And it mattered little that the ceremony fell short of strict standards for establishing a feudal relationship, since the Arnaldi never performed the act of homage: in the words of fellow citizen Daniele dall'Aqua, *fidelitas* was the same as homage.[88]

Even then, in 1452, the Arnaldi were not consistently styled *nobiles*. No single event made them noble. Over the years they stockpiled potential qualifications, adding claim to claim, until the cumulative power of these requisites reached critical mass. Nobility itself was too fluid to permit any clearer understanding.

Noble Is as Noble Does

The single point of consensus in the debate over nobility was the ultimate sanction of public opinion *(fama)*. A noble was one generally deemed noble. This was inherent in the humanist argument for *virtù* as primary qualification: in the absence of a moral tribunal, only public acknowledgment of a noble soul sealed nobility. The figure of Lorenzo de' Medici, in Poggio's dialogue, appealed to "what the crowd holds, which has the greatest authority in matters of this sort." Cristoforo Landino agreed.[89] Bartolus, who otherwise insisted on definite concession by a superior authority, admitted that an individual could be deemed noble simply because "he is called or considered noble." The quality of nobility that makes a person distinct from plebeians, he noted, should be understood "according to our common understanding" or "according to our customs," and always required public acceptance.[90]

The crowd might accept something other than formal title. If a noble had to act nobly, the opposite equation might hold true: sustained noble manners could lead to public acknowledgment of nobility. Bartolus thought so: a generation or two of worthy living could purge the stain of *rusticitas*. Giovanni Conversini listed mores among the primary qualifications for nobility. Cristoforo Lanfranchini, complaining of wool merchants who bought the trappings of knighthood and unworthily claimed its status, tacitly admitted that many successfully did so. So did later aristocrats in Verona, blasting those who simply assumed honorific titles and waited a few years until pretended eminence was generally accepted.[91]

PATRICIATES required networks of clients, patrons, and allies. Venetian nobles plotted in and out of councils, buying and trading votes and forming factions that resisted attempts to curb electioneering. On the neighborhood level, they used gifts and bequests to build relationships that translated into favors, protection, or support. Public office and entry of underage sons to the Great Council were among the prizes; so were the judicial concessions *(gratiae)* needed to get the errant out of hot water.[92] Florentine moralists stressed the necessity of choosing and keeping friends; *ricordanze* exhaustively recorded co-parentage and marriage alliances, and bitterly recalled the penalties—harsh tax assessments and sentences of exile—which resulted when enemies gained power. Florentine archives are filled with letters of recommendation and supplication, memoirs tracing friendships, betrayals, and vendettas, and treatises extolling *amicitia*.[93]

Patricians in the Veneto certainly knew the mechanisms and the imperatives for utilitarian exchanges. The early Arnaldi adopted a strategy of residential and occupational endogamy, coupled with commensurate dowries, to consolidate horizontal alliances. Later, more ambitious generations preferred neighborhood exogamy and asymmetrical dowries to secure linkages with greater families. Throughout, the family carefully chose co-parents to establish both horizontal and vertical connections that complemented, but did not duplicate, those made by marriage. They cultivated affines, who proved especially useful as mediators, executors, and witnesses. For all families, long-term tolerance of tenant debt reflects strategies for building networks of supporters in the countryside. Veronese patricians had rural employees listed in urban tax rolls—whereby they would pay lower taxes—which had the same effect.

Turbulent municipal politics equally demanded strong friendships. If Venetian magistrates now held supreme authority, that fact only heightened competition for the routine administrative posts that remained to natives. In the urban communes of Vicenza and Padua, if we give credence to official complaints, favoritism and personal influence were all-determining. Councillors stuffed ballot boxes to elect friends and hid enemies' ballots. Corrupt voting for rural vicars put the names of "ignoble and unsuitable" citizens into electoral purses and excluded those "of good condition and reputation."[94] Judges and high-ranking fiscal magistrates were regularly accused of extortion and misuse of office; Vicenza's deputies complained of the "insolence" of officials who ignored their orders. Litigants in civil suits adopted the "bad and enormously corrupt custom" of enlisting the services of powerful citizens "through money, friendship or kinship" to intimidate judges. The mighty Jacopo Muzani beat up inferiors yet went scot-free because friends and relatives sat on criminal courts. To combat what he perceived as endemic factionalism, the Vicentine humanist Ognibene da Lonigo wrote a lengthy and sad plea for "the unity and concord of citizens."[95] In Verona, increasingly contentious eligibility scrutinies likewise required patricians to cultivate friends, protectors, and dependents, lest they suffer political oblivion.

IT MIGHT BE SAID, and not just facetiously, that the Arnaldi finally arrived at the pinnacle of Vicentine society when they started fighting with the mighty Bissari family. When they were simple citizens, and even when documents began to call them *nobiles* with some regularity, the Arnaldi had resolved disputes in a peaceful manner: they arbitrated conflicts with top-ranking patricians Biagio Angiolelli or Tebaldo Loschi, and sought recourse against patrician debtors in civic tribunals.[96] In the summer of 1502, however, Silvestro Arnaldi and his son Andrea brawled with the noble Francesco Bissari and his two sons, with wounds inflicted on both sides. At the podestà's exhortation the Arnaldi and Bissari made formal peace, but soon drew arms once more. Again the podestà stepped in, and the five shook hands and kissed, swore never to offend each other or the other's servants and followers, and promised hefty payments—a thousand ducats for verbal insults and three thousand for injurious deeds—for future infractions. This peace was to be "perpetual, pure, simple, sincere and irrevocable," but apparently broke down within two years: each side petitioned the Venetian Council of Ten for ratification of the earlier truce.[97]

If the Arnaldi felt they had to prove themselves by taking on a top clan, they chose a fine opponent. The Bissari had been prominent for centuries,

and had proven their mettle in a series of plots and feuds. In the Quattrocento the family produced the distinguished jurist-orator Matteo Bissari, and
retained the ancient privilege of leading the bishop's horse in processions.
The family was large and rich, with at least ten households and eight seats
on the city's Great Council; Francesco Bissari's *estimo* ranked him among
the wealthiest 4 percent of city households. Pagliarini listed the Bissari second in the hierarchy of Vicentine nobility.[98] By any standard the Bissari were
old blood and far more important than the Arnaldi, but Silvestro and Andrea fought them to a draw.

Fighting was serious business for the upper ranks. It would be impossible
to prove that they were more violent than other groups, but they had long
enjoyed that image. A "reputation for violence, excessive power put into the
service of particular interests and not the common good" had stimulated an-
timagnate laws in the later thirteenth century.[99] Trecento Florentine chronicles associated organized violence with the *grandi*, humanists associated
wealth with contempt for law, and the figure of the noble predator became
a literary commonplace. A perceived patrician predilection for aggression,
vendetta, hot temper, arrogance, and bloodshed was not, of course, a product of mere thuggery. Honor was a primary qualification for nobility, fully
as strong as any title conferred by an external authority, and the imperative
of personal and family honor had to override civic norms for pacification.
"Everyone in the house must take up arms in the attack," said Baldus, "for
an injury to one discolors the whole house."[100]

In the Quattrocento, the great houses of the Veneto fought without pause.
In Verona, Andrea d'Arco murdered Enrico Dal Brolo in 1464–65; a decade
later Francesco Bollani and Leonardo Malaspina were more creative, hiring
a leading artist to paint obscene images and figures of cuckolds on the walls
of Cristoforo Sagramoso's house. About the same time the Venetian Senate
proceeded against members of the Maffei, da Vico, Brenzone, and Lazise families, who gathered their "servants and associates" to kill Bartolomeo Verari.
At the end of the century the Council of Ten sent an envoy to investigate
and prosecute "many things which disturb the peace of our state," particularly the misdeeds of Pietro Salerno.[101] Padua's Camposampiero and Dotti
gathered private armies for ambush and slaughter, which did not end when
Antonio Dotti was cut down by his own sons. In Friuli, the long conflict between the Savorgnan and della Torre drew toward ghastly climax in civil war
after 1509.[102]

Silvestro Arnaldi, consciously or not, participated in a long Vicentine tradition of patrician feuding. Upper-class blood flowed without cease: Antonio

Angiolelli was cut down by Cristofano Vivaro and Cristoforo Nievo in 1414; Nicolo Braschi was killed by unknowns in the main square in the 1430s. The saintly Lorenzo Giustianiani refused the bishopric of Vicenza in 1433, in part because of the "daily disputes of the noble and powerful" in the city. The situation failed to improve: a sampling of the documentation shows Marco Nievo struck down by Andrea Pagello in 1460; Cristoforo Barbarano wounded by Leonello Nievo in 1473; Francesco Pagello accused of assaulting the podestà's vicar, and various Merzari accused of killing Bernardino da Porto two decades later; Giovanni Loschi murdered by Leonardo Trissino, Girolamo Traversi killed by unknowns, and Leonardo Fabri victim to Antonio Nicolo Loschi, all in 1494; Gregorio Nievo wounded by Gianpiero Barbarano in 1503; and Marco Gallo attacked by Francesco Volpe the next year. Giacomo Trento barely escaped the army of his son-in-law Leonardo Trissino in 1502; three months later he was warned not to pursue his own quarrel with Sebastiano Pagello; two years after that someone threw a spear from the window of his house in an attempt to kill Ludovico Aimerico.[103]

These perpetrators and victims were all born into the great families of the city. While the cases are known because miscreants were prosecuted, either penalties were not severe or pardons and commutations of sentences were easily obtained. Exile proved nearly impossible to enforce: in 1494 Giacomo Poiana, banished from the Venetian dominion, operated in an "audacious and factious manner" from his Vicentine stronghold.[104] Guilty parties suffered no lasting disabilities. They certainly did not suffer shame and the obloquy of fellow citizens: Leonardo Malaspina went on to high office in Verona, Giacomo Trento served as communal deputy and ambassador in the midst of his quarrels, and Jacopo Muzani entered Pagliarini's pantheon of worthies despite his depredations.

Venetian magistrates did what they could, taking the worst offenses into the courts of the capital, ordering potentially factious patricians to desist, and arranging peace among families which, like the Arnaldi and Bissari, agreed to reconciliation. They passed law after law against bearing arms, and tinkered constantly with the law of exile. But local governors had sorely limited resources; one of their only remedies, in fact, was to lift the ban of an exile who returned to kill another outlaw, which only compounded cycles of violence. Moreover, central magistracies frequently overruled outright intervention in the interests of preserving subjects' judicial autonomies, which allowed local private influence to mitigate penalties, and they undercut their own efforts by licensing patricians to bear arms.[105] Despite good intentions, Venetians only put a damper on intrapatriciate violence and rarely prevented the first outbreak of any one conflict. The habit of fighting was too deeply ingrained, too necessary to maintenance of honor, and too obvious a means of self-assertion.

TWO ARNALDI PALACES of the Quattrocento are extant. The first has been dated to around 1440; in that year, Andrea Arnaldi undertook major construction (or reconstruction), making payment for floor planking, an inlaid chest, a small wardrobe, a wooden grate, and a staircase.[106] The facade is well preserved, with a portal and two lines of windows framed in the elaborate tracery of the Venetian Gothic style. The palace is not as large and grand as those of longtime nobles such as the Schio, Valmarana, and Thiene, but still is substantial, freestanding, and strongly individualized compared to the anonymous structures of ordinary citizens. As did older and greater clans, the Arnaldi broke with local tradition and did not provide an external arcade to shelter shops or passers-by: the sheer facade, with barred ground-floor windows and massive portal, kept the public well removed. While the Arnaldi drew up wills and (very occasionally) contracts within the palace, they never used it to store merchandise or meet customers, and reserved domestic space for family and intimates. The palace seems well suited to the first Arnaldi generation, assertive and slightly aloof but far from arrogant.

The next generation found the dwelling inadequate. We can only surmise the cause of their dissatisfaction. The Gothic passed out of fashion, and Arnaldi now inclined to call themselves noble may have wished to declare refinement through new architectural styles. They may have demanded more personal space and privacy than had their fathers and mothers: later patrician palaces in Vicenza were invariably larger than their antecedents. Whatever the reason, at some point in the 1476–89 period Gaspare II and Girolamo hired Lorenzo da Bologna to build a new palace. Lorenzo was the leading architect in the city, "engineer" of the cathedral and the new shrine on Monte Berico, and designer of important family burial chapels, the apse of the Santa Corona, and the new church of S. Rocco. He also erected palaces for great families such as the Valmarana, da Porto, and Thiene. Simply putting him on the job set the Arnaldi in the top ranks of patrons. His project for the Arnaldi did not completely reject its Gothic predecessor: the two shared a common wall, and Lorenzo's facade offered a mirror image of window and door placements. The rooms of the new palace, however, were considerably higher and the windows more massive than those of the original.[107] Later Arnaldi asked for continuity with the dwelling of their ancestors, but also for a grander statement of their own standing.

Evidence for decoration of either palace is scarce. It may, however, be possible to draw an analogy with the palace of Verona's Aleardi family, who were similarly well-to-do but not preeminent socially and whose dwelling in 1407 likewise consisted of basement, ground floor, upper floor of "principal apartments," and attic. An inventory described its furnishings in nearly three hundred lots, some—a chest with towels and linen, three cushions, seven handtowels—combining several items: interior spaces were fully supplied, even crowded. Painted blanket racks, rugs, and devotional images suggest that the Aleardi sought elaborate decoration in addition to comfort. Bedrooms clearly demarcated from common living spaces afforded some measure of personal privacy, though the family slept two or more to a room.[108]

There are hints that in the Veneto, albeit not on the scale of Florence,[109] patrician demand for luxury goods was growing. Elegant ceramics from Bassano and Padua began to reach markets in considerable volume. In Veronese tax rolls, the number of silk workers and goldsmiths doubled, the number of hatmakers rose from zero to seventy-seven, painters tripled their ranks, and those in the paper and book trade more than quadrupled. Much luxury production was destined for export, but some must have passed into the big new palaces. The wealthy also filled their houses with servants: the overall average per household doubled, but patricians hired most of the increase. Herlihy concludes that "the rich were enjoying a more elegant, comfortable and perhaps refined life in 1502 than they had in 1425."[110]

There is also evidence of sumptuary legislation, which is difficult to use but may have indicative value. Paduans would not have passed laws against women's clothes and ornaments if wealthy families did not actually buy such fineries, and constant reenactment of the laws indicates that the wealthy went on buying them, regarding fines as a kind of luxury tax. In 1441 Veronese councils passed a law against women owning more than one silk garment, justifying the move on moral grounds but possibly aiming to protect the city's wool industry. However, an expanded attack on women's luxuries in 1446—the ordinance ran to twenty-two detailed clauses—was soon rescinded because, councillors admitted, it could not be enforced. Venetians would not have passed eight major laws in the 1450–1500 period to prevent the immobilization of precious metals, had there not been strong demand for jewelry and cloths of gold and silver; and they would not have passed eight laws if the wealthy had respected the first.[111]

CHAPTER EIGHT

SPIRITUALITY

AND RELIGION

The Power of Prayer

*B*ARTOLOMEO DAL Bovo three times and Manfredo Repeta once addressed long prayers to Christ. Both focused on Jesus crucified: Repeta meditated at length on his appearance and suffering, while dal Bovo pondered the seven last utterances.[1] The prayers would seem to partake of late medieval Christocentrism, which featured the cult of the Passion, Corpus Domini and other Jesus-directed feasts, and eucharistic devotions.[2] As such the prayers could be placed alongside a number of works that circulated in northern Italy: the Veronese Matteo Bossio's *Sermo in passionem Jesu Christi,*[3] Antonio Cornazzaro's *Vita di Christo,*[4] Ubertino da Casale's *Arbor vitae crucifixae Jesus,*[5] the many works of the Veronese Paolo Maffei (died 1453),[6] Ludolph of Saxony's *Vita Christi,*[7] Domenico Cavalca's *Specchio de croce,*[8] St. Bernard's contemplation of the Passion,[9] and so forth.

The parallel, however, is not exact. Christocentrism paired themes of penitence and imitation: the faithful meditate on the Passion and realize the divide between earthly depravity and divine glory; aware of the greatness of their sin, they are led to contrition and Christ-like mortification, charity, and humility. Lorenzo Giustiniani and others urged the faithful so to immerse themselves in Calvary that they felt themselves crucified.[10] Dal Bovo and Repeta had altogether different intentions. Both addressed a Jesus reigning in heaven: the Passion had happened once and for all, and Christ was now dispenser of favor rather than model for imitation. Repeta wished admission to heaven after forgiveness of the "multitude of my sins," but he did not dwell on his sinfulness. His aim was practical: the prayer *Precor te* that he copied might gain him 6,666 days of indulgence.[11] Dal Bovo desired relief from tribulations, persecutions, and the "wrath of my enemies" as well as entry into paradise: he asked protection from external threats rather than cure of his own vices. Because of Christ's past self-sacrifice and kindness to humanity, these authors hoped for similar grace in the present, but they did not deem self-abasement necessary to obtain it.

A similar pragmatic spirit pervades their prayers to saints. Neither sought imitable models of sainthood: Mary as mother, nurturer, or protector, Bridget as ascetic, Lucy as martyr. They invoked the divine for immediate and direct favor: that Bridget protect against tempest, that Anthony reveal the location of stolen goods, that Sebastian drive away the plague, and that Erasmus provide food, clothes, and material necessities. Dal Bovo's twice-copied poem on Lucy stressed her healing of incurable illness.[12]

A second, specialized type of prayer accompanied the Mass. Dal Bovo and Bartolomeo Muronovo copied prayers to be uttered at elevation of host and chalice, simultaneous with the priest's words of consecration. Similar prayers have been noted for Germany, France, and England from the thirteenth century on. Through these prayers, the laity assumed an active voice in eucharistic devotions and established a separate and largely autonomous type of devotion. This quasi-liturgy was parallel and counterpoint to that of the celebrant: "choreographic directions and verbal cues were provided by the chancel rite, but the script was different."[13]

Congregants thereby transformed eucharistic observance, shifting the focus away from communion to elevation. Indeed, gazing upon and offering prayers to the transsubstantiated body and blood, the laity reduced any need for consumption of the elements, since all sensory reception of Christ was equal. This in turn relieved a tension in sacramental thought. To paraphrase Miri Rubin, potentially contradictory themes attached to the Eucharist: it required confession, which reduced frequency, but was also necessary for salvation, which thus required constant contact.[14] Viewing chalice and host, substituting the sense of sight for that of touch, was as efficacious as eating consecrated bread and obviated the need for frequent confession. It also made the Mass a personalized experience, emphasizing private prayer and downgrading collective reception of the Sacrament by the community.

This did not sit well with many clerics, who viewed lay participation with suspicion. Veronese parish priests complained bitterly that members of one confraternity assisted in the Mass to the extent of singing along with their priest. Preachers grumbled that their flocks no longer bothered to make confession, and that congregations quickly drifted away after elevation.[15] But popular preference could not be gainsayed, and several churchmen supplied private Mass-prayers: Aquinas (perhaps), several popes, and compilers of numerous books of hours. Paolo da Certaldo told his readers to go to confession only once or twice yearly, but to hear Mass and "see our Lord" daily. Communion, in fact, became relatively infrequent precisely when Masses proliferated;[16] the cult of paraliturgical prayer provides a partial explanation for this apparent paradox.

Beyond the sacraments lay sacramentals, objects blessed by a priest that could be taken out of church and used to protect the community—candles to ward off storms, herbs to protect houses, holy water to guard crops, and the like. To Repeta, a figure of the Lamb of God, made of wax, balsam, and oil of chrism, would ease childbirth, repel lightning, guard against shipwreck, induce deathbed redemption, and secure triumph over enemies. Sacramentals preserved the imperative of clerical mediation and so were officially tolerated. There were dangers, however, since in practice it proved difficult to contain protective religion within the realm of the clerical and liturgical. Sacramentals, notes Robert Scribner, "could slide over into the field of magic," and were often controlled and manipulated by the laity.[17]

To keep away storms for a year, said dal Bovo, write down the Gospel for Ascension Day, slip the paper under the altar cloth before that day's Mass, retrieve it afterward, and tie it to the clapper of the church bell.[18] The power of the Mass, then, was appropriated and infused into a material object, joining the Word; both powers were then broadcast with the tolling of the bell. Jesus sacrificed (in the Mass) joined with Jesus ascended (the Gospel text) to protect crops and town. Here the priest was an unwitting accomplice to lay self-help: we are dealing with a quasi-sacramental. As Scribner notes wryly, the belief that lay agency could channel sacred power into the material world constituted "a kind of popular Catholic version of the priesthood of all believers."[19] The Church was aware of usurpation of its jurisdiction, and sometimes cracked down on (mis)use of the Mass to work supplemental magic.[20]

Even more susceptible to lay appropriation were those sacred texts that did not require clerical iteration. Scripture written on paper or parchment could cure sickness or repel evil; examples date from earliest Christianity, and were later found throughout the West. Dal Bovo used snippets of psalms for mundane purposes such as expelling bedbugs, protecting himself in a dispute with kinsmen, hoping for sustenance, preventing miscarriage, and blessing a new house. To find stolen goods, one only had to put a passage of Psalm 144 under the head at bedtime and their location would be revealed in a dream.[21] A Perugian urged that the *Non nobis* (Psalm 113) be written on a piece of bread along with an incantation, and eaten, to cure the bite of a rabid dog. Going a step further, lay people detached portions of the liturgy and recited them as defensive prayer: the Creed, Pater Noster, Ave Maria, Gospel passages, Magnificat, *Nunc dimittis,* and *Miseris mei* warded off enmity and plague, stimulated love for friends, and secured pardon for sins at the point of death. The Athanasian Creed was thought to ease childbirth; Muronovo and dal Bovo copied it into their memoirs.[22]

Sacred history, too, provided a resource that laity could deploy on their own account: prayer summoned the power of past succor and bygone miracles to secure protection in the present. So dal Bovo addressed evil spirits that caused storms: "Coniuro vos," he thundered, and threw against them the facts of creation, Jesus' incarnation, advent, nativity, circumcision, baptism, fasting, Cross, Passion, death, burial, resurrection, and ascension, the coming of the Holy Spirit, and all the saints, angels, martyrs, confessors, and holy virgins. Women in childbirth were eased by an oration recalling that Anne brought forth Mary, Elizabeth brought forth John, and Mary brought forth Jesus, all without pain.[23]

It need not matter that words of power might make no sense. Muddled over centuries by people who did not speak the original language, subjected to truncation or interpolation, wonder-working formulas were often gibberish when they reached the Quattrocento. Still, they had acquired their own authority, independent of their ability to be understood. The prayer that dal Bovo addressed to St. Anthony, for example, consists of utterly disconnected phrases. The text had no less value for that fact: he copied it twice.[24]

Devotions in Veneto memoirs were, on the whole, pragmatic and optimistic. Writers offered remedies for specific problems and expected efficacy. They paid little heed to the pathological causes—temporal corruption or human sinfulness—which made alleviation necessary. Rather, they assumed that the world could be relieved and that laity had the capacity to induce divine intervention. The texts that they copied seldom support the widespread view of a later Middle Ages characterized by pessimism and obsessive guilt, and they seldom echo contemporary preachers' emphasis on the need for a life of penance.[25] Compilers in Verona and Vicenza did not dwell on the macabre, dance of death, fragility of life, or futility of earthly striving. Penitential confraternities flourished in the Trecento and Quattrocento, and—far from being mere social clubs—regularly practiced self-mortification;[26] memorialists, though, cared less for abasing the flesh than curing it. Dal Bovo's oration on Job is a case in point: he offered not meditation on the rottenness of the flesh but a recipe against intestinal worms.[27]

Their vision was not unfailingly rosy. Humans did sin and consequently endure hardship; sin required expiation, and so dal Bovo and Muronovo copied penitential psalms. The latter noted the vicious cycle that trapped humans, as poverty produced humility, which resulted in peace, which brought wealth, which led to *dominatio*, which inspired pride, which generated war, which led back to poverty. The brief passage, however, was immediately followed by great chunks of poetry, a medical opinion, and humanist correspondence: Muronovo raised a gloomy theme but dropped it quickly.[28] So, too, dal Bovo copied four sections of Lothario de' Segni (Innocent III)'s treatise on "contempt for the world."[29] But these passages—on inconveniences of old age, brevity of life, human destiny of hard toil, and cupidity of princes— were simple commonplaces by the later Quattrocento, and hardly constitute a call to renounce the world. Anyway, in quantitative terms dal Bovo's compilation was far more concerned to offer texts to alleviate earthly ills. One set of orations, if recited on rising, might ward off daily troubles altogether.[30] The world was less to be scorned than corrected; the solution to misery was less contrition and/or patient endurance than therapeutic action.

The memoirs offer three hagiographic models of piety. One, Bartolomeo Verità's life of St. Paul the hermit, counseled isolation and asceticism, but its inclusion among otherwise nonpenitential texts may be explained by his fondness for ancient and patristic writings.[31] The two others concerned saints whose missions lay within the world. Agapitus earned martyrdom by refusing to refrain from proclaiming his faith before the crowd, the emperor, and Roman officials. Roch, it is true, sometimes withdrew to do penance, but was better appreciated for service to plague victims. Both were models of activism, not contemplation or renunciation, and both, significantly enough, were laymen.[32]

The Power of Images

Memorialists' interests converged in fondness for the letter of Lentulus,[33] which purports to be a message from a Judean official to the Senate and *populus* of Rome. "There has appeared in these days," it begins, "a man of great power named Jesus Christ who is called by the people a prophet of truth, whom his disciples call the son of God, raising the dead and curing the sick." Its concern, however, is not Jesus' divinity and miracles but physical description of a man of middle height, with hazelnut-brown hair falling straight to the ears and curling thereafter, medium-ruddy face, plain and serene countenance, full bifurcated beard, and grey-green eyes. Comments on his demeanor close out the letter: "terrible in rebuke, calm and loving in admonition, glad, always preserving gravity, who has never been seen to laugh but has cried, . . . grave, spare and modest in conversation among the sons of men."

The epistle was enormously popular from the later Middle Ages on. It achieved widespread circulation in Ludolph of Saxony (Ludolph the Carthusian)'s *Vita Jesu Christi* of the mid-Trecento, known from many manuscripts and from several printed editions.[34] Although Lorenzo Valla denied its authenticity in 1440,[35] copyists and consumers felt otherwise. The letter is probably the most common spiritual text in Veneto libraries and archives.[36] In manuscript form it appears almost without variation; such scribal care is very rare and testifies to the text's solemn authority. It is found in both humanist miscellanies and humble memoirs, testifying to its appeal across the spectrum of the literate.

Scripture was silent regarding Jesus' appearance; to remedy that omission, the letter of Lentulus invited the reader to supply a mental picture. In the words of the pseudo-Bonaventure, "Here one may interpolate a very beautiful meditation of which the Scripture does not speak."[37] That "internal visualization,"[38] in turn, was part of a larger program to draw the faithful closer to the human Lord by encouraging them to participate sensibly in his earthly career through imaging. The *Zardino de oration*, for example, encouraged readers to locate the Passion narrative in "a city that is well known to you. . . . And then too you must shape in your mind some people, people well-known to you, to represent for you the people involved in the Passion,"[39] so that sacred accounts might be memorable and vivid. Since projection of a neighbor's face onto the Savior might seem improper, Lentulus provided the image. Here, too, the laity's role shifted from passive to active, their faith deepened not by simple meditation on the Scripture event but by representation of and sharing in its physical setting and human company.

Several other apocryphal texts promoted sacred imaging. Among them is a pseudo-letter of Pilate to the emperor, excusing his own conduct and placing blame for Jesus' death on the Jews, which dramatized the immediate circumstances of the crucifixion. Dal Bovo and many compilers paired it with the letter of Lentulus.[40] The epistle of Pilate originally formed part of a "gospel of Nicodemus," which vividly narrated the Passion and Jesus' descent into hell; there circulated, as well, separate works on the deeds and death of Pilate that visualized the scriptural account. Other apocryphal texts, such as the legend of St. Veronica and pseudo-Dionysus's letter on the deaths of Peter and Paul, extended imaginative re-creation into the era of the early Church. Kieckhefer notes an "unprecedented torrent of such materials" from the Trecento on.[41]

Other genres of devotional works likewise sought to supplement the Gospels and render them visually accessible through "narrative elaboration and systematic description."[42] Ludolph's *Vita* offered dramatized re-creations of events, as did the pseudo-Bonaventuran *Meditations on the Life of Christ* and other graphic texts. In that literature, the reader is asked to undertake nonmystical meditation, absorbing the scene through all five senses, just as Repeta contemplated the "troubled senses, transfixed heart, wracked body, bloody wounds, spread hands, stretched sinews, clamoring mouth, hoarse voice, pallid face, teary eyes, groaning throat, thirsting lips, bitter taste of salt, thrown-back head" of Jesus on the cross. Vicentine *laude* used the device of direct address, placing the reader in dialogue with Christ amid vivid physical descriptions of the Passion.[43]

Although the Passion was central to this highly charged literature, texts were not exclusively Christocentric. One meditation copied into a Quattrocento Veronese miscellany framed the account of Jesus' last days with the story of Mary Magdalen: her sorrowful conversation with John and the Virgin, her travel to Jerusalem, her place in the crowd before Pilate, her witness of the scourging and crucifixion, and her presence at the resurrection.[44] Use of the second-person familiar voice to address the Magdalen makes the reader a participant and tightens the bond with the saint. Meditations on Mary before the cross, and the common genre of the *planctus* that inscribed Mary's lamentations, equally induced a sense of immediacy and personal witness. Verona's regular staging of the Annunciation to and marriage of Mary, similarly, provided the citizenry with Scripture cast in palpable terms.[45] Preachers' edifying stories *(exempla)*, made vivid by histrionics and costumes, gave visual and narrative form to doctrine in terms even the simplest could grasp.[46] Heaven, purgatory, and hell could also be known in sensory terms, making them directly accessible to the faithful and reducing the divide between life and afterlife.[47]

Painted and carved images, too, re-presented the divine, making sensible that which was concealed by passage of time, scriptural reticence, or distance between earth and heaven. Moreover, images had power to afford moral and spiritual guidance throughout life. In conception, wrote Maffeo Vegio, parents should keep a "seemly picture" in view, so that children begin life under divine tutelage; "deformed and monstrous figures" would enter parents' minds and induce physically or morally deformed offspring.[48] Children should have devotional images to teach and inspire faith, play with holy dolls, and enact make-believe Masses; images of monsters and devils would produce terror and vices in the young.[49] Interactive play was also recommended for adults: the mature Anthony of Padua coddled a figure of the baby Jesus. Images in the house, said Savonarola, focused the mind on God and banished worldly distractions. Pier Paolo Vergerio kept a picture of St. Jerome before him, "and with him present I do not dare to say or do or even think anything evil. Rather, by his exhortation, I am joyfully spurred to good studies and positive expectations." Images could clear the conscience at the end of life: so Giovanni Morelli's dying son embraced a panel of the Madonna with prayers and vows. Even condemned criminals might be saved through timely viewing of an edifying picture.[50]

The learned also worried about misuse. They recognized that the faithful might confuse signifier with signified, and insisted that images were but *simulcra*, visualizations of the divine that must be regarded as distinct from the divine itself. Giovanni Dominici delivered stern injunctions against over-ornamentation and overveneration of images, and Leonardo Bruni warned that the "unlearned mob" might actually adore *simulcra*. San Bernardino gave images a secondary place in devotions, and insisted that reverence was due images only as representations of the divine. Pico denied that images merited *latria*, the highest form of adoration.[51]

They fought an uphill and often losing battle. Firsthand depictions of the holy—the veil of Veronica, pictures of the Virgin painted by St. Luke (in Rome, Bologna, Loreto, and Venice), and the Lucchese crucifix carved by Nicodemus from life[52]—surely were more than *simulcra*, since the artifact had enjoyed direct contact with the holy. When other images wept, moved their eyes, nodded their heads, or sweated,[53] the faithful concluded that the divine was immediately present and regarded them with more than simple respect. Even ordinary images might be imputed with that power which their subjects possessed. This, too, was ancient: by the legend of Volusianus, for example, Tiberius was cured of leprosy when he saw the *vultum Domini* (evidently an image on cloth). Once images were accepted as powerful vehicles of instruction and inspiration, belief in their wonder-working capacity was perhaps inevitable, and certainly grew.[54]

People of the Veneto ignored the cautions of the learned. The commune of Verona ordered that city gates be painted with protective images of Virgin and child, the patron San Zeno, and saints Peter and Christopher. Caterina Zugliano ordered pilgrimage to the miracle-working picture of the Virgin at Monte Ortone. A street-side image of the Virgin saved a Venetian woman from a savage beating, and prayers to it effected over a hundred cures and rescues within eighteen months; soon it inspired construction of the great church of S. Maria dei Miracoli. To cure the "mal de 'l saniotto," wrote dal Bovo, visualize the image of the Virgin nursing her son, "such as one sees in many places." He pointedly prayed to *(ad)* an image of Christ, not before *(coram)* it.[55]

Widespread tendency to view the image as repository of the holy rather than its token created inextricable links between divine and depiction. Iconoclasm, therefore, attacked the sacred itself. Vicentines told the story of an artisan who robbed and killed a companion in the town of Lonigo. Reproved by an accomplice while counting his haul in an abandoned church, he was angered and hit a picture of the sorrowing Madonna in the eye and breast. The image bled copiously and alerted the populace to his hiding place; demons then carried him away.[56] To authorities, failure to protect images risked the vengeance of an offended deity: the community as a whole, and certainly its regime, would suffer from an individual's profanation. Venetian officials vigorously prosecuted such offenses: so the Senate ordered Vicentine governors to use all possible means to respond to a "most impious and desperate crime" against an image of the Virgin in the countryside. In the midst of the Ferrarese wars, a Republic hard strapped for cash proposed melting down a gold-encrusted altarpiece in Verona, but quickly dropped the suggestion when the outraged municipal commune threatened to cede the city to the enemy. Sacred space, by extension, required equally vigilant civil protection: councils of the capital demanded that provincial governors punish the theft of some chalices and a murder in a rural church.[57] For public officials no less than the mass of the faithful, divine honor was vested in canvas and wood, stone and decoration.

Pilgrimage

Three memorialists worshiped afar. Andrea Arnaldi in 1445 visited the shrine at Monte Ortone, south and slightly west of Padua, to fulfil the vow of his dying mother. His son Silvestro joined Manfredo Repeta in 1473 to travel to the Virgin's house at Loreto. Six years later Repeta left for Trent to view the body of the boy Simon, believed to have been ritually murdered by Jews.[58]

Andrea Arnaldi's mother died in November, an unpleasant time to be on the road; he delayed his mission until spring. Repeta enjoyed April weather on his first trip, and made the second in October, also a fine time to be abroad. He took care not to disrupt his family, leaving only when his wife was not pregnant and his children were safely out of the dangerous first year of life. He traveled by horse, with a personal servant. His accounts dwelt less on spiritual benefits of pilgrimage than on the voyage itself, as he carefully noted the mileage between towns but expended few words on his devotions.

That is not to say that pilgrimage was a purely festive or recreational undertaking. Repeta covered thirty-four "miles" daily on the Loreto journey, and twenty-one "miles" daily over rough mountain roads to Trent; his *meia* was much longer than an English mile.[59] The trip was no holiday jaunt. Further, his laborious detailing of the journey's stages may indicate not so much priority given to the mechanics of travel as deep respect for the very purpose of the holy journey. Tracing the route from home to shrine and back again with measured steps, Repeta showed an intuitive sense of the liminoid quality of pilgrimage,[60] the sequential progression from mundane space to holy space and return to the mundane. Andrea Arnaldi, too, saw the voyage as a serious undertaking. His mother had ordered that he carry a candle as tall as himself, both heavy and awkward; he went before the bishop's vicar for dispensation to substitute two smaller candles. He would not change the vow's terms without permission from the highest ecclesiastical authority.

The most commonly adduced motives for pilgrimage, penitence and sickness,[61] were not factors in these voyages. Andrea Arnaldi went to ease his mother's soul, and Repeta had not been profoundly ill. Neither, to judge from spiritual texts copied into their memoirs, was inclined to dwell on innate unworthiness or unworthy deeds. In any case, if they sought cure or penance, there was no need for distant travel. Dozens were healed at the suburban shrine of Monte Berico, and suppliants climbed its hill with bare feet, or on their knees, or naked, or with *disciplina*.[62] Rather, pilgrimage offered spiritual benefits unavailable at home. Vicenza possessed no miracle-working pictures, as Monte Ortone did. The uncorrupted body of little Simon was more tangible and immediate than a relic of a bygone saint and, since the boy was deemed a Christ-figure *(Cristicollis)* crucified by enemies of the faith, was more powerful than ordinary relics. Loreto held the actual house of Mary as well as her image painted from life by St. Luke.

Loreto's artifacts alone did not attract Repeta: he remained for seven days awaiting special papal indulgence "from guilt and penalty." He could apply its benefits to his own soul or that of another. Andrea Arnaldi's trip to Monte Ortone was made on someone else's behalf. Pilgrimage was not purely self-directed, but aspired to grace that might be shared or assigned. Here alone the Veneto case belies the sparkling study of Victor Turner and Edith Turner, which asserts that "pilgrimage is exteriorized mysticism" (and mysticism is personalized devotion), and emphasizes pilgrimage as individual experience.[63] On the contrary, holy travel recapitulated community. Arnaldi reaffirmed bonds between the living and the dead. He and Repeta did not "abandon the tight structures of kinship and locality,"[64] but instead used the occasion to reinforce solidarities of blood and friendship. Andrea Arnaldi traveled with his brother Tommaso and their maternal aunt Guglielma. On both voyages Repeta was accompanied by Gregorio Fracanzani, kinsman to his wife; on the first, he also traveled with Silvestro Arnaldi, cousin to his future son-in-law.

Veneto pilgrims did not abandon older shrines. Testaments still ordered visits to Assisi, Jerusalem, and Compostella. Repeta and Bartolomeo Muronovo copied texts from the *Mirabilia urbis Romae*, which listed holy sites in Rome, and Muronovo included lists of indulgences available from Roman churches, a description of the Holy Land, and verses on Christ's sepulchre in Jerusalem.[65] But memorialists themselves went elsewhere. They shared a widespread preference for peripheral sites, away from political, institutional, or ecclesiastical centers—in anthropological terms, for "far" over familiar, sacred over mundane, pure over impure.[66]

Choice of Monte Ortone, Loreto, and Trent also suggests that they sought novelty. The cult of the wonder-working image in the southern Padovano was scarcely a decade old when Caterina Zugliano ordered her son to carry a huge candle there. The shrine at Loreto, it is true, was very old, as the Virgin's house reached its final site in 1295. Papal indulgences date from 1375. Even then, however, the cult remained regional. It attained peninsula-wide prominence only a century later, as a consequence of papal initiative: a new church was begun in 1470–71, and compilation of the record of the house's translation commenced at that time. Repeta's pilgrimage in 1473, then, owed more to current ecclesiastical promotion than to traditional observance.[67]

Simon of Trent's cult was even more a product of official sponsorship. The boy's body was discovered on 26 March 1475, Easter Sunday, and interrogation and torture of Jewish suspects began the next day and continued unabated for six weeks. Such celerity is rare in Quattrocento criminal justice: authorities clearly realized the event's potential for attracting popular devotion. They also sought to broaden the new cult, churning out publicity for a larger Italian audience. On 15 April the bishop's personal physician Gian Mattia Tiberino wrote a poem-letter to fellow Brescians, outlining what came to be the official version of events. This *Passio beati Simonis pueri Tridentini* appeared in print within a few days; thirteen more editions followed within the year, several in nearby cities of Italy. Tiberino's poetic summary of the supposed martyrdom, the "Sum puer ille Simon" that Repeta copied, followed almost immediately and quickly circulated in Italy and southern Germany.[68]

Those who sought to whip up fury against Jews and, not incidentally, to expand Trent's newly won position as a pilgrimage center, faced occasional opposition from the local archduke, the doge, the emperor and the pope. Bishop Johannes Hinderbach and podestà Giovanni da Salis outflanked enemies by rallying writers to their cause. Shortly after Archduke Sigismund suspended interrogations, Hinderbach asked Raffaele Zovenzoni to compose verses expressing his regrets that he could not now punish the Jews responsible and his complaints against the Jews who stirred Sigismund to block proceedings. Zovenzoni obliged, and became "Hinderbach's ally in promoting Simon's cult in Venice." In the summer of 1475, Hinderbach wrote inflammatory letters to Venice, Vicenza, Innsbruck, and Rome. The campaign was effective: Sigismund backed down. When in mid-July Sixtus IV ordered suspension of the trial until arrival of his envoy in Trent, Hinderbach resisted and continued to drum up support abroad. He wrote a *Historia beati Simonis Tridentini*, subsequently published a *De laudibus et interitu beati Simonis a Judaeis mactati*, and compiled an account of miracles attributed to Simon's body. Throughout 1475 and early 1476 Tiberino also kept busy, producing two *relazioni*, a *Historia*, and a *Historia completa* that were quickly printed in a number of cities, including Verona and Vicenza.[69] This, too, was effective, as the curia allowed trial and executions to proceed.

Writers throughout the Veneto jumped on the bandwagon. In the summer of 1475 Verona's Giorgio Sommariva put a *Tormenti del beato Simone da Trento* into print; he added a *Martirio del beato Simone da Trento*, an *Ennaratio sententiae a serenissima venetorum imperio in infidos Judaeos*, and a related *Martyrium Sebastiani Novelli trucidati a perfidis Judaeis* (concerning another supposed ritual murder). Compatriots Girolamo Campagnola and Leonardo Montagna provided short works. In 1475–76 Vicentines Guglielmo Pagello and Bartolomeo Pagliarini wrote seven letters about Simon, two orations against Jews, and an *apologia* of Hinderbach. The suffragan bishop of Vicenza, Pietro Bruti, published an *Epistola contra Judaeos* in 1477, demanding justice for Simon's murder; when Jews were expelled from Vicenza in 1486, he issued a congratulatory *Victoria contra Judaeos* in 1489. The Vicentine jurist Alessandro Nievo's *consilia* repeated now-frequent themes that Jewish usury was, in a metaphoric sense, simply another form of the bloodletting of Christians. Venetian humanists contributed to the growing bibliography.[70]

The ghastly cult was in no respect spontaneous, and at every stage was managed from above. Still, myriad religious consumers chose to accept it, and Repeta fully endorsed it. In his day in Trent, he went three times to gaze upon the "glorious body"; a single viewing was insufficient to satisfy his longing. He also spoke with the boy's father to gain a firsthand account.

Preachers and Preaching

Chronicles and memoirs singled out three preachers for special mention. Bernardino of Siena preached in Verona from November 1422 to February 1423, and in Vicenza between April and June of that year; he returned to Verona in 1436 or 1437, and to both Verona and Vicenza in 1443. His disciple Giovanni Capistrano remained in Verona for nearly a year (1437–38), sometimes ill in the monastery of Arcarotta but sufficiently strong to preach Advent and Lenten cycles; he returned there in 1451, after twelve days in Vicenza. Bernardino da Feltre preached in Verona four times after 1458, and at least five times in Vicenza and its countryside.[71]

All were Observant Franciscan friars. Secular clergy did not attract attention, if indeed they preached much.[72] Chronicles usually mentioned Conventual friars with disapproval, as spiritually and morally lax, and did not note their preaching. Reformed Dominicans, who shared the spotlight with Observant Franciscans in France and predominated in England,[73] and produced Italian champions Antoninus of Florence and Savonarola, had little impact in the Veneto. The Venetian Ludovico Barbo played a leading role in Dominican reform, but his influence was stronger in Venice and Florence than on the *terraferma:* the movement arrived in Vicenza only in 1464, and did not produce preachers of note.[74] If lay preaching was widespread in the Veneto, as it was in Florence,[75] the fact was not recorded.

The three friars were enormously popular, to judge from chronicles and memoirs. Bernardino of Siena was said to have preached before 25,000 Vicentines on 9 May 1423, before 30,000 at the feast of Corpus Domini, and before 20,000 on 20 June. Capistrano himself, according to Muronovo, twice estimated that 30,000 people, "all the populace of Verona," heard him on the piazza. A further 25,000, it was said, turned out in Vicenza, and "when he went through the city, it was necessary that friars and citizens defend him with clubs in hand, and it was not possible for them to defend him fully, so great was the passion of men and women, citizens and countrymen. Those who touched him considered themselves blessed, and they ripped off pieces of his cloak and kept them with great devotion."[76] As he departed, officials had to close the gates to prevent a massive outflow of people. Bernardino da Feltre's audiences were not counted, but he was said to have delivered ninety sermons before a "great influx of people" during Lent and Eastertide of 1493, and one hundred sermons in 1494.[77]

In the short term, their words moved many listeners to contrition. When Bernardino of Siena convinced Veronese to give up usury, the plague that then ravaged the city suddenly ceased. He induced Paduans to burn vanities in 1425, and a later Franciscan's condemnations persuaded the commune to enact stiff sumptuary laws. In the long term, however, audiences proved less receptive to calls for newness of life. Within a few decades of Bernardino's triumph, admitted his follower and namesake, Veronese had returned to open usury. In 1443 he urged Vicentines to expel Jews from their midst; this in fact happened, but not for forty-three years. Universal condemnation of usury was no more effective than Bernardino da Feltre's plea for a crusade against Turks or his campaigns against luxuries.[78]

Audiences did not ignore content altogether. Andrea Arnaldi, for example, praised the "many good *exempla*" that informed Bernardino of Siena's "fine teaching."[79] These longtime staples of popular homiletics, little stories drawn from hagiography, oral tradition, and contemporary life, dramatized points of doctrine to excite an unlearned audience and make teaching more memorable. Histrionic friars turned them into miniature plays, with props and costumes supplementing the spoken word—"preaching as complete spectacle."[80] A preacher might turgidly expound the theology of purgatory, but audiences preferred the *exemplum* of the Veronese whose spirit returned from the dead to describe the afterlife to skeptical Dominicans.[81] Successful friars avoided brooding on the depraved state of humanity and offered lively anecdotes instead. Bernardino da Feltre, for example, told the story of a Vicentine woman who refused to give up pomp and vanities, and derided those who rebuked her. One day at noon, an arrow from heaven killed her on the spot; the stench of her body was so great that none could approach it, and her tomb had to be sealed with pitch.[82]

Contemporary accounts of preaching in the Veneto, however, emphasized not the message but the messenger. The crowd, it would seem, was stirred less by words than by the cures and prodigies the preacher effected. When Bernardino of Siena came to Vicenza in 1443, chronicles made no mention of his teachings, and instead informed posterity that "he performed great miracles, and in particular revived twelve dead people." It was indeed a miracle, noted one, that Bernardino made peace among the factious citizens of Vicenza. Writers recorded not the themes of Capistrano's sermons but the "very great miracles" that he accomplished, partly by his own sanctity and partly by waving Bernardino's beret over the sick.[83] Later there was compiled a book of 2,547 miracles connected to Bernardino and Capistrano, those performed in person and those accomplished by invocation of their names. Many took place in Verona and Vicenza.[84]

Veneto accounts accurately mark Franciscans' shift in emphasis away from preaching and toward the preacher. Breaking with tradition that only Francis himself was regarded as hero, and an unpretentious one at that, Observants accepted the star system. The prophetic figure, through whom God spoke, gave way to the charismatic figure, personally empowered by God. Capistrano's tireless promotion of Bernardino's cult—waving the beret, and leaving three vials of his blood as relics to fortify Vicentine houses—was symptomatic of the new strategy. Among recent scholars, Andre Vauchez has seen danger in publicity given to the miracle-working preacher, as "apt to degenerate into a cult of personality."[85] At the time, though, writers welcomed it with enthusiasm. Memorialists and chroniclers carefully noted Bernardino's death in 1444, and recorded the massive celebration of his canonization six years later.[86] They made little mention of myriad other preachers who passed through their cities, perhaps full of good doctrine but not deemed holy in their own right.

Knowing the Future

Memorialists wrote to give order to their world. They found meaning and reassurance, in part, by sifting through temporal aspects of existence: genealogy and history taught right lessons from the past, and anagraphy and chronicle isolated what posterity would need to know about the present. They were concerned, as well, to chart an uncertain but menacing future, and they found a measure of control in texts that provided forewarning. Prophecy, divination, and prognostication were highly developed: anxieties were considerable, but so too were remedies.

Shortest and simplest were formulas for locating lost or stolen objects. These suffered opprobrium from a long line of clerics who condemned the use of holy texts to know the future or find lost goods: "the future belongs to God alone." As recently as 1455 the preacher Roberto Caracciolo da Lecce had warned Paduans against the "presumption of knowing future matters," and reproved prayer asking that "unknown things" be revealed. Bartolomeo dal Bovo, however, copied one such prayer twice, and regarded its intended results as miracles.[87]

The "Egyptian Days" text copied by dal Bovo, Andrea Arnaldi, and Bartolomeo Muronovo had greater application in daily affairs. "All Greek authors" deemed two dozen days unpropitious for a long list of activities: bloodletting, building, planting, buying, selling, lingering in a shameful place, indeed initiating "any good action." Penalties were dire. Those who fell ill on these days would not rise from bed; an infant born then would not live, or would live in poverty; a man who took a wife would have no good thereby or would remain with her for a few days only or would live with her in poverty; anyone traveling to a foreign land would perish or not return. In short, the reader should not undertake anything from which he or she might suffer harm.[88]

Texts of Egyptian days are very old, dating back to the third century by one reckoning, and circulated widely as far away as England. They, too, drew the fire of clerics: a thirteenth-century manual included the Egyptian days as a topic for inquisitors to raise with suspected heretics or magicians.[89] Once again, memorialists chose to draw their own lines between the licit and the doubtful, and opted for inclusion. They may even, as seen above, have relied on the Egyptian days in scheduling their marriages.

A third type of text, the almanac, moved the scale of prediction to yearly time. Girolamo Manfredi's *Prognosticum* for 1479 supplied weather forecasts and harvest estimates; Repeta, resident in the countryside and deriving the lion's share of his income from agricultural rents, summarized it in his register. Manfredi also, for urban and cosmopolitan readers, predicted eclipses, plagues, deaths of rulers in Italy and beyond, wars, and diplomacy for nearly every year in the 1475–94 period. Supply met strong demand, as his 1479 *pronostico* appeared in four Latin and one Italian versions, printed in cities from Bologna to Louvain; colleagues published many more.[90]

Almanacs, too, might have been subject to criticism, but knowing meteorological trends was too important to be shut off by clerical quibbling. Anyway memorialists and chroniclers in the Veneto did not use weather and other natural phenomena to delve into the mind of God: their interest was purely material. Unusual freezes, floods, and tempests were marvelous and worth noticing, but no chronicler saw them as evidence for God's wrath or coming trials. Even such prodigies as a plague of locusts or a spate of multiple births in Verona were recorded as curiosities or causes of fluctuations in food prices, not portents.[91] Lower-level prophecy, then, helped people of the Veneto pick their way through imminent opportunities and dangers, and held no implications beyond the ordering of quotidian life.

The same cannot be said of the apocalyptic texts that abound in memoirs and other manuscripts. Heterogenous in content, some were old and cryptic while others foretold specific events; some were purely political and predicted local dynastic changes; others were eschatological and looked to the trials immediately preceding the end of time. They have in common an expectation that the present age was drawing to a close, and that the coming age would produce upheaval in the world order.

Bartolomeo Verità preferred sybilline prophecies, which occupy twenty-eight folios of his *zibaldone*. These came in three types. The prophecy of the Tiburtine sibyl, a Greek text of around 378–390 reworked in Latin versions, anticipated a last emperor from the East who would rule for 112 years in prosperity, destroy pagan temples, and baptize nonbelievers; his reign would provide the calm before the arrival of anti-Christ. The text of the Cumean sibyl, an abbreviation of the Tiburtine that dates from around 1090, interpolated calamities, persecutions of churches, plagues, and famines that would befall humanity during anti-Christ's reign. The *Vaticinium sibillae Erithreae*, dated a century later, thought that the last emperor would arise in the West. The definitive version of around 1252–54 told a long allegorical tale of hens, roosters, eagles et al., referring to events and personalities in the reign of Frederick II; these were commonly updated in later manuscripts to refer to other conflicts.[92] The sibylline texts remained enormously popular in the early Renaissance among scholars such as Coluccio Salutati as well as provincial erudites such as Verità, and are commonly found in Veneto archives.[93]

A second category of prophetic texts consists of those associated with Joachim of Fiore. Repeta copied a fine example, published (so he claimed) by the Venetian Leonardo Giustiniani. Both attributions are spurious. Joachim's fame was such that writers and copyists often attached his name to legitimate their works; he could not have written a work so specific to Italian dynastic struggles of the later Quattrocento. Giustiniani, composer of love poetry and sacred songs, is associated with this prophecy only in Repeta's manuscript, and almost certainly did not write it; his name, too, was borrowed to give authority to the text. Whoever he was, the writer told a strange tale indeed. After the death of the "grand Lombard" before the fiftieth year (alluding to the death of Filippo Maria Visconti in 1447), a man of Romagna (i.e., Francesco Sforza) would come to rule in Milan. Far away, one Constantine would put Greece, Trebisond, Bosnia, Slavonia, and part of Hungary under subjection, then attack Italy and sack Rome in 1477. But a peasant would rise up from the Romagna in the 1480s, liberate Rome, conquer the Turk, and make all people Christian; with his aid, the holy man Zuane would return the Church to its pristine state, forcing cardinals, bishops, priests, and friars to "return to their lands as holy apostles."[94]

A third strand of prophecy foretold deliverance from the northwest. Dal Bovo and Verità cited the impending arrival of King Charles of France, who at age twenty-three could come to Italy with a great army and rule justly for a decade, then pass to Greece and be proclaimed emperor. Killing all who refused to adore Jesus Christ, conquering all by the might of God, Charles would travel to Jerusalem where, after rendering laud to God on Mount Olivet, he would die in great torment at the age of sixty-four. This "Second Charlemagne" legend attributed to Telesphorus of Cosenza—scholars doubt both his name and place of origin—was written in 1378–90 and "enjoyed the greatest vogue of any political prophecy in the fifteenth and sixteenth centuries." Venice was a center for manuscript production.[95]

The sibylline, Joachimite, and Second Charlemagne traditions hardly exhaust the repertoire of prophetic texts. Muronovo copied a long poem on the signs of the Last Judgment. Verità included varied works: on a coming pseudo-pope, future events in Venice and Verona, and the end of the world. Others are found in Veneto archives.[96] Most are apocalyptic but also optimistic, foreseeing overthrow of unjust rulers, reform of the Church, submission of enemies in the East, and conversion of pagans and non-Catholics. They perceive the end of time not in terms of judgment and mass consignment to hell, but as the welcome close of a dismal age that persecuted true religion.

Production of earlier medieval prophecy clustered around moments of extreme tension: loss of the Holy Land, papal-Hohenstaufen wars, Black Death, and papal schism. Ottavia Niccoli has drawn attention to later prophecies, dating from the 1490s, which she associates in part with general apocalypticism and in part with anxieties aroused by the Italian wars.[97] Between these bodies of texts, postdating medieval disasters but predating French invasions, fall a number of Quattrocento manuscripts connected to still another source of popular fear: the Turkish onslaught.

Writers in the Veneto were initially unaware of or indifferent to Turkish advances: Andrea Arnaldi alone reported the fall of Constantinople. None mentioned the outbreak of the first Turkish-Venetian war in 1463, probably because most of its engagements took place in the far-off eastern Mediterranean. Only Repeta noted the Turkish raid on Friuli in 1472. Five years later, however, Turkish cavalry penetrated the borders of the Veneto proper. Heightening local alarm were the deaths of prominent Vicentines and Veronese in the Venetian army. This time provincial writers took notice, inflating estimates of Turkish forces to 6,000, 15,000, or 50,000. Almost immediately the Veronese Giorgio Sommariva and Leonardo Montagna published paired poems in which a personified Friuli warned Italy of the fate that loomed if aid was not given her; dal Bovo promptly copied the doggerel into his manuscript.[98]

Turks, it was widely perceived, threatened not so much Venice's northeast border as Christendom itself. All-out crusade was required, not simply the strengthening of local defenses. In practical terms, crusading spirit may have been weak after 1453:[99] the Diet of Mantua (1459–60) failed to rally support, and Pius II's long-projected armada (1464) never materialized. But failure to mount a universal campaign against the infidel cannot be laid at the feet of the peninsula's writers, who made prodigious efforts to stir the faithful. Bernardo Giustiniani's *Oratio exhortatoria contra turcos*, Lauro Querini's letter to Pius II, Celso Maffei's *Suasoria pro facillima turcorum expugnatione*, Mauro Lupo's *De cruce suscipienda contra infideles*, Andrea Diedo's 1467 *Pro victoria Achayea* (encouraging Venetian fleets in the east), and Bessarione's *Epistola* and *Oratio*[100] sought to prove that the task, while arduous, was yet possible. Letters to and from the sultan, and works about Mohammed—including a spurious testament and several biographies—proved Islam's expansive intent.[101] Popes from Nicholas V to Sixtus IV wrote exhortatory letters that were recopied and rushed into print.[102] Histories of Attila served as pointed allegories of God's use of pagan scourges. Marsilio Ficino, Nicolo Sagundino, and Guillaume Fichet encouraged unity and action, and their works soon reached the Veneto; so did pleas from the Grand Master of Rhodes, Gregorius Tiphernatis, and the bishop of Mitilene.[103]

Prophecy could help. A Bolognese in 1377, for example, gave hope to Christians by foretelling terrible storms, battles, and earthquakes to afflict enemy cities: "strength shall fail among the Saracens, and they shall become one with Christians."[104] In the later Quattrocento, despite recent disasters, prophecy could still provide foreknowledge of victory. To Giovanni Nanni of Viterbo, author of the *De futuris Christianorum triumphis in Saracenos* (1480), the book of Revelation and contemporary astronomy proved the imminent collapse of Turkish power.[105] Others updated sibylline prophecies: the Last Emperor would subdue the Turks as final preparation for his glorious reign.[106] A Venetian text of midcentury, while predicting that the sultan would indeed conquer all Italy (except Venice) and persecute the Church, foresaw that Christ would appear to a holy man in Venice and give him power to work miracles, which would induce the sultan's conversion. The Christian Turk, now accepted as emperor, would give the Holy Land to Venice; the holy man would be elected pope, and the world would live in peace and godly living.[107] Some texts, it is true, struck a note of short-term pessimism. A few sibylline prophecies saw 1453 as opening the final age of calamities; a Venetian work thought that anti-Christ would be born in Babylon as a Turkish subject.[108] At least, in such cases, prophecy reassured the faithful that immediate danger was part of God's master plan, a prelude to eventual glory.

In Vicenza, Manfredo Repeta copied a quasi-prophecy that was at once pragmatic and indirect. In a series of precise tables he calculated the resources of Christian powers, the sultan, and pagans subject to him.[109] At face value the signs were not good. Rulers and states from Scotland to Trebizond could raise 295,500 horses, and their annual income totaled 6,830,000 ducats. Combined Moslem income was 7,730,000 ducats, and their cavalry totaled an even million. But luxuries and household salaries drained the sultan's wealth, and only half his horses were available outside his dominion. Furthermore, Repeta forgot to record income from about half the champions of the faith. Correcting for that omission, Christians were considerably more wealthy and were not far short of horses. To those who witnessed one Turkish victory after another—Friulan raids in 1472, 1477, and 1479, capture of Negroponte in 1470, seige of Scutari in 1474 and 1478, and capture of Croia in 1478—Repeta provided assurance that the Christian side was potentially a match for the hitherto invincible Turk. At least, he implied, it was worth a try at combination.

Parish and Monastery

Contemporary witness and recent research suggest that parish priests would have the least claim on popular loyalties. Many were foreigners, with little grasp of local needs; many came from lands that did not speak the local language. In a sample of Vicentine nominations for 1424–25, for example, fifty of sixty-four benefices were given to clergy from outside the Venetian dominion, with German clergy forming a plurality. Two-thirds of Trevisan clergy came from outside the city and district. In the city of Padua, 78 percent of priests were foreign and 57 percent were from outside the Veneto; in the diocese as a whole, 56 percent of beneficed clergy were non-Paduan, including many from Dalmatia and German-speaking lands. Ten of twenty-four clerics in San Floriano in the Valpolicella, in 1434, were Venetian.[110]

Absenteeism, a consequence of pluralism, benefices held in *commendam*, or simple neglect, was endemic. Nearly a third of Vicentine mansionaries (lower cathedral clergy) were missing when the bishop ordered a survey in 1452–53. Those who remained on the job were frequently unable to administer sacraments or liturgies properly. Visitation records reveal poor spiritual and educational training of Treviso's secular clergy, who rarely preached. Responding to questions of the episcopal vicar of Vicenza in 1460–62, many priests admitted ignorance of the daily office, the formula of consecration, and procedures for confession. Nine of twenty-seven did not know how to celebrate Mass, nine of eleven could not recite the Pater Noster, and six of twenty could not list the sacraments.[111]

Poverty may partially explain this record: ill-paid benefices[112] did not allow leisure for study. Many priests were forced to moonlight, which prevented dutiful celebration of the sacraments. Poverty, however, cannot excuse the dismal moral record uncovered by episcopal interrogators. Visitation registers amply reveal piety and service, it is true, but just as many cases of litigiousness, concubinage, and worse. Pope Eugenius IV had to ask Venetian civil authorities to punish certain Vicentine clerics guilty of "homicide, adultery, robbery or other profane crimes."[113]

Clerical associations, mainly concerned with administration of their pooled patrimonies,[114] did not ameliorate or even address problems of the secular clergy. The few activist bishops made little headway against abuses. Vicenza's Francesco Malipiero (1433–51), for example, has been championed as a tireless reformer, but his primary contribution was reorganization of the episcopal patrimony and he did not seriously attempt to impose discipline on lower clergy. Verona's Ermolao Barbaro, too, has been judged exemplary, but much of his energies were expended in a battle with patricians over tithes and a contentious, fruitless effort to consolidate lesser benefices.[115]

Criticism of parish clergy was widespread. Anticlerical satires must be taken with a grain of salt, since the loutish, grasping, and/or sensual priest is as much literary commonplace as reflection of reality; but *topoi* are seldom drawn from fantasy, and audiences were prepared to accept lampoons as not far-fetched. Reformers, especially Observant mendicants such as Bernardino of Siena, incessantly charged lower seculars with dereliction of duty. The energetic and saintly Lorenzo Giustiniani, refusing the see of Vicenza in part because "the clergy is much disordered," admitted that the situation might be beyond repair.[116]

Nor were laity in the Veneto altogether silent. Bartolomeo Guastaverza of Verona went before a notary to charge that the priest Nicolo had not said Mass before a family altar for four months, and that the bishop refused to discipline or replace him. Bartolomeo dal Bovo's will left ten *lire* to the priest of the family's village of origin, if he were resident; otherwise the money was to be spent on the fabric of the church. Dal Bovo assumed that the in-

cumbent might well be absentee, even though his own family held patronage rights over the benefice.[117] The dissatisfied but inarticulate voted with
their feet. The priest of San Vitale in Verona, supported by the city's clerical congregation, complained bitterly that his flock had abandoned his church
for a neighborhood confraternity.[118] Patterns of testation in Venice hint at
similar erosion of loyalties. Trecento wills concentrated bequests within the
parish and ordered burial in its church, but those of the Quattrocento spread
bequests throughout the city, spoke of membership in city-wide confraternities, and elected burial outside the parish.[119]

Still, to conclude on the basis of such evidence that parish allegiance was
thin or thinning would ignore considerable evidence to the contrary. To Bartolomeo dal Bovo, for example, lay involvement in the affairs of the parish
of S. Pietro Incarnario was routine and compelling. He himself often chat-
ted with the rector concerning its fabric and benefice. As had his father, he
chose burial there, and he built there a monument for the family's dead. In
his wills he listed the parish first in requesting postmortem Masses. A board
of lay governors administered its patrimony; one of its chaplains was elected
by the leader (sindicus), financial officers (raxoneri), and general membership of the neighborhood (tuta la vixinanza de la contrà). If the chaplain failed
to say Masses for the donor's soul, the laity held the right to dismiss him and
elect a replacement. Dal Bovo also served on a three-person committee of
fabricadori that oversaw the church's physical plant. With patronage rights,
administrative authority, elected leadership, and broad participation (one of
the fabricadori was a woman) the lay community held a major stake in parish
affairs. Parishioners would not have served actively if the neighborhood cult
had been meaningless.[120]

The episode may not be anomalous. Parochial election of priests "was
found up and down the peninsula." In Florence, lay residents held patronage
rights in eleven of sixty-two parishes. A recent case study amply demonstrates the close bonds of one Florentine neighborhood with its parish church:
the neighborhood assembly met there, parishioners made frequent bequests to
it, the monks of the church often served as witnesses or procurators, confraternities were based there, the abbot acted as administrator of the gonfalone,
and parishioners built tombs and chapels there. Throughout Tuscany, bequests
to parishes remained stable from the thirteenth through fifteenth centuries,
and greatly outnumbered bequests to monasteries and nunneries.[121]

Perceived shortcomings in the secular priesthood as a whole did not, then,
lead automatically to personal disaffection. Parishioners responded to the
emotional appeals of long-familiar worship space, devotions shared with

neighbors, family burial sites, fiscal and administrative responsibilities, and a sense of residential solidarity. If the priest was flawed, he was still theirs, and they valued their small measure of control over local devotions. They were not, therefore, inclined to accept reforms from above. Padua's laity, for example, vigorously resisted the bishop's efforts to improve the morality and spirituality of parish priests. Lesser clergy in Verona shared 769 tiny benefices, which led to clerical poverty, absenteeism, pluralism, and moonlighting, but Eugenius IV's attempt to consolidate benefices down to a more reasonable figure of 190 was largely blunted by lay outcry.[122]

Ongoing parish loyalty was entirely compatible with extraparochial allegiance, and the faithful of the Veneto indeed diversified their attentions. Their favors, however, were not indiscriminant. Older houses of regulars, especially Benedictines, sputtered along with few vocations and scant bequests, and new congregations of reformed Benedictines made little headway. Verona's S. Maria in Organo, decayed "in spiritual and temporal matters," passed to another order in 1444. Vicenza's convent of S. Pietro, deemed "destitute of proper discipline and regular observance," gathered only a handful of nuns until saved by papal intervention. Benedictines at SS. Felice and Fortunato tried to stimulate revival in 1427 by fortuitous discovery of the patrons' bodies, but the cult never took hold and by 1442 only three monks were resident. The Benedictine priory of S. Silvestro passed under absentee prelates and was abandoned, its buildings "destroyed or nearly so." In Tuscany, bequests to older monasteries fell by half while donations to nunneries fell by two-thirds.[123]

Rather, the laity in the Quattrocento polarized attentions between parishes and mendicant houses. They particularly supported Observant movements, giving derelict convents such as S. Biagio and S. Tommaso in Vicenza to reformed mendicants and dedicating new Observant convents to San Bernardino in Verona and Vicenza. In 1445 the city council of Verona half complained, half rejoiced that the Clarisses had so grown in number that their building was no longer adequate. Third orders attracted considerable recruits and bequests.[124] This matches patterns in Italy at large. Bequests to Tuscan mendicants doubled in the 1275–1425 period, until they exceeded those to all other orders combined. The commune and people of Vigevano favored the Observance, as did Duke Francesco Sforza. During his lifetime San Bernardino saw the number of Observant friars grow from 132 to 4,000, and the number of Observant houses grow from 15 to 300 (618 by the end of the century). In 1451 Giovanni Capistrano claimed 600,000 Observant Franciscan tertiaries.[125]

But growing preference for reformed friars introduced tension into the religious life of the laity. With the exception of S. Bernardino in Verona, new Observant convents in the Veneto never matched traditional centers in magnificence, location, wealth, or prestige. Conventual Augustinians (S. Eufemia in Verona) and Franciscans (S. Lorenzo in Vicenza, S. Fermo in Verona) retained their houses; Conventual Dominicans kept control of Vicenza's S. Corona until 1464 and Verona's S. Anastasia until 1477.[126] The new orders settled in peripheral locations. Vicenza's S. Biagio lay outside city walls, S. Sebastiano (Observant Dominicans) on a hill south of the city, and S. Chiara (ex–S. Tommaso) in a suburb. Verona's Observant Franciscans initially gathered at Arcarotta, on the lightly inhabited left bank of the Adige.[127] So, too, Venice's Observant Franciscans settled at S. Giobbe and Santa Maria Maggiore, both removed from the city center, and did not aspire to rival the Conventuals' glorious church of the Frari.[128]

The laity were forced, then, to choose between Conventuals' prestige and Observants' piety. Patrician testaments are telling: the Verità, Fracastoro, Bovi, and Stoppi usually made bequests to new houses, but ordered burial in the old.[129] Ancient sacred spaces, abundant relics, grandiose Gothic piles, and existing family tombs claimed their postmortem affections more than modest establishments of monks dedicated to simplicity and poverty. The Arnaldi are another case in point. They named their children Bernardino, Chiara, and Francesco, went on pilgrimage to the Observant Augustinian shrine at Monte Ortone, joined Observant Franciscan tertiaries, and praised the preaching of Observants Bernardino of Siena and Giovanni Capistrano, but they baptized children, ordered commemorative Masses, and placed their mortal remains in the cathedral.

Commune and Hierarchy

Muronovo and dal Bovo repeated the claim, attributed to bygone archdeacon Pacifico, that Verona was founded by Noah's son Sem and called by Hebrews a "minor Jerusalem." The designation was made official in 1438, when the city's seal, lost in a Milanese invasion, was replaced with one bearing the motto "Verona, new Jerusalem, its patron holy Zeno." Municipal statutes of 1450 ratified the title.[130] Legend became policy: the city would not yield pride of ancient foundation and sanctity to its neighbors.

Such promotion of spiritual-civic identity preoccupied municipal governments throughout the Quattrocento. A first task was to clean up lists of officially celebrated saints, many imposed by past conquerors: the Visconti, for example, had compelled Vicentines to honor S. Maria della Neve, S. Gallo, and S. Ursula, on whose days Milanese forces won victories in the march on the city. New statutes in 1425 struck them from the calendar. Civic observance thereafter was reserved for saints with special resonance for local patriotism: Michael, on whose day the city was liberated from the tyrant Ezzelino da Romano; Felice, Fortunato, Floriano, Leonzio, and Carpoforo, who lay in Vicentine churches; the nearly eponymous Vincenzo. Veronese statutes, too, ordered celebration of those buried in city churches, plus native-born St. Peter Martyr.[131]

Other municipal cults were similarly nativist. The Vicentine commune organized processions when bones of Leonzio and Carpoforo were "discovered"—significantly, by officials and citizens, not clerics—in a carefully staged ritual of 1455.[132] It built a prominent church in Vincenzo's honor in the center of the city's main piazza; there officially sponsored processions began and ended, from its steps communally sponsored friars preached, and there the Monte di Pietà was eventually located. At the same time the commune resisted cults associated with the city's new ruler, the Venetian Republic. Statutes gave the day of St. Vitale, on which Venetian troops entered Vicenza, only the status of minor feast, one of fifty such days of observation. St. Mark himself, though widely venerated elsewhere in the dominion, was also given only a minor feast. Coins circulating in Verona originally bore the image of St. Mark, but the city—which paid for coinage and hence could choose iconography—gradually replaced it with the image of civic patron San Zeno.[133]

Public officials, not local clerics, sponsored new cults and new convents. When the aptly named Vincenza had visions of the Madonna on Monte Berico, the commune appointed a jurist and notaries to compile a dossier of the appearance and subsequent miracles at the shrine. One of the latter smacks of pure boosterism: a man was undecided about whether to undertake pilgrimage to Rome, Padua, or Compostella, until the Virgin called him to have her image painted at Monte Berico instead. While the Venetian government determined which religious order held sway there, the commune retained patronage rights. Municipal deputies, in 1452, petitioned the pope to place the Girolimini in the flourishing northern shrine of Monte Summano.[134]

Installation of reformers also required license from Venetian or ecclesiastical superiors, but initiative generally came from municipal rather than clerical bodies. The Veronese convent of S. Bernardino, approved by the doge upon petition of communal ambassadors, is a case in point.[135] Bernardino and Giovanni Capistrano received credit for inspiring Observant Franciscan houses in Vicenza, but civil authorities actually set the process in motion. In 1420–21, over two years before Bernardino first preached in the city, the commune applied to the doge to have Observant Franciscans take over the moribund monastery of S. Biagio. Friars arrived in April 1423, preceding Bernardino by a month. The commune sponsored the foundation and paid for the building of a church honoring newly canonized Bernardino in 1451. Clarisses took over the old convent of S. Tommaso (renamed S. Chiara) at the urging of patricians Battista Valmarana and Matteo Bissari. The commune sponsored the final major construction campaign of the century, the church of S. Rocco, and directed the installation there of secular canons from San Giorgio in Alga.[136]

Civic managers also assumed responsibility for safeguarding existing cults and institutions. Communal commissions, working with episcopal officials, directed the distribution of pious bequests to convents, parishes, the poor, and charities such as Verona's Domus Pietatis and Vicenza's Ospedale de' Proti.[137] Vicentine councils in 1409 proposed, and doge and Senate approved, creation of an entirely lay panel (three citizens and a notary) to monitor accounts of monasteries, hospitals, and pious institutions, provide for buildings, furnishings, and books, and ensure due celebration of the divine office.[138] These *provisores ecclesiarum* proved effective on at least two occasions. In 1458 the commune declared that "reformation is greatly needed to avoid the scandals which are daily attributed" to the Conventual Dominican house of S. Corona, owing to the "dishonest and obscene and utterly nonreligious" lives of inmates. The petition took several years to work through the ecclesiastical hierarchy, but at last in 1464 "Conventual friars were chased out of the convent, because they did not keep good lives," and were replaced by Observants. The next year the commune charged that nuns of Araceli "were tending towards a more lax life," and the bishop welcomed the request for reform.[139]

In Verona, too, episcopal oversight was poor, and the commune stepped in to fill the vacuum. In 1407–8, accepting a petition from urban councils, the doge charged that many monasteries, churches, and benefices were heading for ruin, and ordered rectors and three citizens to inquire into their management, particularly whether incumbents were worthy or even resident. Commissioners were to report abuses to the bishop; if the bishop took no action, they were to notify Venice. Expectations that bishops might be indifferent proved justified, and doge and municipal councils reaffirmed the panel's jurisdiction in 1442 but no longer required initial complaint to the bishop. Councils then extended the commission's jurisdiction to rural churches; in 1455 they created a further body to visit hospitals. Henceforth the civil authority could by itself regulate buildings, clerical morals, and the celebration of liturgies. Scathing reports of the poor state of churches accompanied reconfirmations of these agencies in 1471 and 1487, indicating that lay intervention was still necessary.[140]

Local bodies were less successful in efforts to establish some control over the episcopacy. The right of cathedral chapters to elect the ordinary, in abeyance for a century, remained a dead letter. The Senate had nominated candidates for bishoprics from 1363, and after 1404 applied the practice to mainland sees. Actual naming of a bishop remained subject to negotiation and occasional outright confrontation between Venice and Rome, but neither side gave much weight to local preference.

Subjects were not altogether silent. Chapters continued to hold elections, hoping to influence higher decisions or obtain concessions. Sometimes they were successful: when canons chose Francesco Malipiero to the see of Vicenza in 1433, the pope concurred and Malipiero declared that he had accepted the local *postulatio* "because it was canonically and lawfully made." Canons likewise claimed right of election in 1501; their choice was overridden, but the Senate at least insisted that Bishop Pietro Dandolo be resident. They also hoped to curry favor with eventual winners: when Verona's chapter threw its support to Gregorio Correr in 1453, rumor was widespread in Venice that Correr would win and that the chapter was simply backing a likely victor. (Correr, in fact, was not named.) Communes, too, thought it worthwhile to lobby for favorites, claiming a say in the process, even if their wishes were little heeded. In 1438 Veronese councils repeatedly asked the Senate not to name Francesco Condulmer bishop; Condulmer received the see.[141]

Bishops were Venetian patricians, without exception, as were most suffragans, major abbots, and holders of key prelacies. Many ordinary benefices were filled from above. Protest against intrusion of outsiders was never stilled, but did not make headway. Even the Veronese commune's modest request in 1459, that benefices valued under sixty ducats be conferred on local citizens, failed to sway the pope.[142] The Republic, for its part, deflected an early request by the Vicentine commune that clerical "dignities and benefices" be given to natives. Equally common, and shrill, were complaints against nonresident bishops. Here provincial communes held stronger ground: the Republic had promised Vicenza in 1404 and 1406 that "the lord bishop . . . ought to stay and make his residence in the city."[143] The Republic, however, made no effort to enforce the directive. Few bishops lived in their dioceses or made more than occasional visits.

Observers still regarded bishops with considerable awe. Andrea Arnaldi gave considerable detail to Malipiero's splendid installation in 1433; Malipiero's funeral, it is said, cost a sumptuous four hundred ducats, including expenses for thirty uniformed mourners and a fur-trimmed baldachin. A mock battle, scattering of coins to onlookers, and a communal gift of cash and plate worth 287 ducats accompanied entry of his successor Pietro Barbo in 1451; the miter alone was valued at three thousand ducats. Thirty thousand people were said to have attended Battista Zeno's entry Mass in 1477.[144]

Accounts of Barbo's arrival hint at some of the reasons for that attention. Barbo was not only bishop but also, by ancient title attached to the office, duke, count, and marquess. So that no one might miss the point, the commune sponsored a *tableau vivante* with actors dressed in robes appropriate to these ranks, each surrounded by a retinue. The bishop directed the feudal as well as the ecclesiastical realm, and in the specific context of Vicenza he ratified—by investitures of tithes—claims of nobility. Further, Barbo announced an indulgence of one hundred days to those present and those visiting the cathedral on anniversaries of the event. Later bishops multiplied indulgences, offering the laity considerable reassurance for the hereafter.[145] Memorialists appreciated two further ministrations of bishops. They held exclusive power to bestow the sacred oil; Andrea Arnaldi meticulously recorded his children's chrismations. Second, only episcopal blessing fully sanctified worship space. Dal Bovo was pleased when Verona's suffragan laid the first stone of a family chapel, and further honored that Bishop Matteo remained to share a meal and chrismate neighborhood children.[146]

But if memorialists and public officials respected the office and patronage of the episcopacy, they held incumbents in less esteem. Arnaldi pointedly noted that Malipiero was installed in absentia, and subsequently died in Venice: he had largely abandoned his see. The Guastaverza wished it officially recorded, by a notary with *publica auctoritas*, that their bishop refused to dismiss a neglectful priest. Vicenza's *Cronica ad memoriam* did not refrain from comment that Battista Zeno, following a splendid installation, immediately left for Rome and died in Venice. Accounts of the fabulous wealth found in Zeno's many palaces were no more complimentary.

There was much to dislike. Neither Verona nor Vicenza had reformers of the level of Padua's Pietro Barozzi or Treviso's Ludovico Barbo.[147] At best, Malipiero allowed Observant and reformed orders to settle in his diocese, but there is no sign that he pursued clerical improvement on his own. Pietro Emiliani's command to the Vicentine clergy, that they care for parishioners' souls "according to law, and not according to charity,"[148] was scarcely edifying. Medieval bishops were often regarded as saints, and their relics still inspired devotion and miracles,[149] but observers seldom associated their Quattrocento successors with anything more than magnificent attire and splendid retinues.

If the bishop was absent or inactive, that itself was cause for protest. Forthright denunciation fills a 1447 provision of Veronese councils, which established a commission to deal with problems resulting from the bishop's nonresidence and desired "especially that our episcopacy be reformed both in head and members." The suggested solution, that the commune build a palace so fine that the bishop would wish to reside in the city, has more than a whiff of sarcasm. An eventual compromise continued to press local demands: the commune agreed to build or repair the palace, but only if (1) the suffragan were resident; (2) the bishop revoked letters suppressing certain benefices and hospitals; (3) one-third of episcopal income be spent on cathedral fabric; and (4) Veronese citizens be supplied to Veronese benefices. By 1480 the arrangement had broken down due to episcopal recalcitrance, and the commune sent a stiff letter asking that the bishop at least provide a resident suffragan.[150] Ongoing appointment of a civic commission to oversee monasteries testifies that the commune simply did not trust its bishop to carry out his responsibilities.

If the bishop was present or active, he was apt to step on local toes. The Veronese laity, in particular, fiercely resisted perceived episcopal encroachment on nativist rights. It has been noted that the commune in 1440 partly blocked the bishop's efforts to reduce many small benefices and assign their revenues to the local School of Acolytes.[151] Two decades later the commune charged that Ermolao Barbaro had diverted the income of that school to support his staff. This accusation was made in the midst of a bitter controversy between commune and bishop over the latter's attempts to make episcopal feudatories swear allegiance directly to him:[152] fiefs had been divisible, heritable, and alienable for centuries, and resumption of direct suzerainty would have thrown landholding into chaos. Bishop Francesco Condulmer's placement of his personal coat of arms on cathedral columns, declared the city council, "sets a bad example to the city, and is displeasing" in its cult of personality and its intrusion in a specifically Veronese center of worship. Refusal of Condulmer's staff to meet with communal representatives only inflamed local annoyance.[153]

Popes were distant figures. Muronovo recorded papal deaths and elections,[154] but did so only occasionally and overlooked many. Neither he nor other observers mentioned the possible sanctity of popes, their efforts to rebuild the papacy, or their promotion of reform; they are treated as any other territorial ruler. Memoirs gave them none of the detail provided, for better or worse, to bishops. The only holy figures in memoirs are mendicant preachers.

When not taciturn, memorialists took a negative tone. Dal Bovo copied an unflattering verse, the "Risposte of a patriarch of Constantinople to the pontiff in Rome":

> We firmly believe in your power over your subjects,
> We cannot tolerate your arrogance,
> We do not wish to endorse your avarice.[155]

Manfredo Repeta's pseudo-Joachimite prophecy also made pointed criticism. Rome itself would fall to the "barbarous mastiff" from the East, belying any image of the pope as bulwark of the faith. Salvation, instead, would come from a peasant, ignorant of letters and books (perhaps a dig at curial humanist refinement?). After unbelievers were conquered and converted, the final—because most difficult?—task would be return of the Church to its pristine purity. Here the agent would be another peasant, dressed in rough clothes (perhaps a dig at curial elegance?). Under this holy Zuane, present absenteeism and opulence would cease:

> The cardinals, if Joachim does not err,
> Who now abound in luxury and avarice,
> He will make to stay on their lands as holy apostles;
> Bishops and archpriests, all of them,
> Will remain honest under his mantle,
> And so too the other priests and friars, who are so many.[156]

In another poem copied by Repeta, God himself would ultimately deny standing to hierarchy and ecclesiastical jurisprudence:

> The chief judge shall judge the judges.
> Papal rank shall have no bearing,
> Nor that of bishop or cardinal:
> The guilty shall be condemned, whatever sort he is.
> It shall do no good to make allegations,
> Nor make exceptions, nor make defense,
> Nor appeal to the apostolic see:
> The guilty shall be condemned, nor does the judge say why.
> So think on this, you miserables, whoever you are,
> What you shall say to that judge:

> In that place there shall be neither law-book nor Digest,
> And he shall be judge, prosecutor and witness.[157]

These are the sole comments on the upper echelons of the Church, and it may be excessive to conclude widespread antihierarchical sentiment from them. Still, memorialists offered no positive valuations to offset these unflattering judgments of papacy and curia. Often warm toward clergy they knew, ambivalent toward bishops, they grew less forgiving and less interested as their vision moved up the ecclesiastical ladder.

EPILOGUE

THIS BOOK HAS SOUGHT, in part, to restore agency to its subjects. All too often in their quest for generalization historians and social scientists create monolithic cultures, as if authorities on the one hand and impersonal forces on the other imposed behavior on common people. The ordinary sort are perceived as more acted upon than actors, functioning primarily to give concrete realization to models dictated from above and without. Ideology set some bounds; demography, ecology, economic structures, law, and the state set others. The task, therefore, is to look beyond nominal subjects to discern the overarching systems that conditioned their experiences. That is not an approach authorized by the evidence underlying this book.

Even in the most sympathetic treatments of spiritual life, for example, subaltern groups emerge as essentially passive receivers of messages and audiences of ritual.[1] On the contrary, as the Veneto memoirs abundantly demonstrate, devotional writers, preachers, and organizers of ritual provided raw materials from which lay people constructed personalized religious views. Compilers had available a large and growing corpus of patristic and medieval writings, sermons, popular texts, and learned treatises. Since they could scarcely assimilate the whole, they selected among their sources and so were active agents in shaping their devotions. Paraliturgies and spiritual-magical lore often allowed them to bypass clerical mediation altogether. Furthermore, since theologians, canonists, and moralists scarcely constituted a monolithic body, indeed frequently reached polar opposite opinions, the laity enjoyed considerable latitude. Consumers in a largely open ecclesiastical market, they chose freely from a broad range of priest-providers; they played down some widely sanctioned elements (penitential and Marian) and brought some less favored themes (prophetic and magical-medical) to the forefront. What they emphasized was not always what producers of religious guidelines might have wished.

The same was true of other aspects of experience. For example, there existed no single doctrine of marriage, but rather a congeries of more or less approved positions. Divergence of opinion presented alternatives, hence allowing variation in everyday decision making. So families in the Veneto picked and chose among calendrical prohibitions, and emphasized parental controls and consummation far more than did mainstream canonists. Dowry systems, too, offered not overarching norms but a profusion of legitimated strategies that left ample space for maneuver. The very mechanisms by which patricians sought to safeguard the orderly devolution of marital wealth were amply and skillfully deployed, by peasants and debtors, to deflect the claims of superiors. In the marketplace, debt might have been endemic, but techniques for managing and expanding debt provided immensely valuable and varied resources for economic flexibility and patronage. Doctrines of nobility offered not a single source of legitimation but many possible means to social validation; the Arnaldi had to pick their way through a crowded field of opportunities and disabilities.

Higher culture, then, set ranges of options but seldom possessed coercive mechanisms to impose orthodoxy. Some facets of experience, it is true, were beyond personal control. There was little to be done about endemic disease and high mortality. Still, responses to demographic fragility varied widely from place to place, suggesting localized strategies for ensuring biological and social reproduction—very different ages at marriage in Florence, Venice, and the Veneto, for example, or differing rates of nuptuality among different social groups. Drastic changes in fertility rates over the course of the Quattrocento were surely not simply the result of shifting biological parameters, but reflect conscious decisions (a decline in the age of women at marriage, for example) as well. People were aware of their options and the risks inherent in each option, and made their choices accordingly. Perhaps local custom rather than individual preference determined specific choices, but the fact that custom was localized indicates responsiveness to small-scale preference.

This book has also aspired to trust its subjects. Certainly in the public record they were capable of dissembling and deception: a good number of dotal documents cannot be taken at face value, and many if not most documents of land sales conceal loans and do not indicate actual alienation. Still, when they themselves set pen to paper, Veneto memorialists made entries and copied texts that mattered to them. An underlying assumption of this book is that they would not have bothered to write if the exercise was purely fictive. We can, I think, discern their intentions, but we must also accept that they were sincere.

For example, to read through the memoirs is to be reminded of the intensity of spiritual sentiment. In addition to regular traces of devotion that fill their pages—invocation of God and saints, naming of children, reckoning calendrical time by saints' days and daily time by liturgical schedules, calls for divine favor on marriages and the deceased, provision for postmortem rites—memorialists collected pious texts of a heterogenous sort: prayers, prophecies, guides to holy places, hagiography, bits of Scripture, apocrypha, accounts of pilgrimages, sacramentals, poetry, and hymns. They also recorded salient events in local and Roman ecclesiastical life. In the work of Bartolomeo dal Bovo, Manfredo Repeta, and Bartolomeo Verità, spiritual and religious material forms a significant, even preponderant proportion of the whole.

Memorialists must have found these texts meaningful, to devote so much time and ink to their copying. The point may be banal, but merits emphasis. Skepticism and scorn long pushed study of faith and devotion from the historical mainstream, relegating it to canon lawyers, antiquaries, and partisan clerics. The past generation has rediscovered church history, indeed has returned it to the forefront, but for the most part still declines to accept the reality of underlying belief for people in the past. Prevalent is a functionalist approach that views religious practice solely in terms of strategies for pacifying the body social, reinforcing hierarchy, constructing corporate and civic identity, building states, placing excess daughters, impressing restrictive models on women, socializing the young, immortalizing the individual, controlling descendants after death, and so forth. To accept conviction is to engage in self-deception.[2]

Authorities certainly realized the power of devotion and sought to channel it for mundane ends. To give primacy to the utility of religious observance, however, is to ignore cause and elevate effect. People of the fifteenth century practiced religion because they believed in it. They welcomed desirable social consequences, but these were not the intent of worship. Rituals could have had no resonance if participants had not accepted the need for expiation, the efficacy of works of faith, the power of God to heal and make right, and the need for humans to reach out to the divine. If reverence was formulaic and routinized, it was no less honest for that fact.[3]

That memorialists of the Veneto were hard-nosed and self-interested is beyond question. Are we, on that account, to conclude that their more high-minded professions were merely the products of covering ideologies? To do so is to impose arbitrary partiality on the documentary record, accepting cold-blooded materialism at face value but rejecting the idealistic out of hand. To do so is also to introduce a patronizing note, asserting that they did not believe what they so manifestly said they believed. And to do so is, in the end, to assume that self-interest and inspired ideals are ultimately incompatible. The many acts of kindness that emerge from the memoirs, for example, have both a sacred rationale and a mundane purpose. Arbitration pacified family tensions and smoothed the flow of money; it equally served the interests of *caritas*. Stated affection for wives, and calls to protect widows and stray female kin, might indeed have aspired to keep dowries close to home; they equally observed Pauline injunctions. Dowries themselves may seem constrictive, even cynical devices, but those who constituted and protected them claimed to have the welfare of their wives and daughters in mind. If writers chose to emphasize the higher values, we dismiss their professed convictions only at the cost of imposing our own values on them. An empirical approach aims at sympathy—with due caution, to be sure, but with equally guarded confidence that words of sentiment are not altogether remote from actual motivation.

There remains an underlying question: if these were indeed obscure people, living in minor societies, can their experience support any degree of generalization? The least dubious of possible answers rests on this book's comparative approach. Conclusions drawn from the Veneto are matched with conclusions drawn from Florence, Venice, and beyond; when the Veneto provides a match, it helps confirm and universalize positions derived from discrete case studies; when patterns from the Veneto are at variance, they indicate that Italian society as a whole was highly nuanced and that extrapolation from metropolitan models is unwise. Still, a dozen memoirs from two cities cannot themselves support rethinking of the field; nor can they aspire to sketch the experience of provincial societies generally.

Another answer, taking refuge in the very genre of the case study, would evade the question. Examination of a few families in Verona and Vicenza allows small-scale generalization only; future study of other provincial settings will demonstrate whether the Veneto experience is eccentric or representative. The burden of proof lies with eventual synthesis by others. But to say that is to offload responsibility onto a future generation—and it is far from certain that other cities will yield similar texts, or that other historians will choose to undertake comparable studies.

A final answer would deny the question altogether. The essential problem is that faced by microhistories: how can an abundantly documented but sharply circumscribed case study connect to larger contexts? Carlo Ginzburg has tried to do so by means of agile but often problematic leaps from the particular to the general; his refuge in assertion when he cannot provide demonstration has been much criticized, though it is hard to see what alternative he had. More recently, Giovanni Levi has largely given up the attempt at linkage. The specific, he has said, is precisely that: it describes the particular accurately, but cannot and should not serve as the basis for broad generalization because all attempt at universalization is inevitably reductive.[4] This, however, cannot dispel charges that the small-scale case study is potentially only anecdotal, indeed admits charges of nominalism.

The question must remain open. These are indeed modest subjects. Study of Veneto memorialists cannot serve as the basis for grand endeavors, and their experience cannot by itself reshape our understanding of Renaissance society. But those who teach, and those who read reviews of their books, know well that no scholar can predict what audiences will receive from his or her exposition, or how they will use it. The case study offers only hope that its data and positions may yet, in other hands, somehow contribute to larger discussion.

APPENDIX

Table 1.1. Age at First Marriage

Mean Age at First Marriage			
Years	*Men*	*Women*	*Difference*
1425–49	25	21.1	3.9
1450–74	24.3	19.4	4.9
1475–99	28.6	20.7	7.9
1500–	25.8	19.3	6.5
TOTALS	25.9	20.1	5.8

Median Age at First Marriage			
Years	*Men*	*Women*	*Difference*
1425–49	25.5	22.1	3.49
1450–74	25	19	6
1475–99	27.8	20.8	7
1500–	24	19.9	4.1
TOTALS	25	19.7	5.3
N =	21	26	

Note: Including second marriages: men's median 27.5 years, mean 28.1 (*N* = 40); women's median 21, mean 20.9 (*N* = 41). These figures include data from Verona's tax returns *(anagrafi)* as well as memoirs.

Table 1.2. Seasonality of Marriage and *Ductio*

Month	Marriage	Ductio
January	6 (20.7%)	5 (29.4%)
February	3 (10.3%)	3 (17.6%)
March	6 (20.7%)	
April	2 (6.9%)	1 (5.9%)
May		
June	1 (3.4%)	
July	1 (3.4%)	1 (5.9%)
August	1 (3.4%)	1 (5.9%)
September	1 (3.4%)	2 (11.8%)
October	2 (6.9%)	3 (17.6%)
November	5 (17.2%)	1 (5.9%)
December	1 (3.4%)	
TOTALS	29 (100%)	17 (100%)

Table 1.3. Day of Marriage and *Ductio*

Day	Marriage	Ductio
Monday	1 (3.7%)	1 (6.7%)
Tuesday	1 (3.7%)	2 (13.3%)
Wednesday	6 (22.2%)	3 (20%)
Thursday	5 (18.5%)	
Friday	1 (3.7%)	
Saturday	1 (3.7%)	
Sunday	12 (44.4%)	9 (60%)
TOTALS	27 (100%)	15 (100%)

Note: Mean interval between marriage and *ductio:* 8 months
($N = 10$).

Table 1.4. Widowhood

	Men	Women
Number widowed	23 (56.1%)	18 (43.9%)
Duration of widow-hood (in years)	15.2	18.2
Remarriage: yes	8 (44.4%)	2 (11.1%)
no	10 (55.6%)	16 (88.9%)

Table 2.1. Seasonality of Birth and Conception

Month of Birth (Conception)	−1449	1450–99	1500–	Total
January (April)	10 (16.4%)	10 (13.9%)	3 (7.3%)	23 (13.2%)
February (May)	7 (11.5%)	7 (9.7%)	4 (9.8%)	18 (10.3%)
March (June)	8 (13.1%)	7 (9.7%)	6 (14.6%)	21 (12.1%)
April (July)	1 (1.6%)	3 (4.2%)	5 (12.2%)	9 (5.2%)
May (August)	2 (3.3%)	9 (12.5%)	2 (4.9%)	13 (7.5%)
June (September)	5 (8.2%)	7 (9.7%)	4 (9.8%)	16 (9.2%)
July (October)	8 (13.1%)	3 (4.2%)	2 (4.9%)	13 (7.5%)
August (November)	4 (6.6%)	4 (5.6%)	6 (14.6%)	14 (8%)
September (December)	2 (3.3%)	4 (5.6%)	3 (7.3%)	9 (5.2%)
October (January)	8 (13.1%)	4 (5.6%)	3 (7.3%)	15 (8.6%)
November (February)	4 (6.6%)	5 (6.9%)	1 (2.4%)	10 (5.7%)
December (March)	2 (3.3%)	9 (12.5%)	2 (4.9%)	13 (7.5%)
TOTALS	61 (100%)	72 (100%)	41 (100%)	174 (100%)

Notes: Each month would report 8.3 percent of births if births were spaced evenly around the calendar. Data from the Cortusi family of Padua and the da Romagna family of Feltre were added to that from Veronese and Vicentine memoirs.

Table 2.2. Mean Fertility of Women

Years	Number of Children	Interval (in months)	Span (in (months)^a	Number of Cases
–1419	5.8	30.4	143	10
1420–59	7.1	23.3	142	9
1460–	9.6	20.7	178	5
TOTALS	7.1	24.8	150	24

^{a}From birth of first child to birth of last child.

Table 2.3. Baptism

1. Interval between birth and baptism			2. Preferred day of baptism (when not an emergency)	
Same day	3	(9.7%)	Monday	
1–2 days	2	(6.5%)	Tuesday	2 (14.3%)
3–6 days	10	(32.2%)	Wednesday	
7–14 days	14	(45.2%)	Thursday	2 (14.3%)
15–30 days	1	(3.2%)	Friday	
30+ days	1	(3.2%)	Saturday	
			Sunday	10 (71.4%)
TOTAL	31	(100%)		

Table 2.4. Ranking of Male Names in the Vicentine *Estimi*

Name	1453	1460	1477	1505
Giovanni	1	1	1	1
Antonio	2	3	4	4
Bartolomeo	3	2	2	3
Giacomo	4	4	5	6
Pietro	5	7	7	9
Francesco	6	5	3	2
Nicolo	7	6	6	10
Domenico	8	9	9	11
Giovanni Battista	9	8	8	7
Cristoforo	10	10	10	16
Matteo	11	13	11	15
Tommaso	12	14	12	19
Andrea	13	12	16	21
Gaspare	14	16	13	19
Marco	14	16	14	14
Giorgio	16	21	25	26
Michele	17	21	21	33
Alberto	18	11	18	22
Vincenzo	18	15	15	16
Guglielmo	20	20	28	46
Lorenzo	21	18	26	26
Paolo	21	19	17	16
Gerardo	23	25	30	37
Melchiorre	24	29	20	32
Stefano	25	21	21	25
Leonardo	26	24	23	26
Biagio	30	25	29	37
Martino	30	25	39	77
Zanino	30	25	41	46
Simone	30	31	30	23
Alvise	34	31	28	12
Angelo	36	28	34	24
Girolamo	41	56	19	8
Ludovico	61	41	34	13
Agostino	61	47	36	25
Bernardino	—	—	23	5
N =	2195	1751	2255	2344

Note: Those names that appear at least once in the top twenty-five.

Table 2.5. Ranking of Female Names in the Vicentine *Estimi*

Name	1453	1460	1477	1505
Caterina	1	1	1	1
Margarita	2	6	4	7
Bartolomea	3	8	–	–
Lucia	3	2	3	1
Dorotea	5	16	9	–
Tomasina	5	16	–	10
Angela	7	16	4	7
Bona	7	16	–	10
Bonora	7	8	9	–
Magdalena	7	8	4	5
Maria	7	4	1	7
Giovanna	7	4	–	–
Elisabetta	13	3	9	3
Antonia	13	6	–	10
Lucrezia	13	8	–	10
Tadea	16	8	–	–
Anna	16	–	9	4
Agnese	–	8	–	10
Flora	–	16	7	–
Veronica	–	–	7	–
Elena	–	8	–	–
Vincenza	–	8	9	–
Chiara	–	–	9	5
N =	95	86	65	62
Households headed by a woman	4.1%	4.7%	2.8%	2.6%

Note: Those names that appear at least once in the top ten.

Table 2.6. Godparents

	Boys (N = 39)	Girls (N = 36)	Total (N = 75)
Number of godfathers	71 (81.6%)	59 (89.4%)	130 (84.9%)
Number of godmothers	16 (18.4%)	7 (10.6%)	23 (15%)
Number of godparents	87	66	153
Godfathers per child	1.8	1.6	1.7
Godmothers per child	0.4	0.2	0.3
Godparents per child	2.2	1.8	2.0

Table 2.7. The Death of a Parent

Parent	Died during Childhood (2–19 years)	Survived through Childhood
Father	33 (24.8%)	100 (75.2%)
Mother	35 (31.5%)	76 (68.5%)
TOTAL	68 (27.9%)	176 (72.1%)

Note: Excluded were those children who themselves died in infancy (0–1 year), for whom the death of a parent would have had negligible emotional impact.

Table 3.1. Deaths in the Memoirs

Age of Death	Male	Female	Total
1–7 days	6 (7.9%)	3 (5.2%)	9 (6.7%)
1–4 weeks	7 (9.2%)	1 (1.7%)	8 (5.9%)
1–12 months	7 (9.2%)	6 (10.3%)	13 (9.7%)
1–3 years	7 (9.2%)	5 (8.6%)	12 (8.9%)
4–12 years	3 (3.9%)	5 (8.6%)	8 (5.9%)
13–19 years	3 (3.9%)	2 (3.4%)	5 (3.7%)
20–39 years	6 (7.9%)	15 (25.9%)	21 (13.4%)
40–59 years	11 (14.5%)	8 (13.8%)	19 (14.1%)
60+	26 (34.2%)	13 (22.4%)	39 (29.1%)
	N = 76	N = 58	N = 134

Table 3.2. Seasonality of Death

Month	−1449	1450–99	1500–	Total
January		3 (5.6%)	5 (12.8%)	8 (6.7%)
February		4 (7.4%)	5 (12.8%)	9 (7.6%)
March	3 (11.5%)	9 (16.7%)	2 (5.1%)	14 (11.8%)
April	1 (3.8%)	5 (9.3%)	3 (7.7%)	9 (7.6%)
May		5 (9.3%)	1 (2.6%)	6 (5%)
June	1 (3.8%)	1 (1.9%)	3 (7.7%)	5 (4.2%)
July	3 (11.5%)	5 (9.3%)	3 (7.7%)	11 (9.2%)
August	6 (23.1%)	3 (5.6%)	3 (7.7%)	12 (10.1%)
September	6 (23.1%)	6 (11.1%)	8 (20.5%)	20 (16.8%)
October	2 (7.7%)	3 (5.6%)	4 (10.3%)	9 (7.6%)
November	2 (7.7%)	8 (14.8%)	1 (2.6%)	11 (9.2%)
December	2 (7.7%)	2 (3.7%)	1 (2.5%)	5 (4.2%)
	N = 26	N = 54	N = 39	N = 119

Table 3.3. Tax Households of Vicentine Memorialist Families

	1453	1477	1505	% Change
Arnaldi	1	2	3	+ 200%
Feramosca	3	2	6	+ 100%
Repeta	12	15	18	+ 50%
TOTAL	16	19	27	+ 69%

Source: A.S.Vic., *estimo* of 1453, 1477, 1505. The *estimo* of 1460 was excluded because one *quartiere* is missing from the register. In this and the following table, it should be stressed that documents record fiscal rather than residential households.

Table 3.4. Tax Households of Veronese Memorialist Families

	1425	1447	1465	1473	1482	1502
Bovo	6	4	8	7	13	7
Bovi	1	4	6	5	2	8
Fracastoro	2	3	3	3	6	6
Guastaverza	2	5	4	4	3	1
Muronovo	1	1	1	3	2	8
Stoppi			1	2	3	6
Verità	8	8	9	10	2	18
TOTAL	20	25	32	34	41	54

Source: A.S.Ver., *estimo*, regs. 251, 254, 256, 257, 258, 260.

Table 3.5. Average Size of Memorialist Families in
Veronese *Anagrafi*

	−1459	1460–79	1480–99
Size	4.7	5.1	5.3
$N =$	12	20	20

Source: A.S.Ver., Anagrafi Comune 147, 199, 200, 202, 312–15,
481–82, 485–86, 909, 1080–81, 1172, 1197–98, 1199; ivi,
Anagrafi Provincia 223–24, 590, 592–93, 723, 742–44, 774–81.
Only blood kin were counted.

Table 4.1. Household Composition

Type:	
Truncated (no nuclei)	28 (31.1%)
Single nucleus[a]	
Simple nucleus	38 (42.2%)
With widowed mother	9 (10%)
Multiple nuclei	
Fraternal	4 (4.4%)
Vertical[b]	10 (11.1%)
Fraternal and vertical	1 (1.1%)
TOTAL	90
Extension:	
One generation	19 (21.1%)
Two generations	49 (54.4%)
Three generations	22 (24.4%)
TOTAL	90
Fraternal households	9 (10%)
Adult male under paternal roof	21 (23.3%)
Households with strays[c]	10 (11.1%)

Source: From Veronese *anagrafi* of memorialist families.
[a]With or without children and/or unmarried brother(s).
[b]Parents and married son(s).
[c]Persons not in direct male line.

Table 4.2. Family Employees

Years	Number of Households	Male	Female	Number per Household
1400–74	31	23 (43.3%)	30 (56.6%)	1.7
1475–99	21	23 (48.9%)	24 (51.1%)	2.2
1500–	37	71 (61.7%)	44 (38.2%)	3.1
TOTALS	89	117 (54.4%)	98 (45.6%)	2.4

Source: A.S.Ver., Anagrafi, Provincia and Comune: households of memorialist families (excluding children of employees).

Table 4.3. Age of Employees

Age	Male	Female	Total
–14	8 (9.4%)	17 (22.9%)	25 (15.7%)
15–19	17 (20.0%)	16 (21.6%)	33 (20.8%)
20–24	16 (18.8%)	13 (17.6%)	29 (18.2%)
25–29	12 (14.1%)	3 (4.1%)	15 (9.4%)
30–39	6 (7.1%)	9 (12.2%)	15 (9.4%)
40–49	10 (11.8%)	3 (4.1%)	13 (8.2%)
50–59	5 (5.9%)	7 (9.5%)	12 (7.5%)
60–69	6 (7.1%)	4 (5.4%)	10 (6.3%)
70+	5 (5.9%)	2 (2.7%)	7 (4.4%)
TOTALS	85	74	159
Mean	31.1	27.6	29.4
Median	25	20	23

Source: See table 4.2. Numbers are lower than in table 4.1 because many entries did not provide ages.

Table 4.4. Distribution of Households by Neighborhood

Verità	1425	1447	1465	1473	1482	1502
Falsorgo	5	2	1	1	1	1
Ferrabo	1	1	1	1	1	1
S. Zeno Oratorio	3	1				1
S. Michele Porta		1				
S. Zilio		1	2	1	1	1
S. Benedetto		2	4	3	2	1
Pigna			1	1	2	6
S. Toma				1	1	
Ponte Pietra				1	1	
S. Cecilia				1	1	1
S. Maria Antiqua					1	
S. Vitale					1	1
S. Maria Fratta						1
S. Eufemia						2
Chiavica						1
S. Stefano						1

Bovi	1425	1447	1465	1473	1482	1502
S. Sebastiano	1					
S. Eufemia		1	1			
Pigna		1	2	1	1	2
Ponte Pietra		1				
S. Zeno Superiore		1				
S. Fermo			1			
S. Paolo			1	1		
S. Martino Aquario			1	1		
Falsorgo				1		
S. Pietro Incarnario				1		
S. Zilio					1	4
S. Giov. in Valle						1
S. Nazaro						1

Muronovo	1425	1447	1465	1473	1482	1502
S. Paolo	1					
S. Cecilia		1	1	2	1	2
Isola Sotta				1	1	2
S. Vitale						4

Source: A.S.Ver., estimo, regs. 251, 254, 256–58, 260.

Table 4.5. Households of the Dionisi Family

Household	1409	1418	1425	1432	1443	1447	1456	1465	1473	1482	1492	1502
S. Fermo	2	3	2	1	1	1	1	3	1	1	1	
S. M. Organo	2	3										
S. Benedetto	1											
S. Vitale			1	1								
Ognisanti					1		1	1	1	3		
Chiavica							1			1	1	
S. Mateo								1	1	1	1	1
S. Paolo								1	1			1
S. Pietro Incarnario									3			
Ferrabo										1		
S. Salvario										1		
S. Zeno Oratorio										1	1	1
Brà											1	
S. M. Fratta											1	1
S. Marco											1	
Isola Sotto											1	2
S. Pietro											1	
S. Nazaro											1	
Mercato Nuovo												1
Ponte Pietra												1

Source: A.S.Ver., Arch. Dionisi-Piomarta, ms. 439 (tabulating *estimi*).

Table 5.1. Veronese Cloth Production, 1475–78

Years	Panni alti	Panni bassi	Total Number
1475–76	9597 (95.1%)	492 (4.9%)	10089
1476–77	7600 (94.5%)	446 (5.5%)	8046
1477–78	1997 (97.9%)	43 (2.1%)	2040
TOTALS	19194 (95.1%)	981 (4.9%)	20175

Source: From Cipolla, "Relazione," p. 214 (in number of cloths).

Table 6.1. Arnaldi Lands: Types of Rents

Type of Rent	1400–39	1440–59	1460–79	1480–99
Money	10 (19.6%)	63 (43.4%)	25 (56.8%)	90 (71.4%)
Kind	13 (25.5%)	32 (22.1%)	7 (15.9%)	19 (15.1%)
Money/kind	23 (45.1%)	40 (27.6%)	6 (13.6%)	7 (5.6%)
Partiary	1 (1.9%)	5 (3.4%)	6 (13.6%)	10 (7.9%)
Money/kind/partiary	4 (7.8%)	5 (3.4%)	—	—
TOTALS	51	145	44	126

Sources: A.S.Vic., Fondo Piovene Orgian, Arnaldi parchments; ivi, Notarile; ivi, Ufficio del Registro.

Table 6.2. Arnaldi Lands, by Number of Fields

Type of Land	1400–39	1440–59	1460–79	1480–99
Arable	29 (29.6%)	117 (31.9%)	26 (20.6%)	31 (15.7%)
Arable/vine	39 (39.8%)	155 (42.3%)	61 (48.4%)	121 (61.1%)
Pasture	12 (12.2%)	59 (16.1%)	28 (22.2%)	22 (11.1%)
Arable/pasture	15 (15.3%)	21 (5.7%)	8 (6.3%)	18 (9.1%)
Forest/waste	3 (3.1%)	14 (3.8%)	3 (2.4%)	6 (3%)
TOTALS	98	366	126	198

Sources: A.S.Vic., Fondo Piovene Orgian, Arnaldi parchments; ivi, Notarile; ivi, Ufficio del Registro.

Table 7.1. *Estimi* of the Vicentine Council of One Hundred (1453)

Estimo (in lire)	Number of Councillors	Cumulative Number of Councillors	Percentage of Assessed Population at or above This Estimo
15+	2 (2.5%)		0.4%
10–14.75	6 (7.4%)	8 (9.9%)	1.2%
6–9.75	10 (12.3%)	18 (22.2%)	3.0%
4–5.75	9 (11.1%)	27 (33.3%)	4.9%
3–3.75	10 (12.3%)	37 (45.7%)	7.2%
2–2.75	14 (17.3%)	51 (62.9%)	11.7%
1–1.75	23 (28.4%)	74 (91.4%)	23.9%
0.5–0.75	3 (3.7%)	77 (95.1%)	47.3%
0.25	4 (4.9%)	81 (100%)	100%

Sources: Council list from Bertoliana, Arch. Torre 62, ff. 772v–74r; *estimi* of 1453 and 1460. Twenty of 101 councillors could not be located on *estimo* rolls.

Table 7.2. *Estimi* of Vicentine Great Council (1510)

Estimo (in lire)	Number of Councillors	Cumulative Number of Councillors	Percentage of Assessed Population at or above This Estimo
15+	2 (0.5%)		0.3%
10–14.75	10 (2.7%)	12 (3.3%)	0.8%
6–9.75	32 (8.8%)	44 (12.1%)	3.4%
4–5.75	34 (9.3%)	78 (21.4%)	5.8%
3–3.75	23 (6.3%)	101 (27.7%)	8.2%
2–2.75	43 (11.8%)	144 (39.6%)	10.8%
1–1.75	87 (23.9%)	231 (63.5%)	22.7%
0.5–0.75	92 (25.3%)	323 (88.7%)	47.7%
0.25	41 (11.3%)	364 (100%)	100%

Sources: Council list from Rumor, *Blasone vicentino,* pp. 286–94; *estimo* of 1505. Two-hundred sixty-two of 626 councillors could not be located on *estimo* rolls.

Table 7.3. Comparative Wealth of Vicentine Council
of One Hundred (1453) and Great Council (1510)

Estimo	1453	1510
Over L. 7	19.8%	8.8%
L. 3–L. 7	25.9%	17.9%
Under L. 3	54.3%	73.4%

Sources: See tables 7.1–7.2. The divisions correspond to the
Veronese categories of *minores, mediocres,* and *maiores.* These
classifications were also used in compilation of Vicentine
assessments (*Ius municipale,* f. 44v), though wealth thresholds
are not mentioned. Since Vicentine *estimo* procedures were
worked out when the city was under Veronese rule, it is likely
that Vicentines used the same criteria.

Table 7.4. Scrutinies for Eligibility to Veronese Councils

Years	Mean Annual Number of Electors	Mean Annual Number of Candidates
1450–56	20	225
1457–68	98	250
1481–89	105	326
1490–99	110	340
1500–1507	110	311

Source: A.S.Ver., Archivi Privati, Lando, regs. 4–6. The years
1467 and 1469–80 are missing. The number of electors is often
not given, but can be inferred from vote totals.
Note: The year 1462 has been omitted: a new system imposed in
this year only reduced the number of candidates to 120.

Table 7.5. Successes/Failures (Percentage of Successes) of Memorialist Families in Veronese Scrutinies

Family	1457–68	1481–89	1490–99	1500–7
Bovo	10/5 (67%)	7/3 (70%)	10/2 (83%)	8/11 (42%)
Bovi	11/5 (69%)	4/7 (36%)	10/1 (91%)	5/7 (42%)
Fracastoro	15/12 (56%)	26/8 (76%)	32/13 (71%)	27/13 (68%)
Verità	25/26 (49%)	50/20 (71%)	53/21 (72%)	31/26 (54%)
Verità Poeta	2/8 (20%)	1/11 (8%)	0/18 (0%)	0/13 (0%)

Source: Same as table 7.4. The Muronovo and Guastaverza do not appear in the scrutinies. The Verità Poeta have been distinguished from the Verità proper; they were regarded as a separate family in all documents of the era.

Table 7.6. Citation of Arnaldi by Noble Title

Years	Noble	No Title	Number of Documents
1430–39	6.1%	93.9%	114
1440–49	7.5%	92.5%	240
1450–59	20.4%	79.6%	269
1460–69	27.5%	72.5%	51
1470–79	66.7%	33.3%	75
1480–89	85.0%	15.0%	120
1490–99	96.9%	3.1%	96

Sources: A.S.Vic., PO, AP, LAGA and LASA; ivi, Not., registers of Bortolo and Cristoforo Bassan, and Ambrogio Saraceni. Included as noble titles are *egregius, illustris, prudens,* and *providus,* as well as *nobilis.*

NOTES

Abbreviations

    A.S. Pad.: Archivio di Stato di Padova
Bib. Civ.: Biblioteca del Museo Civico
Bib. Univ.: Archivio Universitaria

    A.S. Ven.: Archivio di Stato di Venezia
Marciana: Biblioteca Nazionale Marciana

    A.S. Ven.: Archivio di Stato di Verona
AAC: Antico Archivio del Comune
Anag: Anagrafi
    Com: Comune
    Prov.: Provincia
Perg.: Pergamene
Test: Testamenti
Arch. Cap.: Archivio Capitolare
Bib. Civ.: Biblioteca Civica

    Arch. Cap.: Archivio Capitolare
Arch. Curia: Archivio della Curia Vescovile
A.S. Vic: Archivio di Stato di Vicenza
Not.: Fondo Notarile
PO: Archivio Familiare Piovene Orgian
    153 Ist.: No. 153 Istromenti Arnaldi
    AP: Arnaldi parchments
    LAGA: Liber Actoris Gasparis Arnaldi
    LASA: Liber Acquisti Silvestri Arnaldi
    Vic. 152: Vicenza No. 152 (Istromenti diversi)
Test.: Fondo Testamenti Bombacini
Uff. Reg.: Fondo Ufficio del Registro

Biblioteca Civica Bertoliana
    Arch. Torre: Archivio Torre
    Gonz.: Archivio della Camera Gonzati

Introduction

1. James S. Grubb and Gian Maria Varanini, eds., *Memorie familiari dal Veneto (sec. XV)*, forthcoming. The introduction, to which the reader is referred for more thorough consideration of family chronicles, addresses three linked issues: the uncertain typology of the *libro di famiglia*, why the Veneto produced (or preserved) so few memoirs compared with the huge Tuscan repertoire, and why these families might have chosen to compile domestic accounts.

2. Dennis Romano, in the Syracuse University European History Seminar, February 1994.

3. The *liber* of the Arnaldi is also freestanding, but exists only in two mid-sixteenth-century copies. These were evidently compiled from another source or sources and then arranged in topical order. The original has not been located, but was probably, from the evidence of the other memoirs, an account book or *zibaldone*.

4. The Fracastoro text is now bound with a volume of land accounts, but is of a different size and foliation; its original setting is unknown.

5. Febvre, "Man or Productivity," pp. 1–3; Kuehn, "Reading Microhistory," p. 515.

6. "Discorso inaugurale," p. 11.

7. Quoted in Cipolla, *De imperatore*, unfoliated.

8. Burguière, "Introduction" to Forster and Ranum, eds., *Family and Society*, p. viii.

9. Kent, "Essay" to *Bartolomeo Cederni*, p. 10.

10. Brooke, *Medieval Idea*, p. vii.

11. See Burguière, "Introduction," pp. vii–ix.

12. "Professioni," p. 44; similarly, Duby, *The Knight*, p. 7.

Chapter 1. Marriage

1. Frati, "Ricordanze," pp. 375, 382.

2. Vicentines under age twenty-five could act in court only with a procurator or with special permission of a judge; those under age twenty could not alienate goods without the consent of two kinsmen: *Ius municipale*, ff. 87v–88r, 156r; similarly, *Statuti Veronae*, pp. 138–39.

3. The age when those holding seats on the Council of 500 could actually vote: *Ius municipale*, ff. 11v–12r.

4. Belmont, "Fonction," p. 650; Burguière, "Rituel," pp. 638, 647–48; Klapisch-Zuber, *Women*, pp. 254–57; Duby, *The Knight*, esp. p. 225; idem, *Medieval Marriage*, pp. 11–15.

5. Gaspare I's brother Piero had not married: A.S.Vic., Not., Bortolo Bassan 4531, 22 August 1433 (copy in A.S.Vic., Test., XIX, same date); see also ibid., 4535, 22 May 1437.

6. Branca, preface to Morelli's *Ricordi*, pp. 28–29; Alberti, *Libri*, pp. 124–28; Leverotti, "Linee," p. 200.

7. Esmein, *Mariage*, pp. 85–90; Augustine, *City of God*, XV, 16; Brooke, *Medieval Idea*, ch. 2; Leclercq, *Monks*, chs. 2–3.

8. Kirshner and Molho, "Dowry Fund," p. 435.

9. Wealthy families in Florence had a lower incidence of marriage and a higher incidence of celibacy than the poor: Herlihy and Klapisch-Zuber, *Toscans*, pp. 410–11.

10. Duby, *Medieval Marriage*, pp. 10–11; idem, *The Knight*, pp. 104–5, 274. For Flor-

entine and Limousain strategies similar to that of the Arnaldi, see Sillano's introduction to Chellini's *Ricordanze*, p. 16; Biget and Tricard, "Livres," p. 329.

11. Tabulation from Pagliarini, *Cronicae*, bk. V (extinct families) and bk. VI (extant families).

12. Chojnacki, "'Most Serious Duty,'" p. 147; idem, "Measuring Adulthood," p. 382; idem, "Subaltern Patriarchs," p. 78.

13. Hajnal, "European Marriage Patterns," pp. 101–43.

14. Only fifteen of 24,000 girls in Florence's dowry fund were unmarried, and under 6 percent of Tuscan women in the 1427 *catasto* were "permanent spinsters": Molho, "Professioni," pp. 7, 15; Herlihy, "Deaths," p. 143; Klapisch-Zuber, *Women*, pp. 19–20.

15. Kirshner, *Pursuing Honor*, p. 9.

16. Molho, "Professioni," pp. 6–7, 10–13, 27–32; Brucker, "Monasteries," p. 46. Three Veneto wills specifying alternative bequests for daughters to *maritare vel monachare* indicate that families might pay 10 percent, 13 percent, and 43 percent of marital dowries if daughters chose convents: A.S.Ver., Test. 89, #39; ivi 128, #334; Chojnacki, "'Most Serious Duty,'" p. 150.

17. Repeta, f. 81v; Lorcin, *Vivre*, p. 75. The Repeta case illustrates what Lorcin sees as informal female primogeniture, with the eldest given husbands and the youngest given to God: ibid., p. 79; similarly, Epstein, *Wills*, pp. 77–81.

18. Herlihy, "Generation," p. 359; idem, "Deaths," p. 143; idem, "Vieillir," p. 1346; idem, "Tuscan Town," p. 92; idem and Klapisch-Zuber, *Toscans*, pp. 205, 399; Klapisch-Zuber, "Household," p. 272; idem, "Fiscalité," p. 1328; idem, *Women*, p. 111; Kirshner and Molho, "Dowry Fund," pp. 419, 432–33; idem, "Monte," p. 41, tab. 8; Fabbri, *Alleanza*, pp. 112–16.

19. Chojnacki, "Measuring Adulthood," p. 379. Four Freschi men married around 32 (mean 32.8, median 31.2).

20. Herlihy, "Generation," p. 359; idem, "Vieillir," p. 1346; idem, "Deaths," p. 143; idem, *Medieval Households*, pp. 104–7; Klapisch-Zuber, *Women*, p. 110; Herlihy and Klapisch-Zuber, *Toscans*, pp. 205, 207, and variants on pp. 396–99, 404; Molho, "Professioni," p. 14; Kirshner and Molho, "Dowry Fund," p. 432; idem, "Monte," p. 41 and tab. 8; see also Morrison, Kirshner, and Molho, "Life Cycle Events," p. 487.

21. Kirshner and Molho, "Dowry Fund," pp. 430–31; idem, "Monte," tab. 8; Herlihy, "Vieillir," p. 1349; idem, "Deaths," p. 146.

22. Chojnacki, "'Most Serious Duty,'" pp. 142, 151; idem, "Measuring Adulthood," p. 372. Ten Freschi women, however, married at a mean of slightly over twenty-three years.

23. Herlihy, "Generation," p. 359; idem, "Vieillir," p. 1346; Kirshner and Molho, "Dowry Fund," pp. 432–33; idem, "Monte," p. 41 and tab. 8; Herlihy and Klapisch-Zuber, *Toscans*, pp. 205, 207, 396–99; Klapisch-Zuber, "Household," p. 272; idem, "Fiscalité," p. 1329.

24. Herlihy, "Population," p. 114.

25. Florence had a higher percentage of incomplete or isolated households, a lower incidence of marriage, and a higher incidence of celibates than did the rest of Tuscany: Herlihy and Klapisch-Zuber, *Toscans*, pp. 405–7, 410–11.

26. Herlihy, "Marriage," pp. 10–11; idem, *Medieval Households*, 104–9; idem and Klapisch-Zuber, *Toscans*, pp. 207, 399–400; Leverotti, "Linee," p. 188.

27. Smith, "People," p. 111; idem, "Hypothèses," pp. 109–10; Biget and Tricard, "Livres," pp. 327–29; Roussiaud, "Prostitution," pp. 294–95.

28. Hajnal, "European Marriage Patterns," esp. pp. 101–8.

29. Herlihy, "Tuscan Town," p. 92; idem, "Vieillir," p. 1347; Herlihy and Klapisch-Zuber, *Toscans*, pp. 412–13.

30. Vegio, *De educatione*, I, p. 19; Morelli, *Ricordi*, pp. 111–12, 155; Savonarola, *Trattato*, pp. 6–7, 15–16, 21; Molho, "Deception," pp. 206–10; Fabbri, *Alleanza*, pp. 116–19; Herlihy, "Vieillir," pp. 1342, 1346–47; idem, "Roots," p. 133.

31. Chojnacki, "Measuring Adulthood," p. 373; da Feltre, *Sermoni*, I, p. 396; Monaco, "Aspetti," p. 111; Savonarola, *Trattato*, pp. 6–7, 15–16.

32. Herlihy and Klapisch-Zuber, *Toscans*, pp. 594–95; Klapisch-Zuber, *Women*, p. 186; Chojnacki, "Power," p. 128; idem, "Measuring Adulthood," pp. 374–75; idem, "'Most Serious Duty,'" pp. 142–43.

33. I have found but a single comment, from a friar: da Feltre's "Mo, considera un pocho: ista paupercula dimisit patrem et matrem, fratres suos et domum suam, ubi fuit nutrita, alevata etc." (*Sermoni*, II, p. 142).

34. Herlihy, "Population," tab. 8.

35. Caterina Botarini, Cassandra Revese, Marcella Fracanzani, Simone Revese, Giacomo Cavazzoli, and Giovanna da Schio; Elisabetta dal Gorgo came from a nearby neighborhood: 1453 *estimo*, ff. 5, 8, 9, 32; 1460 *estimo*, ff. 97–98, 101–4, 142.

36. Cohn, *Laboring Classes*, pp. 74–82; see also the praise of Giovanni Morelli (like the Arnaldi, rising but still below the top) for an uncle who "si imparento' nella sua vicinanza e in uno medesimo gonfalone": Pandimiglio, "Giovanni di Pagolo Morelli," pp. 34–35. Hughes, however, sees weak neighborhood ties in all Genoese marriages: "Kinsmen," pp. 97–98, 104.

37. Spouses in the early generation came from families that were considerably less wealthy, ranking at least one or two deciles below the Arnaldi in tax assessments. The explanation seems to lie in the Arnaldi's ambiguous standing—rich but not prominent: they were the wealthiest of their occupational and status group, and had to accept less prosperous in-laws if they were to marry at all. Their economic equals were the lawyers, judges, and nobles, who had a clearly higher social rank and with whom the Arnaldi could not hope to marry.

38. A.S.Vic., Not., Bortolo Bassan 4539, 23 October 1441; A.S.Vic., PO, AP, 17 July 1443.

39. *Matricola* in Bertoliana, Gonz. 535.

40. A.S.Vic., Not., Bortolo Bassan 4542, 22 January 1443; A.S.Vic., PO, LAGA, 11 May 1444; merchant guild records in Bertoliana, Gonz. 309; wool guild *matricola* in Bertoliana, Gonz. 544 (cf. Zanazzo, *Arte*, p. 51).

41. For the wealth and residence of later spouses (Elena Poiana, Bernardino Sesso, Paola Repeta, and Dorotea and Alessandro Thiene), see 1453 *estimo*, ff. 7, 17–18, 44, 88; 1460 *estimo*, ff. 100, 110–11, 122–23, 144; 1477 *estimo*, ff. 6, 10, 12, 18, 103; 1505 *estimo*, ff. 2, 4, 7, 15, 18, 23, 30. For these families' pasts, see Pagliarini, *Cronicae*, bk. VI; Repeta, f. 80v. For the neighborhood exogamy of the Florentine patriciate, see Klapisch-Zuber, *Women*, pp. 81–85; Fabbri, *Alleanza*, pp. 108–10; Cohn, *Laboring Classes*, pp. 57–60.

42. Roper, "Weddings," pp. 62, 65–67, 71.

43. For Florence, see Kuehn, "Reading Microhistory," pp. 520–21; Klapisch-Zuber, *Women*, pp. 182–93; Herlihy and Klapisch-Zuber, *Toscans*, pp. 589–93; for Gaeta and Venice, see Brandileone, *Saggi*, pp. 76–79, 119ff.; for Rome, see ibid., pt. I, ch. 7; Klapisch-Zuber, *Women*, pp. 247–51 and ch. 9. Among Venice's Freschi, the *ductio* was immediate in seven of eight cases.

44. Arnaldi, ff. 2r–v, 5r–v, 10r–11r, 13v–15r; Stoppi, f. 2v; Repeta, f. 81v.

45. Helmholz, *Marriage Litigation*, ch. 2.

46. Brucker, *Giovanni*, pp. 29–33, 49; Ruggiero, "Onore," pp. 756–58; Corazzol and Corrà, *Esperimenti*; Braunstein, "Honneur."

47. Esmein, *Mariage*, I, title I, ch. 1, esp. pp. 108–37; Gaudemet, *Mariage*, pp. 165–77; Dauvillier, *Mariage*, esp. pp. 8–32 and title 2, chs. 1–2; Brooke, *Medieval Idea*, esp. pp. 54–56, 65, 128–38, 152; Sheehan, "Choice," pp. 7, 13–19; Donahue, "Canon Law," pp. 144–45; Besta, *Famiglia*, pp. 70–71; Vaccari, *Matrimonio*, pp. 7–8. For legitimation of hand-touch or ring ceremony (physical analogue to verbal consent), see Besta, *Famiglia*, p. 78; Brandileone, *Saggi*, esp. pp. 246–50, 305–6, 356–64 and pt. II, ch. 2; Rodocanachi, "Mariage," p. 33.

48. Brundage, *Law*, pp. 264, 334, 436, 502, 504; Kirshner, "*Maritus*," pp. 126–36.

49. The Lombard law's *wadia*, a mutual pledge between the groom and the bride's legal guardian at the time of betrothal, came to be associated with the *verba de praesenti* or the placing of the ring: Marongiu, "Matrimonio," p. 65; Brandileone, *Saggi*, pp. 17, 248–49 (reference to Vicenza), 255; Besta, *Famiglia*, pp. 128–29. It appears as *guadia* (verb form *guadiare*) in Veneto documents: *Statuti Veronae*, p. 137; A.S.Vic., PO, AP, 24 November 1466 and 21 November 1433; Arnaldi, f. 14r; *Ius municipale*, ff. 130r, 135r; Brandileone, "Intervento," p. 306.

50. Burguière, "Rituel"; Esmein, *Mariage*, pp. 124–37; Marongiu, "Matrimonio," pp. 52–54.

51. Brandileone, *Saggi*, p. 92 (Gratian); Salvioli, "Benedizione," p. 186 (Peter Lombard).

52. Esmein, *Mariage*, pp. 104–5, 108–19; Dauvillier, *Mariage*, p. 122; Marongiu, "Matrimonio," sec. 3; Guerreau-Jalabert, "Structures," p. 1036. The strength of the *verba de futuro* is seen in the case of the Veronese Giorgio Sommariva, who suffered a seven hundred–ducat fine and eighteen years of exile for marrying his son to an already-betrothed girl: Mistruzzi, "Giorgio Sommariva," pp. 152–53, 180–83.

53. Arnaldi, ff. 5v, 11r, 13v. The sole reference to a woman's consent comes from a Freschi marriage contract (Freschi, f. 109r): "che piacendola dicta dona al prefato Zacharia e lui a ley."

54. Besta, *Famiglia*, p. 130; Esmein, *Mariage*, pp. 153–63; Dauvillier, *Mariage*, p. 40; Sheehan, "Choice," pp. 12–13; Marongiu, "Matrimonio," p. 60.

55. Dauvillier, *Mariage*, pp. 126–29; Marongiu, "Matrimonio," pp. 57–61. Veneto ecclesiastical authorities, anxious to prove free consent, respected protest. Fuscha da Thiene, for example, was betrothed at the age of nine by her brother; when she came of age in 1425 and refused to marry her intended, the bishop agreed that *sponsalia* of underage women "*non conficiunt matrimonium*" and allowed her to marry elsewhere: Vicenza, Arch. Curia, Collatio Beneficiorum I, f. 28v.

56. Arnaldi, ff. 2v, 5v, 11r, 13v, 14v–15r; Muronovo, ff. 74v–75r; similarly, Abbondanza, ed., *Notariato*, pp. 307–8.

57. Dauvillier, *Mariage*, p. 80; Brooke, *Medieval Idea*, pp. 128–29; Besta, *Famiglia*, pp. 84–85.

58. Duby, *The Knight*, pp. 34, 72; Brundage, *Law*, pp. 136–37; Besta, *Famiglia*, pp. 104–9; *Ius municipale*, f. 130r; *Statuti Veronae*, p. 208; Brandileone, *Saggi*, pp. 46–47; Carron, *Enfant*, pp. 31–32.

59. Arnaldi, ff. 11r, 13v, 14v, 15r.

60. Roper, "Weddings," pp. 65–68; Belmont, "Fonction"; Brooke, *Medieval Idea*, pp. 129–34; Brandileone, *Saggi*, pp. 78–79; Klapisch-Zuber, *Women*, pp. 185–87.

61. Antonio dal Bovo married on 16 January 1462 and transferred his bride on 6 February 1463; his son was born on 18 April 1463: dal Bovo, f. 4v. For other regions, see Brandileone, *Saggi*, pp. 305–6; Roper, "Weddings," pp. 88–92; Klapisch-Zuber, *Women*, pp. 186, 189, 191–92. Couples did not wait for transfer in France or early modern England: Burguière, "Rituel," p. 645; Macfarlane, *Marriage*, p. 305.

62. Esmein, *Mariage*, pp. 83–85, 96–97, 99–100, 108–19, 124–37; Brundage, *Law*, pp. 135–37, 436, 502; Dauvillier, *Mariage*, pp. 8, 10–11, 55–63; Gaudemet, *Mariage*, pp. 117–18, 174–77; Salvioli, "Benedizione," pp. 188, 191–92; Marongiu, "Matrimonio," pp. 49, 56–61; Brandileone, *Saggi*, pp. 9, 368; 380; Tamassia, *Famiglia*, pp. 191–93; Duby, *The Knight*, p. 34; Kirshner, "Maritus," pp. 113, 126–36.

63. Belmont, "Fonction," pp. 650–55.

64. Esmein, *Mariage*, pp. 178–85 and ch. 3; Dauvillier, *Mariage*, pp. 23–28, 133–35; Brandileone, *Saggi*, pt. I, chs. 1–2, esp. pp. 29–71, and pt. II, ch. 5; Besta, *Famiglia*, p. 83 and ch. 15; Roper, "Weddings," pp. 66–71; Sheehan, "Choice," p. 15; Brandileone, "Intervento," sec. 1–5.

65. Kirshner, "Maritus," pp. 118–19; Klapisch-Zuber, *Women*, pp. 183–87; Herlihy and Klapisch-Zuber, *Toscans*, p. 591; Brucker, *Giovanni*, p. 83; Brandileone, *Saggi*, pp. 40–42, 65–66; idem, "Intervento," secs. 7, 9, 11–12; Rodocanachi, "Mariage," p. 33; Brundage, *Law*, p. 440; Cherubini, *Signori*, pp. 19–20; Salvioli, "Benedizione," pp. 192–93; see also Laribiere, "Mariage," pp. 337–40.

66. Esmein, *Mariage*, pp. 106–8, 149; Besta, *Famiglia*, p. 122; Gaudemet, *Mariage*, pp. 225–37; Dauvillier, *Mariage*, pp. 23–32, 105–21; Brandileone, *Saggi*, pp. 293–94; Sheehan, "Choice," pp. 25–32; Duby, *Medieval Mariage*, pp. 34, 91; idem, *The Knight*, ch. 9; Jussen, "Parrainage," p. 482; Brooke, *Medieval Idea*, p. 29; in general, Molin and Mutembe, *Rituel*. A Venetian law of 1288 ordered preannouncement of the marriage in the bride's parish church: Cecchetti, "Donna," pp. 313–14.

67. Macfarlane, *Marriage*, p. 310; Helmholz, *Marriage Litigation*, pp. 31, 72; Brooke, *Medieval Idea*, pp. 56–59; Brandileone, "Intervento," pp. 269–70; Brundage, *Law*, pp. 190–91; Salvioli, "Benedizione," pp. 173–79.

68. Marongiu, "Matrimonio," pp. 63–64 (but see Klapisch-Zuber, *Women*, p. 193); Hanawalt, *Ties*, p. 203 (but see Helmholz, *Marriage Litigation*, p. 28; Macfarlane, *Marriage*, p. 310; Goody, *Development*, pp. 148–50; Hilaire, *Regime*, p. 33).

69. Dauvillier, *Mariage*, pp. 105–21; Brooke, *Medieval Idea*, p. 251.

70. Portions of weddings in Gaeta, Venice, and Rome might be performed in church, though the core took place in the bride's house: Brandileone, *Saggi*, pp. 76–79, 90–99, 296–313. The Freschi of Venice, however, invariably married in church.

71. Klapisch-Zuber, *Women*, pp. 193–212 (quote from p. 193), 276; Herlihy and Klapisch-Zuber, *Toscans*, p. 591. For the similar situation in Treviso (though there are

scattered references to Masses or benedictions at the time of marriage), see Pesce, *Chiesa*, pp. 37–38.

72. Stoppi, f. 2v. Published nuptual sermons indicate that Masses were not unknown: Verona, Bib. Civ., Incunaboli 31, 307.

73. Arnaldi, ff. 5v, 10v.

74. Esmein, *Mariage*, pp. 396–98; Brundage, *Law*, pp. 158, 191; Manselli, "Vie," p. 6; Gaudemet, *Mariage*, p. 219.

75. Brundage, *Law*, pp. 91–92, 157; Belmont, "Fonction," p. 650; Payer, *Sex*, pp. 24–25; Duby, *The Knight*, pp. 29, 66–67. For Gaeta, see Brandileone, *Saggi*, pp. 76–77; idem, "Intervento," pp. 354–55; for Venice, see Hughes, "Brideprice," p. 275; Ercole, "Vicende," p. 142; Rodocanachi, "Mariage," p. 42; for Florence and Rome, see Klapisch-Zuber, *Women*, pp. 187–88, 193; for the Limousin, see Biget and Tricard, "Livres," p. 337.

76. Dal Bovo, f. 4v; Muronovo, ff. 45r–50; Arnaldi, ff. 44r–v.

77. *Statuti Veronae*, pp. 136–37; Kirshner, *Pursuing Honor*, p. 2; Bellomo, *Ricerche*, ch. 5.

78. A.S.Vic., PO, AP, 17 August 1457; see also ibid., 27 February 1476. For the imperative of providing a dowry, see Kirshner, *Pursuing Honor*, pp. 8–13; Besta, *Famiglia*, ch. 20, esp. p. 146; Ercole, "Istituto," I, pp. 232–48.

79. On the *exclusio propter dotem*, see Bellomo, *Ricerche*, ch. 6; Dominici, *Regola*, pp. 111–12; Ercole, "Istituto," I, pp. 211–48, 260–61, 286–89; Kuehn, *Law*, ch. 10; Hilaire, *Regime*, pp. 350–67; Klapisch-Zuber, *Women*, pp. 213–18; Goody and Tambiah, *Bridewealth*; Goody, *Development*, pp. 243–61; Herlihy and Klapisch-Zuber, *Toscans*, pp. 543–44; Hughes, "Brideprice."

80. One Verità will named sons and daughters as equal inheritors: A.S.Ver., Perg., Verità #396. On the proportion of the dowry, see Morelli, *Ricordi*, pp. 223, 230; Besta, *Famiglia*, p. 148; Chojnacki, "Dowries," p. 575; idem, "Patrician Women," p. 186; Hughes, "Famiglia," pp. 933–34; Lorcin, *Vivre*, p. 65; Sapori, "Alberti del Giudice," p. 184; Fabbri, *Alleanza*, pp. 64–65; Cohn, *Cult*, p. 197; Bellomo, *Ricerche*, ch. 6, #9.

81. In six cases, *donaria* were valued at 13 percent to 24 percent of the dowry: A.S.Ver., Test., mazzo 79, #27; A.S.Vic., PO, 153 Ist., 12 July 1496; dal Bovo, f. 4r. *Correda* in Venice, on the other hand, could amount to up to one-third of the total settlement: Chojnacki, "Marriage Legislation," p. 165; in Freschi marriages, *roba* averaged 32.8 percent of the total. On extradotal goods, see Kirshner, *Pursuing Honor*, pp. 20–22; Kirshner and Molho, "Abbozzo," pp. 26–27; Caro, "Corredi," pp. 526–38; Hilaire, *Regime*, pp. 102–5.

82. On the decline of husbands' gifts, see Herlihy and Klapisch-Zuber, *Toscans*, p. 590; Vaccari, *Matrimonio*, pp. 61, 89; Hughes, "Brideprice," pp. 277, 284; idem, "Domestic Ideals," pp. 129–30; idem, "Famiglia," p. 933; idem, "Urban Growth," pp. 13ff., 24ff. Florentine husbands, however, provided significant if ill-documented gifts to their wives; Klapisch-Zuber, *Women*, pp. 218–24. On the *donatio propter nuptias* and the husband's contribution, see Vaccari, *Matrimonio*, pt. II, ch. 3, esp. pp. 96–98; Hilaire, *Regime*, pp. 138–46, 167–81, 190–215; Epstein, *Wills*, p. 104; Brandileone, *Donatio*, esp. ch. 4; Besta, *Famiglia*, ch. 21. In the Veneto, the term *donatio propter nuptias* refers not to a husband's gift but to a pledge of his goods for eventual dotal restitution: see next note.

83. In the universal formula, the husband confessed receipt of the dowry, then pledged

an equivalent to the bride's father or brother(s) "iure pignoris et nomine donationis propter nuptias seu contradotis et ad conservationem et pro conservatione dotis"; she then renounced further claims on the patrimony: e.g., A.S.Vic., Not., Bortolo Bassan 4540, 13 April 1442; ibid. 4554, 13 April 1456. Venetian men were obliged actually to deposit a sum equal to the dowry with government officials: Chojnacki, "Patrician Women," pp. 191–92; Crouzet-Pavan, *Espaces*, p. 449.

84. *Ius municipale*, f. 153v; *Statuti Veronae*, p. 137; in general, Kirshner, *"Maritus,"* esp. pp. 112, 116, 123–36; idem, "Materials," p. 185; Ercole, "Istituto," II, pp. 194–222.

85. A.S.Vic., Test., XIX, 22 August 1433.

86. A.S.Vic., Not., Bortolo Bassan 4535, 22 May 1437; ibid. 4539, 23 October 1441; ibid. 4540, 13 April 1442.

87. A.S.Vic., Not., Bortolo Bassan 4549, 9 June 1451, 27 October 1451; A.S.Vic., PO, AP, 13 April 1456.

88. A.S.Vic., PO, AP, 4 May 1461; A.S.Vic., Not., Bortolo Bassan 4559, 26 October 1462; ibid. 4560, 29 August 1463.

89. A.S.Vic., PO, 153 Ist., 12 July 1496, 15 August 1502.

90. A.S.Ver., Test., mazzo 79, #27.

91. *Paradisio*, XV, 103–5.

92. Pullan, *"Scuole,"* p. 284.

93. Stuard, "Dowry Increase," esp. p. 810.

94. Herlihy, "Generation," p. 362; idem, "Marriage Market," pp. 12–18; idem, "Vieillir," pp. 1346–49; idem, *Medieval Households*, p. 102; Herlihy and Klapisch-Zuber, *Toscans*, pp. 414–19. There is corroborating evidence of a surplus of women in Molho, "Professioni," p. 9. Still, the higher rate of women entering convents would have brought sex ratios back in line: see Brucker, "Monasteries," esp. p. 41; Lorcin, *Vivre*, p. 75.

95. "Dowries," esp. pp. 580–90; idem, "Patrician Women," pp. 194–95; idem, "'Most Serious Duty,'" pp. 148–49, 152–53.

96. Hughes, "Brideprice," pp. 288–90; Molho, "Professioni," pp. 27–28; Bourdieu, "Marriage Strategies," esp. p. 124; Goody and Tambiah, *Bridewealth*, pp. 22–29, 52; Goody, *Development*, pp. 255–61.

97. Dominici, *Regola*, pp. 111–12, 177; da Feltre, *Sermoni*, I, p. 396; Conversino, *Rationarium*, XIV, p. 82; da Certaldo, *Libro*, pp. 215, 245–46; Pandimiglio, "Giovanni di Pagolo Morelli," pp. 40–41. Morelli did warn against arranging marriage purely for economic gain, pointing to the harm that would befall the family when a high dowry had to be restored: *Ricordi*, p. 211.

98. A.S.Vic., PO, 153 Ist., 15 August 1502.

99. A.S.Ver., Test., mazzo 89, #39; Varanini, "Famiglia," p. 44. On the unavailing efforts of "old" Venetian houses to limit marriage settlements, in order to block "new" patrician families from offering huge dowries to attract prestigious alliances, see Chojnacki, "Marriage Legislation," pp. 172–77.

100. A.S.Vic., Not., Bartolomeo Bassan 4546, 4 March 1447; A.S.Ver., Test., mazzo 89, #39.

101. Veronese jurist Bartolomeo Cipolla thought that husbands were especially likely to provide dowries or make false dowry confessions when they were rich but common, marrying into the nobility: "Sepe hoc de facto contingit quando dives igno-

bilis et vilis conditionis accipit aliquam uxorem nobilem in causa se nobilitandi et dotat eam sive confiteatur se recepisse dotem quan non recipet." In that case, said Cipolla, the husband's fictitious confession should be accepted at face value when calculating the amount to be restored: *De imperatore*, unfoliated, #34 of list of privileges of nobility.

102. A.S.Vic., PO, 153 Ist., 12 July 1496; A.S.Vic., Not., Antonio Saraceni 4958, 29 July 1497; A.S.Vic., Arch. PO, LASA, f. 30, 9 November 1498; A.S.Vic., Not., Antonio Saraceni 4961, 28 February 1506; ibid. 4969, 9 March 1511. For a twelve-year lag in a Mantuan-Paduan marriage, see Marciana, Lat. XIV, 284 (4300), #6. On long-term payments in Tuscany, see Kirshner, *"Maritus,"* pp. 120–23; Hicks, "Sources," p. 39.

103. Hilaire, *Regime*, pp. 69–80.

104. Stoppi, ff. 3v–4v.

105. This was not the case elsewhere: Crouzet-Pavan, *Espaces*, p. 447; Hughes, "Brideprice," p. 281; Kirshner and Molho, "Dowry Fund," p. 435; idem, "Abbozzo," pp. 27–28.

106. A.S.Vic., PO, AP, 13 April 1456, 13 March 1470. For a similar Paduan case, see Collodo, "Credito," p. 23.

107. Hilaire, *Regime*, pp. 136, 160.

108. Klapisch-Zuber, *Women*, esp. pp. 215, 240; Kirshner and Molho, "Monte," p. 26 and *passim*.

109. In twenty-six cases in which the precise duration of marriage is known, the figure is 21.5 years; if we add thirteen unions in which a minimum duration is known (both spouses are known to be alive at some point after the marriage), the figure rises to 23.6 years. Duration of marriage elsewhere has been little studied. Given a greater age gap between Florentine spouses, we might expect a shorter duration of marriage; a high percentage of women in the 33–42 age group were already widowed, for example: Herlihy and Klapisch-Zuber, *Toscans*, p. 403. English figures are comparable to those of Verona and Vicenza (Bennett, *Women*, p. 143) and slightly higher among early modern aristocrats (Houlbrooke, *English Family*, p. 208).

110. See the warnings of Medick and Sabean: "Introduction," p. 3; "Interest," pp. 10–11.

111. Bovi, f. 13r.

112. Arnaldi, ff. 4v–5r.

113. Brucker, *Society*, ##16, 22; Niccolini di Gambugliano, *Chronicles*, pp. 132–34; Phillips, *Marco Parenti*, pp. 45–46; Franceschi, "Memoire," pp. 1158–59; Tamassia, *Famiglia*, pp. 164–65.

114. Arnaldi, ff. 5v, 9r; similarly, Verità, f. 85r.

115. Luke 18:28–30; Ephesians 5:25; and, in general, Brooke, *Medieval Idea*, pp. 41–47, 54, 256; Macfarlane, *Marriage*, pp. 159, 168. For *affectio*, see Besta, *Famiglia*, pp. 67–69; Brundage, *Law*, ch. 3; Gaudemet, *Mariage*, pp. 156–57; Noonan, "Marital Affection." Andrea Arnaldi's *dilectio* for Caterina Botarini was precisely that which theologians and canonists expected between husband and wife: Duby, *The Knight*, pp. 33, 176, 216; Leclercq, *Monks*, p. 15.

116. Vegio, *De educatione*, I, chs. 3–4; Lugli, *Trattatisti*, pp. 11–13, ch. 3; da Certaldo, *Libro*, pp. 128–29, 137, 239–41; Cohn, *Death*, pp. 30–31, 75–76; Kuehn, "Women," p. 127; Herlihy, *Medieval Households*, pp. 116–18; idem and Klapisch-Zuber, *Toscans*, pp. 586–88; Alberti, *Libri*, pp. 107–8; Branca, preface to Morelli's *Ricordi*, pp. 28–29; Monaco, "Aspetti," pp. 115–16, 120–25; da Feltre, *Sermoni*, II, pp. 118, 142–43.

117. Avesani, "Verona," pp. 162–68; Leclercq, *Monks*, ch. 1; Houlbrooke, *English Family*, pp. 77–78, 102–3, 207–8; Macfarlane, *Marriage*, ch. 9; Herlihy, "Family"; Brooke, *Medieval Idea*, esp. ch. 11; Chojnacki, "Power," pp. 126–29.

118. Stoppi, f. 2r.

119. A.S.Ver., Perg., Guastaverza #26.

120. On preference shown to wives as executors of wills and guardians of children, see Hilaire, *Regime*, pp. 339–42; de Renzo Villata, "Note," pp. 69–75; Lorcin, *Vivre*, pp. 66–71; Epstein, *Wills*, pp. 89–90, 223; for Florentine cases, see Klapisch-Zuber, "Women Servants," p. 59; Morelli, *Ricordi*, pp. 213–18; Niccolini di Gambugliano, *Chronicles*, pp. 124–25. Crabb estimates that 70 percent of Florentine widows were made guardians of their children: "Alessandra Macinghi Strozzi," pp. 50–51.

121. A.S.Vic., Not., Bortolo Bassan 4531, 22 August 1433; ibid., 4560, 29 August 1463; A.S.Ver., Test., mazzo 81, #45. The case of the burning of the Vicentine Gentile Thiene's barn hinged on the possibility of his wife's negligence; but "probatum est quod uxor dicti Gentilis est mulier sapiens et prudens et solecita circa gubernationem domus et familiae." Jurist Alessandro Nievo quoted lengthy testimony that she had managed well, kept doors closed, and instructed servants to guard carefully against fire: witnesses and jurist were evidently much impressed with the woman (*Consilia*, #87).

122. Chojnacki, "Power," pp. 132–37 (quote from p. 135); idem, "'Most Serious Duty,'" p. 145; Rosenthal, "Aristocratic Marriage," pp. 188–91; Hanawalt, *Ties*, pp. 218–19.

123. Division of inheritance from A.S.Vic., Not., Bortolo Bassan 4535, 22 May 1437; financial problems from A.S.Vic., PO, AP, 14 July 1438, 15 May 1441; A.S.Vic., Not., Bortolo Bassan 4537, 10 February 1439; ibid. 4541, 22 November 1442; ibid. 4543, 6 June 1443; ibid. 4547, undated and 1 July 1449; A.S.Vic., PO, LAGA, 26 January 1443, 28 November 1444, 10 June 1449, 26 November 1450, 22 April 1452, 25 February 1455; aid to daughters from Arnaldi, f. 9v; A.S.Vic., PO, AP, 17 August 1457, 27 February 1476.

124. A.S.Vic., Not., Andrea Arnaldi, 18 April 1437; A.S.Vic., PO, AP, 28 February 1438, 20 September 1445; A.S.Vic., Not. Bortolo Bassan 4548, 18 November 1446.

125. Kuehn, "Legal Guardianship," esp. pp. 309–12; Kirshner and Pluss, "Opinions," p. 68; Kirshner, "Materials"; idem, "Wives' Claims," pp. 257–58, 260–61; idem and Molho, "Monte," pp. 26–27; Hughes, "Urban Growth," p. 21; Giardina, *"Advocatus,"* pp. 321–23; Laribiere, "Marriage," pp. 344–45, 356–57; *Ius municipale*, ff. 110v, 114r.

126. Kuehn, "Legal Guardianship," pp. 315–19; Kirshner and Pluss, "Opinions," p. 70; and see da Certaldo, *Libro*, pp. 239–41.

127. *Ius municipale*, ff. 106r–v, 114r.

128. Kirshner, "Wives' Claims," pp. 257–59, 265–302; see also Brandileone, *Donatio*, pp. 81–82; Hilaire, *Regime*, pp. 137, 186; Ercole, "Istituto," II, pp. 182–87.

129. A.S.Vic., PO, AP, 11 September 1451.

130. Kirshner, "Wives' Claims," p. 299; idem and Molho, "Monte," p. 30; Laribiere, "Mariage," p. 347; Kuehn, "Legal Guardianship," p. 326; Rosenthal, "Position," p. 375.

131. *Ius municipale*, ff. 154r–v; A.S.Vic., PO, AP, 5–8 February and 10 April 1483; and see Kirshner, "Wives' Claims," pp. 288–90.

132. *Ius municipale*, f. 154r; *Ius municipale vicentinum* (Vicenza, 1706), pp. 330–31.

133. Bertoliana, Arch. Torre 777, ff. 170v–71r. They might also alienate dotal goods to dower daughters, if husbands were unable to do so.

134. A.S.Ver., Perg., Verità, #389.

135. Kirshner, "Wives' Claims," pp. 296–99; idem, "Materials," esp. p. 206. To prevent abuses, Vicentine statutes forbade a wife to accept possession of her husband's goods unless she formally proved his mismanagement of her dotal goods: *Ius municipale*, ff. 106r–v.

136. Bertoliana, Arch. Torre 61, ff. 76v–77r, 188r–v.

137. Bertoliana, Arch. Torre 61, f. 193v. The principle dates from the early Trecento, when the Venetian government reserved dowries in confiscating and selling rebels' property: Crouzet-Pavan, *Espaces*, p. 921. Dowry rights were also reserved when counterfeiters' goods were seized: A.S.Ven., Capi dei Dieci, Lettere 1, #393. For the parallel Florentine situation, see Kirshner, "Wives' Claims," pp. 276–78.

138. A.S.Ven., Senato Terra 1, f. 189v.

139. *Ius municipale*, f. 78r; see also f. 174r.

140. Molho et al., "Genealogia."

141. Bovi, f. 13r.

142. Arnaldi, ff. 6v, 7r–v, 9v, 11r, 13v, 14r, 25v.

143. Belmont, "Fonction," p. 251; Duby, *Medieval Marriage*, p. 99.

144. Herlihy, *Medieval Households*, pp. 82–88; introduction to Klapisch-Zuber, *Women*, pp. ix–x; and see Houlbrooke, *English Family*, pp. 40–44.

145. Augustine, *City of God*, XV, 16; Herlihy, *Medieval Households*, p. 11; idem and Klapisch-Zuber, *Toscans*, pp. 527–30, 544–45; Leclercq, *Monks*, pp. 20–21; Duby, *The Knight*, p. 11.

146. Arnaldi, ff. 18r, 19v–20r.

147. Chojnacki, "'Most Serious Duty,'" pp. 146–47; Crouzet-Pavan, *Espaces*, pp. 393–94.

148. *Ius municipale*, ff. 102r–103r; *Statuti Veronae*, pp. 150–52.

149. A.S.Vic., Not., Bortolo Bassan 4535, 22 May 1437; ibid. 4537, 10 February 1439; ibid. 4543, 6 June 1443.

150. A.S.Vic., Not., Bortolo Bassan 4549, 9 November 1451.

151. *Ius municipale*, ff. 156r–v.

152. Kuehn, "Women," esp. pp. 131–33; Kirshner, *Pursuing Honor*, p. 15; idem and Molho, "Monte," pp. 30–31.

153. A.S.Vic., Test., XIX, 22 August 1433; ivi, Not., Bortolo Bassan 4545, 18 November 1446; ibid. 4560, 29 August 1463; ivi, PO, AP, 17 August 1457; ivi, Not., Antonio Saraceni 4960, 23 November 1499.

154. Herlihy and Klapisch-Zuber, *Toscans*, pp. 543–44.

155. Chojnacki, "Dowries," esp. pp. 578, 589–98; idem, "Patrician Women," esp. pp. 181, 186–89, 200–201; idem, "Power," pp. 138–39; idem, "'Most Serious Duty,'" p. 139.

156. Arnaldi, ff. 7r–v, 9v.

157. Helmholz, *Marriage Litigation*, ch. 3; for simple repudiation, see Duby, *The Knight*, ch. 1.

158. Esmein, *Mariage*, pp. 117, 123; Dauvillier, *Mariage*, pp. 130, 280; Besta, *Famiglia*, p. 71; Brundage, *Law*, p. 288.

159. Noonan, *Power*, pp. 80–82, 129; Dauvillier, *Mariage*, pp. 280, 286–92, 319–27; Esmein, *Mariage*, pp. 130–32; Phillips, *Putting Asunder*, pp. 26–27; Vaccari, *Matrimonio*, pp. 8, 14–15.

160. Brooke, *Medieval Idea*, p. 55.

161. Leclercq, *Monks*, p. 19; Brooke, *Medieval Idea*, pp. 67–68; Dauvillier, *Mariage*, p. 13; Esmein, *Mariage*, pp. 25–26; Kuehn, "Guardianship," pp. 312–13; Brundage, *Law*, pp. 202–3, 242, 252, 296; Elliott, *Spiritual Marriage*, pp. 67, 78, 244, 248, 251–53; Gaudemet, *Mariage*, pp. 84, 129, 241, 249, 257.

162. Widows far outnumbered widowers elsewhere: Lorcin, *Vivre*, p. 60; Hughes, "Domestic Ideals," pp. 139–40; Herlihy, "Deaths," pp. 143–45; idem, "Marriage," pp. 8–10; idem and Klapisch-Zuber, *Toscans*, pp. 400–412, 608; Crabb, "Alessandra Macinghi Strozzi," p. 49. Of sixty-one households headed by males of memorialist families, 75.4 percent show the first wife still alive, 14.8 percent the wife deceased, and 9.8 percent a second wife: A.S.Ver., Anagrafi, Comune and Provincia. Among the Freschi of Venice, only a quarter of widowers remarried.

163. A.S.Vic., Test. XIX, 22 August 1433; ivi, Not., Bortolo Bassan 4535, 22 May 1437; ibid. 4543, 6 June 1443.

164. Dominici, *Regola*, p. 166; see also Morelli, *Ricordi*, p. 220; Barberino, *Reggimento*, p. VI, esp. p. 132; Paton, *Preaching Friars*, pp. 256–58; Brundage, *Law*, pp. 194–95; Lugli, *Trattatisti*, pp. 27–28 (quote of Nappi), 66.

165. A.S.Ver., Test., mazzo 89, #39; ibid., mazzo 60, #49; similarly, ibid., mazzo 42, #96; ivi, Perg., Verità, ser. III, b. 7, #396.

166. Kirshner, *Pursuing Honor*, pp. 7–8; Herlihy and Klapisch-Zuber, *Toscans*, pp. 610–11; Kuehn, "Guardianship," pp. 331–32; Lorcin, *Vivre*, pp. 38–42, 60; Chojnacki, "Power," esp. pp. 136–37; idem, "Patrician Women," p. 189; Klapisch-Zuber, *Women*, pp. 119–22, 124–30; Sapori, ed., *Libri di commercio dei Peruzzi*, p. 177; Besta, *Famiglia*, ch. 26, esp. p. 189; Tamassia, *Famiglia*, pp. 327–34; Epstein, *Wills*, pp. 91, 103–9; Crouzet-Pavan, *Espaces*, p. 415; Ercole, "Istituto," II, p. 223; Hilaire, *Regime*, pp. 334–46; Esposito Aliano, "Famiglia," p. 209; Cohn, *Cult*, p. 200; Boutrouche, "Origines," p. 259. Some cities preferred the stick rather than the carrot: women who remarried lost guardianship of their children from the first marriage (Hughes, "Domestic Ideals," pp. 140–41; and, in general, de Renzo Villata, "Storia," pp. 69–70).

167. Many Florentines did: see Klapisch-Zuber, *Women*, pp. 122–24.

168. Ibid., p. 120. Remarriage was frequent enough to draw moralists' attention: Barberino, *Reggimento*, VII.

169. Neither case, however, produced estrangement between natal and marital families. For the Fracanzani, see A.S.Vic., PO, AP, 9 January 1465, 16 December 1465, 19 April 1466, 18 February 1467; ivi, Not., Bortolo Bassan 4563, 8 February 1466; ivi, Not., Antonio Saraceni 4960, 23 November 1499; for the dal Gorgo, see ivi, Not., Bortolo Bassan 4560, 29 August 1463; ivi, Uff. Reg., 17 September 1493. For a Verità case of departure, see A.S.Ver., Atti del Consiglio 63, f. 141(bis)r.

170. Kirshner, "Wives' Claims," p. 262; idem and Pluss, "Opinions," pp. 67ff.; Herlihy and Klapisch-Zuber, *Toscans*, pp. 610–11.

171. On the legal doctrine requiring maintenance of widows, see Nicolini, "Trattato," ##17–18, 21–23, 25, 27–28; Bellomo, *Ricerche*, ch. 7, #11.

172. Mantese, *Memorie*, 3, 2, pp. 596–97.

173. Herlihy, *Medieval Households*, p. 155; Herlihy and Klapisch-Zuber, *Toscans*, p. 337.

Chapter 2. Children

1. Alberti, *Libri*, p. 144.

2. Brooke, *Medieval Idea*, p. 58; Payer, *Sex*, p. 24; Duby, *The Knight*, p. 29; Brundage, *Law*, pp. 91–92, 158; Manselli, "Vie," p. 6.

3. Flandrin, "Attitude," pp. 187–88; Le Goff, *Birth*, pp. 187–88.

4. Kirshner and Molho, "Monte," p. 34 and tab. 2; Morrison, Kirshner, and Molho, "Life Cycle Events," pp. 487–92; Albini, "Infanzia," p. 151; Biget and Tricard, "Livres," pp. 339–40.

5. Savonarola, *Trattato*, pp. 19–21; Vegio, *De educatione*, I, p. 19; *Soranus' Gynecology*, p. 39; Alberti, *Libri*, pp. 140–41; Morelli, *Ricordi*, p. 213.

6. Arnaldi, ff. 4v, 9r; Stoppi, f. 2r.

7. Dal Bovo, ff. 29r, 35v, 42r; and see Shahar, *Childhood*, p. 32.

8. Muronovo, f. 51v; dal Bovo, ff. 21r–v, 46r; and see Shahar, *Childhood*, p. 36.

9. Herlihy, "Marriage," pp. 16–17; idem, *Medieval Households*, pp. 146–48; idem and Klapisch-Zuber, *Toscans*, pp. 423–28, 439–42; Cherubino, *Regole*, pp. 72–75, 103–4.

10. Klapisch-Zuber, *Women*, pp. 158–59.

11. Repeta, f. 81r.

12. About 2.5 percent of a sample of 1,814 girls enrolled in the Monte delle doti (Kirshner and Molho, "Dowry Fund," p. 413), and about 3 percent from a larger sample (Molho, "Professioni," p. 9; he includes some girls of unknown status), but under 0.5 percent of Florentines listed in the 1427 *catasto* (Herlihy and Klapisch-Zuber, *Toscans*, pp. 175, 434).

13. Lorcin, "Campagnes," p. 221; Kedar, "Notaries," pp. 92–93.

14. "Aspicias ad hospitalia et vide bastardos a centenara a centenara. . . . Si tot bastardi apparent in hospitalia, pensa quanti ne sono che non se sa nec videntur": quoted in Monaco, "Aspetti," pp. 115–16.

15. Kirshner and Molho, "Dowry Fund," pp. 428–30; Klapisch-Zuber, "Women Servants," pp. 69–70; Fabbri, *Alleanza*, p. 47; Guarducci and Ottanelli, *Servitori*, pp. 74–76; Lorcin, *Vivre*, pp. 91, 96.

16. It was not unknown, however. Girolamo Guastaverza declared that he was "seized by love" *(captus amore)* for the mother of his illegitimate son; since the boy was then out of infancy, the liaison was evidently of some duration: A.S.Ver., Perg., Guastaverza #35, busta 1, #8. Pietro Bovi is mentioned living with his *concubina* Benedetta in 1465 and 1473: ivi, Anagrafi, Comune, 481–82. Gabriele Verità's provision of a pension for the mother of a deceased natural son may also indicate an extended relationship: ivi, Test., mazzo 31, #93. In Florence, legal norms privileged offspring of long-term concubinate over the children of brief flings: Kuehn, *Law*, pp. 160, 181.

17. Herlihy and Klapisch-Zuber, *Toscans*, p. 434; Niccolini di Camugliano, *Chronicles*, p. 128; Fabbri, *Alleanza*, p. 47.

18. Lugli, *Trattatisti*, pp. 27–28; Frati, "Notaio," p. 27; Cherubini, "Proprietà," p. 317.

19. A.S.Ver., Perg., Guastaverza #35, busta 1, #8.

20. *Libro*, p. 101; see also pp. 31–32.

21. *Sermoni*, I, p. 397; see also Cherubino, *Regole*, pp. 32–34.

22. Ercole, "Istituto," I, pp. 234–35; Besta, *Famiglia*, chs. 32–34; Nicolini, "Trattato," ##1, 5; Besta, *Successioni*, sec. 15, esp. p. 80; Niccolai, *Formazione*, II, pp. 152–59.

23. Hurtubise, *Salviati*, p. 88; Pezzarossa, "Introduzione" to Martelli's *Ricordanze*, p. 18; Sapori, ed., *Libri di commercio dei Peruzzi*, pp. 465–66, 511.

24. A.S.Ver., Testamenti, mazzo 102, #187 (Tadea Fracastoro's bequests to two bastards, a niece and a half brother); Lorcin, *Vivre*, pp. 96–98.

25. Legitimation was the preferred means of ensuring family survival when there were no sons, since adoption was rare: Kuehn, *Law*, chs. 6–7.

26. Herlihy and Klapisch-Zuber, *Toscans*, pp. 339, 434.

27. Greci, "Arcimboldi," p. 21.

28. Kirshner and Molho, "Dowry Fund," pp. 426, 429–30; Kirshner and Molho, "Monte," p. 39; Molho, "Professioni," pp. 9–11; Fabbri, *Alleanza*, pp. 48–49; Gavitt, *Charity*, pp. 20, 79, 205–9; Trexler, "Foundlings," pp. 266–70.

29. On the unbaptized, see Le Goff, *Birth*, pp. 71, 263, 275; Dante, *Inferno*, IV, 25–30; Shahar, *Childhood*, p. 45; Paravay, "Angoisse," pp. 87–88.

30. Cohn, *Death*, pp. 75–76 (quoting Catherine of Siena); Dati, *Libro*, pp. 42–43, 77.

31. Verità, ff. 116v–17v; Guastaverza; Stoppi, cover sheet verso. The initial Giovanni of compound names was often dropped, and may have been a provisional prebaptismal marker: Giovanni Andrea Nicoló Arnaldi, for example, was known strictly as Andrea in adult life. For examples elsewhere of baptismal name changing, see Abbondanza, ed., *Notariato*, pp. 309–10; Ortalli, "Notariato," tab. 1.

32. Arnaldi, ff. 2v, 3r, 7v–8r, 12r–v; on emergency baptism, see Jussen, "Parrainage," pp. 482–84; Shahar, *Childhood*, p. 49. Gregorio Dati and the Salviati baptized most of their children within a week (Dati, *Libro*; Hurtubise, *Salviati*, p. 127); custom in Bologna and Perugia was to baptize children within eight to ten days of birth (Ortalli, "Notariato," p. 158; Arnaldi, "Notaio-cronista," pp. 307–8; Abbondanza, ed., *Notariato*, pp. 309–10).

33. Corblet, *Sacrement*, chs. 3–4; Klapisch-Zuber, "Peril," p. 224; Paduan sumptuary restrictions in Bonardi, *Lusso*, pp. 9, 41.

34. Arnaldi, ff. 2v, 3r, 7v, 8r, 9r–v, 11v, 12r–13v.

35. Lynch, *Godparents*, pp. 210–11.

36. Arnaldi, ff. 2v, 3v, 4r, 12r; Bovi, ff. 2v, 3v, 4r–v; dal Bovo, f. 51r. For Sienese episcopal chrismation, see Cherubini, *Signori*, pp. 408–10.

37. Herlihy, "Tuscan Names," p. 561 (quoting San Bernardino).

38. Herlihy, "Tuscan Names," p. 572; Fine, "Heritage," p. 854; Mantese, *Memorie*, 3, 2, pp. 784–87.

39. Guerreau-Jalabert, "Structures," pp. 1035–36; Burguière, "Prenoms," pp. 30–32; Goody, *Development*, p. 201; Fine, "Heritage," pp. 858–61; Postles, "Naming Patterns," pp. 34, 56; Klapisch-Zuber, "Parrains," pp. 51–53; Hanawalt, *Ties*, pp. 173–74.

40. Klapisch-Zuber, *Women*, pp. 287–88, 292; idem, "Attribution," pp. 75–76; idem, "Parrains," pp. 57–58; Fine, "Heritage," pp. 871–72.

41. Herlihy, "Tuscan Names," pp. 566–68; Waley, "Personal Names," pp. 189–90; de la Roncière, "Influence," pp. 27–28; in general, see Corblet, *Histoire*, pp. 231–40.

42. Pagliarini, *Cronicae*, pp. 80–84.

43. Hypocoristics and variants were combined: Zuane and Iohannines were counted as Giovanni. First personal names only were counted, as calculation of the 1453 *estimo* indicated that second (and sometimes third) personal names follow the same frequencies as the first.

44. Klapisch-Zuber, "Ruptures," p. 1226; idem, "Parrains," pp. 52–53, 62; idem, "Constitution," pp. 39–41; idem, "Patroni," p. 192; Hurtubise, *Salviati*, p. 128; Banker, *Death*, p. 179; Kedar, "Genoese Notaries," p. 92; idem, "Noms," pp. 431–36; Epstein, *Wills*, pp. 38–39.

45. On reduction of the stock of names elsewhere, see Klapisch-Zuber, "Parrains," pp. 52–53; Kedar, "Noms," p. 438. The proportion of Vicentines with the top ten names (ca. 54 percent) is roughly that of Florence (Klapisch-Zuber, "Parrains," p. 63) and Genoa (Epstein, *Wills*, pp. 38–39). Concentration of names was much greater in southern France, where half the population held the three or five most frequent names: Lorcin, *Vivre*, p. 160; Chiffoleau, *Comptabilité*, pp. 380–81.

46. As was the case in the Lyonnais: Lorcin, *Vivre*, p. 163.

47. The upper classes of Florence, however, resisted the use of names of recent saints: Klapisch-Zuber, "Attribution," p. 82.

48. Plague saints, Mary and Joseph were not popular in Tuscany either: Herlihy, "Tuscan Names," pp. 579–80; Klapisch-Zuber, "Constitution," pp. 43–44.

49. Klapisch-Zuber, *Women*, p. 308; idem, "Constitution," p. 43; idem, "Patroni," p. 197; Herlihy, "Tuscan Names," p. 574.

50. Bennett, *Women*, p. 69; Klapisch-Zuber, *Women*, pp. 293–94, 307; idem, "Patroni," pp. 197–98; Lorcin, *Vivre*, p. 161; Epstein, *Wills*, pp. 39–40; Pitti, *Ricordi*, in Branca, ed., *Mercanti*, pp. 345–48; Waley, "Personal Names," p. 190.

51. Alberti, *Libri*, pp. 142–44.

52. Varanini, "Famiglia," p. 39; on similar classicism in Treviso, see Pesce, *Chiesa*, I, p. 33.

53. Klapisch-Zuber, *Women*, esp. pp. 295, 299–300, 306; idem, "Ruptures," p. 1227; idem, "Parrains," p. 65; idem, "Attribution," pp. 77–81.

54. Nearly every Arnaldi remade an ancestor, for example: Margarita Bona (for an aunt), Joanna Gaspara (grandfather Gaspare died the year before), Girolamo Francesco (for a brother), Lucia Chiara (cousin Lucia had just entered a convent, a form of death), and so forth. Examples from Veneto memoirs could be multiplied at great length.

55. Dati, *Libro*, pp. 40, 74; Bec, "Introduzione" to Niccolini's *Libro*, pp. 22–23.

56. In Florence, the first personal name usually honored a relative, while the second was drawn from the company of saints: Klapisch-Zuber, *Women*, pp. 293–94; idem, "Attribution," p. 82; idem, "Patroni," pp. 195–96; idem, "Constitution," pp. 41–42. The relative priority of ancestral versus spiritual names is moot, however, since ancestors were themselves named for saints: a given Lucia might honor both the martyr and a dead relative.

57. Arnaldi, ff. 3r–4v, 5r; Freschi, ff. 57v, 58v, 60v; Verità, f. 47r. For a similar Florentine custom, see Klapisch-Zuber, *Women*, p. 292; idem, "Attribution," p. 80.

58. Some 78 percent of Florentine second names honored the saint of the day (or San Romolo, a local favorite): Klapisch-Zuber, "Attribution," p. 82.

59. Klapisch-Zuber, *Women*, p. 306; idem, "Attribution," p. 81. She notes, however, that later Quattrocento families exercised a broader choice of names.

60. Arnaldi, ff. 11v, 12r, 13r–v, 15v, 16v; see in general, Lynch, *Godparents*, pp. 5, 335; Corblet, *Sacrement*, ch. 5 and p. 403; Shuhar, *Childhood*, p. 47; Belmont, "Levana," pp. 1–13.

61. Jussen, "Parrainage," pp. 478–80; Klapisch-Zuber, "Peril," p. 216; idem, "Com-

perage," pp. 64–65; Esmein, *Mariage*, p. 366; Bossy, "Padrini," p. 443; idem, "Blood," p. 133; Lynch, *Godparents*, pp. 172, 191, 201–3, 209, 285; Corblet, *Sacrement*, ch. 7. The commune of Padua also tried to limit the number of godparents as part of its sumptuary legislation: Bonardi, *Lusso*, pp. 9, 41.

62. Calculations exclude emergency baptisms, when anyone at hand (often a midwife) was pressed into service.

63. Klapisch-Zuber, "Parrains," p. 54; idem, "Comperage," p. 64; idem, "Peril," tab. 2.

64. Klapisch-Zuber, "Parrains," pp. 56–57; idem, "Patroni," p. 199.

65. Corblet, *Sacrement*, pp. 194–95, ch. 7.

66. Klapisch-Zuber, "Peril," pp. 217–18 and tab. 1; idem, "Comperage," p. 65; idem, "Parrains," p. 56; see also Tricard, "Memoire," p. 132.

67. Klapisch-Zuber, "Comperage," p. 70; idem, "Peril," pp. 229–30.

68. Veneto memoirs offer no examples. Only rarely were Florentine blood kin or relatives by marriage chosen as godparents: Klapisch-Zuber, *Women*, p. 85; idem, "Peril," p. 218; see also Tricard, "Memoire," p. 134.

69. Bossy, "Padrini," p. 443; idem, "Godparenthood," pp. 194, 198; Lynch, *Godparents*, p. 130.

70. Repeated sponsorship within a family was the case in Florence as well: Klapisch-Zuber, "Comperage," pp. 66–67.

71. *Regola*, pp. 139–40. On the social dimension of godparentage, see Lynch, *Godparents*, pp. 14–15, 165–69, 172, 192–201 and ch. 11; Goody, *Development*, pp. 202–3; Bossy, "Blood," pp. 133–34; idem, "Godparenthood," p. 197.

72. Klapisch-Zuber, "Comperage," p. 61; idem, "Peril," pp. 221–22; idem, "Attribution," p. 76; idem, "Parrains," pp. 59–62; Shahar, *Childhood*, p. 117; Jussen, "Parrainage," pp. 475–76. Corblet (*Sacrement*, p. 197) thinks that godparents' obligation to raise the child in the faith was already fading in the ninth century.

73. The Verità present the sole exception: Giovanni Bevilaqua and Lapo Donato Sagramoso were twice chosen as godfather, and the Verità later arranged marriages to their families.

74. As was the case in Florentine and Lyonnais testaments: Klapisch-Zuber, "Parrains," pp. 60–61; Lorcin, *Vivre*, p. 29.

75. Florentines also chose godparents from a more heterogenous pool—richer and poorer, higher– and lower–ranking—than that with which they contracted marriage. Unlike the Arnaldi, however, they often chose business partners and neighbors to sponsor their children: Weissman, *Ritual Brotherhood*, pp. 16–19; Pezzarossa, "Introduzione" to Martelli's *Ricordanze*, pp. 21–22; idem, "Giovanni di Pagolo Morelli," p. 42; Klapisch-Zuber, *Women*, pp. 89–92; idem, "Comperage," p. 69; idem, "Peril," pp. 227–28; idem, "Parrains," p. 62; idem, "Attribution," p. 76; Kent and Kent, *Neighbours*, pp. 89–90; Jussen, "Parrainage," p. 280.

76. Lynch, *Godparents*, pp. 192–201; Bossy, "Godparenthood," pp. 196–97; idem, "Padrini," pp. 444–45.

77. Pagliarini, *Cronicae*, pp. 329–30, 322–23.

78. Klapisch-Zuber, "Comperage," pp. 71–72 (though she notes a decline in patricians' selection of lower–class godparents). On Florentines' frequent choice of nurses, midwives, tenants, and marginals as co-parents, see idem, "Peril," pp. 218–21; Pandimiglio, "Giovanni di Pagolo Morelli," pp. 43–44.

79. Bossy, "Padrini," p. 445; Corblet, *Sacrement*, pp. 184–85.

80. While condemning wet nursing, however, most authorities acknowledged that especially well-to-do parents would send babies out, and devoted much of their attention to the selection and supervision of the mercenary. See Alberti, *Libri*, pp. 44–46; Ross, "Middle-Class Child," pp. 154–55, 184–90; Fildes, *Wet Nursing*, ch. 1; idem, *Breasts*, pp. 27–32; da Feltre, *Sermoni*, II, p. 15; Savonarola, *Trattato*, pp. 145–48; Paton, *Preaching Friars*, p. 249; Goody, *Development*, pp. 69–70; Le Goff, *Birth*, pp. 187–88; dal Bovo, f. 73r; Vegio, *De educatione*, pp. 20–26 and I, chs. 3–4; Klapisch-Zuber, *Women*, pp. 133–34, 144–45, 161; Lugli, *Trattatisti*, pp. 122–23; King, "Caldiera," p. 45; Herlihy, "Roots," p. 135; idem and Klapisch-Zuber, *Toscans*, pp. 330, 555–56; Dominici, *Regola*, pp. 143–44; *Soranus' Gynecology*, pp. 89–103; Shahar, *Childhood*, pp. 55–76.

81. Guastaverza, f. 12v; Bovi, ff. 2v–3r, 4r; Arnaldi, ff. 7r, 12r, 16v; Repeta, f. 81r. For weaning, see *Soranus' Gynecology*, pp. 118–19; Klapisch-Zuber, *Women*, pp. 155–57; Shahar, *Childhood*, pp. 81–82; Fildes, *Wet Nursing*, p. 59; idem, *Breasts*, pp. 60–61, 66–67.

82. Arnaldi, ff. 3r–v.

83. Muronovo, f. 63r; Repeta, f. 81v; Arnaldi, ff. 16v–17r.

84. Aries, *Centuries*, p. 128; De Mause, *Evolution*; Shorter, *Making*, pp. 169–785; Stone, *Family*, pp. 105–14. For refutations of the Aries thesis, see Shahar, *Childhood*; Gavitt, *Charity*, p. 19 and ch. 6; Weinstein and Bell, *Saints*, chs. 1–2; Goodich, *Birth*, pp. 2–4.

85. King, "Caldiera," pp. 35, 46; Herlihy and Klapisch-Zuber, *Toscans*, pp. 558, 570–71; Houlbrooke, *English Family*, pp. 136–37; though see Pollock, *Forgotten Children*, pp. 51–52.

86. Dominici, *Regola*, pp. 143–44, 150–51; da Feltre, *Sermoni*, II, p. 14; Monaco, "Aspetti," pp. 128–32; see also Bonney, "Jean Gerson," pp. 137–38; Ross, "Middle-Class Child," p. 203.

87. Herlihy, "Family," p. 5; idem, "Making," p. 125.

88. Lugli, *Trattatisti*, pp. 5–10; Salimbene from Paton, *Preaching Friars*, pp. 240, 244, 251.

89. Alberti, *Libri*, pp. 33–35, 46–48; da Certaldo, *Libro*, #156.

90. Banker, "Mourning," pp. 352–57; McClure, *Sorrow*, chs. 2, 5 (quote on pp. 114–15).

91. *Sermoni*, I, pp. 397–401; Monaco, "Aspetti," p. 114.

92. Goodich, "Bartholomaeus Anglicus," p. 80; Epstein, *Wills*, p. 68; di Renzo Villata, "Note," pp. 69–75; Lorcin, "Mere Nature," pp. 33–39.

93. *Ricordi*, esp. pp. 455–56, 476–83, 542.

94. Chojnacki, "'Most Serious Duty,'" pp. 142–43; Herlihy, *Medieval Households*, pp. 125–28; Klapisch-Zuber, *Women*, pp. 114–16; Herlihy and Klapisch-Zuber, *Toscans*, esp. p. 568; Macfarlane, *Marriage*, ch. 4; Houlbrooke, *English Family*, pp. 6–7, 134–37; Pollock, *Forgotten Children*, esp. chs. 1–2; Shuhar, *Childhood*, chs. 5, 7; Gavitt, *Charity*, ch. 5.

95. Herlihy, "Vieillir," pp. 1341–45; idem, "Generation," pp. 360–61; idem, "Roots," pp. 139–40, 144–49; idem and Klapisch-Zuber, *Toscans*, pp. 194, 435–36, 603–6; Ross, "Middle-Class Child," pp. 200–203; Pandimiglio, "Giovanni di Pagolo Morelli," pp. 4–5. For moralists' comments, see Vegio, *De educatione*, II, p. 45 and ch. III; Dominici, *Regola*, pp. 150–51.

96. Herlihy, "Population," p. 114; idem, "Marriage," p. 15; idem and Klapisch-Zuber, *Toscans*, 436.

97. The deaths of seventy-one men and fifty-nine women were recorded; among those under the age of twenty, the figures are thirty boys and nineteen girls.

98. Savonarola, *Trattato*, pp. 54–62; Alberti, *Libri*, p. 134. Preference for sons was widespread: Shahar, *Childhood*, pp. 43–45; Fabbri, *Alleanza*, pp. 75–76.

99. Domenici, *Regola*, p. 137; Vegio, *De educatione*, II, p. 12 and bk. III, ch. 12; da Certaldo, *Libro*, #155. Other writers wanted girls kept semiliterate or illiterate: Klapisch-Zuber, "Chiavi," pp. 776–77.

100. Quoted in Monaco, "Aspetti," p. 119.

101. Trexler, "Infanticide," p. 101; idem, "Foundlings," pp. 266–68; Albini, "Bambini," p. 42; idem, "Infanzia," pp. 154, 157; Sandri, *Ospedale*, pp. 128, 131; Gavitt, *Charity*, pp. 20, 205, 209.

102. Herlihy and Klapisch-Zuber, *Toscans*, pp. 327–38, 342–48; Klapisch-Zuber, *Women*, pp. 98–104.

103. In her testament, dated 21 April 1456, she was described as "aged 16 or so"; she was born on 21 October 1438: Arnaldi, f. 4r; A.S.Vic., Not., Bortolo Bassan 4554, 21 April 1456.

104. Klapisch-Zuber (*Women*, pp. 105, 154–55) thinks that girls were weaned earlier, which reduced their chances for survival, but also that girls were left with a wet nurse longer, which put them at greater risk: the two conclusions seem contradictory. Bennett (*Women*, pp. 68–70) thinks that girls had higher mortality rates because of abuse or neglect, but admits that demographic and court evidence does not indicate bias.

105. Ross, "Middle-Class Child," pp. 207–8.

106. Strozzi, cited in Martines, "Way," pp. 22–23; da Certaldo, *Libro*, #359.

107. Gavitt, *Charity*, ch. 5 (noting on pp. 20, 205, 209 that the proportion of female foundlings was declining); Chojnacki, "Measuring Adulthood," pp. 375–77.

108. A.S.Ver., Test., mazzo 62, #79.

Chapter 3. Death

1. Several children are known only from birth notices; they probably died young, but uncertainty regarding their fates did not allow their inclusion in the sample.

2. Albini, "Infanzia," pp. 153–54; Klapisch-Zuber, *Women*, pp. 146, 151. Shahar estimates a general first-year death rate of two hundred to three hundred per thousand children: *Childhood*, p. 149. Mortality rates in foundling hospitals were about double: Sandri, *Ospedale*, p. 161; Pinto, "Personale," p. 127.

3. Carmichael, "Health Status," pp. 37–38; Albini, "Bambini," p. 26; idem, *Guerra*, pp. 168–70, 178; idem, "Mortalità," p. 129. Florentine girls also suffered continued high mortality in late childhood and adolescence: Kirshner and Molho, "Dowry Fund," p. 413; Morrison et al., "Life Cycle Events," p. 487.

4. Herlihy and Klapisch-Zuber, *Toscans*, p. 452; Albini, *Guerra*, p. 170 (tab. 8). Youth mortality rates in the Veneto may be low because families that produced memoirs were wealthy, while evidence for other cities comes from the entire population; the rich suffered lower early mortality than the poor: Kirshner and Molho, "Dowry Fund,"

p. 414; idem, "Abbozzo," p. 34; Morrison et al., "Life Cycle Events," pp. 487, 491; Houlbrooke, *English Family*, p. 29.

5. Herlihy, "Vieillir," p. 1351; Minois, *History*, p. 215; Biget and Tricard, "Livres," p. 352.

6. Herlihy, "Population," p. 101; Herlihy and Klapisch-Zuber, *Toscans*, pp. 371, 378, 382. Florentine tax records did underreport elderly women: ibid., pp. 199, 337–38. The thesis that women enjoyed a higher life expectancy is argued in Herlihy, "Vieillir," pp. 1350–51; idem, "Life Expectancies," pp. 13–15; Bullough and Brundage, *Sexual Practices*, p. 318.

7. Herlihy and Klapisch-Zuber, *Toscans*, p. 200. In the Veneto, the rate of those who died before age twenty increased between the first and second halves of the century; the deterioration of the mortality rate for girls was modest (34.3 percent versus 38.5 percent), while that for boys was appalling (28.9 percent versus 57.9 percent).

8. Morrison et al., "Epidemics," pp. 532–33; Klapisch-Zuber, *Women*, p. 153; Herlihy and Klapisch-Zuber, *Toscans*, pp. 192, 465. Winter is here defined as January through March, spring as April through June, summer as July through September, and fall as October through December.

9. In Florence, August was the most lethal month in normal years, and June through August the most lethal period in plague years; September brought some respite: Herlihy and Klapisch-Zuber, *Toscans*, pp. 192, 465. The Veneto summer comes later and is less hot and dry, which might delay peaks in mortality.

10. Survey in Ell, "Iron," pp. 445–47. Herlihy ("Deaths," pp. 154–55), Carmichael (*Plague*, pp. 90–93; "Health Status," p. 37), and Herlihy and Klapisch-Zuber (*Toscans*, ch. 16, esp. pp. 446, 459) conclude in the affirmative; Morrison et al. ("Epidemics," p. 533), Ell ("Iron," p. 456), Razi (*Life*, pp. 107–9), Menzioni ("Matrimonio," p. 439) in the negative. Del Panta (*Epidemie*, pp. 40–49) and Albini ("Bambini," pp. 26–28; "Infanzia," p. 154; *Guerra*, pp. 133, 153; "Mortalità," p. 133) think that plague hit older children and adolescents hardest, and spared the very young and the very old.

11. Limousin children's deaths clustered overwhelmingly (69 percent) in July through October: Biget and Tricard, "Livres," p. 345.

12. Del Panta, *Epidemie*, pp. 133–34; Ginatempo, *Crisi*, p. 343; Carmichael, "Plague Legislation," pp. 513–14, 517; Gottfried, *Black Death*, pp. 131–34; Menzione, "Matrimonio," p. 442; Livi Bacci, *Societé*, pp. 41, 101–2.

13. Albini, "Mortalità," pp. 130–31; idem, "Bambini," pp. 28–29; Carmichael, *Plague*, ch. 1; idem, "Health Status"; idem, "Plague Legislation," pp. 515–16; Gottfried, *Epidemic Disease*, pp. 62–63; idem, *Black Death*, pp. 134, 156; Del Panta, *Epidemie*, p. 53.

14. Herlihy, "Population," p. 104; Tagliaferri, *Economia*, p. 49; Collodo, "Artigiani," pp. 424–25; idem, "Note," p. 166; Ginatempo and Sandri, *Italia*, pp. 82–83. Herlihy's figures are too high, since he counted all those listed in urban *anagrafi* as members of urban households; but many dependents are clearly listed as resident on rural estates. Since the proportion of dependents grew over the course of the century, Herlihy's reading would inflate the actual urban population.

15. Grubb, *Firstborn*, pp. 77–79; idem, "Ricerca"; Veronese disincentives to immigration in *Statuti Veronae*, pp. 25–28. In 1422 Vicentine councils, worried that the young were not marrying, ordered election of two "affable mediators" to arrange unions, but

the office is not mentioned after midcentury: Bertoliana, Arch. Torre 777, ff. 170r–71v. From the 1470s on the Venetian government progressively restricted the capacity of mainland rectors to grant tax exemptions to immigrants: Bertoliana, Arch. Torre 59, ff. 108r–v; Venice, Marciana, Ital. VII, 498 (8147), ff. 50r–v, 149v.

16. Barbieri, *Ospedale*, pp. 144–45; Bertoliana, Arch. Torre 213, b. 8, ff. 3r, 6r; similarly, Mainoni, "Sviluppo," pp. 208–14.

17. In addition to works cited in subsequent notes, see Ginatempo and Sandri, *Italia*; Grohmann, *Città*, I, pp. 75–78; Fornasari, "Economia," p. 482; Comba, *Contadini*, pp. 75–76; Epstein, "Cities," p. 17; for the Lyonnais recovery, see Lorcin, *Campagnes*, pp. 221–22.

18. Pinto, "Politica," pp. 30–38; Mazzi, "Peste," pp. 112–14; Carmichael, "Plague Legislation," p. 522; idem, *Plague*, pp. 116–26.

19. Pinto, "Politica," pp. 21–22; Albini, "Mortalità," pp. 123, 134.

20. Mueller, "Peste," p. 93; Herlihy and Klapisch-Zuber, *Toscans*, pp. 182–87; Ginatempo, *Crisi*, III, ch. 2.

21. Herlihy and Klapisch-Zuber, *Toscans*, pp. 187, 472–91; Epstein, "Cities," p. 18; Klapisch-Zuber, "Fiscalité," p. 1321.

22. Repeta, f. 77r; dal Bovo, f. 55r.

23. Dal Bovo, f. 115v. Giovanni Morelli (*Ricordi*, pp. 294–301) and the medical writer Tommaso del Garbo (*Consiglio*, ch. 1) also copied recipes against the plague but admitted that the only real remedy was flight.

24. da Feltre, *Sermoni*, II, p. 271; Carmichael, *Plague*, p. 1; Tenenti, *Senso*, pp. 69–73, 185; Chiffoleau, *Comptabilité*, p. 99; McClure, *Sorrow*, p. 94; Vovelle, *Mort*, p. 91; Herlihy and Klapisch-Zuber, *Toscans*, p. 467; Livi Bacci, *Societé*, pp. 43, 96–100, 109–11; Mazzi, "Peste," pp. 100–13. The life of St. Roch copied by dal Bovo (ff. 73r–77v) offered a powerful *exemplum* of the virtues of remaining with, and ministering to, plague-struck communities.

25. *Ius municipale*, ff. 159v–60r, 162r, 166r; Bertoliana, Arch. Torre 777, ff. 82r–v, 99r. Vicentine dyers secured revocation of restrictive legislation, fulling and saw mills clustered along the city's rivers, horses drank from the Bacchiglione, and butchers worked on a bridge: ibid., f. 133r–v; ivi, Arch. Torre 778, ff. 25v–26r, 61r, 75r–v, 77r; A.S.Vic., PO, AP, 16 August 1484. Veronese initiatives against pollution were not couched in terms of public health (pigs damaged property; use of toxic dyes harmed the reputation of the city's cloth, and butchers threw offal into the Adige): A.S.Ver., AAC, reg. 56, ff. 132v–33v, 139v; ivi, reg. 63, ff. 48v–49r, 129r, 208r. In general, see Carmichael, *Plague*, pp. 99–107; idem, "Plague Legislation," p. 510; Mazzi, "Peste," pp. 108–9.

26. Rumor, ed., *Storia*, pp. 397–98; *Cronica ad memoriam*, p. 16.

27. *Ius municipale*, f. 148v; similarly, *Statuti Veronae*, p. 66.

28. Verità, ff. 17r, 46v, 84v; Arnaldi, ff. 10r, 14r, 15r–16v; Repeta, f. 81r.

29. Repeta, f. 84v; Gottfried, *Epidemic Disease*, ch. 2; Corradi, *Annali*, pp. 251–335.

30. Albini, *Guerra*, pp. 48–56 and ch. 2; idem, "Mortalità," pp. 125–27; *Venezia e la peste*, pp. 84–85; Palmer, "Azione," pp. 103–5; Mueller, "Peste," pp. 93–94; Carmichael, *Plague*, pp. 110–16; idem, "Contagion Theory," pp. 214–19, 231, 251; Livi Bacci, "Societé," pp. 111–22; Cipolla, *Public Health*, pp. 11–31.

31. Mazzi, "Peste," p. 110; Carmichael, *Plague*, pp. 99–107 and ch. 5; Crouzet-Pavan, *Espaces*, pp. 761–62, 864–74.

32. A.S.Ver., AAC, reg. 56, f. 261r; Mantese, *Memorie*, III, 2, p. 677; Bertoliana, Arch. Torre 60, f. 145r; Collodo, "Note," p. 159.

33. Carmichael, *Plague*, pp. 61–62, 90; idem, "Plague Legislation," pp. 513–17; Albini, "Mortalità," pp. 130–31; Gottfried, *Black Death*, pp. 131–34.

34. Mantese, *Memorie*, 3, 2, pp. 433–34, 979, 995; Barbieri, *Ospedale*, pp. 142–45; *Cronica ad memoriam*, pp. 25–26, 36–37; Zironda, *Canonici*, pp. 17–19; A.S.Ver., AAC, reg. 63, f. 217v; de Sandre Gasparini, *Contadini*, p. 125; da Feltre, *Sermoni*, I, p. 277. On art, see Arasse, "Devotion," pp. 141–46; Cole, *Italian Art*, pp. 189, 193–94.

35. Arnaldi, ff. 12v, 13v, 15r–v; Stoppi, f. 2r; Verità, f. 17r.

36. Arnaldi, ff. 8r, 8v, 16v; Muronovo, f. 64r.

37. Luke 16:19–26; 23:39–43; sleep imagery in Acts 7:59; I Thessalonians 4:12–14.

38. Matthew 25:31–46 (and see 8:22; 11:22–24; 12:36; 13:36–43; 24:3–31); John 6:39–40, 44, 55.

39. Aries set the terms of debate, positing a gradual shift in emphasis from final collective judgment to individual judgment at point of death: *Western Attitudes*, pp. 27–33; *Homme*, esp. ch. 3. Gurevic's rebuttal posits continual belief in individualized judgment, comingled with belief in collective judgment: "Conscience," esp. pp. 259–73. A consensus view is offered by Vovelle, *Mort*, pp. 62–67; see also Chiffoleau, *Comptabilité*, p. 431; Rapp, "Reforme," esp. pp. 56–57.

40. Arnaldi, ff. 9r, 15r–v; Verità, ff. 17r, 84v–85r.

41. O'Connor, *Art*, pp. 97–100, 157; Rhodes, *Tipografia*, p. 11; Sartore, "Pessimismo," p. 637; Schutte, *Religious Books*, pp. 280–82; Simoni, "Incunabolo," p. 224.

42. Tenenti, *Senso*, chs. 3–5; idem, *Vie*, chs. 1–2 and appendix B; idem, *Senso*, pp. 91–101; Rapp, "Reforme," p. 59; Delumeau, *Peché*, chs. 2–3; Chiffoleau, *Comptabilité*, pp. 105–16; Vovelle, *Mort*, ch. 6.

43. Weinstein, *"Art,"* pp. 92–98; da Certaldo, *Libro*, ##10, 36, 212, 250; da Feltre, *Sermoni*, III, pp. 17–26, 27–33, 35–40, 41–49, 51–57; in general, O'Connor, *Art*, p. 39.

44. Epstein, *Wills*, pp. 44, 64, 155–60; Lorcin, "Clauses," pp. 287, 295, 312–15; idem, "Trois manieres," pp. 4–11; idem, *Vivre*, pp. 3–4, 140–46; Chiffoleau, "Changer"; idem, *Comptabilité*, pp. viii, 38–41, 126–42; idem, "Usage," p. 251; de Lamothe, "Pieté," p. 18; Vovelle, *Mort*, pp. 150–54; Cohn, *Death*, pp. 59–68; idem, *Cult*, ch. 4; Strocchia, "Death Rites"; idem, "Funerals," p. 154; idem, *Death*, chs. 3, 5; Aries, *Attitudes*, pp. 46–49, 63–64.

45. High funeral expenses from Morelli, *Ricordi*, pp. 203, 227; Niccolini di Camugliano, *Chronicles*, pp. 87–88; idem, "Medieval Florentine," pp. 8–9; Edler de Roover, "Andrea Banchi," p. 279; Goldthwaite, *Private Wealth*, pp. 72–73; Hurtubise, *Salviati*, p. 105; and see Herlihy and Klapisch-Zuber, *Toscans*, p. 612; Strocchia, "Death Rites," pp. 120–22.

46. A.S.Vic., Test., 29 December 1475 (1476 modern style).

47. Cipolla, "Libri," pp. 32, 44.

48. *Ius municipale*, ff. 155r–v (but exempting burials of knights and their wives from limitations); A.S.Ver., AAC, reg. 56, ff. 80r (but cancelled within five years due to protests by the bishop and the order of Hermits: ibid., f. 120r); Strocchia, "Death Rites," p. 130; Bonardi, *Lusso*, pp. 11–12.

49. Fasoli, "Alcune note," p. 121; Bonanno et al., "Legati," p. 215; Edler de Roover, "Andrea Banchi," p. 279; Cohn, *Cult*, pp. 13–14.

50. Bertoliana, Gonz. 309, f. 5v (wool guild); Giacomuzzi, *Influsso*, p. 154; Mantese, *Memorie*, 3, 2, pp. 576–93; Sancassani, *Documenti*, pp. 38, 74–75. On corporate participation in funerals, see Betto, *Collegi*, pp. 25, 122–24; Weissman, *Ritual Brotherhood*, p. 49; Henderson, "Religious Confraternities," pp. 385–89; Barr, "Singing Confraternity," pp. 108–12; Lorcin, "Clauses," pp. 297–300; Banker, *Death*, passim (though participation declined: pp. 80–89); Chiffoleau, *Comptabilité*, pp. 266–87; Pasche, *Salut*, pp. 87–90.

51. Arnaldi, ff. 16v–17r.

52. A.S.Vic., Test., 21 May 1488 (Giovanni fu Simone Thiene), 12 July 1495 (Giovanni fu Clemente Thiene); A.S.Vic., Not., Francesco Sorio 5013, s.d. 25 September 1494 (Monza).

53. A.S.Ver., Test., mazzo 31, #93 (Gabriele Verità); ivi, mazzo 93, #23 (Stoppi); ivi, mazzo 102, #85 (Verità Verità); ivi, mazzo 60, #50 (Paulino); Verona, Biblioteca Civica, ms. 938, f. 51 (San Michele). The eminent Veronese jurist Cristoforo Lanfranchini ordered a funeral "sine ulla pompa," with only a priest, friars, and close kin present: Borelli, "'Doctor,'" p. 158. For a noble Paduan's austere funeral, see de Sandre Gasparini, "Parola," pp. 108–9.

54. Dean, *Land and Power*, p. 63 (Niccolo III d'Este ordered burial in a small-town church "in terra nudum abiectis ambitiosis et superbis pompis"); Phillips, *Marco Parenti*, p. 8; Strocchia, *Death*, pp. 180–88, 209–10; Chiffoleau, *Comptabilité*, pp. 142–43; Swanson, *Church*, p. 267; Pesce, *Chiesa*, p. 51; King, *Venetian Humanism*, p. 38; Bonanno et al., "Legati," p. 215.

55. Arnaldi, ff. 8r, 17r; A.S.Vic., Test., 22 August 1433 (Gaspare I); ivi, Not., Bortolo Bassan 4560, 29 August 1463 (Tommaso); ivi, Not., Antonio Saraceni 4960, 23 November 1499 (Gaspare II).

56. McHam, "Donatello's Tomb," pp. 146, 163–65; Arslan, *Catalogo*, pp. 21, 26–27; Mantese, *Memorie*, 3, 2, pp. 904–5. On the rise of burial *apud sanctos*, with preference for proximity to the high altar, see Aries, *Homme*, p. 84; Chiffoleau, "Changer," pp. 124–25.

57. A.S.Ver., Test., mazzo 31, #93 (Gabriele Verità); ivi, mazzo 60, #49 (Bonaventura Bovi); ivi, mazzo 81, #132 (Bonzanino Muronovo); ivi, mazzo 89, #161 (Giorgio dal Bovo); ivi, mazzo 93, #23 (Alvise Stoppi); ivi, mazzo 102, #85 (Verità Verità); ivi, mazzo 128, #334 (Donato Stoppi).

58. Tenenti, *Senso*, chs. 1, 5; also Burke, "Death," pp. 63–64.

59. Le Goff, *Birth*, pp. 5, 11–12.

60. Ibid., pp. 299, 319, 323–24.

61. Le Goff, "Naissance," p. 9 and *passim*; Aries, "Conception," pp. 81–84; Chaunu, "Mourir," pp. 38–39; Gurevich, "Conscience," pp. 262–66 (and introduction by Le Goff); Boase, *Death*, pp. 46–56.

62. Vovelle, *Mort*, p. 66; Vovelle and Vovelle, *Vision*, pp. 13–15.

63. Verona, Bib. Civ., ms. 938, f. 32. In another example of the permeable boundaries between world and afterworld, the spirit of Verona's "Guy de Tourno" returned from death to dispute with monks: Martin, *Metier*, pp. 493–94, 514. On imaging of purgatory, see Vovelle, *Mort*, pp. 66, 134–39.

64. Le Goff, *Birth*, chs. 1–4; Fumagalli, "Paesaggio," p. 416; Pasche, *Salut*, p. 103; Aries, *Homme*, ch. 4; Vovelle, *Mort*, pp. 64–67. Gregory the Great told the story of a

monk who took money for his own use and died scorned by his brothers. When Gregory took pity on him and ordered thirty days of commemorative Masses, the monk appeared in a vision to testify to the relief he had received: *Dialogi*, IV, ch. 55.

65. Le Goff, *Birth*, pp. 69, 243, 248, 322.

66. Ibid., pp. 92–93, 137–39, 143, 148–49, 161–62, 187–89, 228–29, 254–55, 261–62, 269, 292.

67. Falco, *Disposizioni*, pp. 189–94; Vovelle, *Mort*, pp. 173–74; Repeta, f. 136r.

68. Aries, *Attitudes*, pp. 63–64; Cohn, *Death*, pp. 2, 56–57; Lorcin, *Vivre*, pp. 3–4; idem, "Clauses," p. 287; but see Kuehn, "Law," esp. p. 486.

69. Arnaldi, ff. 6r–v; A.S.Vic., Not., Bortolo Bassan 4531, 22 August 1433; and see Hughes, "Famiglia," pp. 931ff.

70. Mantese, *Memorie*, 3, 2, p. 677; A.S.Vic., Not., Bortolo Bassan 4554, 21 April 1456; ivi, Test., 5 February 1489, 9 June 1492, 12 July 1495; Bertoliana, Arch. Torre 61, ff. 363r–66v. For notarial prompts in Tuscany, see Cohn, *Cult*, pp. 12–13, 15.

71. *Statuti Veronae*, pp. 12, 44, 254–55; A.S.Ver., AAC, reg. 56, ff. 14v, 40v, 124v–25r, 236r–v; ivi, reg. 63, ff. 4v, 138r; Vecchiato, "Fontico," pp. 210–11; Cristofoletti, "Cenni," p. 328.

72. Mantese, *Memorie*, 3, 2, pp. 672–73; Bertoliana, Arch. Torre 61, ff. 67v–70r. For municipal administration of legacies elsewhere, see Pesce, *Chiesa*, pp. 55–59; Lorcin, "Clauses," p. 288; Gavitt, *Charity*, p. 11; Banker, *Death*, p. 142; Albini, "Continuità," pp. 142–43.

73. A.S.Ver., Test., mazzo 46, #10; ivi, mazzo 81, #45; ivi, Perg., Verità, ser. III, b. 7, #396. Vicenza's Francesco Monza left 112 ducats to the poor, two hospitals, and a monastery, and 200 ducats to dower "poor maidens": A.S.Vic., Test., 6 February 1487.

74. Lorcin, *Vivre*, pp. 4, 133–35, 138; idem, "Trois manieres," pp. 4–13; idem, *Campagnes*, p. 423; Vovelle, *Mort*, p. 171; Cohn, *Death*, chs. 2–3, 6, esp. pp. 18–21, 47, 98, 120; Crouzet-Pavan, *Espaces*, pp. 590, 912; Albini, "Continuità," pp. 150–51; Strocchia, *Death*, pp. 208–9; but evidence for strong pious bequests is found in Chiffoleau, *Comptabilité* pp. 219–22, 302–23; Boutruche, "Origines," esp. pp. 162, 177; Bonanno et al., "Legati," pp. 192–93, 198, 218–19.

75. Bertoliana, Gonz. B 224, n. 13 (Thiene); A.S.Vic., Test., 25 March and 21 May 1421; A.S.Ver., Test., mazzo 31, #93 (Verità).

76. A.S.Vic., Test., 22 August 1433 (Gaspare I); ivi, Not., Bortolo Bassan 4535, 22 May 1437 (patrimonial division); ibid. 4560, 29 August 1463 (Tommaso); ivi, Not., Antonio Saraceni 4960, 23 November 1499 (Gaspare II); 1453 Estimo, f. 8; 1460 Estimo, f. 103; 1477 Estimo, f. 6; 1505 Estimo, f. 2.

77. Lorcin, *Vivre*, pp. 150–51; Cohn, *Death*, pp. 18–20, 25–28, 120.

78. Collodo, "Artigiani," p. 120; Borelli, "'Doctor,'" p. 158. On growing harshness to the poor, see Swanson, *Church*, p. 103.

79. A.S.Ver., Test., mazzo 79, #27; ivi, mazzo 81, #12; ivi, mazzo 83, #103.

80. Lorcin, *Vivre*, pp. 148, 151; Cohn, *Death*, pp. 18–24, 120; see also Pasche, *Salut*, p. 93.

81. Bonanno et al., "Legati," pp. 198–201.

82. Banker, *Death*, pp. 79, 131; cf. A.S.Ver., Testamenti, mazzo 31, #93; A.S.Vic., Testamenti, 29 December 1476.

83. A.S.Vic., PO, AP, 23 July 1471; A.S.Ver. Test., mazzo 31, #93; ivi, mazzo 102,

#85; ivi, Perg., Malaspina-Verità, #39; see Lorcin, "Trois manieres," p. 8; Cohn, *Death,*
pp. 50–51.

84. Cohn, *Death,* pp. 32–36; idem, *Cult,* pp. 32–33; Mantese, *Memorie,* 3, 2, pp. 317–23.

85. Lorcin, *Vivre,* p. 148; idem, "Trois manieres," pp. 8–9; Cohn, *Cult,* pp. 36–37;
Bonanno et al., "Legati," pp. 195, 209; da Lamothe, "Pieté," pp. 20–24; Pasche, *Salut,*
p. 74.

86. Mantese, *Memorie,* 3, 2, pp. 401–19, 423–31.

87. Lorcin, *Vivre,* pp. 147–48; idem, "Trois manieres," pp. 10, 13; idem, "Clauses,"
pp. 297, 306–7.

88. Lorcin, *Vivre,* p. 4; idem, "Clauses," p. 320; Fasoli, "Note," p. 7; de Lamothe,
"Pieté," p. 35; Vovelle, *Mort,* p. 172; Chiffoleau, *Comptabilité,* pp. 292–97; Mantese,
Memorie, 3, 2, pp. 372–78, 385–87, 570–76; Collodo, "Artigiani," pp. 418–19.

89. Cohn, *Death,* pp. 18–19, 28–32; Bonanno et al., "Legati," p. 194.

90. A.S.Ver., Test., mazzo 31, #93; ivi, mazzo 81, ##12, 45; ivi, mazzo 89, #39;
A.S.Vic., PO, AP, 17 July 1443; ivi, Uff. Reg., 17 September 1493; ivi, Test., 6 February 1487; Bertoliana, Gonz. B 224, n. 13.

91. A.S.Vic., Test., 16 March and 10 April 1423, 13 June 1425, 20 May 1431, 16 January and 13 February 1437, 27 January 1440, 29 December 1475, 26 July 1484, 5 February 1489, 17 September 1493, 25 September 1494, 28 April 1497; A.S.Ver., Test.,
mazzo 93, #23; ivi, mazzo 102, #86; ivi, mazzo 128, #334; see Cohn, *Cult,* pp. 32–33, 65.

92. Mantese, *Memorie,* 3, 1, pp. 523–25, 675–76.

93. Castellazzi, "Testamento," p. 441; A.S.Ver., Test., mazzo 128, #334. For favor to
poveri vergognosi, see Spicciani, "Aspetti"; idem, *Capitale,* pp. 136–38; Albini, "Continuità," pp. 146–48; Pacini, "Osservanza," p. 90; Dyer, *Standards,* pp. 237–39, 249–
51; da Certaldo, *Libro,* #32.

94. Lorcin, *Vivre,* pp. 136–37; idem, "Clauses," pp. 314–15; idem, "Trois manieres,"
pp. 4–12; Cohn, *Death,* pp. 62–68. For growing demand for Masses, see Vovelle, *Mort,*
pp. 171–73; Chiffoleau, *Comptabilite,* pp. 229, 323–55; idem, "Usage"; Boutruche, "Origines," pp. 163–65; Pasche, *Salut,* pp. 109–15; Epstein, *Wills,* ch. 5; Condini, "Sondaggio," p. 375; Cohn, *Cult,* pp. 206–11; Pesce, *Chiesa,* I, p. 35 (but slight counterevidence
for Florence: Hurtubise, *Salviati,* p. 129; Bonanno et al., "Legati," pp. 192–93).

95. Chiffoleau, *Compatibilité,* p. 40; Pesche, *Salut,* p. 11; Cohn, *Death,* p. 15.

96. Arnaldi, f. 6r–v; A.S.Vic., Not., Bortolo Bassan 4539, 4 August 1441; see also
Repeta, f. 20v; Bertoliana, Gonz., Arch. Feramosca, Catastico #286; A.S.Ver., Perg.,
Guastaverza, b. I, ##13–14, 19, 25. Of the 1,072 documents drawn up by one family of
notaries in Vicenza in the 1476–1520 period, 2 percent are *donationes inter vivos,* twice
the proportion of testaments: A.S.Vic., Not., Bartolomeo, Nicolo and Pace Scroffa.

97. Gavitt, *Charity,* pp. 107–8.

98. Gregory the Great, *Dialogi* IV, ch. 55; Le Goff, *Birth,* pp. 91–95, 146–47, 166,
275–76; Lorcin, "Clauses," pp. 319–21; Chiffoleau, *Comptabilité,* pp. 323–24; Strocchia, *Death,* pp. 207–8.

99. A.S.Vic., Test., 25 September 1494.

100. Le Goff, *Birth,* pp. 124–27, 294.

101. These recalled the Masses that Gregory ordered for the soul of an errant monk:
Dialogi IV, ch. 55. They had different formats in different places, and might take up to
a year to complete: see Le Goff, *Birth,* pp. 92–93; Swanson, *Church,* p. 298; Chiffoleau,

"Usage," p. 238; Pesce, *Chiesa*, p. 36; Vovelle, *Mort*, p. 169; Herbert, "Trentains." They were rare in Florence: Bonanno et al., "Legati," p. 212.

102. A.S.Ver., Test., mazzo 31, #93; also ivi, Perg., Guastaverza, #26; in general, Chiffoleau, *Comptabilité*, p. 326–28.

103. Lorcin, "Trois manieres," pp. 7–12; Fasoli, "Note," pp. 121–22; Chiffoleau, *Comptabilité*, p. 349 (and Le Goff's preface, p. ix); Crouzet-Pavan, *Espaces*, pp. 594–95; Vovelle, *Mort*, p. 173; Swanson, *Church*, pp. 294–98. Cohn, however, sees a growing incidence of perpetual Masses in Tuscany: *Cult*, pp. 206–11. The wealthy in England often endowed perpetual chantries: Bossy, "Blood," p. 136; Swanson, *Church*, pp. 296–99; Rosenthal, *Purchase*, pp. 16–17.

104. Chiffoleau, "Usage"; Swanson, *Church*, p. 298.

105. De Lamothe, "Pieté," p. 14.

106. Arnaldi, ff. 6r–v; A.S.Vic., Not., Bortolo Bassan 4531, 22 August 1433.

107. Mantese, *Memorie*, 3, 2, pp. 596–97.

108. Ibid., 2, pp. 373, 383; Repeta, f. 20v.

109. Cohn, *Death*, pp. 199–201; idem, *Cult*, pp. 197–98; Gottfried, *Epidemic Disease*, pp. 22–23; Pasche, *Salut*, p. 20; Condini, "Sondaggio," p. 373; Gonon, *Institutions*, p. 50.

110. *Ius municipale*, ff. 114r, 153v.

111. *Statuti Veronae*, p. 254; *Ius municipale*, f. 155v; and see Herlihy and Klapisch-Zuber, *Toscans*, p. 612; Strocchia, "Death Rites," pp. 124–40; idem, "Funerals," p. 163; idem, *Death*, pp. 10–12; Fumagalli, "Paesaggio," pp. 421–22; McClure, *Sorrow*, p. 41; Chiffoleau, *Comptabilité*, pp. 133–34; Henderson, "Religious Confraternities," p. 386; Vovelle, *Mort*, p. 160.

112. Aries, *Homme*, p. 79; Cohn, *Death*, pp. 201–2; and see Chiffoleau, "Changer," pp. 125–26.

113. A.S.Ver., Perg., Guastaverza, b. I, #26; A.S.Vic., Test., reg. 21, f. 179v. In general, see Pasche, *Salut*, pp. 52–53; Bonanno et al., "Legati," p. 216; Vovelle, *Mort*, p. 163; Strocchia, *Death*, pp. 168, 198–99.

Chapter 4. Household and Family

1. Herlihy, "Making," p. 118; idem, "Family," pp. 2–4; Bullough, "Social Groupings," esp. pp. 6–7; Besta, *Famiglia*, pp. 15–16.

2. Kuehn, *Law*, p. 172; A.S.Ver., Test., mazzo 81, #45; similarly, ivi, #12 ("in familia dictorum de Bovo").

3. A.S.Ver., AAC, reg. 56, f. 148; see also *Vocabularius*, s.v. domus (defined either "per omnibus cohabitationibus in domo" or *agnatio*); Kent and Kent, *Neighbours*, p. 255; Herlihy, "Family," p. 4; Besta, *Famiglia*, p. 25; Heers, *Family Clans*, pp. 104–5.

4. Bovi, f. 13r; Alberti, *Libri*, p. 226.

5. Kuehn, "Honor," esp. p. 301; Herlihy, "Making," p. 116; idem, "Family," esp. pp. 5–7.

6. *Ius municipale*, ff. 9v, 10r, 12r; Bertoliana, Arch. Torre 167, fasc. 8, ff. 1r–2v; similarly, in Verona (*Statuti Veronae*, pp. 23, 42). For boundaries elsewhere, see Roveda, "Istituzioni," p. 60; Crouzet-Pavan, *Espaces*, pp. 393–94.

7. *Ius municipale*, ff. 114r–v, 156r–v, 61v, 87r, 102r–3r, 131r–v, 144v; Bertoliana, Arch. Torre 60, ff. 129r–v; see also *Statuti Veronae*, pp. 25, 106, 134–35.

8. A.S.Ver., Test., mazzo 31, #93 (Gabriele Verità); ivi, mazzo 102, #85 (Verità Verità); similarly, ivi, mazzo 81, #45 (Aventino Fracastoro); A.S.Vic., Test., 21 May 1488, 28 April 1497.

9. A.S.Ver., Anag. Com. 482; similarly, Girolamo and Donato Stoppi (ivi, Anag. Com. 1082).

10. A.S.Ver., Anag. Prov. 224; similarly, Pierfilippo Muronovo, aged forty-six (ivi, Anag. Com. 1172); Verità Verità, aged forty (ivi, Anag. Com. 312).

11. *Libri*, pp. 149–50, 232–34.

12. Herlihy and Klapisch-Zuber, *Toscans*, pp. 510–11; Tamassia, *Famiglia*, pp. 117; Kent, *Household*, pp. 44–51; Klapisch-Zuber, "Structures," p. 17.

13. The cumulative figure is 5.24 percent for multinuclear *frereches* plus the 1.6 percent of nonnuclear *frereches*, to which we should add some of the 1.2 percent of the laterally extended mononuclear families: Herlihy and Klapisch-Zuber, *Toscans*, pp. 481–86, 497–501; and see Klapisch-Zuber, "Household," pp. 279–80; idem, *Women*, p. 33; idem and Demonet, "Uno pane," esp. pp. 38, 45–46; Herlihy, "Vieillir," p. 1341; idem, "Tuscan Town," p. 87; idem, "Mapping Households," pp. 5–9; Heers, *Family Clans*, p. 69.

14. Herlihy, "Mapping Households," pp. 9–12; idem and Klapisch-Zuber, *Toscans*, pp. 509–10; Klapisch-Zuber, *Women*, pp. 71–72, 285.

15. Laslett, *Household*, esp. pp. ix–xi, 5–9; idem, "Household," esp. p. 139; see also Houlbrooke, *English Family*, pp. 10, 18–20; Bennett, "Tie," pp. 118–19; idem, *Women*, pp. 53–64, 100.

16. Klapisch-Zuber, "Household," pp. 270–72; idem, *Women*, p. 24; idem, "Fiscalité," pp. 1317–19; idem and Demonet, "Uno pane," p. 46.

17. Herlihy, "Mapping Households," p. 15; idem, "Deaths," p. 147; idem, *Medieval Households*, p. 153; idem and Klapisch-Zuber, *Toscans*, pp. 476, 507–8; Klapisch-Zuber, "Household," pp. 276–77; idem and Demonet, "Uno pane," esp. p. 52 and fig. 3.4; Kent, *Household*, p. 24; similarly, in Lucca: Leverotti, "Linee," p. 179. Of 49 Salviati households in the 1,427 catasto, 35 percent were "enlarged" and 20 percent were fraternal joint households: Hurtubise, *Salviati*, p. 82.

18. Herlihy, "Mapping Households," p. 12.

19. Herlihy and Klapisch-Zuber, *Toscans*, pp. 182–83, 211, 512–17; Herlihy, "Mapping Households," p. 6; idem, *Medieval Households*, p. 144.

20. Herlihy, "Tuscan Town," p. 87; idem, "Mapping Households," p. 11; idem and Klapisch-Zuber, *Toscans*, pp. 472–76, 480–84, 498–99, 518; Klapisch-Zuber, "Household," pp. 275, 279; Menzioni, "Matrimonio," pp. 445–46.

21. Hughes, "Domestic Ideals," pp. 118–22; idem, "Urban Growth," p. 122; Heers, *Family Clans*, ch. 6; Carron, *Enfant*, ch. 2, pp. 41–50; Maurel, "Structures," pp. 664–66; Hilaire, *Regime*, pp. 249–76; Laslett, "Introduction" to *Household*, p. 16.

22. Cipolla, "Relazione," p. 212; Herlihy, "Population," pp. 106–9; Bautier, "Feux," pp. 255, 258; Guidoboni, "Terre," p. 801.

23. Bovi, ff. 4v–5r, 6v–7r, 13r, 20v–21r; Stoppi, f. 2r; Repeta, ff. 97v, 131v.

24. Herlihy, "Roots," pp. 135–40, 143–50.

25. Cammarosano, "Aspetti," pp. 428–29; Hughes, "Domestic Ideals," pp. 124–28; idem, "Urban Growth," pp. 21–22.

26. Herlihy and Klapisch-Zuber, *Toscans*, pp. 606–10.

27. A.S.Vic., Not., Bortolo Bassan 4559, 26 October 1462 (Tommaso Arnaldi); A.S.Ver., Test., mazzo 81, #45 (Aventino Fracastoro); in general, Hilaire, *Regime*, pp. 217–48.

28. Cammarosano, "Strutture," p. 423; Hughes, "Urban Growth," pp. 119–21; Kuehn, *Emancipation*, pp. 159–60; Leverotti, "Linee," pp. 197–99.

29. *Ius municipale*, ff. 164v–65r; *Statuti Veronae*, p. 150.

30. *Ius municipale*, f. 11v; Arnaldi, f. 18r; Bertoliana, Arch. Torre 1653, s.d. 30 May 1498.

31. *Ius municipale*, ff. 156r–v, 87v.

32. A.S.Ver., Test., mazzo 31, #93 (Gabriele Verità); ivi, mazzo 79, #27 (Bartolomeo dal Bovo); ivi, mazzo 81, #132 (Bonzanino Muronovo); mazzo 93, #209 (Fracastoro).

33. Kuehn, "Honor," esp. pp. 294–300; Herlihy and Klapisch-Zuber, *Toscans*, pp. 608–9.

34. Chojnacki, "Political Adulthood"; Ruggiero, *Violence*, esp. ch. 5, and *Boundaries*.

35. A.S.Vic., Test., 22 August 1433 (Arnaldi), 3 October 1417 (Domenico da Quinto), 16 March 1423 (Marco da Bolzano), 12 July 1495 (Giovanni Thiene); A.S.Ver., Test., mazzo 60, #49 (Bovi); ivi, mazzo 81, #45 (Fracastoro); ivi, mazzo 89, #39 (Verità).

36. Di Renzo Villata, "Note," pp. 59–60, 64–76; Bullough, "Social Groupings," p. 7; Tamassia, *Famiglia*, p. 339; Besta, *Famiglia*, pp. 231, 242–43.

37. *Ius municipale*, ff. 21r, 49v, 88r, 90v–93r; for the Auditori Nuovi, see Marciana, Ital. VII, 1759 (8419), bk. A, III, 26 July 1472; VII, 21 May 1451; bk. B, rubric 46; Bertoliana, Arch. Torre 59, ff. 11v–12v; in general, Besta, *Famiglia*, pp. 242–43; idem, *Successioni*, ch. 54; Niccolai, *Formazione*, pt. I, ch. 6; de Renzo Villata, "Note," pp. 64–68, 81–89.

38. A.S.Vic., PO, AP, 9 January 1465, 16 December 1465, 19 April 1466, 18 February 1467, 12 November 1467; ivi, Not., Bortolo Bassan 4563, 8 February 1466.

39. A.S.Vic., Not., Bortolo Bassan 4560, 29 August 1463. Gaspare II acted as tutor of his half brother Girolamo until the latter came of age: ibid. 4561, 28 April 1464; A.S.Vic., PO, AP, 16 December 1465, 18 April 1470; ivi, Not., Cristoforo Bassan 37/38, 29 March 1473, 23 February 1481, 27 April 1482.

40. A.S.Vic., Test., 11 September 1430; A.S.Vic., Not., Bortolo Bassan 4549, 27 October 1451; A.S.Vic., PO, AP, 24 January 1453.

41. *Ius municipale*, ff. 156r–v; a model case in A.S.Vic., PO, AP, 7 May 1450.

42. A.S.Vic., PO, AP, 21 January 1466, 5 November 1466, 1 May 1467, 21 May 1467, 23 May 1467, 14 November 1467.

43. A.S.Vic., Not., Bortolo Bassan 4549, 27 October 1451.

44. A.S.Ver., Anag. Prov. 774; Borelli, "'Doctor,'" pp. 156–57; Freschi, ff. 40r, 45r; see also de Martin, "Borghesi," p. 91.

45. Pandimiglio, "Giovanni di Pagolo Morelli," pp. 11–12.

46. Laslett, "Introduction" to *Household*, p. xii.

47. A.S.Vic., PO, AP, 17 August 1457, 27 February 1476; Arnaldi, f. 9v.

48. *Libro*, #293.

49. Alberti, *Libri*, p. 226.

50. Herlihy, "Family," pp. 2–7; Besta, *Famiglia*, pp. 15–16; Vegio, *Vocabularia*, s.v. familia.

51. Arnaldi, f. 16v; Bertoliana, Arch. Torre 349, fasc. 6, ff. 15r–16r.

52. Herlihy, "Population," p. 109; idem and Klapisch-Zuber, *Toscans,* p. 520.

53. Klapisch-Zuber, "Women Servants," pp. 60–65; Romano, *Housecraft,* ch. 3.

54. Donato Stoppi had to offer dowry incentives for women to remain in the house for at least eight years: A.S.Ver., Test., mazzo 128, #334. Florentine women's service was usually transient (Klapisch-Zuber, "Women Servants," pp. 61, 68–71; idem, "Come valutare," p. 43), and Venetian women servants had shorter-term contracts than male colleagues (Romano, *Housecraft,* ch. 4).

55. Quoted in Klapisch-Zuber, "Women Servants," pp. 57–58.

56. *Ius municipale,* ff. 158v–9r; Venetian laws in Romano, "Regulation," p. 663; idem, *Housecraft,* ch. 2.

57. *Ius municipale,* ff. 131r–v; Venetian legislation in Romano, "Regulation," pp. 665–66; Florentine fears of loss of honor in Kuehn, *Law,* pp. 83–88; see Goodich, *"Ancilla,"* pp. 122–23.

58. A.S.Vic., PO, AP, 26 February 1435; Tamassia, *Famiglia,* p. 370.

59. Klapisch-Zuber, *Women,* pp. 106–8, 175–76; Boswell, *Kindness,* pp. 400–403, 420–21; Ruggiero, *Boundaries,* pp. 40–41, 107–8; Guarducci and Ottanelli, *Servitori,* ch. 6. Some 60 percent of abandoned children in Florence were born to servants and slaves, and many of these were probably bastards: Gavitt, *Charity,* p. 20.

60. *Ius municipale,* ff. 130r–v.

61. A.S.Vic., PO, LAGA, 26 February 1435, 13 January 1438, 7 October 1438, 1 June 1439, 6 March 1445. For similar contract language elsewhere, see Heers, *Èsclaves,* pp. 148–50, 155–56; Pinto, "Rapporti," pp. 689–90; Laribiere, "Mariage," p. 344; Tamassia, *Famiglia,* p. 368. Dennis Romano has kindly supplied two Venetian examples of child leases: A.S.Ven., Cancelleria Inferiore, Notai, busta 81, notary Domenico de Philosofis, large protocol, f. 3r; ivi, busta 24, notary Rolandinus de Bernardis, protocol 1409–24, f. 8or.

62. *Ius municipale,* ff. 64r–80v, 103r–5r, 107r–8r, 149v–53v; *Statuti Veronae,* p. 237.

63. Cohn, *Death,* pp. 18–20, 28–32, 55–56, 115–17, 216–17; Lorcin, *Vivre,* pp. 108–13; Romano, *Housecraft,* chs. 4–6.

64. A.S.Ver., Perg. 35 (Guastaverza), vol. I, #26; ivi, Test., mazzo 60, #49; ivi, mazzo 93, #23; ivi, mazzo 81, #12; A.S.Vic., Test., 16 January 1437, 13 February 1437, 27 January 1440. Gabriele Verità provided outright bequests, increases in salary, and cancellation of debts to rural laborers and house servants: A.S.Ver., Test., mazzo 31, #93.

65. A.S.Vic., PO, AP, 21 November 1433.

66. A.S.Ver., Test., mazzo 89, #39. The will was drawn up in 1497; in 1501 Viadana was still in the house, aged seventy (ivi, Anag. Prov. 593). He had been with the family since at least 1492 (ivi, Anag. Prov. 592). Abundancia Bellodo, widow of Gabriele Verità, ordered her grandson to keep a *massaria* in his house: ivi, Pergamene, Malaspina-Verità, b. 18, #39.

67. Besta, *Successioni,* p. 79 and ch. 40; Niccolai, *Formazione,* pp. 122–24.

68. A.S.Vic., Test., 21 May 1421, 21 July 1453; ivi, PO, AP, 23 July 1471; A.S.Ver., Test., mazzo 60, ##49–50; ivi, mazzo 79, #27; ivi, mazzo 81, ##45, 132; ivi, mazzo 93, #209; ivi, mazzo 102, #86.

69. A.S.Vic., Test., 10 April 1423, 28 August 1428, 17 September 1428, 20 May 1431, 27 November 1435, 26 January 1437, 21 September 1440, 18 December 1441, 20 June 1450, 26 July 1484; and see Besta, *Successioni,* pp. 5–6.

70. *Ius municipale*, ff. 114r–v.

71. Herlihy and Klapisch-Zuber, *Toscans*, pp. 471, 493; Klapisch-Zuber, *Women*, pp. 19–20; Hughes, "Urban Growth," p. 117; idem, "Struttura," pp. 934–40; Cammarosano, "Aspetti," pp. 417–20; Herlihy, *Medieval Households*, pp. 88–92; Besta, *Successioni*, chs. 15, 17–19; Niccolai, *Formazione*, p. 19, pt. II, ch. 2, pt. IV, ch. 4, pt. V, ch. 2.

72. Niccolai, *Formazione*, pt. II, ch. 2; Lorcin, *Vivre*, ch. 2; Cohn, *Death*, pp. 135–36; Chiffoleau, *Comptabilité*, p. 69.

73. Kuehn, "Ambiguities," p. 13 (citing Jack Goody).

74. A.S.Vic., Test., 18 December 1441; A.S.Ver., Perg., Verità, ser. III, fasc. 7, #396; A.S.Ver., Test., mazzo 62, #79 (earlier testament in ivi, mazzo 60, #49); ivi, mazzo 93, #209.

75. A.S.Vic., PO, AP, 31 May 1473; A.S.Ver., Test., mazzo 46, ##10, 76; a similar case in ivi, Perg., Guastaverza, b. I, #22. For Venice, see Crouzet-Pavan, *Espaces*, pp. 419, 461. Tuscan daughters were not preferred as heirs to distant male kin, and the incidence of such cases declined: Cohn, *Cult*, p. 197.

76. A.S.Vic., Test., 21 May 1421, 16 March 1423, 10 April 1423, 11 January 1428, 7 November 1441; 17 September 1428 (wife and *nepos*), 20 May 1431; 26 January 1436, 21 September 1440, 20 June 1450 (wife and daughter); Bertoliana, Arch. Thiene, Catastico Conte Adriano, #398. Some 15 percent of male testators in a Milanese sample chose women, generally their wives, as primary heirs: Condini, "Sondaggio," p. 374. In general, see Niccolai, *Formazione*, pp. 170–93; Lorcin, *Vivre*, p. 62.

77. *Ius municipale*, ff. 114r, 153v; Niccolai, *Formazione*, pp. 191–93, 290, 303.

78. A.S.Vic., Test., 9 January 1489.

79. A.S.Ver., Test., mazzo 60, #46 (Verità); A.S.Vic., PO, AP, 17 July 1443; A.S.Vic., Test., 23 July 1430, 21 September 1434, 13 August 1436.

80. A.S.Vic., Test., 20 December 1435, 12 September 1440, 3 July 1476; A.S.Ver., Test., mazzo 102, #187.

81. Bovi, ff. 20v–21v; A.S.Ver., Test., mazzo 60, ##49–50; in general, Besta, *Successioni*, chs. 36, 41–42; Niccolai, *Formazione*, p. 39 and p. IV, ch. 3.

82. A.S.Ver., Test., mazzo 79, #27; ivi, mazzo 81, #12; ivi, mazzo 83, #103.

83. A.S.Vic., Test., 3 October 1417, 16 March 1423, 18 December 1441.

84. A.S.Ver., Test., mazzo 93, #209; ivi, mazzo 102, #85; ivi, Perg., Verità, ser. III, vol. 7, #388; in general, Niccolai, *Formazione*, pp. 28–30; Besta, *Successioni*, pp. 20–27.

85. Only some Veneto testaments referred to *fedecommesso*, but nonalienation clauses are virtually identical throughout. For example, Gabriele Verità and Aventino Fracastoro made similar provisions, but the former explicitly invoked *fideicommissum* and the latter never used the term: A.S.Ver., Test., mazzo 31, #93; ivi, mazzo 81, #45.

86. As against Besta, *Successioni*, chs. 38, 53, esp. p. 173; Tamassia, *Famiglia*, p. 128; Bizzocchi, "Dissoluzione," p. 41.

87. Examples in A.S.Ver., Test., mazzo 31, #93; ivi, mazzo 81, ##45, 132; ivi, mazzo 89, #39; Bertoliana, Arch. Thiene, Catastico Conte Adriano, ##202, 268, 334, 516; A.S.Vic., Test., 13 February 1437, 29 December 1475, 5 February 1489, 25 September 1494. In general, see Epstein, *Wills*, p. 86; Kent, *Household*, pp. 137–41; Cohn, *Death*, pp. 152–53, 191–92; idem, *Cult*, ch. 5; Herlihy and Klapisch-Zuber, *Toscans*, p. 499; Klapisch-Zuber, "State," p. 20.

88. A.S.Vic., Test., 25 March 1421, 11 September 1430, 22 August 1433 (Gaspare

Arnaldi); A.S.Vic., Notarile, Antonio Saraceni 4960, 23 November 1499 (Gaspare II Arnaldi).

89. A.S.Ver., Test., mazzo 31, #93.

90. A common name was not prerequisite to membership in the family. To Manfredo Repeta, the second and third cousins who bore surnames such as Zanfata, Repetini, and Trivisolo still counted among the *caxa di Ropeti*: Repeta, f. 97v.

91. Dal Bovo, f. 51v.

92. Heers, *Clans*, pp. 79, 105–7; Kent and Kent, "Pact."

93. A.S.Vic., Not., Antonio Saraceni 4960, 23 November 1499.

94. Crouzet-Pavan, *Espaces*, pp. 398–409; Hughes, "Struttura," p. 946; Lorcin, *Vivre*, p. 101.

95. A.S.Vic., Test., 22 August 1433; ivi, Not., Bortolo Bassan 4560, 29 August 1463; A.S.Ver., Perg., Verità, reg. III, fasc. 7, #396; ivi, Test., mazzo 31, #93.

96. A.S.Vic., Test., 11 September 1430, 29 December 1475, 5 February 1489, 25 September 1494, 12 July 1495; ivi, Not., Antonio Saraceni 4960, 23 November 1499.

97. Hughes, "Struttura," p. 946; Kent, *Household*, pp. 132–34.

98. A.S.Ver., Test., mazzo 31, #93 (Gabriele Verità); ivi, mazzo 60, #49 (Bonaventura Bovi); ivi, mazzo 79, #27 (Bartolomeo dal Bovo); ivi, mazzo 81, #132 (Bonzanino Muronovo); ivi, mazzo 89, #39 (Pietro Verità); ivi, mazzo 93, #23 (Alvise Stoppi); ivi, mazzo 102, #85 (Verità Verità); A.S.Vic., Test., 22 August 1433, 29 December 1475 (Marco Thiene), 5 February 1489; A.S.Vic., Not., Bortolo Bassan 4560, 29 August 1463; Arnaldi, ff. 8r, 16v–17r. For ego-centered suffrages, see ch. 3. Florentines established commemorative liturgies that proclaimed the names of all the family's dead at regular intervals: Kent, *Household*, pp. 100–102; Kent and Kent, "Pact," p. 346.

99. A.S.Ver., Test., mazzo 79, #27; A.S.Vic., Not., Bortolo Bassan 4535, 22 May 1437; ibid. 4537, 10 February 1439; ibid. 4543, 6 June 1443.

100. Vicenza, Arch. Curia, Feudi, reg. 26, 27 November 1478.

101. A.S.Vic., PO, AP, 9 January 1465; ivi, Not., Bortolo Bassan 4563, 8 February 1466; ivi, Notarile, Cristoforo Bassan 36, 23 February 1481; ibid. 37/38, 29 March 1473, 6 April 1478, 27 April 1482.

102. A.S.Vic., PO, AP, 18 April 1470, 11 June 1487; ivi, Notarile, Cristoforo Bassan 38, 10 September 1477.

103. A.S.Vic., Not., Bortolo Bassan 4563, 26 July 1466; ivi, PO, AP, 30 July 1471, 27 February 1476; ivi, Not., Cristoforo Bassan 37/38, 29 March 1473, 6 April 1478.

104. Stoppi, ff. 3v–9r. For Florence, Hurtubise (*Salviati*, pp. 84–85) and Kent (*Household*) think that family economic consortia were common; Goldthwaite ("Organizzazione economica," pp. 4–9) finds few joint interests.

105. Quoted in Bizzocchi, "Dissoluzione," p. 21; a similar Roman statement is found in Esposito Aliano, "Famiglia," p. 212. For Morelli's bitter denunciation of predatory great-uncles, uncles, and cousins, see *Ricordi*, pp. 146–49, 156, 202–4, 231–32; Pandimiglio, "Giovanni di Pagolo Morelli," pp. 26–28; for disputes between stepsiblings, see Goldthwaite, *Private Wealth*, pp. 75–76; Niccolini di Camugliano, *Chronicles*, p. 122; Bizzocchi, "Dissoluzione," pp. 31–40; for nearly invariable division of households in the second generation, see Klapisch-Zuber and Demonet, "Uno pane," pp. 46–47; Sapori, "Alberti," pp. 185–86; idem, ed., *Alberti del Giudice*, pp. 1340,

1349–50; Bizzocchi, "Dissoluzione," pp. 18–25; Goldthwaite, "Medici Bank," pp. 10–13; Kent, *Household*, p. 32.

106. A.S.Vic., PO, AP, 13 April 1456, 9 January 1465, 13 March 1470; ivi, Not., Bortolo Bassan 4557, 2 May 1460.

107. Goldthwaite, *Private Wealth*, p. 33; Hurtubise, *Salviati*, pp. 70–77; Bizzocchi, "Dissoluzione," p. 15; Kent, *Household*, pp. 49–55, 125 and ch. 5; Kent and Kent, *Neighbours*, p. 2; Weissman, *Ritual Brotherhood*, pp. 13–17; Hughes, "Kinsmen," pp. 98–101; Heers, "Urbanisme," pp. 384–89; Esposito Aliano, "Famiglia," p. 206; Grohmann, "Spazio," pp. 612–13; idem, *Città*, I, p. 162; Crouzet-Pavan, *Espaces*, pp. 378–82 (quote on p. 380). Elsewhere, however (pp. 374, 387–92), the latter notes a lack of "spatial solidarity" in Venetian lineage.

108. Only Vicentines possessed of firm surnames were counted. Toponymic surnames were excluded, as were cases in which a family reported a single household in an *estimo*. The mean index for memorialist families in Verona's *estimi* of 1447 (1.6), 1465 (1.7), 1473 (1.4), 1482 (1.3), and 1502 (1.9) is 1.6 (177 households); the mean index for Vicenza's *estimi* of 1453 (1.6), 1460 (1.6), 1477 (1.8), and 1503 (1.9) is 1.7 (1,159 households).

109. Repeta, ff. 81r–v, 107v.

Chapter 5. Work

1. Luzzatto, "Mercanti," esp. pp. 27–33, 39–41, 47–48.

2. Malanima, "Formazione"; de la Roncière, *Florence*; Epstein, "Regional Fairs"; idem, "Cities."

3. Cherubini, *Signori*, esp. p. 325.

4. Kedar, "Genoese Notaries," pp. 84–88; Hughes, "Ideals," p. 118; Rebora, "Libri," p. 210; Balletto, "Battista de Luco," esp. p. xxvii.

5. Esposito Aliano, "Famiglia," pp. 204–6; Luzzatto, "Attività," esp. pp. 167–69; Goldthwaite, *Private Wealth*, esp. pp. 40–45, 192–93, 236; Starn, "Francesco Guicciardini," esp. p. 418; Branca, "Prefazione" to Morelli's *Ricordi*, p. 10.

6. Bertoliana, Gonzati 309, f. 7v; ibid. 544, ff. 64r, 67r.

7. Zanazzo (*Arte*, pp. 21–22, 32) and Brunello ("Arti," pp. 288–89) argue for a merger of Vicentine *mercatores* and *lanarii* around 1389, but they are belied by separate *matricole* (Bertoliana, Gonz. 309 and 544) that continue into the mid-fifteenth century; see also Pozza, "Corporazioni," pp. 262–64; *Ius municipale*, ff. 15v, 148r. Verona's *ars draperiorum* was distinct from and superior to the *ars scapizatorum*: *Statuti Veronae*, p. 188. For a similar division in Padua, see Cessi, "Privilegia," pp. 305–10.

8. *Statuti Veronae*, pp. 21, 41–43 and *Partes et decreta*, pp. 6–7; A.S.Ver., AAC, 56, ff. 61v, 133v–37r, 139v, 227v; ivi, AAC, 63, ff. 17v, 48v–49r, 245r; Simeoni, *Antichi statuti*, ch. 3; Lecce, *Vicende*, pp. 17–25, 3–43; Varanini, *Comuni*, p. 15; Barbieri, "Economia," pp. 331ff. Veronese councils also elected *officiales garzatorie* to supervise the finishing of cloth. For similar bodies elsewhere, see Ascheri, "Arti," pp. 111–33; Mainoni, "Attività," p. 580; idem, "Mercato," p. 27; Martini, "*Universitas*"; *Corpus statutorum*, "Introduzione"; Luzzatto, "Mercanti," pp. 34–35; Greci, "Forme," p. 94; Broglio d'Ajano, "Industria," pp. 235–36.

9. Zanazzo, *Arte*, pp. 126, 217 and docs. 16, 18, 20, 21, 27, 31, 38, 43, 45–47, 59, 60–62; Rossini and Mazzaoui, "Lana," pp. 187–88, 197; Grubb, *Firstborn*, pp. 67–68, 70; Lecce, *Vicende*, p. 50; Brunello, *Arti*, p. 290. For similar legislation in Milan, see Mainoni, "Mercato," p. 22; idem, "Sviluppo," pp. 215–16. For citizenship inducements, see Bertoliana, Arch. Torre 61, ff. 31v–32r, 71v–72r; ivi, Arch. Torre 164, fasc. 16, ff. 1r–2r; A.S.Ver., AAC, reg. 63, f. 17r.

10. *Statuti Veronae*, pp. 229–30; Zanazzo, *Arte*, docs. 13–14; Borghesini, "Arte," pp. 113, 122, 157–59; Rossini and Mazzaoui, "Lana," p. 187; Lecce, *Vicende*, pp. 48–54; Varanini, *Comuni*, pp. 207–8.

11. Zanazzo, *Arte*, docs. 5, 16–17, 19, 38; A.S.Ven., Senato Terra 1, f. 89r; Rossini and Mazzaoui, "Lana," pp. 196–200; Mainoni, "Mercato," pp. 29, 37; Borghesini, "Arte," pp. 113, 122, 160–62.

12. De Roover, *Medici Bank*, pp. 171–74, 184; Edler de Roover, "Andrea Banchi," pp. 236–56.

13. Sales of semifinished goods throughout A.S.Vic., PO, LAGA (cloth transfer, 12 June 1439; putting out, 3 December 1451); ivi, Not., Bortolo Bassan 4559, 26 January 1462; ibid. 4560, 25 February 1463.

14. Contracts throughout A.S.Vic., PO, LAGA; ivi, PO, AP, 10 May 1451; ivi, Not., Bortolo Bassan 4540, 1 March 1442; ibid. 4548, 15 December 1450; ibid. 4549, 12 May 1451; ivi, Not., Cristoforo Bassan 34, 21 January 1445; statutes on *soccide* in *Ius municipale*, ff. 167r–v.

15. He formed at least two additional large-scale partnerships with Lombard cousins, though their duration and capitalization are unknown: Stoppi, ff. 3v–4v, 5v–7r.

16. Lecce, *Ricerche*, pp. 270–73, 281–82, 303–10; a similar Paduan company is described in Collodo, "Artigianati," pp. 409–10. Arnaldi examples are: A.S.Vic., Not., Bortolo Bassan 4535, 7 December 1437; ibid. 4538, 16 February 1440, 31 March 1440, 27 April 1440, 7 September 1440; ibid. 4540, 27 February 1442; ibid. 4545, 4 October 1446; ibid. 4547, 15 February 1449, 7 November 1449; ibid. 4549, 26 February 1451, 9 October 1451; ibid. 4550, 14 March 1452, 22 August 1452; ibid. 4554, 18 June 1456; ibid. 4555, 9 January 1457; ibid. 4556, 4 August 1459; ibid. 4563, 8 February 1466; ivi, Not., Cristoforo Bassan 34, 10 March 1453, 21 March 1453, 3 March 1459; ibid. 37, 8 June 1457, 29 March 1473; ivi, PO, LAGA, 17 February 1452; ivi, PO, AP, 5 December 1448.

17. Goldthwaite, "Medici Bank," pp. 8–19; idem, "Organizzazione," pp. 6–11; Melis, "Opifici," pp. 238–42; Malanima, "Regione"; Edler de Roover, "Andrea Banchi," pp. 225–29.

18. Mainoni, "Note," pp. 565–67; Miani, "Economie," p. 573.

19. A.S.Vic., Not., Bortolo Bassan 4549, 9 October 1451; ivi, PO, LAGA, 17 February 1452; ivi, Not., Cristoforo Bassan 34, 3 March 1459. For Tuscan profits, see Goldthwaite, *Private Wealth*, pp. 42, 172, 201; Sapori, "Alberti," pp. 166–69, 172–73.

20. The Covoni, for example, bought Paduan linen in Verona (Sapori, ed., *Libro*, pp. 79, 277, 279–80, 282–84); Verona's superior river transport made it a shipping point for both Germany and Venice (Vaccari, "Sguardo," pp. 565–66).

21. Hoshino, *Arte*, pp. 223, 297–98; Dini, "Industria," p. 352.

22. A.S.Ver., AAC, reg. 63, ff. 23v–26r, 167r; Cipolla, "Relazione," p. 185; Lecce, *Vicende*, p. 45.

23. Law, "Verona," pp. 21–22; Lecce, *Vicende*, pp. 54–57; Varanini, "Vicenza," pp. 232–38; idem, *Comuni*, pp. 207–11, 335–37; fierce protest of the 1475 order—even though Verona's cloth paid lower taxes than that of other cities—in A.S.Ver., AAC, reg. 63, ff. 137v–38r. In the wine trade, Veronese protest and evasion maintained traditional export routes and markets; they used the Venetian market when conditions were favorable, and avoided it when taxes and fees were too steep: Varanini, *Comuni*, pp. 167–69.

24. Barbieri, "Produzione," p. 190; Sapori, ed., *Libro*, pp. 80–81, 105, 107, 277–78, 280–81, 289–90; Blanshei, "Population," p. 614; Sapori, *Studi*, p. 455; Hoshino, *Arte*, pp. 251, 273, 288, 291, 297–98; A.S.Ver., AAC, reg. 63, ff. 16v, 29v, 70r, 153r–v, 160r; Ashtor, "Exportation," p. 320.

25. Vaccari, "Sguardo," p. 565; Hoshino, *Arte*, p. 275; Varanini, *Comuni*, pp. 207–8.

26. *Ius municipale*, ff. 167v–68v. In consequence, many outsiders pretended to be Vicentine: Zanazzo, *Arte*, doc. 36.

27. Zanazzo, *Arte*, docs. 11, 29, 60–62; Ashton, "Exportation," pp. 319–20; Hoshino, *Arte*, p. 246; Varanini, "Vicenza," pp. 232–38. The Arnaldi frequently sold wool and cloth to inhabitants of the area around Marostica, close to the Brenta and a center of smuggling: e.g., A.S.Vic., PO, LAGA.

28. Hoshino, *Arte*, pp. 274, 296–98.

29. Soranzo, "Cronaca," pp. 93–97; Lecce, *Vicende*, p. 45.

30. Sapori, ed., *Libro*, pp. 22–23, 79–81, 105, 107, 277–84, 289–90; Lecce, *Ricerche*, pp. 287–89; Sapori, *Studi*, II, p. 981; III, pp. 93–95.

31. Hoshino, *Arte*, pp. 264–65, 291; Barbieri, "Produzione," p. 190; Cherubini, *Signori*, p. 33.

32. Mainoni, "Attività," pp. 578–79; idem, "Mercato," pp. 21, 39; Miani, "Economie," p. 573; Lecce, *Ricerche*, pp. 271, 303.

33. Zanazzo, *Arte*, doc. 12. Prestige is measured by the guilds' position in the marching order of civic processions: Bertoliana, Arch. Torre 777, f. 108r; *Ius municipale*, ff. 147v–48r, 148r–v. In 1425 both furnished members of the elite council of the Anziani; the *lanarii* had not done so earlier: ibid., f. 15v; Brunello, *Arti*, pp. 274–75, 289; Pozza, "Corporazioni," pp. 250, 255–56, 257.

34. Zanazzo, *Arte*, p. xvi; Brunello, *Arti*, p. 290; Vaccari, "Scambi," pp. 565–66; Mazzaoui, *Cotton Industry*, pp. 135–38; Rossini and Mazzaoui, "Lana," pp. 188–97. For the rapid expansion of Milanese wool production in the fifteenth century, see Miani, "Economie," pp. 574–75.

35. Collodo, "Note," p. 180; Mazzaoui, *Cotton Industry*, pp. 133–39; Zanazzo, *Arte*, pp. 6–8, 107ff. The number of workers in the Milanese wool industry also fell, though production of finer stuffs remained strong: Mainoni, "Attività," p. 577; idem, "Sviluppo," pp. 229–31. Florentine decline set in earlier (1370s–1430s): Francheschi, "*Tumulto*," pp. 6–28; Dini, "Industria," pp. 337–38.

36. *Economia*, pp. 140–41, 181–83.

37. Lecce, *Vicende*, pp. 60, 64–85.

38. A.S.Ver., AAC, reg. 63, ff. 38r–39v.

39. Varanini, *Comuni*, pp. 207–8.

40. Zanazzo, *Arte*, pp. 6–8, 99–101; Brunello, *Arti*, pp. 295–96; Mazzaoui, *Cotton Industry*, pp. 132–33; Bertoliana, Arch. Torre 61, ff. 341r–v, 376r–77r; Mantese, *Memorie*, 3, 2, pp. 631–34; *Statuti Veronae, Partes et decreta*, pp. 118–19; Lecce, *Vicende*,

ch. 3. According to Tagliaferri, the number of silk workers in Verona rose from eight in 1409 to sixteen in 1509, compared with upwards of a thousand in the wool trade (*Economia*, pp. 140–43, 181–82), but he counts all unspecified spinners and weavers within the wool industry when they may, in fact, have handled silk.

41. A.S.Vic., PO, LAGA, 9 November 1431.

42. Brunello, *Arti*, pp. 123–27; Mainoni, "Attività," pp. 576–77; Mackenney, *Tradesmen*, pp. 82–83; Banchi, *Arte*, pp. v–xvi; Dini, "Industria," p. 339; Broglio d'Ajano, "Industria," p. 213; Comba, *Contadini*, ch. 10; Corti and da Silva, "Note," p. 310; Francheschi, "Tumulto," pp. 29–31.

43. Maschio, "Peronio," esp. pp. 120–21; A.S.Vic., PO, LAGA, 3 April 1443; *Ius municipale*, ff. 143v; and see the sixteenth-century map reproduced in *Vicenza Illustrata*.

44. A.S.Vic., PO, AP, 4 December 1431, 13 January 1436 *(versus portam sancti Laurentii)*; ivi, Not., Giorgio Serrature 6, 19 January 1432).

45. A.S.Vic., PO, LAGA, 14 February 1439; ivi, Not., Bortolo Bassan 4537, 10 February 1439. The Arnaldi also owned a shop in the lower part *(a capite inferiori)* of the Peronio, toward the *garzerias*, but apparently rented it out: ivi, PO, LAGA, 25 February 1443, 3 April 1443; ivi, PO, AP, 20 February 1449.

46. A.S.Vic., Arch., Piovene Orgian, Arnaldi parchments, 15 April 1452 (catastico 207); ivi, Liber Actoris Gasparis Arnaldi, 22 September 1453.

47. Varanini ("Campagne") thinks it refers to wholesale, Tagliaferri (*Economia*, pp. 139–45) to retail; the Arnaldi, at least, sold from very small to very large quantities.

48. A.S.Vic., PO, LAGA, 12 March 1435, 12 June 1436, 18–24 June 1437, 2 December 1437, 7 February 1443, 4 September 1445, 28 July 1450, 21 January 1452. For *planecia*, see Caro, "Corredi," p. 534.

49. A.S.Vic., PO, LAGA, 7 April 1438, 23 May 1438, 16 October 1452.

50. A.S.Vic., PO, LAGA, 18 January 1442, 22 May 1443, 9 November 1448, 3 December 1448, 14 March 1449.

51. Fustian and *pignolato* are sometimes interchangeable: Mazzaoui, *Cotton Industry*, pp. 69, 84, 90, 164; A.S.Vic., Not., Bortolo Bassan 4553, 1 March 1455; ivi, PO, LAGA, 15 November 1431, 2 July 1438, 6 May 1439, 28 May 1446; ivi, PO, AP, 25 June 1435. *Pignolati* was usually sold by the "piece," of undefined dimensions: ibid., 10 June 1444, 3 September 1444, 2 January 1445, 25 February 1446, 23 April 1446, 5 December 1448, 17 August 1453.

52. A.S.Vic., AP, PO, LAGA, 28 August 1434, 12 June 1436, 20 June 1438, June 1442, 20 November 1443, 11 May 1444, 5 December 1448, 24 May 1449, 11 December 1449.

53. A.S.Vic., Not., Giorgio Serrature 6, 19 January 1432; ivi, Not., Bortolo Bassan 4545, 8 October 1446; ibid. 4557, 22 March 1455; ibid. 4559, 26 January 1462; ibid. 4563, 8 February 1466. ivi, PO, AP, 31 January 1447, 22 April 1469; ivi, PO, LAGA, 9 November 1431, 3 December 1453.

54. A.S.Vic., PO, LAGA, 6 May 1439, 26 April 1446, 25 September 1447, 23 May 1449, 7 July 1449, 1 September 1450, 2 November 1451.

55. A.S.Vic., Not., Bortolo Bassan 4552, 22 March 1455.

56. A.S.Vic., PO, LAGA, 20 August 1436, 21 April 1446, 10 July 1452.

57. A.S.Vic., PO, LAGA, 1 March 1436, 11 May 1444, 26 April 1449, 10 July 1452, 17 February 1459.

58. A.S.Vic., PO, LAGA, 20 August 1436, 2 January 1439, 30 February 1439 (*sic*), 13 March 1439, 2 January 1441, 1 August 1446, 21 November 1448, 24 November 1450, 5 April 1454; ivi, Not., Bortolo Bassan 4551, 8 December 1453.

59. A.S.Vic., Not., Giorgio Serrature 6, 19 January 1432; ivi, PO, AP, 19 June 1437, 14 August 1445; ivi, Not., Bortolo Bassan 4548, 9 March 1450, 4 August 1450; ivi, PO, LAGA, 16 January 1439, 23 September 1441, 5 October 1442, 6 March 1456; ivi, Not., Cristoforo Bassan 34, 2 June 1456.

60. A.S.Vic., PO, LAGA, 1 December 1441, 2 January 1445; ivi, Not., Bortolo Bassan 4550, 14 March 1452.

61. A.S.Vic., PO, LAGA, 1 June 1452; ivi, Not., Bortolo Bassan 4549, 24 September 1451.

62. A.S.Vic., PO, LAGA, 17 March 1440, 9 June 1442, 27 February 1443, 3 October 1444, 16 October 1452, 19 December 1452, 12 April 1453.

63. A.S.Vic., PO, AP, 6 July 1454; ivi, PO, LAGA, 8 July 1452.

64. A.S.Vic., Not., Bortolo Bassan 4553, 1 March 1455; ivi, PO, LAGA, 8 March 1459; ivi, Not., Cristoforo Bassan 37/38, 1477–78.

65. A.S.Vic., Not., Bortolo Bassan 4554, 26 January 1455.

66. Silvestro's career can be reconstructed from a set of *minute* and an account book: A.S.Vic., Notarile, Cristoforo Bassan 38; ivi, PO, Vic. 152; see also ivi, PO, AP, 18 May 1484, 6 January 1502, 26 Feb. 1505; ivi, Not., Antonio Saraceni 4951, 6 June 1492; ibid. 4953, 14 January 1494; ibid. 4960, 6 January 1502.

67. Collodo, "Studio," pp. 178–79.

68. A summary of the literature in Balestracci, "Lavoro."

69. Varanini, *Comuni*, p. 137.

70. Herlihy ("Family and Property," p. 11) sees the lower classes lacking liquidity; Goldthwaite (*Building*, p. 302) disagrees.

71. Herlihy, "Distribution," pp. 138–39, 150–54; idem and Klapisch-Zuber, *Toscans*, ch. 9, esp. pp. 251, 256–59.

72. Soldi Rondinini, "Moneta milanese," pp. 493–94; idem, "Moneta viscontea," pp. 327–34; Mainoni, "Sviluppo," pp. 239–40; Allegra, *Città*, pp. 14–15; and in general Day, "Decline," p. 155; idem, *Market Economy*, pp. 11, 57, 72 (source of quote).

73. Repeta, f. 96v.

74. Mueller, "Imperialismo"; idem, "Considerazioni," pp. 181–82; idem, "Crisi," pp. 543–47; idem, "Guerra"; Soldi Rondinini, "Moneta milanese," pp. 501–2; idem, "Economia," pp. 796–98; and in general Day, *Market Economy*, chs. 1–3.

75. Herlihy and Klapisch-Zuber, *Toscans*, p. 299; Allegra, *Città*, pp. 14–15.

76. A.S.Vic., PO, AP, 5 November 1466, 21 June 1501, 19 February, 19 May, 5 December 1506; ivi, Not., Antonio Saraceni 4961, 12 February 1506, 10 May 1506; ibid. 4962, 5 December 1506; ibid. 4963, 27 May 1507.

77. Varanini, "Fisco," pp. 224–26, 237–45 (reprint in *Comuni*); *Statuti Veronae*, pp. 88–92; Bertoliana, Arch. Torre 787, ff. 3r–4r; *Ius municipale*, ff. 23r–32r, 35v–38r; fines in Bertoliana, Arch. Torre 1108–12.

78. A.S.Vic., Not., Bortolo Bassan 4549, 12 May 1451.

79. Bertoliana, Arch. Torre 61, f. 231r (= Zanazzo, *Arte*, doc. 28); Mackinney, *Tradesmen*, pp. 82–84; Lecce, *Vicende*, p. 44; Varanini, "Fisco," pp. 225–26. This was condemned by St. Antoninus, among others: Spicciani, *Capitale*, p. 147.

80. A.S.Vic., Not., Bortolo Bassan 4547, 1 December 1450; ibid. 4557, 21 March 1460; ibid. 4554, 26 January 1456; ivi, PO, AP, 18 May 1484.

81. A.S.Vic., PO, AP, 5 December 1448; ivi, Not., Bortolo Bassan 4549, 26 February 1451; ibid. 4550, 14 March 1452; ivi, Not., Cristoforo Bassan 34, 10 and 21 March 1453; Lecce, *Ricerche*, pp. 305–6.

82. Malanima, "Proprietà," p. 355; Goldthwaite, "Prezzi."

83. A.S.Vic., PO, AP, 21 August 1495 through 5 December 1506.

84. A.S.Vic., PO, AP, 3 July 1448; ivi, Not., Bortolo Bassan 4547, 21 June 1449.

85. A.S.Vic., PO, LAGA, 16 January 1439.

86. A.S.Vic., PO, AP, 4 May 1461, 1 and 21 May 1467. When the Arnaldi bought land in Villabalzana from a Veronese, they provided 89 percent of the price in credits they were owed in Verona (ibid., 20 February 1449); the figure rose to 99 percent in the purchase of Poiana land a decade later (ivi, Not., Bortolo Bassan 4555–56, 13 April 1459) and 100 percent in a 1484 Marola purchase (ivi, Not., Cristoforo Bassan 38, 4 May 1484).

87. So Jacopo Casone declared a debt of L. 38/5 to Andrea Arnaldi, who had paid L. 7/15 to Desseno Clivone for Jacopo's taxes, s. 23/2 for Jacopo's brother's rent, and L. 3/15 to Cristoforo Muzani for Jacopo's horse; Jacopo owed the rest for goods and services received from Andrea: A.S.Vic., PO, LAGA, 25 February 1443.

88. A.S.Vic., PO, AP, 5 January 1440.

89. A.S.Vic., Not., Bortolo Bassan 4538, 17 November 1440.

90. A.S.Vic., PO, AP, 30 July 1471; similarly, 20 February 1470, 13 January 1474; ivi, Not., Antonio Saraceni 4952, 3 August 1493; ibid. 4959, 15 November 1498.

91. A.S.Vic., Not., Bortolo Bassan 4550, 1 June 1452.

92. Tagliaferri, *Economia*, p. 158.

93. A.S.Vic., PO, LAGA, 12 May 1438; similarly, 30 September 1440, 8 May 1442, 1 September 1450; later examples in ivi, Not., Antonio Saraceni 4951, 21 March and 6 June 1492; ibid. 4955, 1 June 1495; ibid. 4958, 5 August 1497.

94. A.S.Vic., Not., Bortolo Bassan 4552, 21 May 1454; ibid. 4551, 1453; ivi, PO, LAGA, 8–10 July 1458.

95. Varanini, "Verona," pp. 210–11; Collodo, "Credito," pp. 14–15; Rossini, "Prestatori," pp. 201, 209.

96. A.S.Vic., PO, LAGA, 2 October 1443; ivi, PO, AP, 24 October 1453; ivi, Not., Bortolo Bassan 4551, 8 and 11 December 1453; Veronese examples cited in Varanini, "Campagne," pp. 196, 209, 213. For loans *ad terminum* elsewhere, see Mainoni, "Sviluppo," p. 241; Cammarosano, "Campagne senesi," pp. 165–69.

97. Dianin, *San Bernardino*, pp. 39–42, 48–51; Hofer, *Giovanni da Capestrano*, pp. 209–12; da Feltre, *Sermoni*, I, p. 277; see also II, p. 271; Meneghin, *Bernardino da Feltre*, pp. 385–86; Brogliato, *750 anni*, pp. 76–79. For condemnations of usury elsewhere, see the bibliography in Kirshner, "Franco Sacchetti"; Soldi Rondinini, "Economia," pp. 808–9; Spicciani, *Capitale*, pp. 147–50; da Certaldo, *Libro*, #173.

98. A.S.Ven., Senato Terra 4, f. 7v.

99. Bertoliana, Arch. Torre 59, f. 355v (but soon relaxed to permit *patroni* to accept equivalents in kind, despite time lag and price change, though monetary profit was illicit: ibid., ff. 188r–v; ivi, Arch. Torre 61, ff. 212r, 256r–v).

100. Bertoliana, Arch. Torre 59, ff. 86r–87v, 188v–89r, 338v. For similar legislation in Siena, see Pinto, "Note," p. 12.

101. Quoted in Luzzatto, "Attività," p. 176.

102. Collodo, "Credito," pp. 9–11; Fiumi, *Storia*, pp. 95–97.

103. A.S.Ver., Test., mazzo 89, #161 (Giorgio Bovi). Cohn thinks restitution gradually declined in Siena (*Death*, pp. 51–53, 100), but Fiumi thinks it was frequent (*Storia*, pp. 97–102).

104. A.S.Vic, Not., Bortolo Bassan 4553, 19 March 1455.

105. Quoted in Spicciani, *Capitale*, p. 27.

106. For Lombardy, see Violante, "Studio," pp. 643–47; Mainoni, "Sviluppo," p. 241; Greci, "Arcimboldi," p. 20; for Tuscany, see Pinto, "Note," pp. 4–5; Polica, "'Reconversion,'" p. 676; Wickham, "Vendite," pp. 372–73; for Padua, see Antoniazzi Villa, "Attività," pp. 209–10; Collodo, "Credito," pp. 4–5.

107. Corazzol, "Interessi," pp. 185–88; idem, *Fitti*, pp. 13–48; idem, "Diffusione," pp. 103–26; idem, "Prestatori," pp. 456–59.

108. A.S.Vic., PO, AP, 28 February 1438, 7 October 1452; ivi, Not., Bortolo Bassan 4543, 10 January 1444; ibid. 4544, 13 August 1445.

109. Corazzol, *Fitti*, ch. 3; idem, "Interessi," esp. p. 185.

110. Villa, "Attitività," pp. 209–10; Collodo, "Credito," pp. 6–7, 13–17; Caliaro, "Prestito," pp. 114–15; Rossini, "Prestatori," pp. 204, 210; Violante, "Prestiti," p. 648; Kotelnikova, "Operazioni," pp. 71–72.

111. Goldthwaite, "Medici Bank," p. 14; Edler de Roover, "Andrea Banchi," p. 228; Sapori, *Studi*, pp. 197, 236; Sillano, "Introduzione" to Chellini's *Ricordanze*, pp. 42, 93; Luzzatto, "Tasso," pp. 192–94; Ioly Zorattini, "Ebrei," p. 222; Fornasari, "Economia," pp. 487–88.

112. Corazzol, "Interessi," pp. 187–88; idem, "Diffusione," pp. 104, 124; idem, *Fitti*, ch. 4, esp. pp. 65–69.

113. Bertoliana, Gonz. 533, f. 132r; A.S.Vic., Collegio dei Notai 51, ff. 47r, 49r, 61r; matriculation from Bertoliana, Gonz. 535, ff. 62r, 76v; A.S.Vic., Collegio dei Notai 89, s.d. 1424.

114. A.S.Ver., Collegio dei Notai 6, ff. 1r, 6r, 8r, 9v–10r, 19r, 34r, 37v, 41v, 43v, 45r, 49r, 53v, 65r, 71r, 76r; Sancassani, *Documenti*, pp. 133, 145, 150–52; Bovi from ivi, Anag. Prov. 590 and Test., mazzo 62, #79. Dal Bovo's occupation may be inferred from his title *ser*, commonly applied to notaries (ivi, Anag. Com. 909).

115. Vicentine processional rankings in Bertoliana, Arch. Torre 777, ff. 108r–v; ivi, Arch. Torre 318, fasc. 2, f. 11r; *Ius municipale*, ff. 147v–48v. Earlier Veronese notaries formed an *ars* and marched with guilds, but in 1438 the corporation was retitled a college and grouped with physicians and judges: *Statuti Veronae*, p. 188; Sancassani, "Notai," p. 255.

116. *Statuti . . . MCCLXIV*, p. 72; Brunello, *Arti*, pp. 274–75; *Ius municipale*, f. 15v.

117. Sancassani, *Documenti*, pp. 35, 37, 42–43, 65–69, 71–74, 83, 85. For standards and status elsewhere, see "*Notai*," pp. 37–38 and ch. 2; Verde, "Nota," pp. 377–78; Costamagna, *Notaio*, chs. 1, 3; Sarti, *Notai*, rubric LXI; Martines, *Lawyers*, pp. 34–40; Petrucci, *Notarii*, pp. 29–35; Nicolai Petronio, "Notariato," pp. 645, 655; Liva, *Notariato*, p. 146.

118. A.S.Vic., Collegio dei Notai 89, s.d. 1 April 1421; Bertoliana, Gonz. 535, ff. 47r, 50v, 57r, 59r–60v, 96r, 99v, 102v; minimum age from ivi, Gonz. 533, f 78r; ivi, Gonz. 187, f. 8r. For enrollment of underage notaries elsewhere, see Valori, "Famiglia," p. 292; Liva, *Notariato*, p. 159.

119. Bertoliana, Gonz. 535, ff. 101r, 111v, 120r, 124r, 126r–v, 130r; A.S.Vic., Collegio dei Notai 91, s.d. 1444.

120. Bertoliana, Gonz. 535, ff. 129v ff. Reduced fees for sons of *module* notaries date at least to 1412: A.S.Vic., Collegio dei Notai 89, f. 266r. On privileged entry of notaries' sons elsewhere, see Kedar, "Genoese Notaries," p. 73; Calleri, *Arte*, p. 31; Puncuh, "Statuti," p. 271; Betto, *Collegi*, pp. 24–25, 29–30, 116.

121. A.S.Vic., Collegio dei Notai 91, 1444; Feramosca, s.d. 1466.

122. A.S.Vic., Collegio dei Notai 114. For the imperial notariate elsewhere, see *Notaio*, pp. 24–25; Calleri, *Arte*, p. 29; Betto, *Collegi*, p. 94; Tamassia, *Famiglia*, p. 101; Aubenas, *Notariat*, p. 73; Liva, *Notariato*, pp. 150–55.

123. Sancassani, *Documenti*, pp. 44, 91–92; Bertoliana, Gonz. 533, ff. 94r–v, 164v–66r; A.S.Vic., Collegio dei Notai 89, f. 343v.

124. A.S.Ver., Collegio dei notai, reg. 6; *Statuti Veronae*, pp. 29–30, 50, 56, 72, 85; Cristofoletti, "Cenni," pp. 326, 329; Sancassani, *Documenti*, p. 36; for Treviso, see Betto, *Collegi*, pp. 22, 27 and rubrics 23–24, 33.

125. Bertoliana, Gonz. 533, rubrics 28, 81–82, 107, 127 and ff. 106r–87, 115v–18r; *Ius municipale*, ff. 23r, 52v–56r, 58r–v, 118v–20v; A.S.Vic., Collegio dei Notai 91 (election to college office). For collegiate privileges elsewhere, see Kedar, "Genoese Notaries," pp. 75–76; Puncuh, "Statuti," p. 272; Calleri, *Arti*, chs. 8–9; Ferraro, *Family*, p. 65.

126. Sancassani, *Documenti*, pp. 15, 18, 37, 46, 65, 68–69, 87, 101–3; *Statuti Veronae*, pp. 35–36.

127. Arnaldi, ff. 19r–20r; Bertoliana, Gonz. 535, ff. 26v, 44r, 46v, 106r, 111v, 130r, 133v.

128. A.S.Vic., PO, LAGA, 15 April 1441, 20 June 1453; rules allowing substitution in Marciana, Latin V, 124 (2639), 1r–4r (notaries of Marostica); Bertoliana, Gonz. 187, ff. 1r–31r.

129. Bertoliana, Gonz. 533, rubrics 107, 188.

130. *Ius municipale*, ff. 47r–52r.

131. L. Cristofoletti, "Registro dei documenti del Collegio dei notai," in Bertoliana, Gonz. 1517, s.d. 1429, 1430, 1436, 1453, 1468, 1496; Bertoliana, Arch. Torre 61, ff. 183r–v; A.S.Ven., Senato Terra 3, f. 63v; Bertoliana, Arch. Torre 59, ff. 307v–8r; Betto, *Collegi*, pp. 95–96.

132. Knapton, "Condanna," pp. 322–23; Fasoli, "Notaio," pp. 128–29, 133–34; Liva, *Notariato*, p. 184; *Notaio*, p. 28; Martines, *Lawyers*, pp. 46–49.

133. A.S.Vic., Collegio dei Notai, regs. 38, 45; Bertoliana, Gonz. 533, ff. 76v–162v.

134. A.S.Vic., Not., Andrea Arnaldi 11.

135. A.S.Vic., Not., Bortolo Bassan 4524–63.

136. Sancassani, *Documenti*, p. 18; *Statuti Veronae*, pp. 67–71; Vicentine standards in *Ius municipale*, ff. 49r–52r, 53v. The three stages of redaction were standard, though local time limits for each stage varied: *Notaio*, pp. 19, 45–46; Calleri, *Arte*, ch. 10; Costamagna, *Notaio*, ch. 2; Petrucci, "Modello," pp. 130–31; Sarti, *Notai*, p. xxviii; Liva, *Notariato*, III, sec. 2.

137. *Statuti Veronae*, pp. 72–78; *Ius municipale*, ff. 52v–56r.

138. A.S.Ver., Collegio dei Notai, reg. 6, f. 4v; see also Calleri, *Arte*, plates 4, 8.

139. *in unione secum stantis et habitantis ac in notariato facientis*: A.S.Vic., Not., Bortolo Bassan 4541, 20 November 1442.

140. A.S.Vic., PO, LAGA, 6 May 1439; ivi, PO, AP, 26 September 1442 (redacted by

Tommaso Arnaldi, involving Andrea Arnaldi). Co-parent Gaspare Tomasini and cousin Cardino Feramosca drew up several Arnaldi documents in 1430–50, and son-in-law Simone Revese did so frequently after 1448.

141. A.S.Vic., PO, AP, 11 June 1448, 23 November 1465.

142. E.g., A.S.Vic., Not., Cristoforo Bassan 37/38, 27 January 1480.

143. In a typical instance, he did not fill in any details of a land sale but instead ended abruptly with the comment "in forma consueta prout ad carta 30 in prima facie usque ad verba 'promisitque dictus' exclusive mutatis tamen mutandis, deinde sic compleatur . . .": A.S.Vic., Not., Antonio Saraceni 4955, 1 June 1495.

144. A.S.Vic., PO, LAGA, 12 July 1440; see also ibid., 18 August 1442, 25 September 1447. For Florence, see *Notaio*, p. 52.

145. Tagliaferri, *Economia*, p. 132. Vicentine calculations are made from 142 cases of notaries whose registers survive (i.e., the practicing notariate) and whose *estimi* can be located.

146. "Studio," p. 173; in general, Petrucci, *Notarii*, p. 36.

147. Bertoliana, Arch. Torre 61, ff. 22v–24v; *Ius municipale*, ff. 86v–88r.

148. A.S.Vic., PO, AP, 13 May 1436; similarly, ibid., 11 January 1489, 9–11 September 1487, 16 May 1489; ivi, LAGA, 29 January 1440, 3 October 1443.

149. A.S.Vic., PO, AP, LAGA, 18 June 1437; similarly, 27 February 1443; ivi, PO, AP, 24 October 1457.

150. A.S.Vic. PO, LAGA, 31 March 1439, 12 July 1440, 17 September 1440, 30 September 1440, 7 August 1441, 16 June 1444, 2 July 1445, 26 October 1445, 6 September 1446; ivi, PO, AP, 14 May 1449, 21 October 1486; ivi, Not., Cristoforo Bassan 38, 10 September 1477.

151. A.S.Vic., PO, LAGA, 20 April 1435, 6 February 1441.

152. A.S.Vic., Not., Bortolo Bassan 4544, 13 November 1445; ivi, PO, LAGA, 17 September 1440, 27 February 1443; ivi, Not., Cristoforo Bassan 37/38, 27 January 1480, 10 February 1480; PO, AP, 10 December 1495; ivi, Not., Antonio Saraceni 4956, 1 and 5 January 1496.

153. A.S.Vic., PO, AP, 30–31 January 1438, 5 January 1440.

154. A.S.Vic., PO, LAGA, 29 January 1440, 31 January 1443, 25 February 1443, 27 January 1444, 23 September 1445 (all in the one to four ducat range), 21 November 1442, 9 June 1438, 18 October 1441, 3 September 1443.

155. A.S.Vic., PO, AP, 29 September 1359–14 December 1360, 10 August 1363, 2 July 1364.

156. A.S.Vic., PO, LAGA, 2 April 1442, 1 June 1452; ivi, PO, AP, 14 May 1449, 16 May 1454 (*colte* of 1445); ivi, Not., Bortolo Bassan 4548, 2 December 1450; ibid., 4549, 24 September 1451.

157. Bertoliana, Arch. Torre 59, ff. 349r–v.

158. Bertoliana, Arch. Torre 59, ff. 136r–v; ivi, Arch. Torre 61, ff. 196v–97r, ff. 220v–21.

159. A.S.Ven., Senato Terra 5, f. 183v; ibid. 7, ff. 113r, 130r.

160. A.S.Vic., Not., Bortolo Bassan 4547, 26 February 1449; ibid., 4549, January 1451 and 4 May 1451.

161. A.S.Pad., Archivi Famigli Diversi, Obizzi 223.

162. A.S.Vic., Not., Bortolo Aviano 4760, fasc. 1, f. 48r; ivi, PO, AP, 12 January and 7 August 1497.

Chapter 6. Land

1. Mazzi and Raveggi, *Uomini*, pp. 60–67; Pinto, "Rapporti," pp. 683–85; idem, "Ordinamento," pp. 223–27; idem, "Campagne," pp. 137–43; idem, "Indebitamento," pp. 3–5; idem, "Strutture," pp. 84–85; idem, "Impruneta," pp. 2–7; Ginatempo, *Crisi*, pp. 336, 340 and *passim;* Cherubini, "Considerazioni," pp. 73–74; idem, "Proprietà," pp. 22–28; idem, "Campagne," ch. 6; idem and Francovich, "Insediamenti," pp. 883–89; Kotelnikova, "Evoluzione," pp. 7–8. In a single (and partial) dissent, Luzzatti thinks that considerable common land and peasant ownership remained in Pisa: "Contratti," p. 572.

2. Chiappa Mauri, "Riflessioni," pp. 127–28; Grohmann, *Città*, I, pp. 161–62, 168 and II, pp. 613–14; Cherubini, *Signori*, ch. 2, sec. 3; Lorcin, *Campagnes*, pp. 383–410.

3. Varanini, "Campagne," pp. 199, 231–42; de Sandre Gasparini, *Contadini*, pp. 37ff.

4. A.S.Ven., Senato Terra 1, f. 189v; *Jus municipale Vicentinum* (Vicenza, 1706), pp. 330–31.

5. A.S.Vic., Not., Antonio Saraceni 4959, October 1498.

6. Collodo, "Credito," pp. 23, 38.

7. Polica, "'Reconversion,'" pp. 676–78.

8. In one complex but routine case, the Arnaldi divided the collateral into thirty shares that the borrower redeemed piecemeal over the course of a decade: A.S.Vic., PO, AP, 15–18 February 1471; ivi, Not., Cristoforo Bassan 35, 6 November 1475, 12 April 1477; ibid. 36, 1478, 2 January 1481.

9. A.S.Vic., Notarile, Bortolo Bassan 4544, 13 August 1445; ibid. 4545, 28 June 1446; ibid. 4553, 6 February 1455; ibid 4556, 7 June 1459; ibid. 4557, 1 May 1460; ibid. 4558, 31 March 1461; ibid. 4559, 14 January 1462; ibid. 4560, 19 February and 2 August 1463; ivi, Not., Cristoforo Bassan 36, 31 December 1478 (with ibid. 35, 22 March 1471); ibid. 35, 6 November 1475 (with ibid. 35, 12 April 1477; ibid. 36, 2 January 1481; ivi, PO, AP, 15–18 February 1471); ibid. 36, 27 May 1477, 31 December 1478 (with ibid. 35, 29 May 1472); ibid. 35, 6 April 1474 (with ibid. 37/38, 29 March 1479); ibid. 36, 3 April 1479; ibid. 38, 23 March 1481, 1 January 1482, 26 August 1483, 3 September 1484, 10 January 1486; francation from PO, AP, 14 November 1503, 28 March 1504.

10. Greci, "Proprietà," p. 13.

11. Grubb, "Mondo," p. 87 and tab. 1.

12. Sancassani, "Beni"; Lazzarini, "Beni"; A.S.Ver., Archivetti Privati, #6 (Auricalco), folder on Verità transactions.

13. A.S.Ven., Governatori delle pubbliche entrate 170, ff. 1r–62r; Grubb, "Patriciate," p. 164; A.S.Vic., Not., Bortolo Bassan 4542, 19 November 1443.

14. A.S.Vic., Not., Bortolo Bassan 4546, 16 June 1447; ibid. 4556, 13 April 1459; ivi, PO, AP, 20 February 1449.

15. A.S.Vic., PO, AP, 10 December 1495; ivi, Not., Antonio Saraceni 4956, 1 January 1496.

16. Grubb, "Patrimonio," pp. 265–67.

17. A.S.Vic., PO, AP, 7 May 1450, 15–18 February 1471; ivi, Not., Cristoforo Bassan 35, 5 May 1471.

18. A.S.Vic., PO, AP, 1 September 1453, 9 February 1454, 27 February 1454, 19 February 1459, 26 May 1470; ivi, Not. Bortolo Bassan 4555, 10 September 1457; Vicenza,

Arch. Cap., Libro Primo Magre, ff. 72r–v; see also Varanini, "Famiglia," pp. 46–47; Rossini, "Amministrazione," pp. 96–97; Chiappa Mauri, "Riflessioni," pp. 129–30; Greci, "Arcimboldi," pp. 15ff.; Cherubini, *Signori,* p. 79.

19. Grohmann, "Spazio," pp. 608–9; idem, *Città,* I, p. 161 and II, pp. 613–14; Puppi, "Funzioni," pp. 91–92; Hicks, "Sienese Society," p. 416; Polica, "'Reconversion,'" esp. p. 679; Puppi, "Funzione," pp. 91–92; Mometto, *Azienda,* ch. 1; Pinto, "Landed Property," pp. 81–83. For the background to this debate—intended to demonstrate Italy's failed transition from feudalism to capitalism, as the bourgeoisie betrayed its commercial vocation in a "return to the land" and sought integration into an older, ongoing feudal aristocracy—see Jones, "Leggenda"; Bordone, "Tema."

20. *Nobiltà,* p. 77; idem, "Considerazioni"; similarly, Greci, "Arcimboldi," pp. 12–15.

21. Collodo, "Credito," p. 6 (and case studies on pp. 6–53); Pinto, "Note," p. 3; idem, "Impruneta," pp. 4–7; Varanini, "Vicenza," pp. 227–30; Grubb, "Mondo," esp. pp. 106–12.

22. Wickham, "Vendite," pp. 356–57; contributions of Harvey, Razi, and Ruiz in *Quaderni Storici* 65 (1987); Harvey, *Peasant Land Market;* Smith, *Land.*

23. A.S.Vic., PO, AP, 21 August 1495–5 December 1506.

24. Herlihy and Klapisch-Zuber, *Toscans,* pp. 268–71; Pinto, "Mezzadria poderale," pp. 460–62; Luzzatti, "Toscana"; idem, "Contratti"; Malanima, "Proprietà," p. 348; Leverotti, "Linee," p. 199; Grohmann, *Città,* II, p. 878; Desplanques, *Campagnes,* pp. 482–83; Cherubini, *Signori,* pp. 92–96.

25. Mirri, "Contadini," pp. 32–39; Kotelnikova, "Evoluzione," esp. pp. 9–12; Herlihy and Klapisch-Zuber, *Toscans,* p. 274; Pinto, "Impruneta," p. 30.

26. Luzzatti, "Toscana," pp. 319–44; Montanari, "Livello," pp. 580–90; Piccinini, "Mezzadri," esp. pp. 7, 22; Anselmi, "Organizzazione," p. 809; idem, "Insediamenti," p. 68; idem, "Piovi," p. 208; Cherubini, "Campagne," ch. 7; Malanima, "Regione," p. 245; Pinto, "Rapporti," pp. 683–85; idem, "Campagne," p. 146; idem, "Impruneta," pp. 1, 10–11, 31; idem, "Strutture," pp. 84–85; Cherubini, "Proprietà," pp. 28–32; Desplanques, "Case," p. 189; Comba, "Origini," pp. 382–89; Polica, "'Reconversion,'" pp. 669, 671, 682. Chiappa Mauri lightly critiqued the tendency to identify all Tuscany with *mezzadria* (and to lack sharecropping is "not backwards, just different"): "Proposito," pp. 122–23.

27. Angiolini, "Ceti"; Kotelnikova, "Evoluzione," pp. 2–3; idem, *Mondo,* esp. pp. 5–18, 276–317; idem, "Condizione," esp. p. 99; idem, "Ruolo," esp. pp. 420–26; Bordone, "Tema"; Mirri, "Contadini," pp. 42–49 and *passim.* A key subtheme is the *mezzadria's* only occasional use of salaried labor, which blocked the rise of a rural proletariat: Kotelnikova, *Mondo,* pp. 317–27; Piccinini, "Mezzadri," esp. ch. 4; Pinto, "Rapporti," pp. 686–93; idem, "Ordinamento," pp. 230–32; Varanini, "Organizzazione," pp. 117–26; idem, "Note sul lavoro"; Modzelewski, "Vicende," pp. 41–62.

28. Varanini, "Organizzazione," esp. pp. 105–11; idem, "Note sul lavoro," pp. 232–37; idem, "Campagne," esp. pp. 190–242; idem, "Esempio," pp. 25–26, 32–34, 47–69.

29. Varanini, "Esempio," pp. 16, 20–22; Lecce, "Beni," pp. 63, 85–86; Rossini, "Amministrazione," pp. 92, 104–5.

30. The Arnaldi archive and notarial documents in the 1400–1499 period give information on 4,853 pieces of cultivated property; the average piece totaled 4.24 *campi.* The Lisiera average is about 4 *campi,* and that of Dueville (excluding a few large waste

plots) about 3 *campi*: Grubb, "Mondo," p. 82; idem, "Patrimonio," tab. 1–2. Varanini ("Organizzazione," p. 105) thinks the Vicentine *campo* corresponded to the Veronese measure of 0.3003 hectares.

31. A.S.Ver., AAC, reg. 63, f. 166r; Varanini, "Esempio," pp. 29–30; idem, "Campagne," pp. 199–214; idem, "Note sul lavoro," p. 238; Lecce, "Beni," p. 59; Rossini, "Amministrazione," p. 81. Padua, where shorter–term *fitti* predominated, may represent an exception; in Friuli, long-term tenures were the norm: Collodo, "Credito," pp. 14–16; De Sandre Gasparini, *Contadini*, pp. 51–58; Cammarosano, *Campagne friulane*, p. 53.

32. A.S.Vic., PO, AP, 1 December 1450, 19 November 1451, 9 February 1454; ivi, LAGA, 23 March 1454. Partiary tenures were also rare in Padua and Friuli: de Sandre Gasparini, *Contadini*, p. 58; Cammarosano, *Campagne friulane*, chs. 2–4.

33. "Emphiteosis dicitur etiam locatio in perpetuam pro uno nummo annuatim solvendo": Baldus, quoted in Bertrachini, *Repertorium*, s.v. emphiteosis.

34. Cariota-Ferrara, *Enfiteusi*, chs. 1–2; discussion of the two *dominia* in Kuehn, *Law*, pp. 108–9.

35. *Ius municipale*, f. 150r; *Statuti Veronae*, pp. 16–17; Ferrari, "Campagna," p. 14; Cariota-Ferrara, *Enfiteusi*, pp. 67–68, 90–92.

36. A.S.Ver., Pergamene, Malaspina-Verità, busta 18, ##47–48; A.S.Vic., PO, AP, 4 December 1431, 2 January 1441, 24 January 1453, 1 September 1453, 9–27 February 1454, 26 May 1470, 19 February 1459; ivi, Not. Bortolo Bassan 4555, 10 September 1457; Vicenza, Arch. Cap., Libro Primo Magre, ff. 72r–v.

37. Cariota-Ferrara, *Enfiteusi*, p. 43.

38. A.S.Vic., Not., Antonio Saraceni 4956, 1–5 January 1496; ibid. 4964, 7 June 1507; ivi, PO, AP, 14 May 1468, 21 February 1471, 10 January 1489, 10 May 1491, 10 December 1495, 9 July 1500.

39. Cariota-Ferrara, *Entifeusi*, pp. 74–78; *Ius municipale*, ff. 150r–51r.

40. Bertoliana, Arch. Torre 59, ff. 110r–11r, 244v–45r, 262v–63v; Rossini, "Amministrazione," p. 116; in general, Grossi, *Locatio*, pp. 101–36.

41. A.S.Vic. PO, AP, 1 March 1498; similarly, 27 May 1505; ivi, Not., Antonio Saraceni 4966, 21 August 1508.

42. Bertoliana, Arch. Torre 777, f. 62r; ivi, 776, f. 27v; Mantese, *Memorie*, 3, 1, pp. 475–76, 503, 511–12.

43. Varanini, "Campagne," p. 207; Grubb, "Patrimonio," pp. 261–62; idem, "Mondo," tab. 2–3; Mometto, *Azienda*, pp. 63–65; de Sandre Gasparini, *Contadini*, pp. 21–38; Cammarosano, *Campagne friulane*, p. 49.

44. Pinto, "Strutture," pp. 79–80; idem, "Forme," pp. 262–71.

45. *Vocabularius*, s.v. emphiteosis; in general, see Cariota-Ferrara, *Enfiteusi*, pp. 30–31, 79; Rossini, "Amministrazione," p. 98; Lecce, "Beni," p. 77; Grossi, *Locatio*, pp. 247–58; Cherubini, *Signori*, pp. 345–48. On the Tuscan trend to rents in kind see Pinto, "Forme," p. 273.

46. *Statuti Veronae, Partes et decreta*, pp. 21–22.

47. Reduced rents in A.S.Vic., Not., Bortolo Bassan 4546, 21 March 1449; ibid. 4547, 2 September 1449; ivi, Not., Cristoforo Bassan 38, 15 May 1483; ivi, Not., Antonio Saraceni 4956, 24 January 1508; increase in ivi, PO, AP, 3 April 1481.

48. A.S.Ver., Perg., Guastaverza, busta 35, #30; A.S.Vic., PO, AP, 6 June 1447, 24 Jan-

uary 1453, 1 September 1453, 4 February 1454, 27 February 1454, 19 February 1459, 9 January 1465, 26 January 1470, 3 April 1481; ivi, Notarile, Bortolo Bassan 4531, 22 January 1433; ibid., 4546, 21 March 1449; Vicenza, Arch. Cap., Libro Primo Magre, ff. 72r–v; for Padua, see Rigon, *Clero*, p. 205.

49. In addition to works on Tuscany cited throughout this chapter, for Lombardy, see Miani, "Economie," pp. 577–78; Chiappa Mauri, "Riflessioni," pp. 123–30; idem, "Linee," pp. 527–36; idem, "Trasformazioni," pp. 409–22; Chittolini, "Origini," pp. 828–36; Lanconelli, "Contratti agrari," p. 641; Comba, "Origini medievali," pp. 382–89; Giorgetti, "Contratti agrari," pp. 724–27; Chittolini, "Avvicendamenti"; Greci, "Proprietà," pp. 15–17; see also Cazzola, "Produzione"; Grohmann, *Città*, II, pp. 613–29.

50. Varanini, "Campagne," pp. 194–95, 232; idem, "Esempio," pp. 68–69; Grubb, "Patrimonio," pp. 272–73.

51. A.S.Vic., PO, AP, 11 September 1451; ivi, PO, LAGA, 30 January, 16 February, and 27 June 1458, 1 March 1459; ivi, Not., Bortolo Bassan 4559, 14 January 1462; Trecento *gastaldi* from Grubb, "Mondo," pp. 90–91; Varanini, "Organizzazione," p. 104.

52. A.S.Vic., PO, AP, 29 December 1484; similarly, ibid., 21 August 1495, 9 July 1500; ivi, Not., Antonio Saraceni 4955, 4 November 1495. Verona's Trivelli, whose lands were dispersed in the Trecento, later concentrated on a few sites in the Valpolicella: de Martini, "Borghesi," pp. 96–97.

53. Grubb, "Mondo," tabs. 2–4; idem, "Feudo," tabs. 1–2; Mometto, *Azienda*, pp. 91–99. The Veneto's move to diversified production came a half century or more later than in other regions: Pini, "Viticoltùra," pp. 867, 881–82; idem, *Vite*, pp. 142, 168; Chiappa Mauri, "Trasformazione," pp. 422–24; de la Roncière, "Vignoble," pp. 142–47.

54. Leicht, "Contratto," esp. pp. 18–19; Caciorgna, "Vite," pp. 163–64; Montanari, "Livello," pp. 588–90.

55. References to improved cultivation in A.S.Vic., PO, AP, 12 May 1412, 17 November 1414, 25 September 1428, 30 August 1434, 13 January 1436, 4 March 1441, 15 May 1441, 28 December 1448, 13 November 1449, 30 December 1455, 24 October 1457, 23 July 1471, 3 April 1481, 3 January 1491; ivi, PO, LAGA, 21 February 1452; ivi, Not., Bortolo Bassan 4546, 21 March 1449; ibid. 4547, 21 July 1449; ibid. 4549, 25 May 1451; ibid. 4553, 14 January 1455; ibid. 4554, 19 June 1456; ibid. 4556, 15 February 1459; see also Varanini, "Organizzazione," pp. 114–15; idem, "Campagne," pp. 222–30.

56. Bertoliana, Arch. Torre 313, f. 10r; *Ius municipale*, ff. 210v–11r; Bertoliana, Arch Torre 59, ff. 77r–78v; Grubb, *Firstborn*, pp. 114–15; Lecce, *Vicende*, pp. 63–64; Mometto, *Azienda*, chs. 2, 4.

57. A.S.Vic., PO, AP, 5 November 1427, 20 January 1440, 22 May 1448; ivi, PO, LAGA, 16 October 1452; ivi, Not., Cristoforo Bassan 37/38, 23 March 1479.

58. A.S.Vic., Not., Bortolo Bassan 4550, 26 January 1452; ibid. 4551, 8 December 1453; Grubb, "Patrimonio," pp. 273–76. On improvement leases (most short-term and/or partiary), see Cammarosano, *Campagne friulane*, pp. 88–90; Cazzola, "Produzione," pp. 267–68; Roveda, "Istituzioni," p. 57; Caciorgna, "Vite," pp. 163–64; Chiappa Mauri, "Trasformazioni," p. 412; Mometto, *Azienda*, pp. 87–90.

59. Varanini, "Esempio," pp. 47–76; Cammarosano, "Campagne senesi," pp. 167–68; de Sandre Gasparini, *Contadini*, ch. 2; Modzelewski, "Vicende," pp. 41–62; but see examples of a lack of innovation in Lecce, "Beni," pp. 66, 72–76, 85–86; Rossini, "Amministrazione," pp. 98, 107–12, 118.

60. Mantese, *Memorie*, 3, 2, pp. 260–66, 443, 611–12.

61. A.S.Vic., PO, AP, 12 December 1447; see Mometto, *Azienda*, p. 52.

62. Pinto, "Rapporti," pp. 684–93; idem, "Note"; idem, "Campagne," pp. 137–43, 148ff; idem, "Ordinamento," pp. 223–27, 243–44; idem, "Forme," pp. 284–96; Kotelnikova, "Rendita," pp. 105–12; idem, *Mondo;* idem, "Evoluzione," pp. 1–2, 9–34; Cherubini, "Mezzadria," pp. 139–41; idem, "Considerazioni," pp. 73–74 and *passim;* idem, "Proprietà," pp. 22–32; idem, "Campagne," chs. 5–6, 10; idem and Francovich, "Insediamenti," pp. 883–901; Cammarosano, "Campagne senesi," pp. 181, 200; Herlihy, "Impruneta," pp. 259–60, 267–70; idem, "Tuscan Town," p. 86; idem and Klapisch-Zuber, *Toscans*, pp. 261–63, 273–74, 277–79; Piccinni, "Mezzadri," pp. 666–72; idem, *Seminare*, chs. 2, 5; Isaacs, "Campagne," pp. 389–93; Ginatempo, *Crisi*, pt. III, chs. 1–2; Polica, "'Reconversion,'" p. 691.

63. Varanini, "Organizzazione," pp. 111–12; idem, "Campagne," pp. 193, 219, 231–42; idem, "Esempio," pp. 73–76, 93–98; Grubb, "Mondo," pp. 108–12; Cammarosano, *Campagne friulane*, p. 104; Law, "Venezia," pp. 10–15; idem, "Differentiis."

64. Grubb, "Patrimonio," p. 272; A.S.Vic., Not., Bortolo Bassan 4530, 11 December 1432; A.S.Vic., PO, AP, 5 February and 10 April 1483, 8 February 1483; common lands from Bertoliana, Arch. Torre 373, fasc. 11, 22 January 1457, 14–15 March 1458, 9 October 1459, 26 April 1475, 20 December 1500.

65. A.S.Vic., PO, AP, 24 July 1449, 13 January 1450, 9 May 1450, 7–12 October 1450, 1 December 1450, 1 March 1451, 28 March 1452; ivi, Not., Cristoforo Bassan 38, 10 September 1477.

66. A.S.Ver., Perg., Verità, ser. III. busta 7, #389.

67. Osheim, "Countrymen," pp. 322, 330–33.

68. *Ius municipale*, ff. 35v–38r, 90v–91r, 112v–13v, 149v–51r; *Statuti Veronae*, pp. 112–16.

69. A.S.Vic., PO, AP, 31 January 1447; similarly, 12 November 1360.

70. A.S.Vic., Not., Bortolo Bassan 4539, 26 October 1441; Osheim, "Countrymen," pp. 328, 335.

71. A.S.Vic., PO, AP, 2 May and 22 August 1489; ivi, Pogg. No. 1.

72. Varanini, *Comuni*, pp. 156–59.

73. Bertoliana, Arch. Torre 1108–12; Grubb, "Mondo," p. 109.

74. *Ius Municipale*, f. 104r; Monaco, *Aspetti*, p. 122. Women also appeared as *nuntia* of male debtors in civil suits: A.S.Vic., PO, LAGA, 10 October 1431, 13–22 March 1432.

75. *Ius municipale*, f. 59v; *Statuti Veronae*, p. 118.

76. *Jus municipale vicentinum* (Vicenza, 1707), pp. 330–31; A.S.Vic., Senato Terra 1, f. 189v.

77. Hilaire, *Regime*, pp. 137–46, 167–81; Kirshner, "Wives' Claims," pp. 276–78; Ercole, "Istituto," II, p. 252.

78. *Jus municipale vicentinum* (Vicenza, 1706), pp. 330–31.

79. Bertoliana, Arch. Torre 59, f. 181r; A.S.Ven., Senato Terra 2, f. 72v. This principle overturned a Vicentine statute of 1311 that all *rustici* of a village were liable for individual debts: Bertoliana, Gonzati 566, bk. IV, rubric 100.

80. A.S.Ven., Senato Terra 4, ff. 94v, 183v; *Statuti Veronae*, p. 117 and *Partes et de-*

creta, pp. 19, 21; Varanini, *Comuni*, pp. 159–60. These laws and that of 1448 were repeated in 1476: Bertoliana, Arch. Torre 59, ff. 181r–v, 302v–3r.

81. A.S.Ven., Avogadori di Comun 3583, fasc. 2, ff. 302r, 316r; *Statuti Veronae, Partes et decreta*, p. 25.

82. Bertoliana, Arch. Torre 59, ff. 116r–17v; Leicht, "Condizione," p. 187; *Statuti Veronae, Partes et decreta*, pp. 29, 32–33; in general, Varanini, "Campagne," p. 249.

83. Osheim, "Countrymen," pp. 317–18, 334; Luzzatti, "Toscana," pp. 290–95.

84. Klapisch-Zuber, *Women*, p. 14.

85. Law, "'Super differentiis,'" pp. 8–15; Varanini, "Campagne," p. 195; Puppi, "Funzioni," p. 92; Marchi, "Letterati," pp. 232–34; Viggiano, *Governanti*, p. 272, n. 190. For Tuscan violence, see Cherubini, "Campagne," pp. 118–20; Piccinni, "Mezzadri," pp. 665–66; idem, *Seminare*, ch. 6; Kotelnikova, *Mondo*, pp. 330–35; in general, Leicht, "Condizione," pp. 182–83, 189–91.

86. Marciana, Latin V, 62 (2356), f. 1r; A.S.Ven., Senato Terra 5, f. 192v; ivi, Senato Terra 8, f. 120v; Grubb, *Firstborn*, ch. 6 and p. 103; Viggiano, *Governanti*, p. 272.

87. A.S.Ven., Senato Terra 1, f. 38v; ivi, Capi dei Dieci, Lettere Ricevute 2, #3.

88. Bertoliana, Arch. Torre 61, ff. 40r–43r (Cogollo); ivi, Gonz. 572, ff. 200v–201r (Mason); ivi, Arch. Torre 59, ff. 213v–15r; A.S.Ven., Capi dei Dieci, Lettere, 1500 #417, 1501 ##108, 132, 1502 ##44, 223, 232; ibid., Lettere di Rettori 223, #24; ivi, Dieci Misti 29, ff. 58v, 77r, 161r–v; ivi, Senato Terra 14, ff. 198r, 199v; ivi, Capi dei Dieci, Lettere, 1502 #176 and ibid. 223, ##15, 17; ivi, Dieci Misti 29, f. 19r (Marostica); on exiles, see Grubb, *Firstborn*, pp. 106–7.

89. Bertoliana, Arch. Torre 777, ff. 95v–96v; ivi, Arch. Torre 61, ff. 118v–21r; ivi, Arch. Torre 59, f. 66r; A.S.Ver., Atti del Consiglio 56, f. 62v.

90. Merlini, *Saggio*, p. 187; Alberti, *Libri*, p. 238.

91. Marchi, "Letterati," pp. 232–34; Mistruzzi, "Giorgio Sommariva," pp. 130–31; Merlini, *Saggi*, pp. 47–49. For antirustic comments by Tuscans, see da Certaldo, *Libro*, pp. 91–93; Cherubini, "Campagne," ch. 10; idem, *Italia rurale*, pp. 123–24; idem, *Signori*, pp. 121–23; idem, "Mondo," pp. 422, 425; Tamassia, *Famiglia*, pp. 11–13; Herlihy and Klapisch-Zuber, *Toscans*, p. 598; Pinto, "Campagne," pp. 149, 152–53; idem, "Forme," p. 326; Mazzi and Raveggi, *Uomini*, pp. 20–34; and, in general, Leicht, "Condizione," pp. 183–85.

92. Grubb, "Patrimonio," p. 276.

93. Bertoliana, Arch. Torre 373, fasc. 11, ff. 17r–18r (Scroffa tried to put his workers in the urban *estimo*, and so reduce the village tax base); Varanini, "Regole," pp. 199–200.

94. A.S.Vic., PO, AP, 13 May 1436 (La Longa), 9 September 1487 (Setteca); ivi, LAGA, 1 November 1445 (La Longa).

95. A.S.Vic., PO, LAGA, 20 April 1435, 4 June 1438, 31 March 1439, 29 January and 12 July 1440, 30 September 1440, 18 October 1441, 31 January and 25 February 1443, 3 October 1444, 23 September 1445, 18 January 1446.

96. Muir, *Mad Blood*, ch. 4; Weissman, "Patronage," p. 43; idem, *Ritual Brotherhood*, pp. 35–40; idem, "Importance," pp. 276–78.

97. de Sandre Gasparini, *Contadini*, pp. 79–82; Varanini, "Organizzazione," pp. 111–112; idem, "Esempio," p. 87; Arnaldi extensions in A.S.Vic., PO, AP, 21 October 1480; ivi, Not., Antonio Saraceni 4953, 26 July 1494; ibid. 4959, 15 November 1498.

98. A.S.Vic., PO, AP, 12 December 1447, 4 May 1452, 7 October 1452, 1 September 1453, 9 February 1454, 27 February 1454, 19 February 1459, 8 November 1491; Arch. Cap., Libro Primo Magre, ff. 72r–v.

99. Herlihy, "Family and Property," pp. 13–14; Osheim, "Countrymen," esp. p. 336; Greci, "Proprietà," pp. 26–27.

100. Bordone, "Tema"; Polica, "Basso Medioevo"; and esp. Jones, "Leggenda."

101. Polica, "'Reconversion,'" pp. 655–56.

102. Varanini, "Campagne," pp. 236–42; see also Zalin, "Economia," p. 64; Puppi, "Funzione," pp. 93–94.

103. Alberti, Libri, pp. 234–38; Cherubini, "Campagne," p. 25.

104. Ambrosoli, "'Opus'"; Pini, "Viticoltora," pp. 852–60; Tanaglia, De agricoltura, p. 3; Tateo, "Disputa," p. 386.

105. Varanini, "Organizzazione," pp. 103–4; Grubb, "Patrimonio," p. 260.

106. Kubelik, Villa, pp. 213–14, 793, 814–15; see also Zalin, "Economia," p. 65. Rosci confirms Vicentine primacy in creating and diffusing villa types: "Ville," p. 81.

107. Rosci, "Ville," pp. 78–79.

108. A.S.Vic., PO, LAGA, 28 February 1452, 9 December 1452, 24 March 1453, 14 December 1454, 4 January 1456.

109. Arnaldi, f. 15v; A.S.Vic., PO, AP, 12 August 1471.

110. A.S.Vic., Not., Cristoforo Bassan 34, 20 January 1453; ivi, PO, AP, 14–15 November 1467, 9 January 1471, 12 August 1471; ivi, PO, LAGA, 28 February 1452, 9 December 1452, 24 March 1453, 13 April 1454, 14 December 1454, 4 January 1456; A.S.Ver., Perg., Malaspina-Verità, busta 17, #27; ivi, Perg., Verità, ser. III, busta 7, #387.

111. A.S.Vic., Not., Antonio Saraceni 4966, 7 November 1508; ivi, PO, AP, 6 March 1518; Sanuto, Itinerario, p. 107.

112. Burns, "Opere," pp. 15–16.

Chapter 7. Patriciate and Nobility

1. Lanaro Sartori, "Patriziato," p. 36.

2. Sapori, "Classi," pp. 308–9.

3. Besozzi, "'Matricula,'" pp. 274–84 and tab. I; Mainoni, "Attività," pp. 582–83.

4. Ascheri, "Arti," pp. 16–19, 46–49 (but an opposite judgment in Hicks, "Sienese Society," pp. 415–16).

5. Battistella, "Comune," I, pp. 277–84; II, pp. 95, 102; Ventura, Nobiltà, pp. 126–38; Betto, Collegi, pp. 106–29.

6. Pagliarini, Cronicae, pp. 35, 41, 47–48; Descriptio nobilium familiarum in Mantese, Memorie, 2, pp. 538–39.

7. Ventura, Nobiltà, pp. 119–20; Varanini, "Vicenza," pp. 184–85.

8. Rubinstein, "Oligarchy," pp. 99–108; quotes from Brucker, Civic World, pp. 31–32, 283, 458; Najemy, Corporation, pp. 51, 115, 307.

9. Ventura, Nobiltà, pp. 65–66; Berengo, Nobili, pp. 31, 236.

10. Ius municipale, ff. 16r, 33r–v, 34v, 38r, 44r, 52v, 56r.

11. Ius municipale, ff. 96v–97r, 129v–31v; Bertoliana, Arch. Torre 60, ff. 128r–v; ivi, Gonz. 571, ff. 147v–48r; ivi, Arch. Torre 61, ff. 373r–75v.

12. da Nono, De generatione, esp. ff. 30r, 31v, 57r, 59v, 60v–61r; in general, Grubb, "Introduzione" to Memorie.

13. Appended to Godi's *Cronaca*, pp. 21–26.

14. Pagliarini, *Cronicae*, bk. VI.

15. Jones, "Leggenda"; critiques by Polica, "Basso Medioevo"; Angiolini, "Ceti"; Bordone, "Tema."

16. Berengo, "Patriziato," esp. pp. 493–98.

17. Quoted in Bennett, *Women*, p. 59.

18. Herlihy, "Tuscan Town," pp. 97–103; idem, "Vieillir," p. 1352.

19. Lorcin, *Campagnes*, pp. 225–27.

20. Lorcin, *Vivre*, pp. 75–77.

21. Brucker, "Monasteries," pp. 45–50.

22. Pagliarini, *Cronicae*, bk. I; Collodo, "Credito," pp. 6–71; Kohl, "Government," pp. 214, 219.

23. Bertoliana, Gonzati 570, f. 1r; Godi, *Cronaca*, p. 20; Pagliarini, *Cronicae*, bks. V–VI.

24. Dean, *Land*, pp. 90–91.

25. Pagliarini, *Cronicae*, bk. VI; see also the list of "Familiae quae aliunde Vicentiam habitatum venerunt," appended to Godi, *Cronaca*, pp. 25–26; Varanini, "Vicenza," pp. 187–203; influx of newcomers into Scaligeri courts in idem, *Scaligeri*, pp. 16–25, 50–51.

26. Bertoliana, Gonz. 566, ff. 116r–17v (1321: Albertus de Arnaldo and Jacobinus q. Petri Solerii); Arch. Torre 35, #45 (1337: Petrus Arnaldi Solerii); A.S.Vic., Corp. Sopp., S. Bartolomeo, reg. 12, #1689 (1346; Litaldus and Zenus Johannis Litaldini were probably members of the family: see A.S.Vic., PO, AP, 14 January 1300; Bertoliana, Gonz. 187, f. 38v; ivi, Gonz. 188, ff. 9v, 27v, 37v, 47v, 71r–v, 99v, 113v, 124r–v, 134r–v, 140v; A.S.Vic., Collegio dei Notai 50).

27. Arnaldi, f. 18r; Bertoliana, Gonz. 535, f. 52v; A.S.Vic., PO, AP, 23 February 1439, 26 September 1442, 12 February 1449; College offices in A.S.Vic., Collegio dei Notai, 91; communal offices in ivi, reg. 9; Bertoliana, Arch. Torre 62, ff. 772v–74r.

28. Gaspare II from Feramosca, s.d. 1482; 1510 council list in Rumor, *Blasone*, pp. 286–94; vicariates in Bertoliana, Arch. Torre 309, fasc. 7. s.d. 1518; *Ius municipale*, f. 187r.

29. Ventura, *Nobiltà*, chs. 1–2 (quotes from pp. 1, 51–52).

30. Law, "Venice," esp. pp. 71–77, 81–86, 89, 93–101; idem, "Verona," pp. 27–28; Varanini, *Comuni*, pp. 187–96; Lanaro Sartori, "Patriziato," pp. 36–38; Viggiano, *Governanti*, pp. 189–90; Giuliani Bossetti, "Transformazione," pp. 45–47; Bertoliana, Arch. Torre 217, fasc. 3, ff. 6r–9v; Ventura, *Nobiltà*, pp. 80–84; copies of the Veronese acts in A.S.Ver., Archivi Privati, Lando, busta 3.

31. Law, "Venice," pp. 75, 89–91; Varanini, "Note," pp. 5–15, quote on p. 24; idem, *Comuni*, pp. 188–96; Lanaro Sartori, "Patriziato," pp. 38–44; Giuliani Bossetti, "Trasformazione," pp. 44–51; Ventura, *Nobiltà*, pp. 26–33, 93–96.

32. *Statuti . . . MCCLXIV*, p. 71; Bertoliana, Gonz. 566, bk. I, rubric 26 (1311 statutes); ivi, Gonz. 568, bk. I, rubric 44 (1339 statutes); *Ius municipale*, f. 11r.

33. Ventura, *Nobiltà*, pp. 14–19, 60–61, 112–13.

34. Arnaldi, f. 18; A.S.Vic., PO, LASA, 25 May 1495.

35. *Ius municipale*, ff. 12r, 15v, 22v–23r; 1520 complaint from Bertoliana, Arch. Torre 62, ff. 496r–98r, rubrics 2–3.

36. Ventura, *Nobiltà*, pp. 80–84, 133; Kohl, "Government," pp. 215–17.

37. *Ius municipale*, ff. 8r–12v.

38. Grubb, *Firstborn*, pp. 77–79; Law, "Venezia," pp. 17–31.

39. Bertoliana, Arch. Torre 60, ff. 84r, 96r–v; Ventura, *Nobiltà*, pp. 112–13.

40. "Patriziato," p. 44.

41. Varanini, "Note," pp. 25–26; Ventura, *Nobiltà*, pp. 100–104.

42. The single attendible population figure is 19,000 urban residents in 1483 (Sanuto, *Itinerario*, p. 108), which translates into about 4,750 households; each *estimo* listed about 2,400 households.

43. Rumor, *Blasone*, pp. 287, 290.

44. Ventura, *Nobiltà*, pp. 61–66, 80–84.

45. Varanini, "Note," p. 5; idem, "Famiglia," pp. 32–35, 43; de Martin, "Borghesi." For an influx of new blood in Rovereto, see Knapton, "Condanna," p. 319. Of Pisan officeholding families in 1542–46, only 4.8 percent came from the old nobility and a total of 11.4 percent from families politically active during the Trecento; only 12.1 percent of the elite *riformatori* were traditional nobles, and only 21.2 percent came from families active during the Trecento: Luzzatti, "Famiglie," pp. 447–48.

46. Lanaro Sartori, "Patriziato," pp. 38–43; *Statuti Veronae*, pp. 22–23.

47. A.S.Ver., Estimo, reg. 256, f. 44v; reg. 257, f. 39v, reg. 258, f. 43r.

48. Ventura, *Nobiltà*, p. 122.

49. Franzina, *Vicenza*, p. 321; Berengo, "Patriziato."

50. Bartolus, *De dignitatibus*, ##61–62; repeated in Bartolus, *Repertorium*, s.v. nobilitas; Alvarotti, *Super feudis*, ff. 57v–58r; *Vocabularius*, s.v. nobilitas; dall'Aqua, *Vocabularius*, s.v. nobilitas; Cipolla, *De imperatore*, unfoliated, #10 in list of qualifications of nobility.

51. Bartolus, *De dignitatibus*, #93.

52. Bertoliana, Gonz. 166, ff. 51r–55r; Arnaldi, f. 26r; Alvarotti, *Super feudis*, f. 88r; imperial passages and ennoblements in Grubb, *Firstborn*, pp. 36–39; Bartolomeo Cipolla's *lux unica mundi* in Varanini, *Comuni*, p. 413 (but noting Gian Maria Filelfo's and Cristoforo Schioppa's disparagement of imperial nobilization).

53. Grubb, *Firstborn*, p. 38; Marciana, Latin X, 148 (3332), ff. 57r, 63v, 70v; Verona, Bib. Civ., ms. 896, f. 30r; ivi, ms. 1017, f. 80v; ivi, ms. 2092, ff. 213r, 217r, 220v–21r.

54. Grubb, *Firstborn*, p. 38; Mantese, *Memorie*, 3, 2, pp. 775, 779–80, 804–5; Bertoliana, Gonz. 460, ff. 22v–25r; ivi, Gonz. 2819, fasc. II, p. 24; Repeta, f. 97r; Rumor, *Blasone*, pp. 295–96; Marciana, Ital. VI, 30 (5891); *Cronica ad memoriam*, s.d. 1452, 1489.

55. Cristiani, *Nobiltà*, pp. 31–32, 36–37, 72–78, 89–90; idem, "Valore," pp. 366–69 (quote on p. 369); Tagliaferri, *Economia*, p. 126.

56. Salvemini, "Dignità," esp. pp. 110–34; Cristiani, "Valore," p. 369; Donati, *Idea*, pp. 6–7; Pezzarossa, "Introduzione" to Martelli's *Ricordanze*, pp. 27–28.

57. Bartolus, *De dignitatibus*, ff. 46r–v; Marrara, *Riseduti*, pp. 12–13; Donati, *Idea*, pp. 6–7.

58. dall'Aqua, *Vocabularius*, s.v. miles; *Vocabularius*, s.v. miles; Savonarola from Ventura, *Nobiltà*, pp. 291–92; Lanfranchini, *Utrum preferendus sit*, ##53–54; Bolognini, *Additio* to Omodei's *Utrum praeferendus sit*, ##92–93.

59. Lanfranchini, *Utrum preferendus sit*, ##37–39; Bolognini, *Additio* to Omodei's *Utrum praeferendus sit*, ##57, 66.

60. Bartolus, *De dignitatibus*, ##35, 102; Bartolus, *Repertorium*, s.v. dignitas; da Platea, *Repertorium*, s.v. nobilitas.

61. Bartolus, *De dignitatibus*, ##36, 45, 77–78, 82; Cipolla, *De imperatore*, unfoliated, ##18–19 in list of qualifications for nobility.

62. Bartolus, *De dignitatibus*, ##35, 69–70, 102; Bartolus, *Repertorium*, s.v. dignitas; Cipolla, *De imperatore*, unfoliated, ##3, 12, 19, 22–23 in list of qualifications for nobility.

63. Law, "Venice," p. 78; Hurtubise, *Salviati*, p. 197.

64. Bartolus, *De dignitatibus*, #10; Bertrachini, *Repertorium*, s.v. nobilitas; Del Monte, *Repertorium*, s.v. nobilitas; da Platea, *Repertorium*, s.v. Doctor; Bartolus, *Repertorium*, s.v. doctor; Lanfranchini, *Utrum preferendus sit*, #19; Cipolla, *De imperatore*, unfoliated, #4 in list of qualifications for nobility ("litterati"); Omodei, *Utrum praeferendus sit*, ##20–22, 28, 34; Bolognini, *Additio* to Omodei, ##50, 76; Malaspina from Castellazzi, "Testamento," p. 441.

65. Garin, *Umanesimo*, pp. 38–46; idem, *Filosofia*, pp. 209–13; idem, *Disputa*; Witt, *Hercules*, ch. 12; Martino da Lodi, *Additio* to Bartolus's *De dignitatibus*; Lanfranchini, *Utrum preferendus sit*; Omodei, *Utrum praeferendus sit* (with *Additio* by Bolognini).

66. Varanini, "Famiglia," pp. 36–39; A.S.Ver., Anag. Prov. 592–93 (Girolamo Verità); *matricula* of Vicenza's College of Jurists from Bertoliana, Gonz. 579, ff. 3r–v; ivi, Not., Cristoforo Bassan 38, 27 April 1482; ivi, PO, AP, 11 June 1487.

67. Betto, *Collegi*, p. 116; Bertoliana, Gonz. 533, ff. 164v–66r; Sancassani, *Documenti*, pp. 29, 36–37, 68, 71–74.

68. Tamassia, *Famiglia*, p. 100; Bolognini's *Additio* to Omodei, #79.

69. *Cronicae*, p. 366.

70. Donati, *Idea*, p. 3; Baron, "Franciscan Poverty," pp. 5–17, 26–29, 35–36.

71. *De dignitatibus*, #47.

72. Tateo, "Disputa," pp. 358–419; Donati, *Idea*, pp. 9–16; Garin, *Umanesimo*, pp. 54–58, 104–5; Baron, "Franciscan Poverty," pp. 17–26, 32–33; Lanfranchini, *Utrum preferendus sit*, ##53–57; Cipolla, *De imperatore*, unfoliated, ##1–2, 4–5 in list of qualifications for nobility.

73. Bertrachini, *Repertorium*, s.v. dignitas, nobilitas; Lanfranchini, *Utrum preferendus sit*, ##31–36, 42; Borelli, "'Doctor,'" p. 163; Tateo, "Disputa," pp. 366–68; in general, Alessio, "Riflessioni."

74. Cristofoletti, "Cenni," pp. 326–29; Bertoliana, Gonz. 533, ff. 164v–66r; Battistella, "Comune," II, p. 102.

75. *De dignitatibus*, #52.

76. Verona, Bib. Civ., ms. 2833, ff. 44v–45r.

77. King, "Caldiera," p. 33.

78. Donati, *Idea*, p. 19; Letzen, introduction to Landino's *De vera nobilitate*, p. 3.

79. Bartolus, *De dignitatibus*, ##53, 55, 62, 64, 77–78, 93, 102; Baldus, quoted in Alvarotti, *Super feudis*, f. 57v, and in Cipolla, *De imperatore*, ##12, 22 in list of qualifications of nobility; in general, Donati, *Idea*, pp. 10–12, 15–16; Tateo, "Disputa," pp. 359–89; Cipolla, *De imperatore*, unfoliated, ##1–3, 5, 12–13, 15, 17, 19, 22–24, 26 in list of qualifications for nobility; King, *Venetian Humanism*, pp. 118–21; Kristeller, introduction to *Lauro Quirini*, pp. 37–41; Lanfranchini, *Utrum preferendus sit*, ##56–60; Conversino, *Rationarium*, p. 55 and pt. III.

80. Bartolus, *De dignitatibus*, #48; Donati, *Idea*, pp. 9–10.

81. *Cronicae*, pp. 360, 370.

82. Fasoli, "Conti," pp. 230–37; Lampertico, *Proemio* to *Statuti . . . MCCLXIV,* pp. xix–xxix; similarly, in Treviso and Feltre: Rasi, "Rapporti," pp. 113–20; Biscaro, "Temporalità," pp. 8–20.

83. Vicenza, Arch. Curia, Feudi, reg. 22, ff. 36v–37v, 40r–v; ivi, reg. 23, ff. 99r–v, 100r; ivi, reg. 24, reg. 44r, 80v–81r; ivi, reg. 25, ff. 207r–8v; ivi, reg. 26, ff. 59r–60r; ivi, reg. 26, s.d. 10 February 1494; ivi, reg. 27, ff. 11r–v, 66r; ivi, reg. 28, f. 181r; in general, Tabacco, "Aristocrazia," p. 710.

84. Varanini, *Comuni,* pp. 380–81.

85. Quoted in Lanfranchini, *Utrum preferendus sit,* #32.

86. Pagliarini, *Cronicae,* pp. 24–25, 27–29, 53–54; *Cronica ad memoriam,* pp. 21–22.

87. Quoted in Cipolla, *De imperatore,* unfoliated.

88. Dall'Aqua, *Vocabularius,* s.v. Feudum.

89. Trinkaus, *Adversity's Noblemen,* p. 53; Tateo, "Disputa," pp. 374–77, 411–12.

90. Donati, *Idea,* p. 6; Bartolus, *Repertorium,* s.v. nobilitas; Bartolus, *De dignitatibus,* ##44–46, 89.

91. Bartolus, *De dignitatibus,* #52; Lanfranchini, *Utrum preferendus sit,* ##53–54; Berengo, "Patriziato," p. 498.

92. Chojnacki, "Political Adulthood," esp. pp. 799–809; idem, "Dowries," esp. pp. 589–97; idem, "Patrician Women"; Romano, *"Quod sibi fiat gratia"*; idem, *Patricians,* ch. 6; Finlay, *Politics,* esp. secs. II, IV; Queller, *Venetian Patriciate*; idem and Swietek, "Myth."

93. Klapisch-Zuber, *Women,* ch. 4; Pandimiglio, "Giovanni di Pagolo Morelli," pp. 28–53; Kent and Kent, *Neighbours,* esp. pp. 5, 89–93; Kent, "Dynamics," esp. p. 64; Weissman, "Patronage"; idem, *Ritual Brotherhood,* esp. pp. 23–40; and, in general, Heers, *Family Clans,* ch. 2; Hughes, "Kinsmen"; Allegra, *Città*; Bertelli, *Potere.*

94. Bertoliana, Arch. Torre 1653, s.d. 30 May 1498; ivi, Arch. Torre 61, ff. 373r–75v (= A.S.Ven., Senato Terra 12, ff. 131v–33r); A.S.Ven., Avogadori di Comun 3583, 156r–v; Padua from Ventura, *Nobiltà,* pp. 86–88.

95. Bertoliana, Arch. Torre 645, #92; ivi, Arch. Torre 62, ff. 422r–v; ivi, Arch. Torre 59, f. 91v; Grubb, *Firstborn,* pp. 94–95; Marciana, Latin XIV, 244 (4681), ff. 43r–60v.

96. A.S. Vic., Not., Bortolo Bassan 4553, 11 and 30 April 1455 (Angiolelli); ivi, PO, LAGA, 9 September 1455 (Loschi); lawsuits involving patricians in ivi, PO, AP, 4 September 1471, 13 April 1472, 19 August 1493, 9 January 1497, 3 April 1498, 4 September 1498; ivi, Magistrature Giudiziarie, Varie, reg. 45, fasc. 21.

97. A.S. Vic., PO, AP, 17 August and 12 November 1502, 11 November 1504.

98. 1505 *estimo,* ff. 2, 16, 34; Rumor, *Blasone,* pp. 286–94; Pagliarini, *Cronicae,* s.v. Bissari; Mantese, *Memorie,* 3, 2, s.v. Bissari; *Cronica ad memoriam,* pp. 22, 31, 57.

99. Klapisch-Zuber, "Ruptures," pp. 1207–9.

100. Herlihy, "Roots," pp. 137–39; Tamassia, *Famiglia,* p. 62; Heers, *Family Clans,* pp. 107–8 (quote on p. 110); Cherubini, *Signori,* pp. 32–33; Hughes, "Family Structures," pp. 7–8.

101. Mistruzzi, "Giorgio Sommariva," pp. 133–34; Simeoni, "Vendetta," pp. 252–53; Viggiano, *Governanti,* pp. 251, 272.

102. Camposampiero and Dotti from Bertoliana, Arch. Torre 59, ff. 213v–15r; Grubb, *Firstborn,* p. 104; Friuli from Muir, *Mad Blood.*

103. Grubb, *Firstborn,* pp. 94, 103–4; *Cronica ad memoriam,* p. 27; Mantese, *Me-*

morie, 3, 2, p. 455 (Braschi); Mantese, "Correnti," p. 116 (Giustiniani); Bertoliana, Arch. Torre 61, ff. 135v–36r (Marco Nievo; see also A.S.Ven., Avogaria di Comun3583, ff. 191v, 197v, 218v, 351v, 378r); ivi, Arch. Torre 1655, ##150, 153 (Nievo and Gallo); Viggiano, *Governanti*, p. 81 (1493 accusations); A.S.Ven., Senato Terra 12, f. 83r (1494 murders); ivi, Dieci Misti 29, ff. 129v, 161v, and ivi, Avogaria di Comun 3372, s.d. 13 March 1505 (Trento); from Bertoliana, Arch. Torre 349, fasc. 6, ff. 15r–16r (Thiene-Toso riots; similarly, Arch. Torre 348, fasc. 1, ff. 1r–4r).

104. Viggiano, *Governanti*, p. 249; on the law of exile, see Grubb, *Firstborn*, pp. 104, 106–8.

105. Grubb, *Firstborn*, ch. 9; legislation in Bertoliana, Arch. Torre 60, ff. 128r–v; ivi, Arch. Torre 59, ff. 66r, 133v–34r, 178r; arms permissions in Bertoliana, Gonzati Do 36, f. 54v; ivi, Arch. Torre 60, f. 251v.

106. A.S.Vic., PO, LAGA, 13 January 1440; dating from Barbieri, *Pittori*, pp. 9–10.

107. Barbieri, *Pittori*, pp. 9–13; Lorenzoni, *Lorenzo*, pp. 17–32 (though with reserve that the palace is by Lorenzo); Barbieri, "Architettura," p. 174; Cevese, "Architettura," pp. 201–2.

108. Cipolla, "Libri," pp. 32–39, 45–53.

109. Goldthwaite, "Renaissance Economy," pp. 659–73.

110. Tagliaferri, *Economia*, pp. 140–53; Herlihy, "Population," pp. 109, 111–12, 115–16 (quote on p. 112).

111. Bonardi, *Lusso*, pp. 12–20, chs. 2–4 and appendixes 1–10; A.S.Ver., AAC, reg. 56, ff. 154r, 187r; Lecce, *Vicende*, pp. 42–43; Mueller, "Crisi," p. 546; in general, Hughes, "Sumptuary Law," esp. pp. 71, 81.

Chapter 8. Spirituality and Religion

1. Dal Bovo, ff. 27v–28v, 38r–39v; Repeta, unbound folio preceding f. 136r.

2. Swanson, *Church*, p. 276; Rubin, *Corpus Christi*, chs. 3–5; Kieckhefer, *Unquiet Souls*, chs. 3–4; Mantese, *Memorie*, 3, 2, pp. 584–89.

3. Bologna, 1495: copy in Verona, Bib. Civ., Incunabolo 180; cf. Giuliari, *Letteratura*, ##272–73.

4. Venice, 1492: copy in Verona, Bib. Civ., Incunabolo 327; see also Schutte, *Religious Books*, p. 149.

5. Venice, 1485: copies in Verona, Bib. Civ., Incunaboli 555, 595.

6. Petrocchi, *Storia*, pp. 127–37.

7. Many editions; copy in Verona, Bib. Civ., Incunabolo 776.

8. Verona, Bib. Civ., mss. 2825, 107; see also Schutte, *Religious Books*, pp. 127–28.

9. Verona, Bib. Civ., ms. 493; see also the anonymous hymn to Christ crucified: ivi, ms. 505.

10. Weissman, "Sacred Eloquence," pp. 256–61; Petrocchi, *Storia*, p. 101; Kieckhefer, *Unquiet Souls*, pp. 91–98, 104–7.

11. Vovelle, *Mort*, p. 174.

12. Repeta, f. 81r; dal Bovo, ff. 1v, 29r–v, 37v, 78r–v, 79r.

13. Dal Bovo, f. 46v; Muronovo, f. 13v; quote from Swanson, *Church*, p. 277; Rubin, *Corpus Christi*, pp. 155–63; Zika, "Hosts"; Reinburg, "Liturgy," pp. 532–37; Grendi, "Societa," p. 516.

14. Rubin, *Corpus Christi*, pp. 150ff.

15. De Sandre Gasparini, "Confraternite," pp. 314–16; Paton, *Preaching Friars*, p. 310.

16. Rubin, *Corpus Christi*, pp. 155–63; da Certaldo, *Libro*, pp. 222–23, #345; Pesce, *Chiesa*, I, pp. 36–37.

17. Scribner, "Cosmic Order"; idem, "Reformation," pp. 479–83 (quote on p. 480); see dal Bovo, f. 29v; Repeta, f. 79r.

18. Dal Bovo, f. 46r. On the use of bells to protect against storms and lightning, see Scribner, "Reformation," p. 483.

19. Scribner, "Cosmic Order," p. 24.

20. A Venetian priest, asked by a merchant whose ship had not reached port to put a paper with the name of St. Christopher on the altar while saying Mass, was accused of magic before Vatican courts: Brucker, "Religious Sensibilities," p. 24.

21. Dal Bovo, ff. 8r, 35r–v, 45r; Abbondanza, ed., *Notariato*, pp. 314–15. In general, Finucane, *Miracles*, p. 63; Grattan and Singer, *Anglo-Saxon Magic*, esp. pp. 10–11, 44–45; Kieckhefer, *Magic*, ch. 4; Monter, *Ritual*, p. 32; Flint, *Rise*, ch. 9. Right use of psalms was outlined in *Modus psallendi* texts: Muronovo, ff. 28r–29v.

22. Muronovo, f. 51v; dal Bovo, ff. 21r–v, 43v; Shahar, *Childhood*, p. 36; recitation and *expositio* of liturgical texts in dal Bovo, ff. 2r, 9r–11v; Muronovo, ff. 18v, 21r, 51r.

23. Dal Bovo, ff. 35v, 46r.

24. Dal Bovo, ff. 37v, 78v; and see Flint, *Rise*, pp. 311–20; Grattan and Singer, *Anglo-Saxon Magic*, pp. 11, 45.

25. Delumeau, *Peché* and *Peur*; Kieckhefer, *Unquiet Souls*, chs. 1, 3, 5; Paton, *Preaching Friars*, ch. 2; Branca, "Introduzione" to *Mercanti*, pp. xxxii–xxxiv; Weissman, "Sacred Eloquence," pp. 256–61; Sartore, "Pessimismo." Petrocchi, however, sees fifteenth-century spirituality as marked by optimism: *Storia*, p. 151; see also Pesce, *Chiesa*, pp. 45–54, 72.

26. Pacini, "Fermenti," pp. 71–72; Henderson, "Penitence," esp. pp. 233–34; Pullan, "*Scuole*," p. 274; Mantese, "'Fratres'"; de Sandre Gasparini, "Confraternità di S. Giovanni Evangelista," esp. pp. 773–74; idem, 'Cura animarum.'"

27. Dal Bovo, f. 34v.

28. Muronovo, ff. 10v–14v.

29. Dal Bovo, ff. 47v–48r.

30. Dal Bovo, f. 43v; similarly, da Certaldo, *Libro*, p. 121, #148.

31. Verità, ff. 13r–16v.

32. Dal Bovo, ff. 70r–77v. For the cult of Roch, strong in the region after a *vita* by Francesco Diedo (1479) and translation of his body to Venice (1485), see Dormeir, "Nuovi culti," pp. 319–20; Pullan, "*Scuole*," p. 273; Schutte, *Religious Books*, pp. 164–65, 316; Baretano, *Cronica*, s.a. 1485; *Cronica ad memoriam*, pp. 36–37; *Cronicha che comenza*, p. 8. Vauchez notes a trend toward "clericalization" of sainthood in the later Middle Ages, but Italian saints were more likely lay than was the case elsewhere: *Sainteté*, pp. 218, 249–54.

33. Arnaldi, f. 21r; dal Bovo, f. 63r; Repeta, f. 94r; Muronovo, f. 52v.

34. The letter has been variously seen as a Greek work, translated into Latin in the thirteenth or fourteenth century, or a twelfth-century work, or a Latin monastic product of ca. 1300: Bardy and Tricot, eds., *Enciclopedia*, pp. 506, 903–4; von Dobschutz,

Christusbilder, pp. 308–9, 326, 330; James, *Apocryphal New Testament*, pp. 477–78; copies of the *Vita Jesu Christi* in Verona, Bib. Civica, Incunaboli 82, 776.

35. Von Dobschutz, *Christusbilder*, pp. 324–25.

36. Marciana, mss. Italian XI, 24 (6620); Italian XI, 126 (6916); Latin I, 72; Latin X, 134; Latin XI, 145; Latin XIV, 106 (6452); Latin XIV, 266 (4502); Latin XIV, 267 (4344); Verona, Bib. Cap., mss. CCVIII, CCXIX, CCXXVIII, CCCXVII, CCCCXCI, DXIX (from indexes); Padua, Bib. Univ., mss. 1001/XXII, 201/XLIV, 2240 (f. 478r), 1139 (ff. 74v–75r), 1291/XXII, 1108 (f. 190r); general list in von Dobschutz, *Christusbilder*, p. 308; see also Bertalot, "Zibaldone." The *Zardino de oration* attributed to Nicolo da Osimo, compiled in 1454 and printed in Venice in 1494, offered a vernacular version: Baxandall, *Painting*, pp. 46, 165–66; Schutte, *Religious Books*, p. 302; copies in Verona, Bib. Civ., Incunaboli 233, 382.

37. Quoted in Miles, *Image*, p. 69; see also Kieckhefer, *Unquiet Souls*, pp. 99–100.

38. Baxandall, *Painting*, p. 45.

39. Quoted in ibid., p. 46.

40. Dal Bovo, ff. 63v–64r; other mss. in Marciana, Latin X, 134, Latin XIV, 106 (6452); Latin XIV, 245 (4682); Latin XIV, 266 (4502); Verona, Bib. Cap., ms. CCXXVIII (from index); Vicenza, Bertoliana 87, ff. 30r–31r; Padua, Bib. Univ., mss. 1001/XXIII, 201/XLIV; Paduan ms. described in Sartore, "Pessimismo," p. 625; see also von Dobschutz, *Christusbilder*, p. 315; James, *Apocryphal New Testament*, p. 146; translation in Schneemelcher, *Apocrypha*, p. 527; printed edition of ca. 1474 from Rhodes, *Tipografia*, pp. 25–26.

41. Tischendorf, *Evangelia*, esp. pp. lxxiv–lxxvii, 333–88, 413–16, 456–58, 471–86; Kieckhefer, *Unquiet Souls*, p. 100; Bainton, *Behold*, p. 14; pseudo-Dionysus in Verona, Bib. Civ., ms. 1188; a *De origine et vita Pilati* in Verona, Bib. Cap., ms. CCXXVIII, ff. 13–17.

42. Kieckhefer, *Unquiet Souls*, p. 102.

43. Repeta, unbound folio preceding f. 136r; Vitaliani, "Contributo"; Auzzas, "Miscellanea." A brief hymn to the crucified Jesus moves systematically through the parts of the dying body and is replete with details of the pierced feet, flowing blood "which pays for all our sins," and so forth: Verona, Bib. Civ., ms. 505 (and see also ms. 653).

44. Verona, Bib. Civ., ms. 507, ff. 173r–79r; see also the *Legenda di Maria Madalena* in Verona, Bib. Cap., ms. DCCXLI.

45. Verona, Bib. Civ., ms. 438, ff. 42–43.

46. Martin, *Metier*, ch. 12, esp. pp. 518–19; Schmitt, *Precheurs*.

47. Accounts of heaven from Boase, *Death*, p. 19; cf. the copy of Bartolomeo Rimbertino's *De deliciis sensibilis paradisi* (Venice, 1498) in Verona, Bib. Civ., Incunabolo 18; a work with the same title by Verona's Celso Maffei (mid-Quattrocento) was printed in Verona in 1504 (Baxandall, *Painting*, pp. 104, 172–73); pseudo-Ambrosian *De paradiso* in Marciana, Latin Z 47 (1498); see also Gatto, "Voyage." Accounts of purgatory in Verona, Bib. Civ., ms. 938, f. 32; Gregory the Great, *Dialogi*, IV, ch. 36; Klapisch-Zuber, "Peril," p. 229; Vovelle, *Mort*, pp. 66, 134–39.

48. Vegio, *De educatione*, I, p. 19.

49. Klapisch, *Women*, ch. 14; Vegio, *De educatione*, I, pp. 30–32; Shahar, *Childhood*, p. 116; Dominici, *Regola*, IV, pp. 131–32.

50. Morelli, *Ricordi*, p. 456; Gavitt, *Charity*, p. 294; McManamon, "Vergerio," p. 361; Weinstein, *"Art,"* pp. 92–94, 101–2; Edgerton, *Pictures*, ch. 5; Cole, *Italian Art*, pp. 195–96.

51. Dominici, *Regola*, IV, pp. 132–33; Arasse, "Devotion," pp. 137–38; Trexler, *Public Life*, pp. 54–57.

52. Agresti, *Volto*; Frugoni, "Proposta"; Baxandall, *Painting*, p. 57; Nadi, *Diario*, pp. 77–78; Goffen, *Piety*, p. 142.

53. Spanish examples in Christian, *Apparitions*, Introduction.

54. Bertoliana, Gonz., f. 33r; Turner and Turner, *Image*, pp. 28, 197; see also Vauchez, *Sainteté*, pp. 524–29; Trexler, *Public Life*, pp. 54–73.

55. *Statuti Veronae*, p. 260; Crouzet-Pavan, *Espaces*, ch. 9, esp. pp. 620, 624, 657; dal Bovo, ff. 42v, 46v.

56. Marciana, Italian VI, 312 (5990), ff. 67v–68v. After 1486, 109 miracles were attributed to supplication to this image. In Florence, a madman who defaced images in Orsanmichele was stoned to death by a crowd: Gavitt, *Charity*, p. 296.

57. A.S.Ven., Senato Terra 7, f. 95v; Grubb, *Firstborn*, pp. 129, 179; Law, "Verona," pp. 27–28.

58. Arnaldi, f. 6v; Repeta, f. 91v, 64v.

59. He covered 50 *meia* from Trent to Verona; the current distance is 92 kilometers, or a little less than 60 English miles. From Campiglia to Trent he traveled 77 *meia*; present roads cover 140 kilometers or about 84 English miles. Modern roads are also considerably straighter than the rough tracks of the Quattrocento.

60. Turner and Turner, *Image*, ch. 1.

61. Sigal, *Marcheurs*, ch. 1; Martin, *Metier*, p. 10; Turner and Turner, *Image*, p. 194.

62. Rumor, ed., *Storia*, esp. p. 404, and miracles XV–LIII.

63. Turner and Turner, *Image*, pp. 6–7 (source of quote), 12–13.

64. Ibid., p. 13.

65. Repeta, f. 92r; Muronovo, ff. 81v–86v.

66. Turner and Turner, *Image*, pp. 180, 241.

67. Weil-Garris, *Santa Casa*, pp. 3–4; Grimaldi, *Loreto*, p. 7. On growing Church control of pilgrim cults in the later Middle Ages, see Turner and Turner, *Image*, esp. pp. 25–26, 193–97.

68. Repeta, ff. 64v–65v; Esposito, "Stereotipo," pp. 81–83; Hsia, *Trent*, ch. 6.

69. Esposito, "Sterotipo," pp. 74–88; Hsia, *Trent*, chs. 5, 11 (quote on p. 51); Dormeir, "Nuovi culti," pp. 346–48; Ortalli, "Cronisti," p. 377; Faccioli, *Catalogo*, p. 26; Rhodes, *Tipografia*, p. 26.

70. Colla et al., "Tipografi," pp. 112–15; Ortalli, "Cronisti," p. 377; Rhodes, *Tipografia*, pp. 12, 26; Mantese, *Memorie*, 3, 2, pp. 156–58, 789–90, 795; Ioly Zorattini, "Ebrei," pp. 224–25; Giuliari, *Letteratura*, ##91, 92, 94; Lepori, "Bruto Pietro," pp. 335–37; Campagnola and Montagna from Verona, Bib. Civ., Incunabolo 1193; Venetians from King, *Venetian Humanism*, p. 37; unpublished works in Verona, Bib. Civ., mss. 1054, 1055. For Sommariva, see also Mistruzzi, "Giorgio Sommariva," pp. 141–50, 154–57.

71. Dianin, *San Bernardino*, pp. xx, 23–26, 39–42, 46–51, 65, 71; Brogliato, *750 anni*, pp. 76–88; Mantese, "Fra Bernardino," pp. 78–79; Meneghin, *Bernardino*, pp. 1–4; de Sandre Gasparini, "Parola," pp. 101–3; Pacini, "Osservanza," pp. 87–88, 91.

72. Zarri, "Aspetti," p. 212.

73. Martin, *Metier*, ch. 3; Swanson, *Church*, p. 269.

74. Zarri, "Aspetti," p. 220; Zironda, "Aspetti," p. 174; Giacomuzzi, "Influsso," p. xxxii.

75. Weissman, "Sacred Eloquence."

76. Muronovo, f. 66v; *Cronica ad memoriam*, pp. 15–16, 19–21.

77. *Cronica ad memoriam*, p. 45; *Cronicha che comenza*, p. 10; da Feltre, *Sermoni*, I, p. xxxix.

78. Da Feltre, *Sermoni*, I, p. 277; Bonardi, *Lusso*, pp. 4–5. For the content of sermons preached in Verona and Vicenza, see Dianin, *San Bernardino*, pp. 39–42, 48–51; *Cronica ad memoriam*, p. 16; Meneghin, *Bernardino*, pp. 385–86; da Feltre, *Sermoni*, I, p. 277, II, p. 271, III, p. 131.

79. Arnaldi, f. 22r.

80. Vauchez, "Riflessioni," p. 308. On *exempla*, see Schmitt, *Precheurs*, esp. pp. 10–23; Forni, "'Predication,'" pp. 29–31; Paton, *Preaching Friars*, pp. 50–52; Baxandall, *Painting*, pp. 48–49; Martin, *Metier*, ch. 12.

81. Martin, *Metier*, pp. 493–94, 514.

82. Da Feltre, *Sermoni*, III, p. 131.

83. *Cronica ad memoriam*, pp. 16–17, 19–21; *Cronicha che comenza*, pp. 4–5; Baretano, *Cronica*, s.a. 1451; Muronovo, f. 66v; Arnaldi, f. 23r.

84. de Sandre Gasparini, "Parola," pp. 114–16.

85. Vauchez, "Riflessioni," p. 308.

86. Arnaldi, f. 22v; Muronovo, f. 66v; *Cronica ad memoriam*, p. 17; *Cronicha che comenza*, pp. 4–5; Beretano, *Cronica*, s.a. 1444, 1450.

87. Schmitt, "Usage," pp. 356–57; da Lecce, *Quaresimale*, pp. 202–11 (quotes on pp. 203 [from Alexander of Halles], 202); dal Bovo, ff. 37v, 78v. San Bernardino also preached against those using divination to "know the secret things of God": quoted in Paton, *Preaching Friars*, pp. 286–88.

88. Dal Bovo, f. 4v; Muronovo, ff. 45r–50v (folded into a general calendar); Arnaldi, f. 35r.

89. Kieckhefer, *Magic*, pp. 86–87, 181, 190; Finucane, *Miracles*, p. 61; Grattan and Singer, *Magic*, pp. 42–43, 199; Flint, *Rise*, pp. 322–23.

90. Repeta, f. 79v; and see Serra-Zanetti, "Pronostici," esp. pp. 203–4, 208–9; Schutte, *Religious Books*, p. 255. For other almanacs, see Verona, Bib. Civ., Incunaboli 407–8, 433; *Indice generale*, IV, s.v. Girolamo and Scipo Manfredi, Antonio Manlio.

91. Muronovo, ff. 63r–v, 67v, 74r, 75r; Repeta, f. 87r; dal Bovo, f. 45v; for chronicles, see Verona, Bib. Civ., ms. 938, p. 36; *Cronica ad memoriam*, s.d. 1457, 1471, 1472, 1477, 1490.

92. Verità, ff. 34r–43r, 48r–61v, 79r–82r; in general, Alexander, "Diffusion," pp. 56–59, 68–79; Lerner, *Powers*, pp. 45, 54–56; Reeves, *Joachim*, pp. 59–60; idem, *Influence*, pp. 299–306; idem, "Idea," pp. 56 and *passim*.

93. Rusconi, *Attesa*, pp. 22, 85–86, 97, 167; Lerner, *Powers*, pp. 82, 90–91, 119, 139, 152; Reeves, *Influence*, index, s.v. sibyl; see Marciana, Latin XIV, 67 (4706), 268 (4503); Verona, Bib. Civ., ms. 2845; ivi, Incunabolo 536; Verona, Bib. Cap., CCLXVI, ff. 90–92.

94. Repeta, f. 80r (and see notes to the printed edition); other Joachimite prophecies in Marciana, Ital. XI, 53 (6728), Latin XIV, 2 (4590); Domenico Morosini's *Vaticinia sive*

prophetiae abbatis Ioachimi et Anselmi episcopi Marsicani (before 1459) was published in Venice in 1589. On Joachimite prophecies, see Reeves, "Popular Prophecies"; idem, *Joachim*, esp. ch. 2; idem, *Influence*. Many such vernacular prophecies, often quite specific regarding events and dates, circulated in Italy: Rusconi, *Attesa*, pp. 143–63; Tognetti, "Venezia," p. 87.

95. Dal Bovo, f. 57v; Verità, ff. 72r–74r; in general, Reeves, *Influence*, pp. 320–29, 329–30, 343–46 (quote on p. 330); idem, "Idea," pp. 329–32; idem, *Joachim*, pp. 68–70; Lerner, *Powers*, ch. 8; Rusconi, *Attesa*, pp. 171–84; Balestracci, "Memorie," p. 48; Schutte, *Religious Books*, pp. 295–96.

96. Muronovo, ff. 2v–5r; Verità, ff. 62r–71v, 82r–83v and loose folio; see also Marciana, Ital. XI, 6 (7222) ("pronostici vari Greco-Latini"), 124 (6802) ("Fra Zuanne"); Latin XIV, 2 (4590) (various), 267 (4344) #14 (on anti-Christ); other Marciana references in Lerner, *Powers*; Reeves, *Influence* and "Idea."

97. Niccoli, *Prophecy*. See also Muir, "Virgin," p. 27; Crouzet-Pavan, *Espaces*, pp. 318, 692; Volpato, "Predicazione," pp. 123–28. Vincent of Ferrer's *De fine mundi* was published in the Veneto in 1477: Rhodes, *Tipografia*, pp. 3–4.

98. Arnaldi, f. 26v; Repeta, ff. 96v–97r; *Cronica ad memoriam*, pp. 32–33; Baretano, *Cronica*, s.a. 1477; *Cronicha che comenza*, pp. 7–8; dal Bovo, ff. 41r–v.

99. Vaughn, *Europe*, pp. 66–72, 78.

100. Verona, Bib. Civ., Incunaboli 236 (Giustiniani), 163, 183, 252 (Maffei); Marciana, Latin XIV, 265 (4501), ##14 (Querini), 22–23 (Bessarione); Marciana, Latin 295 (4348), #23 (Lupo); Padua, Bib. Civ., ms. BM 139 I (Diedo); Venetian works cited in Fabbri, *Memorialistica*, pp. 15–40, 139–230.

101. Verità, f. 45r; Verona, Bib. Civ., Incunabuli 57, 291; Marciana, Latin XIV, 123 (4662), 268 (4503).

102. Marciana, Z Lat. 397 (1733), 437 (1911); ivi, Latin XIV, 265–66 (4501–2), ##20, 71–72, 78, 87–88; 267 (4344), #22; 295 (4348), #47; Schutte, *Religious Books*, p. 368.

103. Marciana, Latin XIV, 47 (4705) (Attila); Verità, ff. 32r–v (Grand Master); Verona, Bib. Civ., ms. 52 (Fichet); Marciana, Latin XIV, 218 (4677), 244 (4681) (Sagundino), 285 (4301) (Tiphernatis), 265 (4501) #3 (bishop of Mitilene). On Ficino, see Weissman, "Sacred Eloquence," p. 252.

104. Mattiolo, *Cronaca*, pp. 7–9.

105. Cited in Perosa, "Zibaldone," p. 144.

106. Reeves, *Influence*, p. 335 and works cited in index, s.v. Turks.

107. Tognetti, "Venezia," pp. 86–87.

108. Marciana, Latin XIV, 267 (4344), #14.

109. Repeta, ff. 92v–93v. Innocent VIII also calculated forces needed to defeat the Turk: Houseley, *Later Crusades*, p. 114.

110. Zironda, "Aspetti," p. 164; Rigon, *Clero*, pp. 233–37; Gios, "Aspetti," pp. 172–75; Pesce, *Chiesa*, I, p. 388; idem, "Clero," p. 370; Law, "Verona," p. 24.

111. Pesce, *Chiesa*, I, p. 394; idem, "Clero," pp. 369–73; Zironda, "Aspetti," pp. 167–69; Rigon, *Clero*, ch. 8, esp. pp. 220–26.

112. Pesce ("Clero," p. 368) sees Trevisan benefices in poor economic shape; Rigon (*Clero*, ch. 8) reaches more optimistic conclusions for Padua.

113. Pesce, "Clero," pp. 405–10; idem, *Chiesa*, I, p. 426; Rigon, *Clero*, ch. 8; Mantese, *Memorie*, 3, 2, p. 120.

114. On clerical *fratalee*, see Rigon, "Associazionismo"; idem, *Clero*, ch. 8; idem, "Congregazione"; Pesce, *Chiesa*, I, pp. 430–38.

115. Mantese, "Correnti," pp. 118–28.

116. Paton, *Preaching Friars*, p. 34; Mantese, "Correnti," p. 116.

117. A.S.Ver., Perg. #35, Guastaverza, busta I, #25; ivi, Test., mazzo 79, #27.

118. De Sandre Gasparini, "'Cura animarum.'"

119. Crouzet-Pavan, *Espaces*, pp. 590, 621; Muir, "Virgin," pp. 32–33.

120. Dal Bovo, ff. 52r–53r, 54r–55r; A.S.Ver., Test., mazzo 34, #44; mazzo 79, #27; mazzo 81, #12. He also reconstructed the church in the village of Bovo, the family's place of origin, and traveled through city and countryside seeking proof of its patron saint's existence.

121. Hay, *Church*, p. 24; Brucker, "Urban Parishes," pp. 18, 23–25; Kent and Kent, *Neighbours*, pp. 128–35, ch. 3; Cohn, *Cult*, pp. 36–37; see also Swanson, *Church*, pp. 217–19, 257.

122. Gios, "Aspetti"; Hay, *Church*, pp. 22, 57; de Sandre Gasparini, "Studio," p. 112; idem, "Governo," pp. 75–76; Brugnoli, "Aspetto," pp. 360–61.

123. Mantese, "Correnti," pp. 172ff; idem, *Memorie*, 3, 2, pp. 317–23, 331–36, 345–48 and pt. 3; Zironda, "Aspetti," pp. 158–59; Cohn, *Cult*, pp. 36–37.

124. A.S.Ver., AAC, reg. 56, f. 107r; Brogliato, *750 anni*, pp. 497–502.

125. Cohn, *Cult*, pp. 36–37; Bonanno et al., "Legati," p. 209; Andenna, "Ordini"; Dianin, *San Bernardino*, p. 59; Brucker, "Monasteries," pp. 44–46, 51; Rubinstein, "Lay Patronage," pp. 64–69; Zarri, "Aspetti," pp. 223, 232–35; Collodo, "Convento."

126. Alce, "Riforma," p. 339. His dating of Veronese reform may be incorrect, as the *Cronica ad memoriam* (p. 25) asserts that Observants from S. Anastasia arrived in Vicenza in 1464.

127. Mantese, *Memorie*, 3, 2, pp. 978–80 (S. Sebastiano); Zironda, "Aspetti," pp. 159, 174 (SS. Sebastiano, Chiara); Dianin, *San Bernardino*, pp. 67–69 (Arcarotta); A.S.Ver., AAC, reg. 56, f. 256r (S. Eufemia). In Treviso as well Observant Franciscans built from scratch: Pesce, *Chiesa*, I, pp. 542–46. In general, see Zarri, "Aspetti," pp. 235–36.

128. Crouzet-Pavan, *Espaces*, pp. 793, 986.

129. A.S.Vic., Test., mazzo 31, #93 (Gabriele Verità: S. Eufemia), mazzo 60, ##46 (Caterina Verità: S. Fermo), 49 (Bonaventura Bovi: S. Anastasia), mazzo 81, ##45 (Avantino Fracastoro: S. Fermo), 132 (Bonzanino Muronovo: S. Anastasia), mazzo 89, #39 (Pietro Verità: S. Anastasia), mazzo 93, #23 (Alvise Stoppi: S. Anastasia), mazzo 93, #204 (Maddalena Fracastoro: S. Fermo), mazzo 102, #85 (Verità: S. Eufemia), mazzo 128, #134 (Donato Stoppi: S. Anastasia). Only Tadea Fracastoro, in 1510, ordered burial in S. Bernardino: ivi, mazzo 102, #187.

130. Muronovo, f. 23v; dal Bovo, f. 58v; Dianin, *San Bernardino*, p. 73; *Statuti Veronae*, Proemium.

131. *Ius municipale*, ff. 146r–48r; Grubb, *Firstborn*, p. 132; *Statuti Veronae*, pp. 94–96.

132. *Cronica ad memoriam*, pp. 24–27.

133. Grubb, *Firstborn*, p. 132; *Ius municipale*, ff. 146r, 148r; Law, "Verona," p. 32.

134. Cracco, "Saints," pp. 292–95; Rumor, ed., *Storia*, #XVII; Mantese, "Correnti," p. 135; idem, *Memorie*, III, 2 , pp. 385–87; Paduan promotion of local cults in Rigon, "Devotion."

135. de Sandre Gasparini, "Parola," p. 127; Dianin, *San Bernardino*, ch. IV.

136. Brogliato, *750 anni*, pp. 93–95; Mantese, "Fra Bernardino," pp. 78–79; idem, "Correnti," pp. 150–55; Pacini, "Osservanza," pp. 87–89; Zironda, "Aspetti," p. 160; *Cronica ad memoriam*, pp. 20–21; Grubb, *Firstborn*, p. 132.

137. A.S.Ver., AAC, reg. 56, ff. 14v, 40v, 41v–45r, 124r–25r, 236r–v; Bertoliana, Arch. Torre 61, ff. 67v–70r; see also above, ch. 3; and Grubb, *Firstborn*, p. 131.

138. Bertoliana, Arch. Torre 61, ff. 21r–22r. Their jurisdiction was soon restricted to "opulent" houses: ibid., ff. 27v–28v.

139. Mantese, *Memorie storiche*, III, 2, pp. 403–4, 414–15; idem, "Correnti," pp. 155–56, 161; *Cronica ad memoriam*, p. 25; Zironda, "Aspetti," p. 161.

140. Brugnoli, "Aspetto," pp. 359–69; de Sandre Gasparini, "Governo," pp. 76, 85. The latter, however, sees civilian commissions as ineffectual, since episcopal visitations in 1454–58 duplicated what should have been their function.

141. Cenci, "'Probae,'" esp. pp. 320, 379, 389 (for unsuccessful efforts of other cities to lobby the Senate, see pp. 382, 416, 418, 421, 423); Varanini, *Comuni*, p. 379; Zironda, "Aspetti," p. 171; Mantese, "Correnti," pp. 114–16; idem, *Memorie*, III, 2, pp. 120–22.

142. Law, "Verona," p. 24; see also Chittolini, "Stati," p. 183. On Venetian ecclesiastical penetration of the mainland, see ibid., pp. 165–69, 180; Zarri, "Aspetti," pp. 247, 251–52.

143. *Ius municipale*, ff. 182v–83r; *Jus municipale vicentinum* (Venice, 1707), pp. 309, 311.

144. Arnaldi, f. 24r; *Cronica ad memoriam*, pp. 21–23, 25, 26, 31–32, 45–46, 56–57; *Cronicha che comenza*, pp. 5, 7, 11–12.

145. Arnaldi, f. 25v; *Cronica ad memoriam*, pp. 21–23, 31–32, 45–46, 56–57.

146. dal Bovo, f. 51r. On chrismation, see above, ch. 2.

147. Pesce, *Ludovico Barbo*; idem, "Ludovico Barbo"; de Sandre Gasparini, "Studio." For Malipiero, see Zironda, "Aspetti," pp. 158–59 (though Mantese offers a more flattering view: "Correnti," pp. 118–28).

148. Quoted in Cracco, "Periodo," p. 31.

149. Benvenuti Papi, "Pastori," sec. 2; *Cronica ad memoriam*, pp. 35–36.

150. A.S.Ver., AAC, reg. 56, ff. 206r–10v, 237r; ivi, reg. 63, f. 210v.

151. Brugnoli, "Aspetto," pp. 360–61; de Sandre Gasparini, "Studio," p. 112; idem, "Governo," pp. 75–76.

152. Law, "Verona," p. 24; Varanini, *Comuni*, pp. 380–81; de Sandre Gasparini, "Vita," p. 75; idem, "Governo," p. 91; Brugnoli, "Aspetto," p. 362.

153. A.S.Ver., AAC, reg. 56, ff. 180v, 183r–v. Prelates elsewhere felt similar resistance. As Florence's Jacopo Ammanati wrote to the bishop of Constance in 1465, "I am an Italian and I have lived for fourteen years among the subjects of the Church. Believe me, our people doesn't have the same respect for their bishops as you enjoy on the far side of the Alps": quoted in Hay, "Contributo," p. 48.

154. Muronovo, ff. 63r, 69r, 71v, 86v. Repeta compiled a list of popes from Peter to contemporaries (ff. 94v–95v).

155. Dal Bovo, f. 7v.

156. Repeta, f. 80r.

157. Repeta, f. 91v.

Epilogue

1. Petrocchi, *Storia;* Verdon, "Christianity."
2. E.g., Trexler, *Public Life*, p. xviii.
3. Starn, "Francisco Guicciardini," p. 439.
4. Discussion with the audience at the Schouler Lecture, Johns Hopkins University, 1993.

BIBLIOGRAPHY

Memoirs

Arnaldi: Bertoliana, Gonzati 153 (ex. F. 2. 17; 22. 10. 29); partial version in Marciana, Ital. XI, 184 (7414).

Bovi: A. S. Ver., Fondo proveniente dalla Biblioteca Civica, ms. 801 (provisional numbering).

dal Bovo: Verona, Bib. Civ., ms. 827.

Feramosca: Bertoliana, Gonzati 3379 (nineteenth-century *zibaldone* contains scattered notices from Feramosca chronicle memoir).

Fracastoro: A. S. Ver., Malaspina CCXVII bis, 2335.

Freschi: Marciana, Ital. VII, 165 (8867).

Guastaverza: Verona, Bib. Civ., ms. 906.

Muronovo: Milan, Biblioteca Trivulziana, ms. 964.

Repeta: Bertoliana, Gonzati 425 (*catasto* of Manfredo Repeta).

da Romagno: Marciana, ZL 469 (1856), f. 144v.

Stoppi: A. S. Ver., Dionisi-Piomarta 1853.

Trento: Bertoliana, Gonzati 3336, ff. 115r–16r.

Verità: A. S. Ver., Dionisi-Piomarta 1509.

Manuscripts

Padua, Bib. Univ.
   Ms. 55, ff. 14r–66r: Giovanni da Nono, *De generatione aliquorum civium urbis Paduae tam nobilium quam ignobilium.*
Vicenza, A. S. Vic.
   Estimo 2412 (1453, 1460), 2412A (1477), 2414 (1505).

Primary Sources (Published)

Alberti, Leon Battista. *I libri della famiglia.* Edited by Ruggiero Romano and Alberto Tenenti. Turin: Einaudi, 1969.

Alighieri, Dante. *Il convivio.* Edited by G. Busnelli and G. Vandelli. Florence: Le Monnier, 1964.

Alvarotti, Jacopo. *In libro feudorum clarissima lectura* (or *Super feudis*). Lyon, 1535 (also Venice, 1477).

dall'Aqua, Daniele, ed. *Vocabularius iuris . . . correctus per Danielem ab Aqua vicentini iuris doctorem*. Vicenza, 1482.

Barberino (da), Francesco. *Reggimento e costumi di donna*. Edited by Giuseppe E. Sansone. Turin: Loescher-Chiantore, 1957.

Baretano, Bartolomeo. *Cronica ab anno 1444 usque ad annum 1532*. Vicenza, 1890.

Bartolus of Sassoferrato. *De dignitatibus*. In *Commentaria*, IV. Venice, 1581.

———. *Repertorium in lecturas Bartoli*. Venice, 1557.

Bertrachini, Giovanni. *Repertorium utriusque iuris*. Nuremberg, 1483.

Branca, Vittore, ed. *Mercanti scrittori. Ricordi nella Firenze tra Medioevo e Rinascimento*. Milan: Rusconi, 1986.

Certaldo (da), Paolo. *Libro di buoni costumi*. Edited by Alfredo Schiaffini. Florence: Le Monnier, 1945.

Chellini, Giovanni. *Le ricordanze di Giovanni Chellini di S. Miniato medico mercante e umanista (1425–1457)*. Edited by Maria Teresa Sillano. Milan: Franco Angeli, 1984.

Cherubino da Siena. *Regole delle vita matrimoniale*. Edited by Francesco Zambrini and Carlo Negroni. Reprint, Bologna, 1969.

Cipolla, Bartolomeo. *De imperatore militum diligendo*. Rome, ca. 1475 (copy in Washington, D.C. Library of Congress).

Conversino da Ravenna, Giovanni. *Rationarium vite*. Edited by Vittore Nason. Florence: Olschki, 1986.

Corpus statutorum mercatorum Placentiae (secc. XIV–XVIII). Edited by Piero Castignoli and Pierre Racine. Milan: Giuffrè, 1967.

Cronica ad memoriam praeteriti temporis praesentis atque futuri. Edited by G. Mocenico. Vicenza, 1884.

Cronicha che comenza dell'anno 1400. Edited by Domenico Bortolan. Vicenza, 1889.

Dati, Gregorio. *Il libro segreto di Gregorio Dati*. Edited by Carlo Gargiolli. Bologna: Romagnoli, 1869. Reprint, Bologna: Forni, 1968.

Dominici, Giovanni. *Regola del governo di cura familiare*. Edited by Donato Salvi. Florence: Angiolo Garinei, 1860.

da Feltre, Bernardino. *Sermoni del beato Bernardino Tomitano da Feltre nella redazione di fra Bernardino Bulgarino da Brescia minore osservante*. Edited by P. Carlo Varischi da Milano. Milan: Renon, 1964.

del Garbo, Tommaso. *Consiglio contro a pistolenza*. Edited by Pietro Ferrato. Bologna: G. Romagnoli, 1866.

Godi, Antonio. *Cronaca dall'anno MCXCIV all'anno MCCLX*. Edited by Giovanni Soranzo. Rerum Italicarum Scriptores, 2nd ed., tome VIII, 2. Città di Castello, 1909 (with anon. chronicles *Nobiles familiae quae in civitate nostra extinctae sunt, Familiae potentes in urbe* and *Familiae quae aliunde vicentiam habitatum venerunt* in appendix).

Gregory the Great. *Dialogi*. In Migne, *Patrologiae Latinae 77*.

Ius municipale vicentinum cum additione partium illustrissimi dominii. Venice: Bartolomeo Contrini, 1567.

Landino, Cristoforo. *De vera nobilitate*. Edited by Manfred Letzen. Geneva: Droz, 1970.

Lanfranchini, Cristoforo. *Utrum praeferendus sit doctor an miles*. In *Tractatus illus-*

trium in utraque tam pontificii tam caesarei iuris facultate iurisconsultorum (= *Tractatus universi iuris*), XVIII. Venice, 1584.

da Lecce, Roberto (Caracciolo). *Quaresimale padovano 1455*. Edited by Orianna Visani. Padua: Messaggero, 1983.

Martelli, Ugolino di Niccolò. *Ricordanze dal 1433 al 1483*. Edited by Fulvio Pezzarossa. Rome: Edizioni di Storia e Letteratura, 1989.

Mattiolo, Pietro. *Cronaca bolognese*. Edited by C. Ricci. Bologna, 1885.

del Monte, Pietro. *Repertorium utriusque iuris*. Nuremberg, 1476.

Montemagno (da), Buonaccorso. *De nobilitate*. In *Prosatori latini del Quattrocento*, edited by Eugenio Garin, 141–65. Milan Ricciardi, 1952.

Morelli, Giovanni di Pagolo. *Ricordi*. Edited by Vittore Branca. Florence: Le Monnier, 1956.

Nadi, Gaspare. *Diario bolognese*. Edited by C. Ricci and A. Bacchi della Lega. Bologna, 1886. Reprint, Bologna, 1981.

Niccolini, Lapo. *Libro degli affari proprii di casa*. Edited by Christian Bec. Paris: SEVPEN, 1969.

Nievo, Alessandro. *Consilia*. Venice, 1566.

Omodei, Signorolo. *Utrum praeferendus sit doctor an miles*. In *Tractatus universi iuris*, XVIII. Venice, 1584.

Pagliarini, Battista. *Cronicae*. Edited by James S. Grubb. Padua: Antenore, 1991.

Platea (de), Ioannes. *Super tribus ultimis libris codicis*. Lyon(?), 1537.

Quirini, Lauro. *Tre trattati sulla nobiltà*. In *Lauro Quirini umanista*, Edited by K. Krautter, P. O. Kristeller, and H. Roob. Florence: Olschki, 1977.

Rumor, Sebastiano, ed. *Storia documentata del santuario di Monte Berico*. Vicenza: S. Giuseppe, 1911.

Salutati, Coluccio. *De nobilitate legum et medicinae*. Edited by Eugenio Garin. Florence: Vallecchi, 1947.

Sanuto, Marin. *Itinerario di Marin Sanuto per la terraferma veneziana nell'anno MCCCCLXXXIII*. Edited by Rawdon Brown. Padua: Seminario, 1847.

Sapori, Armando, ed. *I libri degli Alberti Del Giudici*. Milan: A. Garzanti, 1952.

———. *I libri di commercio dei Peruzzi*. Milan: Fratelli Treves, 1934.

———. *Libro giallo della compagnia dei Covoni*. Milan: Cisalpino, 1970.

Sarti, Nicoletta, ed. *Gli statuti della società dei notai di Bologna dell'anno 1336*. Milan: Giuffrè, 1988.

Savonarola, Michele. *Il trattato ginecologico-pediatrico in volgare (Ad mulieres ferrarienses de regimine pregnantium et noviter natorum usque ad septennium)*. Edited by Luigi Belloni. Milan, 1952.

———. *I trattati in volgare della peste e dell'acqua ardente*. Edited by Luigi Belloni. Rome, 1953.

(Soranus of Ephesus). *Soranus' Gynecology*. Translated by Owsei Temkin. Baltimore: Johns Hopkins University Press, 1991.

Statuta notariorum de collegio civitatis Vicentiae. Venice: Joannes Gryphius, 1566.

Statuti del comune di Vicenza MCCLXIV. Edited by Fedele Lampertico. Deputazione veneta di storia patria, *Monumenti storici*, ser. II, *Statuti*, 1. Venice, 1886.

Statutorum magnificae civitatis Veronae libri quinque. Venice: Leonardo Tivano, 1747. (Cited as *Statuti Veronae*.)

Tanaglia, Michelangelo. *De agricultura*. Edited by Aurelio Roncaglia. Bologna: Palmaverde, 1953.

Vegio, Maffeo. *De educatione liberorum et eorum claris moribus libri sex*. Edited by Sister Maria Walburg Fanning (I–III) and Sister Anne Stanislaus Sullivan (IV–VI). Washington, D.C.: The Catholic University of America, 1933–36.

———. *Vocabularia ex iure civili excerpta*. Vicenza: Phillipus Albinus, 1477.

Vocabularius utriusque iuris tam civilis quam canonici. Milan: Ulrich Scinzenzech, 1492. (Also Paris: Petrus de Dru, 1503.)

Secondary Sources

Abbondanza, Roberto, ed. *Il notariato a Perugia*. Rome: Consiglio nazionale del notariato, 1973.

Agresti, Giuliano, et al. *Volto santo*. Lucca: Rugani, 1989.

d'Alatri, Mariano. *Il movimento francescano della penitenza nella società medioevale*. Rome: Istituto Storico dei Cappuccini, 1980.

Alberzoni, Maria Pia, and Onorato Grassi, eds. *La carità a Milano nei secoli XII–XV*. Milan: Jaca Book, 1989.

Albini, Giuliana. "I bambini nella società lombarda del Quattrocento: una realtà ignorata or protetta?" In *La famiglia e la vita quotidiana in Europa dal 400 al 600*, 23–50. Rome, 1986.

———. "Continuità e innovazione: la carità a Milano nel Quattrocento fra tensione private e strategie pubbliche." In *La carità a Milano*, edited by Alberzoni and Grassi, 137–51.

———. *Guerra, fame, peste. Crisi di mortalità e sistema sanitario nella Lombardia tardomedioevale*. Bologna, 1982.

———. "L'infanzia a Milano nel Quattrocento: note sulle registrazioni delle nascite e sugli esposti all'Ospedale Maggiore." *Nuova Rivista Storica* 67, 1–2 (1983): 144–59.

———. "La mortalità in un grande centro urbano nel 400: il caso di Milano." In *Strutture familiari*, edited by Comba et al., 117–34.

Alce, Venturino. "La riforma dell'ordine domenicano nel 400 e nel primo 500 veneto." In *Riforma della chiesa*, 333–43.

Alessio, Franco. "La riflessione sulle 'artes mechanicae.'" In *Lavorare nel Medio Evo*, 257–94. Todi: Accademia Tudertina, 1983.

Alexander, Paul J. "The Diffusion of Byzantine Apocalypses in the Middle Ages and the Beginnings of Joachimism." In *Prophecy and Millenarianism: Essays in Honour of Marjorie Reeves*, edited by Ann Williams, 53–106. London: Longman, 1980.

Allegra, Luciano. *La città verticale: usurai, mercanti e tessitori nella Chieri del Cinquecento*. Milan: Franco Angeli, 1987.

Ambrosoli, Mauro. "L' 'Opus agriculturae' di Palladio: volgarizzamenti e identificazione dell'ambiente naturale fra Tre e Cinquecento." *Quaderni Storici* 52 (1983): 227–54.

Andenna, Giancarlo. "Gli ordini mendicanti, la comunità e la corte sforzesca." In *Metamorfosi di un borgo*, edited by Chittolini, 145–91.

Angiolini, Franco. "I ceti dominanti in Italia tra Medioevo et età moderna: continuità e mutamenti." *Società e Storia* 10 (1980): 909–18.

Anselmi, Sergio. "Insediamenti, agricoltura, proprietà nel ducato roveresco: la cata-stazione del 1489–1490." *Quaderni Storici* 28 (1975): 37–86.

———. "Organizzazione aziendale, colture, rese nelle fattorie malatestiane, 1398–1456." *Quaderni Storici* 39 (1975): 806–27.

———. "Piovi, perticari e buoi da lavoro nell'agricoltura marchigiana del XV secolo." *Quaderni Storici* 31 (1976): 202–28.

Antoniazzi Villa, Anna. "L'attività di prestito in terraferma veneta e negli antichi stati italiani." *Nuova Rivista Storica* 67, 102 (1983): 207–12.

Arasse, Daniel. "Entre devotion et culture: fonctions de l'image religieuse au XVe siecle." In *Faire croire*, 131–46.

Aries, Philippe. *Centuries of Childhood: A Social History of Family Life.* Translated by Robert Baldick: New York: Vintage Books, 1962.

———. "Une conception ancienne de l'au-delà." In *Death in the Middle Ages*, edited by Herman Braet and Werner Verbeke, 78–87. Leuven, 1983.

———. *L'Homme devant la Mort.* Paris: Editions du Seuil, 1977.

———. *Western Attitudes toward Death: From the Middle Ages to the Present.* Baltimore: Johns Hopkins University Press, 1974.

Arnaldi, Girolamo. "Discorso inaugurale." In *Le scuole degli ordini mendicanti (secoli XIII–XIV)*, 9–32. Todi: Accademia Tudertina, 1978.

———. "Il notaio-cronista e le cronache cittadine in Italia." In *La storia del diritto nel quadro delle scienze storiche*, 293–310. Florence: Olschki, 1966.

Arslan, Edoardo. *Catalogo delle cose d'arte e di antichità d'Italia. Vicenza I: Le chiese.* Rome, 1956.

Artigiani e salariati: il mondo del lavoro nell'Italia dei secoli XII–XV. Pistoia: Centro Italiano di Studi e d'Arte, 1984.

Ascheri, Mario. "Arti, mercanti e mercanzie: il caso di Siena." In *Siena nel Rinascimento. Istituzioni e sistema politico.* Siena: Il Leccio, 1985.

Ascheri, Mario, and Donatella Ciampoli, eds. *Siena e il suo territorio nel Rinascimento.* Siena: Il Leccio, 1986.

Ashtor, Eliyahu, "L'exportation de textiles occidentaux dans le Proche Orient musulman au bas Moyen Age (1370–1517)." In *Studi in memoria di Federigo Melis*, 2:303–77.

Aspetti della vita economica medievale: Atti del convegno di studi nel X anniversario della morte di Federigo Melis. Florence: Università degli Studi di Firenze, 1985.

Aubenas, Roger. *Etude sur le notariat provencal.* Aix: Editions du Feu, 1931.

Auzzas, Ginetta. "Una miscellanea ascetica quattrocentesca della Biblioteca Bertoliana di Vicenza (Cod. G.2.8.17)." In *Medioevo e Rinascimento veneto*, edited by Rino Avesani et al., 353–86. Padua: Antenore, 1979.

d'Avach, Pietro. "La *copula perfecta* e la *consummation coniugi* nelle fonti e nelle dottrina canonista classica." *Rivista Italiana per le Scienze Giuridiche* 85 (1949): 163–250.

Avesani, Rino. "Verona nel Quattrocento. La civiltà delle lettere." In *Verona e il suo territorio*, 4, 2. Verona, 1985.

Balletto, Laura. *Battista de Luco mercante genovese del secolo XV e il suo cartolario.* Geneva, 1979.

Bainton, Roland H. *Behold the Christ.* New York: Harper and Row, 1974.

Bairoch, Paul, Jean Batou, and Pierre Chevre. *La population des villes europeennes: banque de données et analyse sommaire des resultats.* Geneva: Droz, 1988.

Balestracci, Duccio. "Le memorie degli altri." In *Cultura e società nell'Italia medievale*, 1:41–58.

———. "Lavoro e povertà in Toscana alla fine del Medioevo." *Studi Storici* 23, 3 (1982): 565–82.

Banchi, Luciano. *L'arte della seta in Siena nei secc. XV e XVI. Statuti e documenti*. Siena, 1881.

Banker, James R. "Death and Christian Charity in the Confraternities of the Upper Tiber Valley." In *Christianity and the Renaissance*, edited by Verdon and Henderson, 302–27.

———. *Death in the Community: Memorialization and Confraternities in an Italian Commune in the Late Middle Ages*. Athens: University of Georgia Press, 1988.

———. "Mourning a Son: Childhood and Paternal Love in the Consolateria of Gianozzo Manetti." *History of Childhood Quarterly* 3, 3 (1976): 351–62.

Barbarano de Mironi, Francesco. *Historia ecclesiastica della città territorio e diocesi di Vicenca*. Vicenza, 1649–1762.

Barbieri, Franco. "L'architettura gotica civile a Vicenza." *Bolletino CISA* 7 (1965): 167–84.

———. "L'immagine urbana dalla rinascenza alla 'età dei lumi.'" In *Storia di Vicenza*, edited by Barbieri and Preto, 3/2: 211–79.

———. "L'ospedale e l'oratorio dei SS. Maria e Cristoforo a S. Marcello; La chiesa di S. Rocco." In *Vicenza Illustrata*, edited by Neri Pozza, 141–45. Vicenza: Neri Pozza, 1976.

———. *Pittori di Vicenza 1480–1520*. Vicenza: Neri Pozza, 1981.

Barbieri, Franco, and Paolo Preto, eds. *Storia di Vicenza*, III, *L'età della repubblica veneta (1404–1797)*. 2 vols. Vicenza: Neri Pozza, 1989.

Barbieri, Gino. "La produzione delle lane italiane dall'età dei comuni al secolo XVIII." *Economia e Storia* 2 (1973): 177–200.

———. "Economia, finanza e tenore di vita nella Verona scaligera." In *Gli Scaligeri*, edited by Varanini, 329–41.

Bardy, G., and A. Tricot, eds. *Enciclopedia cristologica*. Alba: Edizioni Paoline, 1960.

Baron, Hans. "Franciscan Poverty and Civic Wealth as Factors in the Rise of Humanistic Thought." *Speculum* 13, 1 (1938): 1–37.

Barr, Cyrilla. "A Renaissance Artist in the Service of a Singing Confraternity." In *Life and Death in Fifteenth-Century Florence*, edited by Tetel et al., 105–19.

Baschet, Jerome. "Les conceptions de l'enfer en France au XIVe siècle: imaginaire et pouvoir." *Annales E.S.C.* 40, 1 (1985): 185–207.

Battistella, Ruggiero. "Il comune di Treviso e la cavalleria." *Nuovo Archivio Veneto*, n.s., 7 (1904): 273–87; n.s., 8 (1904): 95–127.

Bautier, Robert-Henri. "Feux, population et structure sociale au milieu du XVe siècle: l'exemple de Carpentras." *Annales E.S.C.* 14, 2 (1959): 255–68.

Baxandall, Michael. *Painting and Experience in Fifteenth-Century Italy*. 2nd ed. Oxford: Oxford University Press, 1988.

Beck, Patrick. "Les noms de bapteme en Bourgogne à la fin du Moyen Age." In *Le prenom*, edited by Dupaquier et al., 161–67.

Bellomo, Manlio. *Problemi del diritto familiare nell'età dei comuni*. Milan: Giuffrè, 1968.

———. *Ricerche sui rapporti patrimoniali tra coniugi*. Milan: Giuffrè, 1961.

Belmont, Nicole. "La fonction symbolique du cortege dans les rituels populaires du mariage." *Annales E.S.C.* 33, 3 (1978): 650–55.

———. "Levana: or, How to Raise Up Children." In *Family and Society*, edited by Forster and Ranum, 1–15.

Bennett, Judith M. "The Tie That Binds: Peasant Marriages and Families in Late Medieval England." *Journal of Interdisciplinary History* 15, 1 (1984): 111–29.

———. *Women in the Medieval English Countryside: Gender and Household in Brigstock before the Plague.* New York: Oxford University Press, 1987.

Benvenuti Papi, Anna. "In castro poenitantiae." *Santità e società femminile nell'Italia medievale.* Florence: Olschki, 1990.

———. "La famiglia e le donne nel Rinascimento fiorentino." *Quaderni Storici* 24, 2 (1989): 646–51.

———. *Pastori di popolo: storie e leggende di vescovi e di città nell'Italia medievale.* Florence: Arnaud, 1988.

Berengo, Marino. *Nobili e mercanti nella Lucca del Cinquecento.* Turin: Einaudi, 1965.

———. "Patriziato e nobiltà: il caso veronese." *Rivista Storica Italiana* 87 (1975): 493–517.

Bertalot, Ludwig. "Uno zibaldone umanistico latino del Quattrocento a Parma." In *Studien zum italienischen und deutschen Humanismus*, 241–64. Rome: Edizione di Storia e Letteratura, 1975.

Bertelli, Sergio. *Il potere oligarchico nello stato-città medievale.* Florence: Nuova Italia, 1978.

Besozzi, Leonida. "La 'matricula' delle famiglie nobili di Milano e Carlo Borromeo." *Archivio Storico Lombardo*, ser. II, 1 (1984): 273–330.

Besta, Enrico. *La famiglia nella storia del diritto italiano.* Milan: Giuffrè, 1962.

———. *Le successioni nella storia del diritto italiano.* Reprint, Milan: Giuffrè, 1961.

Betto, Bianca. *I collegi dei notai, dei giudici, dei medici e dei nobili in Treviso (secc. XIII–XVI)*, Deputazione Veneta di Storia Patria, *Miscellanea di studi e memorie* 19. Venice, 1981.

Biget, Jean-Louis, and Jean Tricard. "Livres de raison et demographie familiale en Limousin au XVe siècle." *Annales de Demographie Historique* (1981): 321–63.

Biraben, Jean-Noel. *Les hommes et la peste en France et dans les pays europeens et mediterraneens.* Paris–The Hague: Mouton, 1975.

Biscaro, Gerolamo. "Le temporalità del vescovo di Treviso dal sec. IX al XIII." *Archivio Veneto*, ser. 5, 18 (1936): 1–72.

Bizzocchi, Roberto. "La dissoluzione di un clan familiare: i Buondelmonti di Firenze nei secoli XV e XVI." *Archivio Storico Italiano* 140 (1982): 3–43.

Blanshei, Sarah Rubin. "Population, Wealth and Patronage in Medieval and Renaissance Perugia." *Journal of Interdisciplinary History* 9, 4 (1979): 597–619.

Boase, T. S. R. *Death in the Middle Ages: Mortality, Judgment and Remembrance.* New York: McGraw-Hill, 1972.

Bonanno, Claudio, Metello Bonanno, and Luciana Pellegrini. "I legati 'pro anima' ed il problema della salvezza nei testamenti fiorentini della seconda metà del Trecento." *Ricerche Storiche* 15 (1985): 183–220.

Bonardi, Antonio. *Il lusso di altri tempi in Padova. Studio storico con documenti inediti*, Deputazione veneta di storia patria, *Miscellanea di storia veneta*, ser. 3, 2. Venice, 1910.

Bonney, Francoise. "Jean Gerson: un nouveau regard sur l'enfance." *Annales de demographie historique* (1973): 137–42.

Bordone, Renato. "Tema cittadino e 'ritorno alla terra' nella storiografia comunale recente." *Quaderni Storici* 52 (1983): 255–77.

Borelli, Giorgio. "'Doctor an miles': aspetti della ideologia nobiliare nell'opera del giurista Cristoforo Lanfranchini." *Nuova Rivista Storica* 73, 1–2 (1989): 151–68.

Borghesini, M. *L'arte della lana in Padova durante il governo della Repubblica Di Venezia (1405–1797)*, Deputazione veneta di storia patria, *Miscellanea di studi e memorie*, 10: Venice, 1964.

Bossy, John. "Blood and Baptism: Kinship, Community and Christianity in Western Europe from the Fourteenth to the Seventeenth Centuries." In *Sanctity and Secularity: The Church and the World*, edited by Derek Baker, 124–43. Oxford: Oxford University Press, 1973.

———. "Godparenthood: The Fortunes of a Social Institution in Early Modern Christianity." In *Religion and Society in Early Modern Europe*, edited by Kaspar von Greyerz, 194–201. London: George Allen and Unwin, 1984.

———. "Padrini e madrine: un'istituzione sociale de cristianesimo popolare in occidente." *Quaderni Storici* 40 (1979): 440–49.

Boswell, John. *The Kindness of Strangers: The Abandonment of Children in Western Europe from Late Antiquity to the Renaissance.* New York: Pantheon, 1988.

Bourdieu, Pierre. "Marriage Strategies as Strategies of Social Reproduction." In *Family and Society*, edited by Forster and Ranum, 117–44.

Boutruche, Robert. "Aux origines d'une crise nobiliaire: donations pieuses et pratiques successorales en Bordelais du XIIIe au XVIe siècle." *Annales d'Histoire Sociale* 1 (1939): 161–77, 257–77.

Brandileone, Francesco. "L'intervento dello stato nella celebrazione del matrimonio in Italia prima del Concilio di Trento." Accademia de' Lincei, *Memorie* (1910): 269–390.

———. *Saggi sulla storia della celebrazione del matrimonio in Italia.* Milan: Hoepli, 1906.

———. "Studi preliminari sullo svolgimento storico dei rapporti patrimoniale fra coniugi in Italia." In *Scritti di storia del diritto privato italiano*, edited by Giuseppe Ermini, 1:229–319. Bologna: Nicola Zanichelli, 1931.

———. *Sulla storia e la natura della donatio propter nuptias.* Bologna: Zanichelli, 1892.

Braunstein, Philippe. "L'honneur perdu de Fiorenza dalla Croce." *Annales E.S.C.* 40, 1 (1985): 227–34.

Brogliano d'Ajano, L. "L'industria della seta a Venezia." In *Storia dell'economia italiana*, edited by Carlo M. Cipolla, 1:209–62. Turin, 1959.

Brogliato, Bortolo. *750 anni di presenza francescana nel vicentino.* Vicenza: LIEF, 1982.

Brooke, Christopher N. L. *The Medieval Idea of Marriage.* Oxford: Oxford University Press, 1989.

Brucker, Gene. *The Civic World of Early Renaissance Florence.* Princeton: Princeton University Press, 1977.

———. *Giovanni and Lusanna: Love and Marriage in Renaissance Florence.* Berkeley: University of California Press, 1986.

———. "Monasteries, Friaries, and Nunneries in Quattrocento Florence." In *Christianity and the Renaissance*, edited by Verdon and Henderson, 41–62.

———. "Religious Sensibilities in Early Modern Europe: Examples from the Records of the Holy Penitentiary." *Historical Reflections/Reflexions Historiques* 15, 1 (1988): 13–25.

———. "Urban Parishes and Their Clergy in Quattrocento Florence: A Preliminary 'Sondage.'" *Renaissance Studies in Honor of Craig Hugh Smyth,* 1:17–27. Florence: Giunti Barbera, 1985.

Brucker, Gene, ed. *The Society of Renaissance Florence: A Documentary Study.* New York: Harper and Row, 1971.

Brugnoli, Pierpaolo. "Un aspetto delle controversie fra clero e città nella Verona del secolo decimoquinto." *Aevum* 39 (1965): 357–69.

Brundage, James A. *Law, Sex, and Christian Society in Medieval Europe.* Chicago: University of Chicago Press, 1987.

Brunello, Franco. *Arti e mestieri a Venezia nel Medioevo e nel Rinascimento.* Vicenza: Neri Pozza, 1981.

———. "Arti e mestieri, corporazioni artigiane, arte della lana, arte della seta." In *Storia di Vicenza,* edited by Barbieri and Preto, 3/1:273–300.

Bullough, D. A. "Early Medieval Social Groupings: The Terminology of Kinship." *Past and Present* 45 (1969): 3–18.

Bullough, Vern L., and James A. Brundage. *Sexual Practices and the Medieval Church.* Buffalo, N.Y., 1982.

Burguière, Andre. "Prenoms et parenté." In *Le prenom,* edited by Dupaquier et al., 29–35.

———. "Le rituel du mariage en France: pratiques ecclesiastiques et pratiques populaires (XVI–XVIII siècle)." *Annales E.S.C.* 33, 3 (1978): 637–49.

Burke, Peter. "Death in the Renaissance, 1347–1656." In *Dies illa: Death in the Middle Ages,* edited by Jane H. M. Taylor, 59–65. Liverpool: Francis Cairns, 1984.

Burns, Howard. "Le opere minori del Palladio." *Bolletino CISA* 21 (1979): 9–34.

Caciorgna, Maria Teresa. "Vite e vino a Velletri alla fine del Trecento." In *Cultura e società nell'Italia medievale,* 1:157–70.

Caliaro, Espedito. "Il prestito ad interesse a Vicenza tra XII e XIII secolo (1184–1222)." *Studi Storici Luigi Simeoni* 33 (1983): 103–20.

Calleri, Luigi. *L'arte dei giudici e notai a Firenze nell'età comunale e nel suo statuto del 1344.* Milan, 1966.

Cammarosano, Paolo. "Aspetti delle strutture familiari nelle città dell'Italia comunale (secoli XII–XIV)." *Studi Medievali,* ser. 3, 16 (1975): 417–35.

———. *Le compagne nell'età comunale.* Turin: Loescher, 1974.

———. "Le campagne senesi dalla fine del secolo XII agli inizi del Trecento: dinamica interna e forme del dominio cittadino." In *Contadini e proprietari nella Toscana moderna,* 153–222.

Cammarosano, Paolo, ed. *Le campagne friulane nel tardo medioevo.* Udine: Casamassima, 1985.

Carile, Antonio, *La cronachistica veneziana (secoli XIII–XVI) di fronte alla spartizione della Romania nel 1204.* Florence: Olschki, 1969.

Cariota-Ferrara, Luigi. *L'enfiteusi.* Turin: UTET, 1951.

Carmichael, Ann G. "Contagion Theory and Contagion Practice in Fifteenth-Century Milan." *Renaissance Quarterly* 44, 2 (1991): 213–56.

———. "The Health Status of Florentines in the Fifteenth Century." In *Life and Death in Fifteenth-Century Florence,* edited by Tetel et al., 28–45.

————. *Plague and the Poor in Renaissance Florence.* Cambridge: Cambridge University Press, 1986.

————. "Plague Legislation in the Italian Renaissance." *Bulletin of the History of Medicine* 57 (1984): 508–25.

Caro, Anna. "Per la storia della società milanese: i corredi nuziali nell'ultima età viscontea e nel periodo della repubblica ambrosiana (1433–1450), dagli atti del notaio Protaso Sansoni." *Nuova Rivista Storica* 65 (1981): 521–50.

Carron, Roland. *Enfant et parenté dans la France medievale (XIe–XIIIe siècles).* Geneva: Droz, 1989.

Castellazzi, Laura. "Il testamento di Spinetta Malaspina e la fondazione dell'ospedale per i nobili poveri a S. Giovanni in Sacco." In *Gli Scaligeri,* edited by Varanini, 441–45.

Cazzola, Franco. "Produzione agricola e rendimenti unitari dei cereali nel Ferrarese a metà Quattrocento: la castalderia di Casaglia (1451–1459)." In *Studi in memoria di Luigi Dal Pane,* 239–300. Bologna: CLEUB, 1982.

Cecchetti, Bartolomeo. "La donna nel Medioevo a Venezia." *Archivio Veneto* 31 (1886): 33–69, 307–45.

Cenci, Cesare. "Senato veneto: 'probae' ai benefizi ecclesiastici." In *Promozioni agli ordini sacri a Bologna e alle dignità ecclesiastiche nel Veneto nei secoli XIV–XV,* edited by Celestino Piana and Cesare Cenci, 311–454. Quaracchi: Collegio San Bonaventura, 1968.

Cessi, Roberto. "Per la storia delle corporazioni dei mercanti di panni e della lana in Padova nei secoli XIII e XIV," and "Un privilegio dell'arte dei drappieri in Padova." In *Padova medioevale: studi e documenti,* edited by Donato Gallo, 1:299–304, 305–17. Padua: Erredici, 1985.

Cevese, Renato. "L'architettura vicentina del primo rinascimento." *Bolletino CISA* (1964): 199–213.

————. *Ville della provincia di Vicenza.* 2nd ed. Milan: Rusconi, 1980.

————. *Ville vicentine.* Milan: Domus, 1957.

Chartier, Roger. "Les arts de mourir, 1450–1600." *Annales E.S.C.* 31, 1 (1976): 51–75.

Chaunu, Pierre. "Mourir à Paris (XVIe–XVIIe–XVIIIe siècles)." *Annales E.S.C.* 31, 1 (1976): 29–50.

Cherubini, Giovanni. "Artigiani e salariati nelle città italiane del tardo Medioevo." In *Aspetti della vita economica medievale,* 707–27.

————. "Le campagne italiane dall'XI al XV secolo." In *Storia d'Italia,* edited by Giuseppe Galasso, 265–448. Turin: UTET, 1981.

————. *L'Italia rurale del basso Medioevo.* Bari: Laterza, 1985.

————. "I lavoratori nell'Italia dei secoli XIII–XV: considerazioni storiografiche e prospettive di ricerca." In *Artigiani e salariati,* 1–26.

————. "La mezzadria toscana delle origini." In *Contadini e proprietari nella Toscana moderna,* 131–52.

————. "Il mondo contadino nella novellistica italiana dei secoli XIV e XV. Una novella di Gentile Sermini." In *Medioevo rurale. Sulle tracce della civiltà contadina,* edited by Vito Fumagalli and Gabriella Rossetti, 417–35. Bologna: Mulino, 1980.

————. "Qualche considerazioni sulle campagne dell'Italia centro-settentrionale (XI–XV)." *Rivista Storica Italiana* 79, 1 (1967): 111–57.

————. "La proprietà fondiaria nei secoli XV–XVI nella storiografia italiana." *Società e Storia* 1 (1978): 9–33.

————. *Signori contadini borghesi: ricerche sulla società italiana del basso medioevo.* Florence: La Nuova Italia, 1974.

Cherubini, Giovanni, and Riccardo Francovich. "Forme e vicende degli insediamenti nella campagna toscana dei secoli XIII–XV." *Quaderni Storici* 8, 3 (1973): 877–904.

Chiappa Mauri, Luisa. "A proposito di due recenti pubblicazioni sulle campagne toscane nel tardo Medio Evo." *Società e Storia* 19 (1983): 121–28.

————. "Linee di tendenza nell'agricoltura lodigiana dei secoli XV e XVI: la possessione di Valera Fratta." *Società e Storia* 25 (1984): 517–38.

————. "Riflessioni sulle campagne lombarde del Quattro-Cinquecento." *Nuova Rivista Storica* 69 (1985): 123–30.

————. "Le trasformazioni nell'area lombarda." In *Le Italie del tardo Medioevo*, edited by Sergio Gensini, 409–32. Pisa: Pacini, 1990.

Chiffoleau, Jacques. "Ce qui fait changer la mort dans la region d'Avignon à la fin du Moyen Age." In *Death in the Middle Ages*, edited by Herman Braet and Werner Verbeke, 117–33. Leuven: Leuven University Press, 1983. (Italian translation in *Quaderni Storici* 50 [1982]: 449–63.)

————. *La comptibilité de l'audelà. Les hommes, la mort e la religion dans la region d'Avignon à la fin du Moyen Age (vers 1320–vers 1480).* Rome: Ècole Francaise de Rome, 1980.

————. "Sur l'usage obsessionnel de la messe pour les morts à la fin du Moyen Age." In *Faire croire*, 236–56.

Chittolini, Giorgio. "Alle origini delle 'grandi aziende' della bassa lombarda." *Quaderni Storici* 13 (1978): 828–44.

————. "Avvicendamenti e paesaggio agrario nella pianura irrigua lombarda (secoli XV–XVI)." In *Agricoltura e trasformazione dell'ambiente (secoli XIII–XVIII)*, edited by Annalisa Guarducci, 555–66. Florence: Le Monnier, 1984.

————. "Stati regionali e istituzioni ecclesiastiche nell'Italia centrosettentrionale del Quattrocento." In *Storia d'Italia, Annali* 9, edited by Giorgio Chittolini and Giovanni Miccoli, 147–93. Turin: Einaudi, 1986.

Chittolini, Giorgio, ed. *Metamorfosi di un borgo. Vigevano in età visconto-sforzesca.* Milan: Franco Angeli, 1992.

Chojnacki, Stanley. "Dowries and Kinsmen in Early Renaissance Venice." *Journal of Interdisciplinary History* 5, 4 (1975): 571–600.

————. "Marriage Legislation and Patrician Society in Fifteenth-Century Venice." In *Law, Custom and the Social Fabric in Medieval Europe*, edited by Bernard S. Bachrach and David Nicholas, 163–84. Kalamazoo: Medieval Institute, 1990.

————. "Measuring Adulthood: Adolescence and Gender in Renaissance Venice." *Journal of Family History* 17, 4 (1992): 371–95.

————. "'The Most Serious Duty.' Motherhood, Gender, and Patrician Culture in Renaissance Venice." In *Refiguring Woman: Perspectives on Gender and the Italian Renaissance*, edited by Marilyn Migiel and Juliana Schiesari, 133–54. Ithaca: Cornell University Press, 1991.

————. "Patrician Women in Early Reinassance Venice." *Studies in the Renaissance* 21 (1974): 176–203.

————. "The Power of Love: Wives and Husbands in Late Medieval Venice." In *Women and Power in the Middle Ages*, edited by Mary Erler and Maryanne Kowaleski, 126–48. Athens: University of Georgia Press, 1988.

————. "Subaltern Patriarchs: Patrician Bachelors in Renaissance Venice." In *Medieval Masculinities: Regarding Men in the Middle Ages*, edited by Clare A. Lees, 73–90. Minneapolis: University of Minnesota Press, 1994.

Christian, William A. *Apparitions in Late Medieval and Renaissance Spain*. Princeton: Princeton University Press, 1981.

Cipolla, Carlo. "Libri e mobili di casa Aleardi al principio del sec. XV." *Archivio Veneto* 24 (1882): 28–53.

————. "La relazione di Giorgio Sommariva sullo stato di Verona e del veronese (1478)." *Nuovo Archivio Veneto* 6 (1893): 161–214.

Cipolla, Carlo M. *Public Health and the Medical Profession in the Renaissance*. Cambridge: Cambridge University Press, 1976.

Cohen, Elizabeth S. "Honor and Gender in the Streets of Early Modern Rome." *Journal of Interdisciplinary History* 22, 4 (1992): 597–625.

Cohn, Samuel K., Jr. *The Cult of Remembrance and the Black Death: Six Renaissance Cities in Central Italy*. Baltimore: Johns Hopkins University Press, 1992.

————. *Death and Property in Siena, 1205–1800: Strategies for the Afterlife*. Baltimore: Johns Hopkins University Press, 1988.

————. *The Laboring Classes in Renaissance Florence*. New York: Academic Press, 1980.

Cole, Bruce. *Italian Art 1250–1550: The Relation of Renaissance Art to Life and Society*. New York: Harper and Row, 1987.

Colla, Angelo. "Tipografi, editori e librai." In *Storia di Vicenza*, edited by Barbieri and Preto, 3/2:109–62.

Collodo, Silvana. "Artigiani e salariati a Padova verso la metà del Quattrocento: il maestro cartaro Nicolò di Antonio da Fabriano." *Critica Storica* 13, 3 (1976): 408–28.

————. "Il convento di S. Francesco e l'osservanza francescana a Padova nel '400." In *Riforma della chiesa*, 359–69.

————. "Credito, movimento della proprietà fondiaria e selezione sociale a Padova nel Trecento." *Archivio Storico Italiano* 141, 1 (1983): 3–71.

————. "Note per lo studio della popolazione e della società di Padova nel Quattrocento." In *Viridarium floridum: Studi di storia veneta offerti dagli allievi a Paolo Sambin*, edited by Maria Chiara Billanovich, Giorgio Cracco, and Antonio Rigon, 159–89. Padua: Antenore, 1984.

Comba, Rinaldo. *Contadini, signori e mercanti nel Piemonte medievale*. Rome: Laterza, 1988.

————. "Le origini medievali dall'assetto insediativo moderno nelle campagne italiane." In *Storia d'Italia*, Annali 8: 369–414. Turin: Einaudi, 1985.

Comba, Rinaldo, Gabriella Piccini, and Giuliano Pinto, eds. *Strutture familiari, epidemie, migrazioni nell'Italia medievale*. Naples: Edizione Scientifiche, 1984.

Condini, Luca. "Un sondaggio fra i testamenti milanesi del secondo Quattrocento." *Archivio Storico Lombardo*, ser. 11, 8 (1991): 367–89.

Contadini e proprietari nella Toscana moderna, vol. 1, *Dal Medioevo all'età moderna*. Florence: Olschki, 1979.

Corazzol, Gigi. *Fitti e livelli a grano. Un aspetto del credito rurale nel Veneto del '500*. Milan: Franco Angeli, 1979.

————. "Interessi in natura e interessi in denari a Venezia nel secondo Cinquecento." *Società e Storia* 27 (1985): 185–89.

———. "Prestatori e contadini nella campagna feltrina intorno alla prima metà del '500." *Quaderni Storici* 26 (1974): 445–500.

———. "Sulla diffusione dei livelli a frumento tra il patriziato veneziano nella seconda metà del '500." *Studi Veneziani,* n.s., 6 (1982): 103–27.

Corazzol, Gigi, and Loredana Corrà. *Esperimenti d'amore. Fatti di giovani nel Veneto del Cinquecento.* Vicenza: Odeonlibri, 1981.

Corblet, Jules. *Histoire dogmatique, liturgique et archeologique du sacrement de bapteme.* Paris, 1882.

Corradi, Alfonso. *Annali delle epidemie occorse in Italia dalle prime memorie fino al 1850,* I. Bologna: Gamberini e Parmeggiani, 1865.

Corti, Gino, and J.-Gentil da Silva. "Note sur la production de la soie à Florence au XVe siècle." *Annales E.S.C.* 20 (1965): 309–11.

Costamagna, G. *Il notaio a Genova tra prestigio e potere.* Rome, 1970.

Crabb, Ann Morton. "How Typical Was Alessandra Macinghi Strozzi of Fifteenth-Century Florentine Widows?" In *Upon My Husband's Death,* edited by Mirrer, 47–68.

Cracco, Giorgio. "Il periodo vicentino di S. Lorenzo Giustiniani." *Odeo Olimpico* 17–18 (1981–82): 29–32.

———. "Des saints aux sanctuaires: hypothese d'une evolution en terre venetienne." In *Faire croire,* 279–97. (Translated as "Dai santi ai santuari: un'ipotesi di evoluzione in ambito veneto." In *Studi sul medioevo veneto,* edited by Giorgio Cracco, Andrea Castagnetti, and Silvana Collodo, 25–42. Turin, 1981.)

Cristiani, Emilio. *Nobiltà e popolo nel comune di Pisa. Dalle origini del podestariato alla signoria dei Donoratico.* Naples, 1962.

———. "Sul valore politico del cavalierato nella Firenze dei secoli XIII e XIV." *Studi Medievali,* ser. 3, 3 (1962): 365–71.

Cristofoletti, Luigi. "Cenni storici sull'antico collegio dei notari della città di Verona (1220–1806)." *Archivio Veneto* 16 (1878): 325–39; 18 (1879): 70–108.

Crouzet-Pavan, Elisabeth. "Un fiore del male: i giovani nelle società urbane italiana (secoli XIV–XV)." In *Storia dei giovani,* edited by Giovanni Levi and Jean-Claude Schmitt, 1:211–77. Rome: Laterza, 1992.

———. *'Sopre le acque salse.' Espaces, pouvoir et societé à Venise à la fin du Moyen Age.* Rome: Ecole Francaise de Rome, 1992.

Cultura e società nell'Italia medievale: Studi per Paolo Brezzi. Rome: Istituto Storico Italiano per il Medio Evo, 1988.

Dauvillier, J. *Le mariage dans le droit classique de l'Eglise depuis le Decret de Gratian (1140) jusqu'à la mort de Clement V (1314).* Paris, 1933.

Day, John. "The Decline of a Money Economy: Sardinia in the Late Middle Ages." In *Studi in memoria di Federigo Melis,* 3:155–76.

———. *The Medieval Market Economy.* Oxford: Basil Blackwell, 1987.

Dean, Trevor. *Land and Power in Late Medieval Ferrara: The Rule of the Este, 1350–1450.* Cambridge: Cambridge University Press, 1988.

Delumeau, Jean. *Le peché e la peur: la culpabilisation en Occident (XIIIe–XVIIIe siècles).* Paris: Fayard, 1983.

———. *La peur en Occident en Occident, XIVe–XVIIe siècles: une cité assiegée.* Paris: Fayard, 1978.

Denley, Peter, and Caroline Elam, eds. *Florence and Italy: Renaissance Studies in Honour of Nicolai Rubinstein*. London: Westfield College, 1988.

Desplanques, Henri. *Campagnes ombriennes. Contribution à l'étude des paysages ruraux en Italie centrale*. Paris: Colin, 1969.

———. "Le case della mezzadria." In *La casa rurale in Italia*, edited by Giuseppe Barbieri and Lucio Gambi, 189–216. Florence: Olschki, 1970.

Dianin, Gian Maria. *San Bernardino da Siena a Verona e nel Veneto*. Verona: San Bernardino, 1981.

Dini, Bruno. "L'industria tessile italiana nel tardo Medioevo." In *Le Italie del tardo Medioevo*, edited by Sergio Gensini, 321–59. Pisa: Pacini, 1990.

———. "I lavoratori dell'arte della lana a Firenze nel XIV e XV secolo." In *Artigiani e salariati*, 27–68.

Donahue, Charles, Jr. "The Canon Law on the Formation of Marriage and Social Practice in the Later Middle Ages." *Journal of Family History* 8 (1983): 144–55.

Donati, Claudio. *L'idea di nobiltà in Italia (secoli XIV–XVIII)*. Bari: Laterza, 1988.

Dormeir, Heinrich. "Nuovi culti di santi intorno al 1500 nelle citta' della Germania meridionale. Circostanze religiose, sociale e materiale della loro introduzione e affermazione." In *Strutture ecclesiastiche in Italia e in Germania prima della Riforma*, edited by Paolo Prodi and Peter Johanek, 317–52. Bologna: Il Mulino, 1984.

Duby, Georges. *The Knight, the Lady and the Priest: The Making of Modern Marriage in Medieval France*. New York: Pantheon, 1983.

———. *Medieval Marriage: Two Models from Twelfth-Century France*. Baltimore: Johns Hopkins University Press, 1978.

Dupaquier, Jacques, Alain Bideau, and Marie-Elizabeth Ducreux, eds. *Le prenom. Mode et histoire*. Paris: Ecole des Hautes Etudes en Sciences Sociales, 1980.

Dyer, Christopher. *Standards of Living in the Later Middle Ages: Social Change in England ca. 1200–1520*. Cambridge: Cambridge University Press, 1989.

Edgerton, Samuel Y., Jr. *Pictures and Punishment: Art and Criminal Prosecution during the Florentine Renaissance*. Ithaca: Cornell University Press, 1985.

Edler de Roover, Florence. "Andrea Banchi, Florentine Silk Manufacturer and Merchant in the Fifteenth Century." *Studies in Medieval and Renaissance History* 3 (1966): 221–86.

Ell, Stephen R. "Iron in Two Seventeenth-Century Plague Epidemics." *Journal of Interdisciplinary History* 15, 3 (1985): 445–57.

Elliott, Dyan. *Spiritual Marriage: Sexual Abstinence in Medieval Wedlock*. Princeton: Princeton University Press, 1993.

Epstein, S. R. "Cities, Regions and the Late Medieval Crisis: Sicily and Tuscany Compared." *Past and Present* 130 (1991): 3–50.

———. "Regional Fairs, Institutional Innovation and Economic Growth in Late Medieval Europe." *Working Papers in Economic History* 11 (1992): 1–38.

Epstein, Steven. *Wills and Wealth in Medieval Genoa, 1150–1250*. Cambridge: Harvard University Press, 1984.

Ercole, Francesco. "L'istituto dotale nella pratica e nella legislazione statutaria dell'Italia superiore." *Rivista italiana per le scienze giuridiche* 45 (1908): 191–302; 46 (1910): 167–257.

————. "Vicende storiche della dote romana nella pratica medievale dell'Italia superiore." *Archivio Giuridico* 80–81 (1908): 34–148.

Esmein, A. *Le mariage en droit canonique.* Paris, 1891. Reprint, New York: Burt Franklin, 1968.

Esposito, Anna. "Lo stereotipo dell'omicidio rituale nei processi tridentini e il culto del 'beato' Simone." In *Processi contro gli ebrei di Trento (1475–1478),* edited by Anna Esposito and Diego Quaglioni, 53–95. Padua: CEDAM, 1990.

Esposito Aliano, Anna. "Famiglia, mercanzia e libri nel testamento di Andrea Santacroce (1471)." In *Aspetti della vita economica e culturale a Roma nel Quattrocento,* 195–220. Rome: Istituto di Studi Romani, 1981.

Fabbri, Lorenzo. *Alleanza matrimoniale e patriziato nella Firenze del '400. Studio sulla famiglia Strozzi.* Florence: Olschki, 1991.

Fabbri, Renata. *Per la memorialistica veneziana in latino del Quattrocento.* Padua: Antenore, 1988.

Faccioli, Giovanni Tomasso. *Catalogo regionato de' libri stampati in Vicenza e suo territorio nel secolo XV.* Vicenza, 1796.

Faire croire: modalités de la diffusion e de la reception des messages religieux du XIIe au XVe siècle. Rome: École Francaise de Rome, 1981.

Falco, Mario. *Le disposizioni 'pro anima'. Fondamenti dottrinali e forme giuridiche.* Turin: Bocca, 1911.

Fasoli, Gina. "Il notaio nella vita cittadina bolognese (secc. XII–XV)." In *Notariato medievale bolognese,* 2:121–42. Rome: Consiglio nazionale del notariato, 1977.

————. "Per la storia di Vicenza dal IX al XII secolo: Conti, vescovi, vescovi conti." *Archivio Veneto,* ser. 5, 36–41 (1945–47): 208–42.

Fasoli, Sara. "Alcune note" to Chiffoleau, *La comptabilité de l'audelà. Nuova Rivista Storica* 69 (1985): 120–22.

Fasolo, Giulio. *Le ville del vicentino.* Vicenza, 1929.

Febvre, Lucien. "Man or Productivity." In *Rural Society in France: Selections from the Annales E.S.C.,* edited by Robert Forster and Orest Ranum, 1–5. Baltimore: Johns Hopkins University Press, 1977.

Ferrari, Ciro. "La Campagna di Verona all'epoca veneziana." In Deputazione di Storia Patria per le Venezie, *Miscellanae di Storia Veneta,* ser. 4, 4 (1930).

Ferraro, Joanne M. *Family and Public Life in Brescia, 1580–1650. The Foundations of Power in the Venetian State.* Cambridge: Cambridge University Press, 1993.

Fildes, Valerie A. *Breasts, Bottles and Babies: A History of Infant Feeding.* Edinburgh: Edinburgh University Press, 1986.

————. *Wet Nursing: A History from Antiquity to the Present.* Oxford: Basil Blackwell, 1988.

Fine, Agnes. "L'heritage du nom de bapteme." *Annales E.S.C.* 42, 4 (1987): 853–77.

Finlay, Robert. *Politics in Renaissance Venice.* New Brunswick: Rutgers University Press, 1980.

Finucane, Ronald C. *Miracles and Pilgrims: Popular Beliefs in Medieval England.* Totowa: Rowman and Littlefield, 1977.

Fiumi, Enrico. *Storia economica e sociale di S. Gimignano.* Florence: Olschki, 1961.

Flandrin, Jean-Louis. "L'attitude à l'egard du petit enfant et les conduites sexuelles dans la civilisation occidentale: structures anciennes et evolution." *Annales du demographie historique* (1973): 143–210.

Flint, Valerie I. J. *The Rise of Magic in Early Medieval Europe.* Princeton: Princeton University Press, 1991.

Fornasari, Massimo. "Economia e credito a Bologna nel Quattrocento: la fondazione del Monte di Pieta'." *Società e Storia* 61 (1993): 475–502.

Forni, Alberto. "La 'nouvelle predication' des disciples de Fouques de Neuilly: intentions, techniques et reactions." In *Faire croire*, 19–37.

Franceschi, Franco. "La memoire des *laboratores* à Florence au debut du XVe siècle." *Annales E.S.C.* 45, 5 (1990): 1143–68.

———. *Oltre il "Tumulto." I lavoratori fiorentini dell'Arte della Lana fra Tre e Quattrocento.* Florence: Olschki, 1993.

Franzina, Emilio. *Vicenza. Storia di una città.* Vicenza: Neri Pozza, 1980.

Frati, Ludovico. "Un notaio poeta bolognese del Quattrocento." *La Rassegna Nazionale* 25, 130 (1903): 26–43.

———. "Ricordanze domestiche di notai bolognesi." *Archivio Storico Italiano* 41 (1908): 371–83.

Frugoni, Chiara. "Una proposta per il Volto Santo." In *Il Volto Santo, storia e culto,* edited by Clara Baracchini and Maria Teresa Filieri, 15–48. Lucca, 1982.

Fumagalli, Camillo. *Il diritto di fraterna nella giurisprudenza da Accursio alla codificazione.* Turin: Bocca, 1912.

Fumagalli, Vito. "Il paesaggio dei morti: luoghi d'incontro tra i morti e i vivi sulla terra nel medioevo." *Quaderni Storici* 50 (1982): 411–25.

Garin, Eugenio. *La filosofia.* Milan: Vallardi, 1947.

———. *L'umanesimo italiano.* Bari: Laterza, 1965.

Garin, Eugenio, ed. *La disputa delle arti nel Quattrocento.* Florence: Valsecchi, 1947.

Gatto, Giuseppe. "Le voyage au paradis. La christianisation des traditions folkloriques au Moyen Age." *Annales E.S.C.* 34, 5 (1979): 929–42.

Gaudemet, Jean. *Le mariage en Occident. Les moeurs et le droit.* Paris: Cerf, 1987.

Gavitt, Philip. *Charity and Children in Renaissance Florence: The Ospedale degli Innocenti, 1410–1536.* Ann Arbor: University of Michigan Press, 1990.

Giacomuzzi, Luciano. *Influsso francescano su vita cristiana e pensiero spirituale.* Vicenza, 1982.

———. *Vita cristiana e pensiero spirituale a Vicenza dal 1400 al 1600.* Rome, 1972.

Giardina, Camillo. "*Advocatus* e *mundoaldus* nel Veneto e nella Val d'Aosta." In *Studi in onore di Amintore Fanfani*, 1:317–25.

Ginatempo, Maria. *Crisi di un territorio: il popolamento della Toscana senese alla fine del Medioevo.* Florence: Olschki, 1988.

Ginatempo, Maria, and Lucia Sandri. *L'Italia delle città: il popolamento urbano tra Medioevo e Rinascimento (secoli XIII–XVI).* Florence: Le Lettere, 1990.

Giorgetti, Giovanni. "Contratti agrari e rapporti sociali nelle campagne." In *Storia d'Italia*, 5:701–60. Turin: Einaudi, 1973.

Gios, Pierantonio. "Aspetti di vita religiosa e sociale a Padova durante l'episcopato di Fantino Dandolo (1448–1456)." In *Riforma della chiesa*, 161–204.

Giuliani Bossetti, Alda. "La trasformazione aristocratica dei consigli di Verona durante il dominio veneziano." *Studi Storici Veronesi* 3 (1951–52): 41–59.

Giuliari, Giambattista. *Della letteratura veronese al cadere del secolo XV.* Bologna: Fava et Garagnani, 1876.

Goffen, Rona. *Piety and Patronage in Renaissance Venice: Bellini, Titian and the Franciscans.* New Haven: Yale University Press, 1986.

Goldthwaite, Richard A. *The Building of Renaissance Florence.* Baltimore: Johns Hopkins University Press, 1980.

———. "The Medici Bank and the World of Florentine Capitalism." *Past and Present* 114 (1987): 3–31.

———. "Organizzazione economica e struttura famigliare." In *I ceti dirigenti nella Toscana tardo comunale, 1–13.* Florence: Francesco Papafava, 1983.

———. "I prezzi del grano a Firenze dal XIV al XVI secolo." *Quaderni Storici* 10 (1975): 5–36.

———. *Private Wealth in Renaissance Florence: A Study of Four Families.* Princeton: Princeton University Press, 1968.

———. "The Renaissance Economy: The Preconditions for Luxury Consumption." In *Aspetti della vita economica medievale,* 659–75.

Gonon, Marguerite. *Les institutions et la societé en Forez au XIVe siècle d'apres les testaments.* Forez: Association des Chartes, 1960.

Goodich, Michael. "*Ancilla Dei:* The Servant as Saint in the Late Middle Ages." In *Women of the Medieval World: Essays in Honor of John H. Mundy,* edited by Julius Kirshner and Suzanne F. Wemple, 119–36. Oxford: Basil Blackwell, 1985.

———. "Bartholomaeus Anglicus on Child-Rearing." *History of Childhood Quarterly* 3, 1 (1975): 75–84.

———. *From Birth to Old Age: The Human Life Cycle in Medieval Thought, 1250–1350.* Lanham, Md.: University Press of America, 1989.

Goody, Jack. *The Development of the Family and Marriage in Europe.* Cambridge: Cambridge University Press, 1983.

Goody, John R., and S. J. Tambiah. *Bridewealth and Dowry.* Cambridge: Harvard University Press, 1973.

Gottfried, Robert S. *The Black Death: Natural and Human Disaster in Medieval Europe.* New York: Free Press, 1983.

———. *Epidemic Disease in Fifteenth Century England.* New Brunswick: Rutgers University Press, 1978.

Grattan, J. H. G., and Charles Singer. *Anglo-Saxon Magic and Medicine.* Oxford: Oxford University Press, 1952.

Greci, Roberto. "Forme di organizzazione del lavoro nelle città italiane tra età comunale e signorie." In *Le città in Italia e Germania nel Medio Evo: cultura, istituzioni, vita religiosa,* edited by R. Elze and Gina Fasoli, 81–117. Trent, 1981.

———. "Proprietà immobiliari, mobiltà, carriere di una famiglia parmense del tardo medioevo: gli Arcimboldi." *Quaderni Storici* 67 (1988): 9–36.

———. "Una proprietà laica del parmense nella prima metà del Quattrocento: i beni di Pierto Rossi in Basilicanova e Mamiano." *Nuova Rivista Storica* 66, 102 (1982): 1–36.

Grendi, Edoardo. "La società dei giovani a Genova fra il 1460 e la riforma del 1528." *Quaderni Storici* 80 (1992): 509–28.

Grimaldi, Floriano. *Loreto: basilica, Santa Casa.* Bologna: Calderini, 1975.

Grohmann, Alberto. *Città e territorio tra medioevo ed età moderna (Perugia, secc. XIII–XVI)*. Perugia: Volumnia, 1981.

———. "Spazio urbano e struttura economica a Perugia nel sec. XV." In *Aspetti della vita economica medievale*, 606–23.

Grossi, Paolo. *Locatio ad longum tempus*. Naples: Morano, 1963.

Grubb, James S. *Firstborn of Venice: Vicenza in the Early Renaissance State*. Baltimore: Johns Hopkins University Press, 1988.

———. "Il Mondo di Lisiera nel Quattrocento." in *Lisiera: storia e cultura di una comunità veneta*, edited by Claudio Povolo, 75–124. Vicenza, 1982.

———. "Patriciate and *Estimo* in Quattrocento Vicenza." In *Il sistema fiscale veneto: problemi e aspetti (XV–XVIII secolo)*, edited by Giorgio Borelli, Paola Lanaro, and Francesco Vecchiato, 147–73. Verona: Libreria Editrice Universitaria, 1982.

———. "Patrimonio, feudo e giurisdizione: la signoria dei Monza a Dueville nel secolo XV." In *Dueville: storia e identificazione di una comunità del passato*, edited by Claudio Povolo, 253–306. Vicenza: Neri Pozza, 1985.

———. "Alla ricerca delle prerogative locali: la cittadinanza a Vicenza, 1404–1509." *Civis: Studi e Testi* 8, 24 (1984): 177–92.

Guarducci, P., and V. Ottanelli. *I servitori domestici della casa borghese toscana nel basso Medio Evo*. Florence: Olschki, 1982.

Guerreau-Jalabert, Anita. "Sur les structures de parenté dans l'Europe medievale." *Annales E.S.C.* 36, 6 (1981): 1028–49.

Guidoboni, Emanuela. "Terre, villaggi e famiglie del Polesine di Casaglia fra XV e XVI secolo." *Società e Storia* 14 (1981): 791–847.

Gurevich, Aaron J. "Au Moyen Age: Conscience individuelle et image de l'au-delà." *Annales E.S.C.* 37, 2 (1982): 255–75.

Hajnal, J. "European Marriage Patterns in Perspective." In *Population in History: Essays in Historical Demography*, edited by D. V. Glass and D. E. C. Eversley, 101–43. London: Edward Arnold, 1965.

Hanawalt, Barbara A. *The Ties That Bound: Peasant Families in Medieval England*. New York: Oxford University Press, 1986.

Harvey, P. D. A. *The Peasant Land Market in Medieval England*. Oxford: Oxford University Press, 1984.

Hay, Denys. *The Church in Italy in the Fifteenth Century*. Cambridge: Cambridge University Press, 1977.

———. "Il contributo italiana alla riforma istituzionale della Chiesa prima della Riforma." In *Strutture ecclesiastiche in Italia e in Germania prima della Riforma*, edited by Paolo Prodi and Peter Johanek, 39–49. Bologna: Il Mulino, 1984.

Heers, Jacques. *Èsclaves et domestiques au moyen-age dans le monde mediterranean:* Paris, 1981.

———. *Family Clans in the Middle Ages*. Amsterdam: North-Holland, 1977.

———. "Urbanisme et structure sociale à Genes au Moyen-Age." In *Studi in onore di Amintore Fanfani*, 1: 371–412.

Helmholz, R. H. *Marriage Litigation in Medieval England*. Cambridge: Cambridge University Press, 1974.

Henderson, John. "Penitence and the Laity in Fifteenth-Century Florence." In *Christianity and the Renaissance*, edited by Verdon and Henderson, 229–49.

———. "Religious Confraternities and Death in Early Renaissance Florence." In *Florence and Italy,* edited by Denley and Elam, 383–94.

Herbert, R. J. "Les trentains gregoriens sous forme de cycles liturgiques." *Revue Benedictine* 81 (1971): 108–22.

Herlihy, David. "Deaths, Marriages, Births and the Tuscan Economy (ca. 1300–1550). In *Population Patterns in the Past,* edited by Ronald Demos Lee, 135–64. New York: Seminar Press, 1977.

———. "The Distribution of Wealth in a Renaissance Community: Florence 1427." In *Towns in Societies: Essays in Economic History and Historical Sociology,* edited by Philip Abrams and E. A. Wrigley, 131–57. Cambridge University Press, 1978.

———. "Family." *The American Historical Review* 96, 1 (1991): 1–16.

———. "Family and Property in Renaissance Florence." In *The Medieval City,* edited by Harry A. Miskimin et al., 3–24. New Haven: Yale University Press, 1977.

———. "The Florentine Merchant Family of the Middle Ages." In *Studi di storia economica toscana nel Medioevo e nel Rinascimento,* 179–201. Pisa: Pacini, 1987.

———. "The Generation in Medieval History." *Viator* 5 (1974): 347–64.

———. "Life Expectancies for Women in Medieval Society." In *The Role of Woman in the Middle Ages,* edited by Rosemarie Thee Morewedge, 1–22. Albany: SUNY Press, 1975.

———. "The Making of the Medieval Family: Symmetry, Structure and Sentiment." *Journal of Family History* 8 (1983): 116–30.

———. "Mapping Households in Medieval Italy." *Catholic Historical Review* 58 (1972): 1–24.

———. "Marriage at Pistoia in the Fifteenth Century." *Bulletino Storico Pistoiese,* ser. 3, 7 (1972): 3–21.

———. *Medieval Households.* Cambridge: Harvard University Press, 1985.

———. "The Medieval Marriage Market." *Journal of Medieval and Renaissance Studies* 6 (1976): 3–27.

———. "The Population of Verona in the First Century of Venetian Rule." In *Renaissance Venice,* edited by J. R. Hale, 91–120. London: Faber and Faber, 1973.

———. "Santa Maria Impruneta: A Rural Commune in the Late Middle Ages." In *Florentine Studies: Politics and Society in Renaissance Florence,* edited by Nicolai Rubinstein, 242–76. London: Faber and Faber, 1968.

———. "Some Psychological and Social Roots of Violence in the Tuscan Cities." In *Violence and Civil Disorder in Italian Cities, 1200–1500,* edited by Lauro Martines, 129–54. Berkeley: University of California Press, 1972.

———. "Tuscan Names, 1200–1530." *Renaissance Quarterly* 41, 4 (1988): 561–82.

———. "The Tuscan Town in the Quattrocento: A Demographic Profile." *Medievalia et Humanistica,* n.s., 1 (1970): 81–109.

———. "Vieillir à Florence au Quattrocento." *Annales E. S. C.* 24 (1969): 1338–52.

Herlihy, David, and Christiane Klapisch-Zuber. *Les toscans et leurs familles: une etude du catasto de 1427.* Paris: Ecole des hautes etudes en sciences sociales, 1978.

Hicks, David L. "Sienese Society in the Renaissance." *Comparative Studies in Society and History* 2 (1959–60): 412–20.

———. "Sources of Wealth in Renaissance Siena: Businessmen and Landowners." *Bolletino Senese di Storia Patria* 93 (1986): 9–42.

Hilaire, Jean. *Le regime des biens entre epoux dans la region de Montpellier au debut du XIIIe siècle à la fin du XVIe siècle.* Montpellier: Causse, Graille & Castelnau, 1957.

Hofer, Giovanni. *Giovanni da Capestrano.* L'Aquila, 1955.

Hoshino, Hidetoshi. *L'arte della lana in Firenza nel basso Medioevo.* Florence: Olschki, 1981.

Houlbrooke, Ralph. *The English Family 1450–1700.* London: Longman, 1984.

Houseley, Norman. *The Later Crusades, 1274–1580: From Lyons to Alcazar.* Oxford: Oxford University Press, 1992.

Hsia, R. Po-Chia. *Trent 1475: Stories of a Ritual Murder Trial.* New Haven: Yale University Press (with Yeshiva University Library), 1992.

Hughes, Diane Owen. "From Brideprice to Dowry in Mediterranean Europe." *Journal of Family History* 3, 3 (1978): 262–96.

———. "Domestic Ideals and Social Behavior: Evidence from Medieval Genoa." In *The Family in History,* edited by Charles E. Rosenberg, 115–43. Philadelphia: University of Pennsylvania Press, 1975.

———. "La famiglia e le donne nel Rinascimento fiorentino." *Quaderni Storici* 24, 2 (1989): 629–34.

———. "Kinsmen and Neighbors in Medieval Genoa." In *The Medieval City,* edited by Miskimin et al., 95–111.

———. "Struttura familiare e sistemi di successione ereditaria nei testamenti dell'Europa medievale." *Quaderni Storici* 33 (1976): 929–52.

———. "Sumptuary Law and Social Relations in Renaissance Italy." In *Disputes and Settlements: Law and Human Relations in the West,* edited by John Bossy, 69–99. Cambridge: Cambridge University Press, 1983.

———. "Urban Growth and Family Structure in Medieval Genoa." In *Towns in Societies: Essays in Economic History and Historical Sociology,* edited by Philip Abrams and E. A. Wrigley, 105–30. Cambridge: Cambridge University Press, 1978. (Reprinted from *Past and Present* 66 [1975]: 3–28.)

Hurtubise, Pierre. *Une famille-temoin: Les Salviati.* Vatican: Biblioteca Apostolica Vaticana, 1985.

Hyde, J. K. *Padua in the Age of Dante.* Manchester: Manchester University Press, 1966.

Ioly Zorattini, Pier Cesare. "Gli ebrei durante la dominazione veneziana." In *Storia di Vicenza,* edited by Barbieri and Preto, 3/1:221–29.

Isaacs, Ann Katherine. "Le campagne senesi fra Quattro e Cinquecento: regime fondiario e governo signorile." In *Contadini e proprietari nella Toscana moderna,* 377–404.

James, Montague Rhodes. *The Apocryphal New Testament.* Oxford: Clarendon, 1989.

Jones, Philip. "Economia e società nell'Italia medievale: la leggenda della borghesia." *Storia d'Italia, Annali,* 1: 187–372. Turin: Einaudi, 1978.

Jussen, Bernhard. "Le parrainage à la fin du Moyen Age: savoir public, attentes theologiques et usages sociaux." *Annales E.S.C.* 47, 2 (1992): 467–502.

Kedar, Benjamin Z. "The Genoese Notaries of 1382: The Anatomy of an Urban Occupational Group." In *The Medieval City,* edited by Miskimin et al., 73–94.

———. "Noms de saints et mentalité populaire à Genes au XIVe siecle." *Le Moyen Age* 73, 3–4 (1967): 431–46.

Kent, D. V. "The Dynamic of Power in Cosimo de' Medici's Florence." In *Patronage, Art and Society,* edited by Kent and Simons, 63–78.

Kent, D. V., and F. W. Kent. *Neighbors and Neighborhood in Renaissance Florence: The District of the Red Lion in the Fifteenth Century.* Locust Valley, N.Y.: J. J. Augustin, 1982.

Kent, D. V., and F. W. Kent. "A Self-Disciplining Pact Made by the Peruzzi Family of Florence (June 1433)." *Renaissance Quarterly* 34, 3 (1981).

Kent, F. W. "Essay." In Gino Corti with F. W. Kent, *Bartolomeo Cederni and His Friends: Letters to an Obscure Florentine.* Florence: Olschki, 1991.

Kent, Francis William. *Household and Lineage in Renaissance Florence: The Family Life of the Capponi, Ginori and Rucellai.* Princeton: Princeton University Press, 1977.

———. "Ties of Neighbourhood and Patronage in Quattrocento Florence." In *Patronage, Art and Society,* edited by Kent and Simons, 79–98.

Kent, Francis William, and Patricia Simons, eds. (with J. C. Eade). *Patronage, Art and Society in Renaissance Italy.* Oxford: Clarendon, 1987.

Kieckhefer, Richard. *Magic in the Middle Ages.* Cambridge: Cambridge University Press, 1990.

———. *Unquiet Souls: Fourteenth-Century Saints and Their Religious Milieu.* Chicago: University of Chicago Press, 1984.

King, Margaret Leah. "Caldiera and the Barbaros on Marriage and the Family: Humanist Reflections of Venetian Realities." *Journal of Medieval and Renaissance Studies* 6 (1976): 19–48.

———. *Venetian Humanism in an Age of Patrician Dominance.* Princeton: Princeton University Press, 1986.

Kirshner, Julius. "*Maritus lucretur dotem uxoris sue premortue* in Late Medieval Florence." *Zeitschrift der Savigny-Stiftung für Rechtgeschichte,* Kanonistische Abteilung 77 (1991): 111–55.

———. "Materials for a Gilded Cage: Non-Dotal Assets in Florence, 1300–1500." In *The Family in Italy from Antiquity to the Present,* edited by David I. Kertzer and Richard P. Saller, 187–207. New Haven: Yale University Press, 1991.

———. *Pursuing Honor while Avoiding Sin: The 'Monte delle doti' of Florence,* Quaderni di *Studi Senesi.* Milan: Giuffre, 1978.

———. "'Ubi est ille?' Franco Sacchetti on the Monte Comune of Florence." *Speculum* 59, 3 (1984): 554–84.

———. "Wives' Claims against Insolvent Husbands in Late Medieval Italy." In *Women of the Medieval World: Essays in Honor of John H. Mundy,* edited by Julius Kirshner and Suzanne F. Wemple, 256–303. Oxford: Basil Blackwell, 1985.

Kirshner, Julius, and Anthony Molho. "The Dowry Fund and the Marriage Market in Early *Quattrocento* Florence." *Journal of Modern History* 50 (1978): 403–38.

Kirshner, Julius, and Anthony Molho. "Il monte delle doti a Firenze dalla sua fondazione nel 1425 alla metà del sedicesimo secolo: abbozzo di una ricerca." *Ricerche Storiche,* n.s., 10 (1980): 21–47.

Kirshner, Julius, and Jacques Pluss. "Two Fourteenth-Century Opinions on Dowries, Paraphernalia and Non-dotal Goods." *Bulletin of Medieval Canon Law,* n.s., 8 (1979): 65–77.

Klapisch-Zuber, Christiane. "L'attribution d'un prenom à l'enfant en Toscane à la fin du Moyen Age." In *L'Enfant en Moyen Age. Acts du Colloque d'Aix en Provence,* 73–84. Aix en Provence, 1980.

———. "Le chiavi fiorentine di Barbablù: l'apprendimento della lettura a Firenze nel XV secolo." *Quaderni Storici* 57 (1984): 765–92.

———. "Constitution et variations temporelles des stocks de prenoms." In *Le prenom*, edited by Dupaquier et al., 37–47.

———. "Comperage et clientelisme à Florence (1360–1520)." *Ricerche Storiche* 15, 1 (1985): 61–74.

———. "Fiscalité et demographie en Toscane (1427–1430)." *Annales E.S.C.* 24 (1969): 1313–37.

———. "Household and Family in Tuscany in 1427." In *Household and Family in Past Time*, edited by Peter Laslett and Richard Wall, 267–81. Cambridge: Cambridge University Press, 1972.

———. "L'invention du passé familial à Florence (XIVe–XVe siècles)." In *Temps, memoire, tradition au Moyen Age*, 97–118. Aix-en-Provence, 1983.

———. "Parrains et filleuls. Une approche comparée de la France, l'Angleterre et l'Italie medievale." *Medieval Prosopography* 6, 2 (1985): 51–77.

———. "Patroni celesti per bambini e bambine al momento del battesimo (Firenze, secc. XIV–XV)." In *La ragnatela dei rapporti. Patronage e reti di relazione nella storia delle donne*, edited by Lucia Ferrante, Maura Palazzi, and Gianna Panata, 191–200. Turin: Rosenberg and Sellier, 1988.

———. "Au peril des commeres. L'alliance spirituelle par les femmes à Florence." In *Femmes Mariages Lignages (XIIe–XIVe siecles. Melanges offerts à Georges Duby*, 215–32. Brussels: De Boeck, 1992.

———. "Ruptures de parenté et changements d'identité chez les magnats florentins du XIVe siècle." *Annales E.S.C.* 43, 5 (1988): 1206–39.

———. "Un salario o l'onore: come valutare le donne fiorentine del XIV–XV secolo." *Quaderni Storici* 79 (1992): 41–49.

———. "Structures demographiques et structures familiales." In *Strutture familiari*, edited by Comba et al., 11–18.

———. "Women Servants in Florence during the Fourteenth and Fifteenth Centuries." In *Women and Work in Preindustrial Europe*, edited by Barbara A. Hanawalt, 56–80. Bloomington: Indiana University Press, 1986.

———. *Women, Family and Ritual in Renaissance Italy*. Chicago: University of Chicago Press, 1985.

Klapisch-Zuber, Christiane, and Michel Demonet. "'A uno pane e uno vino': la famille toscane au debut du XVe siècle." *Annales E.S.C.* 27 (1972): 873–901.

Knapton, Michael. "La condanna penale di Alvise Querini, ex rettore di Rovereto (1477): solo un'altra smentita del mito di Venezia?" *Atti dell'Accademia rovertana degli Agiati*, ser. 6, 28 (1988): 303–32.

Kohl, Benjamin G. "Government and Society in Renaissance Padua." *Journal of Medieval and Renaissance Studies* 2, 2 (1972): 205–21.

Kotelnikova, Liubov A. "Artigiani-affittuari nelle città e nelle campagne toscane del XV–XVI secolo." In *Aspetti della vita economica medievale*, 747–58.

———. "Condizione economica dei mezzadri toscani nel secolo XV." In *Domanda e consumi, livelli e strutture (nei secoli XIII–XVIII)*, edited by Vera Barbagli Bagnoli, 93–99. Florence: Olschki, 1978.

———. "L'evoluzione della rendita fondiaria in Toscana sulle terre dei cittadini e della chiesa (secoli XIV–XV)." *Società e Storia* 23 (1984): 1–43.

———. *Mondo contadino e città in Italia dall'XI al XIV secolo.* Bologna: Mulino, 1975.

———. "Le operazioni di credito e di usura nei secoli XI–XIV e la loro importanza per i contadini toscani." In *Credito, banche e investimenti,* edited by Anna Vannini Marx, 71–73.

———. "Rendita in natura e rendita in denaro nell'Italia medievale (secoli IX–XV)." In *Storia d'Italia, Annali* 6:94–112. Turin: Einaudi, 1983.

———. "Il ruolo dello sviluppo delle città e delle relazioni mercantili-monetarie nei mutamenti delle condizioni economiche e sociali dei contadini toscani nei secoli XII–XV." In *Studi in memoria di Federigo Melis,* 1:409–31. Naples: Giannini, 1978.

Kubelik, Martin. *Die Villa im Veneto: Zur typologischen Entwicklung im Quattrocento.* Munich: Suddeutscher Verlag, 1977.

Kuehn, Thomas. "Some Ambiguities of Female Inheritance Ideology in the Renaissance." *Continuity and Change* 2, 1 (1987): 11–36.

———. "Arbitration and Law in Renaissance Florence." *Renaissance and Reformation,* n.s., II, 4 (1987): 289–319.

———. "'Cum consensu mundualdi': Legal Guardianship of Women in Quattrocento Florence." *Viator* 13 (1982): 309–33.

———. *Emancipation in Late Medieval Florence.* New Brunswick: Rutgers University Press, 1982.

———. "Honor and Conflict in a Fifteenth Century Florentine Family." *Ricerche Storiche* 10, 3 (1980).

———. "Law, Death and Heirs in the Renaissance: Repudiation of Inheritance in Florence." *Renaissance Quarterly* 45, 3 (1992): 484–516.

———. *Law, Family and Women: Toward a Legal Anthropology of Renaissance Italy.* Chicago: University of Chicago Press, 1991.

———. "Reading Microhistory: The Example of *Giovanni and Lusanna.*" *Journal of Modern History* 61 (1989): 512–34.

———. "Some Ambiguities of Female Inheritance Ideology in the Renaissance." *Continuity and Change* 2, 1 (1987): 11–36.

———. "Women, Marriage and *Patria potestas* in Late Medieval Florence." *Revue d'Histoire du Droit* 49 (1981): 127–47.

Laconelli, Angela. "Contratti agrari e rapporti di lavoro nell'Italia medievale." *Studi Storici* 23, 3 (1982): 639–46.

de Lamothe, Marie-Simon. "Pieté et charité publique à Toulouse de la fin du XIIIe siècle au milieu du XVe siècle d'apres les testaments." *Annales du Midi* (1974): 5–39.

Lanaro Sartori, Paola. "Un patriziato in formazione: l'esempio veronese del '400." In *Il primo dominio veneziano,* 35–51.

Laribiere, Genevieve. "Le mariage à Toulouse aux XIVe et XVe siècles." *Annales du Midi* 79 (1967): 335–61.

Laslett, Peter. "Preface" and "Introduction." In *Household and Family in Past Time,* edited by Peter Laslett and Richard Wall, ix–xii, 1–73. Cambridge: Cambridge University Press, 1972.

———. "Servi e servizio nella struttura sociale europea." *Quaderni Storici* 68 (1988): 345–54.

Law, John Easton. "Il Quattrocento a Venezia." In *Il secolo del primato italiano: il Quattrocento*. Milan: TETI, 1988.

———. "'Super differentiis agitatis venetiis inter districtuales et civitatem.' Venezia, Verona e il contado nel '400." *Archivio Veneto*, ser. 5, 151 (1981): 5–32.

———. "Venice and the 'Closing' of the Veronese Constitution in 1405." *Studi Veneziani*, n.s., 1 (1977): 69–103.

———. "Venice, Verona and the della Scala after 1405." *Atti e Memorie*, ser. 6, 29 (1977–78): 157–85.

———. "Verona e il dominio veneziano: gli inizi." In *Il primo dominio veneziano*, 17–33.

Lazzarini, Vittore. "Beni carraresi e proprietari veneziani." In *Studi in onore di Gino Luzzato*, 1:274–88. Milan, 1950.

Lecce, Michele. "I beni terrieri di un antico istituto ospitaliero veronese (secoli XII–XVIII)." In *Studi in onore di Amintore Fanfani*, 3:53–181. Milan, 1962.

———. *Ricerche di storia economica medioevale e moderna*. Verona, 1975.

———. *Vicende dell'industria della lana e della seta a Verona dalle origini al XVI secolo*. Verona, 1955.

Leclercq, Jean. *Monks on Marriage: A Twelfth-Century View*. New York: Seabury Press, 1982.

Le Goff, Jacques. *The Birth of Purgatory*. Chicago: University of Chicago Press, 1984.

———. "La naissance du Purgatoire (XII–XIII siècles)." In *La Mort en Moyen Age*, 7–10.

Leicht, Pier Silverio. "Condizione delle classi agricole lavoratrici nel Rinascimento. I movimenti revoluzionarii del Cinquecento. La crisi del Cinquecento." In *Operai artigiani agricoltori in Italia dal secolo VI al XVI*, 177–92. Milan: Giuffrè, 1946.

———. "Un contratto agrario dei paesi latini mediterranei." In *Studi in onore di Gino Luzzatto*, 1:18–29.

Lepori, F. "Bruto Pietro." *Dizionario biografico degli italiani*, 14:735–37. Rome, 1972.

Lerner, Robert E. *The Powers of Prophecy: The Cedar of Lebanon Vision from the Mongol Onslaught to the Dawn of the Enlightenment*. Berkeley: University of California Press, 1983.

Leverotti, Franca. "Dalla famiglia stretta alla famiglia larga. Linee di evoluzione e tendenze della famiglia rurale lucchese (secoli XIV–XV)." *Studi Storici* 30 (1989): 171–202.

Liva, Alberto. *Notariato e documento notarile a Milano dall'Alto Medioevo alla fine del Settecento*. Rome: Consiglio Nazionale del Notariato, 1979.

Livi Bacci, Massimo. *La societé italienne devant les crises de mortalité*. Florence, 1978.

Lorcin, Marie-Therese. *Les campagnes de la region lyonnaise aux XIVe et XVe siècles*. Lyon: Bosc, 1974.

———. "Les clauses religieuses dans les testaments du plat pays lyonnais aux XIVe et XVe siècles." *Le Moyen Age* 27, 2 (1972): 287–323.

———. "Mere Nature et le devoir social. La mere et l'enfant dans l'oeuvre de Christine de Pizan." *Revue Historique* 571 (1989): 29–44.

———. "Trois manieres d'enterrement à Lyon de 1300 à 1500." *Revue Historique* 261 (1979): 3–15.

———. "Le vignoble et les vignerons du Lyonnais aux XIVe et XVe siècles." In *Le vin au moyen age: production et producteurs*, 15–37. Grenoble, 1978.

———. *Vivre et mourir en Lyonnais à la fin du Moyen Age*. Paris: CNRS, 1981.

Lorenzoni, Giovanni. *Lorenzo da Bologna*. Vicenza: Neri Pozza, 1963.

Lugli, Vittorio. *I trattatisti della famiglia nel Quattrocento*. Bologna: Formiggini, 1909.

Luzzatti, Michele. "Contratti agrari e rapporti di produzione nelle campagne pisane dal XIII al XVI secolo." In *Studi in memoria di Federigo Melis*, 1:569–84. Naples: Giannini, 1978.

———. "Famiglie nobili e famiglie mercantili a Pisa e in Toscana nel Basso Medioevo." *Rivista Storica Italia NA* 86 (1974): 441–59.

———. "Toscana senza mezzadria. Il caso pisano alla fine del Medio Evo." In *Contadini e proprietari nella Toscana moderna*, 279–344.

Luzzatto, Gino. "L'attività commerciale di un patriziato veneziano del Quattrocento." In *Studi di storia economica veneziana*, 167–93. Padua, 1954.

———. "Piccoli e grandi mercanti nelle città italiane del Rinascimento." *In onore e ricordo di Giuseppe Prato*, 27–49. Turin: Istituto Superiore, 1931.

———. "Tasso d'interesse e usura a Venezia nei secoli XIII–XV." In *Miscellanea in onore di Roberto Cessi*, 2:191–202. Rome, 1958.

Lynch, Joseph H. *Godparents and Kinship in Early Medieval Europe*. Princeton: Princeton University Press, 1986.

Macfarlane, Alan. *Marriage and Love in England: Modes of Reproduction 1300–1840*. Oxford: Basil Blackwell, 1986.

Mackenney, Richard. *Tradesmen and Traders: The World of the Guilds in Venice and Europe, c. 1250–c. 1650*. London: Croom Helm, 1987.

Mainoni, Patrizia. "L'attività mercantile e le casate milanesi nel secondo Quattrocento." In *Milano nell'età di Ludovico il Moro*, 2:575–84. Milan: Archivio Storico Civico e Biblioteca Trivulziana, 1983.

———. "Il mercato della lana a Milano dal XIV al XV secolo. Prime indagine." *Archivio Storico Lombardo*, ser. 11, 1 (1984): 20–43.

———. "Note per uno studio sulle società commerciali a Milano nel XV secolo." *Nuova Rivista Storica* 66 (1982): 564–68.

———. "'Viglaebium opibus primum.' Uno sviluppo economico nel Quattrocento lombardo." In *Metamorfosi di un borgo*, edited by Chittolini, 193–266.

Malanima, Paolo. "La formazione di una regione economica: la Toscana nei secoli XIII–XV." *Società e Storia* 20 (1983): 229–70.

———. "La proprietà fiorentina e la diffusione della mezzadria nel contado pisano nei secoli XV e XVI." In *Contadini e proprietari nella Toscana moderna*, 345–76.

Manselli, Raoul. "Vie familiale et ethique sexuelle dans les penitentiels." In *Famille et parenté dans l'Occident medieval*, 363–78. Rome: Ècole Francaise de Rome, 1977.

Mantese, Giovanni. "Correnti riformistiche a Vicenza nel primo Quattrocento." In *Scritti scelti di storia vicentina*, 1:113–85. Vicenza, 1982. (Also *Studi in onore di Federico M. Mistrorigo*, 835–939. Vicenza, 1958.)

———. "Frà Bernardino a Vicenza." In *Vicenza illustrata*, edited by Neri Pozza, 78–79. Vicenza: Neri Pozza, 1976.

———. "'Fratres et sorores de poenitentia' di S. Francesco in Vicenza dal XIII al XV secolo." In *Miscellanea Gilles Gerard Meerssman*, 695–714. Padua: Antenore, 1970.

———. *Memorie storiche della chiesa vicentina*, 3, 1: Vicenza: Istituto S. Gaetano, 1958; 3, 2: Vicenza: Neri Pozza, 1964.

⸻. *L'osservanza francescana del secolo XV a Vicenza nel generale contesto dell'osservanza monastico vicentino*. Vicenza, 1988.

Marchi, Gian Paolo. "Letterati in villa." In *La villa nel veronese*, edited by Viviani, 231–51.

Marongiu, A. "Matrimonio medievale e matrimonio postmedievale: spunti storico-critici." *Rivista di Storia del Diritto Italiano* 57 (1984): 5–119.

Marrara, Danilo. *Riseduti e nobiltà: profilo storico-istituzionale di un'oligarchia toscana nei secoli XVI–XVIII*. Pisa: Pacini, 1976.

Martin, Hervé. *Le metier de predicateur en France septentrionale à la fin du Moyen Age (1350–1520)*. Paris: Editions du Cerf, 1988.

Martines, Lauro. *Lawyers and Statecraft in Renaissance Florence*. Princeton: Princeton University Press, 1968.

⸻. "A Way of Looking at Women in Renaissance Florence." *Journal of Medieval and Renaissance Studies* 4, 1 (1974): 15–28.

Martini, Giuseppe. "*L'universitas mercatorum* di Milano e i suoi rapporti col potere politico (secoli XIII–XV)." In *Studi di storia medievale e moderna per Ernesto Sestan*, 1:219–58.

de Martini, Monica. "Da borghesi a patrizi. I Trivelli di Verona nel Trecento e Quattrocento." *Studi Storici Luigi Simeoni* 38 (1988): 83–107.

Maschio, Ruggero. "Il Peronio di Vicenza." In *Vicenza illustrata*, edited by Neri Pozza, 117–23. Vicenza: Neri Pozza, 1976.

Maurel, Christian. "Structures familiales et solidarites lignageres à Marseille au XVe siècle: autour de l'ascension social des Forbin." *Annales E.S.C.* 41, 3 (1986): 657–81.

de Mause, Lloyd. *The History of Childhood: The Evolution of Parent-Child Relationships as a Factor in History*. London: Souvenir Press, 1976.

Mazzaoui, Maureen Fennell. *The Italian Cotton Industry in the Later Middle Ages*. Cambridge: Cambridge University Press, 1981.

Mazzi, Maria Serena. "La peste a Firenze nel Quattrocento." In *Strutture familiari*, edited by Comba et al., 91–115.

Mazzi, Maria Serena, and Sergio Raveggi. *Gli uomini e le cose nelle campagne fiorentine del Quattrocento*. Florence: Olschki, 1983.

McClure, George W. *Sorrow and Consolation in Italian Humanism*. Princeton: Princeton University Press, 1991.

McHam, Sarah Blake. "Donatello's Tomb of Pope John XXIII." In *Life and Death in Fifteenth-Century Florence*, edited by Tetel et al., 146–73.

McManamon, John M. "Pier Paolo Vergerio (The Elder) and the Beginnings of the Humanist Cult of Jerome." *Catholic Historical Review* 81, 4 (1985):353–71.

Medick, Hans, and David Warren Sabean. "Introduction" and "Interest and Emotion in Family and Kinship Studies: A Critique of Social History and Anthropology." In *Interest and Emotion: Essays on the Study of Family and Kinship*, edited by Hans Medick and David Warren Sabean, 1–8, 9–27. Cambridge: Cambridge University Press, 1984.

Melis, Federigo. "Gli opifici lanieri toscani dei secoli XIII–XVI." In *Produzione commercio e consumo*, edited by Marco Spallanzani, 237–43.

Meneghin, Vittorino. *Bernardino da Feltre e i Monti di Pietà*. Vicenza: LIEF, 1974.

Menzioni, Andrea. "Schemi di matrimonio e mortalità di sessi: una transizione fra medioevo ed età moderna?" *Società e Storia* 12 (1981): 435–47.

Merlini, Domenico. *Saggio di ricerche sulla satira contro il villano.* Turin: Loescher, 1894.

Miani, Gemma. "L'economie lombarde aux XIVe et XVe siècles: une exception à la regle?" *Annales E.S.C.* 19 (1964): 569–79.

Miles, Margaret R. *Image as Insight: Visual Understanding in Western Christianity and Secular Culture.* Boston: Beacon Press, 1985.

Minois, Georges. *History of Old Age: From Antiquity to the Renaissance.* Chicago: University of Chicago Press, 1989.

Mirrer, Louise, ed. *Upon My Husband's Death: Widows in the Literature and Histories of Medieval Europe.* Ann Arbor: University of Michigan Press, 1992.

Mirri, Mario. "Contadini e proprietari nella Toscana moderna." In *Contadini e proprietari nella Toscana moderna,* 9–130.

Mistruzzi, Vittorio. "Giorgio Sommariva rimatore veronese del secolo XV." *Archivio Veneto* 6 (1924): 115–202.

Modzelewski, Karel. "Le vicende della 'pars dominica' nei beni fondiari del monastero di S. Zaccaria a Venezia (sec. X–XIV)." *Bolletino dell'Istituto di Storia della Società e dello Stato Veneziano* 4 (1962): 42–79; 5 (1963): 15–63.

Molho, Anthony. "Deception and Marriage Strategy in Renaissance Florence: The Case of Women's Ages." *Renaissance Quarterly* 41, 2 (1988): 193–217.

———. "*Tamquam vere mortua.* Le professioni religiose femminili nella Firenze del tardo medioevo." *Società e Storia* 43 (1989): 1–44.

Molho, Anthony, Roberto Barducci, Gabriella Battista, and Francesco Donnini. "Genealogia e parentado. Memorie del potere nella Firenze tardo medievale. Il caso di Giovanni Rucellai." *Quaderni Storici* 86 (1994): 365–403.

Molin, Jean-Baptiste, and Protais Mutembe. *Le rituel du mariage en France du XIIe au XVI siecle.* Paris: Beauchesne, 1974.

Mometto, Piergiovanni. *L'azienda agricola Barbarigo a Carpi. Gestione economica ed evoluzione sociale sulle terre di un villaggio della bassa pianura veronese (1443–1539).* Venice: Il Cardo, 1992.

Monaco, Michele. "Aspetti di vita privata e pubblica nelle città italiane centro-settentrionali durante il XV secolo nelle prediche del beato Bernardino da Feltre, francescano dell'Osservanza." In *L'Uomo e la storia: studi storici in onore di Massimo Petrocchi,* 1:77–196. Rome: Edizioni di Storia e Letteratura, 1983.

Montanari, Massimo. "Dal livello alla mezzadria: l'evoluzione dei patti colonici nella Romagna medievale." *Nuova Rivista Storica* 68 (1984): 579–92.

Monter, E. William. *Ritual, Myth and Magic in Early Modern Europe.* Columbus: Ohio University Press, 1984.

Morrison, Alan S., Julius Kirshner, and Anthony Molho. "Epidemics in Renaissance Florence." *American Journal of Public Health* 75, 5 (1985): 528–35.

———. "Life Cycle Events in 15th Century Florence: Records of the *Monte delle doti.*" *American Journal of Epidemiology* 106, 6 (1977): 487–92.

La mort en Moyen Age. Strasbourg, 1977.

Mueller, Reinhold C. "Alcune considerazioni sui significati di moneta." *Società e Storia* 27 (1985): 177–84.

———. "Bank Money in Venice to the Mid-Fifteenth Century." In *La moneta nell'economia europea: secc. XIII–XVIII,* edited by Vera Barbagli Bagnoli, 77–104. Florence: Le Monnier, 1981.

―――. "La crisi economico-monetaria veneziano di metà Quattrocento nel contesto generale." In *Aspetti della vita economica medievale*, 541–56.

―――. "Guerra monetaria tra Venezia e Milano nel Quattrocento." In *La zecca di Milano*, edited by Giovanni Gorini, 341–55. Milan: Società Numismatica Italiana, 1984.

―――. "L'imperialismo monetario veneziano nel Quattrocento." *Società e Storia* 8 (1980): 277–97.

―――. "Peste e demografia: Medioevo e Rinascimento." In *Venezia e la peste 1348/1797*, 93–95.

Muir, Edward. *Mad Blood Stirring: Vendetta and Factions in Friuli during the Renaissance*. Baltimore: Johns Hopkins University Press, 1993.

―――. "The Virgin on the Street Corner: The Place of the Sacred in Italian Cities." In *Religion and Culture in the Renaissance and Reformation*, edited by Steven Ozment, 25–40. Kirkville, Mo.: Sixteenth Century Journal Publications, 1989.

Najemy, John M. *Corporation and Consensus in Florentine Electoral Politics, 1280–1400*. Chapel Hill: University of North Carolina Press, 1982.

Niccolai, Franco. *La formazione del diritto successorio negli statuti del territorio lombardo-tosco*. Milan: Giuffrè, 1940.

Niccoli, Ottavia. *Prophecy and People in Renaissance Italy*. Princeton: Princeton University Press, 1990.

Niccolini di Camugliano, Ginevra. *The Chronicles of a Florentine Family, 1200–1470*. London: Jonathan Cape, 1933.

―――. "A Medieval Florentine: His Family and His Possessions." *American Historical Review* 31 (1925): 1–19.

Nicolai Petronio, Giovanna. "Notariato aretino tra medioevo ed età moderna: collegio, statuti e matricole dal 1339 al 1739." In *Studi in onore di Leopoldo Sandri*, 2: 633–60. Rome, 1983.

Nicolini, Ugo. "Il trattato 'De alimentis' di Martino da Fano." Reprinted in *Scritti di storia del diritto italiano*, 303–35. Milan: Vita e Pensiero, 1983.

Noonan, John T., Jr. "Marital Affection in the Canonists." *Studia Gratiana* 12 (1967): 479–509.

―――. "Power to Choose." *Viator* 4 (1973): 419–34.

―――. *Power to Dissolve: Lawyers and Marriages in the Courts of the Roman Curia*. Cambridge, Mass.: Belknap Press, 1972.

Il notaio nella civiltà fiorentina (secc. XIII–XVI). Florence: Valsecchi, 1984.

O'Connor, Mary Catharine. *The Art of Dying Well: The Development of the Ars moriendi*. New York: Columbia University Press, 1942.

Orme, Nicholas. "Children and the Church in Medieval England." *Journal of Ecclesiastical History* 45, 4 (1994).

Ortalli, Gherardo. "Notariato e storiografia in Bologna nei secoli XIII–XVI." In *Notariato medievale bolognese*, 2:143–89. Rome: Consiglio nazionale del notariato, 1977.

―――. "Cronisti e storici del Quattrocento e del Cinquecento." In *Storia di Vicenza*, edited by Barbieri and Preto 3/1:353–80.

Osheim, Duane J. "Countrymen and the Law in Late-Medieval Tuscany." *Speculum* 64 (1989): 317–37.

Pacini, Gian Piero. "Fermenti religiosi e aggregazione devote del laicato nella chiesa vicentina dal sec. XII al sec. XV." In *Santità e religiosità*, edited by Zironda, 59–78.

———. "L'osservanza francescana a Vicenza." In *Santità e religiosità,* edited by Zironda, 87–95.

Palmer, Richard J. "L'azione della Repubblica di Venezia nel controllo della peste." In *Venezia e la peste 1348/1797,* 103–8.

Pandemiglio, Leonida. "Giovanni di Pagolo Morelli e le strutture familiari." *Archivio Storico Italiano* 136 (1978): 3–88.

Del Panta, Lorenzo. "Cronologia e diffusione delle crisi di mortalità in Toscana dalla fine del XIV agli inizi del XIX secolo." *Ricerche Storiche* 7, 2 (1977): 293–343.

———. *Le epidemie nella storia demografica italitna (secoli XIV–XIX).* Turin: Loescher, 1980.

Paravay, Pierette. "Angoisse collective et miracles au seuil de la mort: resurrections et baptemes d'enfants mort-nés en Dauphiné au XVeme siècle." In *La mort au Moyen Age,* 87–102.

Pasche, Veronique. *"Pour le salut de mon ame."* Les Lausannois face à la morte *(XIVe siecle).* Lausanne: Universite de Lausanne, 1989.

Paton, Bernadette. *Preaching Friars and the Civic Ethos: Siena, 1380–1480.* London: Queen Mary and Westfield College, 1992.

———. *Custodians of the Civic Conscience: Preaching Friars and the Communal Ethos in Late Medieval Siena.* Oxford: Academic Publishers, 1989.

Payer, Pierre J. *Sex and the Penitentials: The Development of a Sexual Code.* Toronto: University of Toronto Press, 1984.

Perosa, Alessandro. "Lo zibaldone di Giovanni Rucellai." In *Giovanni Rucellai ed il suo zibaldone,* 2:99–152. London: The Warburg Institute, 1981.

Pesce, Luigi. *La chiesa di Treviso nel primo Quattrocento.* Rome: Herder, 1987.

———. "Il clero secolare della diocesi di Treviso nel primo Quattrocento." In *Pievi, parrochie e clero,* edited by Paolo Sambin, 361–425.

———. "Ludovico Barbo vescovo riformatore." In *Riforma della chiesa,* 135–59.

———. *Ludovico Barbo vescovo di Treviso (1437–1443). Cura pastorale, riforma della Chiesa, spiritualità.* Padua: Antenore, 1969.

Petrocchi, Massimo. *Storia della spiritualità italiana (secc. XIII–XV).* Rome: Edizioni di Storia e Letteratura, 1984.

Petrucci, Armando. "Modello notarile e testualità." In *Il notariato nella civiltà toscana,* 123–45. Rome: Consiglio nazionale del notariato, 1965.

Petrucci, Armando, ed. *Notarii: documenti per la storia del notariato italiano.* Milan: Giuffrè, 1958.

Phillips, Mark. *The Memoir of Marco Parenti: A Life in Medici Florence.* Princeton: Princeton University Press, 1987.

Phillips, Roderick. *Putting Asunder: A History of Divorce in Western Society.* Cambridge: Cambridge University Press, 1988.

Piccinni, Gabriella. "I mezzadri di fronte al fisco. Primo esame della normativa senese del Quattrocento." In *Cultura e società nell'Italia medievale,* 2:665–82.

———. *"Seminare fruttare raccogliere:" mezzadri e salariati sulle terre di Monte Oliveto Maggiore (1374–1430).* Milan: Feltrinelli, 1982.

Pini, Antonio Ivano. *Vite e vine nel Medioevo.* Bologna: CLEUP, 1989.

———. "La viticoltura italiana nel Medioevo. Coltura della vite e consumo del vino a Bologna dal X al XV secolo." *Studi Medievali,* ser. 3, 15 (1974): 795–884.

Pinto, Giuliano. "Le campagne e la 'crisi'." *Storia della Società Italiana*, 7:121–56. Milan, 1982.

———. "Forme di conduzione e rendita fondiaria nel contado fiorentino (secoli XIV e XV): le terre dell'Ospedale di San Gallo." In *Studi di storia medievale e moderna per Ernesto Sestan*, 1:259–337. Florence: Olschki, 1980.

———. "'Honour' and 'Profit': Landed Property and Trade in Medieval Siena." In *City and Countryside in Late Medieval and Renaissance Italy: Essays Presented to Philip Jones*, edited by Trevor Dean and Chris Wickham, 81–91. London: Hambledon, 1990.

———. "L'Impruneta e Firenze: contadini e proprietari, assetto delle colture e consumi (secoli XIII–XV)." In *Impruneta: una pieve, un paese*, 1–31. Florence: Salimbeni, 1983.

———. "Mezzadria poderale, contadini e proprietari nel catasto fiorentino del 1427." *Società e Storia* 12 (1981): 459–68.

———. "Note sull'indebitamento contadino e lo sviluppo della proprietà fondiaria cittadina nella Toscana tardomedievale." *Ricerche Storiche*, n.s., 10 (1980): 3–19.

———. "Ordinamento colturale e proprietà fondiaria cittadina nella Toscana del tardo Medio Evo." In *Contadini e proprietari nella Toscana moderna*, 223–78.

———. "Personale, balie e salariati dell'ospedale de San Gallo." *Ricerche Storiche* 2 (1974): 113–68.

———. "La politica demografica delle città." In *Strutture familiari*, edited by Comba et al., 19–43.

———. "I rapporti di lavoro nelle campagne senesi fra XIII e XIV secolo. Una nota sul contratto di famulato." In *Cultura e società nell'Italia medievale*, 2:683–95.

———. "Le strutture ambientali e le basi dell'economia rurale" (3–92), "Le colture cerealicole" (93–156), "La mezzadria delle origini: dimore contadine e infrastrutture agricole" (225–46), and "Forme di conduzione e rendita fondiaria nel contado fiorentino: le terre dell'ospedale di San Gallo" (247–29). In *La Toscana nel tardo Medioevo: Ambiente, economia rurale, società*. Florence: Sansoni, 1982.

Polica, Sante. "An attempted 'Recoversion' of Wealth in XVth Century Lucca: The Lands of Michele di Giovanni Guinigi." *Journal of European Economic History* 9, 3 (1980): 655–99.

———. "Basso Medioevo e Rinascimento: 'rifeudalizzazione' e 'transizione'." *Bolletino dell'Istituto Storico Italiano per il Medioevo e Archivio Muratoriano* 88 (1979): 287–316.

Pollock, Linda A. *Forgotten Children: Parent-Child Relations from 1500 to 1900*. Cambridge: Cambridge University Press, 1983.

Postles, D. A. "Personal Naming Patterns of Peasants and Burgesses in Late Medieval England." *Medieval Prosopography* 12, 1 (1991): 29–56.

Pozza, Felice. "Le corporazioni d'arte e mestiere a Vicenza." *Nuovo Archivio Veneto* 10 (1895): 247–311.

Il primo dominio veneziano a Verona (1405–1509). Verona: Accademia di Agricoltura Scienze e Lettere di Verona, 1991.

Pullan, Brian. "The *Scuole Grandi* of Venice: Some Further Thoughts." In *Christianity and the Renaissance*, edited by Verdon and Henderson, 272–301.

Puncuh, Dino. "Gli statuti del collegio dei notai genovesi nel secolo XV." In *Miscellanea di storia ligure in memoria di Giorgio Falco*, 265–310. Genoa, 1966.

Puppi, Leonello. "Funzioni e originalità delle ville veronesi." In *La villa nel veronese*, edited by Viviani, 87–140.

Queller, Donald E. *The Venetian Patriciate: Reality versus Myth*. Urbana: University of Illinois Press, 1986.

Queller, Donald E., and Francis R. Swietek. "The Myth of the Venetian Patriciate: Electoral Corruption in Medieval Venice." In *Two Studies on Venetian Government*, edited by Donald E. Queller. Geneva: Droz, 1977.

Rapp, Francis. "La reforme religieuse et la meditation de la mort à la fin du Moyen Age." In *La mort au Moyen Age*, 53–66.

Rasi, Pietro. "I rapporti fra l'autorità ecclesiastica e l'autorità civile in Feltre (1404–1565)." *Archivio Veneto*, ser. 5, 13 (1933): 82–127.

Razi, Zvi. *Life, Marriage and Death in Medieval Parish: Economy, Society and Demography in Halesowen 1270–1400*. Cambridge: Cambridge University Press, 1980.

Rebora, Giovanni. "Libri di conti di mercanti genovesi nel secolo XV." In *Atti del III convegon internazionale di studi colombiani*, 199–218. Genoa: Civico Istituto Colombiano, 1979.

Reeves, Marjorie E. *The Influence of Prophecy in the Later Middle Ages: A Study in Joachimism*. Oxford: Clarendon, 1969.

———. *Joachim of Fiore and the Prophetic Future*. New York: Harper and Row, 1977.

———. "Joachimist Influences on the Idea of a Last World Emperor." *Traditio* 17 (1961): 323–70.

———. "Some Popular Prophecies from the Fourteenth to the Seventeenth Centuries." In *Popular Belief and Practice*, edited by G. J. Cuming and Derek Baker, 107–34. Cambridge: Cambridge University Press, 1972.

Reinburg, Virginia. "Liturgy and the Laity in Late Medieval and Reformation France." *Sixteenth Century Journal* 23, 3 (1992): 526–47.

di Renzo Villata, Maria Gigliola. "Note per la storia della tutela nell'Italia del Renascimento." In *La famiglia e la vita quotidiana in Europa dal '400 al '600*, 59–95. Rome, 1986.

Rhodes, Dennis E. *La tipografia nel secolo XV a Vicenza, Santorso e Torrebelvicino*. Vicenza: Accademia Olimpica, n.d. (Extract of *Odeo Olimpico 19–20*.)

Riforma della chiesa, cultura e spiritualità nel Quattrocento veneto. Cesena, 1984.

Rigon, Antonio. "L'associazionismo del clero in una città medioevale. Origini e primi sviluppi della 'fratalea cappellanorum' di Padova (XII–XIII sec.)." In *Pievi, parrochie e clero*, edited by Paolo Sambin, 95–180.

———. *Clero e città. 'Fratalea cappellanorum', parroci, cura d'anime in Padova dal XII al XV secolo*. Padua: Istituto per la Storia Ecclesiastica Padovana, 1988.

———. "La congregazione del clero intrinseco di Verona e i suoi statuti (1323)." In *Gli Scaligeri*, edited by Varanini, 427–30.

———. "Devotion et patriotisme communal dans la genese et la diffusion d'un culte: le bienheureux Antoine de Padoue surnominé le 'Pellegrino' (+1267)." In *Faire croire*, 259–78.

Rodocanachi, Emanuele. "Le mariage en Italie à l'epoque de la Renaissance." *Revue des Questions Historiques*, n.s., 32 (1904): 29–60.

Romano, Dennis. *Housecraft and Statecraft: Domestic Service in Renaissance Venice, 1400–1600*. Baltimore: Johns Hopkins University Press, 1996.

———. "*Quod sibi fiat gratia*: Adjustment of Penalties and the Exercise of Influence in Early Renaissance Venice." *Journal of Medieval and Renaissance Studies* 13, 2 (1983): 251–68.

———. "The Regulation of Domestic Service in Renaissance Venice." *Sixteenth Century Journal* 21, 4 (1991): 661–77.

de la Roncière, Charles. *Florence centre regional aux XIV siècle*. Aix en Provence: SODED, 1976.

———. "L'influence des Franciscains dans la campagne de Florence au XIVe siècle." *Melanges de l'École Francaise de Rome: Moyen Age-Temps Modernes* 87 (1975): 27–102.

———. "Le vignoble florentin et ses transformations au XIVe siècle." In *Le vin au moyen age: production et producteurs*, 125–58. Grenoble, 1978.

de Roover, Raymond. *The Rise and Decline of the Medici Bank 1397–1494*. New York: Norton, 1966.

Roper, Lyndal. "'Going to Church and Street': Weddings in Reformation Augsburg." *Past and Present* 106 (1985): 62–101.

Rosci, Marco. "Ville rustiche del Quattrocento veneto." *Bolletino CISA* 11 (1969): 78–82.

Rosenthal, Elaine G. "The Position of Women in Renaissance Florence: Neither Autonomy nor Subjection." In *Florence and Italy: Renaissance Studies in Honour of Nicolai Rubinstein*, edited by Peter Denley and Caroline Elam, 369–81. London: Westfield College, 1988.

Rosenthal, Joel T. "Aristocratic Marriage and the English Peerage, 1350–1500: Social Institution and Personal Bond." *Journal of Medieval History* 10 (1984): 181–94.

———. *The Purchase of Paradise: Gift Giving and the Aristocracy 1307–1485*. Toronto: University of Toronto Press, 1972.

Ross, James Bruce. "The Middle-Class Child in Urban Italy, Fourteenth to Early Sixteenth Century." In *The History of Childhood*, edited by Lloyd deMause, 183–228. New York: The Psychohistory Press, 1974.

Rossini, Egidio. "L'amministrazione del patrimonio fondiario di una pieve nel secolo XV: Isola della Scala di Verona." *Archivio Veneto*, ser. 5, 125 (1985): 79–120.

———. "Prestatori di danaro a Verona nella prima metà del secolo XIV." *Studi Storici Luigi Simeoni* 33 (1983): 201–13.

Rossini, Egidio, and Maureen Fennell Mazzaoui. "La lana come materia prima nel veneto sud-occidentale (secc. XIII–XV)." In *La lana come materia prima*, edited by Marco Spallanzani, 185–201.

Roussiaud, Jacques. "Prostitution, jeunesse et societé dans les villes du sud-est au XV siècle." *Annales E.S.C.* 31, 2 (1976): 289–325.

Roveda, Enrico. "Istituzioni politiche e gruppi sociali nel Quattrocento." In *Metamorfosi di un borgo*, edited by Chittolini, 55–107.

Rubin, Miri. *Corpus Christi: The Eucharist in Late Medieval Culture*. Cambridge: Cambridge University Press, 1991.

Rubinstein, Nicolai. "Lay Patronage and Observant Reform in Fifteenth-Century Florence." In *Christianity and the Renaissance*, edited by Verdon and Henderson, 63–82.

———. "Oligarchy and Democracy in Fifteenth Century Florence." In *Florence and Venice: Comparisons and Relations*, 1:99–112. Florence, 1979.

Ruggiero, Guido. *The Boundaries of Eros: Sex Crime and Sexuality in Renaissance Venice*. New York: Oxford University Press, 1985.

———. "'Piu che la vita caro': onore, matrimonio e reputazione femminile nel tardo rinascimento." *Quaderni Storici* 22, 3 (1987): 753–75.

———. *Violence in Early Renaissance Venice*. New Brunswick: Rutgers University Press, 1980.

Rumor, Sebastiano. *Il blasone vicentino descritto ed illustrato*. Venice, 1899.

Rusconi, Roberto. *L'attesa della fine. Crisi della società, profezia ed apocalisse in Italia al tempo della Grande Scisma d'Occidente*. Rome, 1979.

Salvemini, Gaetano. "La dignità cavalleresca nel comune di Firenze." In *Opere* 1, 2, edited by Ernesto Sestan. Milan: Feltrinelli, 1972.

Salvioli, Giuseppe. "La benedizione nuziale fino al concilio di Trento. " *Archivio Giuridico* 53 (1894): 173–97.

Sambin, Paolo, ed. *Pievi, parrocchie e clero nel veneto dal X al XV secolo*. Deputazione di Storia Patria per le Venezie, *Miscellanea di Studi e Memorie* 24. Venice, 1987.

———. *Saggi di storia ecclesiastica veneta*. Venice, 1954.

Sancassani, Giulio. "Aspetti giuridici nella vita ecclesiastica della città." In *Chiese e monasteri a Verona*, edited by Giorgio Borelli, 229–37. Verona, 1980.

———. "I beni della fattoria scaligera e la loro liquidazione ad opera della Repubblica Veneta, 1405–1417." *Nova Historia* 12, 1 (1960).

———. "I notai di Verona: tasse e tariffe." In *Il sistema fiscale veneto: problemi e aspetti*, edited by Giorgio Borelli, Paola Lanaro, and Francesco Vecchiato, 253–74. Verona: Libreria Editrice Universitaria, 1982.

Sancassani, Giulio, ed. *Documenti sul notariato veronese durante il dominio veneto*. Milan: Giuffrè, 1987.

de Sandre Gasparini, Giuseppina. "Confraternite e 'cura animarum' nei primi decenni del Quattrocento. I disciplinati e la parrocchia di S. Vitale in Verona." In *Pievi, parrochie e clero*, edited by Paolo Sambin, 289–360.

———. "La confraternità di S. Giovanni Evangelista della morte in Padova e una 'riforma' ispirata del vescovo Pietro Barozzi (1502)." *Miscellanea Gilles Gerard Meersseman*, 765–815. Padua: Antenore, 1970.

———. *Contadini, chiesa, confraternità in un paese veneto di bonifica: Villa del Bosco nel '400*. 2nd ed. Verona: Libreria Universitaria, 1987.

———. "Governo della diocesi e 'cura animarum' nei primi anni di episcopato di Ermolao Barbaro vescovo di Verona (1453–1471): prime note." In *Il primo dominio veneziano*, 73–92.

———. "La parola e le opere. Predicazione di S. Giovanni da Capestrano a Verona." *Venezie francescane*, n.s., 6, 1 (1989): 101–30.

———. "Uno studio sull'episcopato padovano di Pietro Barozzi (1487–1507) e altri contributi sui vescovi veneti nel Quattrocento. Problemi e linee di ricerca." *Rivista di Storia della Chiesa in Italia* 34, 1 (1980): 81–122.

———. "Vita religiosa in Valpolicella nella visita di Ermolao Barbaro." *Annuario Storico della Valpolicella* (1986–87): 75–94.

Sandri, Lucia. *L'ospedale di S. Maria della Scala di San Gimignano nel Quattrocento: contributo alla storia dell'infanzia abbandonata*. Florence, 1982.

Sapori, Armando. "Gli Alberti del Giudice di Firenze." In *Studi in onore di Gino Luzzatto*, 1:161–92.

———. "Classi sociali fra il secolo XI e il XV (si puo' parlare di un 'patriziato'?)" In *Studi di storia economica*, 3:307–11. Florence: Sansoni, 1967.

———. *Studi di storia economica (secc. XIII–XIV–XV)*. 2nd ed. 3 vols. Florence: Sansoni, 1955–67.

Sarti, Nicoletta. *Gli statuti della società dei notai di Bologna dell'anno 1336.* Milan: Giuffrè, 1988.

Sartore, Terenzio. "Pessimismo cristiano nei versi di una miscellanea umanistica." In *Miscellanea Gilles Gerard Meersman*, 2:619–58. Padua: Antenore, 1970.

Schmitt, Jean-Claude. "Du bon usage du 'Credo.'" In *Faire croire*, 337–61.

Schmitt, Jean-Claude, ed. *Precheurs d'exemples. Recits de predicateurs du Moyen Age.* Paris: Stock/Moyen Age, 1985.

Schneemelcher, Wilhelm. *New Testament Apocrypha.* Louisville: Westminster/John Knox Press, 1991.

Schutte, Anne Jacobson. *Printed Italian Vernacular Religious Books, 1465–1550: A Finding List.* Geneva: Droz, 1983.

Scribner, Robert W. "Cosmic Order and Daily Life: Sacred and Secular in Pre-Industrial German Society." In *Religion and Society in Early Modern Europe, 1500–1800*, edited by Kaspar von Greyerz, 17–32. London: George Allen and Unwin, 1984.

———. "The Reformation, Popular Magic, and the 'Disenchantment of the World.'" *Journal of Interdisciplinary History* 23, 3 (1993): 475–94.

Serra-Zanetti, Alberto. "I pronostici di Girolamo Manfredi." In *Studi riminesi e bibliografici in onore di Carlo Lucchesi*, 195–213. Faenza, 1952.

Shahar, Shulamith. *Childhood in the Middle Ages.* London: Routledge, 1990.

Sheehan, Michael S. "Choice of Marriage Partner in the Middle Ages: Development and Mode of Application of a Theory of Marriage." *Studies in Medieval and Renaissance History*, n.s., 1 (1978): 3–33.

Shorter, Edward. *The Making of the Modern Family.* New York: Basic Books, 1975.

Sigal, Pierre Andre. *Les marcheurs de Dieu. Pelerinages et pelerins au Moyen Age.* Paris, 1974.

Simeoni, Luigi. *Gli antichi statuti delle arti veronesi secondo la revisione scaligera del 1319*, R. Deputazione Veneta di Storia Patria, *Monumenti*, ser. 2, 4. Venice, 1914.

———. "Una vendetta signorile nel '400 e il pittore Francesco Benaglio." *Nuovo Archivio Veneto*, n.s., 5 (1903): 252–58.

Simoni, Pino. "L'incunabolo veronese 'Ars moriendi.'" *Miscellanea Storica* 1, 1–2 (1992): 221–35.

Smith, Richard M. "Hypothèses sur la nuptialité en Angleterre aux XIII–XIV siècles." *Annales E.S.C.* 28, 1 (1983): 107–35.

———. *Land, Kinship and Life Cycle.* Cambridge: Cambridge University Press, 1984.

———. "The People of Tuscany and Their Families in the Fifteenth Century: Medieval or Mediterranean?" *Journal of Family History* 6, 1 (1981): 107–28.

Soldi Rondinini, Gigliola. "La moneta milanese dal 1450 al 1499: aspetti e problemi." In *Aspetti della vita economica medievale*, 491–514.

———. "La moneta viscontea nella pratica e nella dottrina (prima metà del secolo XV)." In *La Zecca di Milano*, edited by Giovanni Gorini. Milan, 1984.

———. "Le opere di carità a Milano: gli interventi dei Visconti." In *La carità a Milano*, edited by Alberzoni and Grassi, 123–35.

———. "Per la storia della moneta medioevale: economia, politica, dottrina nel caso di Milano alla fine del Quattrocento." In *Cultura e società nell'Italia medievale*, 2:795–809.

Soranzo, Giovanni. "Di una cronaca sconosciuta del secolo XV e del suo anonimo autore." *Nuovo Archivio Veneto*, n.s., 13 (1907): 68–103.

Spallanzani, M., ed. *La lana come materia prima. I fenomeni della sua produzione e circolazione nei secoli XIII–XVIII*. Florence: Olschki, 1974.

———. *Produzione commercio e consumo dei panni di lana*. Florence: Olschki, 1976.

Spicciani, Amleto. "Aspetti finanziari dell'assistenza e stuttura cetuale dei poveri vergognosi fiorentini al tempo del Savonarola (1487–1498)." In *Studi di storia economica toscana nel Medioevo e nel Rinascimento*, 321–46. Pisa: Pacini, 1987.

———. *Capitale e interesse tra mercatura e povertà nei teologi e canonisti dei secoli XIII–XV*. Rome: Jouvence, 1990.

Starn, Randolph. "Francesco Guicciardini and His Brothers." In *Renaissance Studies in Honor of Hans Baron*, edited by Anthony Molho and John A. Tedeschi, 409–44. DeKalb: Northern Illinois Press, 1971.

Stone, Lawrence. *The Family, Sex and Marriage in England 1500–1800*. New York: Harper and Row, 1977.

Stopani, Renato. *Medievali 'case da signore' nella campagna fiorentina*. Florence: Salimbeni, 1977.

Strocchia, Sharon T. *Death and Ritual in Renaissance Florence*. Baltimore: Johns Hopkins University Press, 1992.

———. "Death Rites and the Ritual Family in Renaissance Florence." In *Life and Death in Fifteenth-Century Florence*, edited by Tetel et al., 120–45.

———. "Funerals and the Politics of Gender in Early Renaissance Florence." In *Refiguring Woman: Perspectives on Gender and the Italian Renaissance*, edited by Marilyn Migiel and Juliana Schiesari, 155–68. Ithaca: Cornell University Press, 1991.

Stuard, Susan Mosher. "Dowry Increase and Increments in Wealth in Medieval Ragusa (Dubrovnik)." *Journal of Economic History* 41, 4 (1981): 795–811.

Stuard, Susan Mosher, ed. *Women in Medieval Society*. Philadelphia: University of Pennsylvania Press, 1976.

Studi in memoria di Federigo Melis. Naples: Giannini, 1978.

Studi in onore di Amintore Fanfani. Milan: Giuffrè, 1962.

Studi in onore di Gino Luzzatto. Milan: Giuffrè, 1949.

Swanson, R. N. *Church and Society in Late Medieval England*. Oxford: Basil Blackwell, 1989.

Tabacco, Giovanni. "Interpretazioni e ricerche sull'aristocrazia comunale di Pisa." *Studi Medievali*, ser. 3, 3 (1962): 707–27.

Tagliaferri, Amelio. *L'economia veronese secondo gli estimi dal 1409 al 1635*. Milan: Giuffrè, 1966.

Tamassia, Nino. *La famiglia italiana nei secoli decimoquinto e decimosesto*. Milan: R. Sandron, 1910.

Tateo, Francesco. "La disputa della nobiltà." In *Tradizione e realtà nell'umanesimo italiano*, 355–421. Bari: Dedalo, 1967.

Tenenti, Alberto. "L'ideologia della famiglia fiorentina nel Quattro e Cinquecento." In *La famiglia e la vita quotidiana in Europa dal '400 al '600*, 97–107. Rome, 1986.

———. *Il senso della morte e l'amore della vita nel Rinascimento (Francia e Italia)*. Turin, 1957.

———. *La vie et la mort à travers l'art du XVe siècle*. Paris: A. Colin, 1952.

Tetel, Marcel, Ronald G. Witt, and Rona Goffen, eds. *Life and Death in Fifteenth-Century Florence*. Durham: Duke University Press, 1989.

Tischendorf, Constantinus. *Evangelia Apocrypha*. Leipzig: Hermann Meldelssohn, 1876.

Tognetti, Giampaolo. "Venezia e le profezie sulla conversione dei Turchi." In *Venezia e i Turchi. Scontri e confronti di due civilta'*, 86–90. Milan: Electa, 1985.

Trexler, Richard C. "Charity and the Defence of Urban Elites in the Italian Communes." In *The Rich, the Well Born, and the Powerful*, edited by Frederic Cople Jaher, 64–109. Urbana: University of Illinois Press, 1973.

———. "The Foundlings of Florence, 1395–1455." *History of Childhood Quarterly* 1, 2 (1973): 259–84.

———. "Infanticide in Florence: New Sources and First Results." *History of Childhood Quarterly* 1, 1 (1973): 98–116.

———. *Public Life in Renaissance Florence*. New York: Academic Press, 1980.

Tricard, Jean. "La memoire des Benoist: livre de raison et memoire familiale au XVe siècle." In *Temps, memoire, tradition au Moyen Age*, 119–40. Aix-en-Provence, 1983.

Trinkaus, Charles Edward. *Adversity's Noblemen: The Italian Humanists on Happiness*. New York, 1940.

Turner, Victor, and Edith Turner. *Image and Pilgrimage in Christian Culture: Anthropological Perspectives*. Oxford: Basil Blackwell, 1978.

Vaccari, Pietro. *Il matrimonio canonico*. Milan: Edizioni Universitarie Malfasi, 1950.

———. *Il matrimonio germanico ed il matrimonio romano nel medio evo italiano*. Pavia: Viscontea, n.d.

———. "Uno sguardo ai nuovi rapporti di scambi commerciali fra Lombardia e Venezia nei secoli XIV e XV." In *Studi in onore di Amintore Fanfani*, 3:561–75.

Valori, Alessandro. "Famiglia e memoria. Luca da Panzano dal suo 'Libro di Ricordi': uno studio sulle relazioni familiari nello specchio della scrittura." *Archivio Storico Italiano* 102, 560 (1994): 261–97.

Vannini Marx, Anna, ed. *Credito banche e investimenti (secc. XIII–XX)*. Florence: Le Monnier, 1985.

Varanini, Gian Maria. "Le campagne veronesi del '400 fra tradizione e innovazione." In *Uomini e civiltà agraria in territorio veronese*, 187–262. Verona: Banca Popolare di Verona, 1982.

———. "La classe dirigente veronese e la congiura di Fregnano della Scala (1354)." *Studi Storici Luigi Simeoni* 24 (1984): 9–66.

———. *Comuni cittadini e stato regionale. Ricerche sulla Terraferma veneta nel Quattrocento*. Verona: Libreria Editrice Universitaria, 1992.

———. "Un esempio di ristrutturazione agraria quattrocentesca nella 'bassa' veronese: il monastero di S. Maria in Organo e le terre di Roncanova." *Studi Storici Veronese Luigi Simeoni* 30–31 (1980–81): 1–104.

———. "La famiglia Pindemonte di Verona: le origini e le prime generazioni (secc. XIV–XV)." In *Villa Pindemonte a Isola della Scala*, 31–54. Verona, 1987.

———. "Tra fisco e credito: note sulle Camere dei pegni nelle città veneto del Quattrocento." *Studi Storici Luigi Simeoni* 33 (1983): 215–46.

———. "Note sui consigli civici veronesi (secoli XIV–XV). In margine ad uno studio di J. E. Law." *Archivio Veneto,* ser. 5, 147 (1979): 5–32.

———. "Note sul lavoro salariato in una grande azienda della pianura veneta: le terre della famiglia Proto a Bolzano Vicentino nella seconda metà del Trecento." In *Le prestazioni d'opera nelle campagne italiane del Medioevo,* 231–47. Bologna: CLUEB, 1987.

———. "Organizzazione aziendale e società rurale nella pianura veneta: le terre della famiglia Proti a Bolzano Vicentino nella seconda metà del Trecento." In *Bolzano vicentino: dimensione del sociale e vita economica in un villaggio della pianura vicentino (secoli XIV–XIX),* edited by Claudio Povolo, 95–140. Bolzano vicentino, 1985.

———. "Le regole del bosco di Negrar (Valpolicella) e appunti su beni e pratiche agrarie comunitarie nel veronese (XV–XVI sec.)." *Archivio Veneto,* ser. 5, 121 (1983): 95–114.

———. "Gli Scaligeri, i ceto dirigente veronese, l'elite 'internazionale'." In *Gli Scaligeri,* edited by Varanini, 113–24.

———. "Vicenza nel Trecento. Istituzioni, classe dirigente, economia." In *Storia di Vicenza,* 2, *L'età medievale,* edited by Giorgio Cracco, 139–245. Vicenza: Neri Pozza, 1988.

Varanini, Gian Maria, ed. *Gli Scaligeri 1277–1387.* Verona: Arnaldo Mondadori, 1988.

Vauchez, Andre. "Alcune riflessioni sul movimento dell'Osservanza in Italia nel secolo XV." In *Ordini mendicanti e società italiana, XIII–XV secolo,* 306–10. Milan: Il Saggiatore, 1990.

———. "Presentation." In *Faire croire,* 7–16.

———. *La sainteté en Occident aux derniers siècles du Moyen Age d'apres les proces de canonisation et les documents hagiographiques.* Rome: Ècole Francais de Rome, 1981.

Vaughan, Dorothy. *Europe and the Turk: A Pattern of Alliances, 1350–1700.* Liverpool: Liverpool University Press, 1954.

Vecchiato, Lanfrancho. "Il fontico dei poveri e le delibere 'pro pauperibus' negli atti del consiglio di Verona (secoli XV–XVII)." *Economia e Storia* 2 (1973): 201–31.

Venezia e i Turchi. Scontri e confronti di due civiltà. Milan: Electa, 1985.

Venezia e la peste 1348/1797. Venice, 1979.

Ventura, Angelo. "Aspetti storico-economico della villa veneta." *Bolletino CISA* 11 (1969): 65–77.

———. "Considerazioni sull'agricoltura veneta e sulla accumulazione originaria del capitale nei secoli XVI e XVII." *Studi Storici* 9 (1968): 674–722.

———. *Nobiltà e popolo nella societa' veneta del '400 e '500.* Bari: Laterza, 1964.

Verde, Armando F. "Nota su notai e lo studio fiorentino della fine del '400." In *Il notariato nella civiltà toscana,* edited by Mario Montorzi, 365–89. Rome: Consiglio Nazionale del Notariato, 1985.

Verdon, Timothy. "Christianity, the Renaissance, and the Study of History." In *Christianity and the Renaissance,* edited by Verdon and Henderson, 1–37.

Verdon, Timothy, and John Henderson, eds. *Christianity and the Renaissance: Image and Religious Imagination in the Quattrocento.* Syracuse: Syracuse University Press, 1990.

Viggiano, Alfredo. *Governanti e governati. Legittimità del potere ed esercizio dell'autorità sovrana nello Stato veneto della prima età moderna.* Treviso: Edizioni Canova, 1993.

Violante, Cinzio. "Per lo studio dei prestiti dissimulati in territorio milanese (secoli X–XI)." In *Studi in onore di Amintore Fanfani,* 1:641–735.

Vitaliani, Domenico. "Contributo alla storia della lauda sacra nel Veneto." *Atti e Memorie,* ser. 4, 14 (1914): 179–209.

Viviani, Giuseppe Franco, ed. *La villa nel veronese.* Verona: Banca Mutua Popolare, 1975.

Volpato, Antonio. "La predicazione penitenziale-apocalittica nell'attività di due predicatori del 1473." *Bulletino dell'Istituto Storico Italiano per il Medio Evo e Archivio Muratoriano* 82 (1970): 113–28.

von Dobschutz, Ernst. *Christusbilder. Untersuchunger zur christliche Legende.* Leipzig: J. C. Hinrichs, 1899.

Vovelle, Gaby and Michel. *Vision de la mort et de l'au-delà en Provence.* Paris: Armand Colin, 1970.

Vovelle, Michel. *La mort et l'Occident de 1300 à nos jours.* Paris: Gallimard, 1983.

Waley, Pamela. "Personal Names in Siena, 1285." In *Florence and Italy: Renaissance Studies in Honour of Nicolai Rubinstein,* 187–91. London: Westfield College, 1988.

Wall, Richard. "Introduction." In *Family Forms in Historic Europe,* edited by Jean Robin and Peter Laslett, 1–63. Cambridge: Cambridge University Press, 1983.

Weil-Garris, Kathleen. *The Santa Casa di Loreto: Problems in Cinquecento Sculpture.* New York: Garland, 1977.

Weinstein, Donald. "*The Art of Dying Well* and Popular Piety in the Preaching and Thought of Girolamo Savonarola." In *Life and Death in Fifteenth-Century Florence,* edited by Tetel et al., 88–104.

Weinstein, Donald, and Rudolph M. Bell. *Saints and Society: The Two Worlds of Western Christendom, 1000–1700.* Chicago: University of Chicago Press, 1982.

Weissman, Ronald F. E. "The Importance of Being Ambiguous: Social Relations, Individualism, and Identity in Renaissance Florence." In *Urban Life in the Renaissance,* edited by Susan Zimmerman and Ronald F. E. Weissman, 269–80. Newark: University of Delaware Press, 1989.

———. "Sacred Eloquence: Humanist Preaching and Lay Piety in Renaissance Florence." In *Christianity and the Renaissance,* edited by Verdon and Henderson, 250–71.

———. "Taking Patronage Seriously: Mediterranean Values and Renaissance Society." In *Patronage, Art and Society,* edited by Kent and Simons, 25–46.

———. *Ritual Brotherhood in Renaissance Florence.* New York: Academic Press, 1982.

Wells, Robert V. "Marriage Seasonals in Early America: Comparisons and Comments." *Journal of Interdisciplinary History* 18, 2 (1987): 299–307.

Wickham, Chris. "Vendite di terra e mercato della terra in Toscana nel secolo XI." *Quaderni Storici* 65 (1987): 355–77.

Witt, Ronald G. *Hercules at the Crossroads: The Life, Works and Thought of Coluccio Salutati.* Durham: Duke University Press, 1983.

Zalin, Giovanni. "Economia agraria e insediamento di villa tra Medioevo e Rinascimento." In *La villa nel veronese,* edited by Viviani, 51–86.

Zanazzo, G. B. *L'arte della lana in Vicenza (secc. XIIX–XV)*, Deputazione veneta di storia patria, Miscellanea di storia veneta, ser. 3, 6. Venice, 1914.

Zarri, Gabriella. "Aspetti dello sviluppo degli Ordini religiosi in Italia tra Quattro e Cinquecento," In *Strutture ecclesiastiche in Italia e in Germania prima della Riforma*, edited by Paolo Prodi and Peter Johanek, 207–57. Bologna: Il Mulino, 1984.

Zika, Charles. "Hosts, Processions and Pilgrimages in Fifteenth-Century Germany." *Past and Present* 118 (1988): 25–64.

Zironda, Renato. "Aspetti del clero secolare e regolare della chiesa vicentina dal 1404 al 1563." In *Storia di Vicenza*, edited by Barbieri and Preto, 3/1:157–77.

———. *I canonici secolari di San Giorgio in Alga a San Rocco di Vicenza (1486–1668)*. Vicenza: ESCA, 1988.

Zironda, Renato, ed. *Santità e religiosità nella diocesi di Vicenza*. Vicenza: Biblioteca Civica Bertoliana, 1991.

INDEX

adolescence, 52, 54, 88–91, 96. *See also* coming of age; mortality, adolescent; violence, youthful

affines and cognates, 26–29, 83–84, 103–4, 126, 179; and arbitration, 27, 28, 84; and inheritance, 27, 28, 90, 98–99

Agapitus, St., 52, 189

Aimerico, Ludovico, 182

Alberico da Settefrati, 34

Alberti, Leon Battista, xv; on children, 34, 52, 54–55, 55–56; on the household, 83, 86; on land, 154; on marriage, 17, 21; on servants, 95–96

Albertus Magnus, 5–6, 30, 73

Aleardi family, 69, 184

Alexander III, 9, 12, 21, 30

almanacs. *See* prophecy, almanacs

Angiolelli family, 162; Antonio, 181–82; Biagio, 180

Anguissola family, 162, 169; Gabriele, 150

Anthony, St., 43, 44, 186, 192

Antoninus, St., 197, 271n. 79

dall'Aqua, Daniele, 178

Aquinas, St. Thomas, 30, 73, 187

arbitration, 27, 28–29, 84, 103, 219

d'Arco, Andrea, 181

Aristotle: on conception, 35; on marriage, 6; on nobility, 174, 176

arms and insignia, 102–3

Arnaldi family, ix, 2, 3, 4, 6–7, 16, 17–18, 19, 21, 26–27, 29, 40, 41, 43, 45, 49–50, 51, 63, 70, 74, 84–85, 93, 104, 106, 107, 108, 111, 112, 115, 116, 118, 119, 129, 134, 135, 136, 137, 138, 140, 142, 143, 144, 146, 153, 154–55, 156, 159, 161, 162, 169, 170, 174, 176, 177, 179, 182, 208; Alvise Giovanni,

28, 57, 126; Andrea I, 1, 2, 9, 13, 20, 21, 23, 25–26, 28, 31, 41, 42, 51, 57, 63–64, 71, 81, 84–85, 87, 90, 92, 94, 96, 100, 102, 105, 108, 109, 113–15, 119–20, 123–24, 126, 127–28, 130–31, 135, 143, 145, 152, 155, 156, 162–63, 171, 177–78, 183, 193–95, 198, 200, 202, 212, 274–75n. 140; Andrea II, 18, 50, 155, 164, 180–81; Angela Chiara, 10, 19, 47, 51, 57, 105; Antonio, 57; Bartolomea, 94; Battista, 2, 15, 23, 28, 42, 85, 94–95, 102, 124; Cassandra, 19, 47; Caterina Chiara, 47, 55; Chiara Julia, 55; Gaspare I, 1, 16, 22, 31, 74, 75, 78, 80–81, 84, 91, 92, 97, 102, 103, 104, 113, 142, 238n. 5, 265–66n. 88; Gaspare II, 1, 8, 11, 15, 22, 28, 32, 76, 92, 103, 104, 126, 156, 163, 183, 266n. 88; Giovanna Gaspara, 40, 47, 51, 57, 251n. 54; Giovanni Francesco Bernardino, 57; Girolamo, 57, 64, 104, 193, 251n. 54; Isabeta, 94; Laura, 18; Lucia, 11, 251n. 54; Maddalena, 55; Margarita Bona, 10, 13, 40, 41, 42, 57, 251n. 54; Melchiorre, 47; Michele, 47; Paola Martina, 47, 55; Pietro, 94, 138n. 5; Renaldo, 51, 64–65, 70, 95; Silvestro, 18, 19, 20, 32, 41, 42, 47, 51, 70, 71, 84–85, 90, 92–93, 94, 103, 104, 105, 115, 117, 119, 123–24, 126, 132, 133–34, 140, 143, 146, 147–48, 155, 156, 164, 176, 180–81, 193, 195; Tommaso, 2, 10, 15, 22, 23, 28, 32, 47, 55, 64, 75–76, 87, 92, 93, 94, 102, 103, 105, 113–14, 119–20, 122, 123–24, 128, 130, 145, 146, 156, 177–78, 195, 263n. 27, 274–75n. 140; Ursula Imperatrice, 41, 46, 47, 55, 56, 63–64. *See also* Botarini family, Caterina; Fracanzani family, Marcella; dal Gorgo family, Elisabetta;

337

Library of Congress Cataloging-in-Publication Data

Grubb, James S., 1952–
    Provincial families of the Renaissance : private and public life
in the Veneto / James S. Grubb.
        p.   cm.
    Includes bibliographical references and index.
    ISBN 0-8018-5321-4 (alk. paper)
        1. Family—Italy—Veneto—History. 2. Elite (Social sciences)—
Italy—Veneto—History. 3. Veneto (Italy)—Social life and
customs. 4. Veneto (Italy)—History. I. Title.
HQ630.15.V46G78   1996
306.85'0945'3—dc20   95-53072